How to Use the Maps in *Western Civilization: A Brief History, Fourth Edition*

Here are some basic map concepts that will help you to get the most out of the maps in this textbook.

- Always look at the scale, which allows you to determine the distance in miles or kilometers between locations on the map.

- Examine the legend carefully. It explains the colors and symbols used on the map.

- Note the locations of mountains, rivers, oceans, and other geographic features, and consider how these would affect such human activities as agriculture, commerce, travel, and warfare.

- Read the map caption thoroughly. It provides important information, sometimes not covered in the text itself, and poses a thought question to encourage you to think beyond the mere appearance of the map and make connections across chapters, regions, and concepts.

- Several "spot maps" appear in each chapter, to allow you to view in detail smaller areas that may not be apparent in larger maps. For example, a spot map in Chapter 1 lets you zoom in on Hammurabi's Empire.

- Many of the text's maps also carry a globe icon alongside the title, which indicates that the map appears in interactive form on the text's website:

http://www.thomsonedu.com/history/spielvogel

D1379219

Western Civilization: A Brief History

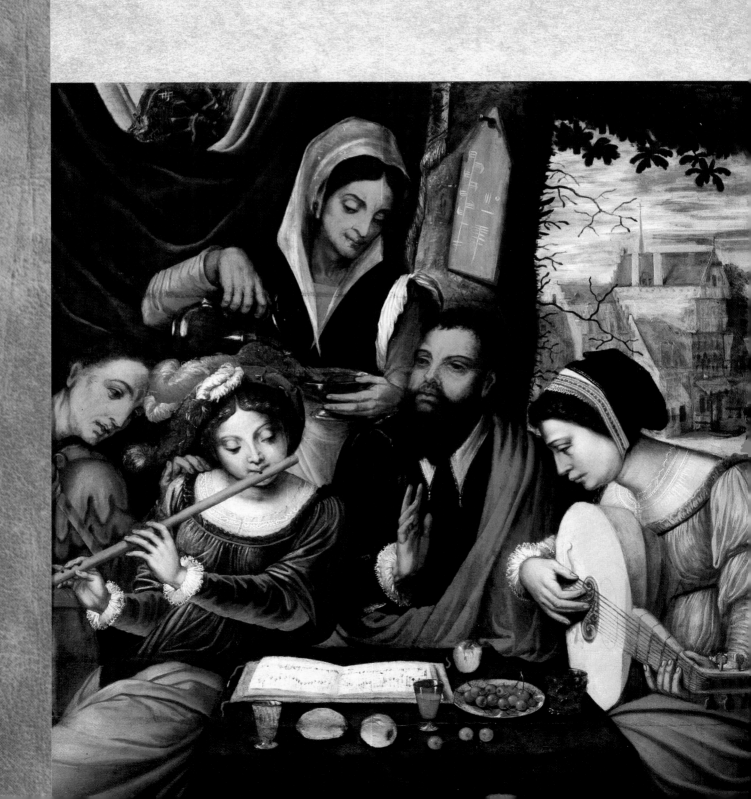

VOLUME I: TO 1715
FOURTH EDITION

WESTERN CIVILIZATION: A BRIEF HISTORY

JACKSON J. SPIELVOGEL

The Pennsylvania State University

THOMSON
WADSWORTH

Australia • Brazil • Canada • Mexico • Singapore • Spain
United Kingdom • United States

THOMSON
★
™
WADSWORTH

Publisher *Clark Baxter*
Senior Acquisitions Editor *Ashley Dodge*
Development Editor *Margaret McAndrew Beasley*
Assistant Editor *Kristen Tatroe*
Editorial Assistant *Ashley Spicer*
Associate Development Project Manager *Lee McCracken*
Senior Marketing Manager *Janise Fry*
Marketing Assistant *Teresa Jessen*
Senior Marketing Communications Manager *Tami Strang*
Content Project Managers *Katy German, Karol Jurado*
Creative Director *Rob Hugel*
Executive Art Director *Maria Epes*
Senior Print Buyer *Karen Hunt*

Production Service *Jonathan Peck, Dovetail Publishing Services*
Text Designer *Kathleen Cunningham*
Photo Researcher *Abigail Baxter*
Copy Editor *Bruce Emmer*
Permissions Editor *Sarah D'Stair*
Cover Designer *Kathleen Cunningham*
Cover Image *A detail from* The Pleasures of a Prodigal Son, Circle of Paul Coeck, *Museo Correr, Venice, Italy,* © *Cameraphoto Arte, Venice, Italy/Art Resource, NY*
Cover Printer *Courier Corporation/Kendallville*
Compositor *International Typesetting and Composition*
Printer *Courier Corporation/Kendallville*

Printed in the United States of America
1 2 3 4 5 6 7 11 10 09 08 07

For more information about our products, contact us at:
Thomson Learning Academic Resource Center
1-800-423-0563
For permission to use material from this text or product, submit a request online at http://www.thomsonrights.com.
Any additional questions about permissions can be submitted by e-mail to thomsonrights@thomson.com.

Library of Congress Control Number: 2006939650

Student Edition:
ISBN-13: 978-0-495-09974-1
ISBN-10: 0-495-09974-0

Thomson Higher Education
10 Davis Drive
Belmont, CA 94002-3098
USA

ABOUT THE AUTHOR

$\mathcal{J}$ACKSON J. SPIELVOGEL is associate professor emeritus of history at The Pennsylvania State University. He received his Ph.D. from The Ohio State University, where he specialized in Reformation history under Harold J. Grimm. His articles and reviews have appeared in such journals as *Moreana, Journal of General Education, Catholic Historical Review, Archiv für Reformationsgeschichte,* and *American Historical Review.* He has also contributed chapters or articles to *The Social History of the Reformation, The Holy Roman Empire: A Dictionary Handbook,* the *Simon Wiesenthal Center Annual of Holocaust Studies,* and *Utopian Studies.* His work has been supported by fellowships from the Fulbright Foundation and the Foundation for Reformation Research. At Penn State, he helped inaugurate the Western civilization courses as well as a popular course on Nazi Germany. His book *Hitler and Nazi Germany* was published in 1987 (fifth edition, 2005). He is the author of *Western Civilization,* first published in 1991 (sixth edition, 2006) and the coauthor (with William Duiker) of *World History,* first published in 1994 (fifth edition, 2007). Professor Spielvogel has won five major universitywide teaching awards. During the year 1988–1989, he held the Penn State Teaching Fellowship, the university's most prestigious teaching award. In 1996, he won the Dean Arthur Ray Warnock Award for Outstanding Faculty Member, and in 2000, he received the Schreyer Honors College Excellence in Teaching Award.

$\mathcal{T}$o Diane,
whose love and support made it all possible
J.J.S.

BRIEF CONTENTS

DETAILED CONTENTS

MAPS

CHRONOLOGIES

DOCUMENTS

These pages constitute an extension of the copyright page. We have made every effort to trace the ownership of all copyrighted material and to secure permission from copyright holders. In the event of any question arising as to the use of any material, we will be pleased to make the necessary corrections in future printings. Thanks are due to the following authors, publishers, and agents for permission to use the material indicated.

PREFACE

We are often reminded how important it is to understand today's world if we are to deal with our growing number of challenges. And yet that understanding will be incomplete if we in the Western world do not comprehend the meaning of Western civilization and the role it has played in the world. Despite modern progress, we still greatly reflect our religious traditions, our political systems and theories, our economic and social structures, and our cultural heritage. I have written this brief history of Western civilization to assist a new generation of students in learning more about the past that has shaped them and the world in which they live.

For the fourth edition, as in the third, I have added considerable new material on world history to show the impact other parts of the world have had on the West. Certainly, the terrorist attacks on the World Trade Center towers in New York and the Pentagon outside Washington, D.C., on September 11, 2001, have dramatized the intricate relationship between the West and the rest of the world. In this edition, I have attempted to show not only how Western civilization has affected the rest of the world but also how it has been influenced since its beginnings by contact with other peoples around the world.

Another of my goals was to write a well-balanced work in which the political, economic, social, religious, intellectual, cultural, and military aspects of Western civilization would be integrated into a chronologically ordered synthesis. Moreover, I wanted to avoid the approach that is quite common in other brief histories of Western civilization—an approach that makes them collections of facts with little continuity from section to section. Instead, I sought to keep the story in history. Narrative history effectively transmits the knowledge of the past and is the form that best enables students to remember and understand the past. At the same time, I have not overlooked the need for the kind of historical analysis that makes students aware that historians often disagree in their interpretations of the past.

Features of the Text

To enliven the past and let readers see for themselves the materials that historians use to create their pictures of the past, I have included in each chapter **primary sources** (boxed documents) that are keyed to the discussion in the text. The documents include examples of the religious, artistic, intellectual, social, economic, and political aspects of Western life. Such varied sources as a description of the life of an upper-class Roman, advice from a Carolingian

mother to her son, marriage negotiations in Renaissance Italy, a debate in the Reformation era, and the diary of a German soldier at Stalingrad all reveal in vivid fashion what Western civilization meant to the individual men and women who shaped it by their activities.

Each chapter has a **lengthy introduction and conclusion** to help maintain the continuity of the narrative and to provide a synthesis of important themes. Anecdotes in the chapter introductions convey more dramatically the major theme or themes of each chapter. **Detailed chronologies** reinforce the events discussed in the text, and **illustrated timelines** at the end of each chapter enable students to see at a glance the major developments of an era. Many of the timelines have been revised to show parallel developments in different cultures or nations. An **annotated bibliography** at the end of each chapter reviews the most recent literature on each period and also points readers to some of the older "classic" works in each field.

Updated maps and illustrations serve to deepen readers' understanding of the text. **Detailed map captions** are designed to enrich students' awareness of the importance of geography to history, and numerous spot maps enable students to see at a glance the region or subject being discussed in the text. To facilitate understanding of cultural movements, illustrations of artistic works discussed in the text are placed near the discussions. **Chapter outlines and focus questions, including critical thinking questions,** at the beginning of each chapter give students a useful overview and guide them to the main subjects of each chapter. A **glossary of important terms** (now boldfaced within the text) and a **pronunciation guide** are included to maximize reader comprehension and aid in review.

New to This Edition

As preparation for the revision of *Western Civilization: A Brief History,* I reexamined the entire book and analyzed the comments and reviews of colleagues who have found the book to be a useful instrument for introducing their students to the history of Western civilization. In making revisions for the fourth edition, I sought to build on the strengths of the first three editions and above all to maintain the balance, synthesis, and narrative qualities that characterized those editions. To keep up with the ever-growing body of historical scholarship, new or revised material has been added throughout the book on many topics, including Paleolithic painting; Hammurabi; the Hittites; the Hanging Gardens of Babylon; Athenian democracy; the decline of the Greek city-states; Greek interaction with India; Hellenistic monarchies; the Celts and their threat to the Hellenistic kingdoms; Hannibal;. Greek influence on the Romans; Cicero; crises in the third century; late antiquity; Germans during the Late Roman Empire; the end of the Roman Empire; the cultural shift brought by the conversion of Europe to Christianity; Augustine and Boethius; Islam; Alcuin and the Carolingian Renaissance; Muslim libraries and intellectual life; revival of Roman law; cross-cultural contacts between Western and Eastern translators and scholars; aristocratic women; the reconquest of Spain; the Hundred Years' War; the Great Schism; the Serb-Ottoman conflict in the fourteenth century; expansion of the Ottoman Empire and the fall of Constantinople; Michelangelo; Wyclif; Luther; Zwingli; the theology of the Anabaptists; the Council of Trent; the revived papacy in the Catholic Reformation; Jesuit missionaries to Asia; the slave trade; decline of the Ming in China; European ideas of cultural superiority; chemistry in the Scientific Revolution; Tahiti and Diderot; deism; Baron d'Holbach's atheism; the role of social divisions in the American Revolution; revolt in Saint-Domingue; the military conquests of Napoleon; Germaine de Staël; industrialization on the European continent; Chartism; Napoleon III's imperialistic adventure in Mexico; Florence Nightingale and nursing in the Crimean War; the spread of industrialization to Japan; the political history of Britain, Italy, Austria-Hungary, Russia, and France in the nineteenth century; causal factors in the rise of imperialism; Africa and Asia before imperialism; the response to imperialism by indigenous peoples; World War I as a global conflict; the Stalinist era; the Japanese home front in World War II; decolonization; the Cold War; women in the Soviet Union and Eastern Europe; politics since 1989; the reunification of Germany; the disintegration of Yugoslavia; and art, varieties of religious life, and science and popular culture since the 1970s. Throughout the revising process, I rewrote some sections and added many new subheadings to facilitate comprehension of the content of the chapters.

Chapters 6 and 7 were reorganized; Chapter 6 now focuses on the Roman Empire to 284, and Chapter 7 is a mostly new chapter on late antiquity and the emergence of the medieval world. The post–World War II material in Chapters 28 and 29 was reorganized to make the chapters chronologically consistent. Chapter 29 was also expanded and updated. New sections were added to a number of chapters: "Transformation of the Roman World: Crises in the Third Century" in Chapter 6; "The Spread of Industrialization to Japan" in Chapter 23; "The Casualties of War" in Chapter 25; "European States and the World: The Colonial Empires" in Chapter 26; "The Path to War in Asia" and "The New Order in Asia" in Chapter 27; "Europe and the World: Decolonization" in Chapter 28; and "The Unification of Europe" and "Postmodern Thought" in Chapter 29. The Suggestions for Further Reading at the end of each chapter were updated, and new illustrations were added throughout the book.

The enthusiastic response to the primary sources (boxed documents) led me to evaluate the content of each document carefully and add new documents throughout the text, including "An Italian Banker Discusses Trading Between Europe and China"; "The Childhood of Catherine the Great"; and "Soldier and Peasant Voices in the Russian Revolution." I also added questions to help guide students in analyzing the documents.

Because courses in Western civilization at American and Canadian colleges and universities follow different chronological divisions, a one-volume edition and a two-volume edition of this text are available to fit the needs of instructors. Teaching and learning ancillaries include the following:

For the Instructor

Instructor's Resource CD-ROM with ExamView® Includes the Instructor's Manual, Test Bank, Resource Integration Grid, ExamView® testing, and PowerPoint® slides with lecture outlines and images that can be used as offered, or customized by importing personal lecture slides or other material. ExamView allows instructors to create, deliver, and customize tests and study guides (both print and online) in minutes with this easy-to-use assessment and tutorial system. Instructors can build tests with as many as 250 questions using up to 12 question types. Using ExamView's complete word-processing capabilities, they can enter an unlimited number of new questions or edit existing ones.

ThomsonNOW This powerful and interactive web-based resource allows instructors to manage large classes with ease—student results flow directly to an instructor's gradebook—and it allows students to gauge their own unique study needs through pre-tests, personalized study plans, and more. Visit www.thomsonedu.com/thomsonnow

Full-Color Map Acetate Package Includes all maps from the text and other sources. More than 100 images. Map commentary is provided by James Harrison, Siena College.

History Video Library A completely new selection of videos for this edition, from *Films from the Humanities & Sciences* and other sources. Over fifty titles to choose from, with coverage spanning from "Egypt: A Gift to Civilization" to "Children of the Holocaust." Available to qualified adoptions.

Music of Western Civilization Available free to adopters, and for a small fee to students, this CD contains many of the musical selections highlighted in the text and provides a broad sampling of the important musical pieces of Western civilization.

JoinIn™ on TurningPoint® Combined with a choice of keypad systems, *JoinIn* turns PowerPoint® applications into audience response software. With a click on a hand-held device, students can respond to multiple choice questions, short polls, interactive exercises, and peer review questions. Instructors can take attendance, check student comprehension of concepts, collect student demographics to better assess student needs, and even administer quizzes. This tool is available to qualified adopters.

For the Student

Map Exercise Workbook   Prepared by Cynthia Kosso, Northern Arizona University. Thoroughly revised and upgraded. Over twenty maps and exercises ask students to identify important cities and countries. Available in two volumes.

MapTutor CD-ROM   This interactive map tutorial helps students learn geography by having them locate geographical features, regions, cities, and sociopolitical movements. Each map exercise is accompanied by questions that test their knowledge and promote critical thinking. Animations vividly show movement such as the conquests of the Romans, the spread of Christianity, invasions, medieval trade routes, and the spread of the Black Death.

Document Exercise Workbook   Prepared by Donna Van Raaphorst, Cuyahoga Community College. A collection of exercises based around primary sources. Available in two volumes.

Magellan Atlas of Western Civilization   Available to bundle with any Western civilization text; contains forty-four full-color historical maps, including "The Conflict in Afghanistan, 2001" and "States of the World, 2001."

Gregory, Documents of Western Civilization   This reader can accompany any Western civilization text. Contains a broad selection of carefully chosen documents.

InfoTrac® College Edition   A Wadsworth exclusive. Students receive four months of real-time access to InfoTrac College Editions' online database of continuously updated, full-length articles from more than 900 journals and periodicals. By doing a simply keyword search, users can quickly generate a powerful list of related articles from thousands of possibilities, then select relevant articles to explore or print out for reference or further study. For professors, InfoTrac articles offer opportunities to ignite discussions or augment their lectures with the latest developments in the discipline. For students, InfoTrac's virtual library allows Internet access to sources that extend their learning far beyond the pages of a text.

Wadsworth History Resource Center

http://history.wadsworth.com

Both instructors and students will enjoy the Wadsworth History Resource Center, with access to the chapter-by-chapter resources for Spielvogel's Western civilization texts. Text-specific content for students includes interactive maps, interactive timelines, simulations, "At the Movies" film activities, tutorial quizzes, glossary, hyperlinks, InfoTrac exercises, and Internet activities. Instructors also have access to the Instructor's Manual, lesson plans, and PowerPoint slides (access code required). From the History home page, instructors and students can access many selections, such as an Internet Guide for History, a career center, lessons on surfing the Web, the World History image bank, and links to great history-related Web sites.

ACKNOWLEDGMENTS

I would like to thank the many teachers and students who have used the first three editions of *Western Civilization: A Brief History*. I am gratified by their enthusiastic response to a textbook that was intended to put the story back in history and capture the imagination of the reader. I especially thank the many teachers and students who made the effort to contact me personally to share their enthusiasm. I am deeply grateful to John Soares for his assistance in preparing the map captions and to Charmarie Blaisdell of Northeastern University for her detailed suggestions on women's history. Daniel Haxall and Kathryn Spielvogel of The Pennsylvania State University provided valuable assistance with materials on postwar art, popular culture, and Postmodern art and thought. Thanks to Wadsworth's comprehensive review process, many historians were asked to evaluate my manuscript and review each edition. I am grateful to the following for the innumerable suggestions for previous editions, which have greatly improved my work:

Paul Allen
University of Utah

Gerald Anderson
North Dakota State University

Susan L. H. Anderson
Campbell University

Letizia Argenteri
University of San Diego

Roy A. Austensen
Illinois State University

James A. Baer
Northern Virginia Community College–Alexandria

James T. Baker
Western Kentucky University

Patrick Bass
Morningside College

John F. Battick
University of Maine

Frederic J. Baumgartner
Virginia Polytechnic Institute

Phillip N. Bebb
Ohio University

Anthony Bedford
Modesto Junior College

F. E. Beemon
Middle Tennessee State University

Joel Benson
Northwest Missouri State University

Leonard R. Berlanstein
University of Virginia

Douglas T. Bisson
Belmont University

Charmarie Blaisdell
Northeastern University

Stephen H. Blumm
Montgomery County Community College

Hugh S. Bonar
California State University

Werner Braatz
University of Wisconsin–Oshkosh

Alfred S. Bradford
University of Missouri

Maryann E. Brink
College of William & Mary

Blaine T. Browne
Broward Community College

J. Holden Camp, Jr.
Hillyer College, University of Hartford

Jack Cargill
Rutgers University

Martha Carlin
University of Wisconsin–Milwaukee

Elizabeth Carney
Clemson University

Kevin K. Carroll
Arizona State University

Yuan-Ling Chao
Middle Tennessee State University

Eric H. Cline
Xavier University

Robert Cole
Utah State University

William J. Connell
Rutgers University

Nancy Conradt
College of DuPage

Marc Cooper
Southwest Missouri State

Richard A. Cosgrove
University of Arizona

David A. Crain
South Dakota State University

Michael A. Crane Jr. (student)
Everett Community College

Steve Culbertson
Owens Community College

Luanne Dagley
Pellissippi State Technical Community College

Michael F. Doyle
Ocean County College

Michael Duckett
Dawson College

Roxanne Easley
Central Washington University

James W. Ermatinger
University of Nebraska–Kearney

Charles T. Evans
Northern Virginia Community College

Porter Ewing
Los Angeles City College

Carla Falkner
*Northeast Mississippi
Community College*

Steven Fanning
University of Illinois–Chicago

Ellsworth Faris
*California State
University–Chico*

Gary B. Ferngren
Oregon State University

Mary Helen Finnerty
Westchester Community College

A. Z. Freeman
Robinson College

Marsha Frey
Kansas State University

Frank J. Frost
*University of California–Santa
Barbara*

Frank Garosi
*California State
University–Sacramento*

Lorettann Gascard
Franklin Pierce College

Richard M. Golden
University of North Texas

Manuel G. Gonzales
Diablo Valley College

Amy G. Gordon
Denison University

Richard J. Grace
Providence College

Hanns Gross
Loyola University

John F. Guilmartin
Ohio State University

Jeffrey S. Hamilton
Gustavus Adolphus College

J. Drew Harrington
Western Kentucky University

James Harrison
Siena College

A. J. Heisserer
University of Oklahoma

Rowena Hernández-Múzquiz
Old Dominion University

Betsey Hertzler
Mesa Community College

Robert Herzstein
University of South Carolina

Shirley Hickson
North Greenville College

Martha L. Hildreth
University of Nevada

Boyd H. Hill, Jr.
University of Colorado–Boulder

Michael Hofstetter
Bethany College

Donald C. Holsinger
Seattle Pacific University

Frank L. Holt
University of Houston

W. Robert Houston
University of South Alabama

Paul Hughes
*Sussex County Community
College*

Richard A. Jackson
University of Houston

Fred Jewell
Harding University

Jenny M. Jochens
Towson State University

William M. Johnston
University of Massachusetts

Allen E. Jones
Troy State University

Jeffrey A. Kaufmann
Muscatine Community College

David O. Kieft
University of Minnesota

Patricia Killen
Pacific Lutheran University

William E. Kinsella Jr.
*Northern Virginia Community
College–Annandale*

James M. Kittelson
Ohio State University

Doug Klepper
Santa Fe Community College

Cynthia Kosso
Northern Arizona University

Clayton Miles Lehmann
University of South Dakota

Diana Chen Lin
Indiana University, Northwest

Ursula W. MacAffer
*Hudson Valley Community
College*

Harold Marcuse
*University of California–Santa
Barbara*

Mavis Mate
University of Oregon

T. Ronald Melton
Brewton Parker College

Jack Allen Meyer
University of South Carolina

Eugene W. Miller Jr.
*The Pennsylvania State
University–Hazleton*

David Mock
Tallahassee Community College

John Patrick Montano
University of Delaware

Rex Morrow
Trident Technical College

Thomas M. Mulhern
University of North Dakota

Pierce Mullen
Montana State University

Frederick I. Murphy
Western Kentucky University

William M. Murray
University of South Florida

Otto M. Nelson
Texas Tech University

Sam Nelson
Willmar Community College

John A. Nichols
Slippery Rock University

Lisa Nofzinger
*Albuquerque Technical
Vocational Institute*

Chris Oldstone-Moore
Augustana College

Donald Ostrowski
Harvard University

James O. Overfield
University of Vermont

Matthew L. Panczyk
Bergen Community College

Kathleen Parrow
Black Hills State University

Carla Rahn Phillips
University of Minnesota

Keith Pickus
Wichita State University

Linda J. Piper
University of Georgia

Janet Polasky
University of New Hampshire

Thomas W. Porter
Randolph-Macon College

Charles A. Povlovich
*California State
University–Fullerton*

Nancy Rachels
Hillsborough CommunityCollege

Charles Rearick
University of Massachusetts–Amherst

Jerome V. Reel Jr.
Clemson University

Paul Reuter
Jefferson State Community College

Joseph Robertson
Gadsden State Community College

Jonathan Roth
San Jose State University

Constance M. Rousseau
Providence College

Julius R. Ruff
Marquette University

Richard Saller
University of Chicago

Magdalena Sanchez
Texas Christian University

Jack Schanfield
Suffolk County Community College

Roger Schlesinger
Washington State University

Joanne Schneider
Rhode Island College

Thomas C. Schunk
University of Wisconsin–Oshkosh

Denise Scifres
Hinds Community College

Kyle C. Sessions
Illinois State University

Linda Simmons
Northern Virginia Community College–Manassas

Donald V. Sippel
Rhode Island College

Glen Spann
Asbury College

John W. Steinberg
Georgia Southern University

Paul W. Strait
Florida State University

James E. Straukamp
California State University–Sacramento

Brian E. Strayer
Andrews University

Fred Suppe
Ball State University

Roger Tate
Somerset Community College

Tom Taylor
Seattle University

Jack W. Thacker
Western Kentucky University

David S. Trask
Guilford Technical Community College

Thomas Turley
Santa Clara University

John G. Tuthill
University of Guam

Maarten Ultee
University of Alabama

Donna L. Van Raaphorst
Cuyahoga Community College

Allen M. Ward
University of Connecticut

Richard D. Weigel
Western Kentucky University

Michael Weiss
Linn-Benton Community College

Richard S. Williams
Washington State University

Arthur H. Williamson
California State University–Sacramento

Katherine Workman
Wright State University

Judith T. Wozniak
Cleveland State University

Walter J. Wussow
University of Wisconsin–Eau Claire

Edwin M. Yamauchi
Miami University

The following individuals contributed suggestions for the fourth edition:

Robert L. Bergman
Glendale Community College

Michael Clinton
Gwynedd Mercy College

Caitlin Corning
George Fox University

Marion F. Deshmukh
George Mason University

Laura Dull
Delta College

Eve Fisher
South Dakota State University

Lucien Frary
Rider University

Derek Hastings
Oakland University

David R. C. Hudson
Texas A&M University

George Kaloudis
Rivier College

Mark Klobas
Scottsdale Community College

Anthony Makowski
Delaware County Community College

Tom Maulucci
State University of New York–Fredonia

David Mock
Tallahassee Community College

Heather O'Grady-Evans
Elmira College

Jonathan Perry
University of Central Florida

Bonnie F. Saunders
Glendale Community College

Richard Schellhammer
University of West Alabama

Colleen M. Shaughnessy Zeena
Endicott College

Douglas R. Skopp
State University of New York–Plattsburgh

Ruth Suyama
Los Angeles Mission College

Janet A. Thompson
Tallahassee Community College

Thomas Turley
Santa Clara University

Nancy G. Vavra
University of Colorado–Boulder

The editors at Thomson Wadsworth have been both help-ful and congenial at all times. I especially wish to thank Clark Baxter, whose clever wit, wisdom, gentle prodding, and good friendship have added much depth to our work-ing relationship. Margaret Beasley thoughtfully, wisely, effi-ciently, and pleasantly guided the overall development of the fourth edition. I also want to express my gratitude to Jon Peck, of Dovetail Publishing Services, whose good humor, well-advised suggestions, and generous verbal sup-port made the production process such a delight. Bruce Emmer, an outstanding copyeditor, taught me much about the fine points of the English language. Abbie Baxter provided valuable assistance in obtaining permissions for the illus-trations and also made superb suggestions for new illus-trations.

Above all, I thank my family for their support. The gifts of love, laughter, and patience from my daughters, Jennifer and Kathryn; my sons, Eric and Christian; my daughters-in-law, Liz and Laurie; and my son-in-law, Daniel, were enormously appreciated. My wife and best friend, Diane, contributed editorial assistance, wise counsel, good humor, and the loving support that made it possible for me to accomplish a project of this magnitude. I could not have written the book without her.

INTRODUCTION TO
STUDENTS OF WESTERN CIVILIZATION

*C*ivilization, as historians define it, first emerged between five and six thousand years ago when people in different parts of the world began to live in organized communities with distinct political, military, economic, and social structures. Religious, intellectual, and artistic activities assumed important roles in these early societies. The focus of this book is on Western civilization, a civilization that many people identify with the continent of Europe.

Defining Western Civilization

Western civilization itself has evolved considerably over the centuries. Most historians trace the origins of Western civilization to the classical world of Rome and Greece and even farther back to the Mediterranean basin, including lands in North Africa and the Middle East. Nevertheless, people in these civilizations viewed themselves as subjects of states or empires, not as members of Western civilization. Later, with the rise of Christianity, peoples in Europe began to identify themselves as part of a civilization different from others, such as that of Islam, leading to a concept of a Western civilization different from other civilizations. In the fifteenth century, Renaissance intellectuals began to identify this civilization not only with Christianity but also with the intellectual and political achievements of the ancient Greeks and Romans.

Important to the development of the idea of a distinct Western civilization were encounters with other peoples. Between 700 and 1500, encounters with the world of Islam helped define the West. But after 1500, as European ships began to move into other parts of the world, encounters with peoples in Asia, Africa, and the Americas not only had an impact on the civilizations found there but also affected how people in the West defined themselves. At the same time, as they set up colonies, Europeans began to transplant a sense of Western identity to other areas of the world, especially North America and parts of Latin America, that have come to be considered part of Western civilization.

As the concept of Western civilization has evolved over the centuries, so have the values and unique features associated with that civilization. Science played a crucial role in the development of modern Western civilization. The societies of the Greeks, the Romans, and the medieval Europeans were based largely on a belief in the existence of a spiritual order; a dramatic departure to a natural or material view of the universe occurred in the seventeenth-century Scientific Revolution. Science and technology have been important in the growth of today's modern and largely secular Western civilization, although antecedents to scientific development also existed in Greek and medieval thought and practice, and spirituality remains a component of the Western world today.

Many historians have viewed the concept of political liberty, belief in the fundamental value of every individual, and a rational outlook based on a system of logical, analytical thought as unique aspects of Western civilization. Of course, the West has also witnessed horrendous negations of liberty, individualism, and reason. Racism, slavery, violence, world wars, totalitarian regimes—these, too, form part of the complex story of what constitutes Western civilization.

The Dating of Time

In our examination of Western civilization, we need also to be aware of the dating of time. In recording the past, historians try to determine the exact time when events occurred. World War II in Europe, for example, began on September 1, 1939, when Hitler sent German troops into Poland, and ended on May 7, 1945, when Germany surrendered. By using dates, historians can place events in order and try to determine the development of patterns over periods of time.

If someone asked you when you were born, you would reply with a number, such as 1987. In the United States, we would all accept that number without question because it is part of the dating system followed in the Western world (Europe and the Western Hemisphere). In this system, events are dated by counting backward or forward from the birth of Jesus Christ (assumed to be the year 1). An event that took place four hundred years before the birth of Jesus would be dated 400 B.C. (before Christ). Dates after the birth of Jesus are labeled A.D. These letters stand for the Latin words *anno Domini,* which mean "in the year of the Lord." Thus an event that took place two hundred years after the birth of Jesus is written A.D. 200, or "in the year of the Lord 200." It can also be written as 200, just as you would not give your birth year as A.D. 1987 but simply as 1987. Historians also make use of other terms to refer to time. A decade is ten years, a century is one hundred years, and a millennium is one thousand years. Thus "the fourth century B.C." refers to the fourth period of one hundred years counting backward from 1, the assumed date of the birth of Jesus. Since the first century B.C. would be the years 100 B.C. to 1 B.C., the fourth century B.C. would be the years 400 B.C. to 301 B.C. We could say, then, that an event in 350 B.C. took place in the fourth century B.C.

"The fourth century A.D." refers to the fourth period of one hundred years after the birth of Jesus. Since the first period of one hundred years would be the years 1 to 100, the fourth period or fourth century would be the years 301 to 400. We could say, then, that an event in 350 took place in the fourth century. Likewise, the first millennium B.C. refers to the years 1000 B.C. to 1 B.C.; the second millennium A.D. refers to the years 1001 to 2000. Some historians now prefer to use the abbreviations B.C.E. ("before the Common Era") and C.E. ("Common Era") instead of B.C. and A.D. This is especially true of world historians, who prefer to use symbols that are not so Western- or Christian-oriented. The dates, of course, remain the same. Thus 1950 B.C.E. and 1950 B.C. would be the same year. In keeping with current usage by many historians of Western civilization, this book uses the notations B.C. and A.D.

The dating of events can also vary from people to people. Most people in the Western world use the Western calendar, also known as the Gregorian calendar after Pope Gregory XIII, who refined it in 1582. The Hebrew calendar uses a different system in which the year 1 is the equivalent of the Western year 3760 B.C., considered to be the date of the creation of the world according to the Bible. Thus the Western year 2006 is the year 5766 on the Hebrew calendar. The Islamic calendar begins year 1 on the day Muhammad fled Mecca, which is the year 622 on the Western calendar.

1

THE ANCIENT NEAR EAST: THE FIRST CIVILIZATIONS

CHAPTER OUTLINE AND FOCUS QUESTIONS

The First Humans

☐ Where did the Neolithic agricultural revolution occur, and how did it affect the lives of men and women?

The Emergence of Civilization

☐ What are the characteristics of civilization, and what are some explanations for why early civilizations emerged?

Civilization in Mesopotamia

☐ How are the chief characteristics of civilization evident in ancient Mesopotamia?

Egyptian Civilization: "The Gift of the Nile"

☐ What are the basic features of the three major periods of Egyptian history? What elements of continuity are there in the three periods? What are their major differences?

CRITICAL THINKING

☐ In what ways were the civilizations of Mesopotamia and Egypt alike? In what ways were they different?

Ruins of the ancient Sumerian city of Uruk

© Nik Wheeler / CORBIS

𝓘N 1849, A DARING YOUNG Englishman made a hazardous journey into the deserts and swamps of southern Iraq. Moving south down the banks of the Euphrates River while braving high winds and temperatures that reached 120 degrees Fahrenheit, William Loftus led a small expedition in search of the roots of civilization. As he said, "From our childhood we have been led to regard this place as the cradle of the human race."

Guided by native Arabs into the southernmost reaches of Iraq, Loftus and his small group of explorers were soon overwhelmed by what they saw. He wrote, "I know of nothing more exciting or impressive than the first sight of one of these great piles, looming in solitary grandeur from the surrounding plains and marshes." One of these piles, known to the natives as the mound of Warka, contained the ruins of Uruk, one of the first cities in the world and part of the world's first civilization.

Southern Iraq, known to ancient peoples as Mesopotamia, was one area in the world where civilization began. Western civilization can be traced back to the ancient Near East, where people in Mesopotamia and Egypt developed organized societies and created the ideas and institutions that we associate with civilization. The later Greeks and

Romans, who played such a crucial role in the development of Western civilization, were themselves nourished and influenced by these older societies in the Near East. It is appropriate, therefore, to begin our story of Western civilization in the ancient Near East with the early civilizations of Mesopotamia and Egypt. Before considering them, however, we must briefly examine prehistory and observe how human beings made the shift from hunting and gathering to agricultural communities and ultimately to cities and civilization.✦

CHRONOLOGY **The First Humans**

Australopithecines	flourished c. 2–4 million years ago
Homo erectus	flourished c. 100,000–1.5 million years ago
Homo sapiens	
Neanderthals	flourished c. 100,000–30,000 B.C.
Homo sapiens sapiens	emerged c. 200,000 B.C.

The First Humans

Historians rely primarily on documents to create their pictures of the past, but no written records exist for the prehistory of humankind. In their absence, the story of early humanity depends on archaeological and, more recently, biological information, which anthropologists and archaeologists use to formulate theories about our early past.

The earliest humanlike creatures—known as hominids—existed in Africa as long as three to four million years ago. Known as Australopithecines, they flourished in East and South Africa and were the first hominids to make simple stone tools.

A second stage in early human development occurred around 1.5 million years ago when HOMO ERECTUS ("upright human being") emerged. *Homo erectus* made use of larger and more varied tools and was the first hominid to leave Africa and to move into both Europe and Asia.

Around 250,000 years ago, a third and crucial stage in human development began with the emergence of *Homo sapiens* ("wise human being"). By 100,000 B.C., two groups of *Homo sapiens* had developed. One type was the Neanderthal, whose remains were first found in the Neander valley in Germany. Neanderthal remains have since been found in both Europe and the Middle East and have been dated to between 100,000 and 30,000 B.C. Neanderthals relied on a variety of stone tools and were the first early people to bury their dead.

The first anatomically modern humans, known as *Homo sapiens sapiens* ("wise, wise human being"), appeared in Africa between 200,000 and 150,000 years ago. Recent evidence indicates that they began to spread outside Africa around 70,000 years ago. Map 1.1 shows probable dates for different movements, although many of these are still controversial. By 30,000 B.C., *Homo sapiens sapiens* had replaced the Neanderthals, who had largely become extinct, and by 10,000 B.C., members of the *Homo sapiens sapiens* species could be found throughout the world. By that time, it was the only human species left. All humans today, be they Europeans, Australian aborigines, or Africans, belong to the same subspecies.

The Hunter-Gatherers of the Old Stone Age

One of the basic distinguishing features of the human species is the ability to make tools. The earliest tools were made of stone, and the term **Paleolithic** (Greek for "old stone") **Age** is used to designate this early period of human history (c. 2,500,000–10,000 B.C.).

For hundreds of thousands of years, humans relied on hunting and gathering for their daily food. Paleolithic peoples had a close relationship with the world around them, and over a period of time, they came to know which animals to hunt and which plants to eat. They did not know how to grow crops or raise animals, however. They gathered wild nuts, berries, fruits, and a variety of wild grains and green plants. Around the world, they hunted and consumed different animals, including buffalo, horses, bison, wild goats, and reindeer. In coastal areas, fish were a rich source of nourishment.

The hunting of animals and the gathering of wild plants no doubt led to certain patterns of living. Archaeologists and anthropologists have speculated that Paleolithic people lived in small bands of twenty to thirty. They were nomadic, moving from place to place to follow animal migrations and vegetation cycles. Hunting depended on careful observation of animal behavior patterns and required a group effort for success. Over the years, tools became more refined and more useful. The invention of the spear, and later the bow and arrow, made hunting considerably easier. Harpoons and fishhooks made of bone increased the catch of fish.

Both men and women were responsible for finding food—the chief work of Paleolithic people. Since women bore and raised the children, they generally stayed close to the camps, but they played an important role in acquiring food by gathering berries, nuts, and grains. Men hunted wild animals, an activity that took them far from camp. Because both men and women played important roles in providing for the band's survival, scientists believe that a rough equality existed between men and women. Indeed, some speculate that both men and women made the decisions that affected the activities of the Paleolithic band.

Some groups of Paleolithic peoples, especially those who lived in cold climates, found shelter in caves. Over time, they created new types of shelter as well. Perhaps the most common was a simple structure of wood poles or sticks covered with animal hides. The systematic use of fire, which archaeologists believe began around 500,000 years ago, made it possible for the caves and human-made structures to have a source of light and

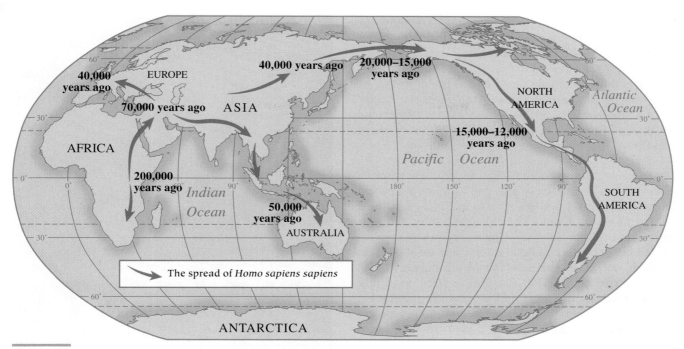

MAP 1.1 **The Spread of *Homo sapiens sapiens*.** *Homo sapiens sapiens* spread from Africa beginning about 70,000 years ago. Living and traveling in small groups, these anatomically modern humans were hunter-gatherers. Although groups of people advanced beyond their old hunting grounds at a rate of only 2 or 3 miles per generation, this was enough to populate the world in tens of thousands of years. **?** Given that some diffusion of humans occurred during ice ages, how would such climate change affect humans and their movements, especially from Asia to Australia and Asia to North America? **View an animated version of this map or related maps at** http://thomsonedu.com/history/spielvogel

heat. Fire also enabled early humans to cook their food, making it taste better, last longer, and in the case of some plants, such as wild grain, easier to chew and digest.

The making of tools and the use of fire—two important technological innovations of Paleolithic peoples—remind us how crucial the ability to adapt was to human survival. But Paleolithic peoples did more than just survive. The cave paintings of large animals found in southwestern France and northern Spain bear witness to the cultural activity of Paleolithic peoples. A cave discovered in southern France in 1994 (known as the Chauvet Cave, after the leader of the expedition that found it) contains more than three hundred paintings of lions, oxen, owls, panthers, and other animals. Most of these are animals that Paleolithic people did not hunt, which suggests to some scholars that the paintings were made for religious or even decorative purposes. The discoverers were overwhelmed by what they saw: "There was a moment of ecstasy. . . . They overflowed with joy and emotion. . . . These were moments of indescribable madness."[1]

The Neolithic Revolution (c. 10,000–4000 B.C.)

The end of the last ice age around 10,000 B.C. was followed by what is called the **Neolithic Revolution**, a significant change in living patterns that occurred in the New Stone Age (*Neolithic* is Greek for "new stone"). The name New Stone Age is misleading, however. Although Neolithic peoples made a new type of polished stone ax, this was not the major change that occurred after 10,000 B.C.

An Agricultural Revolution The biggest change was the shift from hunting animals and gathering plants for sustenance to producing food by systematic agriculture. The planting of grains and vegetables provided a regular supply of food, while the taming of animals, such as sheep, goats, cattle, and pigs, added a steady source of meat, milk, and fibers such as wool for clothing. Larger animals could also be used as beasts of burden. The growing of crops and the taming of food-producing animals created a new relationship between humans and nature. Historians speak of this as an agricultural revolution. Revolutionary change is dramatic and requires great effort, but the ability to acquire food on a regular basis gave humans greater control over their environment. It also allowed them to give up their nomadic ways of life and begin to live in settled communities.

Systematic agriculture probably developed independently between 8000 and 7000 B.C. in various parts of the world. Different plants were cultivated in each: wheat, barley, and lentils in the Near East; rice and millet in southern Asia; millet and yams in western Africa; and beans, potatoes, and corn in the Americas. The Neolithic agricultural revolution needed a favorable environment. In the Near East, the upland areas above the Fertile Crescent (present-day northern Iraq and southern Turkey) were more conducive to systematic farming than the river valleys. This region received the necessary rainfall and was the home of two wild plant species (barley and wheat) and four wild animal species (pigs, cows, goats, and sheep) that humans eventually domesticated.

Consequences of the Neolithic Revolution The growing of crops on a regular basis gave rise to more permanent settlements, which historians refer to as Neolithic farming villages or towns. One of the oldest and most extensive agricultural villages was Çatal Hüyük, located in modern-day Turkey. Its walls enclosed 32 acres, and its population probably reached six thousand inhabitants during its high point from 6700 to 5700 B.C. People lived in simple mudbrick houses that were built so close to one another that there were few streets. To get to their homes, people had to walk along the rooftops and then enter the house through a hole in the roof.

Archaeologists have discovered twelve cultivated products in Çatal Hüyük, including fruits, nuts, and three kinds of wheat. Artisans made weapons and jewelry that were traded with neighboring people. Religious shrines housing figures of gods and goddesses have been found at Çatal Hüyük, as have a number of female statuettes. Molded with noticeably large breasts and buttocks, these "earth mothers" perhaps symbolically represented the fertility of both "mother earth" and human mothers. The shrines and the statues point to the role of religion in the lives of these Neolithic peoples.

The Neolithic Revolution had far-reaching consequences. Once people settled in villages or towns, they built permanent houses for protection and other structures for the storage of goods. As organized communities stockpiled food and accumulated material goods, they began to engage in trade. People also began to specialize in certain crafts, and a division of labor developed. Pottery was made from clay and baked in a fire to make it hard. The pots were used for cooking and to store grains. Woven baskets were also used for storage. Stone tools became refined as flint blades were employed to make sickles and hoes for use in the fields. In the course of the Neolithic Age, many of the food plants still in use today began to be cultivated. Moreover, fibers from plants such as flax were used to make thread that was woven into cloth.

The change to systematic agriculture in the Neolithic Age also had consequences for the relationship between men and women. Men assumed the primary responsibility for working in the fields and herding animals, jobs that kept them away from the home. Although women also worked in the fields, many remained behind to care for the children, weave clothes, and perform other tasks that required labor close to home. In time, as work outside the home was increasingly perceived as more

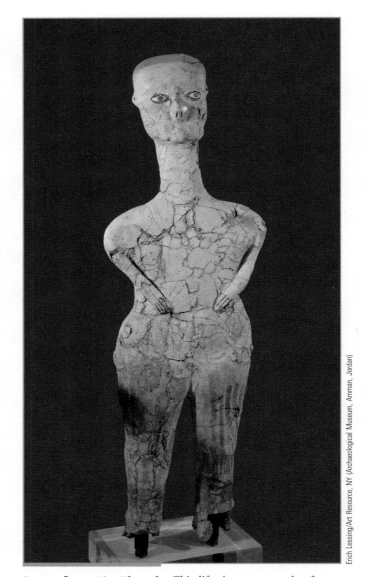

Statue from Ain Ghazal. This life-size statue made of plaster, sand, and crushed chalk dating from 6500 B.C. was discovered in 1984 in Ain Ghazal, an archaeological site near Amman, Jordan. It is among the oldest known statues of the human figure. Although it appears lifelike, its features are considered generic rather than a portrait of an individual face. The purpose and meaning of this sculpture may never be known.

important than work done at home, men came to play the more dominant role in society, a basic pattern that would persist until our own times.

Other patterns set in the Neolithic Age also proved to be enduring elements of human history. Fixed dwellings, domesticated animals, regular farming, a division of labor, men holding power—all of these are part of the human story. For all of our modern scientific and technological progress, human survival still depends on the growing and storing of food, an accomplishment of people in the Neolithic Age. The Neolithic Revolution was truly a turning point in human history.

New Developments Between 4000 and 3000 B.C., significant technical developments began to transform the Neolithic towns. The invention of writing enabled records to be kept, and the use of metals marked a new level of human control over the environment and its resources. Already before 4000 B.C., craftspeople had discovered that certain rocks could be heated to liquefy metals embedded in them. The metals could then be cast in molds to produce tools and weapons that were more refined than stone instruments. Although copper was the first metal to be made into tools, after 4000 B.C., craftspeople in western Asia discovered that combining copper and tin created bronze, a much harder and more durable metal than copper. Its widespread use has led historians to call the period from around 3000 to 1200 B.C. the **Bronze Age**; thereafter, bronze was increasingly replaced by iron.

At first, Neolithic settlements were mere villages. But as their inhabitants mastered the art of farming, more complex human societies began to emerge. As wealth increased, these societies began to develop armies and to build walled towns and cities. By the beginning of the Bronze Age, the concentration of larger numbers of people in the river valleys of Mesopotamia and Egypt was leading to a whole new pattern for human life.

The Emergence of Civilization

As we have seen, early human beings formed small groups that developed a simple culture that enabled them to survive. As human societies grew and developed greater complexity, a new form of human existence—called *civilization*—came into being. A **civilization** is a complex culture in which large numbers of human beings share a number of common elements. Historians have identified a number of basic characteristics of civilization. These include (1) an urban focus: cities became the centers of political, economic, social, cultural, and religious development; (2) a distinct religious structure: the gods were deemed crucial to the community's success, and professional priestly classes regulated relations with the gods; (3) new political and military structures: an organized government bureaucracy arose to meet the administrative demands of the growing population, and armies were organized to gain land and power; (4) a new social structure based on economic power: while kings and an upper class of priests, political leaders, and warriors dominated, there also existed a large group of free men (farmers, artisans, craftspeople) and at the very bottom, socially, a class of slaves; (5) the development of writing: kings, priests, merchants, and artisans used writing to keep records; and (6) new forms of significant artistic and intellectual activity: for example, monumental architectural structures, usually religious, occupied a prominent place in urban environments.

The civilizations that developed in Mesopotamia and Egypt, the forerunners of Western civilization, will be examined in detail in this chapter. But civilization also developed independently in other parts of the world. Between 3000 and 1500 B.C., the valleys of the Indus River in India supported a flourishing civilization that extended hundreds of miles from the Himalayas to the coast of the Arabian Sea. Two major cities, Harappa and Mohenjo-Daro, were at the heart of this South Asian civilization. Many written records of the Indus valley civilization exist, but their language has not yet been deciphered. This Indus valley civilization carried on extensive trade with cities in Mesopotamia.

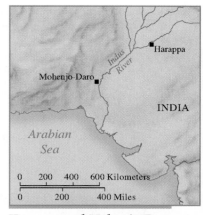

Harappa and Mohenjo-Daro

Another river valley civilization emerged along the Yellow River in northern China about 4,000 years ago. Under the Shang dynasty of kings, which ruled from 1750 to 1122 B.C., this civilization contained impressive cities with huge city walls, royal palaces, and large royal tombs. A system of irrigation enabled this early Chinese civilization to maintain a prosperous farming society ruled by an aristocratic class whose major concern was war.

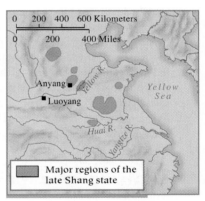

The Yellow River, China

Scholars have believed for a long time that civilization emerged only in four areas, in the fertile river valleys of the Tigris and Euphrates, the Nile, the Indus, and the Yellow River—that is, in Mesopotamia, Egypt, India, and China. Recently, however, archaeologists have discovered two other early civilizations. One of these flourished in Central Asia (in what are now the republics of Turkmenistan and Uzbekistan) around 4,000 years ago. People in this civilization built mudbrick buildings, raised sheep and goats, had bronze tools, used a system of irrigation to grow wheat and barley, and had a writing system.

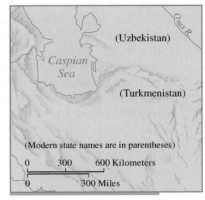

Central Asian Civilization

Another early civilization was discovered in the Supe River valley of Peru. At the center of this civilization was

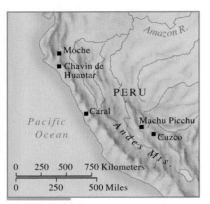

Caral, Peru

the city of Caral, which flourished around 2600 B.C. It contained buildings for officials, apartment buildings, and grand residences, all built of stone. The inhabitants of Caral also developed a system of irrigation by diverting a river more than a mile upstream into their fields.

Why early civilizations developed remains difficult to explain. One theory maintains that challenges forced human beings to make efforts that resulted in the rise of civilization. Some scholars have argued that material forces, such as the growth of food surpluses, made possible the specialization of labor and development of large communities with bureaucratic organization. But the area of the Fertile Crescent (see Map 1.2), in which Mesopotamian civilization emerged, was not naturally conducive to agriculture. Abundant food could be produced only with a massive human effort to manage the water, an undertaking that required organization and led to civilized societies. Other historians have argued that nonmaterial forces, primarily religious, provided the sense of unity and purpose that made such organized living possible. And some scholars doubt that we will ever discover the actual causes of early civilization.

Civilization in Mesopotamia

The Greeks spoke of the valley between the Tigris and Euphrates rivers as Mesopotamia, the "land between the rivers." The region receives little rain, but the soil of the plain of southern Mesopotamia was enlarged and enriched over the years by layers of silt deposited by the rivers. In late spring, the Tigris and Euphrates overflow their banks and deposit their fertile silt, but since this flooding depends on the melting of snows in the upland mountains where the rivers begin, it is irregular and sometimes catastrophic. In such circumstances, farming could be accomplished only with human intervention in the form of irrigation and drainage ditches. A complex system was required to control the flow of the rivers and produce the crops. Large-scale irrigation made possible the expansion of agriculture in this region, and the abundant food provided the material base for the emergence of civilization in Mesopotamia.

The City-States of Ancient Mesopotamia

The creators of Mesopotamian civilization were the Sumerians, a people whose origins remain unclear. By 3000

B.C., they had established a number of independent cities in southern Mesopotamia, including Eridu, Ur, Uruk, Umma, and Lagash. As cities expanded in size, they came to exercise political and economic control over the surrounding countryside, forming city-states. These city-states were the basic units of Sumerian civilization.

Sumerian Cities Sumerian cities were surrounded by walls. Uruk, for example, occupied an area of approximately 1,000 acres encircled by a wall 6 miles long with defense towers located every 30 to 35 feet along the wall. City dwellings, built of sun-dried bricks, included both the small flats of peasants and the larger dwellings of the civic and priestly officials. Although Mesopotamia had little stone or wood for building purposes, it did have plenty of mud. Mudbricks, easily shaped by hand, were left to bake in the hot sun until they were hard enough to use for building. People in Mesopotamia were remarkably inventive with mudbricks, constructing some of the largest brick buildings in the world.

The most prominent building in a Sumerian city was the temple, which was dedicated to the chief god or goddess of the city and often built atop a massive stepped tower called a **ziggurat**. The Sumerians believed that gods and goddesses owned the cities, and much wealth was used to build temples as well as elaborate houses for the priests and priestesses who served the gods. Priests and priestesses, who supervised the temples and their property, had great power. The temples owned much of the city land and livestock and served not only as the physical center of the city but also its economic and political center. In fact, historians believe that in the early stages of the city-states, priests and priestesses played an important role in ruling. The Sumerians believed that the gods ruled the cities, making the state a theocracy (government by a divine authority). Eventually, however, ruling power was shared with worldly figures known as kings.

Kingship Sumerians viewed kingship as divine in origin; they believed kings derived their power from the gods and were the agents of the gods. As one person said in a petition to his king: "You in your judgment, you are the son of Anu [god of the sky]; your commands, like the word of a god, cannot be reversed; your words, like rain pouring down from heaven, are without number."[2] Regardless of their origins, kings had power—they led armies, initiated legislation, supervised the building of public works, provided courts, and organized workers for the irrigation projects on which Mesopotamian agriculture depended. The army, the government bureaucracy, and the priests and priestesses all aided the kings in their rule.

Economy and Society The economy of the Sumerian city-states was primarily agricultural, but commerce and industry became important as well. The people of

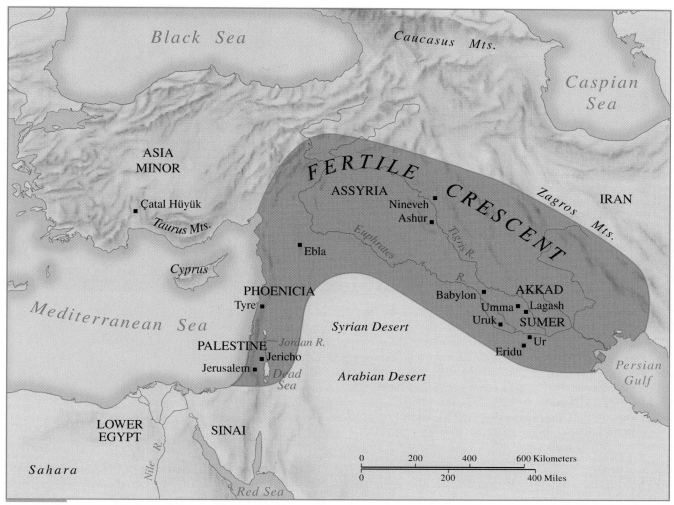

MAP 1.2 **The Ancient Near East.** The Fertile Crescent encompassed land with access to water. Employing flood management and irrigation systems, the peoples of the region established civilizations based on agriculture. These civilizations developed writing, law codes, and economic specialization. **?** What geographical aspects of the Mesopotamian city-states made conflict between them likely? **✐** **View an animated version of this map or related maps at** http://thomsonedu.com/history/spielvogel

Mesopotamia produced woolen textiles, pottery, and metalwork. Foreign trade, which was primarily a royal monopoly, could be extensive. Royal officials imported luxury items, such as copper and tin, aromatic woods, and fruit trees, in exchange for dried fish, wool, barley, wheat, and goods produced by Mesopotamian metalworkers. Traders traveled by land to the Mediterranean in the west and by sea to India in the east. The invention of the wheel around 3000 B.C. led to carts with wheels that made the transport of goods easier.

Sumerian city-states contained three major social groups: nobles, commoners, and slaves. Nobles included royal and priestly officials and their families. Commoners included the nobles' clients who worked for the palace and temple estates and other free citizens who worked as farmers, merchants, fishers, scribes, and craftspeople. At least 90 percent of the population were farmers. They could exchange their crops for the goods of the artisans in town markets. Slaves belonged to palace officials, who used them mostly in building projects; temple officials, who used mostly female slaves to weave cloth and grind grain; and rich landowners, who used them for farming and domestic work.

Empires in Ancient Mesopotamia

As the number of Sumerian city-states grew and the states expanded, conflicts arose as city-state fought city-state for control of land and water. The fortunes of various city-states rose and fell over the centuries. The constant wars, with their burning and sacking of cities, left many Sumerians in deep despair, as is evident in the words of this Sumerian poem from the city of Ur: "Ur is destroyed,

The "Royal Standard" of Ur. This detail is from the "Royal Standard" of Ur, a box dating from around 2700 B.C. that was discovered in a stone tomb from the royal cemetery of the Sumerian city-state of Ur. The scenes on one side of the box depict the activities of the king and his military forces. Shown in the bottom panel are four Sumerian battle chariots. Each chariot held two men, one who held the reins and the other armed with a spear for combat. A special compartment in the chariot held a number of spears. The charging chariots are seen defeating the enemy. In the middle band, the Sumerian soldiers round up the captured enemies. In the top band, the captives are presented to the king, who has alighted from his chariot and is shown standing above all the others in the center of the panel.

bitter is its lament. The country's blood now fills its holes like hot bronze in a mold. Bodies dissolve like fat in the sun. Our temple is destroyed; the gods have abandoned us, like migrating birds. Smoke lies on our city like a shroud."

Located on the flat land of Mesopotamia, the Sumerian city-states were also open to invasion. To the north of the Sumerian city-states lived the Akkadians. We call them a Semitic people because of the type of language they spoke (see Table 1.1). Around 2340 B.C., Sargon, leader of the Akkadians, overran the Sumerian city-states and established an empire that included most of Mesopotamia as well as lands westward to the Mediterranean. But the Akkadian empire eventually disintegrated, and its end by 2100 B.C. brought a return to the system of warring city-states until Ur-Nammu of Ur succeeded in reunifying most of Mesopotamia. But this final flowering of Sumerian

culture collapsed with the coming of the Amorites. Under Hammurabi, the Amorites, or Old Babylonians, a large group of Semitic-speaking seminomads, created a new empire.

Hammurabi (1792–1750 B.C.) employed a well-disciplined army of foot soldiers who carried axes, spears, and copper or bronze daggers. He learned to divide his opponents and subdue them one by one. Using such methods, he gained control of Sumer and Akkad and reunified Mesopotamia almost to the old borders created by Sargon of Akkad. After his conquests, he called himself "the sun of Babylon, the king who has made the four quarters of the world subservient," and established a new capital at Babylon, north of Akkad. He also built temples, defensive walls, and irrigation canals; encouraged trade; and brought about an economic revival. Indeed, Hammurabi saw himself as a shepherd to his people: "I am indeed the shepherd who brings

TABLE 1.1   Some Semitic Languages

Akkadian	*Canaanitic*
Arabic	Hebrew
Aramaic	*Phoenician*
Assyrian	*Syriac*
Babylonian	

NOTE: Languages in italic type are no longer spoken.

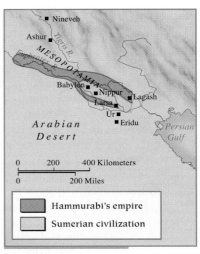

Hammurabi's Empire

THE CODE OF HAMMURABI

ammurabi's is the most complete Mesopotamian law code, although not the earliest. It was inscribed on a stone stele topped by a bas-relief picturing Hammurabi receiving the inspiration for the law code from the sun god Shamash, who was also the god of justice. The law code emphasizes the principle of an eye for an eye and punishments that vary according to social status. Punishments could be severe. The following examples illustrate these concerns.

The Code of Hammurabi

25. If fire broke out in a free man's house and a free man, who went to extinguish it, cast his eye on the goods of the owner of the house and has appropriated the goods of the owner of the house, that free man shall be thrown into that fire.

129. If the wife of a free man has been caught while lying with another man, they shall bind them and throw them into the water. If the husband of the woman wishes to spare his wife, then the king in turn may spare his subject.

131. If a free man's wife was accused by her husband, but she was not caught while lying with another man, she shall make affirmation by god and return to her house.

196. If a free man has destroyed the eye of a member of the aristocracy, they shall destroy his eye.

198. If he has destroyed the eye of a commoner or broken the bone of a commoner, he shall pay one mina of silver.

199. If he has destroyed the eye of a free man's slave or broken the bone of a free man's slave, he shall pay one-half his value.

209. If a free man struck another free man's daughter and has caused her to have a miscarriage, he shall pay ten shekels of silver for her fetus.

210. If that woman has died, they shall put his daughter to death.

211. If by a blow he has caused a commoner's daughter to have a miscarriage, he shall pay five shekels of silver.

212. If that woman has died, he shall pay one-half mina of silver.

213. If he struck a free man's female slave and has caused her to have a miscarriage, he shall pay two shekels of silver.

214. If that female slave has died, he shall pay one-third mina of silver.

What do these points of law from the Code of Hammurabi reveal to you about Mesopotamian society?

peace, whose scepter is just. My benevolent shade was spread over my city. I held the people of the lands of Sumer and Akkad safely on my lap."[3] Hammurabi left his dynasty strong enough that it survived until the 1550s B.C. when the Kassites from the northeast took over.

The Code of Hammurabi Hammurabi is best remembered for his law code, a collection of 282 laws. For centuries, laws had regulated people's relationships with one another in the lands of Mesopotamia, but only fragments of these earlier codes survive. Although many scholars today view Hammurabi's collection less as a code of laws and more as the attempt of Hammurabi to portray himself as the source of justice to the people, the code still gives us a glimpse of the Babylonian society of his time (see the box above).

The Code of Hammurabi reveals a society with a system of strict justice. Penalties for criminal offenses were severe and varied according to the social class of the victim. A crime against a member of the upper class (a noble) was punished more severely than the same offense against a member of the lower class. Moreover, the principle of "an eye for an eye, a tooth for a tooth" was fundamental to this system of justice. This meant that punishments should fit the crime: "If a freeman has destroyed the eye of a member of the aristocracy, they shall destroy his eye." Hammurabi's code also had an

impact on legal ideas in southwestern Asia for hundreds of years, as the following verse from the Hebrew Bible demonstrates: "If anyone injures his neighbor, whatever he has done must be done to him: fracture for fracture, eye for eye, tooth for tooth. As he has injured the other, so he is to be injured" (Leviticus 24:19–20).

Hammurabi's code took the responsibilities of public officials very seriously. The governor of an area and city officials were expected to catch burglars. If they failed to do so, the officials in the district where the crime was committed had to replace the lost property. If murderers were not found, the officials had to pay a fine to the relatives of the murdered person.

The law code also furthered the proper performance of work with what amounted to consumer protection laws. Builders were held responsible for the buildings they constructed. If a house collapsed and caused the death of the owner, the builder was put to death. If the collapse caused the death of the son of the owner, the son of the builder was put to death. If goods were destroyed by the collapse, they had to be replaced and the house itself reconstructed at the builder's expense.

The largest number of laws in the Code of Hammurabi focused on marriage and the family. Parents arranged marriages for their children. After marriage, the parties involved signed a marriage contract; without it, no one was considered legally married. The husband provided a bridal payment, and the woman's parents were responsible for a dowry to the new husband.

As in many patriarchal societies, women had far fewer privileges and rights in marriage than men. A woman's place was in the home, and failure to fulfill her expected duties was grounds for divorce. If she was not able to bear children, her husband could divorce her, but he did have to return the dowry to her family. If his wife tried to leave home to engage in business, thus neglecting her house, her husband could divorce her and did not have to repay the dowry. Furthermore, a wife who was a "gadabout, . . . neglecting her house [and] humiliating her husband," could be drowned. We do know that in practice not all women remained at home. Some worked in the fields and others in business, where they were especially prominent in the running of taverns.

Women were guaranteed some rights, however. If a woman was divorced without good reason, she received the dowry back. A woman could seek divorce and get her dowry back if her husband was unable to show that she had done anything wrong. In theory, a wife was guaranteed use of her husband's property in the event of his death. The mother could also decide which of her sons would receive an inheritance.

Sexual relations were strictly regulated as well. Husbands, but not wives, were permitted sexual activity outside marriage. A wife and her lover caught committing adultery were pitched into the river, although if the husband pardoned his wife, the king could pardon the guilty man. Incest was strictly forbidden. If a father had incestuous relations with his daughter, he would be banished. Incest between a son and mother resulted in both being burned.

Fathers ruled their children as well as their wives. Obedience was duly expected: "If a son has struck his father, they shall cut off his hand." If a son committed a serious enough offense, his father could disinherit him, although fathers were not permitted to disinherit their sons arbitrarily.

The Culture of Mesopotamia

A spiritual worldview was of fundamental importance to Mesopotamian culture. To the peoples of Mesopotamia, the gods were living realities who affected all aspects of life. It was crucial, therefore, that the correct hierarchies be observed. Leaders could prepare armies for war, but success depended on a favorable relationship with the gods. This helps explain the importance of the priestly class and is the reason why even the kings took great care to dedicate offerings and monuments to the gods.

The Importance of Religion The Mesopotamians viewed their city-states as earthly copies of a divine model and order. Each city-state was sacred because it was linked to a god or goddess. Hence Nippur, the earliest center of Sumerian religion, was dedicated to Enlil, the god of wind. Moreover, located at the heart of each city-state was a temple complex. Occupying several acres, this sacred area consisted of a ziggurat with a temple at the top dedicated to the god or goddess who owned the city. The temple complex was the true center of the community. The main god or goddess dwelt there symbolically in the form of a statue, and the ceremony of dedication included a ritual that linked the statue to the god or goddess and thus supposedly harnessed the power of the deity for the city's benefit. Considerable wealth was poured into the construction of temples and other buildings used for the residences of priests and priestesses who helped the gods. Although the gods literally owned the city, the temple complex used only part of the land and rented out the remainder. The temples dominated individual and commercial life, an indication of the close relationship between Mesopotamian religion and culture.

The physical environment had an obvious impact on the Mesopotamian view of the universe. Ferocious floods, heavy downpours, scorching winds, and oppressive humidity were all part of the local climate. These conditions and the resulting famines easily convinced Mesopotamians that this world was controlled by supernatural forces and that the days of human beings "are numbered; whatever he may do, he is but wind," as *The Epic of Gilgamesh* laments. In the presence of nature, Mesopotamians could easily feel helpless, as this poem relates:

> *The rampant flood which no man can oppose,*
> *Which shakes the heavens and causes earth to tremble,*
> *In an appalling blanket folds mother and child,*
> *Beats down the canebrake's full luxuriant greenery,*
> *And drowns the harvest in its time of ripeness.*[4]

The Mesopotamians discerned cosmic rhythms in the universe and accepted its order but perceived that it was not completely safe because of the presence of willful, powerful cosmic powers that they identified with gods and goddesses.

With its numerous gods and goddesses animating all aspects of the universe, Mesopotamian religion was **polytheistic**. The four most important deities were An, Enlil, Enki, and Ninhursaga. An was the god of the sky and hence the most important force in the universe. Since his basic essence was authority, he was also viewed as the source or active principle of all authority, including the earthly power of rulers and fathers alike. Enlil, god of wind, was considered the second greatest power of the visible universe. In charge of the wind and thus an expression of the legitimate use of force, Enlil became the symbol of the proper use of force on earth as well. Enki was god of the earth. Since the earth was the source of life-giving waters, Enki was also god of rivers, wells, and canals. More generally, he represented the waters of creativity and was responsible for inventions and crafts. Ninhursaga began as a goddess associated with soil, mountains, and vegetation. Eventually, however, she was worshiped as a mother goddess, a "mother of all children," who manifested her power by giving birth to kings and conferring the royal insignia on them.

Human beings' relationship with their gods was based on subservience since, according to Sumerian myth, human beings were created to do the manual labor the gods were unwilling to do for themselves. Moreover, humans were insecure because they could never be sure what the gods would do. But humans did make attempts to circumvent or relieve their anxiety by discovering the intentions of the gods; these efforts gave rise to the development of the arts of **divination**.

Divination took a variety of forms. A common form, at least for kings and priests who could afford it, in-volved killing animals, such as sheep or goats, and examining their livers or other organs. Supposedly, features seen in the organs of the sacrificed animals foretold events to come. One handbook predicted that if the animal organ had shape x, the outcome of the military campaign would be y. Private individuals relied on cheaper divinatory techniques. These included interpreting patterns of smoke from burning incense or the pattern formed when oil was poured into water. The Mesopotamian arts of divination arose out of the desire to discover the purposes of the gods: if people could decipher the signs that foretold events, the events would be predictable, and humans could act wisely.

The Cultivation of New Arts and Sciences The realization of writing's great potential was another aspect of Mesopotamian culture. The oldest Mesopotamian texts date to around 3000 B.C. and were written by the Sumerians, who used a **cuneiform** ("wedge-shaped") system of writing. Using a reed stylus, they made wedge-shaped impressions on clay tablets, which were then baked or dried in the sun. Once dried, these tablets were virtually indestructible, and the several hundred thousand that have been discovered have served as a valuable source of information for modern scholars. Sumerian writing evolved from pictures of physical objects to simplified and stylized signs, leading eventually to a phonetic system that made possible the written expression of abstract ideas.

Mesopotamian peoples used writing primarily for record keeping. They also produced monumental texts, documents that were intended to last forever, such as

The Development of Cuneiform Writing. Pictured here is the cone of Uruinimgina, an example of cuneiform writing from an early Sumerian dynasty. The inscription announces reductions in taxes. The table shows the development of writing from pictographic signs to cuneiform characters.

	star	?sun over horizon	?stream	ear of barley	bull's head	bowl	head + bowl	lower leg	?shrouded body
Pictographic sign, c. 3100 B.C.									
Interpretation	star	?sun over horizon	?stream	ear of barley	bull's head	bowl	head + bowl	lower leg	?shrouded body
Cuneiform sign, c. 2400 B.C.									
Cuneiform sign c. 700 B.C. (turned through 90°)									
Phonetic value*	dingir, an	u_4, ud	a	še	gu_4	nig_2, ninda	ku_2	du, gin, gub	lu_2
Meaning	god, sky	day, sun	water, seed, son	barley	ox	food, bread	to eat	to walk, to stand	man

*Some signs have more than one phonetic value and some sounds are represented by more than one sign; for example, u_4 means the fourth sign with the value u.

Courtesy Andromeda Oxford Limited, Oxford, England (Louvre, Paris)

THE GREAT FLOOD

The great poem of Mesopotamian literature, *The Epic of Gilgamesh,* includes an account by Utnapishtim (a Mesopotamian forerunner of the biblical Noah), who had built a ship and survived the flood unleashed by the gods to destroy humankind. This selection recounts how the god Ea advised Utnapishtim to build a boat and how he came to land his boat at the end of the flood. In this section, Utnapishtim is telling his story to Gilgamesh.

The Epic of Gilgamesh

"In those days the world teemed, the people multiplied, the world bellowed like a wild bull, and the great god was aroused by the clamor. Enlil heard the clamor and he said to the gods in council, 'The uproar of mankind is intolerable and sleep is no longer possible by reason of the babel.' So the gods agreed to exterminate mankind. Enlil did this, but Ea [Sumerian Enki, god of the waters] because of his oath warned me in a dream . . . , 'Tear down your house and build a boat, abandon possessions and look for life, despise worldly goods and save your soul alive. Tear down your house, I say, and build a boat. . . . Then take up into the boat the seed of all living creatures. . . .' [Utnapishtim did as he was told, and then the destruction came.]

"For six days and six nights the winds blew, torrent and tempest and flood overwhelmed the world, tempest and flood raged together like warring hosts. When the seventh day dawned the storm from the south subsided, the sea grew calm, the flood was stifled; I looked at the face of the world and there was silence, all mankind was turned to clay. The surface of the sea stretched as flat as a rooftop; I opened a hatch and the light fell on my face. Then I bowed low, I sat down and I wept, the tears streamed down my face, for on every side was the waste of water. I looked for land in vain, but fourteen leagues distant there appeared a mountain, and there the boat grounded; on the mountain of Nisir the boat held fast, she held fast and did not budge. . . . When the seventh day dawned I loosed a dove and let her go. She flew away, but finding no resting-place she returned. Then I loosed a swallow, and she flew away but finding no resting-place she returned. I loosed a raven, she saw that the waters had retreated, she ate, she flew around, she cawed, and she did not come back. Then I threw everything open to the four winds, I made a sacrifice and poured out a libation on the mountain top."

What does this selection from The Epic of Gilgamesh *tell you about the relationship between the Mesopotamians and their gods? How might you explain the difference between this account and the biblical flood story in* Genesis?

---

inscriptions etched in stone on statues and royal buildings. Numerous texts were prepared for teaching purposes. Schools for scribes were in operation by 2500 B.C. They were necessary because much time was needed to master the cuneiform system of writing. The primary goal of scribal education was to produce professionally trained scribes for careers in the temples and palaces, the military, and government. Pupils were male and primarily from wealthy families.

Writing was important because it enabled a society to keep records and maintain knowledge of previous practices and events. Writing also made it possible for people to communicate ideas in new ways, which is especially evident in Mesopotamian literary works. The most famous piece of Mesopotamian literature was *The Epic of Gilgamesh,* an elaborate poem that records the exploits of a legendary king of Uruk. Gilgamesh—wise, strong, and perfect in body, part man, part god—befriends a hairy beast named Enkidu. Together they set off in pursuit of heroic deeds. When Enkidu dies, Gilgamesh experiences the pain of mortality and embarks on a search for the secret of immortality. But his efforts fail (see the box above), and Gilgamesh remains mortal. The desire for immortality, one of humankind's great searches, ends in complete frustration. Everlasting life, this Mesopotamian epic makes clear, is only for the gods.

Mesopotamians also made outstanding achievements in mathematics and astronomy. In math, the Sumerians devised a number system based on 60, using combinations of 6 and 10 for practical solutions. Geometry was used to measure fields and erect buildings. In astronomy, the Sumerians made use of units of 60 and charted the heavenly constellations. Their calendar was based on twelve lunar months and was brought into harmony with the solar year by adding an extra month from time to time.

Egyptian Civilization: "The Gift of the Nile"

Although contemporaneous with Mesopotamia, civilization in Egypt evolved along somewhat different lines. Of central importance to the development of Egyptian civilization was the Nile River. That the Egyptian people recognized its significance is apparent in this Hymn to the Nile (also see the box on p. 13): "The bringer of food, rich in provisions, creator of all good, lord of majesty, sweet of fragrance. . . . He who . . . fills the magazines, makes the granaries wide, and gives things to the poor. He who makes every beloved tree to grow. . . ."[5] Egypt, like Mesopotamia, was a river valley civilization.

SIGNIFICANCE OF THE NILE RIVER AND THE PHARAOH

Two of the most important sources of life for the ancient Egyptians were the Nile River and the pharaoh. Egyptians perceived that the Nile River made possible the abundant food that was a major source of their well-being. This *Hymn to the Nile*, probably from the nineteenth and twentieth dynasties in the New Kingdom, expresses the gratitude Egyptians felt for the Nile.

Hymn to the Nile

> Hail to you, O Nile, that issues from the earth and comes to keep Egypt alive! . . .
>
> He that waters the meadows which Re created, in order to keep every kid alive.
>
> He that makes to drink the desert and the place distant from water: that is his dew coming down from heaven. . . .
>
> The lord of fishes, he who makes the marsh-birds to go upstream. . . .
>
> He who makes barley and brings emmer [wheat] into being, that he may make the temples festive.
>
> If he is sluggish, then nostrils are stopped up, and everybody is poor. . . .
>
> When he rises, then the land is in jubilation, then every belly is in joy, every backbone takes on laughter, and every tooth is exposed.
>
> The bringer of good, rich in provisions, creator of all good, lord of majesty, sweet of fragrance. . . .
>
> He who makes every beloved tree to grow, without lack of them.

The Egyptian king, or pharaoh, was viewed as a god and the absolute ruler of Egypt. His significance and the gratitude of the Egyptian people for his existence are evident in this hymn from the reign of Sesotris III (c. 1880–1840 B.C.).

Hymn to the Pharaoh

> He has come unto us that he may carry away Upper Egypt; the double diadem [crown of Upper and Lower Egypt] has rested on his head.
>
> He has come unto us and has united the Two Lands; he has mingled the reed with the bee [symbols of Lower and Upper Egypt].
>
> He has come unto us and has brought the Black Land under his sway; he has apportioned to himself the Red Land.
>
> He has come unto us and has taken the Two Lands under his protection; he has given peace to the Two Riverbanks.
>
> He has come unto us and has made Egypt to live; he has banished its suffering.
>
> He has come unto us and has made the people to live; he has caused the throat of the subjects to breathe. . . .
>
> He has come unto us and has done battle for his boundaries; he has delivered them that were robbed.

How do these hymns underscore the importance to Egyptian civilization of the Nile River and the institution of the pharaoh?

The Impact of Geography

The Nile is a unique river, beginning in the heart of Africa and coursing northward for thousands of miles. It is the longest river in the world. Thanks to the Nile, an area several miles wide on both banks of the river was capable of producing abundant harvests. The "miracle" of the Nile was its annual flooding. The river rose in the summer from rains in Central Africa, crested in Egypt in September and October, and left a deposit of silt that enriched the soil. The Egyptians called this fertile land the "Black Land" because it was dark from the silt and the lush crops that grew on it. Beyond these narrow strips of fertile fields lay the deserts (the "Red Land").

Unlike the floods of Mesopotamia's rivers, the flooding of the Nile was gradual and usually predictable, and the river itself was seen as life-enhancing, not life-threatening. Although a system of organized irrigation was still necessary, the small villages along the Nile could make the effort without the massive state intervention that was required in Mesopotamia. Egyptian civilization consequently tended to remain more rural, with many small population centers congregated along a narrow band on both sides of the Nile. About 100 miles before it empties into the Mediterranean, the river splits into two major branches, forming the delta, a triangular-shaped territory called Lower Egypt to distinguish it from Upper Egypt, the land upstream to the south (see Map 1.3). Egypt's important cities developed at the tip of the delta. Even today, most of Egypt's people are crowded along the banks of the Nile River.

The surpluses of food that Egyptian farmers grew in the fertile Nile valley made Egypt prosperous. But the Nile also served a unifying factor in Egyptian history. In

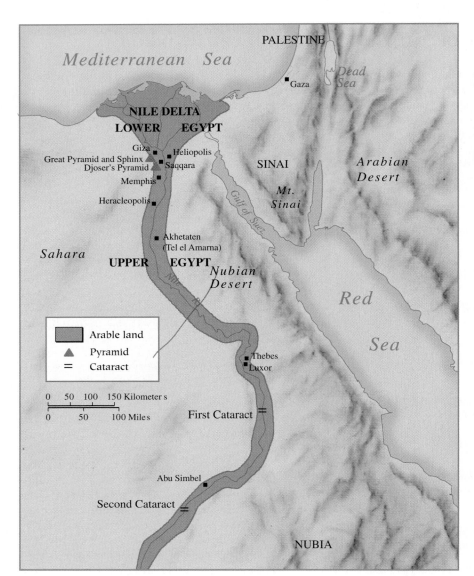

MAP 1.3 **Ancient Egypt.**
Egyptian civilization centered on the life-giving water and flood silts of the Nile River, with most of the population living in Lower Egypt, where the river splits to form the Nile delta. Most of the pyramids, built during the Old Kingdom, are clustered at the entrance to the delta. **?** How did the lands to the east and west of the river make invasions of Egypt difficult? 🖛 **View an animated version of this map or related maps at** http://thomsonedu.com/history/spielvogel

ancient times, the Nile was the fastest way to travel through the land, making both transportation and communication easier. Winds from the north pushed sailboats south, and the current of the Nile carried them north. Often when they headed downstream (north), people used long poles or paddles to propel their boats forward.

Unlike Mesopotamia, which was subject to constant invasion, Egypt was blessed by natural barriers that fostered isolation, protected it from invasion, and gave it a sense of security. These barriers included the deserts to the west and east; the cataracts (rapids) on the southern part of the Nile, which made defense relatively easy; and the Mediterranean Sea to the north. These barriers, however, did not prevent the development of trade.

In essence, Egyptian geography and topography played important roles in the early history of the country. The regularity of the Nile floods and the relative isolation of the Egyptians created a sense of security that was accompanied by a feeling of changelessness. Egyptian civilization was characterized by a remarkable degree of continuity over thousands of years. It was no accident that Egyptians believed in cyclical rather than linear progress. Just as the sun passed through its daily cycle and the Nile its annual overflow, Egyptian kings reaffirmed the basic, unchanging principles of justice at the beginning of each new cycle of rule.

The Old and Middle Kingdoms

The basic framework for the study of Egyptian history was provided by Manetho, an Egyptian priest and historian who lived in the early third century B.C. He divided Egyptian history into thirty-one dynasties of kings. Using Manetho's and other lists of kings, modern historians have divided Egyptian history into three major periods known as the Old Kingdom, the Middle Kingdom, and the New Kingdom. These were periods of long-term stability characterized by strong monarchical authority, competent bureaucracy, freedom from invasion, the construction of temples and pyramids, and

CHRONOLOGY	The Egyptians	
Early Dynastic Period (dynasties 1–2)		c. 3100–2686 B.C.
Old Kingdom (dynasties 3–6)		c. 2686–2125 B.C.
First Intermediate Period (dynasties 7–10)		c. 2125–2055 B.C.
Middle Kingdom (dynasties 11–12)		c. 2055–1650 B.C.
Second Intermediate Period (dynasties 13–17)		c. 1650–1550 B.C.
New Kingdom (dynasties 18–20)		c. 1550–1070 B.C.
Postempire Egypt (dynasties 21–31)		1070–30 B.C.

considerable intellectual and cultural activity. But between the periods of stability were times of political chaos known as the Intermediate Periods, characterized by weak political structures and rivalry for leadership, invasions, a decline in building activity, and a restructuring of society.

According to the Egyptians' own tradition, their land consisted initially of numerous populated areas ruled by tribal chieftains. Around 3100 B.C., the first Egyptian royal dynasty, under a king called Menes, united Upper and Lower Egypt into a single kingdom. Henceforth the king would be called "King of Upper and Lower Egypt," and the royal crown would be a double diadem, signifying the unification of all Egypt. Just as the Nile served to unite Upper and Lower Egypt physically, kingship served to unite the two areas politically.

The Old Kingdom The Old Kingdom encompassed the third through sixth dynasties of Egyptian kings, lasting from around 2686 to 2125 B.C. It was an age of prosperity and splendor, made visible in the construction of the greatest and largest pyramids in Egypt's history. The capital of the Old Kingdom was located at Memphis, south of the delta.

Kingship was a divine institution in ancient Egypt and formed part of a universal cosmic scheme (see the box on p. 13): "What is the king of Upper and Lower Egypt? He is a god by whose dealings one lives, the father and mother of all men, alone by himself, without an equal."[6] In obeying their king, subjects helped maintain the cosmic order. A breakdown in royal power could only mean that citizens were offending divinity and weakening the universal structure. Among the various titles of Egyptian kings, pharaoh (originally meaning "great house" or "palace") eventually came to be the most common.

Although they possessed absolute power, Egyptian kings were supposed to rule not arbitrarily but according to set principles. The chief principle was called *Ma'at,* a spiritual precept that conveyed the idea of truth and justice, especially right order and harmony. To ancient Egyptians, this fundamental order and harmony had existed throughout the universe since the beginning of

time. Pharaohs were the divine instruments who maintained it and were themselves subject to it.

Although theoretically absolute in their power, in practice Egyptian kings did not rule alone. Initially, members of the king's family performed administrative tasks, but by the fourth dynasty, a bureaucracy with regular procedures had developed. Especially important was the office of vizier, "steward of the whole land." Directly responsible to the king, the vizier was in charge of the bureaucracy, with its numerous departments, including police, justice, river transport, and public works. Agriculture and the treasury were the most important departments. Agriculture was, of course, the backbone of Egyptian prosperity, and the treasury collected taxes, which were paid in kind. A careful assessment of land and tenants was undertaken to provide the tax base.

For administrative purposes, Egypt was divided into provinces or nomes, as they were later called by the Greeks—twenty-two in Upper and twenty in Lower Egypt. A governor, called by the Greeks a nomarch, was head of each nome and was responsible to the king and vizier. Nomarchs, however, tended to build up large holdings of land and power within their nomes, creating a potential rivalry with the pharaohs.

The Middle Kingdom Despite the theory of divine order, the Old Kingdom eventually collapsed, ushering in a period of chaos. Eventually, a new royal dynasty managed to pacify all Egypt and inaugurated the Middle Kingdom, a new period of stability lasting from around 2055 to 1650 B.C. Several factors contributed to its vitality. The nome structure was reorganized. The boundaries of each nome were now settled precisely, and the obligations of the nomes to the state were clearly delineated. Nomarchs were confirmed as hereditary officeholders but with the understanding that their duties must be performed faithfully. These included the collection of taxes for the state and the recruitment of labor forces for royal projects, such as stone quarrying.

The Middle Kingdom was characterized by a new concern on the part of the pharaohs for the people. In the Old Kingdom, the pharaoh had been viewed as an inaccessible god-king. Now he was portrayed as the shepherd of his people with the responsibility to build public works and provide for the public welfare. As one pharaoh expressed it, "He [a particular god] created me as one who should do that which he had done, and to carry out that which he commanded should be done. He appointed me herdsman of this land, for he knew who would keep it in order for him."[7]

Society and Economy in Ancient Egypt

Egyptian society had a simple structure in the Old and Middle Kingdoms; basically, it was organized along hierarchical lines with the god-king at the top. The king was surrounded by an upper class of nobles and priests who participated in the elaborate rituals of life that surrounded the pharaoh. This ruling class ran the government and managed its own landed estates, which provided much of its wealth.

Below the upper classes were merchants and artisans. Merchants engaged in active trade up and down the Nile as well as in town and village markets. Some merchants also engaged in international trade; they were sent by the king to Crete and Syria, where they obtained wood and other products. Expeditions traveled into Nubia for ivory and down the Red Sea to Punt for incense and spices. Egyptian artisans displayed unusually high standards of craftsmanship and beauty and produced an incredible variety of goods: stone dishes; beautifully painted boxes made of clay; wooden furniture; gold, silver, and copper tools and containers; paper and rope made of papyrus; and linen clothing.

The largest number of people in Egypt simply worked the land. In theory, the king owned all the land but granted portions of it to his subjects. Large sections were in the possession of nobles and the temple complexes. Most of the lower classes were serfs or common people who were bound to the land and cultivated the estates. They paid taxes in the form of crops to the king, nobles, and priests, lived in small villages or towns, and provided military service and forced labor for building projects.

The Culture of Egypt

Egypt produced a culture that dazzled and awed its later conquerors. The Egyptians' technical achievements alone, especially visible in the construction of the pyramids, demonstrated a measure of skill unique in the world at that time. To the Egyptians, all of these achievements were part of a cosmic order suffused with the presence of the divine.

Spiritual Life in Egyptian Society The Egyptians had no word for religion because it was an inseparable element of existence in the world in which they lived. The Egyptians had a remarkable number of gods associated with heavenly bodies and natural forces. Two groups, sun gods and land gods, came to have special prominence, hardly unusual in view of the importance to Egypt's well-being of the sun, the river, and the fertile land along its banks. The sun was the source of life and hence worthy of worship. A sun cult developed, and the sun god took on different forms and names, depending on his specific function. He was worshiped as Atum in human form and as Re, who had a human body but the head of a falcon. The pharaoh took the title "Son of Re" because he was regarded as the earthly embodiment of Re.

River and land deities included Osiris and Isis with their child Horus, who was related to the Nile and to the sun as well. Osiris became especially important as a symbol of resurrection. A famous Egyptian myth told of the struggle between Osiris, who brought civilization to Egypt, and his evil brother Seth, who killed him, cut his body into fourteen parts, and tossed them into the Nile. Osiris's faithful wife, Isis, found the pieces and, with help from other gods, restored Osiris to life. As a symbol of resurrection and as judge of the dead, Osiris took on an important role for the Egyptians. By identifying with Osiris, one could hope to gain new life, just as Osiris had done. The dead, embalmed and mummified, were placed in tombs (in the case of kings, in pyramidal tombs), given the name of Osiris, and by a process of magical identification became Osiris. Like Osiris, they would then be reborn. The flood of the Nile and the new life it brought to Egypt were symbolized by Isis gathering all of Osiris' parts together and were celebrated each spring in the festival of the new land.

Later Egyptian spiritual practice began to emphasize morality by stressing Osiris' role as judge of the dead. The dead were asked to give an account of their earthly deeds to show whether they deserved a reward. Other means were also employed to gain immortality. Magical incantations, preserved in the *Book of the Dead*, were used to ensure a favorable journey to a happy afterlife. Specific instructions explained what to do when confronted by the judge of the dead. These instructions had two aspects. The negative confession gave a detailed list of what one had not done:

> *I have not committed evil against men.*
> *I have not mistreated cattle.*
> *I have not blasphemed a god. . . .*
> *I have not done violence to a poor man. . . .*
> *I have not made anyone sick. . . .*
> *I have not killed. . . .*
> *I have not caused anyone suffering. . . .*
> *I have not had sexual relations with a boy.*
> *I have not defiled myself.*[8]

Later the supplicant made a speech listing his good actions: "I have done that which men said and that with which gods are content. . . . I have given bread to the hungry, water to the thirsty, clothing to the naked, and a ferry-boat to him who was marooned. I have provided divine offerings for the gods and mortuary offerings for the dead."[9]

The Pyramids One of the great achievements of Egyptian civilization, the building of pyramids, occurred in the time of the Old Kingdom. Pyramids were not built in isolation but as part of a larger complex dedicated to the dead—in effect, a city of the dead. The area included a large pyramid for the king's burial, smaller pyramids for his family, and mastabas, rectangular structures with flat roofs, as tombs for the pharaoh's noble officials. The tombs were well prepared for their residents. The rooms were furnished and stocked with numerous supplies, including chairs, boats, chests, weapons, games, dishes, and a variety of foods. The Egyptians believed that human beings had two bodies, a physical one and a

Osiris as Judge of the Dead.   According to the *Book of the Dead*, after making a denial of offenses (the "negative confession"), the deceased experienced the "weighing of the heart." Shown here is a judgment scene from the *Book of the Dead* of Hunefer, a royal scribe who died around 1285 B.C. Hunefer's heart is placed on one side of a balance scale; on the other side is the feather of Ma'at, the goddess of truth. For Hunefer, heart and feather are of equal weight, so the god Anubis ushers him into the presence of Osiris, seated on his throne at the right. A "swallowing monster," a hybrid creature of crocodile, lion, and hippopotamus, stood ready at the scale to devour the deceased if he failed the test.

spiritual one, which they called the *ka*. If the physical body was properly preserved (that is, mummified) and the tomb furnished with all the various objects of regular life, the *ka* could return and continue its life despite the death of the physical body.

To preserve the physical body after death, the Egyptians practiced mummification, a process of slowly drying a dead body to prevent it from rotting. Special workshops, run by priests, performed this procedure, primarily for the wealthy families who could afford it. According to Herodotus, an ancient Greek historian (see Chapter 3) who visited Egypt around 450 B.C., "The most refined method is as follows: first of all they draw out the brain through the nostrils with an iron hook. . . . Then they make an incision in the flank with a sharp Ethiopian stone through which they extract all the internal organs."[10] The liver, lungs, stomach, and intestines were placed in four special jars that were put in the tomb with the mummy. The priests then covered the corpse with a natural salt that absorbed the body's water. Later, they filled the body with spices and wrapped it with layers of linen soaked in resin. At the end of the process, which took about seventy days, a lifelike mask was placed over the head and shoulders of the mummy, which was then sealed in a case and placed in its tomb in a pyramid.

The largest and most magnificent of all the pyramids was built under King Khufu. Constructed at Giza around 2540 B.C., this famous Great Pyramid covers 13 acres, measures 756 feet at each side of its base, and stands 481 feet high. Its four sides are almost precisely oriented to the four points of the compass. The interior included a grand gallery to the burial chamber, which was built of granite with a lidless sarcophagus for the pharaoh's body. The Great Pyramid still stands as a visible symbol of the power of Egyptian kings and the spiritual conviction that underlay Egyptian society. No later pyramid ever matched its size or splendor. But an Egyptian pyramid was not just the king's tomb; it was also an important symbol of royal power. It could be seen for miles as a visible reminder of the glory and might of the ruler, who was a living god on earth.

Art and Writing   Commissioned by kings or nobles for use in temples and tombs, Egyptian art was largely functional. Wall paintings and statues of gods and kings in temples served a strictly spiritual purpose. They were an integral part of the performance of ritual, which was thought necessary to preserve the cosmic order and hence the well-being of Egypt. Likewise, the mural scenes and sculptured figures found in the tombs had a specific

The Pyramids at Giza. The three pyramids at Giza, across the Nile River from Cairo, are the most famous in Egypt. At the rear is the largest of the three pyramids—the Great Pyramid of Khufu. Next to it is the pyramid of Khafre. In the foreground is the smaller pyramid of Menkaure standing behind the even smaller pyramids for the pharaohs' wives. Covering almost 13 acres, the Great Pyramid of Khufu is immense. It is estimated that the Great Pyramid contains 2.3 million stone blocks, each weighing about 2.5 tons.

function. They were supposed to aid the journey of the deceased into the afterworld.

Egyptian art was also formulaic. Artists and sculptors were expected to observe a strict canon of proportions that determined both form and presentation. This canon gave Egyptian art a distinctive appearance for thousands of years. Especially characteristic was the convention of combining the profile, semiprofile, and frontal views of the human body in relief work and painting in order to represent each part of the body accurately. The result was an art that was highly stylized yet still allowed distinctive features to be displayed.

Writing in Egypt emerged during the first two dynasties. The Greeks later labeled Egyptian writing **hieroglyphics**, meaning "priest carvings" or "sacred writings." Hieroglyphs were symbols that depicted objects and had a sacred value at the same time. Although hieroglyphs were later simplified into two scripts for writing purposes, they never developed into an alphabet. Egyptian hieroglyphs were initially carved in stone, but later the two simplified scripts were written on papyrus, a paper made from the papyrus reed that grew along the Nile. Most of the ancient Egyptian literature that has come down to us was written on papyrus rolls and wooden tablets.

Chaos and a New Order: The New Kingdom

The Middle Kingdom was brought to an end by a new period of instability. An incursion into the delta region by a people known as the Hyksos initiated this second age of chaos. The Hyksos, a Semitic-speaking people, infiltrated Egypt in the seventeenth century B.C. and

came to dominate much of Egypt. However, the presence of the Hyksos was not entirely negative for Egypt. They taught the Egyptians to make bronze for use in new agricultural tools and weapons. The Hyksos also brought new aspects of warfare to Egypt, including the horse-drawn war chariot, a heavier sword, and the compound bow. Eventually, a new line of pharaohs—the eighteenth dynasty—made use of the new weapons to throw off Hyksos domination, reunite Egypt, establish the New Kingdom (c. 1550–1070 B.C.), and launch the Egyptians along a new militaristic and imperialistic path. During the period of the New Kingdom, Egypt became the most powerful state in the Middle East. The Egyptians occupied Palestine and Syria but permitted local princes to rule under Egyptian control. Egyptian armies also moved westward into Libya and expanded Egypt's border to the south by conquering the African kingdom of Nubia.

The eighteenth dynasty was not without its own troubles, however. Amenhotep IV (c. 1364–1347 B.C.) introduced the worship of Aten, god of the sun disk, as the chief god and pursued his worship with great enthusiasm. Changing his own name to Akhenaten ("it is well with Aten"), the pharaoh closed the temples of other gods and especially endeavored to lessen the power of Amon-Re and his priesthood at Thebes. Akhenaten strove to reduce the priests' influence by replacing Thebes as the capital of Egypt with Akhetaten ("dedicated to Aten"), a new city located near modern Tel el Amarna, 200 miles north of Thebes.

Akhenaten's attempt at religious change failed. It was too much to ask Egyptians to ignore their traditional ways and beliefs, especially since they saw the destruction of the old gods as subversive of the very cosmic order on which Egypt's survival and continuing prosperity depended. Moreover, the priests at Thebes were unalterably opposed to the changes, which diminished their influence and power. At the same time, Akhenaten's preoccupation with religion caused him to ignore foreign affairs and led to the loss of both Syria and Palestine. Akhenaten's changes were soon undone after his death by those who influenced his successor, the boy-pharaoh Tutankhamen (1347–1338 B.C.). Tutankhamen returned the government to Thebes and restored the old gods. The Aten experiment had failed to take hold, and the eighteenth dynasty itself came to an end in 1333 B.C.

The nineteenth dynasty managed to restore Egyptian power one more time. Under Rameses II (c. 1279–1213 B.C.), the Egyptians regained control of Palestine but were unable to reestablish the borders of their earlier empire. New invasions in the thirteenth century by the "Sea Peoples," as the Egyptians called them, destroyed Egyptian power in Palestine and drove the Egyptians back within their old frontiers. The days of Egyptian empire were ended, and the New Kingdom itself expired with the end of the twentieth dynasty in 1070 B.C. For the next thousand years, despite periodical revivals of strength, Egypt was dominated by Libyans, Nubians, Persians, and finally Macedonians after the conquest of Alexander the Great (see Chapter 4). In the first century B.C., Egypt became a province in Rome's mighty empire.

Daily Life in Ancient Egypt: Family and Marriage

Ancient Egyptians had a very positive attitude toward daily life on earth and followed the advice of the wisdom literature, which suggested that people marry young and establish a home and family. Monogamy was the general rule, although a husband was allowed to keep additional wives if his first wife was childless. Pharaohs were entitled to harems; the queen, however, was acknowledged as the Great Wife, with a status higher than that of the other wives. The husband was master in the house, but wives were very much respected and in charge of the household and education of the children. From a book of wise sayings came this advice:

> If you are a man of standing, you should found your household and love your wife at home as is fitting. Fill her belly; clothe her back. Ointment is the prescription for her body. Make her heart glad as long as you live. She is a profitable field for her lord. You should not contend with her at law, and keep her far from gaining control. . . . Let her heart be soothed through what may accrue to you; it means keeping her long in your house.[11]

Women's property and inheritance remained in their hands, even in marriage. Although most careers and public offices were closed to women, some did operate businesses. Peasant women worked long hours in the

The Egyptian Diet. The diet of the upper and lower classes in ancient Egypt varied considerably. Meat and fowl, including beef, goat, pork, goose, and pigeons, were on the tables of the rich. Although done for sport as well as food, hunting waterfowl in the stands of papyrus reeds that grew along the river's banks was a favourite pastime of the Egyptian upper classes. Shown on the left is a hunting scene from the eighteenth-dynasty tomb of Nebamun in Thebes. Nebamun, a nobleman, is seen standing in his boat using his throwstick to hunt birds. He holds three birds in his right hand while a cat retrieves two in its claws and holds the wings of another in its teeth. The basic diet of the poor consisted chiefly of bread, and the baking of bread was an important task in all households. The tomb painting on the right from the eighteenth-century dynasty tomb of Mennah shows two men carrying grain while slave girls fight over leftovers in the background.

A FATHER'S ADVICE

*U*pper-class Egyptians enjoyed compiling collections of wise sayings to provide guidance for leading an upright and successful life. This excerpt is taken from *The Instruction of the Vizier Ptah-hotep* and dates from around 2450 B.C. The vizier was the pharaoh's chief official. In this selection, Ptah-hotep advises his son on how to be a successful official.

The Instruction of the Vizier Ptah-hotep

Then he said to his son:

Let not your heart be puffed-up because of your knowledge; be not confident because you are a wise man. Take counsel with the ignorant as well as the wise. The full limits of skill cannot be attained, and there is no skilled man equipped to his full advantage. Good speech is more hidden than the emerald, but it may be found with maidservants at the grindstones. . . .

If you are a leader commanding the affairs of the multitude, seek out for yourself every beneficial deed, until it may be that your own affairs are without wrong. Justice is great, and its appropriateness is lasting; it has been disturbed since the time of him who made it, whereas there is punishment for him who passes over its laws. It is the right path before him who knows nothing. Wrongdoing has never brought its undertaking into port. It may be that it is fraud that gains riches, but the strength of justice is that it lasts. . . .

If you are a man of intimacy, whom one great man sends to another, be thoroughly reliable when he sends you. Carry out the errand for him as he has spoken. Do not be reserved about what is said to you, and beware of any act of forgetfulness. Grasp hold of truth, and do not exceed it. Mere gratification is by no means to be repeated. Struggle against making words worse, thus making one great man hostile to another through vulgar speech. . . .

If you are a man of standing and found a household and produce a son who is pleasing to god, if he is correct and inclines toward your ways and listens to your instruction, while his manners in your house are fitting, and if he takes care of your property as it should be, seek out for him every useful action. He is your son, . . . you should not cut your heart off from him.

But a man's seed often creates enmity. If he goes astray and transgresses your plans and does not carry out your instruction, so that his manners in your household are wretched, and he rebels against all that you say, while his mouth runs on in the most wretched talk, quite apart from his experience, while he possesses nothing, you should cast him off: he is not your son at all. He was not really born to you. Thus you enslave him entirely according to his own speech. He is one whom god has condemned in the very womb. . . .

What does this passage reveal about Egyptian bureaucrats?

---

fields and at numerous domestic tasks, especially weaving cloth. Upper-class women could function as priestesses, and a few queens even became pharaohs in their own right. Most famous was Hatshepsut in the New Kingdom. She served as regent for her stepson Thutmosis III but assumed the throne for herself and remained in power until her death.

Hatshepsut's reign was a prosperous one, as is especially evident in her building activity. She is most famous for the temple dedicated to herself at Deir el Bahri on the west bank of the Nile at Thebes. As pharaoh, Hatshepsut sent out military expeditions, encouraged mining, fostered agriculture, and sent a trading expedition to lower Africa. Because pharaohs were almost always male, Hatshepsut's official statues show her clothed and bearded like a king. She was referred to as "His Majesty." That Hatshepsut was aware of her unusual position is evident from an inscription she had placed on one of her temples. It read, "Now my heart turns to and fro, in thinking what will the people say, they who shall see my monument in after years, and shall speak of what I have done."

Marriages were arranged by parents. The primary concerns were family and property, and clearly the chief purpose of marriage was to produce children, especially sons (see the box above). From the New Kingdom came this piece of wisdom: "Take to yourself a wife while you are a youth, that she may produce a son for you."[12] Only sons could carry on the family name. Daughters were not slighted, however. Numerous tomb paintings show the close and affectionate relationship parents had with both sons and daughters. Although marriages were arranged, some of the surviving love poems from ancient Egypt indicate an element of romance in some marriages. Marriages could and did end in divorce, which was allowed, apparently with compensation for the wife. Adultery, however, was strictly prohibited, and punishments were severe, especially for women, who could have their noses cut off or be burned at the stake.

CONCLUSION

Although early civilizations emerged in different parts of the world, the foundations of Western civilization were laid by the Mesopotamians and Egyptians. They developed cities and struggled with the problems of organized states. They developed writing to keep records and created literature. They constructed monumental architecture to please their gods, symbolize their power, and preserve their culture for all time. They developed new political, military, social, and religious structures to deal with the basic problems of human existence and organization. These first literate civilizations left detailed records that allow us to view how they grappled with three of the fundamental problems that humans have pondered: the nature of human relationships, the nature of the universe, and the role of divine forces in the cosmos. Although later peoples in Western civilization would provide different answers from those of the Mesopotamians and Egyptians, it was they who first posed the questions, gave answers, and wrote them down. Human memory begins with these two civilizations.

By the middle of the second millennium B.C., the creative impulse of the Mesopotamian and Egyptian civilizations was beginning to wane. The invasion of the Sea Peoples around 1200 B.C. ushered in a whole new pattern of petty states and new kingdoms that would lead to the largest empires the ancient Near East had seen.

TIMELINE

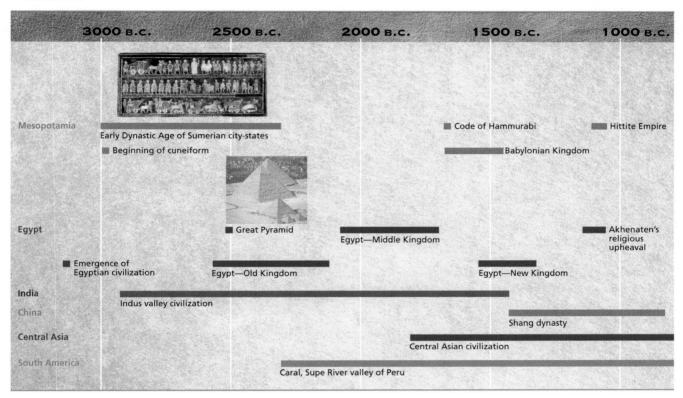

NOTES

1. J.-M. Chauvet et al., *Dawn of Art: The Chauvet Cave* (New York, 1996), pp. 49–50.
2. Quoted in A. Kuhrt, *The Ancient Near East, c. 3000–330 B.C.* (London, 1995), vol. 1, p. 68.
3. Quoted in M. van de Mieroop, *A History of the Ancient Near East, ca. 3000–323 B.C.* (Oxford, 2004), p. 106.
4. T. Jacobsen, "Mesopotamia," in H. Frankfort et al., *Before Philosophy* (Baltimore, 1949), p. 139.
5. J. B. Pritchard, *Ancient Near Eastern Texts,* 3d ed. (Princeton, N.J., 1969), p. 372.
6. Quoted in M. Covensky, *The Ancient Near Eastern Tradition* (New York, 1966), p. 51.
7. Quoted in B. G. Trigger, B. J. Kemp, D. O'Connor, and A. B. Lloyd, *Ancient Egypt: A Social History* (Cambridge, 1983), p. 74.
8. Pritchard, *Ancient Near Eastern Texts*, p. 34.
9. Ibid., p. 36.
10. Quoted in R.-M. Hagen and R. Hagen, *Egypt: People, Gods, Pharaohs* (Cologne, 2002), p. 148.
11. Pritchard, *Ancient Near Eastern Texts,* p. 413.
12. Ibid., p. 420.

SUGGESTIONS FOR FURTHER READING

For a beautifully illustrated introduction to the ancient world, see *Past Worlds: The Times Atlas of Archaeology* (Maplewood, N.J., 1988), written by an international group of scholars. A detailed history of the ancient world with chapters written by different specialists is available in the twelve volumes of *The Cambridge Ancient History,* now in its third edition. A less detailed but sound survey can be found in

L. De Blois and R. J. van der Spek, *An Introduction to the Ancient World,* trans. S. Mellor (London, 1997). The following works are of considerable value in examining the prehistory of humankind: R. Leakey, *The Making of Mankind* (London, 1981); R. J. Wenke, *Patterns in Prehistory: Humankind's First Three Million Years,* 4th ed. (New York, 1999); P. Mellars and C. Stringer, *The Human Revolution* (Edinburgh, 1989); and D. O. Henry, *From Foraging to Agriculture* (Philadelphia, 1989). For a study of the role of women in early human society, see E. Barber, *Women's Work: The First 20,000 Years* (New York, 1994).

Excellent reference tools on the ancient Near East can be found in P. Bienkowski and A. Milward, eds., *Dictionary of the Ancient Near East* (Philadelphia, 2000), and G. Leick, *Who's Who in the Ancient Near East* (London, 1999). General surveys of Mesopotamia and Egypt include A. B. Knapp, *The History and Culture of Ancient Western Asia and Egypt* (Chicago, 1987), and W. von Soden, *The Ancient Orient: An Introduction to the Study of the Ancient Near East* (Grand Rapids, Mich., 1994). For a detailed survey, see A. Kuhrt, *The Ancient Near East, c. 3000–330 B.C.,* 2 vols. (London, 1995). A brief recent survey can be found in M. van de Mieroop, *A History of the Ancient Near East, ca. 3000–323 B.C.* (Oxford, 2004). H.W.F. Saggs, *Babylonians* (Norman, Okla., 1995), and G. Leick, *The Babylonians* (London, 2003), provide an overview of the peoples of ancient Mesopotamia. On the economic and social history of the ancient Near East, see D. C. Snell, *Life in the Ancient Near East* (New Haven, Conn., 1997).

General works on ancient Mesopotamia include J. N. Postgate, *Early Mesopotamia: Society and Economy at the Dawn of History* (London, 1992), and A. L. Oppenheim, *Ancient Mesopotamia,* 2d ed. (Chicago, 1977). A beautifully illustrated survey can be found in M. Roaf, *Cultural Atlas of Mesopotamia and the Ancient Near East* (New York, 1996). The world of the Sumerians has been well described in S. N. Kramer, *The Sumerians* (Chicago, 1963) and *History Begins at Sumer* (New York, 1959). See also the summary of the historical and archaeological evidence by H. Crawford, *Sumer and the Sumerians* (Cambridge, 1991). The fundamental work on the spiritual perspective of ancient Mesopotamia is T. Jacobsen, *The Treasures of Darkness: A History of Mesopotamian Religion* (New Haven, Conn., 1976). On daily life, see S. Bertman, *Handbook to Life in Ancient Mesopotamia* (New York, 2003).

For a good introduction to ancient Egypt, see the beautifully illustrated works by M. Hayes, *The Egyptians* (New York, 1997), and D. P. Silverman, ed., *Ancient Egypt* (New York, 1997). Other general surveys include I. Shaw, ed., *The Oxford History of Ancient Egypt* (New York, 2000); N. Grant, *The Egyptians* (New York, 1996); and N. Grimal, *A History of Ancient Egypt,* trans. I. Shaw (Oxford, 1992). On Akhenaten and his religious changes, see D. Redford, *Akhenaten: The Heretic King* (Princeton, N.J., 1984). Egyptian religion is covered in S. Quirke, *Ancient Egyptian Religion* (London, 1992). On Egyptian culture in general, see J. A. Wilson, *The Culture of Ancient Egypt* (Chicago, 1956). An important study on women is G. Robins, *Women in Ancient Egypt* (Cambridge, Mass., 1993). Daily life can be examined in E. Strouhal, *Life of the Ancient Egyptians* (Norman, Okla., 1992).

Thomson NOW! Enter *ThomsonNOW* using the access card that is available for *Western Civilization: A Brief History.* *ThomsonNOW* will help you understand this chapter with lesson plans generated for your needs. In addition, you can read the following documents, and many more, online:

Enuma Elish
Herodotus, *History,* Book 2, Chapters 124–127

WESTERN CIVILIZATION RESOURCES

Visit the Web site for *Western Civilization: A Brief History* for resources specific to this book:

http://www.thomsonedu.com/history/spielvogel

For a variety of tools to help you succeed in this course, visit the Western Civilization Resource Center at

http://history.wadsworth.com/spielvogel

Included are quizzes, images, documents, interactive simulations, maps and timelines, movie explorations, and a wealth of other sources.

THE ANCIENT NEAR EAST: PEOPLES AND EMPIRES

CHAPTER OUTLINE
AND FOCUS QUESTIONS

On the Fringes of Civilization

⊡ What is the significance of Indo-European–speaking peoples?

The Hebrews: "The Children of Israel"

⊡ In what ways was the Jewish faith unique in the ancient Near East, and how did it evolve over time? Who were the neighbors of the Israelites, and what was their significance?

The Assyrian Empire

⊡ What methods and institutions did the Assyrians use to amass and maintain their empire?

The Persian Empire

⊡ What methods and institutions did the Persians use to amass and maintain their empire, and how did these differ from those of the Assyrians?

CRITICAL THINKING

⊡ What is the relationship between the political history of the Israelites and the evolution of their religious beliefs?

A medieval Italian manuscript version of the judgment of Solomon

Alinari/Regione Umbria/Art Resource, NY (Archivio di Stato, Gubbio, Italy)

*A*ROUND 970 B.C., Solomon came to the throne of Israel, a small state in western Asia. He was lacking in military prowess but excelled in many other ways. Through trade and a series of foreign alliances, he created a strong, flourishing state. But he was especially famed for his skill as a judge. When two women came before him, each claiming that the same infant was her natural child, Solomon ordered his servant to cut the child in half and give half to each woman. The first woman objected: "Please, my lord, give her the living baby! Don't kill him!" The second woman replied, "Neither I nor you shall have him. Cut him in two!" Then Solomon rendered his judgment: "Give the living baby to the first woman. Do not kill him; she is his mother." According to the biblical account, "When all Israel heard the verdict the king had given, they held the king in awe, because they saw that he had wisdom from God to administer justice." After Solomon's death, Israel's power began to crumble. But how had such a small nation been able to survive as long as it did in a Near East dominated by mighty empires?

The weakening of Egypt around 1200 B.C. left no dominant powers in the Near East, allowing a patchwork of petty kingdoms and city-states to emerge, especially in Syria and

Palestine. One of these small states, the Hebrew nation known as Israel, has played a role in Western civilization completely disproportionate to its size. The Hebrews played a minor part in the politics of the ancient Near East, but their spiritual heritage, in the form of Judeo-Christian values, is one of the basic pillars of Western civilization.

The small states did not last. Ever since the first city-states had arisen in the Near East around 3000 B.C., there had been an ongoing movement toward the creation of larger territorial states with more sophisticated systems of control. This process reached a high point in the first millennium B.C. with the appearance of vast empires. Between 1000 and 500 B.C., the Assyrians, the Chaldeans, and the Persians all forged empires that encompassed large areas of the ancient Near East. Each had impressive and grandiose capital cities that emphasized the power and wealth of its rulers. Each brought peace and order for a time by employing new administrative techniques. Each eventually fell to other conquerors. In the long run, these large empires had less impact on Western civilization than the Hebrew people. In human history, the power of ideas is often more significant than the power of empires.

On the Fringes of Civilization

Our story of the beginnings of Western civilization has been dominated so far by Mesopotamia and Egypt. But significant developments were also taking place on the fringes of these civilizations. Farming had spread into the Balkan peninsula of Europe by 6500 B.C., and by 4000 B.C. it was well established in southern France, central Europe, and the coastal regions of the Mediterranean. Although migrating farmers from the Near East may have brought some farming techniques into Europe, historians now believe that the Neolithic peoples of Europe domesticated animals and began to farm largely on their own.

One outstanding feature of late Neolithic Europe was the building of megalithic structures. *Megalith* is Greek for "large stone." Radiocarbon dating, a technique that allows scientists to determine the age of objects, shows that the first megalithic structures were built around 4000 B.C., more than a thousand years before the great pyramids were built in Egypt. Between 3200 and 1500 B.C., standing stones that were placed in circles or lined up in rows were erected throughout the British Isles and northwestern France. Other megalithic constructions have been found as far north as Scandinavia and as far south as the islands of Corsica, Sardinia, and Malta. Some archaeologists have demonstrated that the stone circles were used as observatories to detect not only such simple astronomical phenomena as the midwinter and midsummer sunrises but also such sophisticated observations as the major and minor standstills of the moon.

By far the most famous of these megalithic constructions is Stonehenge in England. Stonehenge consists

Stonehenge. The Bronze Age in northwestern Europe is known for its megaliths, or large standing stones. Between 3200 and 1500 B.C., standing stones arranged in circles or lined up in rows were erected throughout the British Isles and northwestern France. The most famous of these megalithic constructions is Stonehenge in England.

of a series of concentric rings of standing stones. Its construction sometime between 2100 and 1900 B.C. was no small accomplishment. The eighty bluestones used at Stonehenge, for example, weigh 4 tons each and were transported to the site from their original source 135 miles away. Like other megalithic structures, Stonehenge indicates a remarkable awareness of astronomy on the part of its builders, as well as an impressive coordination of workers.

The Impact of the Indo-Europeans

For many historians, both the details of construction and the purpose of the megalithic structures of Europe remain a mystery. Also puzzling is the role of Indo-European people. The name *Indo-European* refers to people who used a language derived from a single parent tongue. Indo-European languages include Greek, Latin, Persian, Sanskrit, and the Germanic languages (see Table 2.1). It has been suggested that the original Indo-European-speaking peoples were based somewhere in the steppe region north of the Black Sea or in southwestern Asia, in modern Iran or Afghanistan. Although there had

TABLE 2.1 Some Indo-European Languages

SUBFAMILY	LANGUAGES
Indo-Iranian	*Sanskrit*, Persian
Balto-Slavic	Russian, Serbo-Croatian, Czech, Polish, Lithuanian
Hellenic	Greek
Italic	*Latin*, Romance languages (French, Italian, Spanish, Portuguese, Romanian)
Celtic	Irish, Gaelic
Germanic	Swedish, Danish, Norwegian, German, Dutch, English

NOTE: Languages in italic type are no longer spoken.

been earlier migrations, around 2000 B.C. these people began major nomadic movements into Europe (including present-day Italy and Greece), India, and western Asia. One group of Indo-Europeans who moved into Asia Minor and Anatolia (modern Turkey) around 1750 B.C. coalesced with the native peoples to form the Hittite kingdom with its capital at Hattusha (Bogazköy in modern Turkey).

Starting around 1600 B.C., the Hittites assembled their own empire in western Asia and even threatened the power of the Egyptians. The Hittites were the first of the Indo-European peoples to make use of iron, enabling them to construct weapons that were stronger and cheaper to make because of the widespread availability of iron ore. Hittite power faltered around 1200 B.C., in part due to internal problems but also as a result of attacks from the west by the Sea Peoples, groups of unknown origin who moved across the Mediterranean in the late thirteenth and early twelfth centuries B.C., and also by an aggressive tribe known as the Gasga, who raided Hittite cities. By 1190 B.C., Hittite power was at an end.

During its heyday, however, the Hittite Empire was one of the great powers in western Asia. The Hittite ruler, known as the Great King, controlled the core areas of the kingdom but in western and southern Anatolia and Syria allowed local rulers to swear allegiance to him as vassals. Constant squabbling over succession to the throne, however, tended to weaken royal authority at times.

During its height, the Hittite Empire also demonstrated an interesting ability to assimilate other cultures into its own. In languages, literature, art, law, and religion, the Hittites borrowed much from Mesopotamia as well as the native peoples that they had subdued. Recent scholarship has stressed the important role of the Hittites in transmitting Mesopotamian culture, as they transformed it, to later Western civilization in the Mediterranean area, especially to the Mycenaean Greeks (See Chapter 3).

The crumbling of the Hittite kingdom and the weakening of Egypt after 1200 B.C. left a power vacuum in western Asia, allowing a patchwork of petty kingdoms and city-states to emerge, especially in the area at the eastern end of the Mediterranean Sea. The Hebrews were one of these peoples.

The Hebrews: "The Children of Israel"

The Hebrews were a Semitic-speaking people who had a tradition concerning their origins and history that was eventually written down as part of the Hebrew Bible, known to Christians as the Old Testament. Describing themselves originally as nomads organized in clans, the Hebrews' tradition states that they were descendants of the patriarch Abraham, who had migrated from Mesopotamia to Palestine, where they became identified as the "Children of Israel." Again according to tradition, a drought in Palestine caused many Hebrews to migrate to Egypt, where they lived peacefully until they were enslaved by pharaohs who used them as laborers on building projects. These Hebrews remained in bondage until Moses led them eastward out of Egypt in the Exodus, which some historians have argued would have occurred in the first half of the thirteenth century B.C. According to the biblical account, the Hebrews then wandered for many years in the desert until they entered Palestine. Organized into twelve tribes, they became embroiled in conflict with the Philistines, a people who had settled in the coastal area of Palestine but were beginning to move into the inland areas.

Many scholars today doubt that the early books of the Hebrew Bible reflect the true history of the early Israelites. They argue that the early books of the Bible, written centuries after the events described, preserve only what the Israelites came to believe about themselves and that recent archaeological evidence often contradicts the details of the biblical account. Some of these scholars have even argued that the Israelites were not nomadic invaders but indigenous peoples in the Palestinian hill country. What is generally agreed, however, is that between 1200 and 1000 B.C., the Israelites emerged as a distinct group of people, possibly organized in tribes or a league of tribes, who established a united kingdom known as Israel.

The United Kingdom

The first king of the Israelites was Saul (c. 1020–1000 B.C.), who initially achieved some success in the ongoing struggle with the Philistines. But after his death in a disastrous battle with this enemy, a brief period of anarchy ensued until one of Saul's lieutenants, David (c. 1000–970 B.C.), reunited the Israelites, defeated the Philistines, and established control over all of Palestine (see Map 2.1). According to the biblical account, some of his conquests led to harsh treatment for the conquered people: "David also defeated the Moabites. He made them lie down on the ground and measured them off with a length of cord. Every two lengths of them were put to death, and the third length was allowed to live. So the Moabites became subject to David and brought tribute."[1] Among David's conquests was the city of

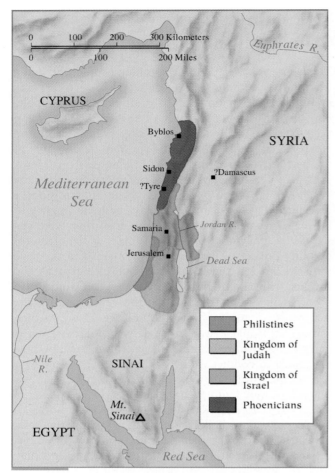

MAP 2.1 **Palestine in the First Millennium** B.C. United under Saul, David, and Solomon, greater Israel split into two states—Israel and Judah—after the death of Solomon. With power divided, the Israelites could not resist invasions that dispersed many Jews from Palestine. Some, such as the "ten lost tribes," never returned. Others were sent to Babylon but were later allowed to return under the rule of the Persians. **?** Why was Israel more vulnerable to the Assyrian Empire than Judah was?

View an animated version of this map or related maps at
http://thomsonedu.com/history/spielvogel

Jerusalem, which he made into the capital of a united kingdom. David centralized Israel's political organization and accelerated the integration of the Israelites into a settled community based on farming and urban life.

David's son Solomon (c. 970–930 B.C.) did even more to strengthen royal power. He expanded the political and military establishments and was especially active in extending the trading activities of the Israelites. Solomon is best known for his building projects, of which the most famous was the Temple in Jerusalem. The Israelites viewed the Temple as the symbolic center of their religion and hence of the kingdom of Israel itself. The Temple now housed the Ark of the Covenant, a holy chest containing the sacred relics of the Hebrew religion and, symbolically, the throne of the invisible God of Israel. Under Solomon, ancient Israel was at the height

Erich Lessing/Art Resource, NY (British Museum, London)

Exiles from Judah. The Assyrians overran the kingdom of Israel in 722 or 721 B.C., destroyed the capital city of Samaria, and then began an assault on the kingdom of Judah. In this eighth-century relief from the palace of Sennacherib at Nineveh, captives with animals and baggage are shown on their way into exile after the Assyrian conquest of the fortified town of Lachish in Judah in 701 B.C. A woman and child have been allowed to travel on the cart. The Assyrians failed, however, to take Jerusalem, and Judah remained independent, although it was forced to pay tribute to the Assyrians.

of its power, but his efforts to extend royal power throughout his kingdom led to dissatisfaction among some of his subjects.

The Divided Kingdom

After Solomon's death, tensions in Israel between the northern and southern tribes led to the establishment of two separate kingdoms—the kingdom of Israel, composed of the ten northern tribes, with its capital eventually at Samaria, and the southern kingdom of Judah, consisting of two tribes, with its capital at Jerusalem. In 722 or 721 B.C., the Assyrians destroyed Samaria, overran the kingdom of Israel, and deported many Israelites to other parts of the Assyrian Empire. These dispersed Israelites (the "ten lost tribes") merged with neighboring peoples and gradually lost their identity.

The southern kingdom of Judah was also forced to pay tribute to Assyria but managed to retain its independence as Assyrian power declined. A new enemy, however, appeared on the horizon. The Chaldeans brought the final destruction of Assyria, conquered the kingdom of Judah, and completely destroyed Jerusalem in 586 B.C. Many people from Judah were deported to Babylonia; the memory of their exile is still evoked in the stirring words of Psalm 137:

> *By the rivers of Babylon, we sat and wept when we*
> *remembered Zion....*

Saul—first king	c. 1020–1000 B.C.
King David	c. 1000–970 B.C.
King Solomon	c. 970–930 B.C.
Northern kingdom of Israel destroyed by Assyria	722 or 721 B.C.
Southern kingdom of Judah falls to Chaldeans; destruction of Jerusalem	586 B.C.
Return of exiles to Jerusalem	538 B.C.

*How can we sing the songs of the Lord while in a
foreign land?*

*If I forget you, O Jerusalem, may my right hand forget
its skill.*

*May my tongue cling to the roof of my mouth if I do
not remember you, if I do not consider Jerusalem
my highest joy.[2]*

But the Babylonian captivity of the people of Judah did not last. A new set of conquerors, the Persians, destroyed the Chaldean kingdom but allowed the people of Judah to return to Jerusalem and rebuild their city and temple. The revived kingdom of Judah remained under Persian control until the conquests of Alexander the Great in the fourth century B.C. The people of Judah survived, eventually becoming known as the Jews and giving their name to Judaism, the religion of Yahweh, the Jewish God.

The Spiritual Dimensions of Israel

The spiritual perspective of the Israelites evolved over time. Early Israelites probably worshiped many gods, including nature spirits dwelling in trees and rocks. For some Israelites, Yahweh was the chief god of Israel, but many, including kings of Israel and Judah, worshiped other gods as well. It was among the Babylonian exiles that Yahweh, the God of Israel, came to be regarded as the only God. After the return of these exiles to Judah, their point of view eventually became dominant, and pure **monotheism**, or the belief that there is only one God for all peoples, came to be the major tenet of Judaism.

"I Am the Lord Your God": Ruler of the World   According to the Jewish conception, there is but one God, whom the Jews called Yahweh. God is the creator of the world and everything in it. Indeed, Yahweh means "he causes to be." To the Jews, the gods of all other peoples were idols. The Jewish God ruled the world; he was subject to nothing. All peoples were his servants, whether they knew it or not. This God was also transcendent. He had created nature but was not in nature. The stars, moon, rivers, wind, and other natural phenomena were not divinities or suffused with divinity, as other peoples of the ancient Near East believed, but they were God's handiwork. All of God's creations could be admired for their awesome beauty but not worshiped as gods.

This omnipotent creator of the universe was not removed from the life he had created, however, but was a just and good God who expected goodness from his people. If they did not obey his will, they would be punished. But he was also a God of mercy and love: "The Lord is gracious and compassionate, slow to anger and rich in love. The Lord is good to all; he has compassion on all he has made."[3] Despite the powerful dimensions of God as creator and sustainer of the universe, the Jewish message also emphasized that each person could have a personal relationship with this powerful being. As the psalmist sang, "My help comes from the Lord, the Maker of heaven and earth. He will not let your foot slip—he who watches over you will not slumber."[4]

"You Only Have I Chosen": Covenant and Law   Three aspects of the Hebrew religious tradition had special significance: the covenant, law, and the prophets. The Israelites believed that during the Exodus from Egypt, when Moses supposedly led his people out of bondage into the "promised land," a special event occurred that determined the Jewish experience for all time. According to tradition, God entered into a covenant or contract with the tribes of Israel who believed that Yahweh had spoken to them through Moses (see the box on p. 28). The Israelites promised to obey Yahweh and follow his law. In return, Yahweh promised to take special care of his chosen people, "a peculiar treasure unto me above all people."

This covenant between Yahweh and his chosen people could be fulfilled, however, only by obedience to the law of God. Law became a crucial element of the Jewish world and had a number of different dimensions. In some instances, it set forth specific requirements, such as payments for offenses. Most important, since the major characteristic of God was his goodness, ethical concerns stood at the center of the law. Sometimes these took the form of specific standards of moral behavior: "You shall not murder. You shall not commit adultery. You shall not steal."[5] But these concerns were also expressed in decrees that regulated the economic, social, and political life of the community since God's laws of morality applied to all areas of life. These laws made no class distinctions and emphasized the protection of the poor, widows, orphans, and slaves.

The Prophets   The Israelites believed that certain religious leaders or "holy men," called prophets, were sent by God to serve as his voice to his people. The golden age of the prophets began in the mid-eighth century B.C. and continued during the time when the people of Israel and Judah were threatened by Assyrian and Chaldean conquerors. These "men of God" went through the land warning the Israelites that they had failed to keep God's commandments and would be punished for breaking the

The Covenant and the Law: The Book of Exodus

*D*uring the Exodus from Egypt, the Hebrews are said to have made a covenant with Yahweh. They agreed to obey their God and follow his law. In return, Yahweh promised to take special care of his chosen people. This selection from the biblical book of Exodus describes the making of the covenant and God's commandments to the Hebrews.

Exodus 19:1–8

In the third month after the Israelites left Egypt—on the very day—they came to the Desert of Sinai. After they set out from Rephidim, they entered the desert of Sinai, and Israel camped there in the desert in front of the mountain. Then Moses went up to God, and the Lord, called to him from the mountain, and said, "This is what you are to say to the house of Jacob and what you are to tell the people of Israel: 'You yourselves have seen what I did to Egypt, and how I carried you on eagles's wings and brought you to myself. Now if you obey me fully and keep my covenant, then out of all nations you will be my treasured possession. Although the whole earth is mine, you will be for me a kingdom of priests and a holy nation.' These are the words you are to speak to the Israelites." So Moses went back and summoned the elders of the people and set before them all the words the Lord had commanded him to speak. The people all responded together, "We will do everything the Lord has said." So Moses brought their answer back to the Lord.

Exodus 20:1–17

And God spoke all these words, "I am the Lord your God, who brought you out of Egypt, out of the land of slavery. You shall have no other gods before me. You shall not make for yourself an idol in the form of anything in heaven above or on the earth beneath or in the waters below. You shall not bow down to them or worship them; for I, the Lord your God, am a jealous God, punishing the children for the sin of the fathers to the third and fourth generation of those who hate, but showing love to a thousand generations of those who love me and keep my commandments. You shall not misuse the name of the Lord your God, for the Lord will not hold anyone guiltless who misuse his name. Remember the Sabbath day by keeping it holy. Six days you shall labor and do all your work, but the seventh day is a Sabbath to the Lord your God. On it you shall not do any work, neither you, nor your son or daughter, nor your manservant or maidservant, nor your animals, nor the alien within your gates. For in six days the Lord made the heavens and the earth, the sea, and all that is in them, but he rested on the seventh day. Therefore the Lord blessed the Sabbath day and made it holy. Honor your father and your mother, so that you may live long in the land the Lord your God is giving you. You shall not murder. You shall not commit adultery. You shall not steal. You shall not give false testimony against your neighbor. You shall not covet your neighbor's house. You shall not covet your neighbor's wife, or his manservant or maidservant, his ox or donkey, or anything that belongs to your neighbor.

What was the nature of the covenant between Yahweh and the Hebrews? What was its moral significance for the Hebrew people? How might you explain its differences from Hammurabi's Code?

---

covenant: "I will punish you for all your iniquities." Amos prophesied the fall of the northern kingdom of Israel to Assyria; twenty years later, Isaiah said the kingdom of Judah too would fall (see the box on p. 29).

Out of the words of the prophets came new concepts that enriched the Jewish tradition and ultimately Western civilization, including a notion of universalism and a yearning for social justice. Although the Jews' religious practices gave them a sense of separateness from other peoples, the prophets transcended this by embracing a concern for all humanity. All nations would someday come to the God of Israel: "All the earth shall worship you." A universal community of all people under God would someday be established by Israel's effort. This vision encompassed the elimination of war and the establishment of peace for all the nations of the world. In the words of the prophet Isaiah: "He will judge between the nations and will settle disputes for many people. They will beat their swords into plowshares and their spears into pruning hooks. Nation will not take up sword against nation, nor will they train for war anymore."[6]

The prophets also cried out against social injustice. They condemned the rich for causing the poor to suffer, denounced luxuries as worthless, and warned of dire punishments for these sins. God's command was to live justly, share with one's neighbors, care for the poor and the unfortunate, and act with compassion. When God's command was not followed, the social fabric of the community was threatened. These proclamations by Israel's prophets became a source for Western ideals of social justice, even if they have never been perfectly realized.

Although the prophets eventually developed a sense of universalism, the demands of the Jewish religion—the obligation to obey their God—encouraged a separation between the Jews and their non-Jewish neighbors. Unlike most other peoples of the Near East, Jews could not simply be amalgamated into a community by accepting the gods of their conquerors and their neighbors. To remain faithful to the demands of their God, they might even have to refuse loyalty to political leaders.

THE HEBREW PROPHETS: MICAH, ISAIAH, AND AMOS

The Hebrew prophets warned the Israelites that they must obey God's commandments or face being punished for breaking their covenant with God. These selections from the biblical prophets Micah, Isaiah, and Amos make clear that God's punishment would fall on the Israelites for their sins. Even the Assyrians, as Isaiah indicated, would be used as God's instrument to punish them.

Micah 6:9–16

Listen! The Lord is calling to the city—and to fear your name is wisdom—"Heed the rod and the One who appointed it. Am I still to forget, O wicked house, your ill-gotten treasures . . . ? Shall I acquit a man with dishonest scales, with a bag of false weights? Her rich men are violent; her people are liars and their tongues speak deceitfully. Therefore, I have begun to destroy you, to ruin you because of your sins. You will eat but not be satisfied; your stomach will still be empty. You will store up but save nothing, because what you save I will give to the sword. You will plant but not harvest; you will press olives but not use the oil on yourselves, you will crush grapes but not drink the wine. . . . Therefore I will give you over to ruin and your people to derision; you will bear the scorn of the nations."

Isaiah 10:1–6

Woe to those who make unjust laws, to those who issue oppressive decrees, to deprive the poor of their rights and withhold justice from the oppressed of my people, making their prey and robbing the fatherless. What will you do on the day of reckoning, when disaster comes from afar? To whom will you run for help? Where will you leave your riches? Nothing will remain but to cringe among the captives or fall among the slain. Yet for all this, his anger is not turned away, his hand is still upraised. "Woe to the Assyrian, the rod of my anger, in whose hand is the club of my wrath! I send him against a godless nation, I dispatch him against a people who anger me, to seize loot and snatch plunder, and to trample them down like mud in the streets."

Amos 3:1–2

Hear this word the Lord has spoken against you, O people of Israel—against the whole family I brought up out of Egypt: "You only have I chosen of all the families of the earth; therefore, I will punish you for all your sins."

What did the Hebrew prophets focus on as the transgressions of the Hebrew people? What do these selections tell you about the nature of the Hebrews as a "chosen" people?

Bridgeman-Giraudon/Art Resource, NY (National & University Library, Jerusalem)

The Neighbors of the Israelites

The Israelites were not the only people living in Palestine. The Philistines, who invaded from the sea, established five towns on the coastal plain of the region. They settled down as farmers and eventually entered into conflict with the Israelites. Although the Philistines were newcomers to the area, the Phoenicians had resided there for some time but now found themselves with a new independence. A Semitic-speaking people, the Phoenicians resided along the Mediterranean coast on a narrow band of land 120 miles long. They had rebuilt their major cities after destruction by the Sea Peoples. Their newfound political independence helped the Phoenicians expand the trade that was already the foundation of their prosperity. In fact, the Phoenician city of Byblos had been the principal distribution center for Egyptian papyrus outside Egypt (the Greek word for book, *biblos*, is derived from the name Byblos).

Hebrew Law. Because of the supposed covenant between Yahweh and the Israelites, law became an important part of Jewish life. Seen here is a twelfth-century manuscript page of the *Mishneh Torah*, a fourteen-volume study of all of Jewish law by Moses Maimonides, the foremost Jewish philosopher of the Middle Ages.

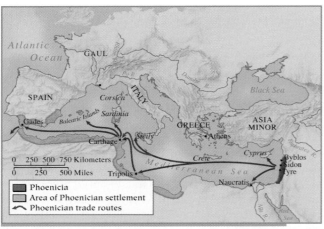

Phoenician Colonies and Trade Routes, c. 800 B.C.

The chief cities of Phoenicia—Byblos, Tyre, and Sidon—were ports on the eastern Mediterranean, but they also served as distribution centers for the lands to the east in Mesopotamia. The Phoenicians themselves produced a number of goods for foreign markets, including purple dye, glass, wine, and lumber from the famous cedars of Lebanon. In addition, the Phoenicians improved their ships and became great international sea traders. They charted new routes, not only in the Mediterranean but also in the Atlantic Ocean, where they sailed south along the west coast of Africa. The Phoenicians established a number of colonies in the western Mediterranean, including settlements in southern Spain, Sicily, and Sardinia. Carthage, the Phoenicians' most famous colony, was located on the North African coast.

Culturally, the Phoenicians are best known as transmitters. Instead of using pictographs or signs to represent whole words and syllables as the Mesopotamians and Egyptians did, the Phoenicians simplified their writing by using twenty-two different signs to represent the sounds of their speech. These twenty-two characters or letters could be used to spell out all the words in the Phoenician language. Although the Phoenicians were not the only people to invent an alphabet, theirs would have special significance because it was eventually passed on to the Greeks. The Phoenicians achieved much while independent, but they ultimately fell subject to the Assyrians, Chaldeans, and Persians.

The Assyrian Empire

The existence of independent states in Palestine was possible only because of the power vacuum existing in the ancient Near East after the demise of the Hittite kingdom and the weakening of Egypt. But this condition did not last; new empires soon came to dominate vast stretches of the ancient Near East. The first of these empires emerged in Assyria, an area whose location on the upper Tigris River brought it into both cultural and political contact with southern Mesopotamia.

Although part of Mesopotamia, Assyria, with its hills and adequate, if not ample, rainfall, had a different terrain and climate. The Assyrians were a Semitic-speaking people who exploited the use of iron weapons to establish an empire by 700 B.C. that included Mesopotamia, parts of the Iranian plateau, sections of Asia Minor, Syria, Palestine, and Egypt down to Thebes (see Map 2.2). Ashurbanipal (669–626 B.C.) was one of the strongest Assyrian rulers, but it was already becoming apparent during his reign that the Assyrian Empire was greatly overextended. Internal strife intensified as powerful Assyrian nobles gained control of vast territories and waged their own private military campaigns. Moreover, subject peoples, such as the Babylonians, greatly resented Assyrian rule and rebelled against it. Soon after Ashurbanipal's reign, the Assyrian Empire began to disintegrate rapidly. The capital city of Nineveh fell to a coalition of Chaldeans and Medes in 612 B.C., and in 605 B.C. the rest of the empire was finally divided between the coalition powers.

Organization of the Empire

At its height, the Assyrian Empire was ruled by kings whose power was considered absolute. Under their leadership, the empire became well organized. By eliminating governorships held by nobles on a hereditary basis and instituting a new hierarchy of local officials directly responsible to the king, the Assyrian kings gained greater control over the resources of the empire. The Assyrians also developed an efficient system of communication to administer their empire more effectively. A network of posting stages was established throughout the empire that used relays of horses (mules or donkeys in mountainous terrain) to carry messages. The system was so effective that a provincial governor anywhere in the empire (except Egypt) could send a query and receive an answer from the king within a week.

The Assyrian Military Machine

The ability of the Assyrians to conquer and maintain an empire was due to a combination of factors. Over many years of practice, the Assyrians developed effective military leaders and fighters. They were able to enlist and deploy troops numbering in the hundreds of thousands, although most campaigns were not conducted on such a large scale. In 845 B.C., an Assyrian army of 120,000 men crossed the Euphrates on a campaign. Size alone was not decisive, however. The Assyrian army was extremely well organized and disciplined. It included a standing army of infantrymen as its core, accompanied by cavalrymen and horse-drawn war chariots that were used as mobile platforms for shooting arrows. Moreover, the Assyrians had the advantage of having the first large armies equipped with iron weapons. The Hittites had been the first to develop iron metallurgy, but iron came to be used extensively only after new methods for hardening it became common after 1000 B.C.

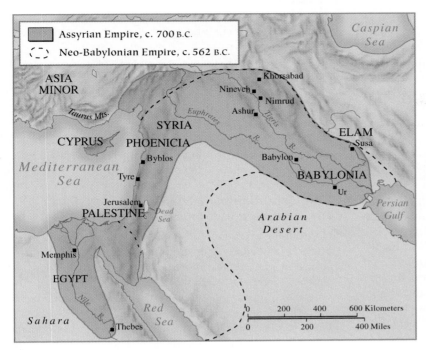

MAP 2.2 The Assyrian and Neo-Babylonian Empires. The Assyrian Empire expanded in large part due to its brutal military methods. It maintained its rule through use of a common language and religion, along with extremely violent suppression of internal revolts. It was overthrown by Chaldeans in Babylonia, leading to the Neo-Babylonian Empire epitomized by Nebuchadnezzar. ❓ Why was control of Babylonia crucial to both empires? 🖱 **View an animated version of this map or related maps at** http://thomsonedu.com/history/spielvogel

Another factor in the army's success was its ability to use various military tactics (see the box on p. 32). The Assyrians were skilled at waging guerrilla war in the mountains and set battles on open ground and were especially renowned for siege warfare. They would hammer a city's walls with heavy, wheeled siege towers and armored battering rams while sappers dug tunnels to undermine the walls' foundations and cause them to collapse. The besieging Assyrian armies learned to cut off supplies so effectively that if a city did not fall to them, the inhabitants could be starved into submission.

A final factor in the effectiveness of the Assyrian military machine was its ability to create a climate of terror as an instrument of war. The Assyrians became famous for their terror tactics, although some historians believe that their policies were no worse than those of other conquerors. As a matter of regular policy, the Assyrians laid waste the land in which they were fighting, smashing dams, looting and destroying towns, setting crops on fire, and cutting down trees, particularly fruit trees. The Assyrians were especially known for committing atrocities on their captives. King Ashurnasirpal recorded this account of his treatment of prisoners:

> 3000 of their combat troops I felled with weapons. . . . Many of the captives taken from them I burned in a fire. Many I took alive; from some of these I cut off their hands to the wrist, from others I cut off their noses, ears and fingers; I put out the eyes of many of the soldiers. . . . I burned their young men and women to death.[7]

After conquering another city, the same king wrote: "I fixed up a pile of corpses in front of the city's gate. I flayed the nobles, as many as had rebelled, and spread their skins out on the piles. . . . I flayed many within my land and spread their skins out on the walls."[8] (Obviously not a king to play games with!) Note that this policy of extreme cruelty to prisoners was not used against all enemies but was reserved primarily for those who were already part of the empire and then rebelled against Assyrian rule.

Assyrian Society and Culture

Unlike the Hebrews, the Assyrians were not fearful of mixing with other peoples. In fact, the Assyrian policy of deporting many prisoners of newly conquered territories to Assyria created a polyglot society in which ethnic differences were not very important. It has been estimated that over a period of three centuries, between four and five million people were deported to Assyria, resulting in a population that was very racially and linguistically mixed. What gave identity to the Assyrians themselves was their language, although even that was akin to that of their southern neighbors in Babylonia, who also spoke a Semitic tongue. Religion was also a cohesive force. Assyria was literally "the land of Ashur," a reference to its chief god. The king, as the human representative of the god Ashur, provided a unifying focus.

Agriculture formed the principal basis of Assyrian life. Assyria was a land of farming villages with relatively few significant cities, especially in comparison to southern Mesopotamia. Unlike the river valleys, where farming required the minute organization of large numbers of people to control irrigation, Assyrian farms received sufficient moisture from regular rainfall.

Trade was second to agriculture in economic importance. For internal trade, metals, such as gold, silver, copper, and bronze, were used as a medium of exchange. Various agricultural products also served as a form of payment or exchange. Because of their geographical

THE ASSYRIAN MILITARY MACHINE

The Assyrians won a reputation for having a mighty military machine. They were able to use a variety of military tactics and were successful whether they were employing guerrilla warfare, fighting set battles, or laying siege to cities. In these three selections, Assyrian kings describe their military conquests.

King Sennacherib (704–681 B.C.) Describes a Battle with the Elamites in 691

At the command of the god Ashur, the great Lord, I rushed upon the enemy like the approach of a hurricane. . . . I put them to rout and turned them back. I transfixed the troops of the enemy with javelins and arrows. . . . I cut their throats like sheep. . . . My prancing steeds, trained to harness, plunged into their welling blood as into a river; the wheels of my battle chariot were bespattered with blood and filth. I filled the plain with the corpses of their warriors like herbage. . . . As to the sheikhs of the Chaldeans, panic from my onslaught overwhelmed them like a demon. They abandoned their tents and fled for their lives, crushing the corpses of their troop as they went. . . . In their terror they passed scalding urine and voided their excrement into their chariots.

King Sennacherib Describes His Siege of Jerusalem (701 B.C.)

As to Hezekiah, the Jew, he did not submit to my yoke, I laid siege to forty-six of his strong cities, walled forts and to the countless small villages in their vicinity, and conquered them by means of well-stamped earth-ramps, and battering-rams brought thus near to the walls combined with the attack by foot soldiers, using mines, breeches as well as sapper work. I drove out of them 200,150 people, young and old, male and female, horses, mules, donkeys, camels, big and small cattle beyond counting, and considered them booty. Himself I made a prisoner in Jerusalem, his royal residence, like a bird in a cage. I surrounded him with earthwork in order to molest those who were leaving his city's gate.

King Ashurbanipal (669–626 B.C.) Describes His Treatment of Conquered Babylon

I tore out the tongues of those whose slanderous mouths had uttered blasphemies against my god Ashur and had plotted against me, his god-fearing prince; I defeated them completely. The others, I smashed alive with the very same statues of protective deities with which they had smashed my own grandfather Sennacherib—now finally as a belated burial sacrifice for his soul. I fed their corpses, cut into small pieces, to dogs, pigs, . . . vultures, the birds of the sky and also the fish of the ocean. After I had performed this and thus made quiet again the hearts of the great gods, my lords, I removed the corpses of those whom the pestilence had felled, whose leftovers after the dogs and pigs had fed on them were obstructing the streets, filling the places of Babylon, and of those who had lost their lives through the terrible famine.

As seen in their own descriptions, what did Assyrian kings believe was important for military success? Do you think their accounts may be exaggerated? Why?

---

location, the Assyrians served as middlemen and participated in an international trade in which they imported timber, wine, and precious metals and stones while exporting textiles produced in palaces, temples, and private villas.

Assyrian culture was a hybrid. The Assyrians assimilated much of Mesopotamian civilization and saw themselves as guardians of Sumerian and Babylonian culture. Ashurbanipal, for example, established a large library at Nineveh that included the available works of Mesopotamian history. Assyrian religion reflected this assimilation of other cultures as well. Although the Assyrians' national god Ashur was their chief deity, virtually all the other gods and goddesses were Mesopotamian.

Among the best-known objects of Assyrian art are the relief sculptures found in the royal palaces in three of the Assyrian capital cities, Nimrud, Nineveh, and Khorsabad. These reliefs, which were begun in the ninth century B.C. and reached their high point in the reign of Ashurbanipal in the seventh, depicted two different kinds of subject matter: ritual or ceremonial scenes, revolving around the person of the king, and scenes of hunting and war. The latter show realistic action scenes of the king and his warriors engaged in battle or hunting animals, especially lions. These pictures depict a strongly masculine world where discipline, brute force, and toughness are the enduring values, indeed, the very values of the Assyrian military monarchy.

The Persian Empire

The Chaldeans, a Semitic-speaking people, had gained ascendancy in Babylonia by the seventh century and came to form the chief resistance to Assyrian control of Mesopotamia. After the collapse of the Assyrian Empire, the Chaldeans, under their king Nebuchadnezzar II (605–562 B.C.), regained for Babylonia a position as the leading power in the ancient Near East.

Nebuchadnezzar rebuilt Babylon as the center of his empire, giving it a reputation as one of the great cities of the ancient world. Babylon was surrounded by great walls, 8 miles in length, encircled by a moat filled by the Euphrates River. The city was adorned with temples and

King Ashurbanipal's Lion Hunt. This relief, sculptured on alabaster as a decoration for the northern palace in Nineveh, depicts King Ashurbanipal engaged in a lion hunt. Lion hunts were not conducted in the wild but under controlled circumstances. The king and his retainers faced lions released from cages in an arena. The purpose was to glorify the king as a conqueror of the king of beasts. Relief sculpture, one of the best-known forms of Assyrian art, reached its high point under Ashurbanipal at about the time that the Assyrian Empire began to disintegrate.

palaces; most famous of all were the Hanging Gardens, known as one of the Seven Wonders of the ancient world. These were supposedly built to satisfy Nebuchadnezzar's wife, a princess from the land of Media, who missed the mountains of her homeland. A series of terraces led to a plateau, an artificial mountain, at the top of which grew the lush gardens irrigated by water piped to the top. According to the account of a first-century A.D. author, the impression of the gardens from a distance was quite remarkable:

> On the top of the citadel are the hanging gardens, a wonder celebrated in the tales of the Greeks. . . . Columns of stone were set up to sustain the whole work, and on these was laid a floor of squared blocks, strong enough to hold the earth which is thrown upon it to a great depth, as well as the water with which they irrigate the soil; and the structure supports trees of such great size that the thickness of their trunks equals a measure of eight cubits [about 12 feet]. They tower to a height of fifty feet, and they yield as much fruit as if they were growing in their native soil. . . . To those who look upon the trees from a distance, real woods seem to be overhanging their native mountains.[9]

But the splendor of the Neo-Babylonian Empire proved to be short-lived when Babylon fell to the Persians in 539 B.C.

The Persians were an Indo-European–speaking people who lived in southwestern Iran. Primarily nomadic, the Persians were organized in tribes or clans led by petty kings assisted by a group of warriors who formed a class of nobles. At the beginning of the seventh century B.C., the Persians became unified under the Achaemenid dynasty, based in Persis in southern Iran. One of the dynasty's members, Cyrus (559–530 B.C.), created a powerful Persian state that rearranged the political map of the ancient Near East.

Cyrus the Great

In 550 B.C., Cyrus established Persian control over Media, making it the first Persian **satrapy** or province. Three years later, Cyrus defeated the prosperous Lydian kingdom in western Asia Minor, and Lydia became another Persian satrapy. Cyrus' forces then went on to conquer the Greek city-states that had been established on the Ionian coast. Cyrus then turned eastward, subduing the eastern part of the Iranian plateau, Sogdiana, and even western India. His eastern frontiers secured, Cyrus entered Mesopotamia in 539 and captured Babylon. His treatment of Babylonia showed remarkable restraint and wisdom. Babylonia was made into a Persian province under a Persian satrap, but many government officials were kept in their positions. Cyrus took the title "King of All, Great King, Mighty King, King of Babylon, King of the Land of Sumer and Akkad, King of the Four Rims [of the earth], the Son of Cambyses the Great King, King of Anshan"[10] and insisted that he stood in the ancient, unbroken line of Babylonian kings. By appealing to the vanity of the Babylonians, he won their loyalty. Cyrus also issued an edict permitting the Jews, who had been brought to Babylon in the sixth century B.C., to return to Jerusalem with their sacred temple objects and to rebuild their temple as well.

To his contemporaries, Cyrus the Great was deserving of his epithet. The Greek historian Herodotus recounted that the Persians viewed him as a "father," a ruler who was "gentle, and procured them all manner of goods."[11] Certainly, Cyrus must have been an unusual ruler for his time, a man who demonstrated considerable wisdom and compassion in the conquest and organization of his empire. Cyrus gained the favor of the priesthoods in his conquered lands by restoring temples

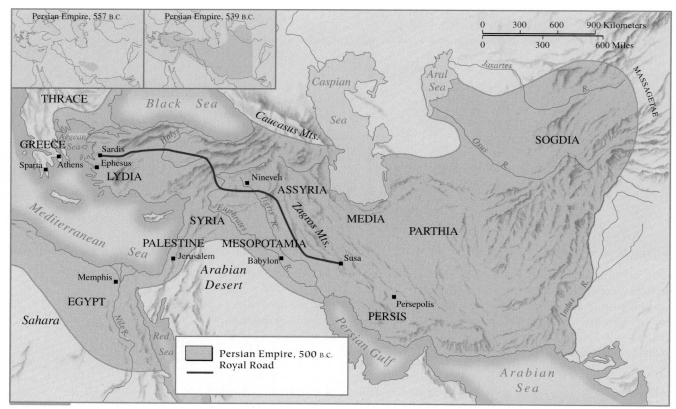

MAP 2.3 The Persian Empire at the Time of Darius. Cyrus the Great united the Persians and led them in successful conquest of much of the Near East. By the time of Darius, the Persian Empire was the largest the world had yet seen. The Persians allowed religious tolerance and gave some government positions to natives of conquered territories. **?** How did Persian policies attempt to overcome the difficulties of governing far-flung provinces? **View an animated version of this map or related maps at** http://thomsonedu.com/history/spielvogel

and permitting religious toleration. He won approval by using not only Persians but also native peoples as government officials in their own states. Unlike the Assyrian rulers of an earlier empire, he had a reputation for mercy. Medes, Babylonians, and Hebrews all accepted him as their legitimate ruler. Indeed, the Hebrews regarded him as the anointed one of God:

> I am the Lord who says of Cyrus, "He is my shepherd and will accomplish all that I please"; he will say of Jerusalem, "Let it be rebuilt"; and of the temple, "Let its foundations be laid." This is what the Lord says to his anointed, to Cyrus, whose right hand I take hold of to subdue nations before him.[12]

Cyrus had a genuine respect for ancient civilizations—in building his palaces, he made use of Assyrian, Babylonian, Egyptian, and Lydian practices.

Expanding the Empire

Cyrus' successors extended the territory of the Persian Empire. His son Cambyses (530–522 B.C.) undertook a successful invasion of Egypt and made it into a satrapy with Memphis as its capital. Darius (521–486 B.C.) added

a new Persian province in western India that extended to the Indus River and moved into Europe proper, conquering Thrace and making the Macedonian king a vassal (see Map 2.3). A revolt of the Ionian Greek cities in 499 B.C. resulted in temporary freedom for these communities in western Asia Minor. Aid from the Greek mainland, most notably from Athens, encouraged the Ionians to invade Lydia and burn Sardis, center of the Lydian satrapy. This event led to Darius' involvement with the mainland Greeks. After reestablishing control of the Ionian Greek cities, Darius undertook an invasion of the Greek mainland, which culminated in the famous Athenian victory in the Battle of Marathon in 490 B.C. (see Chapter 3).

Governing the Empire

By the reign of Darius, the Persians had created the largest empire the world had yet seen. It not only included all the old centers of power in the Near East, Egypt, Mesopotamia, and Assyria but also extended into Thrace and Asia Minor in the west and into India in the east. For administrative purposes, the empire had been divided into around twenty satrapies. Each of these provinces was ruled by a governor or satrap, literally a "protector of the kingdom." Although Darius had not introduced the system of satrapies, he organized it more rationally. He created a sensible system for calculating the tribute that each satrapy owed to the central government and gave satraps specific civil and military duties. They collected tributes, were responsible for justice and security, raised military levies for the royal army, and normally commanded the military forces within their satrapies. In terms of real power, the satraps were miniature kings with courts imitative of the Great King's.

From the time of Darius on, satraps were men of Persian descent. The major satrapies were given to princes of the royal family, and their position became essentially hereditary. The minor satrapies were placed in the hands of Persian nobles. Their offices, too, tended to pass from father to son. The hereditary nature of the governors' offices made it necessary to provide some checks on their power. Consequently, royal officials at the satrapal courts acted as spies for the Great King.

An efficient system of communication was crucial to sustaining the Persian Empire. Well-maintained roads facilitated the rapid transit of military and government personnel. One in particular, the so-called Royal Road, stretched from Sardis, the center of Lydia in Asia Minor, to Susa, the chief capital of the Persian Empire. Like the Assyrians, the Persians established staging posts equipped with fresh horses for the king's messengers.

The Great King Darius

In this vast administrative system, the Persian king occupied an exalted position. All subjects were the king's

Darius, the Great King.   Darius ruled the Persian Empire from 521 to 486 B.C. He is shown here on his throne in Persepolis, a new capital city that he built. In his right hand, Darius holds the royal staff, in his left, a lotus blossom with two buds, a symbol of royalty.

servants, and he was the source of all justice, possessing the power of life and death over everyone. Persian kings were largely secluded and not easily accessible. They resided in a series of splendid palaces. Darius in particular was a palace builder on a grand scale. His description of the construction of a palace in the chief Persian capital of Susa demonstrated what a truly international empire Persia was:

This is the . . . palace which at Susa I built. From afar its ornamentation was brought. . . . The cedar timber was brought from a mountain named Lebanon; the Assyrians brought it to Babylon, and from Babylon the Carians and Ionians brought it to Susa. Teakwood was brought from Gandara and from Carmania. The gold which was used here was brought from Sardis and from Bactria. The stone—lapis lazuli and carnelian—was brought from Sogdiana. . . . The silver and copper were brought from Egypt. The ornamentation with which the wall was

Image credit: © Art Archive/Dagli Orti

A DINNER WITH THE PERSIAN KING

The Persian kings lived in luxury as a result of their conquests and ability to levy taxes from their conquered subjects. In this selection, we read a description of how a Persian king dined with his numerous guests.

Athenaeus, The Deipnosophists

Heracleides of Cumae, author of the *Persian History*, writes in the second book of the work entitled *Equipment*: "All who attend upon the Persian kings when they dine first bathe themselves and then serve in white clothes, and spend nearly half the day on preparations for the dinner. Of those who are invited to eat with the king, some dine outdoors, in full sight of anyone who wishes to look on; others dine indoors in the king's company. Yet even these do not eat in his presence, for there are two rooms opposite each other, in one of which the king has his meal, in the other the invited guests. The king can see them through the curtain at the door, but they cannot see him. Sometimes, however, on the occasion of a public holiday, all dine in a single room with the king, in the great hall. And whenever the king commands a symposium [drinking-bout following the dinner], which he does often, he has about a dozen companions at the drinking. When they have finished dinner, that is the king by himself, the guests in the other room, these fellow-drinkers are summoned by one of the eunuchs; and entering they drink with him, though even they do not have the same wine; moreover, they sit on the floor, while he reclines on a couch supported by feet of gold, and they depart after having drunk to excess. In most cases the king breakfasts and dines alone, but sometimes his wife and some of his sons dine with him. And throughout the dinner his concubines sing and play the lyre; one of them is the soloist, the others sing in chorus. And so ... the 'king's dinner,' as it is called, will appear prodigal to one who merely hears about it, but when one examines it carefully it will be found to have been got up with economy and even with parsimony; and the same is true of the dinners among other Persians of high station. For one thousand animals are slaughtered daily for the king; these comprise horses, camels, oxen, asses, deer, and most of the small animals; many birds are also consumed, including Arabian ostriches—and the creature is large—geese, and cocks. And of all these only moderate portions are served to each of the king's guests, and each of them may carry home whatever he leaves untouched at the meal. But the greater part of these meats and other foods are taken into the courtyard for the bodyguard and light-armed troopers maintained by the king; there they divide all the half-eaten remnants of meat and bread and share them in equal portions. . . ."

What does this description of a royal dinner tell you about the nature of Persian kingship?

---

adorned was brought from Ionia. The ivory was brought from Ethiopia, from India, and from Arachosia. The stone pillars were brought from ... Elam. The artisans who dressed the stone were Ionians and Sardians. The goldsmiths who wrought the gold were Medes and Egyptians. ... Those who worked the baked brick [with figures] were Babylonians. The men who adorned the wall were Medes and Egyptians. At Susa here a splendid work was ordered; very splendid did it turn out.[13]

But Darius was unhappy with Susa. He did not really consider it his homeland, and it was oppressively hot in the summer months. He built another residence at Persepolis, a new capital located to the southeast of the old one at a higher elevation.

The policies of Darius also tended to widen the gap between the king and his subjects. As the Great King himself said of all his subjects, "What was said to them by me, night and day it was done."[14] Over a period of time, the Great Kings in their greed came to hoard immense quantities of gold and silver in the various treasuries located in the capital cities. Both their hoarding of wealth and their later overtaxation of their subjects are seen as crucial factors in the ultimate weakening of the Persian Empire (see the box above).

In its heyday, however, the empire stood supreme, and much of its power depended on the military. By the time of Darius, the Persian monarchs had created a standing army of professional soldiers. This army was truly international, composed of contingents from the various peoples who made up the empire. At its core was a cavalry force of ten thousand and an elite infantry force of ten thousand Medes and Persians known as the Immortals because they were never allowed to fall below ten thousand in number. When one was killed, he was immediately replaced. The Persians made effective use of their cavalry, especially for operating behind enemy lines and breaking up lines of communication.

Persian Religion

Of all the Persians' cultural contributions, the most original was their religion, **Zoroastrianism**. According to Persian tradition, its founder, Zoroaster, was born in 660 B.C. After a period of wandering and solitude, he experienced revelations that caused him to be revered as a prophet of the "true religion." His teachings were eventually written down in the third century A.D. in the *Zend Avesta*.

Like the Hebrews', Zoroaster's spiritual message was monotheistic. To Zoroaster, Ahuramazda was the only god, and the religion he preached was the only perfect

Chuzeville/Réunion des Musées Nationaux/Art Resource, NY (Louvre, Paris, France)

Archers of the Persian Guard. One of the main pillars supporting the Persian Empire was the military. This frieze, composed of enameled brick, depicts members of the famous infantry force known as the Immortals, so called because their number was never allowed to drop below ten thousand. Anyone killed would be replaced immediately. The men in the frieze carry the standard lance and bow and arrow of the infantry.

one. Ahuramazda (the "Wise Lord") was the supreme deity who brought all things into being:

> This I ask of You, O Ahuramazda; answer me well:
> Who at the Creation was the first father of Justice?–
> Who assigned their path to the sun and the stars?–
> Who decreed the waxing and waning of the moon, if
>   it was not You?–. . .
> Who has fixed the earth below, and the heaven above
>   with its clouds that it might not be moved?–
> Who has appointed the waters and the green things
>   upon the earth?–
> Who has harnessed to the wind and the clouds their
>   steeds?–. . .
> Thus do I strive to recognize in You, O Wise One,
> Together with the Holy Spirit, the Creator of all
>   things.[15]

According to Zoroaster, Ahuramazda also possessed abstract qualities or states that all humans should aspire to, such as good thought, right, and piety. Although Ahuramazda was supreme, he was not unopposed. At the beginning of the world, the good spirit of Ahuramazda was opposed by the evil spirit, known as Ahriman.

Humans also played a role in this cosmic struggle between good and evil. Ahuramazda, the creator, gave all humans free will and the power to choose between right and wrong. The good person chooses the right way of Ahuramazda. Zoroaster taught that there would be an end to the struggle between good and evil. Ahuramazda would eventually triumph, and at the last judgment at the end of the world, the final separation of good and evil would occur. Individuals, too, would be judged. Each soul faced a final evaluation of its actions. If a person had performed good deeds, he or she would achieve paradise; if evil deeds, the soul would be thrown into an abyss of torment.

CONCLUSION

Around 1200 B.C., the decline of the Hittites and the Egyptians had created a void that allowed a number of small states to emerge and flourish temporarily. All of them were eventually overshadowed by the rise of the great empires of the Assyrians, Chaldeans, and Persians. The Assyrian Empire was the first to unite almost all of the ancient Near East. Even larger, however, was the empire of the Great Kings of Persia. Although it owed much to the administrative organization created by the Assyrians, the Persian Empire had its own peculiar strengths. Persian rule was tolerant as well as efficient. Conquered peoples were allowed to keep their own religions, customs, and methods of doing business. The many years of peace that the Persian Empire brought to the Near East facilitated trade and the general well-being of its peoples. It is no wonder that many peoples expressed their gratitude for being subjects of the Great Kings of Persia.

The Hebrews were one of these peoples. They created no empire and were dominated by the Assyrians, Chaldeans, and Persians. Nevertheless, they left a spiritual legacy that influenced much of the later development of Western civilization. The evolution of Hebrew monotheism helped Judaism become one of the world's great religions; it influenced the development of both Christianity and Islam. When we speak of the Judeo-Christian heritage of Western civilization, we refer not only to the concept of monotheism but also to ideas of law, morality, and social justice that have become important parts of Western culture.

On the western fringes of the Persian Empire, another relatively small group of people, the Greeks, were evolving cultural and political ideals that would also have an important impact on Western civilization. It is to the Greeks that we now turn.

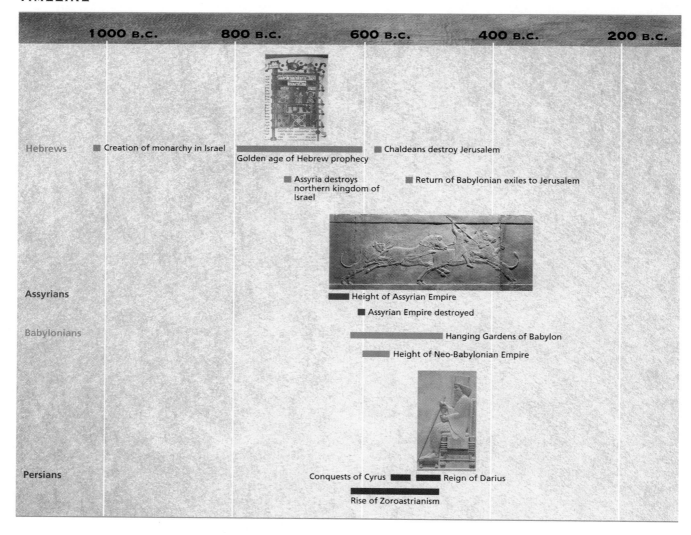

1000 B.C.　　　800 B.C.　　　600 B.C.　　　400 B.C.　　　200 B.C.

Hebrews

■ Creation of monarchy in Israel

Golden age of Hebrew prophecy

■ Chaldeans destroy Jerusalem

■ Assyria destroys northern kingdom of Israel

■ Return of Babylonian exiles to Jerusalem

Assyrians

Height of Assyrian Empire

■ Assyrian Empire destroyed

Babylonians

Hanging Gardens of Babylon

Height of Neo-Babylonian Empire

Persians

Conquests of Cyrus　　Reign of Darius

Rise of Zoroastrianism

NOTES

1. 2 Samuel 8:2.
2. Psalms 137:1, 4–6.
3. Psalms 145:8–9.
4. Psalms 121:2–3.
5. Exodus 20:13–15.
6. Isaiah 2:4.
7. Quoted in H.W.F. Saggs, *The Might That Was Assyria* (London, 1984), p. 261.
8. Ibid., p. 262.
9. J. C. Rolfe, trans., *Quintus Curtius I* (Cambridge, Mass., 1971), pp. 337–339.
10. Quoted in J. M. Cook, *The Persian Empire* (New York, 1983), p. 32.
11. Herodotus, *The Persian Wars*, trans. G. Rawlinson (New York, 1942), p. 257.
12. Isaiah 44:28, 45:1.
13. Quoted in A. T. Olmstead, *History of the Persian Empire* (Chicago, 1948), p. 168.
14. Quoted in Cook, *The Persian Empire*, p. 76.
15. Yasna 44:3–4, 7, as quoted in A. C. Bouquet, *Sacred Books of the World* (Harmondsworth, England, 1954), pp. 111–112.

SUGGESTIONS FOR FURTHER READING

On the Sea Peoples, see the standard work by **N. Sandars**, *The Sea Peoples: Warriors of the Ancient Mediterranean* (London, 1978). Surveys on the Hittites can be found in **O. R. Gurney**, *The Hittites*, rev. ed. (Harmondsworth, England, 1990), and **T. Bryce**, *The Kingdom of the Hittites* (Oxford, 1998). See also **T. Bryce**, *Life and Society in the Hittite World* (Oxford, 2002). For an excellent general survey of the material covered in this chapter, see **A. Kuhrt**, *The Ancient Near East, c. 3000–330 B.C.,* vol. 2 (London, 1995), and **M. van de Mieroop**, *A History of the Ancient Near East, ca. 3000–323 B.C.* (Oxford, 2004).

　　There is an enormous literature on ancient Israel. Two good studies on the archaeological aspects are **A. Mazar**, *Archaeology of the Land of the Bible* (New York, 1992), and **A. Ben-Tor**, ed., *The Archaeology of Ancient Israel* (New Haven, Conn., 1992). For historical narratives, see especially **J. Bright**, *A History of Israel*, 3d ed. (Philadelphia, 1981), a fundamental study; **J. M. Miller and J. H. Hayes**, *A History of Ancient Israel and Judah* (Philadelphia, 1986); **M. Grant**, *The History of Ancient Israel* (New York, 1984); and **H. Shanks**, *Ancient Israel: A Short History from Abraham to the Roman Destruction of the Temple* (Englewood Cliffs, N.J., 1988). For a new perspective, see **N. P. Lemche**, *Ancient Israel: A New History of Israelite Society* (Sheffield, England, 1988). On the origins of the Israelites, see **W. G. Dever**, *Who Were the Early Israelites and Where Did They Come From?* (Grand Rapids, Mich., 2003).

For general studies on the religion of the Hebrews, see **R. Albertz**, *A History of Israelite Religion in the Old Testament Period* (Louisville, Ky., 1994), and **W. J. Doorly**, *The Religion of Israel* (New York, 1997). The role of the prophets is given a new interpretation in **N. Podhoretz**, *The Prophets* (New York, 2002).

For a good account of Phoenician domestic and overseas expansion, see **D. Harden**, *The Phoenicians*, rev. ed. (Harmondsworth, England, 1980). See also **M. E. Aubet**, *The Phoenicians and the West: Politics, Colonies and Trade* (Cambridge, 1993), and **G. Markoe**, *Phoenicians* (London, 2000), on Phoenician society.

A detailed account of Assyrian history is **H.W.F. Saggs**, *The Might That Was Assyria* (London, 1984). **A. T. Olmstead**, *History of Assyria* (Chicago, 1975), is a basic survey of the Assyrian Empire. The Neo-Babylonian Empire can be examined in **H. W. F. Saggs**, *Babylonians* (Norman, Okla., 1995).

The classic work on the Persian Empire is **A. T. Olmstead**, *History of the Persian Empire* (Chicago, 1948), but **J. M. Cook**, *The Persian Empire* (New York, 1983), provides new material and fresh interpretations. Also of value is **J. Curtis**, *Ancient Persia* (Cambridge, Mass., 1990). On the history of Zoroastrianism, see **S. A. Nigosian**, *The Zoroastrian Faith: Tradition and Modern Research* (New York, 1993).

Thomson NOW! Enter *ThomsonNOW* using the access card that is available for *Western Civilization: A Brief History*. *ThomsonNOW* will help you understand this chapter with lesson plans generated for your needs. In addition, you can read the following documents, and many more, online:

Book of Ezra
(Old Testament), Baal Myth of Ugarit

WESTERN CIVILIZATION RESOURCES

Visit the Web site for *Western Civilization: A Brief History* for resources specific to this book:

http://www.thomsonedu.com/history/spielvogel

For a variety of tools to help you succeed in this course, visit the Western Civilization Resource Center at

http://history.wadsworth.com/spielvogel

Included are quizzes, images, documents, interactive simulations, maps and timelines, movie explorations, and a wealth of other sources.

THE CIVILIZATION OF THE GREEKS

CHAPTER OUTLINE AND FOCUS QUESTIONS

Early Greece

▢ How did the geography of Greece affect Greek history?

The Greeks in a Dark Age (c. 1100–c. 750 B.C.)

▢ Why was Homer used as the basis for Greek education?

The World of the Greek City-States (c. 750–c. 500 B.C.)

▢ What was the *polis*, or city-state, and how did the major city-states of Athens and Sparta differ?

The High Point of Greek Civilization: Classical Greece

▢ What did the Greek mean by *democracy*, and in what ways was the Athenian political system a democracy?

The Culture and Society of Classical Greece

▢ Upon what ideals was classical Greek art based, and how were these ideals expressed? What questions did the Greek philosophers pose, and what answers did they suggest?

CRITICAL THINKING

▢ Why is the civilization of the Greeks considered the cornerstone of the Western intellectual tradition?

A bust of Pericles

British Museum, London/The Bridgeman Art Library International

$\mathcal{I}$N 431 B.C., **WAR ERUPTED** as two very different Greek city-states—Athens and Sparta—fought for domination of the Greek world. The people of Athens felt secure behind their walls and in the first winter of the war held a public funeral to honor those who had died in battle. On the day of the ceremony, the citizens of Athens joined in a procession, with the relatives of the dead wailing for their loved ones. As was the custom in Athens, one leading citizen was asked to address the crowd, and on this day it was Pericles who spoke to the people. He talked about the greatness of Athens and reminded the Athenians of the strength of their political system: "Our constitution," he said, "is called a democracy because power is in the hands not of a minority but of the whole people. When it is a question of settling private disputes, everyone is equal before the law. Just as our political life is free and open, so is our day-to-day life in our relations with each other. . . . Here each individual is interested not only in his own affairs but in the affairs of the state as well."

In this famous Funeral Oration, Pericles gave voice to the ideal of democracy and the importance of the individual. It was the Greeks who constructed the intellectual foundations of our Western heritage. They asked some basic questions about human life that still dominate our own intellectual pursuits: What is the nature of the universe? What is the purpose of human existence? What is our relationship to divine forces? What constitutes a community? What constitutes a state? What is true education? What are the true sources of law? What is truth itself, and how do we realize it? Not only did the Greeks provide answers to these questions, but they created a system of logical, analytical thought to examine them. This rational outlook has remained an important feature of Western civilization.

The remarkable story of ancient Greek civilization begins with the arrival of the first Greeks around 1900 B.C. By the eighth century B.C., the characteristic institution of ancient Greek life, the polis or city-state, had emerged. Greek civilization flourished and reached its height in the Classical era of the fifth century B.C., which has come to be closely identified with the achievements of Athenian democracy.◆

Early Greece

Geography played an important role in Greek history. Compared to the landmasses of Mesopotamia and Egypt, Greece covered a small area. Its mountainous peninsula encompassed only 45,000 square miles of territory, about the same as the state of Louisiana. The mountains and the sea were especially significant. Much of Greece consists of small plains and river valleys surrounded by mountain ranges 8,000 to 10,000 feet high. The mountainous terrain had the effect of isolating Greeks from one another. Consequently, Greek communities tended to follow their own separate paths and develop their own way of life. As time went on, these communities became attached to their independence and were only too willing to fight one another to gain advantage. No doubt the small size of these independent Greek communities fostered participation in political affairs and unique cultural expressions, but the rivalry among these communities also led to the bitter warfare that ultimately devastated Greek society.

The sea also influenced the evolution of Greek society. Greece had a long seacoast, dotted by bays and inlets that provided numerous harbors. The Greeks also inhabited a number of islands to the west, south, and particularly the east of the Greek mainland. It is no accident that the Greeks became seafarers who sailed out into the Aegean and the Mediterranean first to make contact with the outside world and later to establish colonies that would spread Greek civilization throughout the Mediterranean region.

Topography helped determine the major territories into which Greece was ultimately divided. South of the Gulf of Corinth was the Peloponnesus, virtually an island (see Map 3.1). Consisting mostly of hills, mountains, and small valleys, the Peloponnesus was the location of Sparta, as well as the site of Olympia, where famous athletic games were held. Northeast of the Peloponnesus was the Attic peninsula (or Attica), the home of Athens,

hemmed in by mountains to the north and west and surrounded by the sea to the south and east. Northwest of Attica was Boeotia in central Greece with its chief city of Thebes. To the north of Boeotia was Thessaly, which contained the largest plains and became a great producer of grain and horses. To the north of Thessaly lay Macedonia, which was not of much importance in Greek history until 338 B.C., when a Macedonian king, Philip II, conquered the Greeks.

Minoan Crete

The earliest civilization in the Aegean region emerged on the large island of Crete, southeast of the Greek mainland. A Bronze Age civilization that used metals, especially bronze, in making weapons had been established there by 2800 B.C. This forgotten civilization was rediscovered at the turn of the twentieth century by the English archaeologist Arthur Evans, who named it "Minoan" after Minos, a legendary king of Crete. In language and religion, the Minoans were not Greek, although they did have some influence on the peoples of the Greek mainland.

Evans's excavations on Crete at the beginning of the twentieth century led to the discovery of an enormous palace complex at Knossus, near modern Heracleion, that was most likely the center of a far-ranging "sea empire," probably largely commercial. We know from archaeological remains that the people of Minoan Crete were accustomed to sea travel and had made contact with the more advanced civilization of Egypt.

The Minoan civilization reached its height between 2000 and 1450 B.C. The palace at Knossus, the royal seat of the kings, demonstrates the prosperity and power of this civilization. It was an elaborate structure built around a central courtyard and included numerous private living rooms for the royal family and workshops for making decorated vases, small sculptures, and jewelry. Even bathrooms, with elaborate drains, were part of the complex. The rooms were decorated with frescoes in bright colors showing sporting events and naturalistic scenes that have led some observers to conclude that the Cretans had a great love of nature.

The centers of Minoan civilization on Crete suffered a sudden and catastrophic collapse around 1450 B.C. The cause of this destruction has been vigorously debated. Some historians believe that a tsunami triggered by a powerful volcanic eruption on the island of Thera was responsible for the devastation. Most historians, however, maintain that the destruction was the result of invasion and pillage by mainland Greeks known as the Mycenaeans.

The First Greek State: Mycenae

The term *Mycenaean* is derived from Mycenae, a remarkable fortified site first excavated by the amateur German archaeologist Heinrich Schliemann. Mycenae

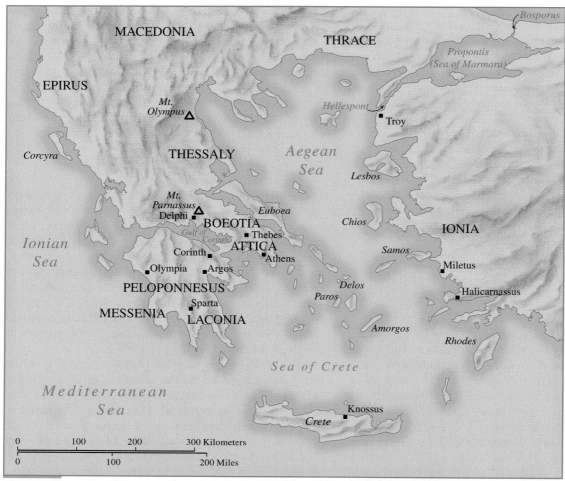

MAP 3.1   Ancient Greece (c. 750–338 B.C.).   Between 750 and 500 B.C., the city-state emerged as the central institution in Greek life and the Greeks' colonization of the Mediterranean and Black Seas. Classical Greece lasted from about 500 to 338 B.C. and marked the high point of Greek civilization in the arts, science, philosophy, and politics but also the period of the Persian Wars and the Peloponnesian War. **?** How does the geography of Greece help explain the rise and development of the Greek city-state? 🕊 **View an animated version of this map or related maps at** http://thomsonedu.com/history/spielvogel

was one center in a Greek civilization that flourished between 1600 and 1100 B.C. The Mycenaean Greeks were part of the Indo-European family of peoples (see Chapter 2) who spread from their original location into southern and western Europe, India, and Iran. One group entered the territory of Greece from the north around 1900 B.C. and managed to gain control of the Greek mainland and develop a civilization.

Mycenaean civilization, which reached its high point between 1400 and 1200 B.C., consisted of a number of powerful monarchies based in fortified palace complexes. Like Mycenae itself, the palaces were built on hills and surrounded by gigantic stone walls. These various centers of power probably formed a loose confederacy of independent states, with Mycenae being the strongest. Next in importance to the kings in these states were the army commanders, priests, and the bureaucrats who kept careful records. The free citizenry included peasants, soldiers,

and artisans, and the lowest rung of the social ladder consisted of serfs and slaves.

The Mycenaeans were, above all, a warrior people who prided themselves on their heroic deeds in battle. Some scholars believe that the Mycenaeans, led by Mycenae itself, spread outward militarily, conquering Crete and making it part of the Mycenaean world. The most famous of all their supposed military adventures has come down to us in the epic poetry of Homer (discussed in the next few pages). Did the Mycenaean Greeks, led by Agamemnon, king of Mycenae, indeed sack the city of Troy on the northwestern coast of Asia Minor around 1250 B.C.,

Minoan Crete and Mycenaean Greece

as Homer described? Since the excavations of Heinrich Schliemann, begun in 1870, scholars have debated this question. Many believe that Homer's account does have a basis in fact.

By the late thirteenth century B.C., Mycenaean Greece was showing signs of serious trouble. Mycenae itself was torched around 1190 B.C., and other Mycenaean centers show similar patterns of destruction as new waves of Greek-speaking invaders moved in from the north. By 1100 B.C., the Mycenaean culture was coming to an end, and the Greek world was entering a new period of considerable insecurity.

The Greeks in a Dark Age (c. 1100–c. 750 B.C.)

After the collapse of Mycenaean civilization, Greece entered a difficult period in which the population declined and food production dropped. Because of the dire conditions and our meager knowledge about the period, historians call it the Dark Age. Not until 850 B.C. did farming revive. At the same time, some new developments were forming the basis for a revived Greece.

During the Dark Age, large numbers of Greeks left the mainland and migrated across the Aegean Sea to various islands and especially to the western shores of Asia Minor, a strip of territory that came to be called Ionia. The Greeks who resided there were called Ionians. Two other major groups of Greeks settled in established parts of Greece. The Aeolian Greeks, located in northern and central Greece, colonized the large island of Lesbos and the adjacent territory of the mainland. The Dorians established themselves in southwestern Greece, especially in the Peloponnesus, as well as on some of the islands in the south Aegean Sea, including Crete.

Other important activities occurred in the Dark Age as well. Greece saw a revival of some trade and some economic activity besides agriculture. Iron came into use for the construction of weapons. And at some point in the eighth century B.C., the Greeks adopted the Phoenician alphabet to give themselves a new system of writing. Near the very end of this Dark Age appeared the work of Homer, who has come to be viewed as one of the greatest poets of all time.

Homer and Homeric Greece

The *Iliad* and the *Odyssey,* the great epic poems of early Greece, were based on stories that had been passed on from generation to generation. It is generally assumed that early in the eighth century B.C., Homer made use of these oral traditions to compose the *Iliad,* his epic of the Trojan War. The war was precipitated by Paris, a prince of Troy, whose kidnapping of Helen, wife of the king of the Greek state of Sparta, outraged all the Greeks. Under the leadership of the Spartan king's brother, Agamemnon

The Slaying of Hector. This scene from a Corinthian Greek vase painting depicts the final battle between Achilles and the Trojan hero Hector, a scene taken from Homer's *Iliad.* The *Iliad* is Homer's masterpiece and was important to later Greeks as a means of teaching the aristocratic values of courage and honor.

of Mycenae, the Greeks attacked Troy. Ten years later, the Greeks finally won and sacked the city.

But the *Iliad* is not so much the story of the war itself as it is the tale of the Greek hero Achilles and how the "wrath of Achilles" led to disaster. As is true of all great literature, the *Iliad* abounds in universal lessons. Underlying them all is the clear message, as one commentator has observed, that "men will still come and go like the generations of leaves in the forest; that [man] will still be weak, and the gods strong and incalculable; that the quality of a man matters more than his achievement; that violence and recklessness will still lead to disaster, and that this will fall on the innocent as well as on the guilty."[1]

The *Odyssey,* Homer's other masterpiece, is an epic romance that recounts the journeys of a Greek hero named Odysseus after the fall of Troy and his ultimate return to his wife. But there is a larger vision here as well: the testing of the heroic stature of Odysseus until, by both cunning and patience, he prevails. In the course of this testing, the underlying moral message is "that virtue is a better policy than vice."[2]

Although the *Iliad* and the *Odyssey* supposedly deal with the heroes of the Mycenaean age of the thirteenth century B.C., many scholars believe that they really describe the social conditions of the Dark Age. According to the Homeric view, Greece was a society based on agriculture in which a landed warrior-aristocracy controlled much wealth and exercised considerable power. Homer's world reflects the values of aristocratic heroes.

Homer's Enduring Importance

This explains the importance of Homer to later generations of Greeks. Homer did not so much record history as make it. The Greeks regarded the *Iliad* and the *Odyssey* as authentic history recorded by one poet, Homer. These masterpieces gave the Greeks an idealized past with a cast of heroes and came to be used as standard texts for the education of generations of Greek males. As one Athenian stated, "My father was anxious to see me develop into a good man . . . and as a means to this end he compelled me to memorize all of Homer."[3] The values Homer taught were essentially the aristocratic values of courage and honor (see the box on p. 45). A hero strives for excellence, which the Greeks called *arete*. In the warrior-aristocratic world of Homer, *arete* is won in struggle or contest. Through his willingness to fight, the hero protects his family and friends, preserves his own honor and that of his family, and earns his reputation.

In the Homeric world, aristocratic women, too, were expected to pursue excellence. Penelope, for example, the wife of Odysseus, the hero of the *Odyssey,* remains faithful to her husband and displays great courage and intelligence in preserving their household during her husband's long absence. Upon his return, Odysseus praises her for her excellence: "Madame, there is not a man in the wide world who could find fault with you. For your fame has reached heaven itself, like that of some perfect king, ruling a populous and mighty state with the fear of god in his heart, and upholding the right."[4] Homer gave the Greeks a model of heroism, honor, and nobility. But in time, as a new world of city-states emerged in Greece, new values of cooperation and community also transformed what the Greeks learned from Homer.

The World of the Greek City-States (c. 750–c. 500 B.C.)

In the eighth century B.C., Greek civilization burst forth with new energies. Two major developments stand out in this era: the evolution of the *polis* as the central institution in Greek life and the Greeks' colonization of the Mediterranean and Black Seas.

The *Polis*

The Greek **polis** (plural, *poleis*) developed slowly during the Dark Age and by the eighth century B.C. had emerged as a truly unique and fundamental institution in Greek society. In a physical sense, the *polis* encompassed a town or city or even a village and its surrounding countryside. But the town or city or village served as the focus or central point where the citizens of the *polis* could assemble for political, social, and religious activities. In some *poleis*, this central meeting point was a hill, which could serve as a place of refuge during an attack and later in some sites came to be the religious center on which temples and public monuments were erected. Below this *acropolis* would be an *agora*, an open place that served both as a place where citizens could assemble and as a market.

Poleis varied greatly in size, from a few square miles to a few hundred square miles. The larger ones were the product of consolidation. The territory of Attica, for example, had once had twelve *poleis* but eventually became a single *polis* (Athens) through a process of amalgamation. The population of Athens grew to about 250,000 by the fifth century B.C. Most *poleis* were much smaller, consisting of only a few hundred to several thousand people.

Although our word *politics* is derived from the Greek term *polis,* the *polis* itself was much more than just a political institution. It was, above all, a community of citizens in which all political, economic, social, cultural, and religious activities were focused. As a community, the *polis* consisted of citizens with political rights (adult males), citizens with no political rights (women and children), and noncitizens (slaves and resident aliens). All citizens of a *polis* possessed basic rights, but these were coupled with responsibilities. The Greek philosopher Aristotle argued that the citizen did not just belong to himself; "we must rather regard every citizen as belonging to the state." The unity of citizens was important and often meant that states would take an active role in directing the patterns of life. However, the loyalty that citizens had to their *poleis* also had a negative side. *Poleis* distrusted one another, and the division of Greece into fiercely patriotic sovereign units helped bring about its ruin. Greece was not a united country but a geographical expression. The cultural unity of the Greeks did not mean much politically.

A New Military System: The Hoplites

As the *polis* developed, so did a new military system. In earlier times, wars in Greece had been fought by aristocratic cavalry soldiers—nobles on horseback. These aristocrats, who were large landowners, also dominated the political life of their *poleis*. But by the end of the eighth century and beginning of the seventh, a new military order came into being that was based on **hoplites,** heavily armed infantrymen who wore bronze or leather helmets, breastplates, and greaves (shin guards). Each carried a round shield, a short sword, and a thrusting spear about 9 feet long. Hoplites advanced into battle as a unit, forming a phalanx (a rectangular formation) in tight order, usually eight ranks deep. As long as the hoplites kept their order, were not outflanked, and did not break, they either secured victory or, at the very least, suffered no harm. The phalanx was easily routed, however, if it broke its order. The safety of the phalanx depended on the solidarity and discipline of its members. As one seventh-century B.C. poet noted, a good hoplite was "a short man firmly placed upon his legs, with a courageous heart, not to be uprooted from the spot where he plants his legs."[5]

The hoplite force had political as well as military repercussions. The aristocratic cavalry was now outdated. Since each hoplite provided his own armor, men of

HOMER'S IDEAL OF EXCELLENCE

The *Iliad* and the *Odyssey* were used as basic texts for the education of Greeks for hundreds of years in antiquity. This passage from the *Iliad,* describing a conversation between Hector, prince of Troy, and his wife, Andromache, illustrates the Greek ideal of gaining honor through combat. At the end of the passage, Homer also reveals what became the Greek attitude toward women: women are supposed to spin and weave and take care of their households and their children.

Homer, *Iliad*

Hector looked at his son and smiled, but said nothing. Andromache, bursting into tears, went up to him and put her hand in his. "Hector," she said, "you are possessed. This bravery of yours will be your end. You do not think of your little boy or your unhappy wife, whom you will make a widow soon. Some day the Achaeans [Greeks] are bound to kill you in a massed attack. And when I lose you I might as well be dead. . . . I have no father, no mother, now. . . . I had seven brothers too at home. In one day all of them went down to Hades' House. The great Achilles of the swift feet killed them all. . . ."

"So you, Hector, are father and mother and brother to me, as well as my beloved husband. Have pity on me now; stay here on the tower; and do not make your boy an orphan and your wife a widow. . . ."

"All that, my dear," said the great Hector of the glittering helmet, "is surely my concern. But if I hid myself like a coward and refused to fight, I could never face the Trojans and the Trojan ladies in their trailing gowns. Besides, it would go against the grain, for I have trained myself always, like a good soldier, to take my place in the front line and win glory for my father and myself. . . ."

As he finished, glorious Hector held out his arms to take his boy. But the child shrank back with a cry to the bosom of his girdled nurse, alarmed by his father's appearance. He was frightened by the bronze of the helmet and the horsehair plume that he saw nodding grimly down at him. His father and his lady mother had to laugh. But noble Hector quickly took his helmet off and put the dazzling thing on the ground. Then he kissed his son, dandled him in his arms, and prayed to Zeus and the other gods: "Zeus; and you other gods, grant that this boy of mine may be, like me, preeminent in Troy; as strong and brave as I; a mighty king of Ilium. May people say, when he comes back from battle, 'Here is a better man than his father.' Let him bring home the bloodstained armor of the enemy he has killed, and make his mother happy."

Hector handed the boy to his wife, who took him to her fragrant breast. She was smiling through her tears, and when her husband saw this he was moved. He stroked her with his hand and said: "My dear, I beg you not to be too much distressed. No one is going to send me down to Hades before my proper time. But Fate is a thing that no man born of woman, coward or hero, can escape. Go home now, and attend to your own work, the loom and the spindle, and see that the maidservants get on with theirs. War is men's business; and this war is the business of every man in Ilium, myself above all."

What important ideals for Greek men and women are revealed in this passage from the Iliad?

---

property, both aristocrats and small farmers, made up the new phalanx. Those who could become hoplites and fight for the state could also challenge aristocratic control.

Colonization and the Growth of Trade

Between 750 and 550 B.C., large numbers of Greeks left to settle in distant lands. Poverty and land hunger created by the growing gulf between rich and poor, overpopulation, and the development of trade were all factors that led to the establishment of colonies. Some Greek colonies were simply trading posts or centers for the transshipment of goods to Greece. Most were larger settlements that included good agricultural land taken from the native populations in those areas. Each colony was founded as a *polis* and was usually independent of the *metropolis* ("mother *polis*") that had established it.

In the western Mediterranean, new Greek settlements were established along the coastline of southern Italy, southern France, eastern Spain, and northern Africa west of Egypt. To the north, the Greeks set up colonies in Thrace, where they sought good farmland to grow grains. Greeks also settled along the shores of the Black Sea and secured the approaches to it with cities on the Hellespont and Bosporus, most noticeably Byzantium, site of the later Constantinople (Istanbul). By establishing these settlements, the Greeks spread their culture throughout the Mediterranean basin. Colonization also led to increased trade and industry. The Greeks on the mainland sent their pottery, wine, and olive oil to these areas; in return, they received grains and metals from the west and fish, timber, wheat, metals, and slaves from the Black Sea region. In many *poleis,* the expansion of trade and industry created a new group of rich men who desired political privileges commensurate with their wealth but found them impossible to gain because of the power of the ruling aristocrats.

Tyranny in the Greek Polis

The desires of these new groups opened the door to the rise of **tyrants** in the seventh and sixth centuries B.C. They

The Hoplite Forces. The Greek hoplites were infantrymen equipped with large round shields and long thrusting spears. In battle, they advanced in tight phalanx formation and were dangerous opponents as long as this formation remained unbroken. This vase painting of the seventh century B.C. shows two groups of hoplite warriors engaged in battle. The piper on the left is leading another line of soldiers preparing to enter the fray.

were not necessarily oppressive or wicked, as our word *tyrant* connotes. Greek tyrants were rulers who seized power by force and who were not subject to the law. Support for the tyrants came from the new rich, who made their money in trade and industry, as well as from poor peasants, who were in debt to landholding aristocrats. Both groups were opposed to the domination of political power by aristocratic **oligarchies**.

Tyrants usually achieved power by a local coup d'état and maintained it by using mercenary soldiers. Once in power, they built marketplaces, temples, and walls that created jobs, glorified the city, and enhanced their own popularity. Tyrants also favored the interests of merchants and traders. Despite these achievements, however, tyranny fell out of favor by the end of the sixth century B.C. Its very nature as a system outside the law seemed contradictory to the ideal of law in a Greek community. Although tyranny did not last, it played a significant role in the course of Greek history by ending the rule of narrow aristocratic oligarchies. The end of tyranny opened the door to greater numbers of people in government. Although this trend culminated in the development of democracy in some communities, in other states expanded

oligarchies of one kind or another managed to remain in power. Greek states exhibited considerable variety in their governmental structures; this can perhaps best be seen by examining the two most famous and most powerful Greek city-states, Sparta and Athens.

Sparta

The Spartans originally occupied four small villages in the southwestern Peloponnesus, in an area known as Laconia, that eventually became unified into a single *polis.* This unification made Sparta a strong community in Laconia and enabled the Spartans to conquer the neighboring Laconians. Many Laconians became *periokoi,* free inhabitants but not citizens who were required to pay taxes and perform military service for Sparta. Other Laconians became **helots** (the name is derived from a Greek word for "capture"). They were bound to the land and forced to work on farms and as household servants for the Spartans.

When the land in Laconia proved unable to maintain the growing number of Spartan citizens, the Spartans looked for land nearby and, beginning around 730 B.C., undertook the conquest of neighboring Messenia despite its larger size and population. Messenia possessed a large, fertile plain ideal for growing grain. After its conquest, which was not completed until the seventh century B.C., the Messenians were made helots and forced to work for the Spartans.

The New Sparta To ensure control over their conquered Laconian and Messenian helots, the Spartans decided to create a military state. By the early sixth century B.C., they had transformed Sparta into a military camp (see the box on p. 48). The lives of all Spartans were now rigidly organized. At birth, each child was examined by state officials who decided whether it was fit to live. Infants judged unfit were left to die. Boys were taken from their mothers at the age of seven and put under control of the state. They lived in military-style barracks, where they were subjected to harsh discipline to make them tough and given an education that stressed military training and obedience to authority. At twenty, Spartan males were enrolled in the army for regular military service. Although allowed to marry, they continued to live in the barracks and ate all their meals in public dining halls with their fellow soldiers. Meals were simple; the famous Spartan black broth consisted of a piece of pork boiled in blood, salt, and vinegar, causing a visitor who ate in a public mess to remark that he now understood why Spartans were not afraid to die. At thirty, Spartan males were allowed to vote in the assembly and live at home, but they stayed in the army until the age of sixty.

While their husbands remained in military barracks until age thirty, Spartan women lived at home. Because of this separation, Spartan women had greater freedom of movement and greater power in the household than was common for women elsewhere in Greece. They were encouraged to exercise and remain fit to bear and raise healthy children. Like the men, Spartan women engaged in athletic exercises in the nude. Many Spartan women upheld the strict Spartan values, expecting their husbands and sons to be brave in war. The story is told that as a Spartan mother was burying her son, an old woman came up to her and said, "You poor woman, what a misfortune." "No," replied the other, "because I bore him so that he might die for Sparta and that is what has happened, as I wished."[6] Another Spartan woman, as she was handing her son his shield, told him to come back carrying his shield or being carried on it.

The Spartan State The Spartan government was headed by two kings, who led the Spartan army on its campaigns. A group of five men, known as the ephors, were elected each year and were responsible for the education of youth and the conduct of all citizens. A council of elders, composed of the two kings and twenty-eight citizens over the age of sixty, decided on the issues that would be presented to an assembly. This assembly of all male citizens did not debate but only voted on the issues put before it by the council of elders.

To make their new military state secure, the Spartans deliberately turned their backs on the outside world. Foreigners, who might bring in new ideas, were discouraged from visiting Sparta. Nor were Spartans, except for military reasons, encouraged to travel abroad where they might pick up new ideas that might prove dangerous to the stability of the state. Likewise, Spartan citizens were discouraged from studying philosophy, literature, or the arts—subjects that might encourage new thoughts. The art of war and of ruling was the Spartan ideal; all other arts were frowned on.

In the sixth century, Sparta used its military might and the fear it inspired to gain greater control of the Peloponnesus by organizing an alliance of almost all the Peloponnesian states. Sparta's strength enabled it to dominate this Peloponnesian League and determine its policies. By 500 B.C., the Spartans had organized a powerful military state that maintained order and stability in the Peloponnesus. Raised from early childhood to believe that total loyalty to the Spartan state was the basic reason for existence, the Spartans viewed their strength as justification for their militaristic ideals and regimented society.

Athens

By 700 B.C., Athens had established a unified *polis* on the peninsula of Attica. Although early Athens had been ruled by a monarchy, by the seventh century it had fallen under the control of its aristocrats. They possessed the best land and controlled political and religious life by means of a council of nobles, assisted by a board of nine archons. Although an assembly of full citizens did exist, it possessed few powers.

Near the end of the seventh century B.C., Athens faced political turmoil because of serious economic problems. Many Athenian farmers found themselves sold into slavery when they were unable to repay the loans they had borrowed from their aristocratic neighbors, pledging themselves as collateral. Over and over, cries arose to cancel the debts and give land to the poor. Athens seemed on the verge of civil war.

The Reforms of Solon The ruling Athenian aristocrats responded to this crisis by choosing Solon, a reform-minded aristocrat, as sole archon in 594 B.C. and giving him full power to make changes. Solon canceled all current land debts, outlawed new loans based on humans as collateral, and freed people who had fallen into slavery for debts. He refused, however, to carry out the redistribution of the land and hence failed to deal with the basic cause of the economic crisis.

Like his economic reforms, Solon's political measures were also a compromise. Though by no means eliminating the power of the aristocracy, they opened the door to the participation of new people, especially the non-aristocratic wealthy, in the government. But Solon's reforms, though popular, did not solve Athens' problems.

THE LYCURGAN REFORMS

To maintain control over the conquered Messenians, the Spartans instituted the reforms that created their military state. These reforms are associated with the name of the lawgiver Lycurgus, although historians are not sure of his historicity. In this account of Lycurgus, the ancient Greek historian Plutarch discusses the effect of these reforms on the treatment and education of boys.

Plutarch, *Lycurgus*

Lycurgus was of another mind; he would not have masters bought out of the market for his young Spartans, . . . nor was it lawful, indeed, for the father himself to breed up the children after his own fancy; but as soon as they were seven years old they were to be enrolled in certain companies and classes, where they all lived under the same order and discipline, doing their exercises and taking their play together. Of these, he who showed the most conduct and courage was made captain; they had their eyes always upon him, obeyed his orders, and underwent patiently whatsoever punishment he inflicted; so that the whole course of their education was one continued exercise of a ready and perfect obedience. The old men, too, were spectators of their performances, and often raised quarrels and disputes among them, to have a good opportunity of finding out their different characters, and of seeing which would be valiant, which a coward, when they should come to more dangerous encounters. Reading and writing they gave them just enough to serve their turn; their chief care was to make them good subjects, and to teach them to endure pain and conquer in battle. To this end, as they grew in years, their discipline was proportionately increased; their heads were close-clipped, they were accustomed to go barefoot, and for the most part to play naked.

After they were twelve years old, they were no longer allowed to wear any undergarments, they had one coat to serve them a year; their bodies were hard and dry, with but little acquaintance of baths and unguents; these human indulgences they were allowed only on some few particular days in the year. They lodged together in little bands upon beds made of the rushes which grew by the banks of the river Eurotas, which they were to break off with their hands with a knife; if it were winter, they mingled some thistledown with their rushes, which it was thought had the property of giving warmth. By the time they were come to this age there was not any of the more hopeful boys who had not a lover to bear him company. The old men, too, had an eye upon them, coming often to the grounds to hear and see them contend either in wit or strength with one another, and this as seriously . . . as if they were their fathers, their tutors, or their magistrates; so that there scarcely was any time or place without someone present to put them in mind of their duty, and punish them if they had neglected it.

[Spartan boys were also encouraged to steal their food.] They stole, too, all other meat they could lay their hands on, looking out and watching all opportunities, when people were asleep or more careless than usual. If they were caught, they were not only punished with whipping, but hunger, too, being reduced to their ordinary allowance, which was but very slender, and so contrived on purpose, that they might set about to help themselves, and be forced to exercise their energy and address. This was the principal design of their hard fare.

What does this passage from Plutarch's account of Lycurgus reveal about the nature of the Spartan state? Why would this whole program have been distasteful to the Athenians?

Aristocratic factions continued to vie for power, and the poorer peasants resented Solon's failure to institute land redistribution. Internal strife finally led to the very institution Solon had hoped to avoid—tyranny. Pisistratus, an aristocrat, seized power in 560 B.C. Pursuing a foreign policy that aided Athenian trade, Pisistratus remained popular with the merchants. But the Athenians rebelled against his son and ended the tyranny in 510 B.C. Although the aristocrats attempted to reestablish an oligarchy, Cleisthenes, another aristocratic reformer, opposed this plan and, with the backing of the Athenian people, gained the upper hand in 508 B.C. The reforms of Cleisthenes now established the basis for Athenian democracy.

The Reforms of Cleisthenes A major aim of Cleisthenes' reforms was to weaken the power of traditional localities and regions, which had provided the foundation for aristocratic strength. He made the *demes*, the villages and townships of Attica, the basic units of political life. Cleisthenes enrolled all the citizens of the demes in ten new tribes, each of which contained inhabitants located in the country districts of Attica, the coastal areas, and Athens. The ten tribes thus contained a cross section of the population and reflected all of Attica, a move that gave local areas a basic role in the political structure. Each of the ten tribes chose fifty members by lot each year for a new Council of Five Hundred, which was responsible for the administration of both foreign and financial affairs and prepared the business that would be handled by the assembly. This assembly of all male citizens had final authority in the passing of laws after free and open debate; thus Cleisthenes' reforms strengthened the central role of the assembly of citizens in the Athenian political system.

The reforms of Cleisthenes created the foundations for Athenian democracy. More changes would come in the fifth century when the Athenians themselves would

Sparta	
Conquest of Messenia	c. 730–710 B.C.
Beginning of Peloponnesian League	c. 560–550 B.C.
Athens	
Solon's reforms	594–593 B.C.
Tyranny of Pisistratus	c. 560–556 and 546–527 B.C.
Deposition of Hippias—end of tyranny	510 B.C.
Cleisthenes' reforms	c. 508–501 B.C.

begin to use the word *democracy* to describe their system (from the Greek words *demos,* "people," and *kratia,* "power," thus "power to the people"). By 500 B.C., Athens was more united than it had ever been and was about to assume a more important role in Greek affairs.

The High Point of Greek Civilization: Classical Greece

Classical Greece is the name given to the period from around 500 B.C. to the conquest of Greece by the Macedonian king Philip II in 338 B.C. It was a time of brilliant achievement, much of it associated with the flowering of democracy in Athens under the leadership of Pericles. Many of the lasting contributions of the Greeks occurred during this period. The age began with a mighty confrontation between the Greek states and the mammoth Persian Empire.

The Challenge of Persia

As Greek civilization expanded throughout the Mediterranean, it was inevitable that it would come into contact with the Persian Empire to the east. The Ionian Greek cities in western Asia Minor had already fallen subject to the Persian Empire by the mid-sixth century B.C. An unsuccessful revolt by the Ionian cities in 499, assisted by the Athenian navy, led the Persian ruler Darius to seek revenge by attacking the mainland Greeks in 490. The Persians landed an army on the plain of Marathon, only 26 miles from Athens. There a mostly Athenian army, though clearly outnumbered, went on the attack and defeated the Persians decisively.

Xerxes, the new Persian monarch after the death of Darius in 486 B.C., vowed revenge and renewed the invasion of Greece. In preparation for the attack, some of the Greek states formed a defensive league under Spartan leadership, while the Athenians pursued a new military policy by developing a navy. By the time of the Persian invasion in 480 B.C., the Athenians had produced a fleet of about two hundred vessels.

Xerxes led a massive invasion force into Greece: close to 150,000 troops, almost seven hundred naval ships, and hundreds of supply ships to keep their large army fed. The Greeks hoped to stop the Persians at the pass of Thermopylae along the main road into central Greece. A Greek force numbering close to nine thousand, under the leadership of the Spartan king Leonidas and his contingent of three hundred Spartans, held off the Persian army for several days. The Spartan troops were especially brave. When told that Persian arrows would darken the sky in battle, one Spartan warrior supposedly responded, "That is good news. We will fight in the shade!" Unfortunately for the Greeks, a traitor told the Persians how to use a mountain path to outflank the Greek force. King Leonidas and the three hundred Spartans fought to the last man.

The Athenians, now threatened by the onslaught of the Persian forces, abandoned their city. While the Persians sacked and burned Athens, the Greek fleet remained offshore near the island of Salamis and challenged the Persian navy to fight. Although the Greeks were outnumbered, they managed to outmaneuver the Persian fleet and utterly defeated it. A few months later, early in 479 B.C., the Greeks formed the largest Greek army seen up to that time and decisively defeated the Persian army at Plataea, northwest of Attica. The Greeks had won the war and were now free to pursue their own destiny.

The Growth of an Athenian Empire in the Age of Pericles

After the defeat of the Persians, Athens stepped in to provide new leadership against the Persians by forming a confederation called the Delian League. Organized in the winter of 478–477 B.C., the Delian League was dominated by the Athenians from the beginning. Its main headquarters was the island of Delos, but its chief officials, including the treasurers and commanders of the fleet, were Athenian. Under the leadership of the Athenians, the Delian League pursued the attack against the Persian Empire. Virtually all of the Greek states in the Aegean were liberated from Persian control. Arguing that the Persian threat was now over, some members of the Delian League wished to withdraw. But the Athenians forced them to remain in the league and to pay tribute. "No secession" became Athenian policy. The Delian League was rapidly becoming the nucleus of an Athenian empire.

At home, Athenians favored the new imperial policy, especially in the 450s B.C., when an aristocrat named Pericles began to play an important political role. Under Pericles, Athens embarked on a policy of expanding democracy at home while severing its ties with Sparta and expanding its new empire abroad. This period of Athenian and Greek history, which historians have subsequently labeled the Age of Pericles, witnessed the height of Athenian power and the culmination of its brilliance as a civilization.

In the Age of Pericles, the Athenians became deeply attached to their democratic system. The sovereignty of the people was embodied in the assembly, which consisted of all male citizens over eighteen years of age. In the 440s, that was probably a group of about 43,000. Not all attended, however, and the number present at the meetings, which were held every ten days on a hillside east of the Acropolis, seldom reached 6,000. The assembly passed all laws and made final decisions on war and foreign policy.

Routine administration of public affairs was handled by a large body of city magistrates, usually chosen by lot without regard to class and usually serving one-year terms. This meant that many male citizens held public office at some time in their lives. A board of ten officials known as generals (*strategoi*) were elected by public vote to guide affairs of state, although their power depended on the respect they had attained. Generals were usually wealthy aristocrats, even though the people were free to select others. The generals could be reelected, enabling individual leaders to play an important political role. Pericles' reelection fifteen times as a general made him one of the leading politicians between 461 and 429 B.C.

All public officials were subject to scrutiny and could be deposed from office if they lost the people's confidence. After 488 B.C., the Athenians occasionally made use of a tactic called ostracism. Members of the assembly could write on a broken pottery fragment (*ostrakon*) the name of the person they most disliked or considered most harmful to the *polis*. A person who received a majority (if at least six thousand votes were cast) was exiled for ten years.

Pericles expanded the Athenians' involvement in democracy, which was what Athenians had come to call their form of government (see the box on p. 51). Power was in the hands of the people: male citizens voted in the assemblies and served as jurors in the courts. Lower-class citizens were now eligible for public offices formerly closed to them. Pericles also introduced state pay for officeholders, including the widely held jury duty. This meant that even poor citizens could hold public office and afford to participate in public affairs. Nevertheless, although the Athenians developed a system of government that was unique in its time in which citizens had equal rights and the people were the government, aristocrats continued to hold the most important offices, and many people, including women, slaves, and foreigners residing in Athens, were not given the same political rights.

The Athenian pursuit of democracy at home was coupled with increasing imperialism abroad. Citing the threat of the Persian fleet in the Aegean, the Athenians moved the Delian League treasury from the island of Delos to Athens itself in 454 B.C. Members were charged a fee (tribute) for the Athenian claim of protection. Pericles also used the money in the league treasury, without the

approval of its members, to build new temples in Athens, an arrogant reminder that the Delian League had become the Athenian Empire. But Athenian imperialism alarmed the other Greek states, and soon all Greece was confronted with a new war.

The Great Peloponnesian War

During the forty years after the defeat of the Persians, the Greek world divided into two major camps: Sparta and its supporters and the Athenian Empire. In his classic *History of the Peloponnesian War,* the great Greek historian Thucydides pointed out that the basic long-range cause of the Peloponnesian War was the fear that Sparta and its allies had of the growing Athenian Empire. Then, too, Athens and Sparta had built two very different kinds of societies, and neither state was able to tolerate the other's system. A series of disputes finally led to the outbreak of war in 431 B.C.

At the beginning of the war, both sides believed they had winning strategies. The Athenians planned to remain behind the protective walls of Athens while the overseas empire and the navy kept them supplied. Pericles knew perfectly well that the Spartans and their allies could beat the Athenians in pitched battles, which was the chief aim of the Spartan strategy. The Spartans and their allies attacked Athens, hoping that the Athenians would send out their army to fight beyond the walls. But Pericles was convinced that Athens was secure behind its walls and retaliated by sending out naval excursions to ravage the seacoast of the Peloponnesus.

In the second year of the war, however, plague devastated the crowded city of Athens and wiped out possibly one-third of the population. Pericles himself died the following year (429 B.C.), a severe loss to Athens. Despite the ravages of the plague, the Athenians fought on in a struggle that dragged on for another twenty-seven years. A crushing blow came in 405 B.C. when the Athenian fleet was destroyed at Aegospotami on the Hellespont. Athens was besieged and surrendered in 404. Its walls were torn down, the navy was disbanded, and the Athenian Empire was destroyed. The great war was finally over.

The Decline of the Greek States (404–338 B.C.)

The Great Peloponnesian War weakened the major Greek states and led to new alliances among the *poleis*. After the defeat of Athens in 404 B.C., the Spartans established control over Greece. Oligarchies of local leaders in cooperation with Spartan garrisons were imposed on states "liberated" from Athenian imperialism. But the harsh policies of the oligarchs soon led to a reaction. In Athens, rebellion enabled the Athenians to reestablish their democracy in 403 B.C. and even to rebuild their navy and again become an important force in the Greek world.

To maintain its newly organized leadership in Greek affairs, Sparta encouraged a Greek crusade against the

ATHENIAN DEMOCRACY: THE FUNERAL ORATION OF PERICLES

In his History of the Peloponnesian War, the Greek historian Thucydides presented his reconstruction of the eulogy given by Pericles in the winter of 431–430 B.C. to honor the Athenians killed in the first campaigns of the Great Peloponnesian War. It is a magnificent, idealized description of the Athenian democracy at its height.

Thucydides, *History of the Peloponnesian War*

Our constitution is called a democracy because power is in the hands not of a minority but of the whole people. When it is a question of settling private disputes, everyone is equal before the law; when it is a question of putting one person before another in positions of public responsibility, what counts is not membership of a particular class, but the actual ability which the man possesses. No one, so long as he has it in him to be of service to the state, is kept in political obscurity because of poverty. And, just as our political life is free and open, so is our day-to-day life in our relations with each other. We do not get into a state with our next-door neighbor if he enjoys himself in his own way, nor do we give him the kind of black looks which, though they do no real harm, still do hurt people's feeling. We are free and tolerant in our private lives; but in public affairs we keep to the law. This is because it commands our deep respect.

We give our obedience to those whom we put in positions of authority, and we obey the laws themselves, especially those which are for the protection of the oppressed, and those unwritten laws which it is an acknowledged shame to break. . . . Here each individual is interested not only in his own affairs but in the affairs of the state as well: even those who are mostly occupied with their own business are extremely well-informed on general politics—this is a peculiarity of ours: we do not say that a man who takes no interest in politics is a man who minds his own business; we say that he has no business here at all. We Athenians, in our own persons, take our decisions on policy or submit them to proper discussions: for we do not think that there is an incompatibility between words and deeds; the worst thing is to rush into action before the consequences have been properly debated. . . . Taking everything together then, I declare that our city is an education to Greece, and I declare that in my opinion each single one of our citizens, in all the manifold aspects of life, is able to show himself the rightful lord and owner of his own person and do this, moreover, with exceptional grace and exceptional versatility. And to show that this is no empty boasting for the present occasion, but real tangible fact, you have only to consider the power which our city possesses and which has been won by those very qualities which I have mentioned.

In the eyes of Pericles, what are the ideals of Athenian democracy? In what ways does Pericles exaggerate his claims? Why would the Athenian passion for debate described by Pericles have been distasteful to the Spartans?

Persians as a common enemy. But the Persians had learned the lessons of Greek politics and offered financial support to Athens and other Greek states to oppose Spartan power within Greece itself, thus beginning a new war that finally ended in 386 B.C.

The city-state of Thebes, in Boeotia, north of Athens, now began to exert its influence. Under the leader Epaminondas, the Thebans dramatically defeated the Spartan army at the Battle of Leuctra in 371 B.C. Spartan power declined, but Theban ascendancy was short-lived. After the death of Epaminondas in the Battle of Mantinea in 362 B.C., the Thebans could no longer dominate Greek politics. Yet the Greek states continued their petty wars, seemingly oblivious to the growing danger to the north, where King Philip II of Macedonia was developing a unified state that would finally end the destructive fratricide of the Greek states by imposing Macedonian authority.

The Culture and Society of Classical Greece

Classical Greece was a time of remarkable intellectual and cultural growth throughout the Greek world, and Peri-

clean Athens was the most important center of classical Greek culture.

The Writing of History

History as we know it, the systematic analysis of past events, was a Greek creation. Herodotus (c. 484–c. 425 B.C.) was the author of *The Persian Wars*, a work commonly regarded as the first real history in Western civilization. The Greek word *historia* (from which we derive our word *history*) means "research" or "investigation," and it is in the opening line of Herodotus' *History* that we find the first recorded use of the word:

> These are the researches [*historia*] of Herodotus of Halicarnassus, which he publishes, in the hope of thereby preserving from decay the remembrance of what men have done, and of preventing the great and wonderful actions of the Greeks and the Barbarians from losing their due meed [reward] of glory; and withal to put on record what were their grounds of feud.[7]

The central theme of Herodotus' work is the conflict between the Greeks and the Persians, which he viewed as a struggle between freedom and despotism. Herodotus traveled extensively and questioned many people to obtain his information. Although he was a master storyteller and sometimes included considerable fanciful material, Herodotus was also capable of exhibiting a critical attitude toward the materials he used.

Thucydides (c. 460–c. 400 B.C.) was a far better historian, indeed, the greatest of the ancient world. Thucydides was an Athenian and a participant in the Peloponnesian War. He had been elected a general, but a defeat in battle led the Athenian assembly to send him into exile, which gave him the opportunity to concentrate on writing his *History of the Peloponnesian War.*

Unlike Herodotus, Thucydides was not concerned with divine forces or gods as causal factors in history. He saw war and politics in purely rational terms, as the activities of human beings. He examined the causes of the Peloponnesian War in a clear and objective fashion, placing much emphasis on the accuracy of his facts. As he stated:

> And with regard to my factual reporting of the events of the war I have made it a principle not to write down the first story that came my way, and not even to be guided by my own general impressions; either I was present myself at the events which I have described or else I heard of them from eyewitnesses whose reports I have checked with as much thoroughness as possible.[8]

Thucydides also provided remarkable insight into the human condition. He believed that political situations recur in similar fashion and that the study of history is therefore of great value in understanding the present.

Greek Drama

Drama, as we know it, was created by the Greeks and was clearly intended to do more than entertain. It was used to educate citizens and was supported by the state for that reason. Plays were presented in outdoor theaters as part of a religious festival. The form of Greek plays remained rather stable. Three male actors who wore masks acted all the parts. A chorus, also male, played the role of groups of people or served as narrators. Action was very limited because the emphasis was on the story and its meaning.

The first Greek dramas were tragedies, plays based on the suffering of a hero and usually ending in disaster. Aeschylus (525–456 B.C.) is the first tragedian whose plays are known to us. Although he wrote ninety tragedies, only seven have survived. As was customary in Greek tragedy, his plots were simple. The entire drama focused on a single tragic event and its meaning. Greek tragedies were sometimes presented in a trilogy (a set of three plays) built around a common theme. The only complete trilogy we possess, called the *Oresteia,* was written by Aeschylus. The theme of this trilogy is derived from Homer. Agamemnon, the king of Mycenae, returns a hero from the defeat of Troy. His wife, Clytemnestra, avenges the sacrificial death of her daughter Iphigenia by murdering Agamemnon, who had been responsible for Iphigenia's death. In the second play of the trilogy, Agamemnon's son Orestes avenges his father by killing his mother. Orestes is now pursued by the Furies, who torment him for killing his mother. Evil acts breed evil acts and suffering is one's lot, suggests Aeschylus. But Orestes is put on trial and acquitted by Athena, the patron goddess of Athens. Personal vendetta has been eliminated, and law has prevailed.

Another great Athenian playwright was Sophocles (c. 496–406 B.C.), whose most famous play was *Oedipus the King.* The oracle of Apollo foretells how a man (Oedipus) will kill his own father and marry his mother. Despite all attempts at prevention, the tragic events occur. Although it appears that Oedipus suffered the fate determined by the gods, Oedipus also accepts that he himself as a free man must bear responsibility for his actions: "It was Apollo, friends, Apollo, that brought this bitter bitterness, my sorrows to completion. But the hand that struck me was none but my own."[9]

The third outstanding Athenian tragedian, Euripides (c. 485–406 B.C.), tried to create more realistic characters. His plots also became more complex and reflected a greater interest in real-life situations. Perhaps the greatest of all his plays was *The Bacchae,* which dealt with the introduction of the hysterical rites associated with Dionysus, god of wine. Euripides is often seen as a skeptic who questioned traditional moral and religious values. Euripides was also critical of the traditional view that war was glorious. He portrayed war as brutal and barbaric.

Greek tragedies dealt with universal themes still relevant in our day. They probed such problems as the nature of good and evil, the conflict between spiritual values and the demands of the state or family, the rights of the individual, the nature of divine forces, and human nature. Over and over, the tragic lesson was repeated: humans were free and yet could operate only within limitations imposed by the gods. The real task was to cultivate the balance and moderation that led to awareness of one's true position. But the pride in human accomplishment and independence is real. As the chorus chants in Sophocles' *Antigone,* "Is there anything more wonderful on earth, our marvelous planet, than the miracle of man?"[10]

Greek comedy developed later than tragedy. The plays of Aristophanes (c. 450–c. 385 B.C.), who used both grotesque masks and obscene jokes to entertain the Athenian audience, are examples of Old Comedy, which was used to attack or savagely satirize both politicians and intellectuals. In *The Clouds,* for example, Aristophanes characterized the philosopher Socrates as the operator of a thought factory where people could learn deceitful ways to handle other people. Of special importance to Aristophanes was his opposition to the Peloponnesian War. *Lysistrata,* performed in 411 B.C., at a time when Athens was in serious danger of losing the war, conveyed a comic but effective message against the war.

The Arts: The Classical Ideal

The arts of the Western world have been largely dominated by the artistic standards established by the Greeks of the Classical period. Classical Greek art did not aim at experimentation for experiment's sake but was concerned with expressing eternally true ideals. The subject matter was the human being, presented as an object of great beauty. The Classical style, based on the ideals of reason, moderation, balance, and harmony in all things, was meant to civilize the emotions.

In architecture, the most important structure was the temple dedicated to a god or goddess. Because Greek religious ceremonies were held at altars in the open air, temples were not used to enclose the faithful, as modern churches are. At the center of Greek temples were walled rooms that housed the statues of deities and treasuries in which gifts to the gods and goddesses were safeguarded. These central rooms were surrounded by a screen of columns that give Greek temples their open structure. The columns were originally made of wood but were changed to limestone in the seventh century and to marble in the fifth century B.C.

Some of the finest examples of Greek Classical architecture were built in fifth-century Athens. The most famous building, regarded as the greatest example of the Classical Greek temple, is the Parthenon, built between 447 and 432 B.C. The master builders Ictinus and Callicrates directed the construction of this temple consecrated to Athena, the patron goddess of Athens. The Parthenon typifies the principles of Classical architecture: the search for calm, clarity, and freedom from superfluous detail. The individual parts of the temple were constructed in accordance with certain mathematical ratios also found in natural phenomena. The architects' concern with these laws of proportion is paralleled by the attempt of Greek philosophers to understand the general laws underlying nature.

Greek sculpture also developed a Classical style that differed significantly from the artificial stiffness of earlier periods. Statues of the male nude, the favorite subject of Greek sculptors, now exhibited more relaxed attitudes; their faces were self-assured; their bodies were flexible and smooth-muscled. Although the figures possessed natural features that made them lifelike, Greek sculptors sought to achieve not realism but a standard of ideal beauty. Polyclitus, a fifth-century sculptor, wrote a treatise (now lost) on a canon of proportions that he illustrated in a work known as the *Doryphoros*. His theory maintained that the use of ideal proportions, based on mathematical ratios found in nature, could produce an ideal human form, beautiful in its perfected and refined features. This search for ideal beauty was the dominant aspect of Classical sculpture.

The Greek Love of Wisdom

Philosophy is a Greek word that literally means "love of wisdom." Early Greek philosophers were concerned with the development of critical or rational thought about the nature of the universe and the place of divine forces in it. The **Sophists,** however, were a group of philosophical teachers in fifth-century Athens who rejected such speculation as foolish; they argued that understanding the universe was beyond the reach of the human mind. It was more important for individuals to improve themselves, so the only worthwhile object of study was human behavior. The Sophists were wandering scholars who sold their services as professional teachers to the young men of Greece, especially those of Athens. The Sophists stressed the importance of **rhetoric** (the art of persuasive speaking) in winning debates and swaying an audience, a skill that was especially valuable in democratic Athens. To the Sophists, there was no absolute right or wrong—what was right for one individual might be wrong for another. True wisdom consisted of being able to perceive and pursue one's own good. Because of these ideas, many people viewed the Sophists as harmful to society and especially dangerous to the values of young people.

One of the critics of the Sophists was Socrates (469–399 B.C.). Because he left no writing of his own, we know about him only from his pupils, especially his most

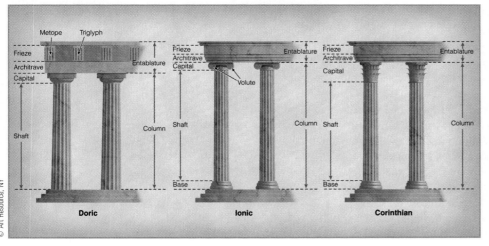

© Art Resource, NY

Doric, Ionic, and Corinthian Orders. The size and shape of a column constituted one of the most important aspects of Greek temple architecture. The Doric order, with plain capitals and no base, developed first in the Dorian Peloponnesus and was rather simple in comparison to the slender Ionic column, which had an elaborate base and spiral-shaped capitals, and the Corinthian column, which featured leaf-shaped capitals.

The Parthenon. The arts in Classical Greece were designed to express the eternal ideals of reason, moderation, symmetry, balance, and harmony. In architecture, the most important form was the temple, and the classic example of this kind of architecture is the Parthenon, built between 447 and 432 B.C. Located on the Acropolis in Athens, the Parthenon was dedicated to Athena, the patron goddess of the city, but it also served as a shining example of the power and wealth of the Athenian Empire.

famous one, Plato. By occupation, Socrates was a stonemason, but his true love was philosophy. He taught a number of pupils, but not for pay, because he believed that the goal of education was only to improve the individual. He made use of a teaching method that is still known by his name. The **Socratic method** employs a question-and-answer technique to lead pupils to see things for themselves using their own reason. Socrates believed that all real knowledge is within each person; only critical examination was needed to call it forth. This was the real task of philosophy, since "the unexamined life is not worth living."

Socrates' questioning of authority led him into trouble. Athens had had a tradition of free thought and inquiry, but defeat in the Peloponnesian War had created an environment much less tolerant of open debate and soul-searching. Socrates was accused and convicted of corrupting the youth of Athens by his teaching. An Athenian jury sentenced him to death.

One of Socrates' disciples was Plato (c. 429–347 B.C.), considered by many the greatest philosopher of Western civilization. Unlike his master Socrates, who wrote nothing, Plato wrote a great deal. He was fascinated with

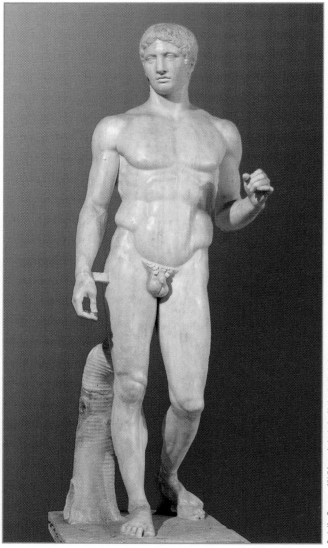

Doryphoros. This statue, known as the *Doryphoros,* or spear carrier, is a Roman copy of the original work by the fifth-century B.C. sculptor Polyclitus, who believed it illustrated the ideal proportions of the human figure. Classical Greek sculpture moved away from the stiffness of earlier figures but retained the young male nude as the favorite subject matter. The statues became more lifelike, with relaxed poses and flexible, smooth-muscled bodies. The aim of sculpture, however, was not simply realism but rather the expression of ideal beauty.

the question of reality: How do we know what is real? According to Plato, a higher world of eternal, unchanging Ideas or Forms has always existed. To know these Forms is to know truth. These ideal Forms constitute reality and can only be apprehended by a trained mind, which, of course, is the goal of philosophy. The objects that we perceive with our senses are simply reflections of the ideal Forms. Hence they are shadows, while reality is found in the Forms themselves.

Plato's ideas of government were set out in a dialogue he titled *The Republic.* Based on his experience in Athens, Plato had come to distrust the workings of democracy. It was obvious to him that individuals could not attain an ethical life unless they lived in a just and rational state. Plato's search for the just state led him to construct an ideal state in which the population was divided into three basic groups. At the top was an upper class, a ruling elite, the philosopher-kings: "Unless either philosophers become kings in their countries or those who are now called kings and rulers come to be sufficiently inspired with a genuine desire for wisdom; unless, that is to say, political power and philosophy meet together . . . there can be no rest from troubles . . . for states, nor yet, as I believe, for all mankind."[11] The second group consisted of citizens who showed courage, the warriors who protected the society. All the rest made up the masses, essentially people driven not by wisdom or courage but by desire. They would be the producers of society—the artisans, tradesmen, and farmers.

In Plato's ideal state, each group fulfilled its assigned role, creating a society that functioned harmoniously. The needs of the community, rather than the happiness of the individual, were Plato's concern, and he focused on the need for the guardians or rulers, above all, to be removed from any concerns for wealth or prestige so that they could strive for what was best for the community. To rid the guardians of these desires, Plato urged that they live together, forgoing both private property and family life. Plato believed that women, too, could be rulers; in this he departed radically from the actual practices of the Greek states.

Plato established a school at Athens known as the Academy. One of his pupils, who studied there for twenty years, was Aristotle (384–322 B.C.), who later became a tutor to Alexander the Great. Aristotle did not accept Plato's theory of ideal Forms. Instead he believed that by examining individual objects, we can perceive their form and arrive at universal principles; however, these principles do not exist as a separate higher world of reality beyond material things but are a part of things themselves. Aristotle's interests, then, lay in analyzing and classifying things based on thorough research and investigation. His interests were wide-ranging, and he wrote treatises on an enormous number of subjects: ethics, logic, politics, poetry, astronomy, geology, biology, and physics.

Like Plato, Aristotle wished for an effective form of government that would rationally direct human affairs. Unlike Plato, he did not seek an ideal state based on the embodiment of an ideal Form of justice; he tried to find the best form of government through a rational examination of existing governments. For his *Politics,* Aristotle examined the constitutions of 158 states and arrived at general categories for organizing governments. He identified three good forms of government: monarchy, aristocracy, and constitutional government. But based on his examination, he warned that monarchy can easily turn into tyranny, aristocracy into oligarchy, and constitutional government into radical democracy or anarchy. He favored constitutional government as the best form for most people.

Aristotle's philosophical and political ideas played an enormous role in the development of Western thought during the Middle Ages (see Chapter 9). So did his ideas on women. Aristotle believed that marriage was meant to provide mutual comfort between man and woman and contributed to the overall happiness of a community: "The community needs both male and female excellences or it can only be half-blessed."[12] Nevertheless, Aristotle maintained that women were biologically inferior to men: "A woman is, as it were, an infertile male. She is female in fact on account of a kind of inadequacy." Therefore, according to Aristotle, women must be subordinated to men, not only in the community but also in marriage: "The association between husband and wife is clearly an aristocracy. The man rules by virtue of merit, and in the sphere that is his by right; but he hands over to this wife such matters as are suitable for her."[13]

Greek Religion

Greek religion was intricately connected to every aspect of daily life; it was both social and practical. Public festivals, which originated in religious practices, served specific functions: boys were prepared to be warriors, girls to be mothers. Since religion was related to every aspect of life, citizens had to have a proper attitude toward the gods. Religion was a civic cult necessary for the well-being of the state. Temples dedicated to a god or goddess were the major buildings in Greek society.

Homer gave an account of the gods that provided Greek religion with a definite structure. Over a period of time, most Greeks came to accept a common religion based on twelve chief gods and goddesses who were thought to live on Mount Olympus, the highest mountain in Greece. Among the twelve were Zeus, the chief deity and father of the gods; Athena, goddess of wisdom and crafts; Apollo, god of the sun and poetry; Aphrodite, goddess of love; and Poseidon, brother of Zeus and god of the seas and earthquakes.

The twelve Olympian gods were common to all Greeks, who thus shared a basic polytheistic religion. Each *polis* usually singled out one of the twelve Olympians as a guardian deity of its community. Athena was the patron goddess of Athens, for example. Because it was desirable to have the gods look favorably on one's activities, ritual assumed enormous proportions in Greek religion. Prayers were often combined with gifts to the gods based on the principle "I give to you, the gods, so that you will give in return." Ritual also meant sacrifices of animals or food. Animals were burned on an altar in front of a temple or a small altar in front of a home.

Festivals also developed as a way to honor the gods and goddesses. Some of these (the Panhellenic celebrations) were important to all Greeks and were held at special locations, such as those dedicated to the worship of Zeus at Olympia or to Apollo at Delphi. Numerous events were held in honor of the gods at the great festivals, including athletic competitions to which all Greeks were invited. The first such games were held at the Olympic festival in 776 B.C. and then held every four years thereafter to honor Zeus. Initially, the Olympic contests consisted of foot races and wrestling, but later, boxing, javelin throwing, and various other contests were added.

The Greeks also had a great desire to know the will of the gods. To do so, they made use of the oracle, a sacred shrine dedicated to a god or goddess who revealed the future. The most famous was the oracle of Apollo at Delphi, located on the side of Mount Parnassus, overlooking the Gulf of Corinth. At Delphi, a priestess listened to questions while in a state of ecstasy that was believed to be induced by Apollo. Her responses were interpreted by the priests and given in verse form to the person asking questions. Representatives of states and individuals traveled to Delphi to consult the oracle of Apollo. States might inquire whether they should undertake a military expedition; individuals might raise such questions as "Heracleidas asks whether he will have offspring from the wife he has now." Responses were often enigmatic and at times even politically motivated. Croesus, the king of Lydia in Asia Minor, who was known for his vast wealth, sent messengers to the oracle at Delphi, asking whether he should go to war with the Persians. The oracle replied that if Croesus attacked the Persians, a mighty empire would be destroyed. Overjoyed to hear these words, Croesus made war on the Persians but was crushed by the enemy forces. A mighty empire was indeed destroyed—his own.

Daily Life in Classical Athens

The Greek city-state was, above all, a male community: only adult male citizens took part in public life. In Athens, this meant the exclusion of women, slaves, and foreign residents, or roughly 85 percent of the population in Attica. Of the 150,000 citizens in Athens, about 43,000 were adult males who exercised political power. Resident foreigners, who numbered about 35,000, received the protection of the laws but were also subject to some of the responsibilities of citizens, namely, military service and the funding of festivals. The remaining social group, the slaves, numbered around 100,000. Most slaves in Athens worked in the home as cooks and maids or toiled in the fields. Some were owned by the state and worked on public construction projects.

Economy and Lifestyle The Athenian economy was largely agricultural but highly diversified. Athenian farmers grew grains, vegetables, and fruit for local consumption; cultivated vines and olive trees for wine and olive oil, which were exportable products; and grazed sheep and goats for wool and milk products. Given the size of its population and the lack of abundant fertile land, Athens had to import between 50 and 80 percent of its grain, a staple in the Athenian diet. Trade was thus highly important to the Athenian economy. The building of the port at Piraeus and the Long Walls (a series of defensive walls nearly 5 miles long connecting Athens and Piraeus) created the physical conditions that made Athens the leading trade center in the fifth-century Greek world.

Artisans were more important to the Athenian economy than their relatively small numbers might suggest. Athens was the chief producer of high-quality painted pottery in the fifth century. Other crafts had moved beyond the small workshop into the factory through the use of slave labor. The shield factory of Lysias, for example, employed 120 slaves. Public works projects also provided jobs for Athenians. The building program of Pericles, financed from the Delian League treasury, made possible the hiring of both skilled and unskilled labor.

The Athenian lifestyle was simple. Houses were furnished with necessities bought from artisans, such as beds, couches, tables, chests, pottery, stools, baskets, and cooking utensils. Wives and slaves made clothes and blankets at home. The Athenian diet was rather plain and relied on such basic foods as barley, wheat, millet, lentils, grapes, figs, olives, almonds, bread made at home, vegetables, eggs, fish, cheese, and chicken. Olive oil was widely used, not only for eating but also for lighting lamps and rubbing on the body after washing and exercise. Although country houses kept animals, they were used for reasons other than their flesh: oxen for plowing, sheep for wool, goats for milk and cheese.

Family and Relationships The family was an important institution in ancient Athens. It was composed of husband, wife, and children (a nuclear family), although other dependent relatives and slaves were also part of the family economic unit. The family's primary social function was to produce new citizens. Strict laws of the fifth century had stipulated that a citizen must be the offspring of a legally acknowledged marriage between two Athenian citizens whose parents were also citizens.

Women were citizens who could participate in most religious cults and festivals but were otherwise excluded from public life. They could not own property beyond personal items and always had a male guardian. The function of the Athenian woman as wife was very clear. Her foremost obligation was to bear children, especially male children who would preserve the family line. The marriage formula that Athenians used put it succinctly: "I give this woman for the procreation of legitimate children." A wife was also expected to take care of her family and her house, either doing the household work herself

HOUSEHOLD MANAGEMENT AND THE ROLE OF THE ATHENIAN WIFE

*I*n fifth-century Athens, a woman's place was in the home. She had two major responsibilities: the bearing and raising children and the management of the household. In his dialogue on estate management, Xenophon relates the instructions of an Attican gentleman to his new wife.

Xenophon, *Oeconomicus*

[Ischomachus addresses his new wife:] For it seems to me, dear, that the gods with great discernment have coupled together male and female, as they are called, chiefly in order that they may form a perfect partnership in mutual service. For, in the first place that the various species of living creatures may not fail, they are joined in wedlock for the production of children. Secondly, offspring to support them in old age is provided by this union, to human beings, at any rate. Thirdly, human beings live not in the open air, like beasts, but obviously need shelter. Nevertheless, those who mean to win stores to fill the covered place, have need of someone to work at the open-air occupations; since plowing, sowing, planting and grazing are all such open-air employments; and these supply the needful food. . . . For he made

the man's body and mind more capable of enduring cold and heat, and journeys and campaigns; and therefore imposed on him the outdoor tasks. To the woman, since he had made her body less capable of such endurance, I take it that God has assigned the indoor tasks. And knowing that he had created in the woman and had imposed on her the nourishment of the infants, he meted out to her a larger portion of affection for newborn babes than to the man. . . .

Your duty will be to remain indoors and send out those servants whose work is outside, and superintend those who are to work indoors, and to receive the incomings, and distribute so much of them as must be spent, and watch over so much as is to be kept in store, and take care that the sum laid by for a year be not spent in a month. And when wool is brought to you, you must see that cloaks are made for those that want them. You must see too that the dry corn is in good condition for making food. One of the duties that fall to you, however, will perhaps seem rather thankless: you will have to see that any servant who is ill is cared for.

What does the selection from Xenophon tell you about the role of women in the Athenian household?

or supervising the slaves who did the actual work (see the box above).

Women were kept under strict control. Since they were married at fourteen or fifteen, they were taught about their responsibilities at an early age. Although many managed to learn to read and play musical instruments, they were often cut off from any formal education. And women were supposed to remain at home, out of sight, except when attending funerals or festivals. If they left the house, they were to be accompanied.

Male homosexuality was also a prominent feature of Athenian life. The Greek homosexual ideal was a rela-

tionship between a mature man and a young male. It is most likely that this was an aristocratic ideal and not one practiced by the common people. Although the relationship was frequently physical, the Greeks also viewed it as educational. The older male (the "lover") won the love of his "beloved" by his value as a teacher and by the devotion he demonstrated in training his charge. In a sense, this love relationship was seen as a way of initiating young men into the male world of political and military dominance. The Greeks did not feel that the coexistence of homosexual and heterosexual predilections created any special problems for individuals or their society.

Erich Lessing/Art Resource, NY (Louvre, Paris)

Women in the Loom Room. In Athens, women were considered citizens and could participate in religious cults and festivals, but they were barred from any political activity. Women were thought to belong in the house, caring for the children and the needs of the household. A principal activity of Greek women was the making of clothes. This scene from the side of a fifth-century B.C. Greek vessel shows one woman spinning and another holding a small hand loom.

TIMELINE

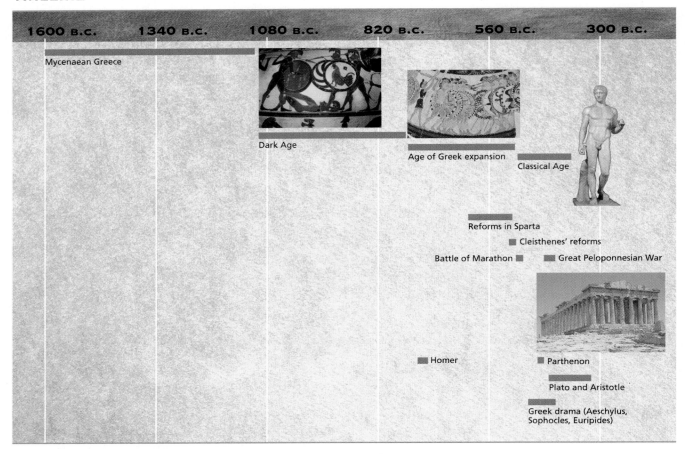

| 1600 B.C. | 1340 B.C. | 1080 B.C. | 820 B.C. | 560 B.C. | 300 B.C. |

Mycenaean Greece

Dark Age

Age of Greek expansion

Classical Age

Reforms in Sparta

Cleisthenes' reforms

Battle of Marathon   Great Peloponnesian War

Homer   Parthenon

Plato and Aristotle

Greek drama (Aeschylus, Sophocles, Euripides)

CONCLUSION

The civilization of the ancient Greeks was the fountainhead of Western culture. Socrates, Plato, and Aristotle established the foundations of Western philosophy. Herodotus and Thucydides created the discipline of history. Our literary forms are largely derived from Greek poetry and drama. Greek notions of harmony, proportion, and beauty have remained the touchstones for all subsequent Western art. A rational method of inquiry, so important to modern science, was conceived in ancient Greece. Many political terms are of Greek origin, and so are our concepts of the rights and duties of citizenship, especially as they were conceived in Athens, the first great democracy. Athens gave the idea of democracy to the Western world.

Especially during their Classical period, the Greeks raised and debated the fundamental questions about the purpose of human existence, the structure of human society, and the nature of the universe that have concerned Western thinkers ever since.

All of these achievements came from a group of small city-states in ancient Greece. And yet Greek civilization also contains an element of tragedy. For all of their brilliant accomplishments, the Greeks were unable to rise above the divisions and rivalries that caused them to fight each other and undermine their own civilization. Of course, their contributions to Western civilization have outlived their political struggles.

NOTES

1. H. D. F. Kitto, *The Greeks* (Harmondsworth, England, 1951), p. 64.
2. Homer, *Odyssey*, trans. E.V. Rieu (Harmondsworth, England, 1946), p. 337.
3. Xenophon, *Symposium*, trans. O. J. Todd (Cambridge, Mass., 1968), III, 5.
4. Homer, *Odyssey*, pp. 290–291.
5. Quoted in T. R. Martin, *Ancient Greece* (New Haven, Conn., 1996), p. 62.
6. Plutarch, quoted in E. Fantham, H. P. Foley, N. B. Kampen, S. B. Pomeroy, and H. A. Shapiro, *Women in the Classical World* (New York, 1994), p. 64.
7. Herodotus, *The Persian Wars*, trans. G. Rawlinson (New York, 1942), p. 3.

8. Thucydides, *History of the Peloponnesian War*, trans. R. Warner (Harmondsworth, England, 1954), p. 24.

9. Sophocles, *Oedipus the King*, trans. D. Grene (Chicago, 1959), pp. 68–69.

10. Sophocles, *Antigone*, trans. D. Taylor (London, 1986), p. 146.

11. Plato, *The Republic*, trans. F. M. Cornford (New York, 1945), pp. 178–179.

12. Aristotle, quoted in S. Blundell, *Women in Ancient Greece* (Cambridge, Mass., 1995), p. 106.

13. Ibid., p. 186.

SUGGESTIONS FOR FURTHER READING

A standard one-volume reference work for Greek history is **J. B. Bury and R. Meiggs**, *A History of Greece to the Death of Alexander the Great*, 4th ed. (New York, 1975). For a beautifully illustrated introduction, see **F. Durando**, *Ancient Greece: The Dawn of the Western World* (New York, 1997). For a brief illustrated introduction, see **J. Camp and E. Fisher**, *The World of the Ancient Greeks* (London, 2002). Other good general introductions to Greek history include **T. R. Martin**, *Ancient Greece* (New Haven, Conn., 1996); **P. Cartledge**, *The Cambridge Illustrated History of Ancient Greece* (Cambridge, 1998); and **W. Donlan et al.**, *Ancient Greece: A Political, Social, and Cultural History* (New York, 1998).

Early Greek history is examined in **O. Murray**, *Early Greece*, 2d ed. (Cambridge, Mass., 1993); **M. I. Finley**, *Early Greece: The Bronze and Archaic Ages*, 2d ed. (New York, 1982); and **J. L. Fitton**, *The Discovery of the Greek Bronze Age* (Cambridge, 1995). On Homer and his world, see the modern classic by **M. I. Finley**, *The World of Odysseus*, 2d ed. (New York, 1979).

General works on Archaic Greece include **A. M. Snodgrass**, *Archaic Greece* (London, 1980), and **M. Grant**, *The Rise of the Greeks* (London, 1987). Economic and social history of the period is covered in **C. Starr**, *The Economic and Social Growth of Early Greece, 800–500 B.C.* (Oxford, 1977). On colonization, see **J. Boardman**, *The Greeks Overseas*, rev. ed. (Baltimore, 1980). On tyranny, see **J. F. McGlew**, *Tyranny and Political Culture in Ancient Greece* (Ithaca, N.Y., 1993). On the culture of Archaic Greece, see **W. Burkert**, *The Orientalizing Revolution: Near Eastern Influence on Greek Culture in the Early Archaic Age* (Cambridge, Mass., 1992). On Sparta, see **P. A. Cartledge**, *Spartan Reflections* (Berkeley, Calif., 2001) and *The Spartans* (New York, 2003). On early Athens, see the still valuable **A. Jones**, *Athenian Democracy* (London, 1957), and **R. Osborne**, *Demos* (New York, 1985). The Persian Wars are examined in **P. Green**, *The Greco-Persian Wars* (Berkeley, Calif., 1996).

A general history of Classical Greece can be found in **J. K. Davies**, *Democracy and Classical Greece*, 2d ed. (Cambridge, Mass., 1993). Valuable works on Athens include **D. Kagan**, *Pericles of Athens and the Birth of Democracy* (New York, 1991); **C. Farrar**, *The Origins of Democratic Thinking: The Invention of Politics in Classical Athens* (Cambridge, 1988); **C. W. Fornara** and **L. J. Samons II**, *Athens from Cleisthenes to Pericles* (Berkeley, Calif., 1991); and

D. Stockton, *The Classical Athenian Democracy* (Oxford, 1990). An interesting work on the intellectual and political history of Athens in the late fifth century B.C. is **M. Munn**, *The School of History: Athens in the Age of Socrates* (Berkeley, Calif., 2000). On the development of the Athenian Empire, see **M. F. McGregor**, *The Athenians and Their Empire* (Vancouver, 1987). The best way to examine the Great Peloponnesian War is to read the work of **Thucydides**, *History of the Peloponnesian War*, trans. **R. Warner** (Harmondsworth, England, 1954). An excellent recent history is **D. Kagan**, *The Peloponnesian War* (New York, 2003). On fourth-century Athens, see **M. H. Hansen**, *The Athenian Democracy in the Age of Demosthenes* (Oxford, 1991).

For a comprehensive history of Greek art, see **M. Robertson**, *A History of Greek Art*, 2 vols. (Cambridge, 1975). On sculpture, see **A. Stewart**, *Greek Sculpture: An Exploration* (New Haven, Conn., 1990). A basic survey of architecture is **H. W. Lawrence**, *Greek Architecture*, rev. ed. (Harmondsworth, England, 1983). On Greek drama, see the general work by **J. De Romilly**, *A Short History of Greek Literature* (Chicago, 1985). On Greek philosophy, a detailed study is available in **W. K. C. Guthrie**, *A History of Greek Philosophy*, 6 vols. (Cambridge, 1962–1981).

On Greek religion, see **J. N. Bremmer**, *Greek Religion* (Oxford, 1994), and **R. Garland**, *Religion and the Greeks* (New York, 1994). On athletic competitions, see **S. G. Miller**, *Ancient Greek Athletics* (New Haven, Conn., 2004).

On the family and women, see **C. B. Patterson**, *The Family in Greek History* (New York, 1998); **E. Fantham et al.**, *Women in the Classical World* (New York, 1994); and **S. Blundell**, *Women in Ancient Greece* (London, 1995). On slavery, see **N.R.E. Fisher**, *Slavery in Classical Greece* (New York, 1995). On homosexuality, see **K. J. Dover**, *Greek Homosexuality* (London, 1978), and **E. Cantarella**, *Bisexuality in the Ancient World* (New Haven, Conn., 1992).

Thomson NOW Enter ThomsonNOW using the access card that is available for *Western Civilization: A Brief History*. ThomsonNOW will help you understand this chapter with lesson plans generated for your needs. In addition, you can read the following documents, and many more, online:

Tyrtaeus, A War Song
Aeschylus, selection from the end of *Agamemnon*
Sophocles, excerpts from *Oedipus the King*
Euripides, excerpt from *Medea*
Plato, excerpts from *Apology* and *Republic*

WESTERN CIVILIZATION RESOURCES

Visit the Web site for *Western Civilization: A Brief History* for resources specific to this book:

http://www.thomsonedu.com/history/spielvogel

For a variety of tools to help you succeed in this course, visit the Western Civilization Resource Center at

http://history.wadsworth.com/spielvogel

Included are quizzes, images, documents, interactive simulations, maps and timelines, movie explorations, and a wealth of other sources.

CHAPTER
4

THE HELLENISTIC WORLD

CHAPTER OUTLINE
AND FOCUS QUESTIONS

Macedonia and the Conquests of Alexander

☐ How was Alexander able to amass his empire, and what might his rule have been like if he had lived longer?

The World of the Hellenistic Kingdoms

☐ What were the main features of the political and military organization of the Hellenistic kingdoms, and how did the new political systems differ from those of the Greek city-states? What were the main social developments in the Hellenistic world?

Culture in the Hellenistic World

☐ What achievements in literature, art, science, and philosophy occurred during the Hellenistic period?

Religion in the Hellenistic World

☐ Which religions were prominent during the Hellenistic period, and what does their popularity suggest about Hellenistic society?

CRITICAL THINKING

☐ How was the Hellenistic period different from the Greek Classical Age?

*Detail of Alexander from the
Battle of Issus mosaic in Pompeii*

Erich Lessing/Art Resource, NY (Museo Archeologico Nazionale, Naples)

$\mathcal{I}$N 334 B.C., **ALEXANDER THE GREAT** led an army of Greeks and Macedonians into western Asia to launch his attack on the Persian Empire. Years of campaigning resulted in the complete defeat of the Persians, and in 327, Alexander and his troops pushed east into India. But two more years of fighting in an exotic and difficult terrain exhausted his troops, who rebelled and refused to go on. Reluctantly, Alexander turned back, leading his men across the arid lands of southern Persia. Conditions in the desert were appalling; the blazing sun and lack of water led to thousands of deaths. At one point, when a group of his soldiers found a little water, they scooped it up in a helmet and gave it to Alexander. Then, according to Arrian, an ancient Greek historian, Alexander, "with a word of thanks for the gift, took the helmet and, in full view of his troops, poured the water on the ground. So extraordinary was the effect of this action that the water wasted by Alexander was as good as a drink for every man in the army." Ever the great military leader, Alexander had found yet another way to inspire his troops.

Alexander the Great was the son of King Philip II of Macedonia, who in 338 B.C. had defeated the Greeks and established his control over the Greek peninsula. When Alexander became king after Philip's death, he led the

Macedonians and Greeks on a spectacular conquest of the Persian Empire, opening the door to the spread of Greek culture throughout the ancient Near East. Greek settlers poured into the lands of the ancient Near East as bureaucrats, traders, soldiers, and scholars. Alexander's triumph gave rise to a new series of kingdoms that blended the achievements of the eastern world with the cultural outlook and attitudes of the Greeks. We use the term **Hellenistic** to designate this new order. The Hellenistic world was the world of Greeks and non-Greek easterners, and it resulted, in its own way, in a remarkable series of accomplishments that are sometimes underestimated. They form the story of this chapter.◆

Macedonia and the Conquests of Alexander

While the Greek city-states were busy fighting each other, to their north a new and ultimately powerful kingdom was emerging. Its people, the Macedonians, were viewed as barbarians by their Greek neighbors to the south. The Macedonians were mostly rural folk and were organized in tribes, not city-states. Not until the end of the fifth century B.C. did Macedonia become an important kingdom. But when Philip II (359–336 B.C.) took control, he turned Macedonia into the chief power of the Greek world.

Philip and the Conquest of Greece

The Greeks had mixed reactions to Philip's growing strength. Some viewed Philip as a savior who would rescue the Greeks from themselves by uniting them. Many Athenians, however, especially the orator Demosthenes, portrayed Philip as ruthless, deceitful, treacherous, and barbaric and called on the Athenians to undertake a struggle against him. In a speech to the Athenian assembly, Demosthenes exclaimed: "[Philip] is not only no Greek, nor related to the Greeks, but not even a barbarian from any place that can be named with honor, but a pestilent knave from Macedonia, from where it was never yet possible to buy a decent slave."

Demosthenes' repeated calls for action, combined with Philip's rapid expansion, finally spurred Athens into action. Allied with a number of other Greek states, Athens fought the Macedonians at the Battle of Chaeronea, near Thebes, in 338 B.C. The Macedonian army crushed the Greeks, and Philip was now free to consolidate his control over the Greek peninsula. The independent Greek *polis*, long the basic political unit of the Greek world, came to an end as Philip formed an alliance of the Greek states that we call the Corinthian League because they met at Corinth. All members took an oath of loyalty: "I swear by Zeus, Earth, Sun, Poseidon, Athena, Ares, and all the gods and goddesses, I will abide by the peace, and I will not break the agreements with

Philip the Macedonian, nor will I take up arms with hostile intent against any one of those who abide by the oaths either by land or by sea."[1]

Although Philip allowed the Greek city-states autonomy in domestic affairs, he retained the general direction of their foreign affairs. Philip insisted that the Greek states end their bitter rivalries and cooperate with him in a war against Persia. Before Philip could undertake his invasion of Asia, however, he was assassinated, leaving the task to his son Alexander.

Alexander the Great

Alexander was only twenty when he became king of Macedonia. The illustrious conqueror was in many ways prepared for kingship by his father, who had taken Alexander along on military campaigns and had given him control of the cavalry at the important Battle of

Alexander the Great. This marble head of Alexander the Great was made in the second or first century B.C. The long hair and tilt of his head reflect the description of Alexander in the literary sources of the time. This portrait shows a youthful and even godlike appearance. Alexander claimed to be descended from Heracles, a Greek hero worshiped as a god, and as pharaoh of Egypt, he gained recognition as a living deity. It is reported that at the base of one of his statues, now lost, in which Alexander was shown gazing at Zeus, were the words "I place the earth under my sway; you, O Zeus, keep Olympus."

Chaeronea. After his father's assassination, Alexander moved quickly to assert his authority, securing the Macedonian frontiers and smothering a rebellion in Greece. He then turned to his father's dream, the invasion of the Persian Empire.

The Conquests of Alexander There is no doubt that Alexander was taking a chance in attacking the Persian Empire. Although weakened in some respects, it was still a strong state. Alexander's fleet was inferior to the Persian navy, and his finances were shaky at best. In the spring of 334 B.C., Alexander entered Asia Minor with an army of some 37,000 men. About half were Macedonians, the rest Greeks and other allies. The cavalry, which would play an important role as a striking force, numbered about 5,000.

His first confrontation with the Persians, in a battle at the Granicus River in 334 B.C. (see Map 4.1), nearly cost him his life but resulted in a major victory. By spring 333, the entire western half of Asia Minor was in Alexander's hands, and the Ionian Greek cities of western Asia Minor had been "liberated" from the Persian oppressor. Meanwhile, the Persian king, Darius III, mobilized his forces to stop Alexander's army. Although the Persian troops outnumbered Alexander's, the Battle of Issus was fought on a narrow field that canceled the advantage of superior numbers and resulted in another Macedonian success. The Persian cause was certainly not helped when Darius made a spectacular exit from the battlefield before it was even clear who would win. After his victory at Issus in 333 B.C., Alexander turned south, and by the winter of 332, Syria, Palestine, and Egypt were under his domination. He took the traditional title of pharaoh of Egypt and founded the first of a series of cities named after him (Alexandria) as the Greek administrative capital of Egypt. It became (and remains today) one of Egypt's and the Mediterranean world's most important cities.

The next year, Alexander renewed his offensive, moving into the territory of the ancient Mesopotamian kingdoms and fighting a decisive battle with the Persians not far from Babylon. At Gaugamela, Alexander's men were clearly outnumbered by the Persian forces, which had established the battle site on a broad, open plain where their war chariots could maneuver to best advantage. Alexander was able to break through the center of the Persian line with his heavy cavalry, followed by the infantry.

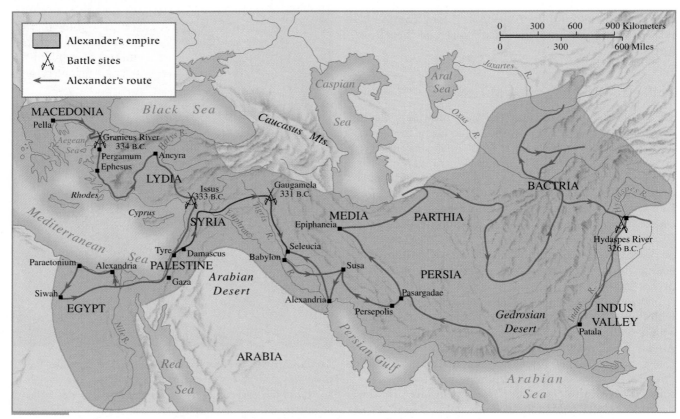

MAP 4.1 **The Conquests of Alexander the Great.** In just twelve years, Alexander the Great conquered vast territories. Dominating lands from west of the Nile to east of the Indus, he brought the Persian Empire, Egypt, and much of the Middle East under his control and laid the foundations for the Hellenistic world. ❓ Approximately how far did he and his troops travel during those twelve years? 🔵 **View an animated version of this map or related map at** http://thomsonedu.com/history/spielvogel

The battle turned into a rout, although Darius managed to escape. After his victory, Alexander entered Babylon and then proceeded to the Persian capitals at Susa and Persepolis, where he acquired the Persian treasuries and took possession of vast quantities of gold and silver.

By 330, Alexander was again on the march. After Darius was killed by one of his own men, Alexander took the title and office of the Great King of the Persians. But he was not content to rest with the spoils of the Persian Empire. During the next three years, he moved east and northeast, as far as modern Pakistan. By summer 327 B.C., he had entered India, which at that time was divided into a number of warring states. In 326 B.C., Alexander and his armies arrived in the plains of northwestern India. At the Battle of the Hydaspes River, Alexander won a brutally fought battle (see the box on p. 64). When Alexander made clear his determination to march east to conquer more of India, his soldiers, weary of campaigning year after year, mutinied and refused to go further. Alexander acceded to their demands and agreed to return, leading his troops through southern Persia across the Gedrosian Desert, where they suffered heavy losses from appalling desert conditions. Alexander and the remnant of his army went to Susa and then Babylon, where he planned still more campaigns. But in June 323 B.C., weakened from wounds, fever, and probably excessive alcohol, he died at the age of thirty-two.

The Legacy of Alexander   Alexander is one of the most puzzling great figures in history. Historians relying on the

CHRONOLOGY	Macedonia and the Conquests of Alexander
Reign of Philip II	359–336 B.C.
Battle of Chaeronea; Philip II conquers Greece	338 B.C.
Reign of Alexander the Great	336–323 B.C.
Alexander invades Asia; Battle of Granicus River	334 B.C.
Battle of Issus	333 B.C.
Battle of Gaugamela	331 B.C.
Fall of Persepolis, the Persian capital	330 B.C.
Alexander enters India	327 B.C.
Battle of Hydaspes River	326 B.C.
Death of Alexander	323 B.C.

same sources give vastly different pictures of him. Some portray him as an idealistic visionary and others as a ruthless Machiavellian. No doubt he was a great military leader—a master of strategy and tactics, fighting in every kind of terrain and facing every kind of opponent. Alexander was a brave and even reckless fighter who was quite willing to lead his men into battle and risk his own life. His example inspired his troops to follow him into unknown lands and difficult situations. We know that he sought to imitate Achilles, the warrior-hero of Homer's *Iliad*, an important ideal in Greek culture. Alexander kept a copy of the *Iliad*—and a dagger—under his pillow. He also

Alexander and Darius at the Battle of Issus.   This late-second- or early-first-century B.C. mosaic from the floor of a Roman villa at Pompeii is thought to be a copy of a panel painting by Philoxenos of Eretria about 310 B.C. The mosaic depicts the battle between Alexander and Darius III, king of Persia, at Issus in 333 B.C. Alexander is seen at left on horseback, recklessly leading his troops into battle. Darius is shown in his chariot, already turning around to flee from the enemy.

Erich Lessing/Art Resource, NY (Museo Archeologico Nazionale, Naples)

ALEXANDER MEETS AN INDIAN KING

In his campaigns in India, Alexander fought a number of difficult battles. At the Battle of the Hydaspes River, he faced a strong opponent in the Indian king Porus. After defeating Porus, Alexander treated him with respect, according to Arrian, Alexander's ancient biographer.

Arrian, *The Campaigns of Alexander*

Throughout the action Porus had proved himself a man indeed, not only as a commander but as a soldier of the truest courage. When he saw his cavalry cut to pieces, most of his infantry dead, and his elephants killed or roaming riderless and bewildered about the field, his behavior was very different from that of the Persian King Darius: unlike Darius, he did not lead the scramble to save his own skin, but so long as a single unit of his men held together, he fought bravely on. It was only when he was himself wounded that he turned the elephant on which he rode and began to withdraw. . . . Alexander, anxious to save the life of this great and gallant soldier, sent . . . [to him] an Indian named Meroes, a man he had been told had long been Porus' friend. Porus listened to Meroes' message, stopped his elephant, and dismounted; he was much distressed by thirst, so when he had revived himself by drinking, he told Meroes to conduct him with all speed to Alexander.

Alexander, informed of his approach, rode out to meet him. . . . When they met, he reined in his horse and looked at his adversary with admiration: he was a magnificent figure of a man, over seven feet high and of great personal beauty; his bearing had lost none of its pride; his air was of one brave man meeting another, of a king in the presence of a king, with whom he had fought honorably for his kingdom.

Alexander was the first to speak. "What," he said, "do you wish that I should do with you?" "Treat me as a king ought," Porus is said to have replied. "For my part," said Alexander, pleased by his answer, "your request shall be granted. But is there not something you would wish for yourself? Ask it." "Everything," said Porus, "is contained in this one request."

The dignity of these words gave Alexander even more pleasure, and he restored to Porus his sovereignty over his subjects, adding to his realm other territory of even greater extent. Thus he did indeed use a brave man as a king ought, and from that time forward found him in every way a loyal friend.

What do we learn from Arrian's account about Alexander's military skills and Indian methods of fighting?

---

claimed to be descended from Heracles, the Greek hero who came to be worshiped as a god. Alexander also aspired to divine honors; as pharaoh of Egypt, he became a living god according to Egyptian tradition and at one point even sent instructions to the Greek cities to "vote him a god."

Regardless of his ideals, motives, or views about himself, one fact stands out: Alexander created a new age, the Hellenistic era. The word *Hellenistic* is derived from a Greek word meaning "to imitate Greeks." It is an appropriate way, then, to describe an age that saw the extension of the Greek language and ideas to the non-Greek world of the Near East. Alexander's destruction of the Persian monarchy had extended Greco-Macedonian rule over an enormous area. It created opportunities for Greek engineers, intellectuals, merchants, soldiers, and administrators. While the Greeks on the mainland might remain committed to the ideals of their city-states, those who followed Alexander and his successors participated in a new political unity based on the principle of monarchy. Alexander had transformed his army from a Macedonian force into an international one, owing loyalty only to himself. His successors used force to establish military monarchies that dominated the Hellenistic world after his death. Autocratic power, based on military strength and pretensions of divine rule, became a regular feature of those Hellenistic monarchies and was part of Alexander's political legacy to the Hellenistic world. His vision of

empire no doubt inspired the Romans, who were the ultimate heirs of Alexander's legacy.

But Alexander also left a cultural legacy. As a result of his conquests, Greek language, art, architecture, and literature spread throughout the Near East. The urban centers of the Hellenistic Age, many founded by Alexander and his successors, became springboards for the diffusion of Greek culture. Alexander had established a number of cities and military colonies named Alexandria to guard strategic points and supervise wide areas. Most of the settlers were Greek mercenaries. It has been estimated that in the course of his campaigns, Alexander summoned 60,000 to 65,000 additional mercenaries from Greece, at least 36,000 of whom took up residence in the garrisons and new cities. While the Greeks spread their culture in the East, they were also inevitably influenced by Eastern ways. Thus Alexander's legacy became one of the hallmarks of the Hellenistic world: the clash and fusion of different cultures.

The World of the Hellenistic Kingdoms

The united empire that Alexander created by his conquests disintegrated after his death. All too soon, Macedonian military leaders were engaged in a struggle for power. By 300 B.C., any hope of unity was dead.

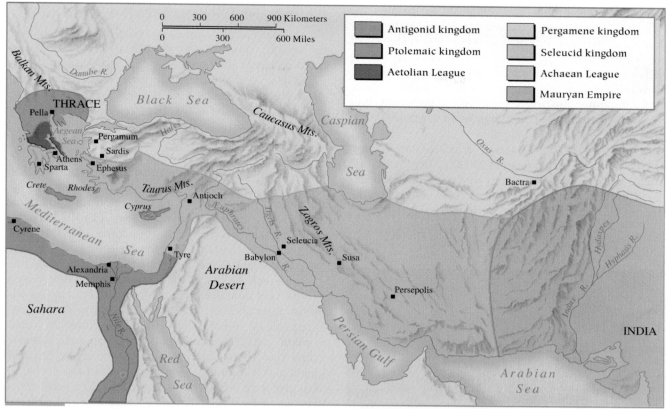

MAP 4.2 **The Hellenistic Kingdoms.** Alexander died unexpectedly at the age of thirty-two and did not designate a successor. Upon his death, his generals struggled for power, eventually establishing four monarchies that spread Hellenistic culture and fostered trade and economic development. ❓ Which kingdom encompassed most of the old Persian Empire? 🌐 **View an animated version of this map or related maps at** http://thomsonedu.com/history/spielvogel

Hellenistic Monarchies

Eventually, four Hellenistic kingdoms emerged as the successors to Alexander (see Map 4.2). In Macedonia, the struggles for power led to the extermination of Alexander's dynasty. Not until 276 B.C. did Antigonus Gonatus, the grandson of one of Alexander's generals, succeed in establishing the Antigonid dynasty as rulers of Macedonia. The Antigonids viewed control of Greece as essential to their power but did not see outright conquest as necessary.

Another Hellenistic monarchy was founded by the general Seleucus, who established the Seleucid dynasty of Syria. This was the largest of the Hellenistic kingdoms and controlled much of the old Persian Empire from Turkey in the west to India in the east, although the Seleucids found it increasingly difficult to maintain control of the eastern territories. In fact, an Indian ruler named Chandragupta Maurya (324–301 B.C.) established a new Indian state, the Mauryan Empire, and drove out the Seleucid forces. However, the Seleucid rulers maintained relations with the Mauryan Empire. Trade was fostered, especially in such luxuries as spices and jewels.

A third Hellenistic kingdom came into being by freeing itself from the Seleucids. This was the kingdom of Pergamum in western Asia Minor under the Attalid dynasty. In 133 B.C., the last member of the Attalid dynasty bequeathed his kingdom to Rome in his will.

The fourth Hellenistic monarchy was Egypt, which had come under the control of Ptolemy, another Macedonian general. Named governor of Egypt after Alexander's death, Ptolemy had established himself as king by 305 B.C., founding the Ptolemaic dynasty of pharaohs. Hellenistic Egypt lasted longer than all the other Hellenistic monarchies; it was not until the reign of Cleopatra VII, who allied herself with the wrong side in the Roman civil wars (see Chapter 5), that Egypt fell to the Romans in 30 B.C.

The Threat from the Celts

The Celts, also known as the Gauls, were a people who had occupied large areas of Europe north of the Alps during the early Iron Age (c. 800–500 B.C.), especially the region to the south and west of the Rhine River, west of the Alps, and north of the Pyrenees (a region known as Gaul).

At the end of the fifth century B.C., possibly as the result of overpopulation, Celtic peoples began to migrate south and east. One group sacked the city of Rome in 390 B.C. (see Chapter 5). After the death of Alexander the Great, other groups of Celts began to threaten the Hellenistic world. Celts attacked Macedonia early in the third century B.C., as one ancient writer reported: "When the defeated Macedonians had fixed themselves within the walls of their cities, the victorious Brennus ravaged the fields of the whole of Macedonia with no one to oppose him."[2] Brennus also led a group of 30,000 Celts into Greece itself and caused considerable damage until being defeated in 278 B.C.

Other groups of Celts later attacked Asia Minor, where Attalus I defeated them in 230 B.C. After his victory, Attalus gained control of much of Asia Minor and declared himself king of Pergamum. Their attacks led the Celts to be feared everywhere in the Hellenistic world.

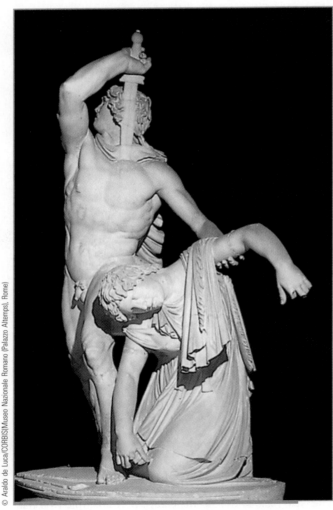

A Celt and His Wife: Better a Martyr than a Slave. This statue of a Celtic chieftain and his wife is a Roman copy of a bronze original that was part of a larger monument erected in the 220s B.C. to commemorate the victory of Attalus I of Pergamum over the Celts, a victory that gave Pergamum control over much of Asia Minor. In this scene, the defeated Celtic leader plunges a sword into his chest just after he has killed his wife to prevent her from being sold into slavery.

Political Institutions

The Hellenistic monarchies provided a sort of stability for several centuries, even though Hellenistic kings refused to accept the new status quo and periodically engaged in wars to alter it. At the same time, an underlying strain always existed between the new Greco-Macedonian ruling class and the native populations. Together these factors generated a certain degree of tension that was never truly ended until the vibrant Roman state to the west stepped in and imposed a new order.

The Hellenistic kingdoms shared a common political system that represented a break with their Greek past. To the Greeks, monarchy was an institution for barbarians, associated in their minds with people like the Persians. Although they retained democratic forms of government in their cities, the Greeks of the Hellenistic world were forced to accept monarchy as a new fact of political life.

Although Alexander the Great had apparently hoped to fuse Greeks and easterners—he used Persians as administrators and encouraged his soldiers to marry easterners, as he himself did—Hellenistic monarchs relied primarily on Greeks and Macedonians to form the new ruling class. It has been estimated that in the Seleucid kingdom, for example, only 2.5 percent of the people in authority were non-Greek, and most of them were commanders of local military units. Those who did advance to important administrative posts had learned Greek (all government business was transacted in Greek) and had become Hellenized in a cultural sense. The policy of excluding non-Greeks from leadership positions, it should be added, was not due to the incompetence of the natives but to the determination of the Greek ruling class to maintain its privileged position. It was the Greco-Macedonian ruling class that provided the only unity in the Hellenistic world.

Hellenistic Cities

Cities played an especially important role in the Hellenistic kingdoms. Throughout his conquests, Alexander had founded a series of new cities and military settlements, and Hellenistic kings did likewise. The new population centers varied considerably in size and importance. Military settlements were meant to maintain order and might consist of only a few hundred men who were strongly dependent on the king. But there were also new independent cities with thousands of inhabitants. Alexandria in Egypt was the largest city in the Mediterranean region by the first century B.C.

Hellenistic rulers encouraged this massive spread of Greek colonists to the Near East because of their intrinsic value to the new monarchies. Greeks (and Macedonians) provided not only a recruiting ground for the army but also a pool of civilian administrators and workers who would contribute to economic development. Even architects, engineers, dramatists, and actors were in demand in the new Greek cities. Many Greeks and Macedonians

© Araldo de Luca/CORBIS(Museo Nazionale Romano (Palazzo Altemps), Rome)

were quick to see the advantages of moving to the new urban centers and gladly sought their fortunes in the Near East. Greeks of all backgrounds joined the exodus, at least until around 250 B.C., when the outpouring began to slow.

In the Hellenistic cities, the culture was primarily Greek. The political institutions of the cities were modeled after those of the Greek *polis*. Greeks of the Classical period would easily have recognized the councils, assemblies, and codes of law. The physical layout of the new cities was also modeled after those of the Greek homeland. Using the traditional rectilinear grid, cities were laid out with temples, altars, and stone theaters.

Many of the new urban centers were completely dominated by Greeks while the native populations remained cut off from all civic institutions. The Greeks commissioned purely Greek sculpture, read literature of the Classical period, and had separate law courts for themselves. Complaints from resentful natives have been recorded. An Egyptian camel driver, for example, complained bitterly that he was not paid regularly because he did "not know how to behave like a Greek." Not only was it difficult for easterners to enter the ranks of the ruling class, but those who did so had to become thoroughly Hellenized. This often required alienation from one's own culture.

The Greeks' belief in their own cultural superiority provided an easy rationalization for their political dominance of the eastern cities. But Greek control of the new cities of the Near East was also necessary because the kings frequently used the cities as instruments of government, enabling them to rule considerable territory without an extensive bureaucracy. At the same time, for security reasons, the Greeks needed the support of the kings. After all, the Hellenistic cities were islands of Greek culture in a sea of non-Greeks. The relationship between rulers and cities, therefore, was a symbiotic one that bore serious consequences for the cities.

In the political system, religious practices, and architecture of their new cities, the Greeks tried to re-create the *poleis* of their homeland. But it was no longer possible to do so. The new cities were not autonomous entities and soon found themselves dependent on the power of the Hellenistic monarchies. Although the kings did not rule the cities directly, they restricted freedom in other ways. Cities knew they could not conduct an independent foreign policy and did not try to do so. The kings also demanded tribute, which could be a heavy burden.

The Greek cities of the Hellenistic era were the chief agents for the spread of Greek culture in the Near East, as far, in fact, as modern Afghanistan and India. These cities were also remarkably vibrant despite their subordination to the Hellenistic monarchies and persisted in being a focal point for the loyalty of their citizens.

Economic Trends in the Hellenistic World

Agriculture was still of primary importance to both the native populations and the new Greek cities of the Hellenistic world. The Greek cities continued their old agrarian patterns. A well-defined citizen body owned land and worked it with the assistance of slaves. But these farms were isolated units in a vast area of land ultimately owned by the king or assigned to large estate owners and worked by native peasants dwelling in villages. Overall, then, neither agricultural patterns nor methods of production underwent significant changes.

Few new products or manufacturing methods were introduced during the Hellenistic era, but the centers of manufacturing shifted significantly. Industry spread from Greece to the east—especially to Asia Minor, Rhodes, and Egypt. New textile centers were set up at Pergamum, while glass and silver crafts were developed in Syria. And busiest of all the cities in manufacturing was Alexandria in Egypt, center of the production of parchment, textiles, linens, oil, metalwork, and glass.

Commerce expanded considerably in the Hellenistic era. Indeed, trading contacts linked much of the Hellenistic world. The decline in the number of political barriers encouraged more commercial traffic. Although Hellenistic monarchs still fought wars, the conquests of Alexander and the policies of his successors made possible greater trade between east and west. Two major trade routes connected the east with the Mediterranean. The central route was the major one and led by sea from India to the Persian Gulf, up the Tigris River to Seleucia, which replaced Babylon as the center for waterborne traffic from the Persian Gulf and overland caravan routes as well. Overland routes from Seleucia then led to Antioch and Ephesus. A southern route wound its way from India by sea but went around Arabia and up the Red Sea to Petra or later Berenice. Caravan routes then led overland to Coptos on the Nile and from there to Alexandria and the Mediterranean.

An incredible variety of products was traded: gold and silver from Spain; iron from northern Armenia; salt from Asia Minor; timber from Macedonia; purple dye from Tyre; ebony, gems, ivory, and spices from India; frankincense (used on altars) from Arabia; slaves from Thrace, Syria, and Asia Minor; fine wines from Syria and western Asia Minor; olive oil from Athens; and numerous exquisite foodstuffs, such as the famous prunes of Damascus. The greatest trade, however, was in the basic staple of life—grain. The great exporting areas were Egypt, Sicily, and the Black Sea region.

New Opportunities For Women

One of the significant features of social life in the Hellenistic world was the emergence of new opportunities for women—at least, for upper-class women—especially in the economic area. Documents show increasing numbers of women involved in managing slaves, selling property, and making loans. Even then, legal contracts in which women were involved had to include their official male guardians, although in numerous instances these men no longer played an important function but were listed only to satisfy legal requirements. In Sparta, women

A New Autonomy for Women

*U*pper-class women made noticeable gains in Hellenistic society. But even in the lives of ordinary women, a new assertiveness came to the fore despite the continuing domination of society by men. The first selection is taken from the letter of a wife to her husband, complaining about his failure to return home. In the second selection, a father complains that his daughter has abandoned him, contrary to Egyptian law providing that children who have been properly raised should support their parents.

Letter from Isias to Hephaistion, 168 B.C.

If you are well and other things are going right, it would accord with the prayer that I make continually to the gods. I myself and the child and all the household are in good health and think of you always. When I received your letter from Horos, in which you announce that you are in detention in the Serapeum at Memphis, for the news that you are well I straightway thanked the gods, but about your not coming home, when all the others who had been secluded there have come, I am ill-pleased, because after having piloted myself and your child through such bad times and been driven to every extremity owing to the price of wheat, I thought that now at least, with you at home, I should enjoy some respite, whereas you have not even thought of coming home nor given any regard to our circumstances, remembering how I was in want of everything while you were still here, not to mention this long lapse of time and these critical days, during which you have sent us nothing. As, moreover, Horos who delivered the letter has brought news of your having been released from detention, I am thoroughly ill-pleased. Notwithstanding, as your mother also is annoyed, for her sake as well as for mine please return to the city, if nothing more pressing holds you back. You will do me a favor by taking care of your bodily health. Farewell.

Letter from Ktesikles to King Ptolemy, 220 B.C.

I am wronged by Dionysios and by Nike my daughter. For though I raised her, my own daughter, and educated her and brought her to maturity, when I was stricken with bodily ill-health and was losing my eyesight, she was not minded to furnish me with any of the necessities of life. When I sought to obtain justice from her in Alexandria, she begged my pardon, and in the eighteenth year she swore me a written royal oath to give me each month twenty drachmas, which she was to earn by her own bodily labor. . . . But now corrupted by Dionysios, who is a comic actor, she does not do for me anything of what was in the written oath, despising my weakness and ill-health. I beg you, therefore, O King, not to allow me to be wronged by my daughter and by Dionysios the actor who corrupted her, but to order Diophanes the strategus [a provincial administrator] to summon them and hear us out; and if I am speaking the truth, let Diophanes deal with her corrupter as seems good to him and compel my daughter Nike to do justice to me. If this is done I shall no longer be wronged but by fleeing to you, O King, I shall obtain justice.

What specific complaints are contained in each letter? What do these complaints reveal about some women in the Hellenistic world?

---

were allowed to own land and manage their own economic affairs. Because many of their husbands were absent or had died in war, many Spartan women became wealthy; females owned 40 percent of the land in Sparta.

Spartan women, however, were an exception, especially on the Greek mainland. Women in Athens, for example, still remained highly restricted and supervised. Although a few philosophers welcomed female participation in men's affairs, many philosophers rejected equality between men and women and asserted that the traditional roles of wives and mothers were most satisfying for women. In her treatise "On Chastity," Phintys wrote that "serving as generals, public officials, and statesmen is appropriate for men," but "keeping house, remaining within, and taking care of husbands belongs to women."[3]

But the opinions of philosophers did not prevent upper-class women from making gains in areas other than the economic sphere (see the box above). New possibilities for females arose when women in some areas of the Hellenistic world were allowed to pursue education in the traditional fields of literature, music, and even athletics. Education, then, provided new opportunities for women: female poets appeared again in the third century B.C., and there are instances of women involved in both scholarly and artistic activities.

The creation of the Hellenistic monarchies, which represented a considerable departure from the world of the *polis*, also gave new scope to the role played by the monarchs' wives, the Hellenistic queens. In Macedonia, a pattern of alliances between mothers and sons provided openings for women to take an active role in politics, especially in political intrigue. In Egypt, opportunities for royal women were even greater because the Ptolemaic rulers reverted to an Egyptian custom of kings marrying their own sisters. Of the first eight Ptolemaic rulers, four wed their sisters. Ptolemy II and his sister-wife Arsinoë II were both worshiped as gods in their lifetimes. Arsinoë played an energetic role in government and was involved in the expansion of the Egyptian navy. She was also the first Egyptian queen whose portrait appeared on coins with her husband. Hellenistic queens also showed an intense interest in culture. They wrote poems, collected art, and corresponded with intellectuals.

Culture in the Hellenistic World

Although the Hellenistic kingdoms encompassed vast areas and many diverse peoples, the Greeks provided a sense of unity as a result of the diffusion of Greek culture throughout the region. The Hellenistic era was a period of considerable cultural accomplishment in many areas—literature, art, science, and philosophy. Although these achievements occurred everywhere in the Hellenistic world, certain centers, especially the great cities of Alexandria and Pergamum, stood out. In both cities, cultural developments were encouraged by the rulers themselves. Rich Hellenistic kings had considerable resources with which to patronize culture.

The Ptolemies in Egypt made Alexandria an especially important cultural center. The library became the largest in ancient times, housing more than half a million scrolls. The museum (literally, "temple of the Muses") created a favorable environment for scholarly research. Alexandria became home to poets, writers, philosophers, and scientists—scholars of all kinds.

New Directions in Literature

The Hellenistic Age produced an enormous quantity of literature, most of which has not survived. Hellenistic monarchs, who held literary talent in high esteem, subsidized writers on a grand scale. The Ptolemaic rulers of Egypt were particularly lavish. The combination of their largess and the famous library drew a host of scholars and authors to Alexandria, including a circle of poets. Theocritus (c. 315–250 B.C.), originally a native of the island of Sicily, wrote "little poems" or idylls dealing with erotic subjects, lovers' complaints, and pastoral themes expressing his love of nature and its beauty.

In the Hellenistic era, Athens remained the theatrical center of the Greek world. As tragedy withered, writers invented New Comedy, which rejected political themes and sought only to entertain and amuse. The Athenian playwright Menander (c. 342–291 B.C.) was perhaps the best representative of New Comedy. Plots were simple: typically, a hero falls in love with a not-really-so-bad prostitute who turns out eventually to be the long-lost daughter of a rich neighbor. The hero marries her, and they live happily ever after.

The Hellenistic period saw a great outpouring of historical and biographical literature. The chief historian of the Hellenistic Age was Polybius (c. 203–c. 120 B.C.), a Greek who lived for some years in Rome. He is regarded as second only to Thucydides among Greek historians. His major work consisted of forty books narrating the history of the "inhabited Mediterranean world" from 221 to 146 B.C. Only the first five books are extant, although long extracts from the other books survive. His history

Portrait of Queen Arsinoë II. Arsinoë II, sister and wife of King Ptolemy II, played an active role in Egyptian political affairs. This statue from the Ptolemaic period depicts the queen in the traditional garb of a pharaoh's wife.

focuses on the growth of Rome from a city-state to a vast empire. It is apparent that Polybius understood the significance of the Romans' achievement. He followed Thucydides in seeking rational motives for historical events. He also approached his sources critically and used firsthand accounts.

Hellenistic Art

In addition to being patrons of literary talent, the Hellenistic monarchs were eager to spend their money to beautify and adorn the cities in their states. The founding of new cities and the rebuilding of old ones provided numerous opportunities for Greek architects and sculptors. The structures of the Greek homeland—gymnasia, baths, theaters, and, of course, temples—lined the streets of these cities. Most noticeable in the temples was the use of the more ornate Corinthian order, which became especially popular during the Hellenistic Age (see the illustration in Chapter 3 on p. 53).

Sculptors were commissioned by Hellenistic kings and rich citizens. Thousands of statues, many paid for by the people honored, were erected in towns and cities all over the Hellenistic world. While maintaining the technical skill of the classical period, Hellenistic sculptors moved away from the idealism of fifth-century classicism to a more emotional and realistic art, seen in numerous statues of old women, drunks, and little children at play.

Alexander the Great's incursion into the western part of India resulted in some Greek cultural influences there, especially during the Hellenistic era. In the first century B.C., Indian sculptors began to create statues of the Buddha. The impact of Greek sculpture was especially evident in the Buddhist statues made in Gandhara, which is today part of Pakistan.

A Golden Age of Science

The Hellenistic era witnessed a more conscious separation of science from philosophy. In Classical Greece, what we would call the physical and life sciences had been divisions of philosophical inquiry. Nevertheless, the Greeks, by the time of Aristotle, had already established an important principle of scientific investigation, empirical research, or systematic observation as the basis for generalization. In the Hellenistic Age, the sciences tended to be studied in their own right.

One of the traditional areas of Greek science was astronomy, and two Alexandrian scholars continued this exploration. Aristarchus of Samos (c. 310–230 B.C.) developed a heliocentric view of the universe, contending that the sun and the fixed stars remained stationary while the earth rotated around the sun in a circular orbit. This view was not widely accepted, and most scholars clung to the earlier geocentric view of the Greeks, which held that the earth was at the center of the universe. Another astronomer, Eratosthenes (c. 275–194 B.C.), determined that the earth was round and calculated the earth's circumference at 24,675 miles, within 200 miles of the actual figure.

A third Alexandrian scholar was Euclid, who lived around 300 B.C. He established a school in Alexandria but is primarily known for his *Elements*. This was a systematic organization of the fundamental elements of geometry as they had already been worked out; it became the standard textbook of plane geometry and was used up to modern times.

The most famous of the scientists of the Hellenistic period, Archimedes (287–212 B.C.), came from the western Mediterranean region. Archimedes was especially

Drunken Old Woman. Hellenistic sculptors no longer tried to capture ideal beauty in their sculpture, a quest that characterized Greek classicism, but moved toward a more emotional and realistic art. This statue of a drunken old woman is typical of this new trend in art. Old and haggard, mired in poverty, she struggles to just go on living.

important for his work on the geometry of spheres and cylinders, for establishing the value of the mathematical constant pi, and for creating the science of hydrostatics. Archimedes was also a practical inventor. He may have devised the so-called Archimedean screw, used to pump water out of mines and to lift irrigation water, as well as a compound pulley for transporting heavy weights. During the Roman siege of his native city of Syracuse, he constructed a number of devices to thwart the attackers. According to Plutarch's account, the Romans became so frightened "that if they did but see a little rope or a piece of wood from the wall, instantly crying out, that there it was again, Archimedes was about to let fly some device at them, they turned their backs and fled."[4] Archimedes' accomplishments inspired a wealth of semilegendary stories. Supposedly, he discovered specific gravity by observing the water he displaced in his bath and became so excited by his realization that he jumped out of the water and ran home naked, shouting "Eureka!" ("I have found it!"). He is said to have emphasized the importance of levers by proclaiming to the king of Syracuse, "Give me a

© Araldo de Luca/CORBIS

Hellenistic Sculpture and a Greek-Style Buddha. Greek architects and sculptors were highly valued throughout the Hellenistic world. Shown on the left is a terra-cotta statuette of a draped young woman, made as a tomb offering near Thebes, probably around 300 B.C. The incursion of Alexander into the western part of India resulted in some Greek cultural influences there. During the first century B.C., Indian sculptors in Gandhara began to make statues of the Buddha in a style that combined Indian and Hellenistic artistic traditions, evident in the stone sculpture of Buddha on the right. Note the wavy hair topped by a bun tied with a ribbon, also a feature of earlier statues of Greek deities. This Buddha is also seen wearing a Greek-style toga.

lever and a place to stand on, and I will move the earth." The king was so impressed that he encouraged Archimedes to lower his sights and build defensive weapons instead.

Philosophy: New Schools of Thought

While Alexandria and Pergamum became the renowned cultural centers of the Hellenistic world, Athens remained the prime center for philosophy and continued to attract the most illustrious philosophers, who chose to establish their schools there. Two entirely new schools of philosophical thought reinforced Athens' reputation as a philosophical center.

Epicureanism Epicurus (341–270 B.C.), the founder of **Epicureanism**, established a school in Athens before 300 B.C.

Epicurus' famous belief in a doctrine of pleasure began with his view of the world. Though he did not deny the existence of the gods, he did not believe they played any active role in the world. The universe ran on its own. This left human beings free to follow self-interest as a basic motivating force. Happiness was the goal of life, and the means to achieving it was the pursuit of pleasure, the only true good. But the pursuit of pleasure was not meant in a physical, hedonistic sense:

When, therefore, we maintain that pleasure is the end, we do not mean the pleasures of profligates and those that consist in sensuality, as is supposed by some who are either ignorant or disagree with us or do not understand, but freedom from pain in the body and from trouble in the mind. For it is not continuous drinkings and revellings, nor the satisfaction of lusts, nor the enjoyment of fish and other luxuries of the

THE STOIC IDEAL OF HARMONY WITH GOD

The Stoic Cleanthes (331–232 B.C.) succeeded Zeno as head of this school of philosophy. One historian of Hellenistic civilization has called this work by Cleanthes the greatest religious hymn in Greek literature. Certainly, it demonstrates that Stoicism, unlike Epicureanism, did have an underlying spiritual foundation. This poem has been compared to the great psalms of the Hebrews.

Cleanthes, *Hymn to Zeus*

Nothing occurs on the earth apart from you, O God,

nor in the heavenly regions nor on the sea,

except what bad men do in their folly;

but you know to make the odd even,

and to harmonize what is dissonant; to you the alien is akin.

And so you have wrought together into one all things that are good and bad,

So that there arises one eternal logos [rationale] of all things,

Which all bad mortals shun and ignore,

Unhappy wretches, ever seeking the possession of good things

They neither see nor hear the universal law of God,

By obeying which they might enjoy a happy life.

Based on Cleanthes' poem, what are some of the beliefs of the Stoics. How do they differ from the beliefs of the Epicureans?

---

wealthy table, which produce a pleasant life, but sober reasoning, searching out the motives for all choice and avoidance, and banishing mere opinions, to which are due the greatest disturbance of the spirit.[5]

Pleasure was not satisfying one's desire in an active, gluttonous fashion but rather freedom from emotional turmoil, freedom from worry, the freedom that came from a mind at rest. To achieve this passive pleasure, one had to free oneself from public activity: "We must release ourselves from the prison of affairs and politics." They were too strenuous to give peace of mind. But this was not a renunciation of all social life, for to Epicurus, a life could be complete only when it was centered on the basic ideal of friendship: "Of all the things which wisdom acquires to produce the blessedness of the complete life, far the greatest is the possession of friendship."[6] Epicurus' own life in Athens was an embodiment of his teachings. He and his friends created their own private community where they could pursue their ideal of true happiness.

Stoicism   Epicureanism was eventually overshadowed by another school of thought known as **Stoicism**, which became the most popular philosophy of the Hellenistic world and later flourished in the Roman Empire as well. It was the product of a teacher named Zeno (335–263 B.C.), who came to Athens and began to teach in a public colonnade known as the Painted Portico (the *Stoa Poikile*—hence *Stoicism*). Like Epicureanism, Stoicism was concerned with how individuals find happiness. But Stoics took a radically different approach to the problem. To them, happiness, the supreme good, could be found only in virtue, which meant essentially living in harmony with the divine will. One achieved happiness by choosing to follow the divine will through the free exercise of one's own will. To the Stoics, the divine will was the same thing as the will of nature because nature was simply a manifestation or expression of the gods. "Living according to nature," therefore, meant following the divine will or the natural laws that the gods established to run the universe.

Virtuous living, then, was living in accordance with the laws of nature or submitting to the divine will (see the box above). This led to the acceptance of whatever one received in life since the divine will for us was by its very nature good. By accepting divine law, people mastered themselves and gained inner peace. Life's problems could not disturb such individuals, and they could bear whatever life offered (hence our word *stoic*).

Unlike Epicureans, Stoics did not believe in the need to separate oneself from the world and politics. Public service was regarded as noble. The real Stoic was a good citizen and could even be a good government official. Because Stoics believed that a divine principle was present throughout the universe, each human being also contained a divine spark. This led to a belief in the oneness of humanity. The world constituted a single society of equal human beings. Although they were not equal in the outer world, because each contained the divine spark, all were free to follow the divine will (what was best for each individual). All persons then, even slaves, though unfree in body, were equal at the level of the soul.

Epicureanism and especially Stoicism appealed to large numbers of people in the Hellenistic world. Both of these philosophies focused primarily on the problem of human happiness. Their popularity would suggest a fundamental change in the character of the Greek lifestyle. In the Classical Greek world, the happiness of individuals and the meaning of life were closely associated with the life of the *polis*. One found fulfillment within the community. In the Hellenistic kingdoms, although the *polis* continued to exist, the sense that one could find satisfaction and fulfillment through life in the *polis* had weakened. Not only did individuals seek new philosophies that offered personal happiness, but in the cosmopolitan world of the Hellenistic states, with their mixtures of peoples, a new openness to thoughts of universality could also emerge. For some people, Stoicism embodied this larger sense of community. The appeal of new philosophies in the Hellenistic era can also be explained by the apparent decline in certain aspects of traditional religion.

Religion in the Hellenistic World

When the Greeks spread throughout the Hellenistic kingdoms, they took their gods with them. Although the construction of temples may have been less important than in classical times, there were still many demonstrations of a lively religious faith. But over a period of time, there was a noticeable decline in the vitality of the traditional Greek Olympian religion. The civic cults based on the traditional gods no longer seemed sufficient to satisfy people's emotional needs.

This left Greeks receptive to the numerous religious cults of the eastern world. The Greeks were always tolerant of other existing religious institutions. Hence in the Hellenistic cities of the Near East, the traditional civic cults of their own gods and foreign cults existed side by side. Alexandria had cults of the traditional Greek gods, Egyptian deities such as Isis and Horus, the Babylonian Astarte, and the Syrian Atargatis.

But for many people, the search for personal meaning remained unfulfilled. Among educated Greeks, the philosophies of Epicureanism and especially Stoicism offered help. Another source of solace came in the form of **mystery religions**.

Mystery Religions

Mystery cults, with their secret initiations and promises of individual salvation, were not new to the Greek world. But the Greeks of the Hellenistic era were strongly influenced by eastern mystery cults, such as those of Egypt, which offered a distinct advantage over the Greek mystery religions. The latter had usually been connected to specific locations (such as Eleusis), which meant that a would-be initiate had to undertake a pilgrimage in order to participate in the rites. In contrast, the eastern mystery religions were readily available since temples to their gods and goddesses were located throughout the Greek cities of the east.

All of the mystery religions were based on the same fundamental premises. Individuals could pursue a path to salvation and achieve eternal life by being initiated into a union with a savior god or goddess who had died and risen again. The ritual of initiation, by which the seeker identified with the god or goddess, was, no doubt, a highly emotional experience.

The Egyptian cult of Isis was one of the most popular of the mystery religions. The cult of Isis was very ancient but became truly universal in Hellenistic times. Isis was the goddess of women, marriage, and children, as one of her hymns states: "I am she whom women call goddess. I ordained that women should be loved by men: I brought wife and husband together, and invented the marriage contract. I ordained that women should bear children."[7] Isis was also portrayed as the giver of civilization who had brought laws and letters to all humankind. The cult of Isis offered a precious commodity to its initiates—the promise of eternal life. In many ways, the mystery religions of the Hellenistic era helped pave the way for Christianity.

The Jews In The Hellenistic World

In observing the similarities among their gods and goddesses, Greeks and easterners tended to assume they were the same beings with different names, giving rise to a process of **syncretism**. But a special position was occupied in the Hellenistic world by the Jews, whose monotheistic religion was exclusive and did not accommodate this kind of fusion of spiritual beings.

The Jewish province of Judaea (which embraced the lands of the old Hebrew Kingdom of Judah) was ruled by the Ptolemies until it fell under the control of the Seleucids by 200 B.C. In the reign of the Seleucid king Antiochus IV (175–163 B.C.), conflict erupted in Judaea. Hellenistic monarchs were generally tolerant of all religions, but problems with Rome prompted Antiochus to try to impose more cultural and religious unity throughout his kingdom. When he sent troops to Jerusalem and seized the Temple, he sparked a Jewish uprising led by Judas Maccabaeus (164 B.C.). The rebels succeeded in recapturing the Temple, a joyous event that has been celebrated every year since in the Jewish holiday of Hanukkah (Hebrew for "rededication"). Although the conflict in Judaea continued, the Seleucids ultimately made concessions and allowed the Jews considerable freedom.

But large numbers of Jews no longer lived in Judaea. There was a large Jewish population in Egypt, particularly in Alexandria, as well as Jewish settlements throughout the cities of Asia Minor and Syria. In each city, Jews generally set up a synagogue and formed a private association for worship as other foreigners did. But some city authorities also allowed the Jews to form a political corporation that gave them greater rights than other resident aliens. Most important, they gained the privilege to live by their own laws and their own judicial system. The Jews were not really interested in citizenship in the cities in which they resided because full citizenship required worship of the city's gods, anathema to Jews, who believed only in Yahweh.

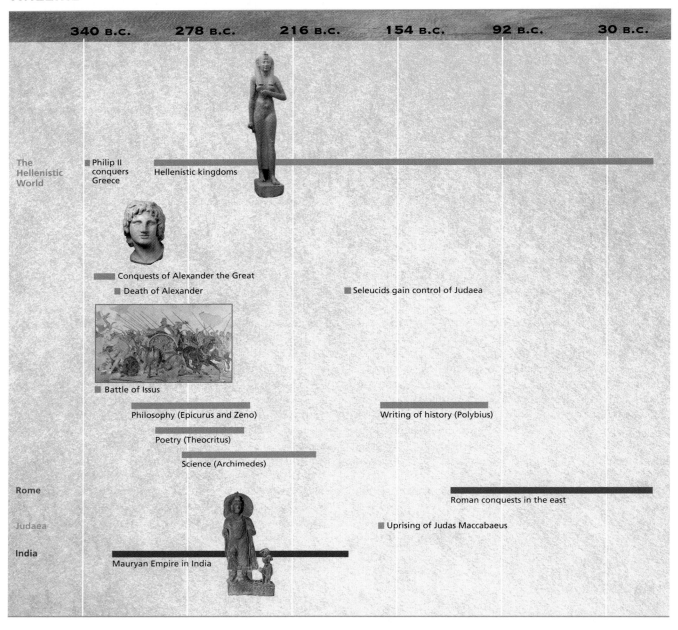

	340 B.C.	278 B.C.	216 B.C.	154 B.C.	92 B.C.	30 B.C.

The Hellenistic World

■ Philip II conquers Greece

Hellenistic kingdoms

Conquests of Alexander the Great

■ Death of Alexander

■ Seleucids gain control of Judaea

■ Battle of Issus

Philosophy (Epicurus and Zeno)

Writing of history (Polybius)

Poetry (Theocritus)

Science (Archimedes)

Rome

Roman conquests in the east

Judaea

■ Uprising of Judas Maccabaeus

India

Mauryan Empire in India

CONCLUSION

Although historians once viewed the Hellenistic era as a period of stagnation after the brilliant Greek civilization of the fifth century B.C., our survey of the Hellenistic world has shown the inaccuracy of that position. The Hellenistic period was vibrant in its own way. New cities arose and flourished. New philosophical ideas captured the minds of many. Significant achievements occurred in art, literature, and science. Greek culture spread throughout the Near East and made an impact wherever it was carried. In some areas of the Hellenistic world, queens played an active role in political life, and many upper-class women found new avenues for expressing themselves.

But serious problems remained. Hellenistic kings continued to engage in inconclusive wars. Much of the formal culture was the special preserve of the Greek conquerors, whose attitude of superiority kept them largely separated from the native masses of the Hellenistic kingdoms. Although the Hellenistic world achieved a degree of political stability, by the late third century B.C. signs of decline were beginning to multiply. Some of the more farsighted perhaps realized the danger presented to the Hellenistic world by the growing power of Rome. The Romans would ultimately inherit Alexander's empire, and we must now turn to them and try to understand what made them such successful conquerors.

NOTES

1. Quoted in S. B. Pomeroy, S. M. Burstein, W. Donlan, and J. T. Roberts, *Ancient Greece: A Political, Social, and Cultural History* (Oxford, 1999), p. 390.
2. Quoted in G. Shipley, *The Greek World After Alexander, 323–30 B.C.* (London, 2000), p. 53.
3. Quoted in M. B. Fant and M. R. Lefkowitz, *Women's Life in Greece and Rome: A Source Book in Translation* (Baltimore, 1992), no. 208.
4. Plutarch, *Life of Marcellus*, trans. J. Dryden (New York, n.d.), p. 378.
5. *Epicurus: The Extant Remains*, trans. C. Bailey (Oxford, 1926), pp. 89–90.
6. Ibid., pp. 115, 101.
7. Quoted in W. W. Tarn, *Hellenistic Civilization* (London, 1930), p. 324.

SUGGESTIONS FOR FURTHER READING

For a general introduction to the Hellenistic era, see **F. W. Walbank**, *The Hellenistic World* (Cambridge, Mass., 1993), and **G. Shipley**, *The Greek World After Alexander, 323–30 B.C.* (New York, 2000). Other studies include **W. W. Tarn** and **G. T. Griffith**, *Hellenistic Civilization*, 3d ed. (London, 1952); **M. Grant**, *From Alexander to Cleopatra: The Hellenistic World* (London, 1982); and **P. Green**, *Alexander to Actium: The Historic Evolution of the Hellenistic Age* (Berkeley, Calif., 1990).

For a good introduction to the early history of Macedonia, see **E. N. Borza**, *In the Shadow of Olympus: The Emergence of Macedon* (Princeton, N.J., 1990), and **R. M. Errington**, *A History of Macedonia* (Berkeley, Calif., 1990). There are considerable differences of opinion on Alexander the Great. Good biographies include **R. L. Fox**, *Alexander the Great* (London, 1973); **P. Cartledge**, *Alexander the Great* (New York, 2004); **N.G.L. Hammond**, *The Genius of Alexander the Great* (Chapel Hill, N.C., 1997); **P. Green**, *Alexander of Macedon* (Berkeley, Calif., 1991); and **G. M. Rogers**, *Alexander: The Ambiguity of Greatness* (New York, 2004).

Studies on the various Hellenistic monarchies include **N.G.L. Hammond** and **F. W. Walbank**, *A History of Macedonia, vol. 3, 336–167 B.C.* (Oxford, 1988); **S. Sherwin-White** and **A. Kuhrt**, *From Samarkand to Sardis: A New Approach to the Seleucid Empire* (Berkeley, Calif., 1993); **N. Lewis**, *Greeks in Ptolemaic Egypt* (Oxford, 1986); and **R. E. Allen**, *The Attalid Kingdom* (Oxford, 1983).

On the Celts, see **B. Cunliffe**, *The Ancient Celts* (London, 1997), and the beautifully illustrated brief study by **J. Davies**, *The Celts* (London, 2000).

A good survey of Hellenistic cities can be found in **A.H.M. Jones**, *The Greek City from Alexander to Justinian* (Oxford, 1940). On economic and social trends, see **M. I. Finley**, *The Ancient Economy*, 2d ed. (London, 1985), and the classic and still indispensable **M. I. Rostovtzeff**, *Social and Economic History of the Hellenistic World*, 3 vols., 2d ed. (Oxford, 1953). Hellenistic women are examined in **S. B. Pomeroy**, *Women in Hellenistic Egypt* (New York, 1984).

For a general introduction to Hellenistic culture, see **J. Onians**, *Art and Thought in the Hellenistic Age* (London, 1979). On art, see **J. J. Pollitt**, *Art in the Hellenistic Age* (New York, 1986). The best general survey of Hellenistic philosophy is **A. A. Long**, *Hellenistic Philosophy: Stoics, Epicureans, Skeptics*, 2d ed. (London, 1986). A superb work on Hellenistic science is **G.E.R. Lloyd**, *Greek Science After Aristotle* (London, 1973).

On various face of Hellenistic religion, see **L. Martin**, *Hellenistic Religions: An Introduction* (New York, 1987), and **R. E. Witt**, *Isis in the Graeco-Roman World* (London, 1971).

On the entry of Rome into the Hellenistic world, see the basic work by **E. S. Gruen**, *The Hellenistic World and the Coming of Rome*, 2 vols. (Berkeley, Calif., 1984).

Thomson **NOW!** Enter *ThomsonNOW* using the access card that is available for *Western Civilization: A Brief History*. *ThomsonNOW* will help you understand this chapter with lesson plans generated for your needs. In addition, you can read the following documents, and many more, online:

Plutarch, Life of Alexander
Aristotle, excerpt from *Nicomachean Ethics*
Aristotle, *Metaphysics*, Chapter 12

WESTERN CIVILIZATION RESOURCES

Visit the Web site for *Western Civilization: A Brief History* for resources specific to this book:

http://www.thomsonedu.com/history/spielvogel

For a variety of tools to help you succeed in this course, visit the Western Civilization Resource Center at

http://history.wadsworth.com/spielvogel

Included are quizzes, images, documents, interactive simulations, maps and timelines, movie explorations, and a wealth of other sources.

THE ROMAN REPUBLIC

Horatius defending the bridge as envisioned by Charles Le Brun, a seventeenth-century French painter

© Dulwich Picture Gallery, London/Bridgeman Art Library

ℰARLY ROMAN HISTORY is filled with legendary tales of the heroes who made Rome great. One of the best known is the story of Horatius at the bridge. Threatened by attack from the neighboring Etruscans, Roman farmers abandoned their fields and moved into the city, where they would be protected by the walls. One weak point in the Roman defenses, however, was a wooden bridge over the Tiber River. Horatius was on guard at the bridge when a sudden assault by the Etruscans caused many Roman troops to throw down their weapons and flee. Horatius urged them to make a stand at the bridge to protect Rome; when they hesitated, as a last resort he told them to destroy the bridge behind him while he held the Etruscans back. Astonished at the sight of a single defender, the confused Etruscans threw their spears at Horatius, who caught them on his shield and barred the way. By the time the Etruscans had regrouped and were about to overwhelm the lone defender, the Roman soldiers brought down the bridge. When Horatius heard the bridge crash into the river behind him, he dived fully armed into the water and swam safely to the other side through a hail of arrows. Rome had been saved by the courageous act of a Roman who knew his duty and was determined to carry it out. Courage, duty, determination—these qualities would also serve the many

Romans who believed that it was their mission to rule nations and peoples.

In the first millennium B.C., a group of Latin-speaking people established a small community on the plain of Latium on the Italian peninsula. This community, called Rome, was one of the numerous communities founded by Latin-speaking peoples throughout Latium and the rest of Italy. Roman history is basically the story of the Romans' conquest of the plain of Latium, then Italy, and finally the entire Mediterranean region. How were the Romans able to do this? The Romans made the right decisions at the right time; in other words, they had political wisdom.

They were also practical. Unlike the Greeks, who reserved their citizenship for small, select groups, the Romans often offered citizenship to the peoples they conquered, thus laying the groundwork for a strong, integrated empire. The Romans also did not hesitate to borrow ideas and culture from the Greeks. Roman strength lay in government, law, and engineering. The Romans knew how to govern people, establish legal structures, and construct the roads that took them to the ends of the known world. Throughout their empire, they carried their law, their political institutions, their engineering skills, and their Latin language. And even after the Romans were gone, those same gifts continued to play an important role in the civilizations that came after them.✦

The Emergence of Rome

Italy is a peninsula extending about 750 miles from north to south (see Map 5.1). It is not very wide, however, averaging about 120 miles across. The Apennine Mountains traverse the peninsula from north to south, forming a ridge down the middle that divides west from east. Nevertheless, Italy has some fairly large fertile plains ideal for farming. Most important were the Po River valley in the north, probably the most fertile agricultural area; the plain of Latium, on which Rome was located; and Campania to the south of Latium. To the east of the Italian peninsula is the Adriatic Sea, and to the west, the Tyrrhenian Sea with the nearby large islands of Corsica and Sardinia. Sicily lies just west of the toe of the boot-shaped Italian peninsula.

Geography had an impact on Roman history. Although the Apennines bisect Italy, they are less rugged than the mountain ranges of Greece and so did not divide the peninsula into many small isolated communities. Italy also possessed considerably more productive farmland than Greece, enabling it to support a large population. Rome's location was favorable from a geographical point of view. Located 18 miles inland on the Tiber River, Rome had access to the sea and yet was far enough inland to be safe from pirates. Built on seven hills, it was easily defended. Situated where the Tiber could be readily forded, Rome became a natural crossing point for north-south traffic in western Italy. All in all, Rome had a good central location in Italy from which to expand.

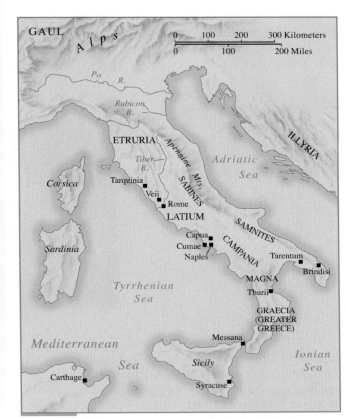

MAP 5.1 **Ancient Italy.** Ancient Italy was home to several groups. Both the Etruscans in the north and the Greeks in the south had a major influence on the development of Rome. ❓ Once Rome conquered the Etruscans, Sabines, Samnites, and other local groups, what aspects of the Italian peninsula helped make it defensible against outside enemies? 👄 **View an animated version of this map or related maps at** http://thomsonedu.com/history/spielvogel

Moreover, the Italian peninsula juts into the Mediterranean, making it an important crossroads between the western and eastern parts of that sea. Once Rome had unified Italy, involvement in affairs throughout the region was natural. And after the Romans had conquered their Mediterranean empire, Italy's central location made their task of governing that empire considerably easier.

The Greeks in Italy

We know little about the Indo-European peoples who moved into Italy during the second half of the second millennium B.C. By the first millennium B.C., other peoples had also settled in Italy, the two most notable being the Greeks and the Etruscans. The Greeks arrived on the Italian peninsula in large numbers during the age of Greek colonization (750–550 B.C.; see Chapter 3). Initially, the Greeks settled in southern Italy and gradually migrated around the coast and up the peninsula as far as Brindisi. They also occupied the eastern two-thirds of Sicily. Ultimately, the Greeks had considerable influence on Rome. They cultivated olives and grapes, passed on

Etruscan Tomb Mural. Like the Egyptians, the Etruscans filled their tombs with furniture, bowls, and other objects of daily life, as well as murals showing diversions experienced in life and awaiting the dead in the afterlife. Shown in this mural found in an Etruscan tomb at Tarquinia are servants and musicians at a banquet. This mural was painted in the first half of the fifth century B.C.

their alphabetic system of writing, and provided artistic and cultural models through their sculpture, architecture, and literature. Indeed, many historians view Roman culture as a continuation of Greek culture. Whereas Greek influence had initially touched Rome indirectly through the Etruscans, the Roman conquest of southern Italy and Sicily brought the Romans into direct contact with Greeks.

The Etruscans

The initial development of Rome was influenced most by the Etruscans, who had settled north of Rome in Etruria. The origins of the Etruscans are not clear, but after 650 B.C., they expanded in Italy and became the dominant cultural and economic force in a number of areas. To the north, they moved into north-central Italy, including the Po valley. To the south, according to Roman tradition and archaeological evidence, they controlled Rome and possibly all of Latium. From Latium they moved south and came into direct conflict with Greek colonists in southern Italy. In the sixth century B.C., the Etruscans were at the height of their power. But by 480 B.C., their power had begun to decline, and by 400 B.C., they were confined to Etruria itself. Later they were invaded by Celts from Gaul and then conquered by the Romans. But by then the Etruscans had made an impact. By transforming villages into towns and cities, they brought urbanization to northern and central Italy (as the Greeks had done in southern Italy). Rome was the Etruscans' most enduring product.

Early Rome

According to Roman legend, Rome was founded by twin brothers, Romulus and Remus, in 753 B.C., and archaeologists

have found that around that time, there was a settlement consisting of huts on the tops of several of Rome's hills. The early Romans, basically a pastoral people, spoke Latin, which, like Greek, belongs to the Indo-European family of languages (see Table 2.1 in Chapter 2). The Roman historical tradition also maintained that early Rome (753–509 B.C.) had been under the control of seven kings and that two of the last three had been Etruscans. Some historians believe that the king list may have some historical accuracy. What is certain is that Rome did fall under the influence of the Etruscans for about one hundred years during the period of the kings.

By the beginning of the sixth century, under Etruscan influence, Rome began to change from a pastoral community to an actual city. The Etruscans were responsible for an outstanding building program. They constructed the first roadbed of the chief street through Rome—the Sacred Way—before 575 B.C. and oversaw the development of temples, markets, shops, streets, and houses. By 509 B.C., the date when the monarchy was supposedly overthrown and a republican form of government was established, a new Rome had emerged, essentially as a result of the fusion of Etruscan and native Roman elements. After Rome had expanded over its seven hills and the valleys in between, the Servian Wall was built to surround the city in the fourth century B.C.

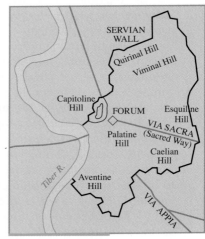

The City of Rome

The Roman Republic (c. 509–264 B.C.)

The transition from a monarchy to a republican government was not easy. Rome felt threatened by enemies from every direction and, in the process of meeting these threats, embarked on a course of military expansion that led to the conquest of the entire Italian peninsula. During this period of expansion in Italy, the Roman Republic developed political institutions that were in many ways determined by the social divisions that existed within the community.

The Roman State

In politics and law, as in conquest, the Romans took a practical approach and fashioned political institutions in response to problems as they arose. Hence it is important to remember that the political institutions we will discuss evolved over a period of centuries.

Political Institutions　The chief executive officers of the Roman Republic were the **consuls** and **praetors.** Two consuls, chosen annually, administered the government and led the Roman army into battle. They possessed *imperium,* or "the right to command." In 366 B.C., a new office, that of the praetor, was created. The praetor also possessed *imperium* and could govern Rome when the consuls were away from the city and could also lead armies. The praetor's primary function, however, was the execution of justice. He was in charge of the civil law as it applied to Roman citizens. In 242 B.C., reflecting Rome's growth, another praetor was added to judge cases in which one or both people were noncitizens.

As Rome expanded into the Mediterranean, additional praetors were established to govern the newly conquered provinces (two in 227, two more in 197). But as the number of provinces continued to grow, the Romans devised a new system in which ex-consuls and ex-praetors who had served their one-year terms were given the title of proconsul and propraetor and sent out as provincial governors. This demonstrates once again the Romans' practical solution to an immediate problem. It was reasonable to assume that officials with governmental experience would make good provincial administrators, although this was not always true in practice due to the opportunities for financial corruption in the provinces.

The Roman state also had administrative officials with specialized duties. **Quaestors** were assigned to assist consuls and praetors in the administration of financial affairs. **Aediles** supervised the public games and watched over the grain supply of the city, a major problem for a rapidly growing urban community that relied on imported grain to feed its population.

The Roman **senate** held an especially important position in the Roman Republic. The senate or council of elders was a select group of about three hundred men who served for life. The senate was not a legislative body and could only advise the magistrates. This advice of the senate was not taken lightly, however, and by the third century B.C. it had virtually the force of law. No doubt the prestige of the senate's members furthered this development. But it also helped that the senate met continuously, while the chief magistrates changed annually and the popular assemblies operated slowly and met only periodically.

The Roman Republic possessed a number of popular assemblies. The most important was the **centuriate assembly,** essentially the Roman army functioning in its political role. Organized by classes based on wealth, it was structured in such a way that the wealthiest citizens always had a majority. The centuriate assembly elected the chief magistrates and passed laws. Another assembly, the council of the plebs, came into being in 471 B.C. as a result of the struggle of the orders (see next section).

The government of the Roman Republic, then, consisted of three major elements. Two consuls and later other elected officials served as magistrates and ran the state. An assembly of adult males (the centuriate assembly), controlled by the wealthiest citizens, elected these officials, while the senate, a small group of large landowners, advised them. The Roman state, then, was an aristocratic republic controlled by a relatively small group of privileged people.

The Struggle of the Orders: Social Divisions in the Roman Republic　The most noticeable element in the social organization of early Rome was the division between two groups—the **patricians** and the **plebeians**. The patrician class in Rome consisted of families who were descended from the original senators appointed during the period of the kings. Their initial prominence was probably due to their wealth as great landowners. Thus patricians constituted an aristocratic governing class. Only they could be consuls, other magistrates, and senators. Through their patronage of large numbers of dependent clients, they could control the centuriate assembly and many other facets of Roman life.

The plebeians constituted the considerably larger group of "independent, unprivileged, poorer, and vulnerable men" as well as large nonpatrician landowners, less wealthy landholders, craftspeople, merchants, and small farmers. Although they were citizens, they did not possess the same rights as the patricians. Both patricians and plebeians could vote, but only the patricians could be elected to governmental offices. Both had the right to make legal contracts and marriages, but intermarriage between patricians and plebeians was forbidden. At the beginning of the fifth century B.C., the plebeians began a struggle to seek both political and social equality with the patricians.

The first success of the plebeians came in 494 B.C., when they withdrew physically from the state. The patricians, realizing that they could not defend Rome by themselves, were forced to compromise. Two new officials known as **tribunes of the plebs** were instituted (later raised to five and then ten in number). These tribunes were given the power to protect plebeians against arrest by patrician

CINCINNATUS SAVES ROME: A ROMAN MORALITY TALE

There is perhaps no better account of how the virtues of duty and simplicity enabled good Roman citizens to prevail during the travails of the fifth century B.C. than Livy's account of Cincinnatus. He was chosen dictator, supposedly in 457 B.C., to defend Rome against the attacks of the Aequi. The position of dictator was a temporary expedient used only in emergencies; the consuls would resign, and a leader with unlimited power would be appointed for a fixed period (usually six months). In this account, Cincinnatus did his duty, defeated the Aequi, and returned to his simple farm in just fifteen days.

Livy, *The Early History of Rome*

The city was thrown into a state of turmoil, and the general alarm was as great as if Rome herself were surrounded. Nautius was sent for, but it was quickly decided that he was not the man to inspire full confidence; the situation evidently called for a dictator, and, with no dissenting voice, Lucius Quinctius Cincinnatus was named for the post.

Now I would solicit the particular attention of those numerous people who imagine that money is everything in this world, and that rank and ability are inseparable from wealth: let them observe that Cincinnatus, the one man in whom Rome reposed all her hope of survival, was at that moment working a little three-acre farm . . . west of the Tiber, just opposite the spot where the shipyards are today. A mission from the city found him at work on his land—digging a ditch, maybe, or plowing. Greetings were exchanged, and he was asked—with a prayer for divine blessing on himself

and his country—to put on his toga and hear the Senate's instructions. This naturally surprised him, and, asking if all were well, he told his wife Racilia to run to their cottage and fetch his toga. The toga was brought, and wiping the grimy sweat from his hands and face he put it on; at once the envoys from the city saluted him, with congratulations, as Dictator, invited him to enter Rome, and informed him of the terrible danger of Municius' army. A state vessel was waiting for him on the river, and on the city bank he was welcomed by his three sons who had come to meet him, then by other kinsmen and friends, and finally by nearly the whole body of senators. Closely attended by all these people and preceded by his lictors he was then escorted to his residence through streets lined with great crowds of common folk who, be it said, were by no means so pleased to see the new Dictator, as they thought his power excessive and dreaded the way in which he was likely to use it.

[Cincinnatus proceeds to raise an army, march out, and defeat the Aequi.]

In Rome the Senate was convened by Quintus Fabius the City Prefect, and a decree was passed inviting Cincinnatus to enter in triumph with his troops. The chariot he rode in was preceded by the enemy commanders and the military standards, and followed by his army loaded with its spoils. . . . Cincinnatus finally resigned after holding office for fifteen days, having originally accepted it for a period of six months.

What values did Livy emphasize in his account of Cincinnatus? How important were those values to Rome's success? Why did Livy say he wrote his history?

---

magistrates. Moreover, after a new popular assembly for plebeians only, called the **council of the plebs**, was created in 471 B.C., the tribunes became responsible for convoking it and placing proposals before it. If adopted, these measures became **plebiscita** ("it is the opinion of the plebs"), but they were binding only on the plebeians, not the patricians. Nevertheless, the council of the plebs gave the plebeians considerable political leverage. After 445 B.C., when a law allowed patricians and plebeians to intermarry, the division between the two groups became less important. In the fourth century B.C., the consulship was opened to the plebeians. The climax of the struggle between the orders came in 287 B.C. with passage of a law that stipulated that all *plebiscita* passed by the council of the plebs had the force of law and were binding on the entire community, including patricians.

The struggle between the orders, then, had a significant impact on the development of the Roman constitution. Plebeians could hold the highest offices of state, they could intermarry with the patricians, and they could pass laws binding on the entire Roman community. Although the struggle had been long, the Romans had handled it by

compromise, not violent revolution. Theoretically, by 287 B.C., all Roman citizens were equal under the law, and all could strive for political office. But in reality, as a result of the right of intermarriage, a select number of patrician and plebeian families formed a new senatorial aristocracy that came to dominate the political offices. The Roman Republic had not become a democracy.

The Roman Conquest of Italy

At the beginning of the Republic, Rome was surrounded by enemies, including the Etruscans to the north and the Sabines, Volscians, and Aequi to the east and south. The Latin communities on the plain of Latium posed an even more immediate threat. If we are to believe Livy, one of the chief ancient sources for the history of the early Roman Republic, Rome was engaged in almost continuous warfare with its neighbors for the next hundred years.

In his account of these years, Livy provided a detailed narrative of Roman efforts. Many of Livy's stories were legendary in character and indeed were modeled on events in Greek history. But Livy, writing in the first

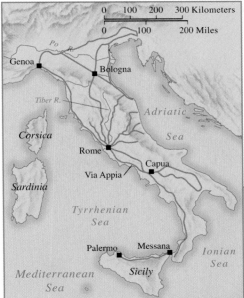

Roman Roads in Italy. The Romans built a remarkable system of roads. After laying a foundation with gravel, which allowed for drainage, the Roman builders placed flagstones, closely fitted together. Unlike other peoples who built similar kinds of roads, the Romans did not follow the contours of the land but made their roads as straight as possible to facilitate communications and transportation, especially for military purposes. Seen here is a view of the Via Appia (Appian Way), built in 312 B.C. under the leadership of the censor and consul Appius Claudius (Roman roads were often named after the great Roman families who encouraged their construction). The Via Appia (shown on the map) was meant to make it easy for Roman armies to march from Rome to the newly conquered city of Capua, a distance of 152 miles.

century B.C., used such stories to teach Romans the moral values and virtues that had made Rome great. These included tenacity, duty, courage, and especially discipline (see the box on p. 80). Indeed, Livy recounted stories of military leaders who executed their own sons for leaving their place in battle, a serious offense, since the success of the hoplite infantry depended on maintaining a precise order. These stories had little basis in fact, but like the story of George Washington and the cherry tree in American history, they provided mythic images to reinforce Roman patriotism.

By 340 B.C., Rome had crushed the Latin states in Latium. During the next fifty years, the Romans waged a fierce struggle with the Samnites, a hill people from the central Apennines, some of whom had settled in Campania, south of Rome. Rome was again victorious. The conquest of the Samnites gave Rome considerable control over a large part of Italy and also brought it into direct contact with the Greek communities of southern Italy. Soon after their conquest of the Samnites, the Romans were involved in hostilities with some of these Greek cities and by 267 B.C. had completed their conquest of southern Italy. After overrunning the remaining Etruscan states to the north in 264 B.C., Rome had conquered all of modern Italy except the extreme north.

To rule Italy, the Romans devised the Roman Confederation. Under this system, Rome allowed some peoples—especially the Latins—to have full Roman citizenship. Most of the remaining communities were made allies. They remained free to run their own local affairs but were required to provide soldiers for Rome. Moreover, the Romans made it clear that loyal allies could improve their status and even aspire to becoming Roman citizens. Thus the Romans had found a way to give conquered peoples a stake in Rome's success.

The Romans' conquest of Italy can hardly be said to be the result of a direct policy of expansion. Much of it was opportunistic. The Romans did not hesitate to act when they felt that their security was threatened. And surrounded by potential enemies, Rome in a sense never felt secure. Yet once embarked on a course of expansion, the Romans pursued consistent policies that help explain their success. The Romans excelled at making wise diplomatic decisions. Though firm and even cruel when necessary—rebellions were put down without mercy—they were also shrewd in extending their citizenship and allowing autonomy in domestic affairs. In addition, the Romans were not only good soldiers but persistent ones as well. The loss of an army or a fleet did not cause them to quit but instead spurred them on to build new armies and new fleets. Finally, the Romans had a practical sense of strategy. As they conquered, they settled Romans and Latins in new communities outside Latium. By 264 B.C., the Romans had established fortified towns at all strategic locations. By building roads to these settlements and connecting them, the Romans assured themselves of an impressive military and communications network that enabled them to rule effectively and efficiently. By insisting on military service from the allies in the Roman

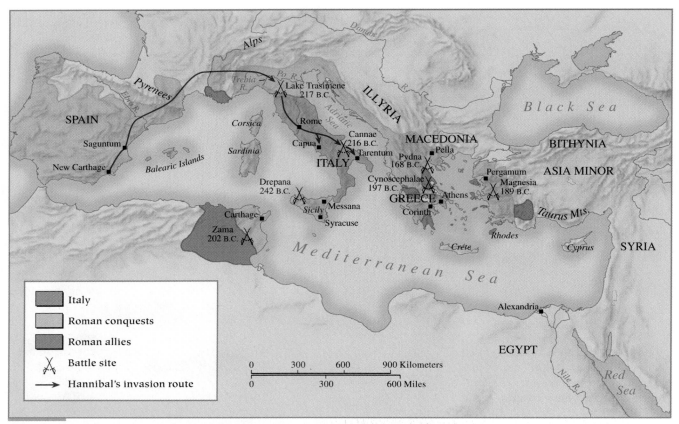

MAP 5.2 Roman Conquests in the Mediterranean, 264–133 B.C. Beginning with the Punic Wars, Rome expanded its holdings, first in the western Mediterranean at the expense of Carthage and later in Greece and western Asia Minor. ❓ What aspects of Mediterranean geography, combined with the territorial holdings and aspirations of Rome and the Carthaginians, made the Punic Wars more likely? 🖜 **View an animated version of this map or related maps at** http://thomsonedu.com/history/spielvogel

Confederation, Rome essentially mobilized the entire military manpower of all Italy for its wars.

The Roman Conquest of the Mediterranean (264–133 B.C.)

After their conquest of the Italian peninsula, the Romans found themselves face to face with a formidable Mediterranean power—Carthage. Founded around 800 B.C. by Phoenicians from Tyre, Carthage in North Africa was located in a favorable position for commanding Mediterranean trade routes and had become an important commercial center (see Map 5.2). It had become politically and militarily strong as well. By the third century B.C., the Carthaginian empire included the coast of northern Africa, southern Spain, Sardinia, Corsica, and western Sicily. With its monopoly of western Mediterranean trade, Carthage was the largest and richest state in the area. The presence of Carthaginians in Sicily made the Romans apprehensive about Carthaginian encroachment on the Italian coast. In 264 B.C., mutual suspicions

drove the two powers into a lengthy struggle for control of the western Mediterranean.

The Struggle with Carthage

The First Punic War (264–241 B.C.) (the Latin word for Phoenician was *Punicus*) began when the Romans decided to intervene in a struggle between two Sicilian cities by sending an army to Sicily. The Carthaginians, who considered Sicily within their own sphere of influence, deemed this just cause for war. In going to war, both sides determined on the conquest of Sicily. The Romans realized that the war would be long and drawn out if they could not supplement land operations with a navy and promptly developed a substantial naval fleet. The Carthaginians, for their part, had difficulty finding enough mercenaries to continue the fight. After a long struggle in which both sides lost battles in northern Africa and Sicily, a Roman fleet defeated the Carthaginian navy off Sicily, and the war quickly came to an end. In 241 B.C., Carthage gave up all rights to Sicily and had to pay an indemnity.

Hannibal and the Second Punic War After the war, Carthage made an unexpected recovery and extended its domains in Spain to compensate for the territory lost to Rome. The Carthaginians proceeded to organize a formidable land army in the event of a second war with Rome, because they realized that defeating Rome on land was essential to victory. When the Romans encouraged one of Carthage's Spanish allies to revolt against Carthage, Hannibal, the greatest of the Carthaginian generals, struck back, beginning the Second Punic War (218–201 B.C.).

This time the Carthaginians decided to bring the war home to the Romans by fighting them in their own backyard. Hannibal went into Spain, moved east, and crossed the Alps with an army of thirty to forty thousand men and six thousand horses and elephants. The Alps took a toll on the Carthaginian army; most of the elephants did not survive the trip. The remaining army, however, posed a real threat. At Cannae in 216 B.C., the Romans lost an army of almost forty thousand men. Rome seemed on the brink of disaster but refused to give up, raised yet another army, and gradually recovered. Although Hannibal remained free to roam in Italy, he had neither the men nor the equipment to lay siege to the major cities, including Rome itself. The Romans began to reconquer some of the Italian cities that had rebelled against Roman rule after Hannibal's successes. More important, the Romans pursued a strategy that aimed at undermining the Carthaginian empire in Spain. By 206 B.C., the Romans had pushed the Carthaginians out of Spain.

The Romans then took the war directly to Carthage. Late in 204 B.C., a Roman army under Publius Cornelius Scipio, later known as Scipio Africanus, moved from Sicily into northern Africa and forced the Carthaginians to recall Hannibal from Italy. At the Battle of Zama in 202 B.C., the Romans decisively defeated Hannibal's forces, and the war was over. Eventually, Hannibal left Carthage and went to help Antiochus, the ruler of the Seleucid kingdom, in his struggle with Rome. After Antiochus made peace with the Romans, Hannibal fled to Bithynia, near the Black Sea. Pursued by the Romans, Hannibal killed himself after saying, "Let us free Rome of her dread of one old man."

By the peace treaty signed in 201 B.C. by the Carthaginians and Romans, Carthage lost Spain, agreed to pay an indemnity, and promised not to go to war without Rome's permission. Spain, like Sicily, Corsica, and Sardinia earlier, was made into a Roman province. Rome had become the dominant power in the western Mediterranean.

The Destruction of Carthage But some Romans wanted even more. A number of prominent Romans, especially the conservative politician Cato, advocated the complete destruction of Carthage. Cato ended every speech he made to the senate with the words, "And I think Carthage must be destroyed." When the Carthaginians technically broke their peace treaty with Rome by going to war against one of Rome's North African allies who had been encroaching on Carthage's home territory, the Romans declared war. Roman forces undertook their third and last war with Carthage (149–146 B.C.). This time Carthage was no match for the Romans, who in 146 B.C. seized this opportunity to carry out the final destruction of Carthage. The territory was made a Roman province called Africa.

The Eastern Mediterranean

During the Punic Wars, Rome had become acutely aware of the Hellenistic states of the eastern Mediterranean when the king of Macedonia made an alliance with Hannibal after the Roman defeat at Cannae. But Rome was preoccupied with the Carthaginians, and it was not until after the defeat of Carthage that Rome became involved in the world of Hellenistic politics as an advocate of the freedom of the Greek states. This support of the Greeks brought the Romans into conflict with both Macedonia and the kingdom of the Seleucids. Roman military victories and diplomatic negotiations rearranged the territorial boundaries of the Hellenistic kingdoms and brought the Greek states their freedom in 196 B.C. For fifty years, the Romans tried to be a power broker in the affairs of the Greeks without direct control of their lands. When the effort failed, the Romans changed their policy.

Macedonia was made a Roman province in 148 B.C., and when some of the Greek states rose in revolt against Rome's restrictive policies, Rome acted decisively. The city of Corinth, leader of the revolt, was destroyed in 146 B.C. to teach the Greeks a lesson, and Greece was placed under the control of the Roman governor of Macedonia. Thirteen years later, in 133 B.C., the king of Pergamum deeded his kingdom to Rome, giving Rome its first province in Asia. Rome was now master of the Mediterranean Sea.

The Nature of Roman Imperialism

Rome's empire was built in three stages: the conquest of Italy, the conflict with Carthage and expansion into the western Mediterranean, and the involvement with and domination of the Hellenistic kingdoms in the eastern Mediterranean. The Romans did not have a master plan for the creation of an empire; as it had been in Italy, much of their continued expansion was opportunistic, in response to perceived threats to their security. The more they expanded, the more threats to their security appeared on the horizon, involving them in yet more conflicts. Indeed, the Romans liked to portray themselves as declaring war only for defensive reasons or to protect allies. That is only part of the story, however. It is likely, as some historians have suggested, that at some point a group of Roman aristocratic leaders emerged who favored expansion both for the glory it offered and for the economic benefits it provided. Certainly, by the second century B.C., aristocratic senators perceived new opportunities for lucrative foreign commands, enormous spoils of war, and an abundant supply of slave labor for their growing landed estates. By that same time, the destruction

CHRONOLOGY	The Roman Conquest of Italy and the Mediterranean	
Defeat of the Latin states		340–338 B.C.
Samnite Wars		343–290 B.C.
Defeat of Greek states in southern Italy		281–267 B.C.
First Punic War		264–241 B.C.
Second Punic War		218–201 B.C.
Battle of Cannae		216 B.C.
Completion of Roman seizure of Spain		206 B.C.
Battle of Zama		202 B.C.
Third Punic War		149–146 B.C.
Incorporation of Macedonia as a Roman province		148 B.C.
Destruction of Carthage		146 B.C.
Roman acquisition of Pergamum		133 B.C.

A Roman Legionary. The Roman legionaries, famed for their courage and tenacity, made possible Roman domination of the Mediterranean Sea. At the time of the Punic Wars, the Roman legionaries wore chain-mail armor and helmets with plumes and carried oval shields. Roman soldiers used heavy javelins and swords were their major weapons. This equipment, which is evident in this reconstruction of a Roman legionary from a museum in Rome, remained standard until the time of Julius Caesar.

of Corinth and Carthage indicated that Roman imperialism had become more arrogant and brutal as well. Rome's foreign success also had enormous repercussions for the internal development of the Roman Republic.

Society and Culture in the Roman World

One of the most noticeable aspects of Roman culture and society is the impact of the Greeks. The Romans had experienced Greek influence early on through the Greek cities in southern Italy. By the end of the third century B.C., however, Greek civilization was playing an ever-increasing role in Roman culture. Greek ambassadors, merchants, and artists traveled to Rome and spread Greek thought and practices. After their conquest of the Hellenistic kingdoms, Roman military commanders shipped Greek manuscripts and artworks back to Rome. Multitudes of educated Greek slaves were used in Roman households. Virtually every area of Roman life, from literature and philosophy to religion and education, was affected by Greek models. Rich Romans hired Greek tutors and sent their sons to Athens to study. As the Roman poet Horace said, "Captive Greece took captive her rude conqueror." Greek thought captivated the less sophisticated Roman mind, and the Romans became willing transmitters of Greek culture—not, however, without some resistance from Romans who had nothing but contempt for Greek politics and who feared the end of old Roman values. Even those who favored Greek culture blamed the Greeks for Rome's new vices, including a taste for luxury and homosexual practices.

Roman Religion

Every aspect of Roman society was permeated with religion. The official state religion focused on the worship of a pantheon of gods and goddesses, including Jupiter, Juno, Minerva, and Mars. As Rome developed and came into contact with other peoples and gods, the community simply adopted new deities. Hence the Greek Hermes became the Roman Mercury. Eventually, a complete amalgamation of Greek and Roman religion occurred, giving the Romans and the Greeks essentially a single "Greco-Roman" religion.

Roman religion focused on the worship of the gods for a very practical reason—human beings were thought to be totally dependent on them. The exact performance of ritual was crucial to establishing a right relationship with the gods. What was true for individuals was also valid for the state: it also had to observe correct ritual to receive its reward. Accurate performance of ritual was performed by a college of priests or pontiffs, who thus bore responsibility for maintaining the right relationship between the state and the gods. If the rituals were performed correctly, the Romans would obtain the "peace of the gods." No doubt the Roman success in creating an empire was a visible confirmation of divine favor. As Cicero, the first-century B.C. politician and writer, claimed, "We have overcome all the nations of the world, because we have realized that the world is directed and governed by the gods."[1]

Just as the state had an official cult, so did families. Because the family was regarded as a small state within the state, it had its own household cults, which included Janus, the spirit of the doorway, and Vesta, goddess of the hearth. Here, too, proper ritual was important, and it was the responsibility of the **paterfamilias** as head of the family to ensure that religious obligations were properly fulfilled.

Religious festivals were an important part of Roman religious practice. There were two kinds: public festivals ordained and paid for by the state and private festivals celebrated by individuals and families. By the mid-second century B.C., six public festivals were celebrated annually, each lasting several days. The practice of holding games also grew out of religious festivals. The games were inaugurated in honor of Jupiter Optimus Maximus ("best and greatest"), the patron deity of Rome, but had become annual events by 366 B.C. In the late Republic, both the number of games and the number of days they lasted were increased. Originally, the games consisted of chariot racing in the Circus Maximus; later, animal hunts and theatrical performances were added. In the empire, gladiatorial contests would become the primary focus (see Chapter 6).

The Growth of Slavery

Slavery was a common institution throughout the ancient world, but no people possessed more slaves or relied so much on slave labor as the Romans eventually did. Before the third century B.C., a small Roman farmer might possess one or two slaves who would help farm his few acres and perform domestic chores. These slaves would most likely be from Italy and be regarded as part of the family household. Only the very rich would have large numbers of slaves.

The Roman conquest of the Mediterranean brought a drastic change in the use of slaves. Large numbers of foreign slaves were brought back to Italy. During the Republic, then, the chief source of slaves was from capture in war, followed by piracy. Of course, the children of slaves also became slaves. While some Roman generals brought back slaves to be sold to benefit the public treasury, ambitious generals of the first century B.C., such as Pompey and Caesar, made personal fortunes by treating slaves captured by their armies as private property.

Slaves were used in many ways in Roman society. The rich, of course, owned the most and the best. In the late Republic, it became a badge of prestige to be attended by many slaves. Greeks were in much demand as tutors, musicians, doctors, and artists. Roman businessmen would employ them as shop assistants or artisans. Slaves were also used as farm laborers; in fact, huge gangs of slaves living in pitiful conditions worked the large landed estates known as **latifundia**. Cato the Elder argued that it was cheaper to work slaves to death and then replace them than to treat them well. Many slaves of all nationalities were used as menial household workers, such

Temple of Portunus. The Romans considered the proper worship of the gods an important key to success. Typical of Roman religious architecture was the small urban temple located in the midst of a crowded commercial center. Pictured here is a rectangular temple built in Rome in the late second or early first century B.C. and dedicated to Portunus, the god of harbors. The temple was located in the cattle market close to the Tiber River.

Household Slaves. It became a sign of status for upper-class Romans to have numerous specialist slaves at work in a household. This wall painting from central Italy depicts an elaborate dressing room where a female slave is arranging a girl's hair while the girl's mother and sister look on.

as cooks, valets, waiters, cleaners, and gardeners. Roads, aqueducts, and other public facilities were constructed by contractors using slave labor. The total number of slaves is difficult to judge—estimates vary from 20 to 30 percent of the population.

It is also difficult to generalize about the treatment of Roman slaves. There are numerous instances of humane treatment by masters and situations where slaves even protected their owners from danger out of gratitude and esteem. But slaves were also subject to severe punishments, torture, abuse, and hard labor that drove some to run away or even revolt against their owners. The Republic had stringent laws against aiding a runaway slave. The murder of a master by a slave might mean the execution of all the other household slaves. Near the end of the second century B.C., large-scale slave revolts occurred in Sicily, where enormous gangs of slaves were subjected to horrible working conditions on large landed estates. Slaves were branded, beaten, inadequately fed, worked in chains, and housed at night in underground prisons. It took three years (135–132 B.C.) to crush a revolt of seventy thousand slaves, and the great revolt on Sicily (104–101 B.C.) involved most of the island and took a Roman army of seventeen thousand men to suppress. The most famous revolt on the Italian peninsula occurred in 73 B.C. Led by Spartacus, a slave who had been a Thracian gladiator, the revolt broke out in southern Italy and involved seventy thousand slaves. Spartacus managed to defeat several Roman armies before he was finally trapped and killed in southern Italy in 71 B.C. Six thousand of his followers were crucified, the traditional form of execution for slaves.

The Roman Family

At the heart of the Roman social structure stood the family, headed by the *paterfamilias*—the dominant male. The household also included the wife, sons with their wives and children, unmarried daughters, and slaves. A family was virtually a small state within the state, and the power of the *paterfamilias* was parallel to that of the state magistrates over the citizens. Like the Greeks, Roman males believed that the weakness of the female sex necessitated male guardians (see the box on p. 87). The *paterfamilias* exercised that authority; on his death, sons or nearest male relatives assumed the role of guardians. By the late Republic, however, although the rights of male guardians remained legally in effect, upper-class women found numerous ways to circumvent the power of their guardians.

Fathers arranged the marriages of daughters, although there are instances of mothers and daughters having influence on the choice. In the Republic, women married *cum manu,* "with legal control" passing from father to husband. By the mid-first century B.C., the dominant practice had changed to *sine manu,* "without legal control," which meant that married daughters officially remained within the father's legal power. Since the fathers of most married women were dead, not being in the "legal control" of a husband made possible independent property rights that forceful women could translate into considerable power within the household and outside it. Traditionally, Roman marriages were intended to be for life, but divorce was introduced in the third century B.C. and became relatively easy to obtain since either party could initiate it and no one needed to prove the breakdown of the marriage. Divorce became especially prevalent in the first century B.C.—a period of political turmoil—when marriages were used to cement political alliances.

Some parents in upper-class families provided education for their daughters. Some girls had private tutors, and others may have gone to primary schools. But at the age when boys were entering secondary schools, girls were pushed into marriage. The legal minimum age was twelve, although fourteen was a more common age in practice. Although some Roman doctors warned that early pregnancies could be dangerous for young girls, early marriages persisted due to the desire to benefit from dowries as soon as possible and the reality of early mortality. A good example is Tullia, Cicero's beloved daughter. She was married at sixteen, widowed at twenty-two, remarried one year later, divorced at twenty-eight, remarried at twenty-nine, and divorced at thirty-three. She died at thirty-four, not unusual for females in Roman society.

The Evolution of Roman Law

One of Rome's chief gifts to the Mediterranean world of its day and to succeeding generations was its development of law. The Twelve Tables of 450 B.C. were the first codification of Roman law (see the box on p. 88), and although inappropriate for later times, they were never officially

CATO THE ELDER ON WOMEN

During the Second Punic War, the Romans enacted the Oppian Law, which limited the amount of gold women could possess and restricted their dress and use of carriages. In 195 B.C., an attempt was made to repeal the law, and women demonstrated in the streets on behalf of the effort. According to the Roman historian Livy, the conservative Roman official Cato the Elder spoke against repeal and against the women favoring it. Although the words are probably not Cato's own, they do reflect a traditional male Roman attitude toward women.

Livy, *The History of Rome*

"If each of us, citizens, had determined to assert his rights and dignity as a husband with respect to his own spouse, we should have less trouble with the sex as a whole; as it is, our liberty, destroyed at home by female violence, even here in the Forum is crushed and trodden underfoot, and because we have not kept them individually under control, we dread them collectively. . . . But from no class is there not the greatest danger if you permit them meetings and gatherings and secret consultations. . . .

"Our ancestors permitted no woman to conduct even personal business without a guardian to intervene in her behalf; they wished them to be under the control of fathers, brothers, husbands; we (Heaven help us!) allow them now even to interfere in public affairs, yes, and to visit the Forum and our informal and formal sessions. What else are they doing now on the streets and at the corners except urging the bill of the tribunes and voting for the repeal of the law?

Give loose rein to their uncontrollable nature and to this untamed creature and expect that they will themselves set bounds to their license; unless you act, this is the least of the things enjoined upon women by custom or law and to which they submit with a feeling of injustice. It is complete liberty or rather, if we wish to speak the truth, complete license that they desire.

"If they win in this, what will they not attempt? Review all the laws with which your forefathers restrained their license and made them subject to their husbands; even with all these bonds you can scarcely control them. What of this? If you suffer them to seize these bonds one by one and wrench themselves free and finally to be placed on a parity with their husbands, do you think you will be able to endure them? The moment they begin to be your equals, they will be your superiors. . . .

"Now they publicly address other women's husbands, and, what is more serious, they beg for law and votes, and from various men they get what they ask. In matters affecting yourself, your property, your children, you, Sir, can be importuned; once the law has ceased to set a limit to your wife's expenditures you will never set it yourself. Do not think, citizens, that the situation which existed before the law was passed will ever return. . . ."

What particular actions on the part of the women protesting this law have angered Cato? What more general concerns does he have about Roman women? What does he believe is women's ultimate goal in regard to men?

---

abrogated and were still memorized by schoolboys in the first century B.C. Civil law derived from the Twelve Tables proved inadequate for later Roman needs, however, and gave way to corrections and additions by the praetors. On taking office, a praetor issued an edict listing his guidelines for dealing with different kinds of legal cases. The praetors were knowledgeable in law, but they also relied on Roman jurists—amateur law experts—for advice in preparing their edicts. The interpretations of the jurists, often embodied in the edicts of the praetors, created a body of legal principles.

In 242 B.C., the Romans appointed a second praetor who was responsible for examining suits between a Roman and a non-Roman as well as between two non-Romans. The Romans found that although some of their rules of law could be used in these cases, special rules were often needed. These rules gave rise to a body of law known as the law of nations, defined by the Romans as "that part of the law which we apply both to ourselves and to foreigners." But the influence of Greek philosophy, primarily Stoicism, led Romans in the late Republic to develop the idea of the law of nature—or universal divine law derived from right reason. The Romans came to view their law of nations as

derived from or identical to this law of nature, thus giving Roman jurists a philosophical justification for systematizing Roman law according to basic principles.

The Development of Literature

The Romans produced little literature before the third century B.C., and the Latin literature that emerged in that century was strongly influenced by Greek models. The demand for plays at public festivals eventually led to a growing number of native playwrights. One of the best known was Plautus (c. 254–184 B.C.), who used plots from Greek New Comedy (see Chapter 4) for his own plays. The actors wore Greek costumes and Greek masks and portrayed the same basic stock characters: lecherous old men, skillful slaves, prostitutes, young men in love. Plautus wrote for the masses and became a very popular playwright in Rome.

In the last century of the Republic, the Romans began to produce a new poetry, less dependent on epic themes and more inclined to personal expression. Latin poets were now able to use various Greek forms to express their own feelings about people, social and political life, and love. The finest example of this can be seen in

THE TWELVE TABLES

In 451 B.C., plebeian pressure led to the creation of a special commission of ten men who were responsible for codifying Rome's laws and making them public. In so doing, the plebeians hoped that they could restrict the arbitrary power of the patrician magistrates, who alone had access to the laws. The Twelve Tables represent the first formal codification of Roman laws and customs. The laws dealt with litigation procedures, debt, family relations, property, and other matters of public and sacred law. The code was inscribed on bronze plaques, which were eventually destroyed. These selections are taken from reconstructions of the code preserved in later writings.

Selections from the Twelve Tables

Table III: Execution; Law of Debt

When a debt has been acknowledged, or judgment about the matter has been pronounced in court, thirty days must be the legitimate time of grace. After that, the debtor may be arrested by laying on of hands. Bring him into court. If he does not satisfy the judgment, or no one in court offers himself as surety in his behalf, the creditor may take the defaulter with him. He may bind him either in stocks or in fetters. . . .

Unless they make a settlement, debtors shall be held in bond for sixty days. During that time they shall be brought before the praetor's court in the meeting place on three successive market days, and the amount for which they are judged liable shall be announced; on the third market day they shall suffer capital punishment or be delivered up for sale abroad, across the Tiber.

Table IV: Rights of Head of Family

Quickly kill . . . a dreadfully deformed child.

If a father three times surrenders a son for sale, the son shall be free from the father.

A child born ten months after the father's death will not be admitted into legal inheritance.

Table V: Guardianship; Succession

Females shall remain in guardianship even when they have attained their majority.

A spendthrift is forbidden to exercise administration over his own goods. . . . A person who, being insane or a spendthrift, is prohibited from administering his own goods shall be under trusteeship of agnates [nearest male relatives].

Table VII: Rights Concerning Land

Branches of a tree may be lopped off all round to a height of more than 15 feet. . . . Should a tree on a neighbor's farm be bent crooked by a wind and lean over your farm, action may be taken for removal of that tree.

It is permitted to gather up fruit falling down on another man's farm.

Table VIII: Torts or Delicts

If any person has sung or composed against another person a song such as was causing slander or insult to another, he shall be clubbed to death.

If a person has maimed another's limb, let there be retaliation in kind unless he makes agreement for settlement with him.

Any person who destroys by burning any building or heap of corn deposited alongside a house shall be bound, scourged, and put to death by burning at the stake, provided that he has committed the said misdeed with malice aforethought, but if he shall have committed it by accident, that is, by negligence, it is ordained that he repair the damage.

Table IX: Public Law

The penalty shall be capital punishment for a judge or arbiter legally appointed who has been found guilty of receiving a bribe for giving a decision.

Table XI: Supplementary Laws

Intermarriage shall not take place between plebeians and patricians.

What do the selections from the Twelve Points reveal about Roman society? In what ways do these points of law differ from those found in the Code of Hammurabi? In what ways are they similar?

---

the work of Catullus (c. 87–54 B.C.), Rome's "best lyric poet" and one of the greatest in world literature.

Catullus became a master at adapting and refining Greek forms of poetry to express his emotions. He wrote a variety of poems on, among other things, political figures, social customs, the use of language, the death of his brother, and the travails of love. Catullus became infatuated with Clodia, the promiscuous sister of a tribune and wife of a provincial governor, and addressed a number of poems to her (he called her Lesbia), describing his passionate love and hatred for her (Clodia had many other lovers besides Catullus):

> *You used to say that you wished to know only Catullus,*
> *Lesbia, and wouldn't take even Jove before me!*
> *I didn't regard you just as my mistress then:*
> *I cherished you as a father does his sons or his*
> *daughters' husbands.*
> *Now that I know you, I burn for you even more fiercely,*
> *though I regard you as almost utterly worthless.*

*How can that be, you ask? It's because such cruelty
forces lust to assume the shrunken place of
affection.*[2]

The ability of Catullus to express in simple fashion his intense feelings and curiosity about himself and his world had a noticeable impact on later Latin poets.

The development of Roman prose was greatly aided by the practice of oratory. Romans had great respect for oratory since the ability to persuade people in public debate meant success in politics. Oratory was brought to perfection in a literary fashion by Cicero (106–43 B.C.), the best exemplar of the literary and intellectual interests of the senatorial elite of the late Republic and, indeed, the greatest prose writer of that period. For Cicero, oratory was not simply skillful speaking. An orator was a statesman, a man who achieved his highest goal by pursuing an active life in public affairs.

Later, when the turmoil of the late Republic forced him into semiretirement politically, Cicero became more interested in the writing of philosophical treatises. He served a most valuable purpose for Roman society by popularizing and making understandable the works of Greek philosophers. In his philosophical works, Cicero, more than anyone else, transmitted the classical intellectual heritage to the Western world. Cicero's original contributions came in the field of politics. His works *On the Laws* and *On the Republic* provided fresh insights into political thought, including the need for a mixed constitution: "a moderate and well-balanced form of government which is a combination of the three simple good forms (monarchy, aristocracy, and democracy) is preferable even to monarchy."[3] His emphasis on the need to pursue an active life to benefit and improve humankind would greatly influence the later Italian Renaissance.

Roman Art

The Romans were also dependent on the Greeks for artistic inspiration. During the third and second centuries B.C., they adopted many features of the Hellenistic style of art. The Romans developed a taste for Greek statues, which they placed not only in public buildings but also in their homes. Once demand outstripped the supply of original works, reproductions of Greek statues became fashionable. The Romans' own portrait sculpture was characterized by an intense realism that included even unpleasant physical details. Wall paintings and frescoes in the houses of the rich realistically depicted landscapes, portraits, and scenes from mythological stories.

The Romans excelled in architecture, a highly practical art. Although they continued to employ Greek styles and made use of colonnades, rectangular structures, and post-and-lintel construction, the Romans were also innovative. They made considerable use of curvilinear forms: the arch, vault, and dome. The Romans were also the first people in antiquity to use concrete on an enormous scale. By combining concrete and curvilinear forms, they were able to construct massive buildings—public baths and amphitheaters, the most famous of which was the Coliseum in Rome, capable of seating fifty thousand spectators. These large buildings were made possible by Roman engineering skills. These same skills were put to use in constructing roads (the Romans built a network of 50,000 miles of roads throughout their empire), aqueducts (in Rome, almost a dozen aqueducts kept a population of one million supplied with water), and bridges.

Values and Attitudes

The Romans were by nature a conservative people. They were very concerned about maintaining the *mos maiorum*, the customs or traditions of their ancestors. They emphasized parental authority and, above all, their obligations to the state. The highest virtue was *pietas*—the dutiful execution of one's obligations to one's fellow citizens, to the gods, and to the state.

By the second century B.C., however, the assembling of an empire had begun to weaken the old values. The Romans began to focus more on affluence, status, and material possessions. Emphasis shifted toward individualism and away from collective well-being, the old public spirit that had served Rome so well. Observers worried about the decline of the old values blamed it on different causes. Some felt that after the destruction of Carthage, the Romans no longer had any strong enemies to challenge them. Others believed that the Romans had simply been overwhelmed by the affluence afforded by the new empire. And some blamed everything on the Greeks for importing ideas and practices baneful to the Romans. Of course, there were also many Romans who, though desirous of maintaining traditional values, were also well aware that the acquisition of an empire had created a new world with new demands and values.

The Decline and Fall of the Roman Republic (133–31 B.C.)

By the mid-second century B.C., Roman domination of the Mediterranean Sea was well established. Yet the process of building an empire had weakened and threatened the internal stability of Rome. This internal instability characterizes the period of Roman history from 133 until 31 B.C., when the armies of Octavian defeated Mark Antony and stood supreme over the Roman world. By that time, the constitution of the Roman Republic was in shambles.

Social, Economic, and Political Problems

By the second century B.C., the senate had become the effective governing body of the Roman state. It consisted of three hundred men, drawn primarily from the landed aristocracy; they remained senators for life and held the chief magistracies of the Republic. During the wars of the third and second centuries, the senate came to exercise enormous power. It directed the wars and took control of both foreign and domestic policy, including financial affairs.

Moreover, the magistracies and senate were increasingly controlled by a relatively select circle of wealthy and powerful families, both patrician and plebeian, called the **nobiles** ("nobles"). In the hundred years from 233 to 133 B.C., 80 percent of the consuls came from twenty-six families; moreover, 50 percent came from only ten families. Hence the *nobiles* constituted a governing oligarchy that managed, through its landed wealth, system of patronage, and intimidation, to maintain its hold over the magistracies and senate and thus guide the destiny of Rome while running the state in its own interests.

By the end of the second century B.C., two types of aristocratic leaders, called the **optimates** ("the best men") and the **populares** ("favoring the people"), became prominent. *Optimates* and *populares* were terms of political rhetoric that were used by individuals within the aristocracy against fellow aristocratic rivals to distinguish one set of tactics from another. The *optimates* controlled the senate and wished to maintain their oligarchical privileges, while the *populares* were usually other ambitious aristocrats who used the people's assemblies as instruments to break the domination of the *optimates*. The conflicts between these two types of aristocratic leaders and their supporters engulfed the first century B.C. in political turmoil.

Of course, the aristocrats formed only a tiny minority of the Roman people. The backbone of the Roman state and army had traditionally been the small farmers. But economic changes that began in the period of the Punic Wars increasingly undermined the position of that group. Their lands had been severely damaged during the Second Punic War when Hannibal invaded Italy. Moreover, in order to win the wars, Rome had to increase the term of military service from two to six years. When they returned home, many farmers found their farms so deteriorated that they chose to sell out instead of remaining on the land. By this time, capitalistic agriculture was also increasing rapidly. Landed aristocrats had been able to develop large estates (the *latifundia*) by taking over state-owned land and by buying out small peasant owners. These large estates relied on slave and tenant labor and frequently concentrated on cash crops, such as grapes for wine, olives, and sheep for wool, which small farmers could not afford to do. Thus the rise of the *latifundia* contributed to the decline in the number of small citizen farmers. Because the latter group traditionally provided the foundation of the Roman army, the number of men available for military service declined. Moreover, many of these small farmers drifted to the cities, especially Rome, forming a large class of day laborers who possessed no property. This new urban proletariat was a highly unstable mass with the potential for much trouble in depressed times.

The Reforms of the Gracchi

In 133 B.C., Tiberius Gracchus, himself a member of the aristocracy and a new tribune, came to believe that the underlying cause of Rome's problems was the decline of the small farmer. Consequently, Tiberius bypassed the senate, where he knew his rivals would oppose his proposal, and had the council of the plebs pass a land reform bill that authorized the government to reclaim public land held by large landowners and to distribute it to landless Romans. Many senators, themselves large landowners whose estates included large tracts of public land, were furious, and a group of them took the law into their own hands and assassinated Tiberius.

The efforts of Tiberius Gracchus were continued by his brother Gaius, elected tribune for both 123 and 122 B.C. Gaius, too, pushed for the distribution of land to displaced farmers. But he broadened his reform program with measures that would benefit the **equestrian order,** a rising group of wealthy people who wanted a share in the political power held by the ruling aristocracy. Many senators, hostile to Gaius' reforms and fearful of his growing popularity, instigated mob action that resulted in the death of the reformer and many of his friends in 121 B.C. The attempts of the Gracchus brothers to bring reforms had opened the door to more instability and further violence.

A New Role for the Roman Army: Marius and Sulla

In the closing years of the second century B.C., a series of military disasters gave rise to a fresh outburst of popular anger against the old leaders of the senate. Military defeats in northern Africa under a senate-appointed general encouraged Marius—a "new man" from the equestrian order—to run for the consulship on a "win the war" campaign slogan. Marius won and became a consul for 107 B.C. Marius took command of the army in Africa and brought the war to a successful conclusion. He was then called on to defeat the Celts, who threatened an invasion of Italy. Marius was made consul for five years, from 104 to 100 B.C., raised a new army, and decisively defeated the Celts, leaving him in a position of personal ascendancy in Rome.

In raising a new army, Marius initiated military reforms that proved to have drastic consequences. The Roman army had traditionally been a conscript army of small landholders. Marius recruited volunteers from both the urban and rural proletariat who possessed no property. These volunteers swore an oath of loyalty to the general, not the senate, and thus inaugurated a professional-type army that might no longer be subject to the state. Moreover, to recruit these men, a general would promise them land, so the generals had to play politics to get legislation passed that would provide the land for their veterans. Marius left a powerful legacy. He had created a new system of military recruitment that placed much power in the hands of the individual generals.

Lucius Cornelius Sulla was the next general to take advantage of the new military system. The senate had placed him in charge of a war in Asia Minor, but when the council of the plebs tried to transfer command of this war to Marius, a civil war ensued. Sulla won and seized Rome itself in 82 B.C. He forced the senate to grant him the title of dictator to "reconstitute the Republic." After conducting a reign of terror to wipe out all opposition, Sulla revised the constitution to restore power to the senate and eliminated most of the powers of the popular assemblies and the tribunes of the plebs. In 79 B.C., believing that he had created a firm foundation for the traditional Republic governed by a powerful senate, he retired. But his real legacy was quite different from what he had intended. His example of using an army to seize power would prove most attractive to ambitious men.

The Collapse of the Republic

For the next fifty years, Roman history would be characterized by two important features: the jostling for power by a number of strong individuals and the civil wars generated by their conflicts. Three men came to hold enormous military and political power—Crassus, Pompey, and Julius Caesar. Crassus, who was known as the richest man in Rome, had successfully put down the major slave rebellion led by Spartacus. Pompey had returned from a successful military command in Spain in 71 B.C. and had been hailed as a military hero. Julius Caesar had been a spokesman for the *populares* from the beginning of his political career and had a military command in Spain. In 60 B.C., Caesar joined with Crassus and Pompey to form a coalition that historians call the First Triumvirate.

Scala/Art Resource, NY (Museo Archeologico Nazionale, Naples)

Caesar. Conqueror of Gaul and member of the First Triumvirate, Julius Caesar is perhaps the best-known figure of the late Republic. Caesar became dictator of Rome in 47 B.C. and after his victories in the civil war was made dictator for life. Some members of the senate who resented his power assassinated him in 44 B.C. Pictured is a marble copy of a bust of Caesar.

Reforms of Tiberius Gracchus	133 B.C.
Reforms of Gaius Gracchus	123–122 B.C.
Marius: First consulship	107 B.C.
Marius: Consecutive consulships	104–100 B.C.
Sulla as dictator	82–79 B.C.
Pompey's command in Spain	77–71 B.C.
Campaign of Crassus against Spartacus	73–71 B.C.
First Triumvirate (Caesar, Pompey, Crassus)	60 B.C.
Caesar in Gaul	59–49 B.C.
Murder of Crassus by Parthians	53 B.C.
Caesar's crossing of the Rubicon	49 B.C.
End of civil war	45 B.C.
Caesar as dictator	47–44 B.C.
Octavian's defeat of Antony at Actium	31 B.C.

Though others had made political deals before, the combined wealth and power of these three men was enormous, enabling them to dominate the political scene and achieve their basic aims: Pompey received lands for his veterans and a command in Spain, Crassus was given a command in Syria, and Caesar was granted a special military command in Gaul (modern France). When Crassus was killed in battle in 53 B.C., his death left two powerful men with armies in direct competition. Caesar had used his time in Gaul wisely. He had conquered all of Gaul and gained fame, wealth, and military experience as well as an army of seasoned veterans who were loyal to him. When leading senators fastened on Pompey as the less harmful to their cause and voted for Caesar to lay down his command and return as a private citizen to Rome, Caesar refused. He chose to keep his army and moved into Italy by illegally crossing the Rubicon, the river that formed the southern boundary of his province. ("Crossing the Rubicon" is a phrase used to this day to mean taking a decisive action and being unable to turn back.) Caesar marched on Rome, starting a civil war between his forces and those of Pompey and his allies. The defeat of Pompey's forces left Caesar in complete control of the Roman government.

Caesar had officially been made dictator in 47 B.C., and three years later, he was made dictator for life. He continued to hold elections for offices but saw to it that his supporters chose the people he recommended. Upon becoming Rome's ruler, he quickly instituted a number of ambitious reforms. He increased the senate to nine hundred members by filling it with many of his supporters and granted citizenship to a number of people in the provinces who had helped him. By establishing colonies of Roman citizens in North Africa, Gaul, and Spain, he initiated a process of Romanization in those areas. He also reorganized the administrative structures of cities in Italy in an attempt to create a sense of order in their government. Caesar was a generous victor and pardoned

THE ASSASSINATION OF JULIUS CAESAR

When it became apparent that Julius Caesar had no intention of restoring the Republic as they conceived it, about sixty senators, many of them his friends or pardoned enemies, formed a conspiracy to assassinate the dictator. It was led by Gaius Cassius and Marcus Brutus, who naively imagined that this act would restore the traditional Republic. The conspirators set the Ides of March (March 15), 44 B.C., as the date for the assassination. Although warned about a plot against his life, Caesar chose to disregard it. This account of his death is taken from his biography by the Greek writer Plutarch.

Plutarch, *Life of Caesar*

Fate, however, is to all appearance more unavoidable than unexpected. For many strange prodigies and apparitions are said to have been observed shortly before this event. . . . One finds it also related by many that a soothsayer bade him [Caesar] prepare for some great danger on the Ides of March. When this day was come, Caesar, as he went to the senate, met this soothsayer, and said to him mockingly, "The Ides of March are come," who answered him calmly, "Yes, they are come, but they are not past. . . ."

All these things might happen by chance. But the place which was destined for the scene of this murder, in which the senate met that day, was the same in which Pompey's statue stood, and was one of the edifices which Pompey had raised and dedicated with his theater to the use of the public, plainly showing that there was something of a supernatural influence which guided the action and ordered it to that particular place. Cassius, just before the act, is said to have looked toward Pompey's statue, and silently implored his assistance. . . . When Caesar entered, the senate stood up to show their respect to him, and of Brutus' confederates, some came about his chair and stood behind it, others met him, pretending to add their petitions to those of Tillius Cimber, in behalf of his brother, who was in exile; and they followed him with their joint applications till he came to his seat. When he sat down, he refused to comply with their requests, and upon their urging him further began to reproach them severely for their demand, when Tillius, laying hold of his robe with both his hands, pulled it down from his neck, which was the signal for the assault. Casca gave him the first cut in the neck, which was not mortal nor dangerous, as coming from one who at the beginning of such a bold action was probably very much disturbed; Caesar immediately turned about, and laid his hand upon the dagger and kept hold of it. And both of them at the same time cried out, he that received the blow, in Latin, "Vile Casca, what does this mean?" and he that gave it, in Greek to his brother, "Brother, help!" Upon this first onset, those who were not privy to the design were astonished, and their horror and amazement at what they saw were so great that they dared not fly nor assist Caesar, nor so much as speak a word. But those who came prepared for the business enclosed him on every side, with their naked daggers in their hands. Which way soever he turned he met with blows, and saw their swords leveled at his face and eyes, and was encompassed like a wild beast in the toils on every side. For it had been agreed they should each of them make a thrust at him, and flesh themselves with his blood: for which reason Brutus also gave him one stab in the groin. Some say that he fought and resisted all the rest, shifting his body to avoid the blows, and calling out for help, but that when he saw Brutus' sword drawn, he covered his face with his robe and submitted, letting himself fall, whether it were by chance or that he was pushed in that direction by his murderers, at the foot of the pedestal on which Pompey's statue stood, and which was thus wetted with his blood. So that Pompey himself seemed to have presided, as it were, over the revenge done upon his adversary, who lay here at his feet, and breathed out his soul through his multitude of wounds, for they say he received three-and-twenty. And the conspirators themselves were many of them wounded by each other while they all leveled their blows at the same person.

What does the account of Caesar's assassination tell you about the character of Julius Caesar?

---

many of the republican leaders who had opposed him, allowing them to return to Rome. He also reformed the calendar by introducing the Egyptian solar year of 365 days (with changes implemented in 1582, it became the basis of our current calendar). He planned much more in the way of building projects and military adventures in the east, but in 44 B.C., a group of leading senators who resented his domination assassinated him in the belief that they had struck a blow for republican liberty (see the box above). In truth, they had set the stage for another civil war that delivered the death blow to the Republic.

Within a few years after Caesar's death, two men had divided the Roman world between them—Octavian, Caesar's heir and grandnephew, taking the west, and Antony, Caesar's ally and assistant, the east. But the empire of the Romans, large as it was, was still too small for two masters, and Octavian and Antony eventually came into conflict. Antony allied himself with the Egyptian queen Cleopatra VII, with whom, like Caesar before him, he fell in love. Octavian began a propaganda campaign, accusing Antony of catering to Cleopatra and giving away Roman territory to this "whore of the east." Finally, at the Battle of Actium in Greece in 31 B.C., Octavian's forces smashed the army and navy of Antony and Cleopatra. Both fled to Egypt, where, according to the account of the Roman historian Florus, they committed suicide a year later:

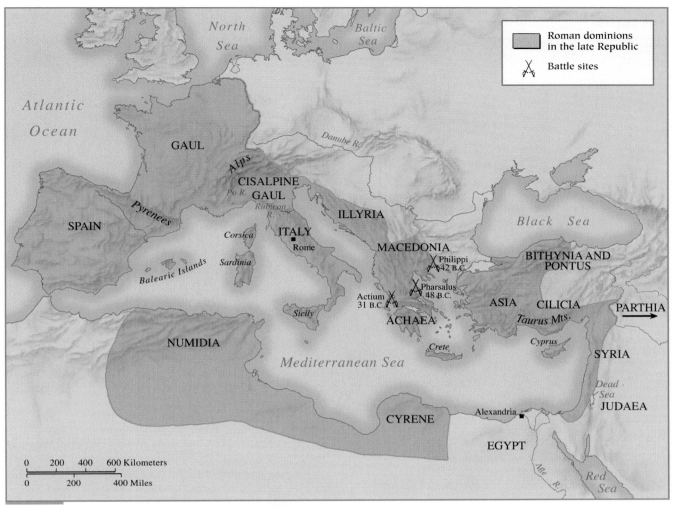

MAP 5.3 **Roman Dominions in the Late Republic, 31 B.C.** Rome expanded its empire not only in response to military threats on its borders but also for increased access to economic resources and markets, in addition to the vanity of conquest itself. ❓ For comparison, look back at Map 5.2. In what areas did the Romans gain the greatest amount of territory, and how?

🐾 **View an animated version of this map or related maps at** http://thomsonedu.com/history/spielvogel

Antony was the first to commit suicide, by the sword. Cleopatra threw herself at Octavian's feet, and tried her best to attract his gaze: in vain, for his self-control was impervious to her beauty. It was not her life she was after, for that had already been granted, but a portion of her kingdom. When she realized this was hopeless and that she had been earmarked to feature in Octavian's triumph in Rome, she took advantage of her guard's carelessness to get herself into the mausoleum, as the royal tomb is called.

Once there, she put on the royal robes which she was accustomed to wear, and lay down in a richly perfumed coffin beside her Antony. Then she applied poisonous snakes to her veins and slipped into death as though into a sleep.[4]

Octavian, at the age of thirty-two, stood supreme over the Roman world (see Map 5.3). The civil wars had ended. And so had the Republic.

CONCLUSION

In the eighth and seventh centuries B.C., the pastoral community of Rome emerged as a city. Between 509 and 264 B.C., the expansion of this city led to the union of almost all of Italy under Rome's control. Even more dramatically, between 264 and 133 B.C., Rome expanded to the west and east and became master of the Mediterranean Sea.

After 133 B.C., however, Rome's republican institutions proved inadequate for the task of ruling an empire. In the breakdown that ensued, ambitious individuals saw op-

portunities for power unparalleled in Roman history and succumbed to the temptations. After a series of bloody civil wars, peace was finally achieved when Octavian defeated Antony and Cleopatra. Octavian's real task was at hand: to create a new system of government that seemed to preserve the Republic while establishing the basis for a new order that would rule the empire in an orderly fashion. Octavian proved equal to the task of establishing a Roman imperial state.

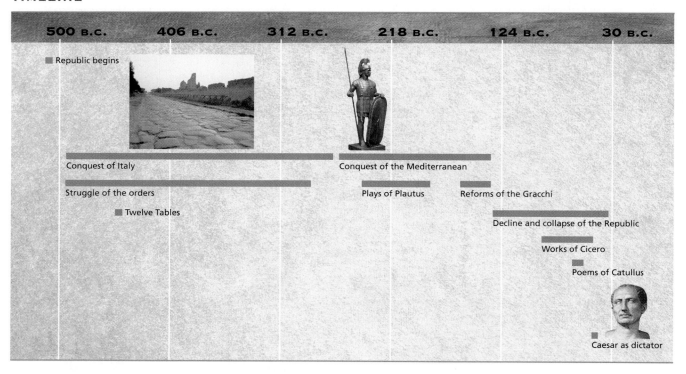

| 500 B.C. | 406 B.C. | 312 B.C. | 218 B.C. | 124 B.C. | 30 B.C. |

Republic begins

Conquest of Italy

Conquest of the Mediterranean

Struggle of the orders

Plays of Plautus

Reforms of the Gracchi

Twelve Tables

Decline and collapse of the Republic

Works of Cicero

Poems of Catullus

Caesar as dictator

NOTES

1. Quoted in C. Starr, *Past and Future in Ancient History* (Lanham, Md., 1987), pp. 38–39.
2. *The Poems of Catullus*, trans. C. Martin (Baltimore, 1990), p. 109.
3. Quoted in A. Everitt, *Cicero* (New York, 2001), p. 181.
4. Florus, *Epitome of Roman History*, trans. E. S. Forster (Cambridge, Mass., 1961), IV, ii, 149–151

SUGGESTIONS FOR FURTHER READING

For a general account of the Roman Republic, see **J. Boardman, J. Griffin, and O. Murray, *eds., The Oxford History of the Roman World*** (Oxford, 1991). Good surveys of Roman history include **M. H. Crawford, *The Roman Republic***, 2d ed. (Cambridge, Mass., 1993); **H. H. Scullard, *History of the Roman World, 753–146 B.C.***, 4th ed. (London, 1978) and ***From the Gracchi to Nero***, 5th ed. (London, 1982); **M. Le Glay, J.-L. Voisin, and Y. Le Bohec, *A History of Rome,*** trans. **A. Nevill,** 2d ed. (Oxford, 2000); **M. T. Boatwright, D. J. Gargola, and R. J. A. Talbert, *The Romans: From Village to Empire*** (New York, 2004); and **A. Kamm, *The Romans*** (London, 1995). For beautifully illustrated surveys, see **J. F. Drinkwater and A. Drummond, *The World of the Romans*** (New York, 1993), and **G. Woolf,** ed., ***Cambridge Illustrated History of the Roman World*** (Cambridge, 2003). The history of early Rome is well covered in **T. J. Cornell, *The Beginnings of Rome: Italy and Rome from the Bronze Age to the Punic Wars (c. 1000–264 B.C.)*** (London, 1995). Aspects of the Roman political structure can be studied in **R. E. Mitchell, *Patricians and Plebeians: The Origin of the Roman State*** (Ithaca, N.Y., 1990). Changes in Rome's economic life can be

examined in **A. H. M. Jones, *The Roman Economy*** (Oxford, 1974). On the Roman social structure, see **G. Alföldy, *The Social History of Rome*** (London, 1985).

A general account of Rome's expansion in the Mediterranean is provided by **R. M. Errington, *The Dawn of Empire: Rome's Rise to World Power*** (Ithaca, N.Y., 1971). On the conquest of Italy, see **J.-M. David, *The Roman Conquest of Italy,*** trans. **A. Nevill** (Oxford, 1996). On Rome's struggle with Carthage, see **N. Bagnall, *The Punic Wars*** (Oxford, 2002), and **A. Goldsworthy, *The Punic Wars*** (New York, 2001). On Roman expansion in the eastern Mediterranean, see **A. N. Sherwin-White, *Roman Foreign Policy in the Greek East*** (London, 1984). On Roman military forces, see **A. Goldsworthy, *The Complete Roman Army*** (London, 2003).

Roman religion can be examined in **J. Liebeschuetz, *Continuity and Change in Roman Religion*** (Oxford, 1979), and **H. H. Scullard, *Festivals and Ceremonies of the Roman Republic*** (Ithaca, N.Y., 1981). A general study of daily life in Rome is available in **F. Dupont, *Daily Life in Ancient Rome*** (Oxford, 1994). On the Roman family, see **S. Dixon, *The Roman Family*** (Baltimore, 1992). Roman women are examined in **R. Baumann, *Women and Politics in Ancient Rome*** (New York, 1995), and **S. Dixon, *The Roman Mother*** (Norman, Okla., 1988). On slavery and its consequences, see **K. R. Bradley, *Slavery and Rebellion in the Roman World, 140–70 B.C.*** (Bloomington, Ind., 1989). For a brief and readable survey of Latin literature, see **R. M. Ogilvie, *Roman Literature and Society*** (Harmondsworth, England, 1980). On Roman art and architecture, see **R. Ling, *Roman Painting*** (New York, 1991); **D. E. Kleiner, *Roman Sculpture*** (New Haven, Conn., 1992); and **M. Wheeler, *Roman Art and Architecture*** (London, 1964).

An excellent account of basic problems in the history of the late Republic can be found in **M. Beard and M. H. Crawford, *Rome in the***

Late Republic (London, 1985). Also valuable are **D. Shotter,** *The Fall of the Roman Republic* (London, 1994), and **E. Hildinger,** *Swords Against the Senate: The Rise of the Roman Army and the Fall of the Republic* (Cambridge, Mass., 2002). Numerous biographies provide many details on the politics of the period. Especially worthwhile are **A. H. Bernstein,** *Tiberius Sempronius Gracchus: Tradition and Apostasy* (Ithaca, N.Y., 1978); **D. Stockton,** *The Gracchi* (Oxford, 1979); **C. Meier,** *Caesar* (London, 1995); **R. Seager,** *Pompey: A Political Biography* (Berkeley, Calif., 1980); and **A. Everitt,** *Cicero* (New York, 2001).

Thomson NOW! Enter *ThomsonNOW* using the access card that is available for *Western Civilization: A Brief History.* *ThomsonNOW* will help you understand this chapter with lesson plans generated for your needs. In addition, you can read the following documents, and many more, online:

Terence, *Phormio*
Plutarch, Life of Caesar
Cicero, Oration in Defense of Aulus Licinius Archias
Cicero, Tusculan Disputations

WESTERN CIVILIZATION RESOURCES

Visit the Web site for *Western Civilization: A Brief History* for resources specific to this book:

http://www.thomsonedu.com/history/spielvogel

For a variety of tools to help you succeed in this course, visit the Western Civilization Resource Center at

http://history.wadsworth.com/spielvogel

Included are quizzes, images, documents, interactive simulations, maps and timelines, movie explorations, and a wealth of other sources.

CHAPTER

THE ROMAN EMPIRE

Hadrian (with outstretched arms) entering Rome

Nimatallah/Art Resource, NY (Palazzo dei Conservatori, Rome)

𝒲ITH THE VICTORIES OF OCTAVIAN, peace finally settled on the Roman world. Although civil conflict still erupted occasionally, the new imperial state constructed by Octavian experienced a period of remarkable stability for the next two hundred years. To the Romans, their divine mission was clearly to rule nations and peoples. Hadrian, an emperor during the second century A.D., was one of many Roman leaders who believed in Rome's mission. He was a strong and intelligent ruler who took his responsibilities seriously. Between 121 and 132, he visited all of the provinces in the empire. According to his Roman biographer, Aelius Spartianus, "Hardly any emperor ever traveled with such speed over so much territory." When he arrived in a province, Hadrian dealt firsthand with any problems and bestowed many favors on the local population. He also worked to establish the boundaries of the provinces and provide for their defense. New fortifications, such as the 80-mile-long Hadrian's Wall across northern Britain, were built to defend the borders. Hadrian insisted on rigid discipline for frontier armies and demanded that the soldiers be kept in training, "just as if war were imminent." He also tried to lead by personal example; according to his biographer, he spent time with the troops and "cheerfully ate out of doors such camp food as bacon, cheese, and vinegar." Moreover, he "would walk as much as twenty miles fully armed."

The Romans imposed their peace on the largest empire established in antiquity. Indeed, Rome's writers proclaimed that "by heaven's will my Rome shall be capital of the world."[1] Rome's writers were not quite accurate, but few Romans were aware of the Han Chinese Empire, which flourished at the same time (202 B.C.–A.D. 221) and extended from Central Asia to the Pacific. Although there was little contact between them, the Han and Roman Empires had remarkable similarities: they lasted for centuries; they had remarkable success in establishing centralized control; and they maintained their law and political institutions, their technical skills, and their languages throughout the empire.

By the third century A.D., however, Rome's ability to rule nations and people began to weaken as the empire began to experience renewed civil war, economic chaos, and invasions. At the same time, Christianity emerged in one of the most remarkable success stories of Western civilization.◆

The Age of Augustus (31 B.C.– A.D. 14)

In 27 B.C., Octavian proclaimed the "restoration of the Republic." He understood that only traditional republican forms would satisfy the senatorial aristocracy. At the same time, Octavian was aware that the Republic could not be fully restored and managed to arrive at a compromise that worked at least during his lifetime. In 27 B.C., the senate awarded him the title of Augustus, "revered one." He preferred the title *princeps,* meaning "chief citizen" or "first among equals." The system of rule that Augustus established is sometimes called the **principate**, conveying the idea of a constitutional monarch as coruler with the senate. But while Augustus worked to maintain this appearance, in reality power was heavily weighted in favor of the *princeps.*

The New Order

In the new constitutional order that Augustus created, the basic governmental structure consisted of the *princeps* (Augustus) and an aristocratic senate. Augustus retained the senate as the chief deliberative body of the Roman state. Its decrees, screened in advance by the *princeps,* now had the effect of law. The title of *princeps* carried no power in itself, but Augustus held the office of consul each year until 23 B.C., when he assumed the power of a tribune, which enabled him to propose laws and veto any item of public business. By observing proper legal forms for his power, Augustus proved highly popular. As the Roman historian Tacitus commented, "Indeed, he attracted everybody's goodwill by the enjoyable gift of peace.... Opposition did not exist."[2] No doubt the ending of the

Augustus. Octavian, Caesar's adopted son, emerged victorious from the civil conflict that rocked the Republic after Caesar's assassination. The senate awarded him the title Augustus. This marble statue from Prima Porta, an idealized portrait, is based on Greek rather than Roman models. The statue was meant to be a propaganda piece, depicting a youthful general addressing his troops. At the bottom stands Cupid, the son of Venus, goddess of love, meant to be a reminder that the Julians, Caesar's family, claimed descent from Venus, thus emphasizing the ruler's divine background.

civil wars had greatly bolstered Augustus' popularity (see the box on p. 98). At the same time, his continuing control of the army, while making possible the Roman peace, was a crucial source of his power.

The Military Augustus was especially eager to stabilize the military and administrative structures of the Roman Empire. The peace of the empire depended on the army, and so did the security of the *princeps.* While primarily responsible for guarding the frontiers of the empire, the

THE ACHIEVEMENTS OF AUGUSTUS

This excerpt is taken from a text written by Augustus and inscribed on a bronze tablet at Rome. Copies of the text were displayed in stone in many provincial capitals. Called "the most famous ancient inscription," the *Res Gestae* of Augustus summarizes his accomplishments in three major areas: his offices, his private expenditures on behalf of the state, and his exploits in war and peace. Though factual in approach, it is a highly subjective account.

Augustus, *Res Gestae*

Below is a copy of the accomplishments of the deified Augustus by which he brought the whole world under the empire of the Roman people, and of the moneys expended by him on the state and the Roman people, as inscribed on two bronze pillars set up in Rome.

1. At the age of nineteen, on my own initiative and at my own expense, I raised an army by means of which I liberated the Republic, which was oppressed by the tyranny of a faction [Mark Antony and his supporters]....

2. Those who assassinated my father [Julius Caesar, his adoptive father] I drove into exile, avenging their crime by due process of law; and afterwards when they waged war against the state, I conquered them twice on the battlefield.

3. I waged many wars throughout the whole world by land and by sea, both civil and foreign, and when victorious I spared all citizens who sought pardon....

5. The dictatorship offered to me ... by the people and the senate, both in my absence and in my presence, I refused to accept....

17. Four times I came to the assistance of the treasury with my own money, transferring to those in charge of the treasury 150,000,000 sesterces. And in the consulship of Marcus Lepidus and Lucius Arruntius I transferred out of my own patrimony 170,000,000 sesterces to the soldiers' bonus fund, which was established on my advice for the purpose of providing bonuses for soldiers who had completed twenty or more years of service....

22. I gave a gladiatorial show three times in my own name, and five times in the names of my sons or grandsons; at these shows about 10,000 fought....

25. I brought peace to the sea by suppressing the pirates. In that war I turned over to their masters for punishment nearly 30,000 slaves who had run away from their owners and taken up arms against the state....

26. I extended the frontiers of all the provinces of the Roman people on whose boundaries were peoples not subject to our empire....

27. I added Egypt to the empire of the Roman people....

28. I established colonies of soldiers in Africa, Sicily, Macedonia, in both Spanish provinces, in Achaea, Asia, Syria, Narbonese Gaul, and Pisidia. Italy, moreover, has twenty-eight colonies established by me, which in my lifetime have grown to be famous and populous....

35. When I held my thirteenth consulship, the senate, the equestrian order, and the entire Roman people gave me the title of "father of the country." ... At the time I wrote this document I was in my seventy-sixth year.

What were the achievements of Augustus? To what extent did these accomplishments create the "job" of being emperor? In what sense could this document be called a piece of propaganda?

army was also used to maintain domestic order within the provinces. Augustus maintained a standing army of twenty-eight legions, or about 150,000 men. Roman legionaries were recruited only from the citizenry and, under Augustus, largely from Italy. Augustus also maintained a large contingent of auxiliary forces—around 130,000—enlisted from the subject peoples. Augustus was also responsible for establishing the **praetorian guard**. Although nominally a military reserve, these "nine cohorts of elite troops," roughly nine thousand men, had the important task of guarding the person of the *princeps*. Eventually the praetorian guard would play a weighty role in making and deposing emperors.

The role of the *princeps* as military commander gave rise to a title by which this ruler eventually came to be known. When victorious, a military commander was acclaimed by his troops as *imperator*. Augustus was so acclaimed on a number of occasions. *Imperator* is our word *emperor*. Although this title was applied to Augustus and his successors, Augustus himself preferred to use the title of *princeps*.

Roman Provinces and Frontiers Augustus inaugurated a new system for governing the provinces. Under the Republic, the senate had appointed the provincial governors. Now certain provinces were allotted to the *princeps*, who assigned deputies known as legates to govern them. These legates were from the senatorial class and held office as long as the emperor chose. The senate continued to designate the governors of the remaining provinces, but the authority of Augustus enabled him to overrule the senatorial governors and establish a uniform imperial policy.

Augustus also stabilized the frontiers of the Roman Empire. He conquered the central and maritime Alps and then expanded Roman control of the Balkan peninsula up to the Danube River. His attempt to conquer Germany failed when three Roman legions under Varus were massacred in A.D. 9 in the Teutoburg Forest by a coalition of German tribes. The defeat severely dampened Augustus' enthusiasm for continued expansion in central Europe. Thereafter, the Romans were content to use the Rhine as the frontier between the Roman province of

Gaul and the German tribes to the east. In fact, Augustus' difficulties had convinced him that "the empire should not be extended beyond its present frontiers."[3] His defeats in Germany taught Augustus that Rome's power was not unlimited. They also left him devastated; for months he beat his head against a door, shouting "Varus, give me back my legions."

Augustan Society

Society in the Early Roman Empire was characterized by a system of social stratification, inherited from the Republic, in which Roman citizens were divided into three basic classes: the senatorial, equestrian, and lower classes. Augustus had accepted the senatorial order as a ruling class for the empire. Senators filled the chief magistracies of the Roman government, held the most important military posts, and governed the provinces. One needed to possess property worth 1 million sesterces (an unskilled laborer in Rome received 3 sesterces a day; a Roman legionary, 900 sesterces a year in pay) to belong to the senatorial order. The equestrian order was open to all Roman citizens of good standing who possessed property valued at 400,000 sesterces. They, too, could now hold military and governmental offices, but the positions open to them were less important than those of the senators.

Citizens not of the senatorial or equestrian order belonged to the lower classes, who made up the overwhelming majority of the free citizens. The diminution of the power of the Roman assemblies ended whatever political power they may have possessed earlier in the Republic. Many of these people were provided with free grain and public spectacles to keep them from creating disturbances. Nevertheless, by gaining wealth and serving as lower officers in the Roman legions, it was sometimes possible for them to advance to the equestrian order.

Augustus' belief that Roman morals had been corrupted during the late Republic led him to initiate social legislation to arrest the decline. He thought that increased luxury had undermined traditional Roman frugality and simplicity and caused a decline in morals, evidenced by easy divorce, a falling birthrate among the upper classes, and lax behavior manifested in hedonistic parties and the love affairs of prominent Romans with fashionable women and elegant boys.

Through his new social legislation, Augustus hoped to restore respectability to the upper classes and reverse the declining birthrate as well. Expenditures for feasts were limited, and other laws made adultery a criminal offense. In fact, Augustus' own daughter Julia was exiled for adultery. Augustus also revised the tax laws to penalize bachelors, widowers, and married persons who had fewer than three children.

The Augustan Age

The Augustan Age was a lengthy one. Augustus died in A.D. 14 after dominating the Roman world for forty-five years. He had created a new order while placating the old by restoring and maintaining traditional values, a fitting combination for a leader whose favorite maxim was "make haste slowly." By the time of his death, his new order was so well established that few agitated for an alternative. Indeed, as the Roman historian Tacitus pointed out, "Actium had been won before the younger men were born. Even most of the older generation had come into a world of civil wars. Practically no one had ever seen truly Republican government.... Political equality was a thing of the past; all eyes watched for imperial commands."[4] The Republic was now only a memory and, given its last century of warfare, an unpleasant one at that. The new order was here to stay.

The Early Empire (14–180)

There was no serious opposition to Augustus' choice of his stepson Tiberius as his successor. By designating a family member as *princeps,* Augustus established the Julio-Claudian dynasty; the next four successors of Augustus were related either to his own family or to that of his wife, Livia.

The Julio-Claudians

Several major tendencies emerged during the reigns of the Julio-Claudians (14–68). In general, more and more of the responsibilities that Augustus had given to the senate tended to be taken over by the emperors, who also instituted an imperial bureaucracy, staffed by talented freedmen, to run the government on a daily basis. As the Julio-Claudian successors of Augustus acted more openly as real rulers rather than "first citizens of the state," the opportunity for arbitrary and corrupt acts also increased. Nero (54–68) freely eliminated people he wanted out of the way, including his own mother, whose murder he arranged. Without troops, the senators proved unable to oppose these excesses. However, Nero's extravagances did provoke a revolt of the Roman legions. Abandoned by the guards, Nero chose to commit suicide by stabbing himself in the throat after uttering his final words, "What an artist the world is losing in me." A new civil war erupted in 69, known as the year of the four emperors. The significance of the year 69 was summed up precisely by Tacitus when he stated that "a well-hidden secret of the principate had been revealed: it was possible, it seemed, for an emperor to be chosen outside Rome."[5]

The Five "Good Emperors" (96–180)

At the beginning of the second century, however, a series of five so-called **good emperors** created a period of peace and prosperity that lasted for almost a hundred years. These men treated the ruling classes with respect, cooperated with the senate, ended arbitrary executions, maintained peace throughout the empire, and supported domestic policies generally beneficial to the empire. Though absolute monarchs, they were known for their tolerance and diplomacy. By adopting capable men as their successors, the first four good emperors reduced the chances of succession problems.

Under the five good emperors, the powers of the emperor continued to be extended at the expense of the senate. Increasingly, imperial officials appointed and directed by the emperor took over the running of the government. The good emperors also extended the scope of imperial administration to areas previously untouched by the imperial government. Trajan (98–117) established a program that provided state funds to assist poor parents in raising and educating their children.

The good emperors were widely praised by their subjects for their extensive building programs. Trajan and Hadrian (117–138) were especially active in constructing public works—aqueducts, bridges, roads, and harbor facilities—throughout the provinces and in Rome. Trajan built a new forum in Rome to provide a setting for his celebrated victory column. Hadrian's Pantheon, a temple of "all the gods," is one of the grandest ancient buildings surviving in Rome.

The Roman Empire at Its Height: Frontiers and Provinces

Although Trajan broke with Augustus' policy of defensive imperialism by extending Roman rule into Dacia (modern Romania), Mesopotamia, and the Sinai peninsula, his conquests represent the high-water mark of Roman expansion (see Map 6.1). His successors recognized that the empire was overextended and pursued a policy of retrenchment. Hadrian withdrew Roman forces from much of Mesopotamia. Although he retained Dacia and Arabia, he went on the defensive in his frontier policy by reinforcing the fortifications along a line connecting the Rhine and Danube Rivers and by building a defensive wall 80 miles long to keep the Scots out of Roman Britain.

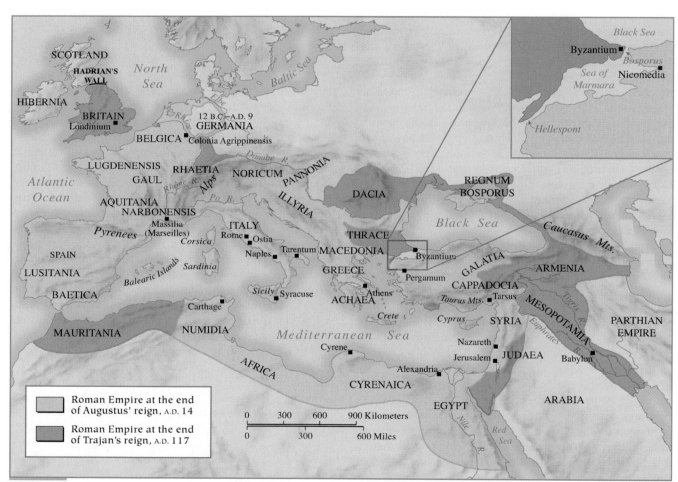

MAP 6.1 **The Roman Empire from Augustus to Trajan (14–117).** Augustus and later emperors continued the expansion of the Roman Empire, adding more resources but also increasing the tasks of administration and keeping the peace. Compare this map with Map 5.3 ❓ Which territories were conquered by Augustus, and which were added by the end of Trajan's reign? ✎ **View an animated version of this map or related maps at** http://thomsonedu.com/history/ spielvogel

By the end of the second century, the vulnerability of the empire had become apparent. Frontiers were stabilized, and the Roman forces were established in permanent bases behind the frontiers. But when one frontier was attacked, troops had to be drawn from other frontiers, leaving them vulnerable to attack. The empire lacked a real strategic reserve, and in the next century its weakness would be ever more apparent.

At its height in the second century, the Roman Empire was one of the greatest states the world had seen. It covered about 3.5 million square miles and had a population, like that of Han China, estimated at more than 50 million. While the emperors and the imperial administration provided a degree of unity, considerable leeway was given to local customs, and the privileges of Roman citizenship were extended to many people throughout the empire. In 212, the emperor Caracalla completed the process by giving Roman citizenship to every free inhabitant of the empire. Latin was the language of the western part of the empire, while Greek was used in the east. Although Roman culture spread to all parts of the empire, there were limits to Romanization because local languages persisted and many of the empire's residents spoke neither Latin nor Greek.

The Importance of Cities The administration and cultural life of the Roman Empire depended greatly on cities and towns. A provincial governor's staff was not large, so local city officials were expected to act as Roman agents in carrying out many government functions, especially those related to taxes. Most towns and cities were not large by modern standards. The biggest was Rome, but there were also some large cities in the east: Alexandria in Egypt numbered over 300,000 inhabitants, Ephesus in Asia Minor had 200,000, Antioch in Syria around 150,000. In the west, cities were usually small, with only a few thousand inhabitants. Cities were important in the spread of Roman culture, law, and the Latin language. They were also uniform in physical appearance with similar temples, markets, amphitheaters, and other public buildings.

Magistrates and town councillors chosen from the ranks of the wealthy upper classes directed municipal administration. These municipal offices were unsalaried but were nevertheless desired by wealthy citizens because they received prestige and power at the local level as well as Roman citizenship. Roman municipal policy effectively tied the upper classes to Roman rule and ensured that these classes would retain control over the rest of the population.

The process of Romanization in the provinces was reflected in significant changes in the governing classes of the empire. In the course of the first century, there was a noticeable decline in the number of senators from Italian families. Increasingly, the Roman senate was being recruited from wealthy provincial equestrian families. The provinces also provided many of the legionaries for the Roman army and, beginning with Trajan, supplied many of the emperors.

Rome in Germany. The Roman army helped bring Roman culture and institutions to the provinces. Local production and trade grew up around the military camps to meet the soldiers' needs, and cities often developed from the bases themselves or from colonies located nearby. Pictured are the remains of the Porta Nigra, the gateway to the Roman city of Augusta Treverorum (modern Trier). In the Early Empire, Trier became the headquarters of the imperial procurator of Belgica and the two Germanies. Its close location to Roman military camps along the Rhine enabled it to flourish as one of the major cities in the western Roman Empire.

Prosperity in the Early Empire

The Early Empire was a period of considerable prosperity. Internal peace resulted in unprecedented levels of trade (see Map 6.2). Merchants from all over the empire came to the chief Italian ports of Puteoli on the Bay of Naples and Ostia at the mouth of the Tiber. Trade extended beyond the Roman boundaries and included even silk goods from China. The importation of large quantities of grain to feed the people of Rome and an incredible quantity of luxury items for the wealthy upper classes in the west led to a steady drain of gold and silver coins from Italy and the west to the eastern part of the empire.

Increased trade helped stimulate manufacturing. The cities of the east still produced the items made in Hellenistic times. The first two centuries of the empire also witnessed the high point of industrial development in Italy. Some industries became concentrated in certain areas, such as bronze work in Capua and pottery in Arretium in Etruria. Other industries, such as brickmaking, were pursued in rural areas on large landed estates. Much production remained small-scale and was done by individual craftsmen, usually freedmen or slaves. In the course of the first century, Italian centers of industry began to experience increasing competition from the provinces.

Despite the extensive trade and commerce, agriculture remained the chief occupation of most people and the underlying basis of Roman prosperity. While the large

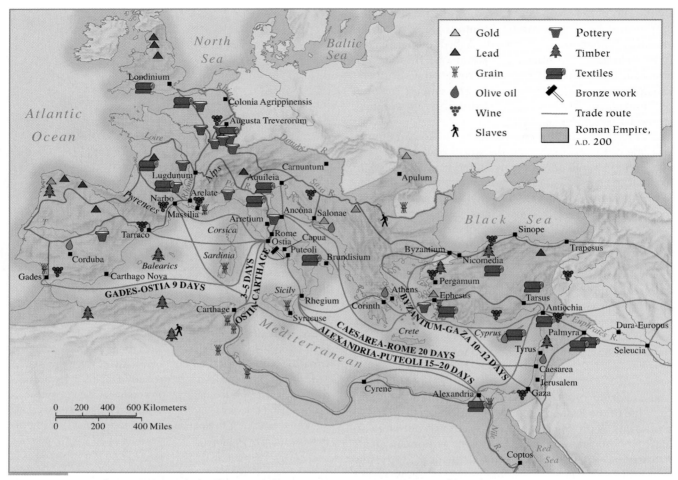

MAP 6.2 **Trade Routes and Products in the Roman Empire, c. 200.** Although still primarily an agrarian economy, the Roman Empire provided the single currency and stable conditions necessary for an expansion of trade in various commodities and products. **?** An extensive system of roads and shipping routes also facilitated trade. What truth is there to the statement "All roads lead to Rome"? 🌐 **View an animated version of this map or related maps at** http://thomsonedu.com/history/spielvogel

landed estates called *latifundia* still dominated agriculture, especially in southern and central Italy, small peasant farms persisted, particularly in Etruria and the Po valley. Although large estates concentrating on sheep and cattle raising used slaves, the lands of some *latifundia* were worked by free tenant farmers who paid rent in labor, produce, or sometimes cash.

In considering the prosperity of the Roman world, it is important to remember the enormous gulf between rich and poor (see the box on p. 103.). The development

Roman Trade. Trade was an important ingredient in the prosperity of the Early Empire. This third-century A.D. Roman mosaic from Sousse, Tunisia, shows workers unloading a cargo of iron ore from a ship.

THE DAILY LIFE OF AN UPPER-CLASS ROMAN

There was an enormous gulf between rich and poor in Roman society. The upper classes lived lives of great leisure and luxury in their villas and on their vast estates. Pliny the Younger (c. 62–c. 113) was an upper-class Roman who rose to the position of governor of Bithynia in Asia Minor. In this excerpt from one of his letters, Pliny describes a typical day vacationing at one of his Italian villas. Although Pliny owned four villas in Italy, he did not belong to the ranks of the really rich in Roman society.

Pliny, Letter to Fuscus Salinator

You want to know how I plan the summer days I spend in Tuscany. I wake when I like, usually about sunrise, often earlier but rarely later. My shutters stay closed, for in the stillness and darkness I feel myself surprisingly detached from any distractions and left to myself in freedom. . . . If I have anything on hand I work it out in my head, choosing and correcting the wording, and the amount I achieve depends on the ease or difficulty with which my thoughts can be marshaled and kept in my head. Then I call my secretary, the shutters are opened, and I dictate what I have put into shape; he goes out, is recalled, and again dismissed. Three or four hours after I first wake (but I don't keep to fixed times) I betake myself according to the weather either to the terrace or the covered arcade, work out the rest of my subject, and dictate it. I go for a drive, and spend the time in the same way as when walking or lying down; my powers of concentration do not flag and are in fact refreshed by the change. After a short sleep and another walk I read a Greek or Latin speech aloud and with emphasis, not so much for the sake of my voice as my digestion, though of course both are strengthened by this. Then I have another walk, am oiled, take exercise, and have a bath. If I am dining alone with my wife or with a few friends, a book is read aloud during the meal and afterward we listen to a comedy or some music; then I walk again with the members of my household, some of whom are educated. Thus the evening is prolonged with varied conversations, and even when the days are at their longest, comes to a satisfying end.

Sometimes I vary this routine, for, if I have spent a long time on my couch or taking a walk, after my siesta and reading I go out on horseback instead of a carriage so as to be quicker and take less time. Part of the day is given up to friends who visit me from neighboring towns and sometimes come to my aid with a welcome interruption when I am tired. Occasionally I go hunting, but not without my notebooks so that I shall have something to bring home even if I catch nothing. I also give some time to my tenants (they think it should be more) and the boorishness of their complaints gives fresh zest to our literary interests and the more civilized pursuits of town.

What does Pliny's letter tell you about the lifestyle of upper-class Romans? Could this lifestyle be related to the decline of the Roman Empire?

---

of towns and cities, so important to the creation of any civilization, is based in large degree on the agricultural surpluses of the countryside. In ancient times, the margin of surplus produced by each farmer was relatively small. Therefore, the upper classes and urban populations had to be supported by the labor of a large number of farmers who never found it easy to produce much more than for themselves. In lean years, when there were no surpluses, the townspeople often took what they wanted, leaving little for the peasants.

Roman Culture and Society in the Early Empire

The high point of Latin literature was reached in the time of Augustus. The literary accomplishments of the Augustan Age were such that the period has been called the golden age of Latin literature.

The Golden Age of Latin Literature

The most distinguished poet of the Augustan Age was Virgil (70–19 B.C.). The son of a small landholder in northern Italy, he welcomed the rule of Augustus and wrote his greatest work in the emperor's honor. Virgil's masterpiece was the *Aeneid*, an epic poem clearly meant to rival the work of Homer. The connection between Troy and Rome is made explicitly. Aeneas, the son of Anchises of Troy, survives the destruction of Troy and eventually settles in Latium; hence Roman civilization is linked to Greek history. The character of Aeneas is portrayed as the ideal Roman—his virtues are duty, piety, and faithfulness. Virgil's overall purpose was to show that Aeneas had fulfilled his mission to establish the Romans in Italy and thereby start Rome on its divine mission to rule the world.

> Let others fashion from bronze more lifelike, breathing images—
> For so they shall—and evoke living faces from marble;
> Others excel as orators, others track with their instruments
> The planets circling in heaven and predict when stars will appear.
> But, Romans, never forget that government is your medium!
> Be this your art:—to practise men in the habit of peace,
> Generosity to the conquered, and firmness against aggressors[6]

OVID AND THE ART OF LOVE

*O*vid has been called the last great poet of the Augustan golden age of literature. One of his most famous works was *The Art of Love,* a guidebook for the seduction of women. Unfortunately for Ovid, the work appeared at a time when Augustus was anxious to improve the morals of the Roman upper class. Augustus considered the work offensive, and Ovid soon found himself in exile.

Ovid, *The Art of Love*

Now I'll teach you how to captivate and hold the woman of your choice. This is the most important part of all my lessons. Lovers of every land, lend an attentive ear to my discourse; let goodwill warm your hearts, for I am going to fulfill the promises I made you.

First of all, be quite sure that there isn't a woman who cannot be won, and make up your mind that you will win her. Only you must prepare the ground. Sooner would the birds cease their song in the springtime, or the grasshopper be silent in the summer, ... than a woman resist the tender wooing of a youthful lover....

Now the first thing you have to do is to get on good terms with the fair one's maid. She can make things easy for you. Find out whether she is fully in her mistress's confidence, and if she knows all about her secret dissipations. Leave no stone unturned to win her over. Once you have her on your side, the rest is easy....

In the first place, it's best to send her a letter, just to pave the way. In it you should tell her how you dote on her; pay her beauty compliments and say all the nice things lovers always say.... Even the gods are moved by the voice of entreaty. And promise, promise, promise. Promises will cost you nothing. Everyone's a millionaire where promises are concerned....

If she refuses your letter and sends it back unread, don't give up; hope for the best and try again....

Don't let your hair stick up in tufts on your head; see that your hair and your beard are decently trimmed. See also that your nails are clean and nicely filed; don't have any hair growing out of your nostrils; take care that your breath is sweet, and don't go about reeking like a billy-goat. All other toilet refinements leave to the women or to perverts....

When you find yourself at a feast where the wine is flowing freely, and where a woman shares the same couch with you, pray to that god whose mysteries are celebrated during the night, that the wine may not overcloud your brain. 'Tis then you may easily hold converse with your mistress in hidden words whereof she will easily divine the meaning....

By subtle flatteries you may be able to steal into her heart, even as the river insensibly overflows the banks which fringe it. Never cease to sing the praises of her face, her hair, her taper fingers and her dainty foot....

Tears, too, are a mighty useful resource in the matter of love. They would melt a diamond. Make a point, therefore, of letting your mistress see your face all wet with tears.

Howbeit, if you can't manage to squeeze out any tears—and they won't always flow just when you want them to—put your finger in your eyes.

What were Ovid's principles of love? Why do you think Augustus found The Art of Love *so offensive?*

As Virgil expressed it, ruling was Rome's gift.

Another prominent Augustan poet was Horace (65–8 B.C.), a friend of Virgil's. Horace was a sophisticated writer whose overriding concern was to point out to his contemporaries the "follies and vices of his age." In the *Satires,* a medley of poems on a variety of subjects, Horace is revealed as a detached observer of human weaknesses. He directed his attacks against movements, not living people, and took on such subjects as sexual immorality, greed, and job dissatisfaction ("How does it happen, Maecenas, that no man alone is content with his lot?"). Horace mostly laughs at the weaknesses of humankind and calls for forbearance: "Supposing my friend has got liquored and wetted my couch, ... is he for such a lapse to be deemed less dear as a friend, or because when hungry he snatched up before me a chicken from my side of the dish?"[7]

Ovid (43 B.C.–A.D. 18) was the last of the great poets of the golden age. He belonged to a youthful, privileged social group in Rome that liked to ridicule old Roman values. In keeping with the spirit of this group, Ovid wrote a frivolous series of love poems known as the *Amores.* Intended to entertain and shock, they achieved their goal.

Another of Ovid's works was *The Art of Love.* This was essentially a takeoff on didactic poems. Whereas authors of earlier didactic poems had written guides to farming, hunting, or some such subject, Ovid's work was a handbook on the seduction of women (see the box above).

The most famous Latin prose work of the golden age was written by the historian Livy (59 B.C.–A.D. 17). Livy's masterpiece was his *History of Rome* from the foundation of the city to 9 B.C. Only 35 of the original 142 books have survived, although we do possess brief summaries of the whole work from other authors. Livy perceived history in terms of moral lessons. He stated in the preface that

> the study of history is the best medicine for a sick mind; for in history you have a record of the infinite variety of human experience plainly set out for all to see; and in that record you can find for yourself and your country both examples and warnings: fine things to take as models, base things, rotten through and through, to avoid.[8]

For Livy, human character was the determining factor in history.

Livy's history celebrated Rome's greatness. He built scene upon scene that not only revealed the character of the chief figures but also demonstrated the virtues that had made Rome great. Of course, he had serious weaknesses as a historian. He was not always concerned about the factual accuracy of his stories. But he was an excellent storyteller, and his work remained the standard history of Rome for centuries.

The Silver Age of Latin Literature

In the history of Latin literature, the century and a half after Augustus is often labeled the "silver age" to indicate that the literary efforts of the period, though good, were not equal to the high standards of the Augustan golden age. The popularity of rhetorical training encouraged the use of clever literary expressions at the expense of original content. A good example of this trend can be found in the works of Seneca.

Educated in Rome, Seneca (c. 4 B.C.–A.D. 65) became strongly attached to the philosophy of Stoicism. In letters written to a young friend, he expressed the basic tenets of Stoicism: living according to nature, accepting events dispassionately as part of the divine plan, and universal love for all humanity. Thus "the first thing philosophy promises us is the feeling of fellowship, of belonging to mankind and being members of a community. . . . Philosophy calls for simple living, not for doing penance, and the simple way of life need not be a crude one."[9] Viewed in retrospect, Seneca displays some glaring inconsistencies. While preaching the virtues of simplicity, he amassed a fortune and was ruthless at times in protecting it. His letters show humanity, benevolence, and fortitude, but his sentiments are often undermined by an attempt to be clever with words.

The greatest historian of the silver age was Tacitus (c. 56–120). His main works included the *Annals* and *Histories,* which presented a narrative account of Roman history from the reign of Tiberius through the assassination of Domitian (14–96). Tacitus believed that history had a moral purpose: "It seems to me a historian's foremost duty to ensure that merit is recorded, and to confront evil deeds and words with the fear of posterity's denunciations."[10] As a member of the senatorial class, Tacitus was disgusted with the abuses of power perpetrated by the emperors and was determined that the "evil deeds" of wicked men would not be forgotten. Many historians believe he went too far in projecting the evils of his own day into his account of the past. His work *Germania* is especially important as a source of information about the early Germans. But it too is colored by Tacitus' attempt to show the Germans as noble savages in comparison with the decadent Romans.

Roman Law

The Early Empire experienced great progress in the study and codification of the law. The second and early third centuries A.D. witnessed the "classical age of Roman law," a period in which a number of great jurists classified and compiled basic legal principles that have proved extremely valuable to the Western world. Most jurists emphasized the emperor as the source of law: "What has pleased the emperor has the force of law."

In the "classical age of Roman law," the identification of the law of nations with natural law led to a concept of natural rights. According to the jurist Ulpian (d. 228), natural rights implied that all men are born equal and should therefore be equal before the law. In practice, however, that principle was not applied. The Romans did, however, establish standards of justice applicable to all people, many of which we would immediately recognize. A person was regarded as innocent until proved otherwise. People accused of wrongdoing were allowed to defend themselves before a judge. A judge was expected to weigh evidence carefully before arriving at a decision. These principles lived on in Western civilization long after the fall of the Roman Empire.

The Upper-Class Roman Family

By the second century A.D., significant changes were occurring in the Roman family. The foundations of the authority of the *paterfamilias* over his family, which had already begun to weaken in the late Republic, were further undermined. The *paterfamilias* no longer had absolute authority over his children; he could no longer sell his children into slavery or have them put to death. Moreover, the husband's absolute authority over his wife also disappeared, a process that had begun in the late Republic. In the Early Empire, the idea of male guardianship continued to weaken significantly, and by the late second century had become a formality.

Upper-class Roman women in the Early Empire had considerable freedom and independence. They had acquired the right to own, inherit, and dispose of property. Upper-class women could attend races, the theater, and events in the amphitheater, although in the latter two places they were forced to sit in sections apart from the men. Moreover, ladies of rank were still accompanied by maids and companions when they went out. Some women operated businesses, such as shipping firms. Women could still not participate in politics, but the Early Empire saw a number of important women who influenced politics through their husbands, including Livia, the wife of Augustus; Agrippina, the mother of Nero; and Plotina, the wife of Trajan.

Imperial Rome

At the center of the colossal Roman Empire was the ancient city of Rome (see Map 6.3). Truly a capital city, Rome had the largest population of any city in the empire. It is estimated that its population was close to one million by the time of Augustus. For anyone with ambitions, Rome was the place to be. A magnet to many people, Rome was extremely cosmopolitan. Nationalities from all over the

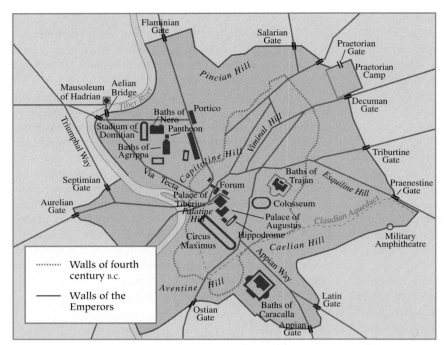

empire resided there, with entire neighborhoods inhabited by specific groups, such as Greeks and Syrians.

Rome was an overcrowded and noisy city. Because of the congestion, cart and wagon traffic was banned from the streets during the day. The noise from the resulting vehicular movement at night often made sleep difficult. Evening pedestrian travel was dangerous. Although Augustus had organized a police force, lone travelers could be assaulted, robbed, or soaked by filth thrown out of the upper-story windows of Rome's massive apartment buildings.

An enormous gulf existed between rich and poor in the city of Rome. While the rich had comfortable villas, the poor lived in apartment blocks called *insulae,* which might be six stories high. Constructed of concrete, they were often poorly built and prone to collapse. The use of wooden beams in the floors and movable stoves, torches, candles, and lamps within the rooms for heat and light made the danger of fire constant. Once started, fires were extremely difficult to put out. The famous conflagration of 64, which Nero was unjustly accused of starting, devastated a good part of the city. Besides the hazards of collapse and fire, living conditions were also poor. High rents forced entire families into one room. The absence of plumbing and central heating made life so uncomfortable that poorer Romans spent most of their time outdoors in the streets.

Fortunately for these people, Rome boasted public buildings unequaled anywhere in the empire. Its temples, forums, markets, baths, theaters, triumphal arches, governmental buildings, and amphitheaters gave parts of the city an appearance of grandeur and magnificence.

Though the center of a great empire, Rome was also a great parasite. Beginning with Augustus, the emperors accepted responsibility for providing food for the urban populace, with about 200,000 people receiving free grain.

Even with the free grain, conditions were grim for the poor. Early in the second century, a Roman doctor noted that rickets was common among children in the city.

In addition to food, entertainment was provided on a grand scale for the inhabitants of Rome. The poet Juvenal said of the Roman masses, "But nowadays, with no vote to sell, their motto is 'Couldn't care less.' Time was when their plebiscite elected generals, heads of state, commanders of legions: but now they've pulled in their horns, there's only two things that concern them: Bread and Circuses."[11] Public spectacles were provided by the emperor and other state officials as part of the great festivals—most of them religious in origin—celebrated by the state. More than one hundred days a year were given over to these public holidays. The festivals included three major types of entertainment. At the Circus Maximus, horse and chariot races attracted hundreds of thousands of spectators, while dramatic and other performances were held in theaters. But the most famous of all the public spectacles were the gladiatorial shows.

The Gladiatorial Shows

The gladiatorial shows were an integral part of Roman society. They took place in amphitheaters, the first permanent one of which had been constructed at Rome in 29 B.C. Perhaps the most famous was the Flavian amphitheater, called the Colosseum, which could seat fifty thousand spectators. Similar amphitheaters were built throughout the empire, with capacities ranging from a few thousand to tens of thousands. In most cities and towns, the amphitheaters were the biggest buildings, rivaled only by the circuses for races and the public baths. Where a society invests its money gives an idea of its

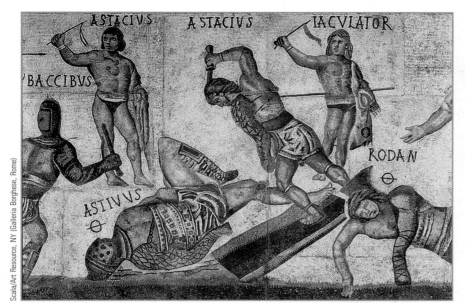

The Gladiatorial Games. Although some gladiators were free men enticed by the possibility of rewards, most were condemned criminals, slaves, or prisoners of war who were trained in special schools. A great gladiator could win his freedom through the games. This mosaic from the fourth century A.D. depicts different aspects of gladiatorial fighting and clearly shows the bloody nature of the games.

priorities. Since the amphitheater was the primary location for the gladiatorial games, it is fair to say that public slaughter was an important part of Roman culture.

Gladiatorial games were held from dawn to dusk. Contests to the death between trained fighters formed the central focus of these games. Most gladiators were slaves or condemned criminals and were trained for combat in special gladiatorial schools.

Gladiatorial games included other forms of entertainment as well. Criminals of all ages and both sexes were sent into the arena without weapons to face certain death from wild animals who would tear them to pieces. Numerous kinds of animal contests were also staged: wild beasts against each other, such as bears against buffaloes; staged hunts with men shooting safely from behind iron bars; and gladiators in the arena with bulls, tigers, and lions. Reportedly, five thousand beasts were killed in one day of games when the emperor Titus inaugurated the Colosseum in A.D. 80. Enormous resources were invested in the capture and shipment of wild animals for slaughter, and whole species were hunted to extinction in parts of the empire.

These bloodthirsty spectacles were wildly popular with the Roman people. The Roman historian Tacitus said, "Few indeed are to be found who talk of any other subjects in their homes, and whenever we enter a classroom, what else is the conversation of the youths."[12] But the gladiatorial games served a purpose beyond mere entertainment. Like the other forms of public entertainment, they fulfilled both a political and a social need by diverting thoughts of the idle masses from political unrest. It was said of the emperor Trajan that he understood that although the distribution of grain and money satisfied the individual, spectacles were necessary for the "contentment of the masses."

Transformation of the Roman World: Crises in the Third Century

At the end of the second century, a number of natural catastrophes struck Rome. Floods of the Tiber, famine, and plague brought back from the east by the army led to considerable loss of population and a shortage of military manpower. To many Romans, these natural disasters seemed to portend an ominous future for Rome, and indeed, in the course of the third century, the Roman Empire came near to collapse.

Political and Military Woes

After a series of civil wars, Septimius Severus (193–211), who was born in North Africa and spoke Latin with an accent, used his legions to seize power. On his deathbed, Septimius Severus advised his sons, "Live in harmony, make the soldiers rich, and don't give a damn for anything else." His advice set the tone for the new dynasty he established. The Severan rulers (193–235) began to create a military monarchy. The army was expanded, soldiers' pay was increased, and military officers were appointed to important government positions. A new stability seemed at hand, but the increased power of the military led new military leaders to aspire to become emperor, and the military monarchy of the Severan rulers degenerated into military anarchy.

For the next fifty years (235–284), the empire was mired in the chaos of continual civil war. Contenders for the imperial throne found that bribing soldiers was an effective way to become emperor. In these five decades, there were twenty-two emperors, only two of whom did

Septimius Severus and His Family. This portrait painted on wood about A.D. 200, found in Egypt, is the only existing painted likeness of a Roman emperor. The emperor is portrayed with gray hair and beard in memory of Marcus Aurelius. To legitimize his authority, Septimius Severus had himself adopted into the Antonine dynasty, calling himself the son of Marcus Aurelius. The emperor stands next to his wife with their two sons in front of them. The face of his son Geta has been blotted out, no doubt by order of the other son standing next to him, Caracalla, who had his brother killed when he succeeded to the throne.

not meet a violent end. At the same time, the empire was beset by a series of invasions, no doubt encouraged by the internal turmoil. In the east, the Sassanid Persians made inroads into Roman territory. A fitting symbol of Rome's crisis was the capture of the Roman emperor, Valerian (253–260), by the Persians and his death in captivity, an event unprecedented in Roman history. Valerian's body was displayed in the chief towns of Persia. Germanic tribes also poured into the empire. The Goths overran the Balkans and moved into Greece and Asia Minor. The Franks advanced into Gaul and Spain. Not until the reign of Aurelian (270–275) were most of the boundaries restored. Although he abandoned the Danubian province of Dacia, Aurelian reconquered Gaul and reestablished order in the east and along the Danube. Grateful citizens hailed him as "restorer of the world."

As civil wars and invasion wore down the central government, provinces began to break away from the empire. A military commander named Postumus seized control of Gaul and then gained the support of Britain and Spain. He defended his "Gallic empire" until he was killed by his own soldiers in 269. In the east, Zenobia, the wife of the ruler of Syria, seized power after his death and then in 270 extended her control over Egypt and much of Asia Minor. In 272, Emperor Aurelian ended this threat to imperial power by defeating Zenobia and her forces in Syria.

Economic and Social Crises

Invasions, civil wars, and plague came close to causing an economic collapse of the Roman Empire in the third century. The population declined drastically, possibly by as much as one-third. There was a noticeable decline in trade and small industry. The labor shortage created by plague affected both military recruiting and the economy. Farm production deteriorated significantly. Fields were ravaged by Germanic tribes and even more often by the defending Roman armies. Many farmers complained that Roman commanders and their soldiers were confiscating produce and livestock. Provincial governors seemed powerless to stop these depredations, and some even joined in the extortion. The monetary system began to show signs of collapse as a result of debased coinage and the beginnings of serious inflation.

Armies were needed more than ever, but financial strains made it difficult to enlist and pay the necessary soldiers. Short of cash, the imperial government paid its soldiers with produce, causing bitter resentment. Whereas in the second century the Roman army had been recruited among the inhabitants of frontier provinces, by the mid-third century the state had to rely on hiring barbarians to fight under Roman commanders. These soldiers had no understanding of Roman traditions and no real attachment to either the empire or the emperors. By the end of the third century, a new political structure would emerge (see Chapter 7).

Transformation of the Roman World: The Rise of Christianity

The advent of Christianity marks a fundamental break with the dominant values of the Greco-Roman world. Christian views of God, human beings, and the world were quite different from those of the Greeks and Romans. Nevertheless, to understand the rise of Christianity, we must first examine both the religious environment of the Roman world and the Jewish background from which Christianity emerged.

The Religious World of the Roman Empire

Augustus had taken a number of steps to revive the Roman state religion, which had declined during the turmoil of the late Republic. The official state religion focused on the worship of a pantheon of gods and goddesses. Observance of proper ritual by state priests theoretically established the proper relationship between Romans and the gods and guaranteed security, peace, and prosperity. The polytheistic Romans were extremely tolerant of other religions. The Romans allowed the worship of native gods and goddesses throughout their provinces and even adopted some of the local gods. In addition, the imperial cult of Rome and Augustus was developed to bolster support for the emperors. After Augustus, deceased emperors deified by the Roman senate were included in the official imperial cult.

The desire for a more emotional spiritual experience led many people to the mystery religions of the Hellenistic east, which flooded into the western Roman world during the Early Empire. The mystery religions offered secret teachings that promised their followers advantages unavailable through Roman religion: an entry into a higher world of reality and the promise of a future life superior to the present one. They also featured elaborate rituals with deep emotional appeal. By participating in their ceremonies and performing their rites, an adherent could achieve communion with spiritual beings and undergo purification that opened the door to life after death.

Although many mystery cults competed for the attention of the Roman world, perhaps the most important was Mithraism. Mithras was the chief agent of Ahuramazda, the supreme god of light in Persian Zoroastrianism (see Chapter 2). In the Roman world, Mithras came to be identified with the sun god and was known by his Roman title, the Unconquered Sun. Mithraism had spread rapidly in Rome and the western provinces by the second century A.D. and was especially favored by soldiers, who viewed Mithras as their patron deity. Mithraists paid homage to the sun on the first day of the week (Sunday), commemorated the sun's birthday around December 25, and celebrated ceremonial meals. All of these practices had parallels in Christianity.

The Jewish Background

In Hellenistic times, the Jewish people had been granted considerable independence by their Seleucid rulers (see Chapter 4). Roman involvement with the Jews began in 63 B.C., and by A.D. 6, Judaea had been made a province and placed under the direction of a Roman procurator. But unrest continued, augmented by divisions among the Jews themselves. The Sadducees favored a rigid adherence to Hebrew law, rejected the possibility of personal immortality, and favored cooperation with the Romans. The Pharisees followed a strict adherence to Jewish ritual, and although they wanted Judaea to be free from Roman control, they did not advocate violent means to achieve this goal. The Essenes were a Jewish sect that lived in a religious community near the Dead Sea. As revealed in the Dead Sea Scrolls, a collection of documents first discovered in 1947, the Essenes, like many other Jews, awaited a Messiah who would save Israel from oppression, usher in the kingdom of God, and establish a true paradise on earth. A fourth group, the Zealots, were militant extremists who advocated the violent overthrow of Roman rule. A Jewish revolt in A.D. 66 was crushed by the Romans four years later. The Jewish Temple in Jerusalem was destroyed, and Roman power once more stood supreme in Judaea.

The Origins of Christianity

In the midst of the confusion and conflict in Judaea, Jesus of Nazareth (c. 6 B.C.–A.D. 30) began his public preaching. Jesus grew up in Galilee, an important center of the militant Zealots. Jesus' message was straightforward. He reassured his fellow Jews that he did not plan to undermine their traditional religion: "Do not think that I have come to abolish the Law or the Prophets; I have not come to abolish them but to fulfill them."[13] According to Jesus, what was important was not strict adherence to the letter of the law and attention to rules and prohibitions but the transformation of the inner person: "So in everything, do to others what you would have them do to you, for this sums up the Law and the Prophets."[14] God's command was simple—to love God and one another: "Love the Lord your God with all your heart and with all your soul and with all your mind and with all your strength. The second is this: Love your neighbor as yourself."[15] In the Sermon on the Mount (see the box on p. 110), Jesus presented the ethical concepts—humility, charity, and brotherly love—that would form the basis for the value system of medieval Western civilization. As we have seen, these were not the values of classical Greco-Roman civilization.

Although some Jews welcomed Jesus as the Messiah who would save Israel from oppression and establish God's kingdom on earth, Jesus spoke of a heavenly kingdom, not an earthly one: "My kingdom is not of this world."[16] In this he disappointed the radicals. At the same time, conservative religious leaders believed that Jesus was another false Messiah who was undermining respect for traditional Jewish religion. To the Roman authorities of Palestine and their local allies, the Nazarene was a potential revolutionary who might transform Jewish expectations of a messianic kingdom into a revolt against Rome. Jesus thus found himself denounced on many sides and was given over to the Roman authorities. The procurator Pontius Pilate ordered his crucifixion. But

CHRISTIAN IDEALS: THE SERMON ON THE MOUNT

Christianity was one of many religions competing for attention in the Roman Empire during the first and second centuries. The rise of Christianity marked a fundamental break with the value system of the upper-class elites who dominated the world of classical antiquity. As these excerpts from the Sermon on the Mount in the Gospel of Matthew illustrate, Christians emphasized humility, charity, brotherly love, and a belief in the inner being and a spiritual kingdom superior to this material world. These values and principles were not those of classical Greco-Roman civilization as exemplified in the words and deeds of its leaders.

The Gospel According to Matthew

Now when he saw the crowds, he went up on a mountainside and sat down. His disciples came to him, and he began to teach them saying:

> *Blessed are the poor in spirit: for theirs is the kingdom of heaven.*
>
> *Blessed are those who mourn: for they will be comforted.*
>
> *Blessed are the meek: for they will inherit the earth.*
>
> *Blessed are those who hunger and thirst for righteousness: for they will be filled.*
>
> *Blessed are the merciful: for they will be shown mercy.*
>
> *Blessed are the pure in heart: for they will see God.*
>
> *Blessed are the peacemakers: for they will be called sons of God.*
>
> *Blessed are those who are persecuted because of righteousness for theirs is the kingdom of heaven....*

You have heard that it was said, "Eye for eye, and tooth for tooth." But I tell you, Do not resist an evil person. If someone strikes you on the right cheek, turn to him the other also....

You have heard that it was said, "Love your neighbor, and hate your enemy." But I tell you, Love your enemies and pray for those who persecute you....

Do not store up for yourselves treasures on earth, where moth and rust destroy, and where thieves break in and steal. But store up for yourselves treasures in heaven, where moth and rust do not destroy, and where thieves do not break in and steal. For where your treasure is, there your heart will be also....

No one can serve two masters. Either he will hate the one and love the other, or he will be devoted to the one and despise the other. You cannot serve both God and Money.

Therefore I tell you, do not worry about your life, what you will eat or drink; or about your body, what you will wear. Is not life more important than food, and the body more important than clothes? Look at the birds of the air; they do not sow or reap to store away in barns, and yet your heavenly Father feeds them. Are you not much more valuable than they?...So do not worry, saying, What shall we eat? or What shall we drink? or What shall we wear? For the pagans run after all these things, and your heavenly Father knows that you need them. But seek first his kingdom and his righteousness, and all these things will be given to you as well.

What were the ideals of early Christianity? How do they differ from the values and principles of classical Greco-Roman civilization?

---

that did not solve the problem. A few loyal disciples spread the story that Jesus had overcome death, had been resurrected, and had then ascended into heaven. The belief in Jesus' resurrection became an important tenet of Christian doctrine. Jesus was now hailed by his followers as the "anointed one" (*Christos* in Greek), the Messiah who would return and usher in the kingdom of God on earth.

The Importance of Paul   Christianity began, then, as a religious movement within Judaism and was viewed that way by Roman authorities for many decades. Although tradition holds that one of Jesus' disciples, Peter, founded the Christian church at Rome, the most important figure in early Christianity after Jesus was Paul of Tarsus (c. 5–c. 67). Paul reached out to non-Jews and transformed Christianity from a Jewish sect into a broader religious movement.

Called the "second founder of Christianity," Paul was a Jewish Roman citizen who had been strongly influenced by Hellenistic Greek culture. He believed that the message

of Jesus should be preached not only to Jews but to Gentiles (non-Jews) as well. Paul was responsible for founding Christian communities throughout Asia Minor and along the shores of the Aegean.

It was Paul who provided a universal foundation for the spread of Jesus' ideas. He taught that Jesus was, in effect, a savior-God, the son of God, who had come to earth to save all humans who were basically sinners as a result of Adam's original sin of disobedience against God. By his death, Jesus had atoned for the sins of all humans and made it possible for all men and women to experience a new beginning with the potential for individual salvation. By accepting Jesus Christ as their Savior, they too could be saved.

The Spread of Christianity   At first, Christianity spread slowly. Although the teachings of early Christianity were mostly disseminated by the preaching of convinced Christians, written materials also appeared. Paul had written a series of letters, or epistles, outlining Christian

Jesus and His Apostles. Pictured is a fourth-century fresco from a Roman catacomb depicting Jesus and his apostles. Catacombs were underground cemeteries where early Christians buried their dead. Christian tradition holds that in times of imperial repression, Christians withdrew to the catacombs to pray and even hide.

beliefs for different Christian communities. Some of Jesus' disciples may also have preserved some of the sayings of the master in writing and would have passed on personal memories that became the basis of the written gospels— the "good news" concerning Jesus—which attempted to provide a record of Jesus' life and teachings and formed the core of the New Testament, the Christian Bible. Although Jerusalem was the first center of Christianity, its destruction by the Romans in A.D. 70 left individual Christian churches with considerable independence. By 100, Christian churches had been established in most of the major cities of the east and in some places in the western part of the empire. Many early Christians came from the ranks of Hellenized Jews and the Greek-speaking populations of the east. But in the second and third centuries, an increasing number of followers came from Latin-speaking people. A Latin translation of the Greek New Testament that appeared soon after 200 aided this process.

Although some of the fundamental values of Christianity differed markedly from those of the Greco-Roman world, the Romans initially did not pay much attention to the Christians, whom they regarded at first as simply another sect of Judaism. The structure of the Roman Empire itself aided the growth of Christianity. Christian missionaries, including some of Jesus' original twelve disciples, or apostles, used Roman roads to travel throughout the empire spreading their "good news."

As the popular appeal of Christianity grew, the Roman attitude toward it began to change. The Romans were tolerant of other religions except when they threatened public order or public morals. Many Romans came to view Christians as harmful to the order of the Roman state. Because Christians held their meetings in secret and seemed to be connected to Christian groups in distant areas, the government could view them as potentially dangerous to the state.

Some Romans felt that Christians were overly exclusive and hence harmful to the community and public order. The Christians did not recognize other gods and therefore abstained from public festivals honoring these divinities. Finally, Christians refused to participate in the worship of the state gods and the imperial cult. Since the Romans regarded these as important to the state, the Christians' refusal undermined the security of the state and hence constituted an act of treason, punishable by death. But to the Christians, who believed there was only one real God, the worship of state gods and the emperors was idolatry and would endanger their own salvation.

Roman persecution of Christians in the first and second centuries was never systematic but sporadic and local. Persecution began during the reign of Nero. After the fire that destroyed much of Rome, the emperor used the Christians as scapegoats, accusing them of arson and hatred of the human race and subjecting them to cruel deaths in Rome. In the second century, Christians were largely ignored as harmless. By the end of the reigns of the five good emperors, Christians still represented a small minority, but one of considerable strength.

The Growth of Christianity

The sporadic persecution of Christians by the Romans in the first and second centuries had done nothing to stop the growth of Christianity. It had, in fact, served to strengthen Christianity as an institution in the second and third centuries by causing it to shed the loose structure of the first century and move toward a more centralized organization of its various church communities. Crucial to this change was the emerging role of the bishops, who began to assume more control over church communities. The Christian church was creating a well-defined hierarchical structure in which the bishops and clergy were salaried officers separate from the laity or regular church members.

Christianity grew slowly in the first century, took root in the second, and had spread widely by the third. Why was Christianity able to attract so many followers? First of all, the Christian message had much to offer the Roman world. The promise of salvation, made possible by Jesus' death and resurrection, had immense appeal in a world full of suffering and injustice. Christianity seemed to imbue life with a meaning and purpose beyond the simple material things of everyday reality. Second, Christianity was not entirely unfamiliar. It could be viewed as simply another eastern mystery religion, offering immortality as the result of the sacrificial death of a savior-God. At the same time, it offered advantages that the other mystery religions lacked. Jesus had been a human figure, not a mythological one, such as Mithras. Moreover, Christianity had universal appeal. Unlike Mithraism, it was not restricted to men. Furthermore, it did not require a painful or expensive initiation rite as other mystery religions did. Initiation was accomplished simply by baptism—a purification by water—by which one entered into direct communion with Jesus. In addition, Christianity gave new meaning to life and offered what the Roman state religions could not— a personal relationship with God and a link to higher worlds.

Finally, Christianity fulfilled the human need to belong. Christians formed communities bound to one another in which people could express their love by helping each other and offering assistance to the poor, the sick, widows, and orphans. Christianity satisfied the need to belong in a way that the huge, impersonal, and remote Roman Empire could never do.

Christianity proved attractive to all classes. The promise of eternal life was for all—rich, poor, aristocrats, slaves, men, and women. As Paul stated in his Epistle to the Colossians: "And [you] have put on the new self, which is being renewed in knowledge in the image of its Creator. Here there is no Greek nor Jew, circumcised or uncircumcised, barbarian, Scythian, slave or free, but Christ is all, and is in all."[17] Although it did not call for revolution or social upheaval, Christianity emphasized a sense of spiritual equality for all people.

Many women, in fact, found that Christianity offered them new roles and new forms of companionship with other women. Christian women fostered the new religion in their own homes and preached their convictions to other people in their towns and villages. Many also died for their faith. Perpetua was an aristocratic woman who converted to Christianity. Her pagan family begged her to renounce her new faith, but she refused. Arrested by the Roman authorities, she chose instead to die for her faith and was one of a group of Christians who were slaughtered by wild beasts in the arena at Carthage on March 7, 203.

As the Christian church became more organized, some emperors in the third century responded with more systematic persecutions, but their schemes failed to work. The last great persecution was by Diocletian at the beginning of the fourth century. But even he had to admit what had become apparent in the course of the third century—Christianity had become too strong to be eradicated by force.

TIMELINE

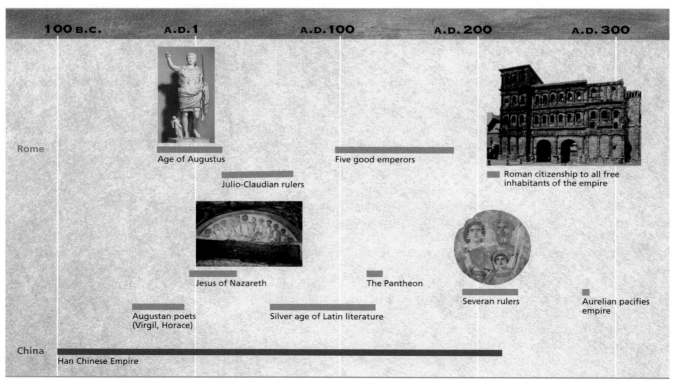

| 100 B.C. | A.D. 1 | A.D. 100 | A.D. 200 | A.D. 300 |

Rome

Age of Augustus

Julio-Claudian rulers

Five good emperors

Roman citizenship to all free inhabitants of the empire

Jesus of Nazareth

The Pantheon

Severan rulers

Aurelian pacifies empire

Augustan poets (Virgil, Horace)

Silver age of Latin literature

China

Han Chinese Empire

CONCLUSION

The Roman Republic had created one of the largest empires in antiquity, but its republican institutions had proved inadequate for the task of ruling an empire. After a series of bloody civil wars, Augustus created a new order that began the Roman Empire, which experienced a lengthy period of peace and prosperity between 14 and 180. During this **Pax Romana**, trade flourished and the provinces were governed efficiently. In addition, within their empire, the Romans developed a remarkable series of achievements that were bequeathed to the future.

These achievements were fundamental to the development of Western civilization. The Romance languages of today (French, Italian, Spanish, Portuguese, and Romanian) are based on Latin. Western practices of impartial justice and trial by jury owe much to Roman law. As great builders, the Romans left monuments to their skills throughout Europe, some of which, including aqueducts and roads, are still in use today. Other monuments provided models for public buildings in the West for hundreds of years. Aspects of Roman administrative practices survived in the Western world for centuries. The Romans also preserved the intellectual heritage of the Greco-Roman world of antiquity.

By the third century A.D., the Roman world was being buffeted by civil wars, invasions, and economic problems. At the same time, a new religion–Christianity–was spreading throughout the empire. As we shall see in the next chapter, the response to these developments slowly transformed the Roman Empire.

NOTES

1. Livy, *The Early History of Rome*, trans. A. de Sélincourt (Harmondsworth, England, 1960), p. 35.
2. Tacitus, *The Annals of Imperial Rome*, trans. M. Grant (Harmondsworth, England, 1956), p. 30.
3. Ibid., p. 37.
4. Ibid., p. 31.
5. Tacitus, *The Histories, trans.* K. Wellesley (Harmondsworth, England, 1964), p. 23.
6. Virgil, *The Aeneid*, trans. C. Day Lewis (Garden City, N.Y., 1952), p. 154.
7. Horace, *Satires,* in *The Complete Works of Horace*, trans. Lord Dunsany and M. Oakley (London, 1961), 1.1, p. 139; 1.3, p. 151.
8. Livy, *Early History of Rome*, p. 18.
9. Seneca, *Letters from a Stoic*, trans. R. Campbell (Harmondsworth, England, 1969), let. 5.
10. Tacitus, *Annals of Imperial Rome*, p. 147.
11. Juvenal, *The Sixteen Satires*, trans. P. Green (Harmondsworth, England, 1967), sat. 10, p. 207.
12. Tacitus, *A Dialogue on Oratory*, in *The Complete Works of Tacitus*, trans. A. Church and W. Brodribb (New York, 1942), 29, p. 758.
13. Matthew 5:17.
14. Matthew 7:12.
15. Mark 12:30–31.
16. John 18:36.
17. Colossians 3:10–11.

SUGGESTIONS FOR FURTHER READING

For a general account of the Roman Empire, see **J. Boardman, J. Griffin, and O. Murray, eds., *The Oxford History of the Roman World*** (Oxford, 1991), and **G. Wolf, ed., *Cambridge Illustrated History of the Roman World*** (Cambridge, 2003). Good surveys of the Early Empire include **P. Garnsey and R. P. Saller, *The Roman Empire: Economy, Society and Culture*** (London, 1987); **C. Wells, *The Roman Empire*,** 2d ed. (London, 1992); **M. Goodman, *The Roman World,*** *44 B.C.–A.D 180* (London, 1997); **J. Wacher, *The Roman Empire*** (London, 1987); and **F. Millar, *The Roman Empire and Its Neighbours*,** 2d ed. (London, 1981).

Studies of Roman emperors of the first and second centuries include **W. Eck, *The Age of Augustus*,** trans. **D. L. Schneider** (Oxford, 2003); **R. Seager, *Tiberius*** (London, 1972); **E. Champlin, *Nero*** (Cambridge, Mass., 2003); **E. Speller, *Following Hadrian*** (Oxford, 2003); and **M. Hammond, *The Antonine Monarchy*** (Rome, 1959). For brief biographies of all the Roman emperors, see **M. Grant, *The Roman Emperors*** (New York, 1985). On the wife of Augustus, see **A. A. Barrett, *Livia: First Lady of Imperial Rome*** (New Haven, Conn., 2002).

The Roman army is examined in **J. B. Campbell, *The Emperor and the Roman Army*** (Oxford, 1984). On the provinces and Roman foreign policy, see **E. N. Luttwak, *The Grand Strategy of the Roman Empire from the First Century A.D. to the Third*** (Baltimore, 1976); **B. Isaac, *The Limits of Empire: The Roman Empire in the East*** (Oxford, 1990); and **S. L. Dyson, *The Creation of the Roman Frontier*** (Princeton, N.J., 1985). On the battle in the Teutoburg Forest, see **P. S. Wells, *The Battle That Stopped Rome: Emperor Augustus, Arminius, and the Slaughter of the Legions in the Teutoburg Forest*** (New York, 2003).

A good survey of Roman literature can be found in **R. M. Ogilvie, *Roman Literature and Society*** (Harmondsworth, England, 1980). More specialized studies include **R. O. Lyne, *The Latin Love Poets from Catullus to Horace*** (Oxford, 1980), and **K. Galinsky, *Augustan Culture*** (Princeton, N.J., 1996).

Various aspects of Roman society are covered in **L. Adkins and R. A. Adkins, *Handbook to Life in Ancient Rome*** (New York, 1994). Also useful on urban life is **J. E. Stambaugh, *The Ancient Roman City*** (Baltimore, 1988). On public festivals, see **P. Veyne, *Bread and Circuses*** (London, 1992). On the gladiators, see **T. Wiedemann, *Emperors and Gladiators*** (New York, 1992). Studies on Roman women include **J.P.V.D. Balsdon, *Roman Women: Their History and Habits*** (London, 1969), and **S. B. Pomeroy, *Goddesses, Whores, Wives, and Slaves: Women in Classical Antiquity*** (New York, 1975), pp. 149–226. On slavery, see **K. Bradley, *Slavery and Society at Rome*** (New York, 1994).

For a general introduction to early Christianity, see **J. Court and K. Court**, *The New Testament World* (Cambridge, 1990). Useful works on early Christianity include **W. A. Meeks**, *The First Urban Christians* (New Haven, Conn., 1983); **W.H.C. Frend**, *The Rise of Christianity* (Philadelphia, 1984); and **R. MacMullen**, *Christianizing the Roman Empire* (New Haven, Conn., 1984). For a detailed analysis of Christianity in the 30s and 40s of the first century A.D., see **J. D. Crossan**, *The Birth of Christianity* (New York, 1998). On Christian women, see **D. M. Scholer, ed.,** *Women in Early Christianity* (New York, 1993), and **R. Kraemer**, *Her Share of the Blessings: Women's Religion Among the Pagans, Jews and Christians in the Graeco-Roman World* (Oxford, 1995).

Thomson NOW! Enter *ThomsonNOW* using the access card that is available for *Western Civilization: A Brief History*. *ThomsonNOW* will help you understand this chapter with lesson plans generated for your needs. In addition, you can read the following documents, and many more, online:

   Virgil, Book 1 of *The Aeneid*
   Horace, Satire 1 of Book 1
   The Gospel of Mark (New Testament)
   Ignatius, "Letter to the Ephesians"

WESTERN CIVILIZATION RESOURCES

Visit the Web site for *Western Civilization: A Brief History* for resources specific to this book:
   http://www.thomsonedu.com/history/spielvogel
For a variety of tools to help you succeed in this course, visit the Western Civilization Resource Center at
   http://history.wadsworth.com/spielvogel
Included are quizzes, images, documents, interactive simulations, maps and timelines, movie explorations, and a wealth of other sources.

LATE ANTIQUITY AND THE EMERGENCE OF THE MEDIEVAL WORLD

*A fourteenth-century French manuscript illustration
of the baptism of Clovis*

Giraudon/The Bridgeman Art Library International (Bibliotheque Municipale, Castres, France)

𝓑Y THE THIRD CENTURY, the third century, the Roman Empire was experiencing a number of problems as well as witnessing the growth of a new religion–Christianity. To restore the empire, the emperors Diocletian and Constantine initiated a number of reforms, and Constantine converted to Christianity, starting a process that gave the Late Empire a new state religion.

After Constantine, the empire continued to survive, but it had to deal repeatedly with incursions of Germanic tribes in the west. By the second half of the fifth century, new political arrangements were undermining the old imperial structure in the west, leading to the emergence of a series of German kingdoms that would form the basis of a new civilization. The Christian church also played a role as it converted these Germanic tribes to its faith.

The conversion to Christianity of the pagan leaders of German tribes was sometimes dramatic, at least as reported by the sixth-century historian Gregory of Tours. Clovis, leader of the Franks, married Clotilde, daughter of the king of the Burgundians. She was a Christian, but Clovis refused her pleas to become a Christian, telling her, "Your god can do nothing." But during a battle with the Alemanni, when

Clovis' army was close to utter destruction, "He saw the danger; his heart was stirred; and he raised his eyes to heaven, saying, 'Jesus Christ, I beseech the glory of your aid. If you shall grant me victory over these enemies, I will believe in you and be baptized in your name.' " When he had uttered these words, the Alemanni began to flee. Clovis soon became a Christian.

While the Germanic kingdoms were establishing roots in the west, the eastern part of the old Roman Empire, increasingly Greek in culture, continued as the Byzantine Empire. Serving as a buffer between Europe and the peoples to the east, the Byzantine or Eastern Roman Empire also preserved the intellectual and legal accomplishments of Greek and Roman antiquity. At the same time, a new culture centered on Islam emerged in the east; it spread through large parts of the old Roman Empire, preserved much of Greek culture, and created its own flourishing civilization. This chapter concerns the dramatic transformations occurring in the Roman world in late antiquity, the heirs of the Roman Empire, and the medieval world they began to create.◆

The Late Roman Empire

At the end of the third and beginning of the fourth centuries, the Roman Empire gained a new lease on life through the efforts of two strong emperors, Diocletian and Constantine, who restored order and stability. The Roman Empire was virtually transformed into a new state: the Late Roman Empire, which included a new governmental structure, a rigid economic and social system, and a new state religion—Christianity.

The Reforms of Diocletian and Constantine

Diocletian had risen through the ranks to become a prominent military leader. After the murder of the emperor Numerian by his praetorian prefect, Diocletian executed the prefect and was then hailed as emperor by his soldiers. Diocletian's own rise to power led him to see the need for a new system for ruling the Roman Empire.

Political Reforms Believing that the empire had grown too large for a single ruler, Diocletian (284–305) divided it into four administrative units (see Map 7.1), each with its own prefect. Despite the appearance of four-man rule, however, Diocletian's military seniority enabled him to claim a higher status and hold the ultimate authority. Constantine (306–337) continued and even expanded the autocratic policies of Diocletian. Both rulers greatly strengthened and enlarged the administrative bureaucracies of the Roman Empire. Henceforth, civil and military bureaucracies were sharply separated. Each contained a hierarchy of officials who exercised control at the various levels. The emperor presided over both hierarchies of officials and served as the only link between them. New titles of nobility—such as *illustres* ("illustrious ones") and

illustrissimi ("most illustrious ones")—were instituted to dignify the holders of positions in the civil and military bureaucracies.

Military Reforms Additional military reforms were also instituted. The army was enlarged to almost 400,000 men, including units filled with Germans. By the end of Constantine's reign, a new organization of the army had also been put in place. Military forces were of two kinds: garrison troops, which were located on the frontiers and intended as a first line of defense against invaders, and mobile units, which were located behind the frontier but could be quickly moved to support frontier troops when the borders were threatened. This gave the empire greater flexibility in responding to invasion.

Economic and Social Trends The political and military reforms of Diocletian and Constantine greatly enlarged two institutions—the army and the civil service—that drained most of the public funds. Though more revenues were needed to pay for the army and bureaucracy, the population was not growing, so the tax base could not be expanded. Diocletian and Constantine devised new economic and social policies to deal with these financial burdens, but like their political policies, they were all based on coercion and loss of individual freedom. To fight **inflation**, Diocletian resorted to issuing a price edict in 301 that established maximum wages and prices for the entire empire, but despite severe penalties, it was unenforceable and failed to work.

Coercion also came to form the underlying basis for numerous occupations in the Late Roman Empire. To ensure the tax base and keep the empire going despite the shortage of labor, the emperors issued edicts that forced people to remain in their designated vocations. Basic jobs, such as bakers and shippers, became hereditary. Free tenant farmers continued to decline and soon found themselves bound to the land by large landowners who took advantage of depressed agricultural conditions to enlarge their landed estates.

In general, the economic and social policies of Diocletian and Constantine were based on an unprecedented degree of control and coercion. Though temporarily successful, such authoritarian policies in the long run stifled the very vitality the Late Empire needed to revive its sagging fortunes.

Constantine's Building Program Constantine was especially interested in building programs despite the strain they placed on the budget. Between 324 and 330, he engaged in his biggest project, the construction of a new capital city in the east, on the site of the Greek city of Byzantium, on the shores of the Bosporus. Named the "city of Constantine," or Constantinople (modern Istanbul), it was developed for defensive reasons; it had an excellent strategic location. Calling it his "New Rome," Constantine endowed the city with a forum, large palaces, and a vast amphitheater. It was officially dedicated on May 11,

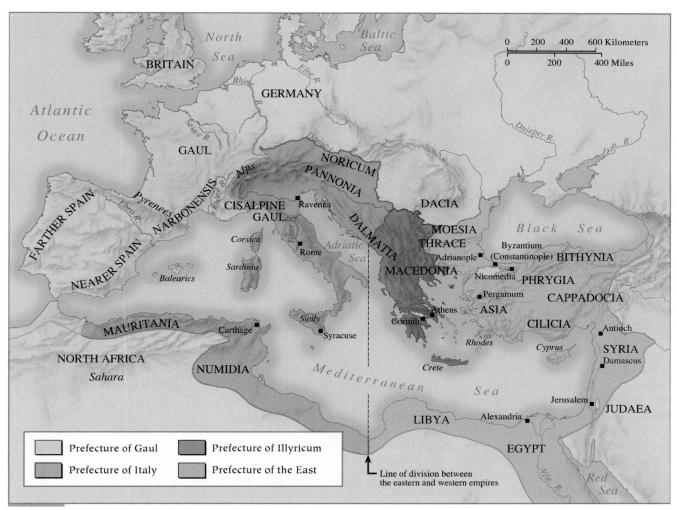

MAP 7.1 Divisions of the Late Roman Empire, c. 300. Diocletian imposed order and a new economic and administrative structure on the Late Empire. He divided the Roman Empire into four regions, each ruled by either an "Augustus" or a "Caesar," although Diocletian retained supreme power. ❓ Compare this map with Map 6.1. How much territory was lost by the time of Diocletian? 🌐 **View an animated version of this map or related maps at** http://thomsonedu.com/history/spielvogel

330, "by the commandment of God," and in the following years, many Christian churches were built there.

The Empire's New Religion

Christianity flourished after Constantine became the first Christian emperor. According to the traditional story, before a crucial battle, he saw a vision of a Christian cross with the writing, "In this sign you will conquer." Having won the battle, the story goes, Constantine was convinced of the power of the Christian God. Although he was not baptized until the end of his life, in 313 he issued the famous Edict of Milan, officially tolerating the existence of Christianity. Under Theodosius "the Great" (378–395), it was made the official religion of the Roman Empire. Christianity had triumphed.

Organization and Religious Disputes By the fourth century, the Christian church had developed a system of government. The Christian community in each city was headed by a bishop, whose area of jurisdiction was known as a bishopric or diocese. The bishoprics of each Roman province were clustered together under the direction of an archbishop. The bishops of four great cities, Rome, Jerusalem, Alexandria, and Antioch, held positions of special power in church affairs because the churches in these cities all asserted that they had been founded by the original apostles sent out by Jesus.

One reason the church needed a more formal organization was the problem of **heresy**. As Christianity developed and spread, contradictory interpretations of important doctrines emerged. Heresy came to be viewed as a teaching different from the official catholic or universal beliefs of the

The Emperor Constantine. Constantine played an important role in restoring order and stability to the Roman Empire at the beginning of the fourth century. This marble head of Constantine, which is 8 feet 6 inches high, was part of an enormous 30-foot-tall seated statue of the emperor in the New Basilica in Rome. Constantine used these awe-inspiring statues throughout the empire to build support for imperial policies by reminding his subjects of his position as an absolute ruler with immense power. With his eyes turned toward heaven Constantine's special relationship with God is made clear.

church. In a world where people were concerned about salvation, the question of whether Jesus' nature was divine or human took on great significance. These doctrinal differences also became political issues, creating political factions that actually warred with one another. It is unlikely that ordinary people understood what these debates meant.

One of the major heresies of the fourth century was **Arianism**, which was a product of the followers of Arius, a priest from Alexandria in Egypt. Arius believed that Jesus Christ had been human and thus not truly God. Arius was opposed by Athanasius, a bishop of Alexandria, who argued that Jesus was human but also truly God. Emperor Constantine, disturbed by the controversy, called the first ecumenical council of the church, a meeting composed of representatives from the entire Christian community. The Council of Nicaea, held in 325, condemned Arianism and stated that Jesus was of "the same substance" as God:

> We believe in one God the Father All-sovereign, maker of all things visible and invisible; And in one Lord Jesus Christ, the Son of God, begotten of the Father, only-begotten, that is, of the substance of the Father, God of God, Light of Light, true God of true God, begotten not made, of one substance with the Father.[1]

The Council of Nicaea did not end the controversy, however; not only did Arianism persist in some parts of the Roman Empire for many years, but many of the Germanic Goths who established states in the west converted to Arian Christianity (see "The Germanic Kingdoms" later in this chapter). As a result of these fourth-century theological controversies, the Roman emperor came to play an increasingly important role in church affairs.

The End of the Western Empire

Constantine had reunited the Roman Empire and restored a semblance of order. After his death, however, the empire continued to divide into western and eastern parts, and by 395, they had become virtually two independent states. In the fifth century, the empire in the east remained intact under the Roman emperor in Constantinople (see "The Byzantine Empire" later in this chapter), but the administrative structure of the empire in the west collapsed and was replaced by a series of Germanic kingdoms.

During the first and second centuries A.D., the Romans had established the Rhine and Danube Rivers as the empire's northern boundary. The Romans called all the peoples to the north of the rivers "Germans" and regarded them as uncivilized barbarians. In fact, the Germans consisted of different groups with their own customs and identities, but these constantly changed as tribes broke up and came together in new configurations. At times, they formed larger confederations under strong warrior leaders. The Germans lived by herding and farming and also traded with people living along the northern frontiers of the Roman Empire.

Although the Romans had established political frontiers along the Rhine and Danube Rivers, Romans and Germans often came into contact across these boundaries. For some time, the Romans had hired Germanic tribes to fight other Germanic tribes that threatened Rome or enlisted groups of Germans to fight for Rome. In any case, until the fourth century, the empire had proved capable of absorbing these people without harm to its political structure. In the second half of the fourth century, however, the situation began to change.

In the late fourth century, the Germanic tribes came under new pressures when the Huns, a fierce tribe of nomads from Asia, moved into the Black Sea region and forced Germanic groups westward. One of the largest groups, which came to be known as the Visigoths, crossed the Danube into German territory and settled down as Roman allies. Ill-treated by Roman officials, the Visigoths soon revolted, and the attempt to stop them at Adrianople in 378 led to a crushing defeat for the Romans. Soon the Visigoths were again on the move. Under their king Alaric, they moved into Italy and sacked Rome in 410. Then, at the urging of the emperor, they moved into Spain and southern Gaul as Roman allies.

The Roman experience with the Visigoths established a precedent. The emperors in the first half of the fifth century made alliances with whole groups of Germanic

Diocletian	284–305
Constantine	306–337
Edict of Milan	313
Construction of Constantinople	324–330
Battle of Adrianople	378
Theodosius the Great	378–395
Division of the empire	395
Alaric and Visigoths sack Rome	410
Roman legions abandon Britain	410
Vandals sack Rome	455
Odoacer deposes Romulus Augustulus	476

peoples, who settled peacefully in the western part of the empire. The Burgundians settled themselves in much of eastern Gaul, just south of another German tribe called the Alemanni. Only the Vandals consistently remained hostile to the Romans. They sacked parts of Gaul and crossed the Pyrenees into Spain. Defeated by incoming Visigoths, the Vandals crossed the Strait of Gibraltar and conquered the province of Africa. In 455, the Vandals even attacked Rome, sacking it more ferociously than the Visigoths had in 410.

Increasingly, German military leaders dominated the imperial courts of the western empire, treating the Roman emperors as puppet rulers under their control. One such German leader finally ended the charade of Roman imperial rule. Odoacer deposed the Roman emperor, Romulus Augustulus, in 476 and began to rule on his own. Meanwhile, the Ostrogoths, another branch of the Goths, under their king Theodoric (493–526), marched into Italy, killed Odoacer, and established control of Italy in 493.

By the end of the fifth century, Roman imperial authority in the west had ceased. Nevertheless, the intellectual, governmental, and cultural traditions of the Late Roman Empire continued to live in the new Germanic kingdoms.

The Germanic Kingdoms

By 500, the western Roman Empire was being replaced politically by a series of kingdoms ruled by German monarchs (see Map 7.2). The pattern of settlement and the fusion of the Romans and Germans took different forms in the various kingdoms.

The Ostrogothic Kingdom of Italy

More than any other Germanic state, the Ostrogothic kingdom of Italy managed to maintain the Roman tradition of government. The Ostrogothic king, Theodoric, had received a Roman education while a hostage in Constantinople. After taking control of Italy, he was eager to create a synthesis of Ostrogothic and Roman practices.

In addition to maintaining the entire structure of imperial Roman government, he established separate systems of rule for the Ostrogoths and the Romans. The Italian population lived under Roman law administered by Roman officials. The Ostrogoths were governed by their own customs and their own officials.

After Theodoric's death in 526, it quickly became apparent that much of his success had been due to the force of his personality. His successors soon found themselves facing opposition from the imperial forces of the Byzantine or eastern Roman Empire. Under Emperor Justinian (527–565) (see "The Byzantine Empire" later in this chapter), Byzantine armies reconquered Italy between 535 and 554, devastating much of the peninsula and in the process destroying Rome as one of the great urban centers of the Mediterranean world. The Byzantine reconquest proved ephemeral, however. Another German tribe, the Lombards, invaded in 568 and conquered much of northern and central Italy. Unlike the Ostrogoths, the Lombards were harsh rulers who cared little for Roman structures and traditions.

The Visigothic Kingdom of Spain

The Visigothic kingdom in Spain demonstrated a number of parallels to the Ostrogothic kingdom of Italy. Both favored coexistence between the Roman and German populations, both featured a warrior caste dominating a larger native population, and both continued to maintain much of the Roman structure of government while largely excluding Romans from power. There were also noticeable differences, however. Laws preventing intermarriage were dropped, and the Visigothic and Hispano-Roman peoples began to blend. A new body of law common to both peoples also developed.

The Visigothic kingdom possessed one fatal weakness. With no established procedure for choosing new rulers, powerful Visigoths fought constantly to lay claim to the kingship. Church officials tried to help develop a sense of order, as this decree illustrates: "No one of us shall dare to seize the kingdom; no one shall arouse sedition among the citizenry; no one shall think of killing the king...." Church edicts failed to stop the feuds, however, and assassinations remained a way of life in Visigothic Spain. In 711, Muslim invaders destroyed the Visigothic kingdom itself (see "The Rise of Islam" later in this chapter).

The Frankish Kingdom

Only one of the German states on the European continent proved long-lasting—the kingdom of the Franks. The establishment of a Frankish kingdom was the work of Clovis (c. 482–511), a member of the Merovingian dynasty who became a Catholic Christian around 500. He was not the first German king to convert to Christianity, but the others had joined the Arian sect of

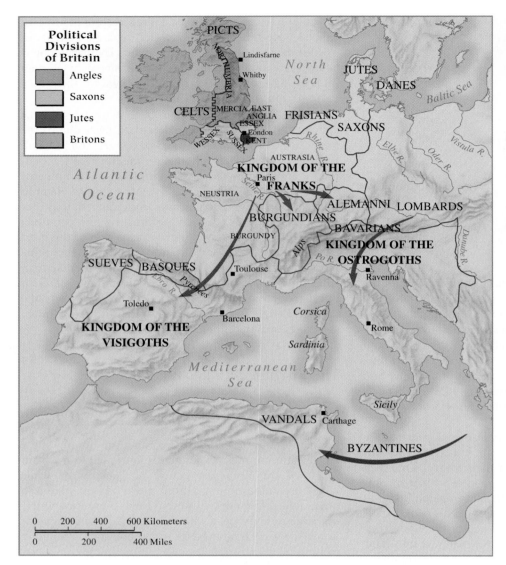

PICTS

Lindisfarne

Whitby

North Sea

JUTES

DANES

Baltic Sea

CELTS   NORTHUMBRIA   MERCIA EAST ANGLIA   FRISIANS

ESSEX

WESSEX   SUSSEX KENT   London

SAXONS

AUSTRASIA   *Rhine R.*   *Elbe R.*   *Oder R.*   *Vistula R.*

KINGDOM OF THE FRANKS   Paris

NEUSTRIA   *Seine R.*   ALEMANNI   LOMBARDS

Atlantic Ocean   BURGUNDIANS   BAVARIANS

BURGUNDY   *Alps*   **KINGDOM OF THE OSTROGOTHS**

SUEVES   BASQUES   Toulouse   *Po R.*   Ravenna

Ebro R.   *Pyrenees*   Barcelona   *Corsica*   Rome

Toledo   *Danube R.*

KINGDOM OF THE VISIGOTHS   *Sardinia*

Mediterranean Sea   *Sicily*

VANDALS   Carthage

BYZANTINES

0	200	400	600 Kilometers
0	200		400 Miles

MAP 7.2 The Germanic Kingdoms of the Old Western Empire. The Germanic tribes filled the power vacuum caused by the demise of the Roman Empire, building states that blended elements of Germanic customs and laws with those of Roman culture, including large-scale conversions to Christianity. The Franks established the most durable of these Germanic states. **?** How did the movements of Franks during this period correspond to the borders of present-day France? **View an animated version of this map or related maps at** http://thomsonedu.com/history/spielvogel

Christianity. The Christian church in Rome, which had become known as the Roman Catholic church, regarded the Arians as heretics, who believed in teachings different from the official church doctrine. Clovis' conversion to Catholic Christianity gained him the support of the Roman Catholic church, which was eager to obtain the friendship of a major Germanic ruler who was a Catholic Christian.

By 510, Clovis had established a powerful new Frankish kingdom stretching from the Pyrenees in the west to German lands in the east (modern-day France and western Germany). After the death of Clovis, however, his sons divided the newly created kingdom, as was the Frankish custom. During the sixth and seventh centuries, the once-united Frankish kingdom came to be partitioned into three major areas: Neustria in northern Gaul; Austrasia, consisting of the ancient Frankish lands on both sides of the Rhine; and the former kingdom of Burgundy.

During this time, the Frankish kingdom witnessed a process of fusion between Gallo-Roman and Frankish cultures and peoples, a process accompanied by a significant decline in Roman standards of civilization and commercial activity. The Franks were warriors and did little to encourage either urban life or trade. By 750, Frankish Gaul was basically an agricultural society in which the old Roman estates of the Late Empire had continued unimpeded. Institutionally, however, Germanic concepts of kingship and customary law replaced the Roman governmental structure.

Anglo-Saxon England

The barbarian pressures on the western Roman Empire had forced the emperors to withdraw the Roman armies and abandon Britain by the beginning of the fifth century. This opened the door to the Angles and Saxons, Germanic tribes from Denmark and northern Germany. Although these same peoples had made plundering raids for the past century, the withdrawal of the Roman armies

Baptism of Clovis. The conversion of Clovis to Roman Catholicism around 500 was an important factor in gaining papal support for his Frankish kingdom. In this illustration from a thirteenth-century Italian manuscript, Clovis is being baptized by Saint Remigius, the bishop of Rheims. Saint Remigius was known as a devout missionary; it was said, "by his signs and miracles, he brought low the heathen altars everywhere."

Theodoric establishes Ostrogothic kingdom in Italy	493
Frankish king Clovis converts to Christianity	c. 500
Reconquest of Italy by Byzantines	535–552
Lombards begin conquest of Italy	568
Muslims shatter Visigoths in Spain	711

out eyes, or slicing off ears and noses. Because this system could easily get out of control, an alternative system arose that made use of a fine called **wergeld**, which was paid by a wrongdoer to the family of the person he had injured or killed. *Wergeld,* which means "man money," was the value of a person in monetary terms. That value varied considerably according to social status. An offense against a nobleman, for example, cost considerably more than one against a freeman or a slave.

Under German customary law, compurgation and the ordeal were the two most commonly used procedures for determining whether an accused person was guilty and should have to pay wergeld. Compurgation was the swearing of an oath by the accused person, backed up by a group of "oath helpers," numbering twelve or twenty-five, who would also swear that the accused person should be believed. The ordeal functioned in a variety of ways, all of which were based on the principle of divine intervention; divine forces (whether pagan or Christian) would not allow an innocent person to be harmed (see the box on p. 122).

The Frankish Family and Marriage For the Franks, like other Germanic peoples, the extended family was at the center of social organization. The Frankish family structure was simple. Males were dominant and made all the important decisions. A woman obeyed her father until she married and then fell under the legal domination of her husband. A widow, however, could hold property without a male guardian. In Frankish law, the wergeld of a wife of childbearing age—of value because she could bring forth children—was considerably higher than that of a man. The law stated, "If any one killed a free woman after she had begun bearing children, he shall be sentenced to 24,000 denars... After she can have no more children, he who kills her shall be sentenced to 8,000 denars."[2]

Because marriage affected the extended family group, fathers or uncles could arrange marriages for the good of the family without considering their children's wishes. Most important was the engagement ceremony in which a prospective son-in-law made a payment symbolizing the purchase of paternal authority over the bride. The essential feature of the marriage itself involved placing the married couple in bed to achieve their physical union. In first marriages, it was considered important that the wife be a virgin, which ensured that any children would

enabled them to make settlements instead. They met with resistance from the Celtic Britons, however, who still controlled the western regions of Cornwall, Wales, and Cumberland at the beginning of the seventh century. The German invaders eventually succeeded in carving out small kingdoms throughout the island, Kent in southeast England being one of them.

The Society of the Germanic Kingdoms

As Germans and Romans intermarried and began to create a new society, some of the social customs of the Germanic people began to play an important role. The crucial social bond among the Germanic peoples was the family, especially the extended or patriarchal family of husbands, wives, children, brothers, sisters, cousins, and grandparents. In addition to working the land together and passing it down to succeeding generations, the extended family provided protection, which was sorely needed in the violent atmosphere of Merovingian times.

The German conception of family affected the way Germanic law treated crime and punishment. In the Roman system, as in our own, a crime such as murder was considered an offense against society or the state and was handled by a court that heard evidence and arrived at a decision. Germanic law tended to be personal. An injury by one person against another could mean a blood feud in which the family of the injured party took revenge on the kin of the wrongdoer. Feuds could lead to savage acts of revenge, such as hacking off hands or feet, gouging

GERMANIC CUSTOMARY LAW: THE ORDEAL

*I*n Germanic customary law, the ordeal came to be a means by which accused persons might clear themselves. Although the ordeal took different forms, all involved a physical trial of some sort, such as holding a red-hot iron. It was believed that God would protect the innocent and allow them to come through the ordeal unharmed. This sixth-century account by Gregory of Tours describes an ordeal by hot water.

Gregory of Tours, "An Ordeal of Hot Water" (c. 580)

An Arian presbyter disputing with a deacon of our religion made venomous assertions against the Son of God and the Holy Ghost, as is the habit of that sect [the Arians]. But when the deacon had discoursed a long time concerning the reasonableness of our faith and the heretic, blinded by the fog of unbelief, continued to reject the truth, . . . the former said: "Why weary ourselves with long discussions? Let acts approve the truth; let a kettle be heated over the fire and someone's ring be thrown into the boiling water. Let him who shall take it from the heated liquid be approved as a follower of the truth, and afterward let the other party be converted to the knowledge of the truth. And do you also understand, O heretic, that this our party will fulfill the conditions with the aid of the Holy Ghost; you shall confess that there is no discordance, no dissimilarity in the Holy Trinity." The heretic consented to the proposition and they separated after appointing the next morning for the trial. But the fervor of faith in which the deacon had first made this suggestion began to cool through the instigation of the enemy. Rising with the dawn he bathed his arm in oil and smeared it with ointment. But nevertheless he made the round of the sacred places and called in prayer on the Lord. . . . About the third hour they met in the market place. The people came together to see the show. A fire was lighted, the kettle was placed upon it, and when it grew very hot the ring was thrown into the boiling water. The deacon invited the heretic to take it out of the water first. But he promptly refused, saying, "You who did propose this trial are the one to take it out." The deacon all of a tremble bared his arm. And when the heretic presbyter saw it besmeared with ointment he cried out: "With magic arts you have thought to protect yourself, that you have made use of these salves, but what you have done will not avail." While they were thus quarreling there came up a deacon from Ravenna named Iacinthus and inquired what the trouble was about. When he learned the truth he drew his arm out from under his robe at once and plunged his right hand into the kettle. Now the ring that had been thrown in was a little thing and very light so that it was thrown about by the water as chaff would be blown about by the wind; and searching for it a long time he found it after about an hour. Meanwhile the flame beneath the kettle blazed up mightily so that the greater heat might make it difficult for the ring to be followed by the hand; but the deacon extracted it at length and suffered no harm, protesting rather that at the bottom the kettle was cold while at the top it was just pleasantly warm. When the heretic beheld this he was greatly confused and audaciously thrust his hand into the kettle saying, "My faith will aid me." As soon as his hand had been thrust in all the flesh was boiled off the bones clear up to the elbow. And so the dispute ended.

What was the purpose of the ordeal of hot water? What does it reveal about the nature of the society that used it?

---

be the husband's. A virgin symbolized the ability of the bloodline to continue. Accordingly, adultery was viewed as pollution of the woman and her offspring, hence poisoning the future. Adulterous wives were severely punished (an adulterous woman could be strangled or even burned alive); adulterous husbands were not. Divorce was relatively simple and was initiated primarily by the husband. Divorced wives simply returned to their families.

For most women in the new Germanic kingdoms, their legal status reflected the material conditions of their lives. Archaeological evidence suggests that most women had life expectancies of only thirty to forty years, and 10 to 15 percent of women died in their childbearing years, no doubt due to complications associated with childbirth. For most women, life consisted of domestic labor: providing food and clothing for the household, caring for the children, and assisting with numerous farming chores. Of all women's labors, the most important was childbearing, because it was indispensable to perpetuating the family and its possessions.

Development of the Christian Church

By the end of the fourth century, Christianity had become the predominant religion of the Roman Empire. As the official Roman state disintegrated, the Christian church played an increasingly important role in the emergence and growth of the new European civilization.

The Power of the Pope

One of the far-reaching developments in the history of the Christian church was the emergence of one bishop—that of Rome—as the recognized leader of the western Christian church. According to church tradition, Jesus had given the keys to the kingdom of heaven to Peter, who was considered the chief apostle and the first bishop of Rome. Subsequent bishops of Rome were considered Peter's successors and came to be known as popes (from

THE LIFE OF SAINT ANTHONY

In the third and early fourth centuries, the lives of martyrs had provided important models for early Christianity. But in the course of the fourth century, monks or desert fathers, who attempted to achieve spiritual perfection through asceticism, the denial of earthly life, and the struggle with demons became the new spiritual ideal for Christians. Consequently, spiritual biographies of early monks became a significant new form of Christian literature. Especially noteworthy was *The Life of Saint Anthony* by Saint Athanasius, the defender of Catholic orthodoxy against the Arians. His work had been translated into Latin before 386. This excerpt describes how Anthony fought off the temptations of Satan.

Athanasius, *The Life of Saint Anthony*

Now when the Enemy [Satan] saw that his craftiness in this matter was without profit, and that the more he brought temptation into Saint Anthony, the more strenuous the saint was in protecting himself against him with the armor of righteousness, he attacked him by means of the vigor of early manhood which is bound up in the nature of our humanity. With the goadings of passion he sued to trouble him by night, and in the daytime also he would vex him and pain him with the same to such an extent that even those who saw him knew from his appearance that he was waging war against the Adversary. But the more the Evil One brought unto him filthy and maddening thoughts, the more Saint Anthony took refuge in prayer and in abundant supplication, and amid them all he remained wholly chaste. And the Evil One was working upon him every shameful deed according to his wont, and at length he even appeared unto Saint Anthony in the form of a woman; and other things which resembled this he performed with ease, for such things are a subject for boasting to him.

But the blessed Anthony knelt down upon his knees on the ground, and prayed before Him who said, "Before you criest unto Me, I will answer you," and said, "O my Lord, this I entreat you. Let not Your love be blotted out from my mind, and behold, I am, by Your grace, innocent before You." And again the Enemy multiplied in him the thoughts of lust, until Saint Anthony became as one who was being burned up, not through the Evil One, but through his own lusts; but he girded himself about with the threat of the thought of the Judgment, and of the torture of Gehenna, and of the worm which does not die. And while meditating on the thoughts which could be directed against the Evil One, he prayed for thoughts which would be hostile to him. Thus, to the reproach and shame of the Enemy, these things could not be performed; for he who imagined that he could be God was made a mock of by a young man, and he who boasted over flesh and blood was vanquished by a man who was clothed with flesh.

Based on the account by Athanasius, how would you characterize the ascetic ideals of early Christian monks? How important were those ideals to the growth of early Christianity?

---

the Latin word *papa*, meaning "father") of the Catholic church.

Although western Christians came to accept the bishop of Rome as head of the church in the fourth and fifth centuries, there was no unanimity on the extent of the powers the pope possessed as a result of this position. Nevertheless, the emergence in the sixth century of a strong pope, Gregory I, known as Gregory the Great, set the papacy and the Roman Catholic church on an energetic path that enabled the church in the seventh and eighth centuries to play an increasingly prominent role in civilizing the Germans and aiding the emergence of a distinctly new European civilization.

As pope, Gregory I (590–604) took charge of Rome and its surrounding area and made it into an administrative unit that eventually came to be known as the Papal States. Gregory also pursued a policy of extending papal authority over the Christian church in the west. He intervened in ecclesiastical conflicts throughout Italy and corresponded with the Frankish rulers, urging them to reform the church in Gaul. He successfully initiated the efforts of missionaries to convert England to Christianity and was especially active in converting the pagan peoples of Germanic Europe. His primary instrument was the monastic movement.

The Monks and Their Missions

A **monk** (Latin *monachus*, meaning "one who lives alone") was a person who sought to live a life divorced from the world, cut off from ordinary human society, in order to pursue an ideal of godliness or total dedication to the will of God. Christian **monasticism** was initially based on the model of the solitary hermit who forsakes all civilized society to pursue spirituality. Saint Anthony (c. 250–350) was a prosperous peasant in Egypt who decided to follow Jesus' injunction in the Gospel of Saint Mark: "Go your way, sell whatsoever you have, and give to the poor, and you shall have treasure in heaven: and come, take up the cross, and follow me." Anthony gave away his 300 acres of land to the poor and went into the desert to pursue his ideal of holiness (see the box above). Others did likewise, often to extremes. Saint Simeon the Stylite lived for three decades in a basket atop a pillar over 60 feet high. These spiritual gymnastics established a new ideal for Christianity. Whereas the early Christian model had been the martyr who died for the faith and achieved eternal life in the process, the new ideal was the monk who died to the world and achieved spiritual life through denial, asceticism, and mystical experience of God.

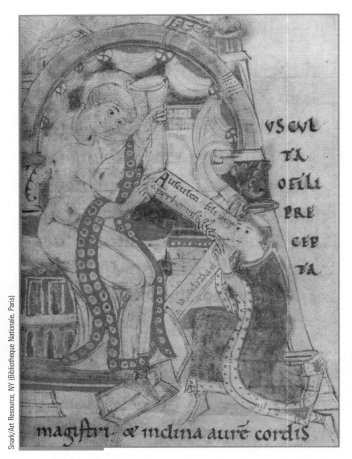

Saint Benedict. Benedict was the author of a set of rules that was instrumental in the development of monastic groups in the Catholic church. Shown in this medieval Latin manuscript is Benedict handing the rules of the Benedictine order to a monk.

These early monks, however, soon found themselves unable to live in solitude. Their feats of holiness attracted followers on a wide scale, and as the monastic ideal spread throughout the east, a new form of monasticism based on the practice of communal life soon became the dominant form. Monastic communities came to be seen as the ideal Christian society that could provide a moral example to the wider society around them.

Benedictine Monasticism Saint Benedict of Nursia (c. 480–c. 543), who founded a monastic house for which he wrote a set of rules sometime between 520 and 530, established the fundamental form of monastic life in the western Christian church. The Benedictine rule came to be used by other monastic groups and was crucial to the growth of monasticism in the western Christian world.

Benedict's rule favored an ideal of moderation. In chapter 40 of the rule, on the amount a monk should drink, this sense of moderation becomes apparent:

> "Every man has his proper gift from God, one after this manner, another after that." And therefore it is with some misgiving that we determine the amount of food for someone

else. Still, having regard for the weakness of some brothers, we believe that a hemina of wine [a quarter liter] per day will suffice for all. Let those, however, to whom God gives the gift of abstinence, know that they shall have their proper reward. But if either the circumstances of the place, the work, or the heat of summer necessitates more, let it lie in the discretion of the abbot to grant it. But let him take care in all things lest satiety or drunkenness supervene.[3]

At the same time, moderation did not preclude a disciplined existence based on the ideals of poverty, chastity, and obedience.

Benedict's rule divided each day into a series of activities, with primary emphasis on prayer and manual labor. Physical work of some kind was required of all monks for several hours a day because idleness was "the enemy of the soul." At the very heart of community practice was prayer, the proper "work of God." While this included private meditation and reading, all monks gathered together seven times during the day for common prayer and chanting of psalms. A Benedictine life was a communal one; monks ate, worked, slept, and worshiped together.

Each Benedictine monastery was strictly ruled by an **abbot**, or "father" of the monastery, who held complete authority over them; unquestioning obedience to the will of the abbot was expected of each monk. Each Benedictine monastery owned lands that enabled it to be a self-sustaining community, isolated from and independent of the world surrounding it. Within the monastery, however, monks were to fulfill their vow of poverty: "Let all things be common to all, as it is written, lest anyone should say that anything is his own or arrogate it to himself."[4] By the eighth century, Benedictine monasticism had spread throughout the west.

Although the original monks were men, women soon followed suit in withdrawing from the world to dedicate themselves to God. The first monastic rule for western women was produced by Caesarius of Arles for his sister in the fifth century. It strongly emphasized a rigid cloistering of these **nuns** to preserve them from dangers.

Monasticism played an indispensable role in early medieval civilization. Monks became the new heroes of Christian civilization. Their dedication to God became the highest ideal of Christian life. Monks copied Latin works and passed on the legacy of the ancient world to Western civilization in its European stage. Moreover, the monks played an increasingly significant role in spreading Christianity to the entire European world.

Monks as Missionaries The British Isles, in particular, became an important center of Christian culture and missionary fervor. After their conversion, the Celts of Ireland and Anglo-Saxons of England created new centers of Christian learning and in turn themselves became enthusiastic missionaries.

By the sixth century, Irish monasticism was a flourishing institution with its own unique characteristics. Unlike Benedictine monasticism, it was strongly ascetic. Monks performed strenuous fasts, prayed and meditated

IRISH MONASTICISM AND THE PENITENTIAL

*I*rish monasticism became well known for its ascetic practices. Much emphasis was placed on careful examination of conscience to determine if one had committed a sin against God. To facilitate this examination, penitentials were developed that listed possible sins with appropriate penances. Penance usually meant fasting a number of days each week on bread and water. Although these penitentials were eventually used throughout Christendom, they were especially important in Irish Christianity. This excerpt from the Penitential of Cummean, an Irish abbot, was written about 650 and demonstrates a distinctive feature of the penitentials, an acute preoccupation with sexual sins.

The Penitential of Cummean

A bishop who commits fornication shall be degraded and shall do penance for twelve years.

A presbyter or a deacon who commits natural fornication, having previously taken the vow of a monk, shall do penance for seven years. He shall ask pardon every hour; he shall perform a special fast during every week except in the days between Easter and Pentecost.

He who defiles his mother shall do penance for three years, with perpetual pilgrimage.

So shall those who commit sodomy do penance every seven years.

He who merely desires in his mind to commit fornication, but is not able, shall do penance for one year, especially in the three forty-day periods.

He who is willingly polluted during sleep shall arise and sing nine psalms in order, kneeling. On the following day, he shall live on bread and water.

A cleric who commits fornication once shall do penance for one year on bread and water; if he begets a son he shall do penance for seven years as an exile; so also a virgin.

He who loves any woman, but is unaware of any evil beyond a few conversations, shall do penance for forty days.

He who is in a state of matrimony ought to be continent during the three forty-day periods and on Saturday and on Sunday, night and day, and in the two appointed week days [Wednesday and Friday], and after conception, and during the entire menstrual period.

After a birth he shall abstain, if it is a son, for thirty-three [days]; if a daughter, for sixty-six [days].

Boys talking alone and transgressing the regulations of the elders [in the monastery], shall be corrected by three special fasts.

Children who imitate acts of fornication, twenty days; if frequently, forty.

But boys of twenty years who practice masturbation together and confess [shall do penance] twenty or forty days before they take communion.

What does the Penitential of Cummean reveal about the nature of Irish monasticism? What do you think was the theory of human sexuality held by early Irish Christianity?

---

frequently under extreme privations, and confessed their sins on a regular basis to their superiors. In fact, Irish monasticism gave rise to the use of penitentials or manuals that provided a guide for examining one's life to see what sins, or offenses against the will of God, one had committed (see the box above). A great love of learning also characterized Irish monasticism. The Irish eagerly absorbed both Latin and Greek culture and fostered education as a major part of their monastic life.

Their emphasis on asceticism led many Irish monks to go into voluntary exile. This "exile for the love of God" was not into isolation, however, but into missionary activity. Irish monks became fervid missionaries. Saint Columba (521–597) left Ireland in 565 as a "pilgrim for Christ" and founded an influential monastic community off the coast of Scotland on the island of Iona. From there Irish missionaries went to northern England to begin the process of converting the Angles and Saxons. Other Irish monks traveled to the European continent. New monasteries founded by the Irish became centers of learning wherever they were located.

At the same time the Irish monks were busy bringing their version of Christianity to the Anglo-Saxons of Britain, Pope Gregory the Great had set into motion an effort to convert England to Roman Christianity. His most important agent was Augustine, a monk from Rome, who arrived in England in 597. England at that time had a number of Germanic kingdoms. Augustine went first to Kent, where he converted King Ethelbert; most of the king's subjects then followed suit. Pope Gregory's conversion techniques emphasized persuasion rather than force, and as seen in this excerpt from one of his letters, he was willing to assimilate old pagan practices in order to coax the pagans into the new faith:

> We wish you [Abbot Mellitus] to inform him [Augustine] that we have been giving careful thought to the affairs of the English, and have come to the conclusion that the temples of the idols among that people should on no account be destroyed. The idols are to be destroyed, but the temples themselves are to be aspersed with holy water, altars set up in them, and relics deposited there. For if these temples are well-built, they must be purified from the worship of demons and dedicated to the service of the true God.[5]

Freed of their pagan past, temples had become churches, as one Christian commentator noted with joy: "The dwelling place of demons has become a house of God. The saving light has come to shine, where shadows covered all. Where sacrifices once took place and idols

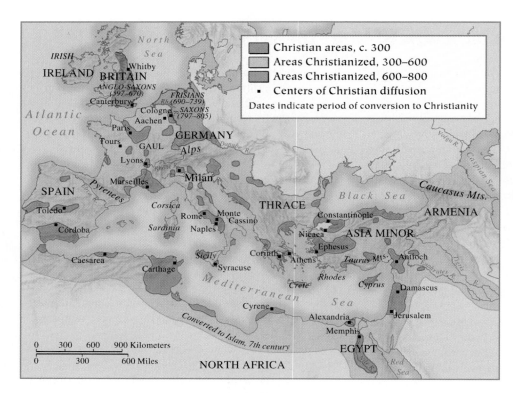

MAP 7.3 **The Spread of Christianity, 400–800.** The Christian church had penetrated much of the Roman Empire by the end of the fifth century. It emerged as a major base of power after the fall of the empire, and it pushed its influence into new areas through the activities of missionaries. ❓ What aspects of geography help explain the relatively late conversions of the Anglo-Saxons in Britain and the Frisians and Saxons east of the Rhine River? 🔎 **View an animated version of this map or related maps at** http:// thomsonedu.com/history/spielvogel

stood, angelic choirs now dance. Where God was angered once, now God is made content."[6] Likewise, old pagan feasts were given new names and incorporated into the Christian calendar. The Christian feast of Christmas, for example, was held on December 25, the day of the pagan celebration of the winter solstice.

As Roman Christianity spread northward in Britain, it encountered Irish Christianity moving southward. Roman Christianity prevailed, although the English church, despite its newfound unity and loyalty to Rome, retained some Irish features. Most important was the concentration on monastic culture with special emphasis on learning and missionary work. By 700, the English church had become the best trained and most learned in western Europe.

Following the Irish example, English monks spread to the European continent to carry on the work of conversion (see Map 7.3). Most important was Boniface (c. 680–755), who undertook the conversion of pagan Germans in Frisia, Bavaria, and Saxony. By 740, Saint Boniface, the "Apostle of the Germans," had become the most famous churchman in Europe. Fourteen years later, he was killed while trying to convert the pagan Frisians. Boniface was a brilliant example of the numerous Irish and English monks whose tireless efforts made Europe the bastion of the Roman Catholic faith.

Women and Monasticism Women played an important role in the monastic missionary movement and the conversion of the Germanic kingdoms. Double monasteries, where both monks and nuns lived in separate houses but attended church services together, were found in both the English and Frankish kingdoms. The monks and nuns followed a common rule under a common head. Frequently, this leader was an **abbess** rather than an abbot. Many of these abbesses belonged to royal houses, especially in Anglo-Saxon England. In the kingdom of Northumbria, for example, Saint Hilda founded the monastery of Whitby in 657. As abbess, she was responsible for giving learning an important role in the life of the monastery; five future bishops were educated under her tutelage. For female intellectuals, monasteries offered opportunities for learning not found elsewhere in the society of their day.

Nuns of the seventh and eighth centuries also played an important role in the spread of Christianity. The great English missionary Boniface relied on nuns in England for books and money. He also asked the abbess of Wimborne to send groups of nuns to establish convents in newly converted German lands. A nun named Leoba established the first convent in Germany at Bischofsheim.

The Path of Celibacy The monastic movement enabled some women to pursue a new path to holiness, Cloisters for both men and women offered the ideal place to practice the new Christian ideal of celibacy. This newfound emphasis on abstaining from sexual relations, especially evident in the emphasis on virginity, created a new image of the human body in late antiquity. To many Greeks and Roman, the human body had been a source of beauty, joy, and pleasure, noticeable in numerous works of art. To many Christians, the body was seen as a hindrance to a spiritual connection with God. The refusal to have sex was a victory over the desires of the flesh and thus an avenue to holiness.

In the fourth and fifth centuries, a cult of virginity also moved beyond the walls of monasteries and convents.

Throughout the Mediterranean world, groups of women got together to study the importance and benefits of celibacy. In Rome, a woman named Marcella supported a group of aristocratic women in their studies of celibacy.

Christianity and Intellectual Life

Many early Christians expressed considerable hostility toward the pagan culture of the classical world. Tertullian (c. 160–c. 225), a Christian writer from Carthage, had proclaimed: "What has Jerusalem to do with Athens, the Church with the Academy, the Christian with the heretic? . . . After Jesus Christ we have no need of speculation, after the Gospel no need of research."[7] To many early Christians, the Bible (see Chapter 6) contained all the knowledge anyone needed. Others, however, thought it was not possible to separate Christian thought from classical traditions and education and encouraged Christianity to absorb the classical heritage. As it spread in the eastern Roman world, Christianity adopted Greek as its language; the New Testament was written in Greek. Christians also turned to Greek thought for help in expressing complicated theological concepts. In many ways, then, Christianity served to preserve Greco-Roman culture.

The work of Augustine (354–430) provides one of the best examples of how Christianity used pagan culture in the service of Christianity. Augustine came to be seen as one of the Latin fathers of the Catholic church, intellectuals who wrote in Latin and profoundly influenced the development of Christian thought in the west.

Born in North Africa, Augustine was reared by his mother, an ardent Christian. He eventually became a professor of rhetoric at Milan in 384. After experiencing a profound and moving religious experience, he gave up his teaching position and went back to North Africa, where he became bishop of Hippo from 396 until his death in 430.

Augustine's most famous work, *The City of God*, was a profound expression of a Christian philosophy of government and history. In it, he theorized on the ideal relations between two kinds of societies existing throughout time—the City of God and the City of the World. Those who loved God would be loyal to the City of God, whose ultimate location was the kingdom of heaven. Earthly society would always be uncertain because of human beings' inclination to sin. And yet the City of the World was still necessary, for it was the duty of rulers to curb the depraved instincts of sinful humans and maintain the peace necessary for Christians to live in the world. Hence Augustine posited that secular government and authority were necessary for the pursuit of the true Christian life on earth; in doing so, he provided a justification for secular political authority that would play an important role in medieval thought.

Another important intellectual of the early church was Jerome (345–420), who pursued literary studies in Rome and became a master of Latin prose. Jerome had mixed feelings about his love for classical studies, however, and like Augustine, he experienced a spiritual conversion after which he tried to dedicate himself more fully to Jesus. Ultimately, Jerome found a compromise by purifying the literature of the pagan world and then using it to further the Christian faith. Jerome was a great scholar, and his extensive knowledge of both Hebrew and Greek enabled him to translate the Old and New Testaments into Latin. In the process, he created the so-called Latin Vulgate, or common text, of the Scriptures that became the standard edition for the Catholic church in the Middle Ages.

Although the Christian church came to accept classical culture, it was not easy to do so in the world of the new German kingdoms. Nevertheless, some Christian scholars managed to keep learning alive. Boethius and Cassiodorus, two important Christian intellectuals, both served as officials of the Ostrogothic king Theodoric. Boethius (c. 480–524) received the traditional education typical of the Roman aristocracy. His most famous work was written in prison, where he was kept for a year by Theodoric on a charge of treason before being executed. This work, *On the Consolation of Philosophy*, is a dialogue between Boethius and philosophy personified as a woman. Philosophy leads Boethius to a clear understanding of true happiness and the highest good, which she equates with God. These are not achieved by outward conditions, since the person who lives virtuously finds happiness within.

Cassiodorus (c. 490–c. 585) also came from an aristocratic Roman family and served as an official of the Ostrogothic king Theodoric. The conflicts that erupted after the death of Theodoric led Cassiodorus to withdraw from public life and retire to his landed estates in southern Italy, where he wrote his final work, *Divine and Human Readings*. This was a compendium of the literature of both Christian and pagan antiquity. Cassiodorus accepted the advice of earlier Christian intellectuals to make use of classical works while treasuring the Scriptures above all else.

Cassiodorus continued the tradition of late antiquity of classifying knowledge according to certain subjects. In assembling his compendium of authors, he followed the works of late ancient authors in placing all secular knowledge into the categories of the seven **liberal arts**, which were divided into two major groups: the *trivium*, consisting of grammar, rhetoric, and dialectic or logic, and the *quadrivium*, consisting of the mathematical subjects of arithmetic, geometry, astronomy, and music. The seven liberal arts would become the cornerstone of education until the seventeenth century.

The Byzantine Empire

As noted earlier, in the fourth century, the western and eastern parts of the Roman Empire began to go their separate ways. As the Germans moved into the western part

Justinian and His Court. Ravenna remained the center of the Byzantine presence in Italy for two hundred years. The Church of San Vitale at Ravenna contains some of the finest examples of sixth-century Byzantine mosaics (artworks created by cementing small colored pieces of glass or rock to a wall or floor). This mosaic depicts the Byzantine emperor Justinian and his court dressed in their elaborate robes. Justinian is seen with soldiers, his staff, and members of the clergy.

Scala/Art Resource, NY (S. Vitale, Ravenna, Italy)

of the empire and established various kingdoms over the course of the next hundred years, the Roman Empire in the east, centered on Constantinople, solidified and prospered.

The Reign of Justinian (527–565)

When he became emperor of the eastern Roman Empire, Justinian was determined to reestablish the Roman Empire in the entire Mediterranean world. His army, commanded by Belisarius, probably the best general of the late Roman world, sailed to North Africa and quickly destroyed the Vandals in two major battles. From North Africa, Belisarius led his forces onto the Italian peninsula and defeated the Ostrogoths. By 552, Justinian appeared to have achieved his goal. His reconstituted empire included Italy, part of Spain, North Africa, Asia Minor, Palestine, and Syria (see Map 7.4). But his success proved fleeting. Only three years after Justinian's death, the Lombards conquered much of Italy. Although the eastern empire maintained the fiction of Italy as a province, its forces were limited to southern and central Italy, Sicily, and some coastal areas.

Justinian's most important contribution was his codification of Roman law. The eastern empire had inherited a vast quantity of legal materials connected to the development of Roman law, which Justinian wished to simplify. The result was the *Corpus Iuris Civilis* (Body of Civil Law), a codification of Roman law that remained in force in the eastern Roman Empire until its end in 1453. And because it was written in Latin (it was in fact the last product of eastern Roman culture to be written in Latin, which was soon replaced by Greek), it was also eventually used in the west and ultimately became the basis of the legal system of all of continental Europe.

Life in Constantinople: The Emperor's Building Program After riots destroyed much of Constantinople in 532, Emperor Justinian rebuilt the city and gave it the appearance it would keep for almost a thousand years. With a population estimated in the hundreds of thousands, Constantinople was the largest city in Europe during the Middle Ages. It viewed itself as the center of an empire and a special Christian city.

Until the twelfth century, Constantinople was Europe's greatest commercial center, the chief marketplace where western and eastern products were exchanged. Highly desired in Europe were the products of the East: silk from China, spices from Southeast Asia and India, jewelry and ivory from India (the latter used by artisans for church items), wheat and furs from southern Russia, and flax and honey from the Balkans. Many of these eastern goods were then shipped to the Mediterranean area and northern Europe. Moreover, imported raw materials were used in Constantinople for local industries. During Justinian's reign, two Christian monks smuggled silkworms from China to begin a Byzantine silk industry. The state controlled the production of silk cloth, and the workshops themselves were housed in Constantinople's royal palace complex. European demand for silk cloth made it the city's most lucrative product.

Much of Constantinople's appearance in the Middle Ages was due to Justinian's program of rebuilding in the sixth century. The city was dominated by an immense palace complex, hundreds of churches, and a huge arena known as the Hippodrome. No residential district was particularly fashionable; palaces, tenements, and slums ranged alongside one another. Justinian added many new buildings. His public works projects included roads, bridges, walls, public baths, law courts, and colossal underground reservoirs to hold the city's water supply. He also built hospitals, schools, monasteries, and churches. Churches were his special passion, and in Constantinople alone he built or rebuilt thirty-four of them. His greatest achievement was the famous Hagia Sophia, the Church of the Holy Wisdom, completed in 537. The center of Hagia Sophia consisted of four large piers crowned by

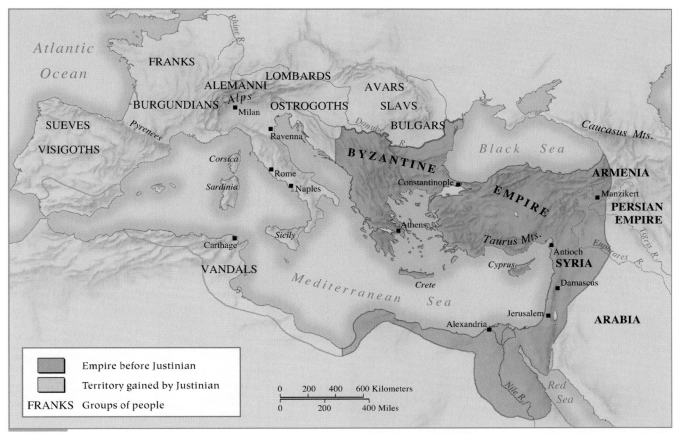

MAP 7.4 **The Byzantine Empire in the Time of Justinian.** The Byzantine emperor Justinian briefly restored much of the Mediterranean portion of the old Roman Empire. His general Belisarius quickly conquered the Vandals in North Africa but wrested Italy from the Ostrogoths only after a long and devastating struggle. **?** Examine Map 6.1. What former Roman territories lay outside Justinian's control? 🌐 **View an animated version of this map or related maps at** http://thomsonedu.com/history/spielvogel

an enormous dome, which seemed to be floating in space. In part this impression was created by ringing the base of the dome with forty-two windows, which allowed an incredible play of light within the cathedral. Light served to remind the worshipers of God. As invisible light illuminates darkness, so too was it believed that invisible spirit illuminates the world.

The Hippodrome was a huge amphitheater, constructed of brick covered by marble, holding between forty and sixty thousand spectators. Although gladiator fights were held there, the main events were the chariot races; twenty-four would usually be presented in one day. The citizens of Constantinople were passionate fans of chariot racing. Successful charioteers were acclaimed as heroes and honored with public statues.

From Eastern Roman to Byzantine Empire

Justinian's accomplishments had been spectacular, but when he died, he left the eastern Roman Empire with serious problems: too much territory to protect far from Constantinople, an empty treasury, a decline in population

after a plague, and renewed threats to its frontiers. In the first half of the seventh century, the empire faced attacks from the Persians to the east and the Slavs to the north.

The most serious challenge to the eastern Roman Empire came from the rise of Islam, which unified the Arab tribes and created a powerful new force that swept through the east (see the next section, "The Rise of Islam"). The defeat of an eastern Roman army at Yarmuk in 636 meant the loss of the provinces of Syria and Palestine. The Arabs also moved into the old Persian Empire and conquered it. Arabs and eastern Roman forces now faced each other along a frontier in southern Asia Minor.

Problems arose along the northern frontier as well, especially in the Balkans, where an Asiatic people known as the Bulgars had arrived earlier in the sixth century. In 679, the Bulgars defeated the eastern Roman forces and took possession of the lower Danube valley, establishing a strong Bulgarian kingdom.

By the beginning of the eighth century, the eastern Roman Empire was greatly diminished in size. Consisting only of the eastern Balkans and Asia Minor, it was no longer a major eastern Mediterranean state. The external

Interior of Hagia Sophia. This view of the interior of the Church of the Holy Wisdom, constructed under Justinian by Anthemius of Tralles and Isidore of Milan, gives an idea of how the windows around the base of the dome produced a special play of light within the cathedral. The pulpits and plaques bearing inscriptions from the Qur'an were introduced when the Turks converted this church to a mosque in the fifteenth century.

challenges had important internal repercussions as well. By the eighth century, the eastern Roman Empire had been transformed into what historians call the Byzantine Empire, a civilization with its own unique character that would last until 1453 (Constantinople was built on the site of an older city named Byzantium—hence the term *Byzantine*).

The Byzantine Empire, c. 750

© Digital Vision/Getty Images

CHRONOLOGY The Byzantine Empire

Reign of Justinian	527–565
Justinian codifies Roman law	529–533
Reconquest of Italy by the Byzantines	535–552
Completion of Hagia Sophia	537
Arab defeat of Byzantines at Yarmuk	636
Defeat by the Bulgars; losses in the Balkans	679

The Byzantine Empire was both a Greek and a Christian state. Increasingly, Latin fell into disuse as Greek became both the common and the official language of the empire. The Byzantine Empire was also built on a faith in Jesus that was shared by almost all of its citizens. An enormous amount of artistic talent was poured into the construction of churches, church ceremonies, and church decoration. Spiritual principles deeply permeated Byzantine art.

The emperor occupied a crucial position in the Byzantine state. Portrayed as chosen by God, the emperor was crowned in sacred ceremonies, and his subjects were expected to prostrate themselves in his presence. His power was considered absolute and was limited in practice only by deposition or assassination. Because the emperor appointed the head of the church (known as the patriarch), he also exercised control over both church and state. The Byzantines believed that God had commanded their state to preserve the true Christian faith. Emperor, clergy, and state officials were all bound together in service to this ideal. It can be said that spiritual values truly held the Byzantine state together.

By 750, it was apparent that two of Rome's heirs, the Germanic kingdoms and the Byzantine Empire, were moving in different directions. Nevertheless, Byzantine influence on the Western world was significant. The images of a Roman imperial state that continued to haunt the west lived on in Byzantium. The legal system of the west owed much to Justinian's codification of Roman law. In addition, the Byzantine Empire served as a buffer state, protecting the west for a long time from incursions from the east. Although the Byzantine Empire would continue to influence the west until its demise in 1453, it went its own way. One of its bitterest enemies was the new power of Islam.

The Rise of Islam

Like the Hebrews and the Assyrians, the Arabs were a Semitic-speaking people of the Near East with a long history. In Roman times, the Arabian peninsula was dominated by Bedouin nomads who moved constantly to find water and food for themselves and their animals. Although some Arabs prospered from trading activities, especially in the north, most Arabs were poor Bedouins, whose tribes were known for their independence, their warlike qualities, and their dislike of urban-dwelling Arabs.

Although these early Arabs were polytheistic, there was a supreme God named Allah (Arabic for "God") who ruled over the other gods. Allah was symbolized by a sacred stone, and each tribe had its own stone. All tribes, however, worshiped a massive black meteorite, the Black Stone, which had been placed in a central shrine called the *Ka'ba* in the city of Mecca.

In the fifth and sixth centuries A.D., the Arabian peninsula took on new importance. As a result of political disorder in Mesopotamia and Egypt, the usual trade routes in the region began to change. A new trade route—from the Mediterranean through Mecca to Yemen and then by ship across the Arabian Sea and the Indian Ocean—became more popular, and communities in that part of the Arabian peninsula, including Mecca, began to prosper from this caravan trade. As a result, tensions arose between the Bedouins in the desert and the increasingly wealthy merchant classes in the towns. Into this intense world came Muhammad.

Muhammad

Born in Mecca to a merchant family, Muhammad (c. 570–632) was orphaned at the age of five. He grew up to become a caravan manager and eventually married a rich widow who was also his employer. In his middle years, he began to experience visions that he believed were inspired by Allah. Muhammad believed that although Allah had already revealed himself in part through Moses and Jesus—and thus through the Hebrew and Christian traditions—the final revelations were now being given to him. Out of these revelations, which were eventually written down, came the Qur'an (or Koran), which contained the guidelines by which followers of Allah were to live. Muhammad's teachings formed the basis for the religion known as Islam, which means "submission to the will of Allah." Allah was the all-powerful being who had created the universe and everything in it. Humans must subject themselves to Allah if they wished to achieve everlasting life. Those who became his followers were called Muslims, meaning "practitioners of Islam."

After receiving the revelations, Muhammad set out to convince the people of Mecca of the truth of his revelations. At first, many thought he was insane, and others feared that his attacks on the corrupt society around him would upset the established social and political order. Discouraged by the failure of the Meccans to accept his message, in 622 Muhammad and some of his closest supporters left the city and moved north to the rival city of Yathrib, later renamed Medina ("city of the Prophet"). The year of the journey to Medina, known in history as the *Hegira* ("departure"), became year 1 in the official calendar of Islam.

Muhammad, who had been invited to the town by a number of prominent residents, soon began to win support from people in Medina as well as from members of Bedouin tribes in the surrounding countryside. From these groups, he formed the first Muslim community (the **umma**). Muslims saw no separation between political and religious authority; submission to the will of Allah meant submission to his Prophet, Muhammad. Muhammad soon became both a religious and political leader. His political and military skills enabled him to put together a reliable military force, with which he returned to Mecca in 630, conquering the city and converting the

Muslims Celebrating the End of Ramadan. Ramadan is the holy month of Islam during which all Muslims must fast from dawn to sunset. Observance of Ramadan is one of the Five Pillars of Islam. Muhammad instituted the fast during his stay at Medina. It was designed to replace the single Jewish Day of Atonement. This Persian miniature depicts Muslims on horseback celebrating the end of Ramadan.

Bibliotheque Nationale, Paris/The Bridgeman Art Library

THE QUR'AN: THE PILGRIMAGE

*T*he Qur'an is the sacred book of the Muslims, comparable to the Bible in Christianity. This selection from Sura 22, titled "Pilgrimage," discusses the importance of making a pilgrimage to Mecca, one of the Five Pillars of Islam. The pilgrim's final destination was the *Ka'ba* at Mecca, containing the Black Stone.

Qur'an, Sura 22: "Pilgrimage"

Exhort all men to make the pilgrimage. They will come to you on foot and on the backs of swift camels from every distant quarter; they will come to avail themselves of many a benefit, and to pronounce on the appointed days the name of God over the cattle which He has given them for food. Eat of their flesh, and feed the poor and the unfortunate.

Then let the pilgrims tidy themselves, make their vows, and circle the Ancient House. Such is God's commandment. He that reveres the sacred rites of God shall fare better in the sight of his Lord.

The flesh of cattle is lawful for you, except for that which has been specified before. Guard yourselves against the filth of idols; and avoid the utterance of falsehoods.

Dedicate yourselves to God, and serve none besides Him. The man who serves other deities besides God is like him who falls from heaven and is snatched by the birds or carried away by the wind to some far-off region. Even such is he.

He that reveres the offerings made to God shows the piety of his heart. Your cattle are useful to you in many ways until the time of their slaughter. Then they are offered for sacrifice at the Ancient House.

For every community We have ordained a ritual, that they may pronounce the name of God over the cattle which He has given them for food. Your God is one God; to Him surrender yourselves. Give good news to the humble, whose hearts are filled with awe at the mention of God; who endure adversity with fortitude, attend to their prayers, and give in alms from what We gave them.

We have made the camels a part of God's rites. They are of much use to you. Pronounce over them the name of God as you draw them up in line and slaughter them; and when they have fallen to the ground eat of their flesh and feed the uncomplaining beggar and the demanding supplicant. Thus have We subjected them to your service, so that you may give thanks.

Their flesh and blood does not reach God; it is your piety that reaches Him. Thus has He subjected them to your service, so that you may give glory to God for guiding you.

Give good news to the righteous. God will ward off evil from true believers. God does not love the treacherous and the thankless.

What is the key purpose of undertaking a pilgrimage to Mecca? What is the historical importance of the sacred stone?

townspeople to the new faith. From Mecca, Muhammad's ideas spread quickly across the Arabian peninsula and within a relatively short time had resulted in both the religious and political unification of Arab society.

The Teachings of Islam

At the heart of Islam was the Qur'an, with the basic message that there is no God but Allah and Muhammad is his Prophet. Essentially, the Qur'an contains Muhammad's revelations of a heavenly book written down by secretaries. Consisting of 114 *suras* (chapters), the Qur'an is the sacred book of Islam, which recorded the beliefs of the Muslims and served as their code of ethics and law.

Islam was a direct and simple faith, emphasizing the need to obey the will of Allah. This meant following a basic ethical code consisting of the **Five Pillars of Islam:** belief in Allah and Muhammad as his Prophet; standard prayer five times a day and public prayer on Friday at midday to worship Allah; observance of the holy month of **Ramadan** (the ninth month on the Muslim calendar) with fasting from dawn to sunset; making a pilgrimage (known as the *hajj*), if possible, to Mecca at least once in one's lifetime (see the box above); and giving alms to the poor and unfortunate. The faithful who observed the law were guaranteed a place in an eternal paradise.

Islam was not just a set of religious beliefs but a way of life as well. After the death of Muhammad, Muslim scholars drew up a law code, called the *Shari'a,* to provide believers with a set of prescriptions to regulate their daily lives. Much of the *Shari'a* was drawn from existing legal regulations or from the *Hadith,* a collection of the sayings of Muhammad that was used to supplement the revelations contained in the Qur'an. Believers were subject to strict guidelines for their behavior. In addition to the Five Pillars, Muslims were forbidden to gamble, to eat pork, to drink alcoholic beverages, and to engage in dishonest behavior. Sexual practices were also strictly regulated. Marriages were to be arranged by parents, and contact between unmarried men and women was discouraged. In accordance with Bedouin custom, males were permitted to have more than one wife, but Muhammad attempted to limit the practice by restricting the number of wives to four.

The Spread of Islam

The death of Muhammad in 632 presented his followers with a dilemma. Muhammad had never named a successor, and although he had several daughters, he left no sons. In a male-oriented society, who would lead the community of the faithful? Shortly after Muhammad's death, some of his closest followers selected Abu Bakr, a wealthy merchant

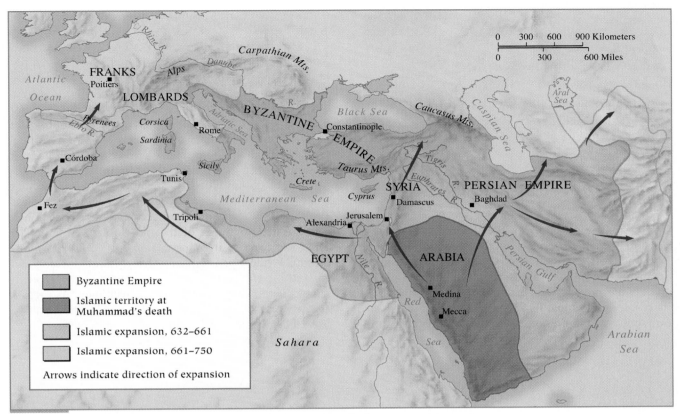

MAP 7.5 The Spread of Islam. Muhammad, the prophet of Islam, engaged in warfare against neighboring tribes. Militaristic expansion continued with great zeal under the Prophet's successors. Islamic rule spread rapidly in the decades after Muhammad's death, stopped finally by the Byzantine Empire and the Franks. ❓ Why was the continuance of the Byzantine Empire a key factor in stopping the spread of Islam into Europe? 🐾 **View an animated version of this map or related maps at** http://thomsonedu.com/history/spielvogel

who was Muhammad's father-in-law, as **caliph**, or temporal leader, of the Islamic community.

Muhammad and the early caliphs who succeeded him took up the Arabic tribal custom of the *razzia* or raid in the struggle against their enemies. Some people refer to this activity as *jihad,* which they misleadingly interpret as "holy war." *Jihad* actually means "striving in the way of the Lord" to achieve personal betterment, which can include a fair, defensive fight to preserve one's life and one's faith. Arab conquests were not carried out to convert others, since conversion to Islam was purely voluntary. Conquered people who did not convert were required only to submit to Muslim rule and pay taxes.

The Byzantines and the Persians were the first to feel the strength of the newly united Arabs. At Yarmuk in 636, the Muslims defeated the Byzantine army, and by 640 they had taken possession of the province of Syria (see Map 7.5). To the east, the Arabs went on to conquer the Persian Empire by 650. In the meantime, by 642, Egypt and other areas of northern Africa had been added to the new Muslim empire. Led by a series of brilliant generals, the Arabs had put together a large and highly motivated army

whose valor was enhanced by the belief that Muslim warriors were guaranteed a place in paradise if they died in battle.

Early caliphs, ruling from Medina, organized their newly conquered territories into taxpaying provinces. By the mid-seventh century, problems arose again over the succession to the Prophet until Ali, Muhammad's son-in-law, was assassinated and the general Muawiya, the governor of Syria and one of Ali's chief rivals, became caliph in 661. He was known for one outstanding virtue: he used force only when necessary. As he said, "I never use my sword when my whip will do, nor my whip when my tongue will do."[8] Muawiya moved quickly to make the caliphate hereditary in his own family, thus establishing the Umayyad dynasty. As one of its first actions, the Umayyad dynasty moved the capital of the Muslim empire from Medina to Damascus in Syria. This internal dissension over the caliphate created a split in Islam between the Shi'ites, or those who accepted only the descendants of Ali, Muhammad's son-in-law, as the true rulers, and the Sunnites, who claimed that the descendants of the Umayyads were the true caliphs. This seventh-century split in Islam has lasted to the present day.

Birth of Muhammad	c. 570
Muhammad's flight from Mecca (*Hegira*)	622
Death of Muhammad	632
Defeat of Byzantines at Yarmuk	636
Seizure of Byzantine provinces of Syria and Egypt	640–642
Defeat of Persians	650
Invasion of Spain	c. 710

Internal dissension, however, did not stop the expansion of Islam. After sweeping across North Africa, the Muslims crossed the Strait of Gibraltar and moved into Spain around 710. The Visigothic kingdom collapsed, and by 725, most of Spain had become a Muslim state with its center at Córdoba. In 732, a Muslim army, making a foray into southern France, was defeated at the Battle of Tours near Poitiers. Muslim expansion in Europe came to a halt.

Meanwhile, in 717, another Muslim force had launched a naval attack on Constantinople with the hope of destroying the Byzantine Empire. In the spring of 718, the Byzantines destroyed the Muslim fleet and saved the Byzantine Empire and indirectly Christian Europe, because the fall of Constantinople would no doubt have opened the door to Muslim invasion of eastern Europe. The Byzantine Empire and Islam now established an uneasy frontier in southern Asia Minor.

The Arab advance had finally come to an end, but not before the southern and eastern Mediterranean parts of the old Roman Empire had been conquered. Islam had become heir to much of the old Roman Empire. The Umayyad dynasty at Damascus now ruled an enormous empire. While expansion had conveyed untold wealth and new ethnic groups into the fold of Islam, it also brought contact with Byzantine and Persian civilization. As a result, the new Arab empire would be influenced by Greek culture as well as the older civilizations of the ancient Near East.

TIMELINE

	250	350	450	550	650	750

Roman Empire — Diocletian and Constantine · Division of the empire · Odoacer deposes Romulus Augustulus

Europe — Germanic kingdoms · Benedictine order established · Lombards begin conquest of Italy

Byzantine Empire — Reign of Justinian · Completion of Hagia Sophia · Arab defeat of Byzantines at Yarmuk · Byzantine losses in the Balkans

Arab Empire — Life of Muhammad · Muhammad's flight to Medina · Muslim entry into Spain · Defeat of Muslims near Poitiers

The period from the mid-third century to the mid-eighth century was both chaotic and creative. During late antiquity, the Roman world of the Mediterranean was gradually transformed. Three new entities fell heir to Roman civilization: the Germanic kingdoms of western Europe, the Byzantine Empire, and Islam. In the west, Roman elements combined with German and Celtic influences; in the east, Greek and eastern elements of late antiquity were of more consequence. Although the Germanic kingdoms of the west and the Byzantine civilization of the east came to share a common bond in Christianity, the faith proved incapable of keeping them in harmony politically, and the two civilizations continued to move apart. But Christianity remained a dominant influence in both civilizations and in the west was especially important as a civilizing agent that brought pagan peoples into the new European civilization that was slowly being born. The rise of Islam, Rome's third heir, resulted in the loss of the southern and eastern Mediterranean portions of the old Roman Empire to a religious power that was neither Roman nor Christian. The new Islamic empire forced Europe back on itself, and slowly there emerged a new culture that became the heart of what we know as Western civilization.

NOTES

1. "The Creed of Nicaea," in H. Bettenson, ed., *Documents of the Christian Church* (London, 1963), p. 35.
2. E. F. Henderson, *Select Historical Documents of the Middle Ages* (London, 1892), p. 181.
3. N. F. Cantor, ed., *The Medieval World, 300–1300* (New York, 1963), p. 104.
4. Ibid. p. 103.
5. Bede, *A History of the English Church and People*, trans. L. Sherley-Price (Harmondsworth, England, 1968), pp. 86–87.
6. Quoted in P. Brown, *The Rise of Western Christendom: Triumph and Adversity, A.D. 200–1000* (Oxford, 1997), p. 98.
7. Tertullian, "The Prescriptions Against the Heretics," in *The Library of Christian Classics*, vol. 5, *Early Latin Theology*, ed. and trans. S. L. Greenslade (Philadelphia, 1956), p. 36.
8. Quoted in A. Goldschmidt Jr., *A Concise History of the Middle East*, 4th ed. (Boulder, Colo., 1991), p. 56.

SUGGESTIONS FOR FURTHER READING

For good introductions to late antiquity, see **P. Brown**, ***The World of Late Antiquity, A.D. 150–750*** (New York, 1989); **J. Moorhead**, ***The Roman Empire Divided, 400–700*** (London, 2001); **A. Cameron**, ***The Mediterranean World in Late Antiquity, A.D. 395–600*** (London, 1993); and **R. Collins**, ***Early Medieval Europe, 300–1000*** (New York, 1991). There is an excellent collection of essays and encyclopedic entries in **G. W. Bowersock**, **P. Brown**, and **O. Grabar**, ***Late Antiquity: A Guide to the Postclassical World*** (Cambridge, Mass., 1999).

On the Late Roman Empire, see **A. Cameron**, ***The Later Roman Empire*** (Cambridge, Mass., 1993). On the fourth century, see **M. Grant**, ***Constantine the Great: The Man and His Times*** (New York, 1993), and **T. D. Barnes**, ***The New Empire of Diocletian and Constantine*** (Cambridge, Mass., 1982). Studies analyzing the aristocratic circles, the barbarian invasions, and the military problem include **E. A. Thompson**, ***Romans and Barbarians*** (Madison, Wis., 1982); **A. Ferrill**, ***The Fall of the Roman Empire: The Military Explanation*** (London, 1986); and **P. Heather**, ***The Fall of the Roman Empire: A New History of Rome and the Barbarians*** (New York, 2006).

For surveys of the German tribes and their migrations, see **T. S. Burns**, ***A History of the Ostrogoths*** (Bloomington, Ind., 1984); **P. Heather**, ***Goths and Romans*** (Oxford, 1991); **E. James**, ***The Franks*** (Oxford, 1988); and **I. N. Wood**, ***Merovingian Kingdoms*** (London, 1994). On the relationship between the Romans and the Germans, see **T. S. Burns**, ***Rome and the Barbarians, 100 B.C.–A.D 400*** (Baltimore, 2003).

For a superb introduction to early Christianity, see **P. Brown**, ***The Rise of Western Christendom: Triumph and Adversity, A.D. 200–1000***, 2d ed. (Oxford, 2002). On Saints Augustine and Jerome, see **H. Chadwick**, ***Augustine*** (Oxford, 1986), and **J.N.D. Kelly**, ***Saint Jerome*** (London, 1975). For a good account of early monasticism, see **C. H. Lawrence**, ***Medieval Monasticism***, 2d ed. (London, 1989). For women in monastic life, see **S. F. Wemple**, ***Women in Frankish Society: Marriage and the Cloister, 500–900*** (Philadelphia, 1981). On women in general, see **G. Clark**, ***Women in Late Antiquity: Pagan and Christian Life-Styles*** (Oxford, 1993).

A brief survey of the development of the papacy can be found in **G. Barraclough**, ***The Medieval Papacy*** (New York, 1968). **J. Richards**, ***The Popes and the Papacy in the Early Middle Ages, 476–752*** (Boston, 1979), is a more detailed study of the early papacy. On Pope Gregory the Great, see **C. Straw**, ***Gregory the Great: Perfection in Imperfection*** (Berkeley, Calif., 1988). On Irish monasticism, see **L. M. Bitel**, ***Isle of the Saints: Monastic Settlement and Christian Community in Early Ireland*** (Ithaca, N.Y., 1990).

Brief but good introductions to Byzantine history can be found in **J. Haldon**, ***Byzantium: A History*** (Charleston, S.C., 2000), and **W. Treadgold**, ***A Concise History of Byzantium*** (London, 2001). For a comprehensive survey of the Byzantine Empire, see **W. Treadgold**, ***A History of the Byzantine State and Society*** (Stanford, Calif., 1997). See also **C. Mango, ed.**, ***The Oxford History of Byzantium*** (Oxford, 2002). On Justinian, see **J. Moorhead**, ***Justinian*** (London, 1995), and **J.A.S. Evans**, ***The Age of Justinian*** (New York, 1996). The role of the Christian church is discussed in **J. Hussey**, ***The Orthodox Church in the Byzantine Empire*** (Oxford, 1986).

Good brief surveys of the Islamic Middle East include **A. Goldschmidt Jr.**, ***A Concise History of the Middle East***, 7th ed. (Boulder, Colo., 2001), and **S. N. Fisher** and **W. Ochsenwald**, ***The Middle East: A History*** (New York, 2003). On the rise of Islam, see **F. E. Peters**, ***Muhammad and the Origins of Islam*** (Albany, N.Y., 1994); **M. Lings**, ***Muhammad: His Life Based on the Earliest Sources***

(New York, 1983); and **F. Donner**, *The Early Islamic Conquests* (Princeton, N.J., 1980).

Thomson NOW! Enter *ThomsonNOW* using the access card that is available for *Western Civilization: A Brief History.* *ThomsonNOW* will help you understand this chapter with lesson plans generated for your needs. In addition, you can read the following documents, and many more, online:

Saint Paul's First Epistle to the Corinthians
Pliny the Younger, Letter 97
Plotinus, excerpts from the first book of the Six Enneads

EUROPEAN CIVILIZATION IN THE EARLY MIDDLE AGES, 750–1000

CHAPTER OUTLINE AND FOCUS QUESTIONS

The World of the Carolingians

▣ How did the political, intellectual, and daily life in the Carolingian Empire represent a fusion of Gallo-Roman, Germanic, and Christian practices?

Disintegration of the Carolingian Empire

▣ What impact did the Vikings have on the history and culture of medieval Europe?

The Emerging World of Lords and Vassals

▣ What was fief-holding, and how was it related to manorialism?

The Zenith of Byzantine Civilization

▣ What were the chief developments in the Byzantine Empire between 750 and 1000?

The Slavic Peoples of Central and Eastern Europe

▣ What patterns of development occurred in central and eastern Europe as a result of the Slavic peoples?

The World of Islam

▣ What were the chief developments in the Islamic world between 750 and 1000?

CRITICAL THINKING

▣ In what ways can it be said the Islamic civilization was superior to the civilization of western Europe in the ninth and tenth centuries?

A medieval French manuscript illustration of the coronation of Charlemagne by Pope Leo III

Scala/Art Resource, NY (Bibliothèque de l'Arsenal, Paris)

𝓘N 800, CHARLEMAGNE, the king of the Franks, journeyed to Rome to help Pope Leo III, who was barely clinging to power in the face of rebellious Romans. On Christmas Day, Charlemagne and his family, attended by Romans, Franks, and even visitors from the Byzantine Empire, crowded into Saint Peter's Basilica to hear Mass. Quite unexpectedly, at least according to a Frankish writer, "as the king rose from praying before the tomb of the blessed apostle Peter, Pope Leo placed a golden crown on his head." In keeping with ancient tradition, the people in the church shouted, "Long life and victory to Charles Augustus, crowned by God the great and pacific Emperor of the Romans." Seemingly, the Roman Empire in the West had been reborn, and Charles had become the first western emperor since 476. But this "Roman emperor" was actually a German king, and he had been crowned by the head of the western Christian church. In truth, the coronation of Charlemagne was a sign not of the rebirth of the Roman Empire but of the emergence of a new European civilization.

By the year of Charlemagne's coronation, the contours of this new European civilization were beginning to emerge in western Europe. Increasingly, Europe would become the focus and center of Western civilization. Building on a fusion of Germanic, Greco-Roman, and Christian elements, the medieval European world first became visible in the Carolingian Empire of Charlemagne. The agrarian foundations of the eighth and ninth centuries proved inadequate to maintain a large monarchical system, however, and a new political and military order based on the decentralization of political power subsequently evolved to become an integral part of the political world of the Middle Ages.

European civilization began on a shaky and uncertain foundation, however. In the ninth century, Vikings, Magyars, and Muslims posed threats that could easily have stifled the new society. But European civilization absorbed the challenges. The Vikings and Magyars were assimilated, and recovery slowly began. By 1000, European civilization was ready to embark on a period of dazzling vitality and expansion.♦

The World of the Carolingians

By the eighth century, the Merovingian dynasty was losing its control of the Frankish lands. Charles Martel, the Carolingian mayor of the palace of Austrasia, became the virtual ruler of these territories. When Charles died in 741, Pepin, his son, deposed the Merovingians and assumed the kingship of the Frankish state, an action approved by the pope. In imitation of an Old Testament practice, Pepin (751–768) was crowned and formally anointed with holy oil by a representative of the pope. The anointing not only symbolized that the king had been entrusted with a sacred office but also provided yet another example of the fusion between Germanic institutions and Christian practices in the Early Middle Ages.

Charlemagne and the Carolingian Empire (768–814)

Pepin was succeeded on the throne of the Frankish kingdom by his son, a dynamic and powerful ruler known to history as Charles the Great, or Charlemagne (*Carolus magnus* in Latin—hence our word *Carolingian*). Charlemagne was a determined and decisive man, intelligent and inquisitive. A fierce warrior, he was also a wise patron of learning and a resolute statesman (see the box on p. 139). He greatly expanded the territory of the Carolingian Empire during his lengthy rule (see Map 8.1).

Expansion of the Carolingian Empire   In the tradition of the Germanic kings, Charlemagne was a determined warrior who undertook fifty-four military campaigns. Even though the Frankish army was relatively small—only eight thousand men gathered each spring for campaigning—supplying it and transporting it to distant areas could still present serious problems. The Frankish army consisted mostly of infantry, with some cavalry armed with swords and spears.

Charlemagne's campaigns took him to many parts of Europe. In 773, Charlemagne led his army into Italy, crushed the Lombards, and took control of the Lombard state. Although his son was crowned king of Italy, Charlemagne was its real ruler. Four years after his invasion of Italy, Charlemagne moved his forces into northern Spain. This campaign proved disappointing: not only did the Basques harass his army as it crossed the Pyrenees on the way home, but they also ambushed and annihilated his rear guard.

Charlemagne was considerably more successful with his eastern campaigns into Germany, especially against the Saxons living between the Elbe River and the North Sea. As Einhard, Charlemagne's biographer, recounted it:

> No war ever undertaken by the Frank nation was carried on with such persistence and bitterness, or cost so much labor, because the Saxons, like almost all the tribes of Germany, were a fierce people, given to the worship of devils, and hostile to our religion, and did not consider it dishonorable to transgress and violate all law, human and divine.[1]

Charlemagne's insistence that the Saxons convert to Christianity simply fueled their resistance. Not until 804, after eighteen campaigns, was Saxony finally pacified and added to the Carolingian domain.

In southeastern Germany, Charlemagne invaded the land of the Bavarians in 787 and brought them into his empire by the following year, an expansion that then brought him into contact with the southern Slavs and the Avars. The latter disappeared from history after their utter devastation at the hands of Charlemagne's army. Now at its height, Charlemagne's empire covered much of western and central Europe; not until the time of Napoleon in the nineteenth century would an empire of this size be seen again in Europe.

Governing the Empire   Charlemagne continued the efforts of his father in organizing the Carolingian kingdom. Because there was no system of public taxation, Charlemagne was dependent on the royal estates for the resources he needed to govern his empire. Food and goods derived from these lands provided support for the king, his household staff, and officials. To keep the nobles in his service, Charlemagne granted part of the royal lands as lifetime holdings to nobles who assisted him.

Besides the household staff, the administration of the empire was accomplished by counts, who were the king's chief representatives in local areas. Counts were members of the nobility who had already existed under the Merovingians. They had come to control public services in their own lands and thus acted as judges, military leaders, and agents of the king. Gradually, as the rule of the Merovingian kings weakened, many counts had simply attached the royal lands and services performed on behalf of the king to their own family possessions.

In an effort to gain greater control over his kingdom, Charlemagne attempted to limit the power of the counts. They were required to serve outside their own family

THE ACHIEVEMENTS OF CHARLEMAGNE

*E*inhard, the biographer of Charlemagne, was born in the valley of the Main River in Germany about 775. Raised and educated in the monastery of Fulda, an important center of learning, he arrived at the court of Charlemagne in 791 or 792. Although he did not achieve high office under Charlemagne, he served as private secretary to Louis the Pious, Charlemagne's son and successor. Einhard's *Life of Charlemagne* was modeled on Suetonius's *Lives of the Caesars*, especially his biography of Augustus. Einhard's work, written between 817 and 830, was the "first medieval biography of a lay figure." In this selection, he discusses some of Charlemagne's accomplishments.

Einhard, *Life of Charlemagne*

Such are the wars, most skillfully planned and successfully fought, which this most powerful king waged during the forty-seven years of his reign. He so largely increased the Frank kingdom, which was already great and strong when he received it at his father's hands, that more than double its former territory was added to it.... He subdued all the wild and barbarous tribes dwelling in Germany between the Rhine and the Vistula, the Ocean and the Danube, all of which speak very much the same language, but differ widely from one another in customs and dress....

He added to the glory of his reign by gaining the good will of several kings and nations.... The Emperors of Constantinople [the Byzantine emperors] sought friendship and alliance with Charles by several embassies; and even when the Greeks [the Byzantines] suspected him of designing to take the empire from them, because of his assumption of the title Emperor, they made a close alliance with him, that he might have no cause of offense. In fact, the power of the Franks was always viewed with a jealous eye, whence the Greek proverb, "Have the Frank for your friend, but not for your neighbor."

This King, who showed himself so great in extending his empire and subduing foreign nations, and was constantly occupied with plans to that end, undertook also very many works calculated to adorn and benefit his kingdom, and brought several of them to completion. Among these, the most deserving of mention are the basilica of the Holy Mother of God at Aix-la-Chapelle, built in the most admirable manner, and a bridge over the Rhine River at Mainz, half a mile long, the breadth of the river at this point.... Above all, sacred buildings were the object of his care throughout his whole kingdom; and whenever he found them falling to ruin from age, he commanded the priests and fathers who had charge of them to repair them, and made sure by commissioners that his instructions were obeyed.... Thus did Charles defend and increase as well as beautify his kingdom....

He cherished with the greatest fervor and devotion the principles of the Christian religion, which had been instilled into him from infancy. Hence it was that he built the beautiful church at Aix-la-Chapelle, which he adorned with gold and silver and lamps, and with rails and doors of solid brass. He had the columns and marbles for this structure brought from Rome and Ravenna, for he could not find such as were suitable elsewhere. He was a constant worshiper at this church as long as his health permitted, going morning and evening, even after nightfall, besides attending mass....

He was very forward in caring for the poor, so much so that he not only made a point of giving in his own country and his own kingdom, but when he discovered that there were Christians living in poverty in Syria, Egypt, and Africa, at Jerusalem, Alexandria, and Carthage, he had compassion on their wants, and used to send money over the seas to them.... He sent great and countless gifts to the popes, and throughout his whole reign the wish that he had nearest at heart was to reestablish the ancient authority of the city of Rome under his care and by his influence, and to defend and protect the Church of St. Peter, and to beautify and enrich it out of his own store above all other churches.

How long did Einhard know Charlemagne? Does this excerpt reflect close, personal knowledge of the man, his court, and his works or hearsay and legend?

lands and were moved about periodically rather than being permitted to remain in a county for life. By making the offices appointive, Charlemagne tried to prevent the counts' children from automatically inheriting their offices. Moreover, as another check on the counts, Charlemagne instituted the *missi dominici* ("messengers of the lord king"), a lay lord and a church official who were sent out to local districts to ensure that the counts were executing the king's wishes.

The Carolingian system was glaringly inefficient. Great distances had to be covered on horseback, making it impossible for Charlemagne and his household staff to exercise much supervision over local affairs. What held the system together was personal loyalty to the king—who was strong enough to ensure loyalty by force when necessary.

Charlemagne also realized that the Catholic church could provide valuable assistance in governing his kingdom. By the end of the seventh century, the system of ecclesiastical government within the Christian church that had been created in the Late Roman Empire had largely disintegrated. Many church offices were not filled or were held by grossly unqualified relatives of the royal family. Both Pepin and his son Charlemagne took up the cause of church reform by creating new bishoprics and archbishoprics, restoring old ones, and seeing to it that the clergy accepted the orders of their superiors and executed their duties.

Charlemagne as Emperor As Charlemagne's power grew, so did his prestige as the most powerful Christian ruler; one monk even wrote of his empire as the "kingdom of Europe."

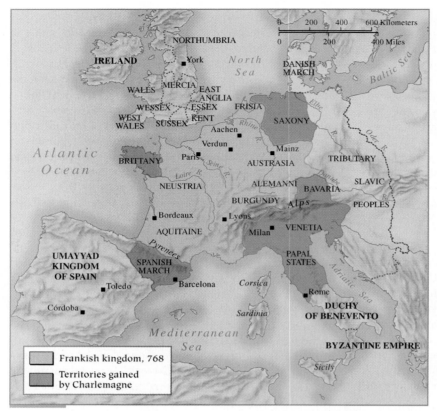

MAP 8.1 **The Carolingian Empire.** Charlemagne inherited the Carolingian Empire from his father, Pepin. He expanded his territories in several directions, creating an empire that would not be rivaled in size until the conquests of Napoleon in the early nineteenth century. ❓ How might Charlemagne's holdings in northern Italy have influenced his relationship with the pope? 🔊 **View an animated version of this map or related maps at** http://thomsonedu.com/history/spielvogel

In 800, Charlemagne acquired a new title—emperor of the Romans—largely as a result of the ever-closer relationship between the papacy and the Frankish monarchs.

Already during the reign of Pepin, an alliance emerged between the kingdom of the Franks and the papacy. The popes welcomed this support, and in the course of the second half of the eighth century, they increasingly severed their ties with the Byzantine Empire and drew closer to the Frankish kingdom. Charlemagne encouraged this development. In 799, after a rebellion against his authority, Pope Leo III (795–816) managed to escape from Rome and flee to safety at Charlemagne's court. Charlemagne offered assistance, and when he went to Rome in November 800 to settle affairs, he was received by the pope like an emperor. On Christmas Day in 800, Pope Leo placed a crown on Charlemagne's head and declared him emperor of the Romans.

The significance of this imperial coronation has been much debated. Charlemagne's biographer Einhard claimed that Charlemagne "at first had such an aversion that he declared that he would not have set foot in the Church the day that it was conferred, although it was a great feast-day, if he could have foreseen the design of the Pope."[2] But Charlemagne also perceived the usefulness of the imperial title; after all, he was now on a level of equality with the Byzantine emperor. Moreover, the papacy now had a defender of great stature, although later popes in the Middle Ages would become involved in fierce struggles with emperors over who possessed the higher power.

In any case, Charlemagne's coronation as Roman emperor demonstrated the strength, even after three hundred years, of the concept of an enduring Roman Empire. More important, it symbolized the fusion of the Roman, Christian, and Germanic elements that constituted the foundation of European civilization. A Germanic king had been crowned emperor of the Romans by the spiritual leader of western Christendom. A new civilization had emerged.

The Carolingian Intellectual Renewal

Charlemagne had a strong desire to revive learning in his kingdom, an attitude that stemmed from his own intellectual curiosity as well as the need to provide educated clergy for the church and literate officials for the government. His efforts led to a revival of learning and culture that some historians have labeled the Carolingian Renaissance, or "rebirth" of learning.

For the most part, the revival of classical studies and the efforts to preserve Latin culture took place in the monasteries, many of which had been established by the Irish and English missionaries of the seventh and eighth centuries. By the ninth century, the work required of Benedictine monks was the copying of manuscripts. Monasteries established *scriptoria*, or writing rooms, where monks copied not only the works of early Christianity, such as the Bible, but also the works of Latin classical authors. The production of manuscripts in Carolingian monastic *scriptoria* was a crucial factor in the preservation of the ancient legacy. About eight thousand manuscripts survive from Carolingian times. Virtually 90 percent of the ancient Roman works that we have today exist because they were copied by Carolingian monks.

Charlemagne personally promoted learning by establishing a palace school and encouraging scholars from all over Europe to come to the Carolingian court. The best known of these scholars was Alcuin from the famous school at York, founded as part of a great revival of learning in the Anglo-Saxon kingdom of Northumbria. From 782 to 796, while serving at Charlemagne's court as an adviser on ecclesiastical affairs, Alcuin also provided

The Coronation of Charlemagne. After a rebellion in 799 forced Pope Leo III to seek refuge at Charlemagne's court, Charlemagne went to Rome to settle the affair. There, on Christmas Day 800, he was crowned emperor of the Romans by the pope. This manuscript illustration shows Leo III placing a crown on Charlemagne's head.

the leadership for the palace school. He concentrated on teaching classical Latin and adopted Cassiodorus' sevenfold division of knowledge known as the liberal arts (see Chapter 7), which became the basis for all later medieval education. All in all, the Carolingian Renaissance played a crucial role in keeping the classical heritage alive as well as maintaining the intellectual life of the Catholic church.

Life in the Carolingian World

In daily life as well as intellectual life, the newly emerging Europe of the Carolingian era witnessed an amalgamation of Roman, Germanic, and Christian practices. These last in particular seem to have exercised an ever-increasing influence.

Family and Marriage   By Carolingian times, the Catholic church had begun to influence Frankish family life and marital and sexual attitudes. Marriages in Frankish society were arranged by fathers or uncles to meet the needs of the extended family. Although wives were expected to be faithful to their husbands, Frankish aristocrats often kept concubines, either slave girls or free women from their estates. Even the "most Christian king" Charlemagne kept a number of concubines.

To limit such sexual license, the church increasingly emphasized its role in marriage and attempted to Christianize it. Although marriage was a civil arrangement, priests tried to add their blessings and strengthen the concept of a special marriage ceremony. To stabilize marriages, the church also began to emphasize **monogamy** and permanence. A Frankish church council in 789 stipulated that marriage was "indissoluble" and condemned the practice of concubinage and easy divorce, and during the reign of Emperor Louis the Pious (814–840), the church formally prohibited divorce. Now a man who married was expected to remain with his wife "even though she were sterile, deformed, old, dirty, drunken, a frequenter of bad company, lascivious, vain, greedy, unfaithful, quarrelsome, abusive . . . , for when that man was free, he freely engaged himself."[3]

The acceptance and spread of the Catholic church's views on the indissolubility of marriage encouraged the development of the **nuclear family** at the expense of the extended family. Although the kin was still an influential social and political force, the conjugal unit came to be seen as the basic unit of society. The new practice of young couples establishing their own households brought a dynamic element to European society. It also had a significant impact on women (see the box on p. 142). In the extended family, the eldest woman controlled all the other female members; in the nuclear family, the wife was still dominated by her husband, but at least she now had control of her own household and children.

Christianity and Sexuality   The early church fathers had stressed that celibacy and complete abstinence from sexual activity constituted an ideal state superior to marriage. Subsequently, the early church gradually developed a case for clerical celibacy, although it proved impossible to enforce in the Early Middle Ages. The early fathers had also emphasized, however, that not all people had the self-discipline to remain celibate. It was thus permissible to marry, as Paul had indicated in his first epistle to the Corinthians:

> It is good for a man not to touch a woman. Nevertheless, to avoid fornication, let every man have his own wife, and let every woman have her own husband. . . . I say therefore to the unmarried and widows, it is good for them if they abide even as I. But if they cannot contain, let them marry: for it is better to marry than to burn.[4]

The church thus viewed marriage as the lesser of two evils; it was a concession to human weakness and fulfilled

ADVICE FROM A CAROLINGIAN MOTHER

*T*he wife of a Carolingian aristocrat bore numerous responsibilities. She was entrusted with the management of the household and even the administration of extensive landed estates while her husband was absent in the royal service or on a military campaign. A wife was also expected to bear larger numbers of children and to supervise their upbringing. This selection by Dhouda, wife of Bernard, marquis of Septimania (in southern France), is taken from a manual she wrote to instruct her son on his duties to his new lord, King Charles the Bald (840–877).

Dhouda of Septimania, *Handbook for William*

Direction on your comportment toward your lord.

You have Charles as your lord; you have him as lord because, as I believe, God and your father, Bernard, have chosen him for you to serve at the beginning of your career, in the flower of your youth. Remember that he comes from a great and noble lineage on both sides of his family. Serve him not only so that you please him in obvious ways, but also as one clearheaded in matters of both body and soul. Be steadfastly and completely loyal to him in all things....

This is why, my son, I urge you to keep this loyalty as long as you live, in your body and in your mind. For the advancement that it brings you will be of great value both to you and to those who in turn serve you. May the madness of treachery never, not once, make you offer an angry insult. May it never give rise in your heart to the idea of being

disloyal to your lord. There is harsh and shameful talk about men who act in this fashion. I do not think that such will befall you or those who fight alongside you because such an attitude has never shown itself among your ancestors. It has not been seen among them, it is not seen now, and it will not be seen in the future.

Be truthful to your lord, my son William, child of their lineage. Be vigilant, energetic, and offer him ready assistance as I have said here. In every matter of importance to royal power take care to show yourself a man of good judgment—in your own thoughts and in public—to the extent that God gives you strength. Read the sayings and the lives of the holy Fathers who have gone before us. You will there discover how you may serve your lord and be faithful to him in all things. When you understand this, devote yourself to the faithful execution of your lord's commands. Look around as well and observe those who fight for him loyally and constantly. Learn from them how you may serve him. Then, informed by their example, with the help and support of God, you will easily reach the celestial goal I have mentioned above. And may your heavenly Lord God be generous and benevolent toward you. May he keep you safe, be your kind leader and your protector. May he deign to assist you in all your actions and be your constant defender.

What advice does Dhouda give her son? What does this selection tell us about aristocratic women in the Early Middle Ages and their relationship with power?

---

the need for companionship, sex, and children. In the church of the Early Middle Ages, it was generally agreed that marriage gave the right to indulge in sexual intercourse. Sex, then, was permissible within marriage, but only so long as it was used for the sole purpose of procreation, not for pleasure. The church condemned all forms of contraception and also strongly condemned abortion, although its prohibition failed to stop either practice. Various herbal potions were available to prohibit conception or cause abortion. The Catholic church accepted only one way to limit children: periodic or total abstinence from intercourse.

The Catholic church's condemnation of sexual activity outside marriage also included homosexuality. Neither Roman religion nor Roman law had recognized any real difference between homosexual and heterosexual eroticism, and the Roman Empire had taken no legal measures against homosexual relations between adults. Later, in the Byzantine Empire, the emperor Justinian in 538 condemned homosexuality, emphasizing that such practices brought down the wrath of God ("we have provoked Him to anger") and endangered the welfare of the state. Justinian recommended that the guilty parties be punished by castration. Although the church in the Early Middle Ages similarly condemned homosexuality,

it also pursued a flexible policy in its treatment of homosexuals. In the Early Middle Ages, homosexuals were treated less harshly than married couples who practiced contraception.

Diet For both rich and poor, the fundamental staple of the Carolingian diet was bread. The aristocratic classes, as well as the monks, consumed it in large quantities. Ovens at the monastery of Saint Gall were able to bake a thousand loaves of bread. Sometimes a gruel made of barley and oats was substituted for bread in the peasant diet.

The upper classes in Carolingian society enjoyed a much more varied diet than the peasants. Pork was the primary meat. Domestic pigs, allowed to run wild in the forests to find their own food, were collected and slaughtered in the fall, then smoked and salted to be eaten during the winter months. Because Carolingian aristocrats were especially fond of roasted meat, hunting wild game became one of their favorite activities. They ate little beef and mutton, however, because cattle were kept as dairy cows and oxen to draw plows, and sheep were raised for wool.

Dairy products became prevalent in the Carolingian diet. Milk, which spoiled rapidly, was made into cheese and butter. Chickens were raised for their eggs. Vegetables also formed a crucial part of the diet of both the rich and the poor. These included legumes, such as beans, peas, and lentils, and roots, such as garlic, onions, and carrots.

Both gluttony and drunkenness were vices shared by many people in Carolingian society. Monastic rations were greatly enlarged in the eighth century to include a daily allotment of 3.7 pounds of bread (nuns were permitted only 3 pounds), 1.5 quarts of wine or ale, 2 to 3 ounces of cheese, and 8 ounces of vegetables (4 for nuns). These rations totaled 6,000 calories a day, and since only heavy and fatty foods—bread, milk, and cheese—were considered nourishing, we begin to understand why some Carolingians were known for their potbellies.

Everyone in Carolingian society, including abbots and monks, drank heavily and often to excess. Taverns became a regular feature of life and were found everywhere: in marketplaces, in pilgrimage centers, and on royal, episcopal, and monastic estates. Drinking contests were not unusual; one penitential stated, "Does drunken bravado encourage you to attempt to outdrink your friends? If so, thirty days's fast."

The aristocrats and monks favored wine above all other beverages, and much care was lavished on its production, especially by monasteries. Ale was especially popular in the northern and eastern parts of the

Carolingian world. Water was also drunk as a beverage, but much care had to be taken to obtain pure sources from wells or clear streams.

Health Medical practice in Carolingian times stressed the use of medicinal herbs and bleeding. Although the latter was practiced regularly, moderation was frequently recommended. Some advised carefulness as well: "Who dares to undertake a bleeding should see to it that his hand does not tremble." Physicians were also available when people faced serious illnesses. Many were clerics, and monasteries trained their own. Monasteries kept medical manuscripts copied from ancient works and grew herbs to provide stocks of medicinal plants. Carolingian medical manuscripts contained descriptions of illnesses, recipes for medical potions, and even gynecological advice, although monks in particular expended little effort on female medical needs.

Physicians of the Early Middle Ages supplemented their medicines and natural practices with appeals for otherworldly help. Magical rites and influences were carried over from pagan times; Germanic tribes had used magical medicine for centuries. But as pagans were converted to Christianity, miraculous healing through the intervention of God, Jesus, or the saints soon replaced pagan practices. Medieval chronicles abound with accounts of people healed by touching a saint's body.

Disintegration of the Carolingian Empire

The Carolingian Empire began to disintegrate soon after Charlemagne's death. Charlemagne was succeeded by his son Louis the Pious (814–840), who was unable to control either the Frankish aristocracy or his own four sons, who fought continually. In 843, after their father's death, the three surviving brothers signed the Treaty of Verdun. This agreement divided the Carolingian Empire among them into three major sections: Charles the Bald (843–877) obtained the west Frankish lands, which formed the core of the eventual kingdom of France; Louis the German (843–876) took the eastern lands, which became Germany; and Lothair (840–855) received the title of emperor and a "Middle Kingdom" extending from the North Sea to Italy, including the Netherlands, the Rhineland, and northern Italy. The territories of the Middle Kingdom became a source of incessant struggle between the other two Frankish rulers and their heirs. Indeed, France

Division of the Carolingian Empire by the Treaty of Verdun, 843

Travelers at an Inn. Inns provided refuge for the many pilgrims, merchants, and others who traveled Europe's dangerous roads in the Middle Ages. In this illustration, two merchants are shown playing backgammon to while away the time.

and Germany would fight over the territories of the Middle Kingdom for centuries.

Although this division of the Carolingian Empire was made for political reasons (dividing landholdings among the male heirs was a traditional Frankish custom), two different cultures began to emerge. By the ninth century, inhabitants of the west Frankish area were speaking a Romance language derived from Latin that became French. Eastern Franks spoke a Germanic dialect. The later kingdoms of France and Germany did not yet exist, however. In the ninth century, the frequent struggles among the numerous heirs of the sons of Louis the Pious led to further disintegration of the Carolingian Empire. In the meantime, while powerful aristocrats acquired even more power in their own local territories at the expense of the squabbling Carolingian rulers, the process of disintegration was abetted by external attacks on various parts of the old Carolingian world.

Invasions of the Ninth and Tenth Centuries

In the ninth and tenth centuries, western Europe was beset by a wave of invasions of several non-Christian peoples—one old enemy, the Muslims, and two new ones, the Magyars and Vikings (see Map 8.2). The Muslims began a new series of attacks in the Mediterranean in the ninth century. They raided the southern coasts of Europe, especially Italy; occupied Sicily; destroyed the Carolingian defenses in northern Spain; and conducted forays into southern France. The Magyars were a people from western

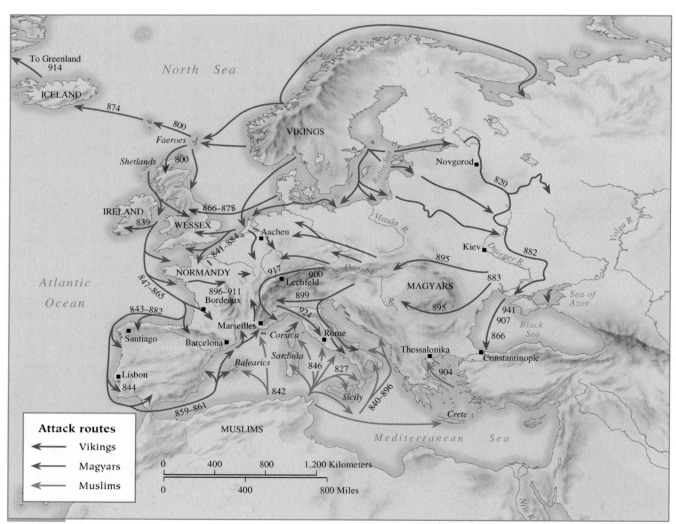

MAP 8.2 Invasions of the Ninth and Tenth Centuries. Attacks by invading Vikings, Magyars, and Muslims terrorized much of Europe in the ninth and tenth centuries, disrupting the economy and spurring the development of fief-holding. The Vikings were the biggest problem, but they eventually formed settlements, converted to Christianity, and were assimilated. ❓ Why was it important for the marauding Vikings to build sound boats and develop good seafaring skills? 🖱 **View an animated version of this map or related maps at** http://thomsonedu.com/history/ spielvogel

Asia who moved into eastern and central Europe at the end of the ninth century. They established themselves on the plains of Hungary and from there made raids into western Europe. The Magyars were finally crushed at the Battle of Lechfeld in Germany in 955. At the end of the tenth century, they were converted to Christianity and settled down to establish the kingdom of Hungary.

The Vikings By far the most devastating and far-reaching attacks of the time came from the Northmen or Norsemen of Scandinavia, also known as the Vikings. The Vikings were a Germanic people who had settled in Scandinavia. Why they invaded other areas of Europe is uncertain. Perhaps overpopulation and the emergence of more effective monarchs in Denmark, Norway, and Sweden caused some of the freedom-loving Scandinavians to seek escape from the growing order. The Vikings' great love of adventure and their search for booty and new avenues of trade may also have been important factors.

Two features of Viking society help explain what the Vikings accomplished. First, they were warriors. And second, they were superb shipbuilders and sailors. Their ships were the best of the period. Long and narrow with beautifully carved arched prows, the Viking "dragon ships" carried about fifty men. Their shallow draft enabled them to sail up European rivers and attack places at some distance inland. Vikings sacked villages and towns, destroyed churches, and easily defeated small local armies. Viking attacks frightened people and led many a clergyman to plead with them to change their behavior and appease God's anger, as is revealed in this sermon in 1014 by an English archbishop:

> Things have not gone well now for a long time at home or abroad, but there has been devastation and persecution in every district again and again, and the English have been for a long time now completely defeated and too greatly disheartened through God's anger; and the pirates [Vikings] so strong with God's consent that often in battle one puts to flight ten, and sometimes less, sometimes more, all because of our sins.... We pay them continually and they humiliate us daily; they ravage and they burn, plunder, and rob and carry on board; and lo, what else is there in all these events except God's anger clear and visible over this people?[5]

Because there were different groups of Scandinavians, Viking expansion varied a great deal. Norwegian Vikings moved into Ireland and western England, while the Danes attacked eastern England, Frisia, and the Rhineland and navigated rivers to enter western Frankish lands. Swedish Vikings dominated the Baltic Sea and progressed into the Slavic areas to the east. Moving into northwestern Russia, they went down the rivers to Novgorod and Kiev and established fortified ports throughout these territories.

Early Viking raids had been carried out largely in the summer; by the mid-ninth century, however, the Northmen had begun to establish winter settlements in Europe from which they could make expeditions to conquer and settle new lands. By 850, groups of Norsemen had settled in Ireland, and the Danes occupied an area known as the

The Pierpont Morgan Library/Art Resource, NY (The Pierpont Morgan Library, New York)

Vikings Attacking England. This illustration from an eleventh-century English manuscript depicts a group of armed Vikings invading England. Two ships have already reached the shore, and a few Vikings are shown walking down a long gangplank onto English soil.

Danelaw in northeast England by 878. Beginning in 911, the ruler of the western Frankish lands gave one band of Vikings land at the mouth of the Seine River, forming a section of France that ultimately became known as Normandy. This policy of settling the Vikings and converting them to Christianity was a deliberate one, since the new inhabitants served as protectors against additional Norseman attacks.

The Vikings were also daring explorers. After 860, they sailed westward in their long ships across the north Atlantic, reaching Iceland in 874. Erik the Red, a Viking exiled from Iceland, traveled even farther west and discovered Greenland in 985. A Viking site in North America was founded in Newfoundland.

By the tenth century, Viking expansion was drawing to a close, but not before Viking settlements had been made in many parts of Europe. Like the Magyars, the Vikings were assimilated into European civilization. Once again, Christianity proved a decisive civilizing force. Europe and Christianity were becoming virtually synonymous.

The Viking raids and settlements also had important political repercussions. The inability of royal authorities to protect their peoples against these incursions caused local populations to turn instead to the local aristocrats who provided security for them. In the process, the landed aristocrats not only increased their strength and prestige but also assumed even more of the functions of local governments that had previously belonged to kings; over time these developments led to a new political and military order.

The Emerging World of Lords and Vassals

The renewed invasions and the disintegration of the Carolingian Empire led to the emergence of a new type of relationship between free individuals. When governments ceased to be able to defend their subjects, it became important to find some powerful lord who could offer protection in exchange for service. The contract sworn between a lord and his subordinate (known as a vassal) is the basis of a form of social organization that later generations of historians called feudalism. But feudalism was never a system, and many historians today prefer to avoid using the term.

Vassalage

The practice of **vassalage** was derived from Germanic society, in which warriors swore an oath of loyalty to their leader. They fought for their chief, and he in turn took care of their needs. By the eighth century, an individual who served a lord in a military capacity was known as a vassal.

With the breakdown of governments, powerful nobles took control of large areas of land. They needed men to fight for them, so the practice arose of giving grants of land to vassals who in return would fight for their lord. The Frankish army had originally consisted of foot soldiers, dressed in coats of mail and armed with swords. But in the eighth century, when larger horses and the stirrup were introduced, a military change began to occur. Earlier, horsemen had been throwers of spears. Now they wore armored coats of mail (the larger horse could carry the weight) and wielded long lances that enabled them to act as battering rams (the stirrups kept them on their horses). For almost five hundred years, warfare in Europe was

dominated by heavily armored cavalry, or knights, as they came to be called. The knights came to have the greatest social prestige and formed the backbone of the European aristocracy.

Of course, a horse, armor, and weapons were expensive to purchase and maintain, and learning to wield these instruments skillfully on horseback took much time and practice. Consequently, lords who wanted men to fight for them had to grant each vassal a piece of land that provided for the support of the vassal and his family. In return, the vassal provided fighting skills. In the Early Middle Ages, when trade was minimal and wealth was

A Medieval Knight. In return for his fighting skills, a knight received a piece of land from his lord that provided for his economic support. Pictured here is a bronze statue of a knight with his equipment. The introduction of the high saddle, stirrup, and larger horses allowed horsemen to wear heavier armor and to wield long lances, vastly improving the fighting ability of the cavalry.

based primarily on land holdings, land became the most important gift a lord could give to a vassal in return for military service.

The relationship between lord and vassal was made official by a public ceremony. To become a vassal, a man performed an act of homage to his lord, as described in this passage from a medieval digest of law:

> The man should put his hands together as a sign of humility, and place them between the two hands of his lord as a token that he vows everything to him and promises faith to him; and the lord should receive him and promise to keep faith with him. Then the man should say: "Sir, I enter your homage and faith and become your man by mouth and hands [that is, by taking the oath and placing his hands between those of the lord], and I swear and promise to keep faith and loyalty to you against all others, and to guard your rights with all my strength."[6]

As in the earlier Germanic band, loyalty to one's lord was the chief virtue.

Fief-Holding

The land granted to a vassal in return for military service came to be known as a **fief.** In time, many vassals who held such grants of land came to exercise rights of jurisdiction or political and legal authority within their fiefs. As the Carolingian world disintegrated politically under the impact of internal dissension and invasions, an increasing number of powerful lords arose. Instead of a single government, many people were now responsible for keeping order.

Fief-holding also became increasingly complicated with the development of **subinfeudation**. The vassals of a king, who were themselves great lords, might also have vassals who would owe them military service in return for a grant of land from their estates. Those vassals, in turn, might likewise have vassals, who at this low level would be simple knights with barely enough land to provide their equipment. The lord-vassal relationship, then, bound together both greater and lesser landowners. At all levels, the lord-vassal

relationship was always an honorable relationship between free men and did not imply any sense of servitude. Since kings could no longer provide security in the midst of the breakdown created by the invasions of the ninth century, the practice of subinfeudation became ever more widespread. With their rights of jurisdiction, fiefs gave lords virtual possession of the rights of government.

The new practice of lordship was basically a product of the Carolingian world, but it also spread to England, Germany, central Europe, and in some form to Italy. Fief-holding came to be characterized by a set of practices that determined the relationship between a lord and his vassal. The major obligation of a vassal to his lord was to perform military service, usually about forty days a year. A vassal was also required to appear at his lord's court when summoned to give advice to the lord. He might also be asked to sit in judgment in a legal case because the important vassals of a lord were peers and only they could judge each other. Finally, vassals were also responsible for aids, or financial payments to the lord on a number of occasions, including the knighting of the lord's eldest son, the marriage of his eldest daughter, and the ransom of the lord's person in the event he was captured.

In turn, a lord had responsibilities toward his vassals. His major obligation was to protect his vassal, either by defending him militarily or by taking his side in a court of law if necessary. The lord was also responsible for the maintenance of the vassal, usually by granting him a fief.

The Manorial System

The landholding class of nobles and knights comprised a military elite whose ability to function as warriors depended on having the leisure time to pursue the arts of war. Landed estates, worked by a dependent peasant class, provided the economic sustenance that made this way of life possible. A **manor** (see Map 8.3) was simply an agricultural estate operated by a lord and worked by peasants.

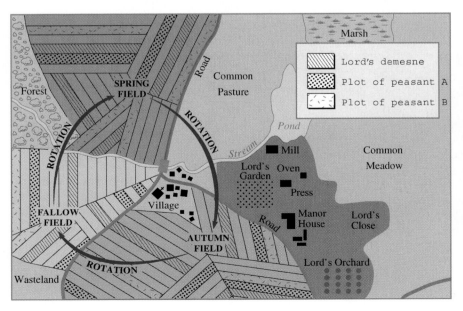

MAP 8.3 A Typical Manor. The manorial system created small, tightly knit communities in which peasants were economically and physically bound to their lord. Crops were rotated, with roughly one-third of the fields lying fallow at any one time, which helped replenish soil nutrients (see Chapter 9). ❓ How does the area of the lord's manor, other buildings, garden, and orchard compare to that of the peasant holdings in the village? 🔊 **View an animated version of this map or related maps at** http://thomsonedu.com/history/spielvogel

Manorialism grew out of the unsettled circumstances of the Early Middle Ages, when small farmers often needed protection or food in a time of bad harvests. Free peasants gave up their freedom to the lords of large landed estates in return for protection and use of the lord's land. Although a large class of free peasants continued to exist, increasing numbers of free peasants became serfs—peasants bound to the land and required to provide labor services, pay rents, and be subject to the lord's jurisdiction. By the ninth century, probably 60 percent of the population of western Europe had become serfs.

Labor services consisted of working the lord's **demesne**, the land retained by the lord, which might consist of one-third to one-half of the cultivated lands scattered throughout the manor. The rest would be used by the peasants for themselves. Building barns and digging ditches were also part of the labor services. Serfs usually worked about three days a week for their lord.

The serfs paid rents by giving the lord a share of every product they raised. Moreover, serfs paid the lord for the use of the manor's common pasturelands, streams, ponds, and surrounding woodlands. For example, if a serf fished in the pond or stream on a manor, he turned over part of the catch to his lord. Peasants were also obliged to pay a tithe (a tenth of their produce) to their local village church.

Lords possessed a variety of legal rights over their serfs as a result of their unfree status. Serfs were legally bound to the lord's lands and could not leave without his permission. Although free to marry, serfs could not marry anyone outside their manor without the lord's approval. Moreover, lords sometimes exercised public rights or political authority on their lands, which gave them the right to try peasants in their own court. In fact, the lord's manorial court provided the only law that most peasants knew. Peasants also had to pay the lord for certain services; for example, they might be required to bring their grain to the lord's mill and pay a fee to have it

ground into flour. Thus the rights a lord possessed on his manor gave him virtual control over both the lives and the property of his serfs.

In the Early Middle Ages, whether free or unfree, a vast majority of men and women, possibly 90 percent, worked the land. Although trade declined precipitously in this period, it never entirely disappeared. Overall, however, compared to the Byzantine Empire or Muslim caliphates, western Europe in the Early Middle Ages was an underdeveloped, predominantly agricultural society.

The Zenith of Byzantine Civilization

In the seventh and eighth centuries, the Byzantine Empire had lost much of its territory to Slavs, Bulgars, and Muslims. By 750, the empire consisted only of Asia Minor, some lands in the Balkans, and the southern coast of Italy. Although Byzantium was beset with internal dissension and invasions in the ninth century, it was able to deal with them and not only endured but even expanded, reaching its high point in the tenth century, which some historians have called the "golden age of Byzantine civilization."

During the reign of Michael III (842–867), the Byzantine Empire continued to be plagued by problems. The Bulgars mounted new attacks, and the Arabs continued to harass the empire. Moreover, a new church problem with political repercussions erupted over differences between the pope as leader of the western Christian church and the patriarch of Constantinople as leader of the eastern (or Orthodox) Christian church. Patriarch Photius condemned the pope as a heretic for accepting a revised form of the Nicene Creed stating that the Holy Spirit proceeded from the Father and the Son instead of "The Holy Spirit, who proceeds from the Father." A council of eastern bishops followed Photius's wishes and excommunicated the pope, creating the so-called Photian schism. Although the differences were later

Peasants in the Manorial System. In the manorial system, peasants were required to provide labor services for their lord. This thirteenth-century illustration shows a group of English peasants harvesting grain. Overseeing them is a bailiff, or manager, who supervised the work of the peasants.

A WESTERN VIEW OF THE BYZANTINE EMPIRE

ℬishop Liudprand of Cremona undertook diplomatic missions to Constantinople on behalf of two western kings, Berengar of Italy and Otto I of Germany. This selection is taken from his description of his mission to the Byzantine emperor Constantine VII in 949 as an envoy for Berengar, king of Italy from 950 until his overthrow by Otto I of Germany in 964. Liudprand had mixed feelings about Byzantium: admiration, yet also envy and hostility because of its superior wealth.

Liudprand of Cremona, *Antapodosis*

Next to the imperial residence at Constantinople there is a palace of remarkable size and beauty which the Greeks called Magnavra...the name being equivalent to "fresh breeze." In order to receive some Spanish envoys, who had recently arrived, as well as myself..., Constantine gave orders that his palace should be got ready....

Before the emperor's seat stood a tree, made of bronze gilded over, whose branches were filled with birds, also made of gilded bronze, which uttered different cries, each according to its varying species. The throne itself was so marvelously fashioned that at one moment it seemed a low structure, and at another it rose high into the air. It was of immense size and was guarded by lions, made either of bronze or of wood covered over with gold, who beat the ground with their tails and gave a dreadful roar with open mouth and quivering tongue. Leaning upon the shoulders of two eunuchs I was brought into the emperor's presence. At my approach the lions began to roar and the birds to cry out, each according to its kind; but I was neither terrified nor surprised, for I had previously made enquiry about all these things from people who were well acquainted with them. So after I had three times made obeisance to the emperor with my face upon the ground, I lifted my head, and behold! The man whom just before I had seen sitting on a moderately elevated seat had now changed his raiment and was sitting on the level of the ceiling. How it was done I could not imagine, unless perhaps he was lifted up by some such sort of device as we use for raising the timbers of a wine press. On that occasion he did not address me personally...but by the intermediary of a secretary he enquired about Berengar's doings and asked after his health. I made a fitting reply and then, at a nod from the interpreter, left his presence and retired to my lodging.

It would give me some pleasure also to record here what I did then for Berengar....The Spanish envoys...had brought handsome gifts from their masters to the emperor Constantine. I for my part had brought nothing from Berengar except a letter and that was full of lies. I was very greatly disturbed and shamed at this and I began to consider anxiously what I had better do. In my doubt and perplexity it finally occurred to me that I might offer the gifts, which on my account I had brought for the emperor, as coming from Berengar, and trick out my humble present with fine words. I therefore presented him with nine excellent curaisses, seven excellent shields with gilded bosses, two silver gift cauldrons, some swords, spears and spits, and what was more precious to the emperor than anything, four carzimasia; that being the Greek name for young eunuchs who have had both their testicles and their penis removed. This operation is performed by traders at Verdun, who take the boys into Spain and make a huge profit.

What impressions of the Byzantine court do you receive from Liudprand of Cremona's account? What is the modern meaning of the word Byzantine? How does this account help explain the modern meaning of the word?

---

papered over, this controversy served to further the division between the eastern and western Christian churches.

The Macedonian Dynasty

The problems that arose during Michael's reign were effectively dealt with by the efforts of a new dynasty of Byzantine emperors, known as the Macedonians (867–1081). This dynastic line managed to repel the external enemies, go over to the offensive, and reestablish domestic order. Supported by the church, the emperors continued to think of the Byzantine Empire as a continuation of the Christian Roman Empire of late antiquity. Although for diplomatic reasons they occasionally recognized the imperial title of western emperors, such as Charlemagne, they still regarded them as little more than barbarian parvenus.

The Macedonian emperors could boast of a remarkable number of achievements in the late ninth and tenth centuries. They worked to strengthen the position of free farmers, who felt threatened by the attempts of landed aristocrats to expand their estates at the expense of the farmers. The emperors were well aware that the free farmers made up the rank and file of the Byzantine cavalry and provided the military strength of the empire. The Macedonian emperors also fostered a burst of economic prosperity by expanding trade relations with western Europe, especially by selling silks and metalworks. Thanks to this prosperity, the city of Constantinople flourished. Foreign visitors continued to be astounded by its size, wealth, and physical surroundings. To western Europeans, it was the stuff of legends and fables (see the box above).

In the midst of this prosperity, Byzantine cultural influence expanded due to the active missionary efforts of eastern Byzantine Christians. Eastern Orthodox Christianity was spread to eastern European peoples, including the Bulgars and the Serbs. Perhaps the greatest missionary success occurred when the prince of Kiev in Russia converted to Christianity in 987.

Under the Macedonian rulers, Byzantium enjoyed a strong civil service, talented emperors, and military advances. In the tenth century, these competent emperors combined with a number of talented generals to mobilize the empire's military resources and take the offensive. The Bulgars were defeated, and both the eastern and western parts of Bulgaria were annexed to the empire. The Byzantines went on to add the islands of Crete and Cyprus to the empire and defeat the Muslim forces in Syria, expanding the empire to the upper Euphrates. By the end of the reign of Basil II (976–1025), the Byzantine Empire was the largest it had been since the beginning of the seventh century.

The Byzantine Empire in 1025

The Slavic Peoples of Central and Eastern Europe

North of Byzantium and east of the Carolingian Empire lay a spacious plain through which a number of Asiatic nomads, including the Huns, Bulgars, Avars, and Magyars, had pushed their way westward, terrorizing and plundering the settled peasant communities. Eastern Europe was ravaged by these successive waves of invaders, who found it relatively easy to create large empires that were in turn overthrown by the next invaders. Over a period of time, the invaders themselves were largely assimilated with the native Slavic peoples of the area.

The Slavs were originally a single people in central Europe who, through mass migrations and nomadic invasions, gradually divided into three major groups: the western, southern, and eastern Slavs (see Map 8.4).

Western Slavs

In the region east of the eastern Frankish or Germanic kingdom emerged the Polish and Bohemian kingdoms of the western Slavs. The Germans assumed responsibility for the conversion of these Slavic peoples since some German emperors considered it their duty to spread Christianity to the barbarians. Of course, it also gave them the opportunity to extend their political authority. German missionaries had converted the Czechs in Bohemia by the end of the ninth century, and a bishopric eventually occupied by a Czech bishop was established at Prague in the tenth. The Slavs in Poland were not converted until the reign of Prince Mieszko (c. 960–992). In 1000, an independent Polish archbishopric was set up at

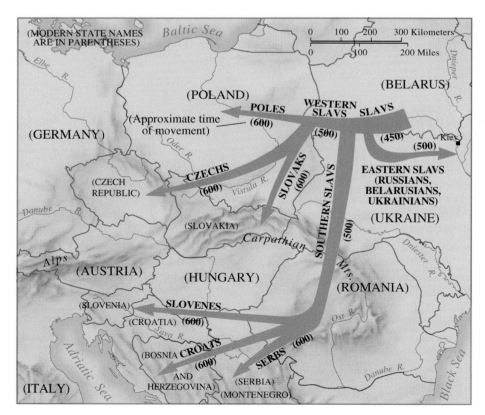

MAP 8.4 **The Migrations of the Slavs.** Originally from east-central Europe, the Slavic people broke into three groups. The western Slavs converted to Catholic Christianity, while the eastern Slavs and southern Slavs, under the influence of the Byzantine Empire, embraced the Eastern Orthodox faith. ❓ What connections do these Slavic migrations have with what we today characterize as eastern Europe? 🔊 **View an animated version of this map or related maps at** http://thomsonedu.com/history/spielvogel

Gniezno by the pope. The non-Slavic kingdom of Hungary, which emerged after the Magyars settled down after their defeat at Lechfeld in 955, was also converted to Christianity by German missionaries. Saint Stephen, king of Hungary from 997 to 1038, facilitated the acceptance of Christianity by his people. The Poles, Czechs, and Hungarians all accepted Catholic or western Christianity and became closely tied to the Roman Catholic church and its Latin culture.

Southern Slavs

The southern and eastern Slavic populations largely took a different path because of their proximity to the Byzantine Empire. The Slavic peoples of Moravia were converted to the Eastern Orthodox Christianity of the Byzantine Empire by two Byzantine missionary brothers, Cyril and Methodius, who began their activities in 863. They created a Slavonic (Cyrillic) alphabet, translated the Bible into Slavonic, and created Slavonic church services. While the southern Slavic peoples accepted Christianity, a split eventually developed between the Croats, who accepted the Roman church, and the Serbs, who remained loyal to eastern Christianity.

Although the Bulgars were originally an Asiatic people who conquered much of the Balkan peninsula, they were eventually absorbed by the larger native south Slavic population. Together, by the ninth century, they formed a largely Slavic Bulgarian kingdom. Although the conversion to Christianity of this state was complicated by the rivalry between the Roman Catholic and Eastern Orthodox churches, the Bulgarians eventually accepted the latter. By the end of the ninth century, they embraced the Slavonic church services earlier developed by Cyril and Methodius. The acceptance of Eastern Orthodoxy by the southern Slavic peoples, the Serbs and Bulgarians, meant that their cultural life was also linked to the Byzantine state.

Eastern Slavs

The eastern Slavic peoples, from whom the modern Russians, White Russians (Belarusians), and Ukrainians are descended, had settled in the territory of present-day Ukraine and European Russia. There, beginning in the late eighth century, they began to contend with Viking invaders. Swedish Vikings, known to the eastern Slavs as Varangians, moved down the extensive network of rivers into the lands of the eastern Slavs in search of booty and new trade routes. After establishing trading links with the Byzantine state, the Varangians built trading settlements, became involved in the civil wars among the Slavic peoples, and eventually came to dominate the native peoples, just as their fellow Vikings were doing in parts of western Europe. According to the traditional version of the story, the semilegendary Rurik secured his ruling dynasty in the Slavic settlement of Novgorod in 862. Rurik and his fellow Vikings were called the Rus, from which Russia, the name eventually attached to the state they founded is derived (see the box on p. 152). Although much about Rurik is unclear, it is certain that his follower Oleg (c. 873–913) took up residence in Kiev and established the Rus state, a union of east Slavic territories known as the principality of Kiev. Oleg's successors extended their control over the eastern Slavs and expanded the territory of Kiev until it encompassed the lands between the Baltic and Black Seas and the Danube and Volga Rivers. By marrying Slavic wives, the Viking ruling class was gradually assimilated into the Slavic population, a process confirmed by their assumption of Slavic names.

The growth of the principality of Kiev attracted religious missionaries, especially from the Byzantine Empire. One Rus ruler, Vladimir (c. 980–1015), married the Byzantine emperor's sister and officially accepted Christianity for himself and his people in 987. His primary motive was probably not a spiritual one. By all accounts, Vladimir was a cruel and vicious man who believed an established church would be helpful in the development of an organized state. From the end of the tenth century on, Byzantine Christianity became the model for Russian religious life, just as Byzantine imperial ideals came to influence the outward forms of Russian political life.

The World of Islam

The Umayyad dynasty of caliphs had established Damascus as the center of an Islamic empire created by Arab expansion in the seventh and eighth centuries. But Umayyad rule created resentment, and the Umayyads also helped bring about their own end by their corrupt behavior. One caliph, for example, supposedly swam in a pool of wine and drank enough of it to lower the wine level considerably. Finally, in 750, Abu al-Abbas, a descendant of the uncle of Muhammad, brought an end to the Umayyad dynasty and established the Abbasid dynasty, which lasted until 1258.

The Abbasid rulers brought much change to the world of Islam. They tried to break down the distinctions between Arab and non-Arab Muslims. All Muslims, regardless of ethnic background, could now hold both civil and military offices. This helped open Islamic life to the influences of the civilizations they had conquered. Many Arabs now began to intermarry with the peoples they had conquered.

In 762, the Abbasids built a new capital city, Baghdad, on the Tigris River far to the east of Damascus. The new capital was well placed. It took advantage of river traffic to the Persian Gulf and was located on the caravan route from the Mediterranean to Central Asia. The move eastward allowed Persian influence to come to the fore, encouraging a new cultural orientation. Under the Abbasids, judges, merchants, and government officials, rather than warriors, were regarded as the ideal citizens.

The new Abbasid dynasty experienced a period of splendid rule well into the ninth century. Best known of

A MUSLIM'S DESCRIPTION OF THE RUS

Despite the difficulties that travel presented, some contact among the various cultures did occur through trade, diplomacy, and the conquest and migration of peoples. This document is a description of the Swedish Rus who eventually merged with the native Slavic peoples to form the principality of Kiev, commonly regarded as the first Russian state. This account was written by Ibn Fadlan, a Muslim diplomat sent from Baghdad in 921 to a settlement on the Volga River. His comments on the filthiness of the Rus reflect the Muslim preoccupation with cleanliness.

Ibn Fadlan, *Description of the Rus*

I saw the Rus folk when they arrived on their trading-mission and settled at the river Atul (Volga). Never had I seen people of more perfect physique. They are tall as date-palms, and reddish in color. They wear neither coat nor kaftan, but each man carried a cape which covers one half of his body, leaving one hand free. No one is ever parted from his axe, sword, and knife. Their swords are Frankish in design, broad, flat, and fluted. Each man has a number of trees, figures, and the like from the fingernails to the neck. Each woman carried on her bosom a container made of iron, silver, copper or gold—its size and substance depending on her man's wealth....

They [the Rus] are the filthiest of God's creatures. They do not wash after discharging their natural functions, neither do they wash their hands after meals. They are as lousy as donkeys. They arrive from their distant river, and there they build big houses on its shores. Ten or twenty of them may live together in one house, and each of them has a couch of his own where he sits and diverts himself with the pretty slave girls whom he had brought along for sale. He will make love with one of them while a comrade looks on; sometimes they indulge in a communal orgy, and, if a customer should turn up to buy a girl, the Rus man will not let her go till he has finished with her.

They wash their hands and faces every day in incredibly filthy water. Every morning the girl brings her master a large bowl of water in which he washes his hands and face and hair, then blows his nose into it and spits into it. When he has finished the girl takes the bowl to his neighbor—who repeats the performance. Thus the bowl goes the rounds of the entire household....

If one of the Rus folk falls sick they put him in a tent by himself and leave bread and water for him. They do not visit him, however, or speak to him, especially if he is a serf. Should he recover he rejoins the others; if he dies they burn him. But if he happens to be a serf they leave him for the dogs and vultures to devour. If they catch a robber they hang him to a tree until he is torn to threads by wind and weather....

What was Ibn Fadlan's impression of the Rus? Why do you think he was so critical of their behavior?

---

the caliphs of the time was Harun al-Rashid (786–809), whose reign is often described as the golden age of the Abbasid caliphate. His son al-Ma'mun (813–833) was a great patron of learning. He founded an astronomical observatory and created a foundation for translating classical Greek works. This was also a period of growing economic prosperity. The Arabs had conquered many of the richest provinces of the old Roman Empire, and they now controlled the trade routes to the east. Baghdad became the center of an enormous trade empire that extended into Europe, Asia, and Africa, greatly adding to the wealth of the Islamic world.

Despite the prosperity, all was not quite well in the empire of the Abbasids. There was much fighting over the succession to the caliphate. When Harun al-Rashid died, his two sons fought to succeed him in a struggle that almost destroyed the city of Baghdad. As the tenth-century Muslim historian al-Mas'udi wrote, "Mansions were destroyed,

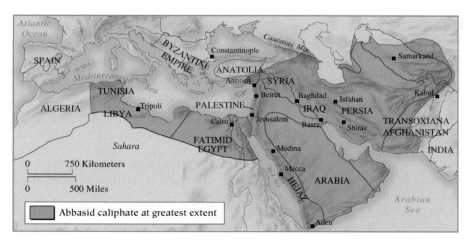

The Abbasid Caliphate at the Height of Its Power

most remarkable monuments obliterated; prices soared. . . . Brother turned his sword against brother, son against father, as some fought for Amin, others for Ma'mun. Houses and palaces fuelled the flames; property was put to the sack."[7]

Vast wealth also gave rise to financial corruption. By awarding important positions to court favorites, the Abbasid caliphs began to undermine the foundations of their own power and become figureheads. Rulers of the provinces of the empire broke away from the control of the caliphs and established their own independent dynasties. In the eighth century, Spain had already established its own caliphate when Abd al-Rahman of the Umayyad dynasty had fled there. In 756, he seized control of southern Spain and then expanded his power into the center of the peninsula. He took the title of emir, or commander, and set up the emirate of al-Andalus (the Arabic name for Spain), with its center at Córdoba. Under Abd-al-Rahman's successors, a unique society developed in which all religions were tolerated. The court also supported writers and artists, creating a brilliant and flourishing culture.

The fragmentation of the Islamic empire accelerated in the tenth century. A caliphate of the Fatimid family was established in Egypt in 973, and an independent dynasty also operated in North Africa. Despite the political disunity of the Islamic world, however, the underlying Islamic civilization was unified by two common bonds: the Qur'an and the Arabic language.

Islamic Civilization

From the beginning of their empire, Muslim Arabs had demonstrated a willingness to absorb the culture of their conquered territories. The Arabs were truly heirs to the remaining Greco-Roman culture of the Roman Empire. Just as readily, they assimilated Byzantine and Persian culture. In the eighth and ninth centuries, numerous Greek, Syrian, and Persian scientific and philosophical works were translated into Arabic. As the chief language in the southern Mediterranean and the Near East and the required language of Muslims, Arabic became a truly international tongue.

The Muslims created a brilliant urban culture at a time when western Europe was predominantly a rural world of petty villages. This can be seen in such new cities as Baghdad and Cairo, but also in Córdoba, the capital of the Umayyad caliphate in Spain. With a population of possibly 100,000, Córdoba was Europe's largest city after Constantinople. It had seventy public libraries, and the number of manuscripts in the caliph's private library reached 400,000. One caliph collected books from different parts of the world and then had them translated into Arabic and Latin. These included works on geography that later proved valuable to Western sailors and merchants. Schools were also established, and the Great Mosque of Córdoba became a center for scholars from all over the Islamic world. Large numbers of women served as teachers and librarians in Córdoba.

CHRONOLOGY **Byzantium, the Slavs, and the Islamic World**

The Byzantine Empire

Michael III	842–867
Macedonian dynasty	867–1081
Basil II	976–1025

The Slavs

Establishment of Novgorod	c. 862
Conversion of Moravian Slavs by Cyril and Methodius	863
Founding of principality of Kiev	c. 873–913
Reign of Prince Mieszko; conversion of Slavs in Poland to Christianity	c. 960–992
Vladimir's conversion to Christianity	987
Saint Stephen, king of Hungary	997–1038

Islam

Overthrow of Umayyad dynasty by Abbasids	750
Creation of emirate of al-Andalus	756
Harun al-Rashid	786–809
Establishment of Fatimid caliphate in Egypt	973

During the first few centuries of the Arab empire, it was the Islamic world that saved and spread the scientific and philosophical works of ancient civilizations. At a time when the ancient Greek philosophers were largely unknown in Europe, key works by Plato and Aristotle were translated into Arabic. They were put in a library called the House of Wisdom in Baghdad, where they were read and studied by Muslim scholars. Texts on mathematics were brought from India. This process was aided by the use of paper. The making of paper was introduced from China in the eighth century, and by the end of the century, paper factories had been established in Baghdad. Booksellers and libraries soon followed. European universities later benefited from this scholarship when these works were translated from Arabic into Latin.

Although Islamic scholars are rightly praised for preserving much of classical knowledge for the West, they also made considerable advances of their own. Nowhere is this more evident than in their contributions to mathematics and the natural sciences. The list of achievements in mathematics and astronomy alone is impressive. The Muslims adopted and passed on the numerical system of India, including the use of the zero. In Europe, it became known as the Arabic system. Al-Khwarizmi, a ninth-century Iranian mathematician, developed the mathematical discipline of algebra. In astronomy, the Muslims were aware that the earth was round, and they set up an observatory at Baghdad to study the stars, many of which they named. They also perfected the astrolabe, an instrument used by sailors to determine their location by observing the positions of heavenly bodies. It was the astrolabe that made it possible for Europeans to sail to the Americas.

© Photodisc Green/Getty Images

Mosque at Córdoba. The first Great Mosque of Córdoba was built by Abd-al-Rahman, founder of the Umayyad dynasty of Spain, in the eighth century. The mosque was later enlarged in the tenth century. Shown here is the interior of the sanctuary, with its two levels of arches. Although the Umayyad caliphs of Damascus were overthrown and replaced by the Abbasid dynasty in the eighth century, the independent Umayyad dynasty in Spain lasted until the eleventh century.

Muslim scholars also made discoveries in chemistry and developed medicine as a field of scientific study. Especially renowned was Ibn Sina (980–1037), known as Avicenna in the West, who wrote a medical encyclopedia that, among other things, stressed the contagious nature of certain diseases and showed how they could be spread by contaminated water supplies. After its translation into Latin, Avicenna's work became a basic medical textbook for medieval European university students. Avicenna was but one of many Arabic scholars whose work was translated into Latin and helped the development of intellectual life in Europe in the twelfth and thirteenth centuries.

TIMELINE

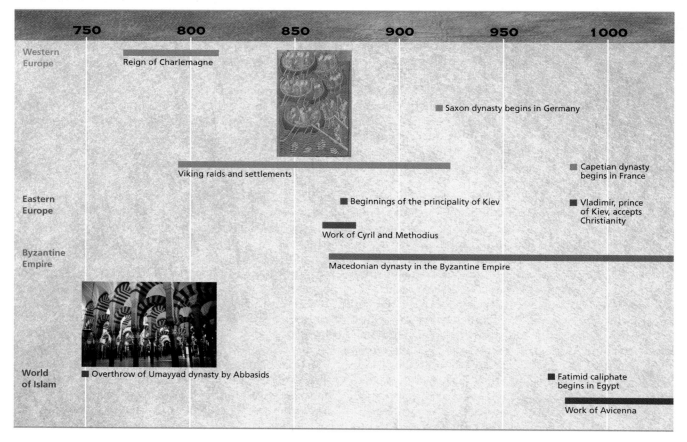

	750	800	850	900	950	1000
Western Europe		Reign of Charlemagne		Saxon dynasty begins in Germany		Capetian dynasty begins in France
		Viking raids and settlements				
Eastern Europe			Beginnings of the principality of Kiev		Vladimir, prince of Kiev, accepts Christianity	
			Work of Cyril and Methodius			
Byzantine Empire			Macedonian dynasty in the Byzantine Empire			
World of Islam		Overthrow of Umayyad dynasty by Abbasids			Fatimid caliphate begins in Egypt	
					Work of Avicenna	

CONCLUSION

After the turmoil of the disintegration of the Roman Empire and the establishment of the Germanic states, a new European civilization began to emerge in the Early Middle Ages. The coronation of Charlemagne, descendant of a Germanic tribe converted to Christianity, as Roman emperor in 800 symbolized the fusion of the three chief components of the new European civilization: the German tribes, the classical tradition, and Christianity. In the long run, the creation of a western empire fostered the idea of a distinct European identity and marked the shift of power from the south to the north. Italy and the Mediterranean had been the center of the Roman Empire. The lands north of the Alps now became the political center of Europe.

With the disintegration of the Carolingian Empire, new political institutions began to develop in Europe, characterized by a decentralization of political control in which lords exercised legal, administrative, and military power. The practice of fief-holding transferred public authority into private hands and provided the security sorely lacking in a time of weak central government and repeated invasions by Muslims, Magyars, and Vikings. While Europe struggled, the Byzantine and Islamic worlds continued to prosper and flourish, the brilliance of their urban cultures standing in marked contrast to the under-developed rural world of Europe. By 1000, however, rural Europe had not only recovered but was beginning to expand in ways undreamed of by previous generations. Europe stood poised for a giant leap.

NOTES

1. Einhard, *The Life of Charlemagne*, trans. S. Turner (Ann Arbor, Mich., 1960), p. 30.
2. Ibid., p. 57
3. Quoted in P. Riché, *Daily Life in the World of Charlemagne*, trans. J. A. McNamara (Philadelphia, 1978), p. 56.
4. 1 Corinthians 7:1–2, 8–9.
5. Quoted in S. Keynes, "The Vikings in England, c. 790–1016," in P. Sawyer, ed., *The Oxford Illustrated History of the Vikings* (Oxford, 1997), p. 81.
6. Quoted in O. Thatcher and E. McNeal, eds., *A Source Book for Medieval History* (New York, 1905), p. 363.
7. al-Mas'udi, *The Meadows of Gold: The Abbasids*, ed. P. Lunde and C. Stone (London, 1989), p. 151.

SUGGESTIONS FOR FURTHER READING

Good general histories of the entire medieval period can be found in **S. Painter and B. Tierney, *Western Europe in the Middle Ages, 300–1475*** (New York, 1983); **E. Peters, *Europe and the Middle Ages*,** 2d ed. (Englewood Cliffs, N.J., 1989); **D. Nicholas, *The Evolution of the Medieval World: Society, Government, and Thought in Europe, 312–1500*** (London, 1993); and **G. Holmes, ed., *The Oxford Illustrated History of Medieval Europe*** (Oxford, 1988). For a good general survey of the social history of the Middle Ages, see **C. B. Bouchard, *Life and Society in the West: Antiquity and the Middle Ages*** (San Diego, Calif., 1988). For a brief history of the period covered in this chapter, see **R. Collins, *Early Medieval Europe, 300–1000*** (New York, 1991). See also the brief work by **B. Rosenwein, *A Short History of the Middle Ages*** (Orchard Park, N.Y., 2002). For a good collection of essays, see **R. McKitterick, ed., *Early Middle Ages: Europe, 400–1000*** (Oxford, 2001).

Carolingian Europe is examined in **P. Riché, *The Carolingians: A Family Who Forged Europe*** (Philadelphia, 1993). On Charlemagne, see **A. Barbero, *Charlemagne: Father of a Continent*,** trans. A Cameron** (Berkeley, Calif., 2004). On Carolingian culture, see ***Carolingian Culture: Emulation and Innovation*** (New York, 1994) and the collection of essays titled ***The Frankish Kings and Culture in the Early Middle Ages*** (Brookfield, Vt., 1995) by **R. McKitterick**.

Various aspects of social life in the Carolingian world are examined in **P. Riché, *Daily Life in the World of Charlemagne*,** trans. **J. A. McNamara** (Philadelphia, 1978); **C. B. Bouchard, *Life and Society in the West: Antiquity and the Middle Ages*** (San Diego, Calif., 1988), ch. 5; and **S. F. Wemple, *Women in Frankish Society: Marriage and the Cloister*** (Philadelphia, 1981). On attitudes toward sexuality in the early Christian church, see the important works by **P. Brown, *The Body and Society*** (New York, 1988), and **E. Pagels, *Adam, Eve, and the Serpent*** (New York, 1988).

The Vikings are examined in **F. D. Logan, *The Vikings in History*,** 2d ed. (London, 1991); **G. Jones, *A History of the Vikings*,** rev. ed. (Oxford, 2001); and **P. Sawyer, ed., *The Oxford Illustrated History of the Vikings*** (New York, 1997).

Two introductory works on fief-holding are **J. R. Strayer, *Feudalism*** (Princeton, N.J., 1985), and the classic work by **M. Bloch, *Feudal Society*,** trans. **L. A. Manyon** (London, 1961). For an important revisionist view, see **S. Reynolds, *Fiefs and Vassals*** (Oxford, 1994).

Byzantine civilization in this period is examined in **R. Jenkins, *Byzantium: The Imperial Centuries, 610–1071*** (New York, 1969), and **W. Treadgold, *The Byzantine Revival, 780–842*** (Stanford, Calif., 1988). On the Slavic peoples of central and eastern Europe, see **F. Dvornik, *The Slavs in European History and Civilization*** (New Brunswick, N.J., 1962); **Z. Vana, *The World of the Ancient Slavs*** (London, 1983); and **S. Franklin** and **J. Shepard, *The Emergence of Rus, 750–1200*** (New York, 1996). The world of Islam in this period is discussed in **H. Kennedy, *The Prophet and the Age of the Caliphates: The Islamic Near East from the Sixth to the Eleventh Century*** (London, 1986), and **J. Lassner, *The Shaping of Abbasid Rule*** (Princeton, N.J., 1980). For a broad view on the relations between Islam and the West, see **B. Lewis, *Islam and the West*** (Oxford, 1994).

Thomson NOW! Enter *ThomsonNOW* using the access card that is available for *Western Civilization: A Brief History*. *ThomsonNOW* will help you understand this chapter with lesson plans generated for your needs. In addition, you can read the following documents, and many more, online:

Saint Benedict, Rule

Saint Finnian of Clonard, Penitential

Einhard, *Life of Charlemagne*

WESTERN CIVILIZATION RESOURCES

Visit the Web site for *Western Civilization: A Brief History* for resources specific to this book:

http://www.thomsonedu.com/history/spielvogel

For a variety of tools to help you succeed in this course, visit the Western Civilization Resource Center at

http://history.wadsworth.com/spielvogel

Included are quizzes, images, documents, interactive simulations, maps and timelines, movie explorations, and a wealth of other sources.

THE RECOVERY AND GROWTH OF EUROPEAN SOCIETY IN THE HIGH MIDDLE AGES

CHAPTER OUTLINE AND FOCUS QUESTIONS

Land and People in the High Middle Ages

☐ What new agricultural practices arose in the High Middle Ages?

☐ What roles did peasants and aristocrats play in the civilization of the High Middle Ages?

The New World of Trade and Cities

☐ What developments contributed to the revival of trade during the High Middle Ages, and what areas were its primary beneficiaries?

☐ What were the major features of medieval cities?

The Intellectual and Artistic World of the High Middle Ages

☐ What were the major intellectual and cultural achievements of European civilization in the High Middle Ages?

CRITICAL THINKING

☐ What is the relationship between economic and social changes and intellectual and artistic developments in the High Middle Ages?

Street scene in a thirteenth-century English town

𝒯HE NEW EUROPEAN CIVILIZATION that had emerged in the ninth and tenth centuries began to come into its own in the eleventh and twelfth centuries as Europeans established new patterns that reached their zenith in the thirteenth century. The High Middle Ages (1000–1300) was a period of recovery and growth for Western civilization, characterized by a greater sense of security and a burst of energy and enthusiasm. New agricultural practices that increased the food supply helped spur a commercial and urban revival that, accompanied by a rising population, gave a new dynamism to a formerly static society.

Townspeople themselves were often great enthusiasts for their new way of life. In the twelfth century, William Fitz-Stephen spoke of London as one of the noble cities of the world: "It is happy in the healthiness of its air, in the Christian religion, in the strength of its defences, the nature of its site, the honor of its citizens, the modesty of its women; pleasant in sports; fruitful of noble men." To Fitz-Stephen, London offered myriad opportunities and pleasures. Fairs and markets were held regularly, and "practically anything that man may need is brought daily not only into special places but even into the open squares." Any man, according to Fitz-Stephen, "if he is healthy and not a good-for-nothing, may earn his living expenses and esteem according to his station." Then, too, there are the happy inhabitants of the city: Where else has one "ever met such a wonderful show of people this side or the other side of the sea"? Sporting events and leisure activities are available in every season of the year: "In Easter holidays they fight battles on water." In summer, "the youths are exercised in leaping, dancing, shooting, wrestling, casting the stone; the maidens dance as long as they can well see." In winter, "when the great fen, or moor, which waters the walls of the city on the north side, is frozen, many young men play upon the ice; some, striding as wide as they may, do slide swiftly."[1] To Fitz-Stephen, "every convenience for human pleasure is known to be at hand" in London. One would hardly know from his cheerful description that medieval cities faced overcrowded conditions, terrible smells from rotting garbage and raw sewage, and the constant challenge of epidemics and fires.

By the twelfth and thirteenth centuries, both the urban centers and the urban population of Europe were experiencing a dramatic expansion. New forms of cultural and intellectual expression also arose in this new urban world. Although European society in the High Middle Ages remained overwhelmingly agricultural, the growth of trade and cities along with the development of a money economy and new commercial practices and institutions constituted a veritable commercial revolution that affected most of Europe.◆

Land and People in the High Middle Ages

In the Early Middle Ages, Europe was a sparsely populated expanse dotted with villages of farmers and warriors and covered with forests, which provided building and heating materials and food in the form of game. The climate had begun to improve around 700 after centuries of wetter and colder conditions, but natural disasters remained a threat. Drought or too much rain could mean bad harvests, famine, and dietary deficiencies that made people susceptible to a wide range of diseases. Life expectancy remained low.

The High Middle Ages, from 1000 to 1300, witnessed continued improvement in climate as a small rise in temperature made for longer and better growing seasons. At the same time, Europe experienced a dramatic increase in population, from 38.5 to 73.5 million people (see Table 9.1). This was physically evident in the growth of agricultural villages, towns, and cities and the increase in land under cultivation.

What accounted for this dramatic rise in population? For one thing, conditions in Europe were more settled and peaceful after the invasions of the Early Middle Ages had stopped. Agricultural production also rose dramatically after 1000. Were it not for this increase in food supplies, the greater population could never have been sustained.

TABLE 9.1 **Population Estimates (in millions), 1000 and 1340**

Area	1000	1340
Mediterranean		
Greece and Balkans	5	6
Italy	5	10
Iberia	7	9
Total	17	25
Western and Central Europe		
France and Low Countries	6	19
British Isles	2	5
Germany and Scandinavia	4	11.5
Total	12	35.5
Eastern Europe		
Russia	6	8
Poland	2	3
Hungary	1.5	2
Total	9.5	13
Total	38.5	73.5

Source: J. C. Russell, *The Control of Late Ancient and Medieval Population* (Philadelphia: American Philosophical Society, 1985) p. 36. These are estimates; some figures, especially those for eastern Europe, could be radically revised by new research.

The New Agriculture

During the High Middle Ages, significant changes occurred in the way Europeans farmed. In addition to the improved growing conditions, another factor in increasing the output of food was the increase in arable land, achieved chiefly by clearing forested areas for cultivation (see the box on p. 159). Land-hungry peasants cut down trees and drained swamps. By the thirteenth century, the total acreage used for farming in Europe was greater than at any time before or since.

Technological Changes Technological changes also furthered the development of agriculture. Many of these depended on the use of iron, which was mined in various areas of Europe. Iron was in demand to make swords and armor as well as scythes, axheads, and hoes for use on farms and saws, hammers, and nails for building purposes. Iron was crucial in making the **carruca,** a heavy, wheeled plow strong enough to turn over the dense clay soil north of the Alps and allow for drainage.

Because of the *carruca*'s weight, six or eight oxen were needed to pull it, but oxen were slow. Two new inventions for the horse made it possible to plow faster. A new horse collar, which appeared in the tenth century, distributed the weight around the shoulders and chest, rather than along the throat, and could be used to hitch up a series of horses, enabling them to pull the heavy new plow faster and cultivate more land. And horseshoes, iron pads nailed to the horses' hooves, gave them better traction in the rocky, clayey soil.

THE ELIMINATION OF MEDIEVAL FORESTS

*O*ne of the interesting environmental changes of the Middle Ages was the elimination of millions of acres of forest to create new areas of arable land and to meet the demand for timber. Timber was used as fuel and to build houses, mills of all kinds, bridges, fortresses, and ships. Incredible quantities of wood were burned to make charcoal for the iron forges. The clearing of the forests caused the price of wood to skyrocket by the thirteenth century. This document from 1140 illustrates the process. Suger, the abbot of Saint-Denis, needed 35-foot beams for the construction of a new church. His master carpenters told him that there were no longer any trees big enough in the area around Paris and that he would have to go far afield to find such tall trees. This selection recounts his efforts.

Suger's Search for Wooden Beams

On a certain night, when I had returned from celebrating Matins [a prayer service], I began to think in bed that I myself should go through all the forests of these parts.... Quickly disposing of all duties and hurrying up in the early morning, we hastened with our carpenters, and with the measurements of the beams, to the forest called Iveline. When we traversed our possession in the Valley of Chevreuse we summoned...the keepers of our own forests as well as men who know about the other woods, and questioned them under oath whether we would find there, no matter with how much trouble, any timbers of that measure. At this they smiled, or rather would have laughed at us if they had dared; they wondered whether we were quite ignorant of the fact that nothing of the kind could be found in the entire region, especially since Milon, the Castellan of Chevreuse,...had left nothing unimpaired or untouched that could be used for palisades and bulwarks while he was long subjected to wars both by our Lord the King and Amaury de Montfort. We however—scorning whatever they might say—began, with the courage of our faith as it were, to search through the woods; and toward the first hour we found one timber adequate to the measure. Why say more? By the ninth hour or sooner, we had, through the thickets, the depths of the forest and the dense, thorny tangles, marked down twelve timbers (for so many were necessary) to the astonishment of all.

What does Suger's search for wooden beams reveal about the environmental problems of the Middle Ages?

The use of the heavy, wheeled plow also led to cooperative agricultural villages. Because iron was expensive, the plow had to be purchased by the entire community. Similarly, an individual family could not afford a team of animals, so villagers shared their beasts. Moreover, the plow's size and weight made it hard to maneuver, so land was cultivated in long strips to minimize the amount of turning that would have to be done.

People in the High Middle Ages learned to harness the power of water and wind to do jobs formerly done by human or animal muscle. Mills, located along streams and powered by the rushing water, were used to grind grains and produce flour. Dams were built to increase the force of the water. Europeans also developed windmills to capture the power of the wind. These two types of mills were the most important inventions for the harnessing of power until the steam engine in the eighteenth century, and their spread had revolutionary consequences for producing more food.

The Three-Field System   The shift from a two-field to a **three-field system** also contributed to the increase in agricultural production. In the Early Middle Ages, it was common to plant one field while allowing another of equal size to lie fallow to regain its fertility. Now estates were divided into three parts. One field was planted in the fall with winter grains, such as rye and wheat, while spring grains, such as oats and barley, and vegetables, such as peas, beans, or lentils, were planted in the second field. The third was allowed to lie fallow. By rotating the fields, only one-third, rather than one-half, of the land lay fallow at any time. The rotation of crops also prevented the soil from being exhausted so quickly, and more crops could now be grown.

By the thirteenth century, increasing demand for agricultural produce in the towns and cities led to higher food prices. This encouraged lords to try to grow more food for profit. One way to do this was to lease their demesne land to their serfs. Labor services were then transformed into money payments or fixed rents, thereby converting many unfree serfs into free peasants. Although many peasants still remained economically dependent on their lords, they were no longer legally tied to the land. Lords, in turn, became collectors of rents rather than operators of manors with both political and legal privileges. The political and legal powers once exercised by lords were increasingly reclaimed by the monarchical states.

Life of the Peasantry

Peasant activities were largely determined by the seasons of the year. Each season brought a new round of tasks appropriate for the time, although some periods were considerably more hectic than others, especially harvest time in August and September. A new cycle began in October, when the peasants prepared the ground for planting winter crops. In February and March, the land was plowed for spring crops—oats, barley, peas, beans, and lentils. Early summer was a comparatively relaxed time, although there was still weeding and sheepshearing

Peasant Activities. The kind of work that European peasants did was dictated by the month and the season. This French calendar of 1460 shows a number of medieval farming activities, including sowing seeds, harvesting crops, pruning plants, shearing sheep, threshing, pressing grapes, and taking care of animals.

Art Resource, NY (Musée Condé, Chantilly, France)

to be done. In every season, serfs worked not only their own land but also the lord's demesne. They also tended the small gardens attached to their dwellings where they grew the vegetables that made up much of their diet.

Religious feast days, Sunday Mass, baptisms, marriages, and funerals all brought peasants into contact with the village church, a crucial part of manorial life. In the village church, the peasant was baptized as an infant, confirmed in his or her faith, sometimes married, and given the sacrament of Holy Communion as well as the last rites of the church before death. The village priest taught the peasants the basic elements of Christianity so that they would gain the Christian's ultimate goal, salvation.

The lifestyle of the peasants was very simple. Their cottages consisted of wood frames with walls made of laths or sticks; the spaces between the laths were stuffed with straw and rubble and then plastered over with clay. Roofs were thatched. The houses of poorer peasants consisted of a single room, but others had at least two rooms—a main room for cooking, eating, and other activities and another room for sleeping. There was little privacy in a medieval peasant household.

Peasant women occupied both an important and a difficult position in manorial society. They were expected to carry and bear their children and at the same time fulfill their obligation to labor in the fields. Their ability to manage the household might determine whether a peasant family would starve or survive in difficult times.

Though simple, a peasant's daily diet was nutritious when food was available. The basic staple of the peasant diet, and the medieval diet in general, was bread. After

the women made dough for the bread, the loaves were baked in community ovens, which were owned by the lord of the manor. Peasant bread generally contained not only wheat and rye but also barley, millet, and oats, giving it a dark appearance and a heavy, hard texture. Bread was supplemented by vegetables from the household gardens, cheese from cow's or goat's milk, nuts and berries from woodlands, and fruits such as apples, pears, and cherries. Chickens provided eggs and sometimes meat.

Grains were important not only for bread but also for making ale. In northern Europe, ale was the most common drink of the poor. If records are accurate, enormous quantities of it were consumed. A monastery in the twelfth century records a daily allotment to the monks of three gallons a day, far above the weekend consumption of many present-day college students. Peasants in the field undoubtedly consumed even more. This high consumption of alcohol might explain the large number of accidental deaths recorded in medieval court records.

The Aristocracy of the High Middle Ages

In the High Middle Ages, European society was dominated by a group of men whose chief preoccupation was warfare—the lords and vassals of medieval society. The lords were the kings, dukes, counts, barons, and viscounts (and even bishops and archbishops) who held extensive lands and considerable political power. They formed an **aristocracy** or nobility that held real political, economic, and social power. Nobles relied for military help on knights, mounted warriors who fought for them in return for

Castle and Aristocrats. This illustration is from the *Très Riches Heures* (Very Sumptuous Hours) of Jean, duke of Berry. The three Limbourg brothers created this "book of hours," which was a book containing prayers to be recited at different times each day. This scene depicts the château at Dourdan, France, and its surrounding lands. In the foreground, elaborately dressed aristocratic men and women are seen amusing themselves.

weapons and daily sustenance. As warriors united by the institution of knighthood, lords and knights came to form a common group, albeit a group with social divisions based on extremes of wealth and landholdings.

Medieval theory maintained that the warlike qualities of the nobility were justified by their role as defenders of society, and the growth of the European nobility in the High Middle Ages was made visible by an increasing number of castles scattered across the landscape. Although castle architecture varied considerably, castles did possess two common features: they were permanent residences for the noble family, its retainers, and servants, and they were defensible fortifications. For defensive purposes, castles were surrounded by open areas and large stone walls. At the heart of the castle was the keep, a large, multistoried building that housed

kitchens, stables, and storerooms; a great hall for visitors, dining, and administrative business; and numerous rooms for sleeping and living. The growing wealth of the High Middle Ages made it possible for the European nobility to build more complex castles with thicker walls and more elaborately decorated interiors. As castles became more sturdily built, they proved to be more easily defended and harder to seize by force.

The Way of the Warrior At the age of seven or eight, the sons of the nobility were sent either to a clerical school to pursue a religious career or to another nobleman's castle, where they prepared for the life of a noble. Their chief lessons were military; they learned how to joust, hunt, ride, and handle weapons properly. After his apprenticeship in knighthood, at about the age of twenty-one, a young man formally entered the adult world in a ceremony of "knighting." A sponsor girded a sword on the young candidate and struck him on the cheek or neck with an open hand (or later touched him three times on the shoulder with the blade of a sword), possibly signifying the passing of the sponsor's military valor to the new knight.

In the eleventh and twelfth centuries, under the influence of the church, an ideal of civilized behavior called **chivalry** gradually evolved among the nobility. Chivalry represented a code of ethics that knights were supposed to uphold. In addition to defending the church and the defenseless, knights were expected to treat captives as honored guests instead of putting them in dungeons. Chivalry also implied that knights should fight only for glory, but this account of a group of English knights by a medieval writer reveals another motive for battle: "The whole city was plundered to the last farthing, and then they proceeded to rob all the churches throughout the city, . . . and seizing gold and silver, cloth of all colors, gold rings, goblets, and precious stones . . . they all returned to their own lords rich men."[2] Apparently, not all chivalric ideals were taken seriously.

After his formal initiation into the world of warriors, a young man returned home to find himself once again subject to his parents' authority. Young men were discouraged from marrying until their fathers died, at which time they could marry and become lords of the castle. Trained to be warriors but with no adult responsibilities, young knights had little to do but fight. As the church stepped up efforts to curb socially destructive fighting in the twelfth century, tournaments began to be organized. Initially, tournaments consisted of the melee, in which warriors on horseback fought with blunted weapons in free-for-all combat. By late in the century, the melee was preceded by the joust, or individual combat between two knights. Gradually, the joust became the main part of the tournament. Knights saw tournaments as an excellent way to train for war. As one knight explained, "A knight cannot distinguish himself in [war] if he has not trained for it in tourneys. He must have seen his blood flow, heard his teeth crack under fist blows, felt his opponent's weight bear down upon him as he lay on the ground and,

WOMEN IN MEDIEVAL THOUGHT

*W*hether a nun or the wife of an aristocrat, towns-man, or peasant, a woman in the Middle Ages was considered inferior to a man and by nature subject to a man's authority. Although there are a number of examples of strong women who ignored such attitudes, church teachings reinforced these notions. The first selection from Gratian, the twelfth-century jurist who wrote the first sys-tematic work on canon law, supports this view. The second selection was written by a wealthy fifty-year-old merchant in Paris who wanted to instruct his fifteen-year-old bride on how to be a good wife.

Gratian, *Decretum*

Women should be subject to their men. The natural order for mankind is that women should serve men and children their parents, for it is just that the lesser serve the greater.

The image of God is in man and it is one. Women were drawn from man, who has God's jurisdiction as if he were God's vicar, because he has the image of one God. Therefore woman is not made in God's image.

Woman's authority is nil; let her in all things be subject to the rule of man.... And neither can she teach, nor be a witness, nor give a guarantee, nor sit in judgment.

Adam was beguiled by Eve, not she by him. It is right that he whom woman led into wrongdoing should have her under his direction, so that he may not fail a second time through female-levity.

A Merchant of Paris on Marriage

I entreat you to keep his linen clean, for this is up to you. Because the care of outside affairs is men's work, a husband must look after these things, and go and come, run here and there in rain, wind, snow, and hail—sometimes wet, some-times dry, sometimes sweating, other times shivering, badly fed, badly housed, badly shod, badly bedded—and nothing harms him because he is cheered by the anticipation of the care his wife will take of him on his return—of the pleasures, joys, and comforts she will provide, or have provided for him in her presence: to have his shoes off before a good fire, to have his feet washed, to have clean shoes and hose, to be well fed, provided with good drink, well served, well honored, well bedded in white sheets and white nightcaps, well covered with good furs, and comforted with other joys and amusements, intimacies, affections, and secrets about which I am silent. And on the next day fresh linen and garments....

Also keep peace with him. Remember the country proverb that says there are three things that drive a good man from his home: a house with a bad roof, a smoking chimney, and a quarrelsome woman. I beg you, in order to preserve your husband's love and good will, be loving, amiable, and sweet with him.... Thus protect and shield your husband from all troubles, give him all the comfort you can think of, wait on him, and have him waited on in your home.... If you do what is said here, he will always have his affection and his heart turned toward you and your service, and he will forsake all other homes, all other women, all other help, and all other households.

What do these two documents reveal about male attitudes toward women in the Middle Ages? How were these atti-tudes justified?

---

after being twenty times unhorsed, have risen twenty times to fight."[3]

Aristocratic Women Although women could legally hold property, most women remained under the control of men—their fathers until they married (usually at the age of fifteen or sixteen) and their husbands after they married. Nevertheless, aristocratic women had numerous opportunities for playing important roles. Because the lord was often away at war, on a Crusade (see Chapter 10), or at court, the lady of the castle had to manage the estate, a considerable responsibility in view of the fact that households, even of lesser aristocrats, could include large numbers of officials and servants. The lady of the castle was also responsible on a regular basis for overseeing the food supply and maintaining all other supplies for the smooth operation of the household.

Although women were expected to be subservient to their husbands (see the box above), there were many strong women who advised and sometimes even dominated their husbands. Perhaps the most famous was Eleanor of Aquitaine (c. 1122–1204), heiress to the duchy of Aquitaine in southwestern France. Married to King Louis VII of France (1137–1180), Eleanor accompanied her husband on a Crusade, but her alleged affair with her uncle during the Crusade led Louis to have their marriage annulled. Eleanor then married Henry, duke of Normandy and count of Anjou, who became King Henry II of England (1154–1189). She took an active role in politics, even assisting her sons in rebelling against Henry in 1173 and 1174.

Blanche of Castile (1188–1252) was another powerful medieval queen. She became regent while her son Louis IX was a boy and ruled France with a powerful hand during much of the 1220s and 1230s. She repelled the attempt of some rebellious French nobles to seize her son, the young king, and defeated Henry III of England when he tried to incite an uprising in France in an attempt to reconquer Normandy. Blanche's political sense was so astute that even when Louis IX came of age, he continued to rely on her as his chief adviser. One medieval chronicler gave her the highest compliment he could think of: "She ruled as a man."

The New World of Trade and Cities

Medieval Europe was an overwhelmingly agrarian society, with most people living in small villages. In the eleventh and twelfth centuries, however, new elements were introduced that began to transform the economic foundation of Western civilization: a revival of trade, considerable expansion in the circulation of money, a restoration of specialized craftspeople and artisans, and the growth and development of towns. These changes were made possible by the new agricultural practices and subsequent increase in food production, which freed some European families from the need to produce their own food. Merchants and artisans could now buy their necessities.

The Revival of Trade

The revival of commercial activity was a gradual process. During the chaotic conditions of the Early Middle Ages, large-scale trade had declined in western Europe except for Byzantine contacts with Italy and the Jewish traders who moved back and forth between the Muslim and Christian worlds. By the end of the tenth century, however, people with both the skills and the products for commercial activity were emerging in Europe.

Cities in Italy assumed a leading role in the revival of trade (see Map 9.1). By the end of the eighth century, Venice, on the northeastern coast, had emerged as a town with close trading ties to the Byzantine Empire. It developed a mercantile fleet and by the end of the tenth century had become the chief western trading center for

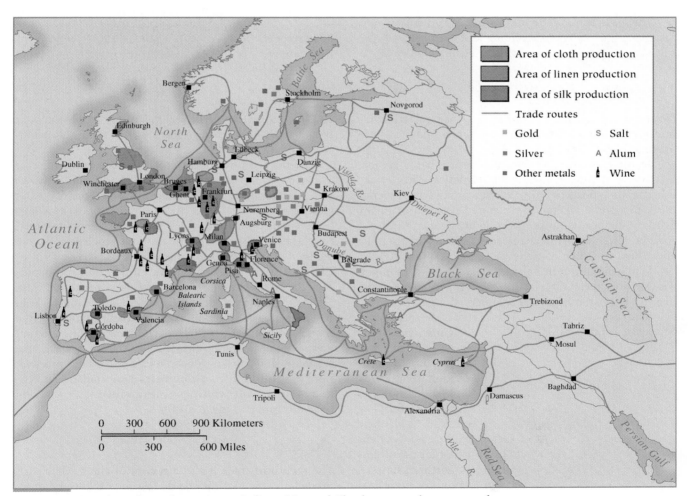

MAP 9.1 Medieval Trade Routes. Italian cities and Flanders were the centers of gradually expanding trade in Europe. They fostered the exchange of goods from the Byzantine Empire and the Far East with those of various regions of Europe. The diminishing threats of violence over time greatly helped trade. ❓ Look at Map 6.2. In what areas had trade expanded, and how can you account for this? 💠 **View an animated version of this map or related maps at** http://thomsonedu.com/history/spielvogel

AN ITALIAN BANKER DISCUSSES TRADING BETWEEN EUROPE AND CHINA

Working on behalf of a banking guild in Florence, Francesco Balducci Pegolotti journeyed to England and Cyprus. As a result of his contacts with many Italian merchants, he acquired considerable information about long-distance trade between Europe and China. In this account, written in 1340, he provides advice for Italian merchants.

Francesco Balducci Pegolotti, *An Account of Traders Between Europe and China*

In the first place, you must let your beard grow long and not shave. And at Tana [modern Rostov] you should furnish yourself with a guide. And you must not try to save money in the matter of guides by taking a bad one instead of a good one. For the additional wages of the good one will not cost you so much as you will save by having him. And besides the guide it will be well to take at least two good menservants who are acquainted with the Turkish tongue....

The road you travel from Tana to China is perfectly safe, whether by day or night, according to what the merchants say who have used it. Only if the merchant, in going or coming, should die upon the road, everything belonging to him will become the possession of the lord in the country in which he dies.... And in like manner if he dies in China.... China is a province which contains a multitude of cities and towns. Among others there is one in particular, that is to say the capital city, to which many merchants are attracted, and in which there is a vast amount of trade; this city is called Khanbaliq [modern Beijing]. And the said city has a circuit of one hundred miles, and is all full of people and houses and of dwellers in the said city....

Whatever silver the merchants may carry with them as far as China, the emperor of China will take from them and put into his treasury. And to merchants who thus bring silver they give that paper money of theirs in exchange... and with this money you can readily buy silk and all other merchandise that you have a desire to buy. And all the people of the country are bound to receive it. And yet you shall not pay a higher price for your goods because your money is of paper.

What were Francesco Pegolotti's impressions of China? Were they positive or negative? Explain your answer.

Byzantine and Islamic commerce. Other coastal communities in western Italy, such as Genoa and Pisa, also opened new trade routes.

In the High Middle Ages, Italian merchants became even more daring in their trade activities. They established trading posts in Cairo, Damascus, and a number of Black Sea ports, where they acquired goods brought by Muslim merchants from India, China, and Southeast Asia. A few Italian merchants even journeyed to India and China in search of trade (see the box above).

While the northern Italian cities were busy trading in the Mediterranean, the towns of Flanders were doing likewise in northern Europe. Flanders, the area along the coast of present-day Belgium and northern France, was known for the production of a much desired, high-quality woolen cloth. The location of Flanders made it a logical entrepôt for the traders of northern Europe. Merchants from England, Scandinavia, France, and Germany converged there to trade their wares for woolen cloth. Flanders prospered in the eleventh and twelfth centuries, and such Flemish towns as Bruges and Ghent became centers for the trade and manufacture of woolen cloth.

By the twelfth century, it was almost inevitable that a regular exchange of goods would develop between Flanders and Italy. To encourage this trade, the counts of Champagne in northern France devised a series of six fairs held annually in the chief towns of their territory. Northern merchants brought the furs, woolen cloth, tin, hemp, and honey of northern Europe to the fairs of Champagne and exchanged them for the cloth and swords of northern Italy and the silks, sugar, and spices of the East.

As trade increased, both gold and silver came to be in demand at fairs and trading markets of all kinds. Slowly, a money economy began to emerge. New trading companies as well as banking firms were set up to manage the exchange and sale of goods. All of these new practices were part of the rise of **commercial capitalism,** an economic system in which people invested in trade and goods in order to make profits.

The Growth of Cities

The revival of trade led to a revival of cities. Merchants needed places where they could live and build warehouses to store their goods. Towns had greatly declined in the Early Middle Ages, especially in Europe north of the Alps. Old Roman cities continued to exist but had dwindled in size and population. With the revival of trade, merchants began to settle in these old cities, followed by craft workers or artisans, people who had developed skills on manors

Flanders as a Trade Center

or elsewhere and now perceived the opportunity to ply their trade producing objects that could be sold by the merchants. In the course of the eleventh and twelfth centuries, the old Roman cities came alive with new residents.

Founding of New Cities and Towns Beginning in the late tenth century, many new cities and towns were founded, particularly in northern Europe. Usually, a group of merchants established a settlement near some fortified stronghold, such as a castle or monastery. The original meaning of the English *borough* or *burgh* and the German *Burg* as a fortress or walled enclosure is still evident in the names of many cities, such as Edinburgh and Hamburg. Castles were particularly favored because they were usually located along major routes of transportation or at the intersection of two important trade routes; the lords of the castle also offered protection. As the settlement prospered and expanded outward, new walls were built to protect it.

Most towns were closely tied to their surrounding territories because they were dependent on the countryside for their food supplies. In addition, they were often part of the territory belonging to a lord and were subject to his jurisdiction. Although lords wanted to treat towns and townspeople as they would their vassals and serfs, cities had totally different needs and a different perspective. Townspeople needed mobility to trade. Consequently, the merchants and artisans of these boroughs and burghs, who came to be called burghers or **bourgeois,** constituted a revolutionary group who needed their own unique laws to meet their requirements. Since the townspeople were profiting from the growth of trade and sale of their products, they were willing to pay for the right to make their own laws and govern themselves. In many instances, lords and kings saw the potential for vast new sources of revenues and were willing to grant (or sell) to the townspeople the liberties they were beginning to demand.

By 1100, burghers were obtaining charters of liberties from their territorial lords that granted them the privileges they wanted, including the right to bequeath goods and sell property, freedom from any military obligation to the lord, written urban law that guaranteed them their freedom, and the right to become a free person after residing a year and a day in the town. The last provision made it possible for a runaway serf who could avoid capture to become a free person in a city. Almost all new urban communities gained these elementary liberties, but only some towns obtained the right to govern themselves by choosing their own officials and administering their own courts of law.

City Governments Over time, medieval cities developed their own governments for running the affairs of the community. Citizens (males who had been born in the city or who had lived there for some time) elected members of a city council that ran the affairs of the city and also served as judges and magistrates. The electoral process was carefully engineered to ensure that only members of the wealthiest and most powerful families, who came to be called the patricians, were elected.

City governments kept close watch over the activities of their community. To care for the welfare of the community, a government might regulate air and water pollution; provide water barrels and delegate responsibility to people in every section of the town to fight fires, which were an ever-present danger; construct warehouses to stockpile grain in the event of food emergencies; and set the standards of weights and measures used in the various local industries. Urban crime was not a major problem in the towns of the High Middle Ages because the relatively small size of communities made it difficult for criminals to operate openly. Nevertheless, medieval urban governments did organize town guards to patrol the streets by night and the city walls by day. People caught committing criminal acts were quickly tried for their offenses. Serious offenses, such as murder, were punished by execution, usually by hanging. Lesser crimes were punished by fines, flogging, or branding.

Medieval cities remained relatively small in comparison to either ancient or modern cities. A large trading city would number about 5,000 inhabitants. By 1300, London was the largest city in England, with almost 40,000 people. On the Continent north of the Alps, only a few great urban centers of commerce, such as Bruges and Ghent, had a population close to that. Italian cities tended to be larger, with Venice, Florence, Genoa, Milan, and Naples numbering almost 100,000 inhabitants each. Even the largest European city, however, seemed insignificant alongside the Byzantine capital of Constantinople or the Arab cities of Damascus, Baghdad, and Cairo. For a long time to come, Europe remained predominantly rural, but in the long run, the rise of towns and the growth of trade laid the foundations for the eventual transformation of Europe from a rural agricultural society to an urban industrial one.

Life in the Medieval City

Medieval towns were surrounded by stone walls that were expensive to build, so the space within was precious and tightly filled. This gave medieval cities their characteristic appearance of narrow, winding streets with houses crowded against each other and the second and third stories of the dwellings built out over the streets. Because dwellings were constructed mostly of wood before the fourteenth century and candles and wood fires were used for light and heat, the danger of fire was great. Medieval cities burned rapidly once a fire started.

Most of the people who lived in cities were merchants involved in trade and artisans engaged in manufacturing of some kind. Generally, merchants and artisans had their own sections within a city. The merchant area included warehouses, inns, and taverns. Artisan sections were usually divided along craft lines; each craft had its own street where its activity was pursued.

Shops in a Medieval Town. Most urban residents were merchants involved in trade and artisans who manufactured a wide variety of products. Master craftsmen had their workshops in the ground-level rooms of their houses. In this illustration, two well-dressed burghers are touring the shopping districts of a French town. Tailors, furriers, a barber, and a grocer (from left to right) are visible at work in their shops.

The physical environment of many medieval cities was not pleasant. They were often dirty and rife with smells from animal and human waste deposited in backyard privies or on the streets. Air pollution was also a fact of life, not only from the ubiquitous wood fires but also from the use of a cheaper fuel, coal, employed industrially by lime burners, brewers, and dyers, as well as by poor people who could not afford to purchase wood. Cities were also unable to stop water pollution, especially from the tanning and animal-slaughtering industries. Butchers dumped blood and waste products from their butchered animals into the river, while tanners threw in tannic acids, dried blood, fat, hair, and wastes.

Because of the pollution, cities were not inclined to use the rivers for drinking water but relied instead on wells. Some communities repaired the system of aqueducts left over from Roman times, and some even constructed new ones. Private and public baths also existed in medieval towns. Paris, for example, had thirty-two public baths for men and women. City laws did not allow lepers and people with "bad reputations" to use them, but such measures did not prevent the public baths from being known for permissiveness. One contemporary commented on what occurred in public bathhouses: "Shameful things. Men make a point of staying all night in the public baths and women at the break of day come in and through 'ignorance' find themselves in the men's rooms."[4] Authorities came under increasing pressure to close the baths

down, and the great plague of the fourteenth century sealed their fate.

There were considerably more men than women in medieval cities. Women, in addition to supervising the household, purchasing food and preparing meals, raising the children, and managing the family finances, were also often expected to help their husbands in their trades. Some women also developed their own trades, such as brewing ale or making glass, to earn extra money. Sometimes when master craftsmen died, their widows carried on their trades. Some women in medieval towns were thus able to lead lives of considerable independence.

Industry in Medieval Cities

The revival of trade enabled cities and towns to become important centers for manufacturing a wide range of products, such as cloth, metalwork, shoes, and leather goods. A host of crafts were carried on in houses along the narrow streets of the medieval cities. From the twelfth century on, artisans began to organize themselves into **guilds,** which came to play a leading role in the economic life of the cities.

By the thirteenth century, virtually every group of craft workers, including tanners, carpenters, and bakers, had its own guild, and specialized groups of merchants, such as dealers in silk, spices, wool, or banking, had guilds as well. Craft guilds directed almost every aspect of the production process. They set standards for the articles produced, specified the methods of production to be used, and fixed the price at which the finished goods could be sold. Guilds also determined the number of men who could enter a specific trade and the procedure they must follow to do so.

A person who wanted to learn a trade first became an apprentice to a master craftsman, usually at around the age of ten. After five to seven years of service, in which they learned their craft, apprentices became journeymen (or journeywomen, although most were male), who then worked for wages for other masters. Journeymen aspired to become masters as well. To do so, they were expected to produce a "masterpiece," a finished piece in their craft that allowed the master craftsmen of the guild to judge whether the journeymen were qualified to become masters and join the guild.

The Intellectual and Artistic World of the High Middle Ages

The High Middle Ages was a time of tremendous intellectual and artistic vitality. The period witnessed the growth of educational institutions, a rebirth of interest in ancient culture, a quickening of theological thought, the development of a vernacular literature, and a burst of activity in architecture. While monks continued to play an important role in intellectual activity, the secular clergy, cities, and courts, whether of kings, princes, or high church officials, began to exert a newfound influence. Especially significant were the new cultural expressions that emerged in towns and cities.

The Rise of Universities

The university as we know it—with faculty, students, and degrees—was a product of the High Middle Ages. The word *university* is derived from the Latin word *universitas*, meaning a corporation or guild, and referred to either a guild of teachers or a guild of students. Medieval universities were educational guilds or corporations that produced educated and trained individuals.

The Origins of Universities The first European university was founded in Bologna, Italy, and coincided with the revival of interest in Roman law, especially the rediscovery of Justinian's *Body of Civil Law*. In the twelfth century, Irnerius (1088–1125), a great teacher of Roman law in Bologna, attracted students from all over Europe. Most of them were laymen, usually older individuals who served as administrators to kings and princes and were eager to learn more about law so they could apply it in their jobs. To protect themselves, students at Bologna formed a guild or *universitas*, which was recognized by Emperor Frederick Barbarossa and given a charter in 1158. Although the faculty also organized itself as a group, the *universitas* of students at Bologna was far more influential. It obtained a promise of freedom for students from

local authorities, regulated the price of books and lodging, and determined the curriculum, fees, and standards for their masters. Teachers were fined if they missed a class or began their lectures late.

In northern Europe, the University of Paris became the first recognized university. A number of teachers or masters who had received licenses to teach from the cathedral school of Notre-Dame in Paris began to take on extra students for a fee. By the end of the twelfth century, these masters teaching at Paris had formed a *universitas* or guild of masters. By 1200, the king of France, Philip Augustus, officially acknowledged the existence of the University of Paris. The University of Oxford in England, organized on the Paris model, appeared in 1208. A migration of scholars from Oxford led to the establishment of Cambridge University the following year. In the Late Middle Ages, kings, popes, and princes vied to found new universities. By the end of the Middle Ages, there were eighty universities in Europe, most of them located in England, France, Italy, and Germany (see Map 9.2).

Teachers and Students in the Medieval University A student's initial studies at a medieval university centered around the traditional liberal arts curriculum, which consisted of grammar, rhetoric, logic, arithmetic, geometry, astronomy, and music. All classes were conducted in Latin, which provided a common means of communication for students, regardless of their country of origin. Basically, medieval university instruction was done by a

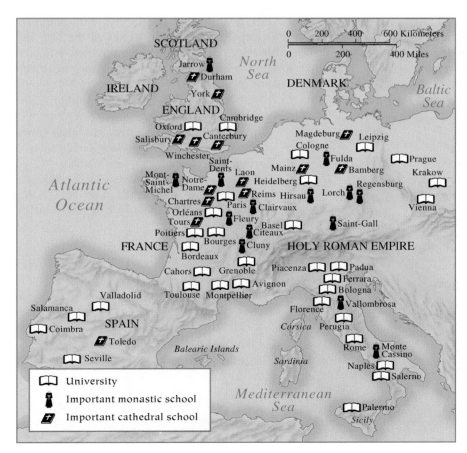

MAP 9.2 Main Intellectual Centers of Medieval Europe. Education in the Early Middle Ages rested primarily with the clergy, especially the monks. Although monastic schools were the centers of learning from the ninth century to the early eleventh, they were surpassed in the course of the eleventh century by the cathedral schools organized by the secular (nonmonastic) clergy. In the twelfth and thirteenth centuries, the universities surpassed both monastic and cathedral schools as intellectual centers. ❓ In what ways did France qualify as the intellectual capital of Europe? 🔎 **View an animated version of this map or related maps at** http://thomsonedu.com/history/spielvogel

lecture method. The word *lecture* is derived from the Latin verb meaning "to read." Before the development of the printing press in the fifteenth century, books were expensive, and few students could afford them, so masters read from a text (such as a collection of laws if the subject were law) and then added their commentaries. No exams were given after a series of lectures, but when a student applied for a degree, he (women did not attend universities in the Middle Ages) was given a comprehensive oral examination by a committee of teachers. These exams were taken after a four- or six-year period of study. The first degree a student could earn was the *artium baccalaureus,* or bachelor of arts; later he might receive an *artium magister,* or master of arts. All degrees were technically licenses to teach, although most students receiving them did not become teachers.

After completing the liberal arts curriculum, a student could go on to study law, medicine, or theology, which was the most highly regarded subject of the medieval curriculum. The study of law, medicine, or theology could take a decade or more. A student who passed his final oral examinations was granted a doctoral degree, which officially allowed him to teach his subject. Students who received degrees from medieval universities could pursue other careers besides teaching that proved to be much more lucrative. A law degree was deemed essential for those who wished to serve as advisers to kings and princes. The growing administrative bureaucracies of popes and kings also demanded a supply of clerks with a university education who could keep records and draw up official documents. Medieval universities provided the teachers, administrators, lawyers, and doctors for medieval society.

Medieval universities shared in the violent atmosphere of the age. Records from courts of law reveal numerous instances of disturbances in European universities. One

German professor was finally dismissed for stabbing one too many of his colleagues in faculty meetings. A student in Bologna was attacked in the classroom by another student armed with a sword. Oxford regulations attempted to dampen the violence by forbidding students to bring weapons to class. Not uncommonly, town and gown struggles ("gown" refers to the academic robe worn by teachers and students) escalated into bloody riots between townspeople and students (see the box on p. 169).

A Revival of Classical Antiquity

Another aspect of the intellectual revival of the High Middle Ages was a resurgence of interest in the works of classical antiquity—the works of the Greeks and Romans. In the twelfth century, western Europe was introduced to a large number of Greek scientific and philosophical works, including those of Galen and Hippocrates on medicine, Ptolemy on astronomy, and Euclid on mathematics. Above all, the West now had available the complete works of Aristotle. During the second half of the twelfth century, all of Aristotle's scientific works were translated into Latin. This great influx of Aristotle's works had an overwhelming impact on the West. He came to be viewed as the "master of those who know," the man who seemed to have understood every field of knowledge.

The recovery of Greek scientific and philosophical works was not a simple process, however. Little knowledge of Greek had survived in Europe. It was through the Muslim world, especially in Spain, that the West recovered the works of Aristotle and other Greeks. The translation of Greek works into Arabic was one aspect of the brilliant Muslim civilization; in the twelfth century, these writings were translated from Arabic into Latin, making them available to the West.

University Classroom. This illustration shows a university classroom in fourteenth-century Germany. As was customary in medieval classrooms, the master is reading from a text. The students vary considerably in age and in the amount of attention they are willing to give the lecturer.

UNIVERSITY STUDENTS AND VIOLENCE AT OXFORD

*M*edieval universities shared in the violent atmosphere of their age. Town-and-gown quarrels often resulted in bloody conflicts, especially during the universities' formative period. This selection is taken from an anonymous description of a student riot at Oxford at the end of the thirteenth century.

A Student Riot at Oxford

[The townsmen] seized and imprisoned all scholars on whom they could lay hands, invaded their inns [halls of residence], made havoc of their goods and trampled their books under foot. In the face of such provocation the Proctors [university officials] sent their assistants about the town, forbidding the students to leave their inns. But all commands and exhortations were in vain. By nine o'clock next morning, bands of scholars were parading the streets in martial array. If the Proctors failed to restrain them, the mayor was equally powerless to restrain his townsmen. The great bell of St. Martin's rang out an alarm; oxhorns were sounded in the streets; messengers were sent into the country to collect rustic allies. The clerks [students and teachers], who numbered three thousand in all, began their attack simultaneously in various quarters. They broke open warehouses in the Spicery, the Cutlery and elsewhere. Armed with bow and arrows, swords and bucklers, slings and stones, they fell upon their opponents. Three they slew, and wounded fifty or more. One band . . . took up a position in High Street between the Churches of St. Mary and All Saints', and attacked the house of a certain Edward Hales. This Hales was a longstanding enemy of the clerks. There were no half measures with him. He seized his crossbow, and from an upper chamber sent an unerring shaft into the eye of the pugnacious rector. The death of their valiant leader caused the clerks to lose heart. They fled, closely pursued by the townsmen and country-folk. Some were struck down in the streets, and others who had taken refuge in the churches were dragged out and driven mercilessly to prison, lashed with thongs and goaded with iron spikes.

Complaints of murder, violence and robbery were lodged straightway with the King by both parties. The townsmen claimed three thousand pounds' damage. The commissioners, however, appointed to decide the matter, condemned them to pay two hundred marks, removed the bailiffs, and banished twelve of the most turbulent citizens from Oxford.

Who do you think was responsible for this conflict between town and gown? Why? Why do you think the king supported the university?

The Islamic world had more to contribute intellectually to the West than translations, however. Scientific work in the ninth and tenth centuries had enabled it to forge far ahead of the Western world, and in the twelfth and thirteenth centuries, Arabic works on physics, mathematics, medicine, and optics became available to the West in Latin translations. Adelard of Bath (1090–1150) was one source of these works. Having traveled throughout the Mediterranean world, he later translated an Arabic version of Euclid's *Elements* (see Chapter 4) into Latin, as well as the mathematical works of al-Khwarizmi (see Chapter 8). Adelard also introduced to Europeans the astrolabe, an Arabic astronomical instrument of great value to sailors.

When Aristotle's works were brought into the West in the second half of the twelfth century, they were accompanied by commentaries written by outstanding Arabic and Jewish philosophers. One example was Ibn-Rushd, also known as Averroës (1126–1198), who lived in Córdoba and composed a systematic commentary on virtually all of Aristotle's surviving works.

The Revival of Roman Law

Another aspect of the revival of classical antiquity was the rediscovery of the great work of Justinian, the *Body of Civil Law*, known to the medieval West before 1100 only at second hand. Initially, teachers of law, such as Irnerius of Bologna, were content merely to explain the meaning of Roman legal terms to their students. Gradually, they became more sophisticated so that by the mid-twelfth century, "doctors of law" had developed commentaries and systematic treatises on the legal texts. Italian cities, above all Pavia and Bologna, became prominent centers for the study of Roman law. By the thirteenth century, Italian jurists were systematizing the various professional commentaries on Roman law into a single commentary known as the ordinary gloss. Study of Roman law at the universities came to consist of learning the text of the law along with this gloss.

The training of students in Roman law at medieval universities led to further application of its principles as these students became judges, lawyers, scribes, and councillors for the towns and monarchies of western Europe. By the beginning of the thirteenth century, the old system of the ordeal was being replaced by a rational decision-making process based on the systematic collection and analysis of evidence, a clear indication of the impact of Roman law on the European legal system.

The Development of Scholasticism

The importance of Christianity in medieval society probably made it certain that theology would play a central role in the European intellectual world. Theology, the formal study of religion, was "queen of the sciences" in the new universities. Beginning in the eleventh century, the effort to apply reason or logical analysis to the church's basic doctrines had a significant impact on the study of theology. The word **scholasticism** is used to refer to the philosophical and theological system of the medieval schools. A primary preoccupation of scholasticism was the attempt to reconcile faith and reason—to demonstrate that what was accepted on faith was in harmony with what could be learned by reason.

Scholasticism had its beginnings in the theological world of the eleventh and twelfth centuries but reached its high point in the thirteenth. The overriding task of scholasticism in the thirteenth century was to harmonize Christian revelation with the work of Aristotle. The great influx of Aristotle's works into the West in the High Middle Ages threw many theologians into consternation. Aristotle was so highly regarded that he was called simply "the Philosopher," yet he had arrived at his conclusions by rational thought—not revelation—and some of his doctrines, such as the mortality of the individual soul, contradicted the teachings of the church. The most famous attempt to reconcile Aristotle and the doctrines of Christianity was that of Saint Thomas Aquinas.

Thomas Aquinas (1225–1274) studied theology at Cologne and Paris and taught at both Naples and Paris, and it was at the latter that he finished his famous *Summa Theologica* (*Summa of Theology*—a summa was a compendium that attempted to bring together all existing knowledge on a given subject). Aquinas' masterpiece was organized according to the dialectical method of the scholastics. Aquinas first posed a question, cited sources that offered opposing opinions on the question, and then resolved them by arriving at his own conclusions. In this fashion, Aquinas raised and discussed some six hundred articles or issues.

Aquinas' reputation derives from his masterful attempt to reconcile faith and reason. He took it for granted that there were truths derived by reason and truths derived by faith. He was certain, however, that the two truths could not be in conflict:

> The light of faith that is freely infused into us does not destroy the light of natural knowledge [reason] implanted in us naturally. For although the natural light of the human mind is insufficient to show us these things made manifest by faith, it is nevertheless impossible that these things which the divine principle gives us by faith are contrary to these implanted in us by nature [reason]. Indeed, were that the case, one or the other would have to be false, and, since both are given to us by God, God would have to be the author of untruth, which is impossible. . . . It is impossible that those things which are of philosophy can be contrary to those things which are of faith.[5]

The natural mind, unaided by faith, could arrive at truths concerning the physical universe. Without the help of God's grace, however, reason alone could not grasp spiritual truths, such as the Trinity (the belief that God, Jesus, and the Holy Spirit are three manifestations of the same unique deity) or the Incarnation (the belief that Jesus in his lifetime was God in human form).

Literature in the High Middle Ages

Latin was the universal language of medieval European civilization. Used in the church and schools, it enabled learned people to communicate anywhere on the Continent. But in the twelfth century, much new literature was being written in the vernacular (the local language, such as Spanish, French, English, or German). A new market for vernacular literature appeared in the twelfth century when educated laypeople at court and in the new urban society sought fresh avenues of entertainment.

Perhaps the most popular vernacular literature of the twelfth century was troubadour poetry, which was chiefly the product of nobles and knights. This poetry focused on the love of a knight for a lady, generally a married noble lady, who inspires him to become a braver knight and a better poet. A good example is found in the laments of the crusading noble Jaufré Rudel, who cherished a dream lady from afar whom he said he would always love but feared he would never meet:

> Most sad, most joyous shall I go away,
> Let me have seen her for a single day,
>   My love afar,
> I shall not see her, for her land and mine
> Are sundered, and the ways are hard to find,
> So many ways, and I shall lose my way,
>   So wills it God.[6]

First appearing in southern France, troubadour poetry soon spread to northern France, Italy, and Germany.

Another type of vernacular literature was the **chanson de geste**, or heroic epic. The earliest and finest example is *The Song of Roland*, which appeared around 1100 and was written in a dialect of French, a language derived from Latin. The *chansons de geste* were written for a male-dominated society. The chief events described in these poems are battles and political contests. Their world is one of combat in which knights fight courageously for their kings and lords. Women play little or no role in this literary genre.

Romanesque Architecture: "A White Mantle of Churches"

The eleventh and twelfth centuries witnessed an explosion of building, both private and public. The construction of castles and churches absorbed most of the surplus resources of medieval society and at the same time reflected its basic preoccupations, God and warfare. The churches were by far the most conspicuous of the public buildings. A chronicler of the eleventh century commented:

> [After the] year of the millennium, which is now about three years past, people all over the world, but especially in Italy and France, began to rebuild their churches. Although most of them were well built and in little need of alterations, Christian nations were rivalling each other to have the most beautiful edifices. One might say the world was shaking herself, throwing off her old garments, and robing herself with a white mantle of

churches. Then nearly all the cathedrals, the monasteries dedicated to different saints, and even the small village chapels were reconstructed more beautifully by the faithful.[7]

Hundreds of new cathedrals, abbeys, and pilgrimage churches, as well as thousands of parish churches in rural villages, were built in the eleventh and twelfth centuries. This building spree reflected a revived religious culture and the increased wealth of the period produced by agriculture, trade, and the growth of cities.

The cathedrals of the eleventh and twelfth centuries were built in the **Romanesque** style, a truly international style. The construction of churches required the services of a cadre of professional master builders whose employment throughout Europe guaranteed international unity in basic features.

Romanesque churches were normally built in the basilica shape used in the construction of churches in the Late Roman Empire. Basilicas were simply rectangular buildings with flat wooden roofs. Elaborating on this basic plan, Romanesque builders made a significant innovation by replacing the flat wooden roof with a long, round stone vault called a barrel vault or a cross vault where two barrel vaults intersected (a vault is simply a curved roof made of masonry). The barrel vault was used when a transept was added to create a church plan in the shape of a cross. Although barrel and cross vaults were technically difficult to construct, they were considered aesthetically pleasing and technically proficient. They also had fine acoustics.

Because stone roofs were extremely heavy, Romanesque churches required massive pillars and walls to hold them up. This left little space for windows, making Romanesque churches quite dark inside. The massive walls and pillars gave Romanesque churches a sense of solidity and a look reminiscent of a fortress.

Barrel Vaulting. The eleventh and twelfth centuries witnessed an explosion of church construction. Using the basilica shape, master builders replaced flat wooden roofs with long, round stone vaults known as barrel vaults. As this illustration of a Romanesque church in Vienne, France, indicates, the barrel vault limited the size of the church and left little room for windows.

The Gothic Cathedral

Begun in the twelfth century and brought to perfection in the thirteenth, the **Gothic** cathedral remains one of the great artistic triumphs of the High Middle Ages. Soaring skyward, as if to reach heaven, it was a fitting symbol for medieval people's preoccupation with God.

Two fundamental innovations of the twelfth century made Gothic cathedrals possible. The combination of ribbed vaults and pointed arches replaced the barrel vault of Romanesque churches and enabled builders to make Gothic churches higher than their Romanesque counterparts. The use of pointed arches and ribbed vaults created an impression of upward movement, a sense of weightless upward thrust that implied the energy of God. Another technical innovation, the flying buttress, basically a heavy arched pier of stone built onto the outside of the walls, made it possible to distribute the weight of the church's vaulted ceilings outward and downward and thus reduce the thickness of the heavy walls used in Romanesque churches to hold the weight of the massive barrel vaults. The thinner walls of Gothic cathedrals could consequently be filled with magnificent stained-glass windows, which created a play of light inside that varied with the sun at different times of the day. The preoccupation with colored light in Gothic cathedrals was inspired by the belief that natural light was a symbol of the divine light of God.

The first fully Gothic church was the abbey church of Saint-Denis near Paris, inspired by its famous Abbot Suger and built between 1140 and 1150. A product of northern France, the Gothic style had spread by the mid-thirteenth century to England, Spain, Germany, and virtually all the rest of Europe. The most brilliant Gothic cathedrals were still to be found in France—in Paris (Notre-Dame), Reims, Amiens, and Chartres.

A Gothic cathedral was the work of an entire community. All classes of society contributed to its construction. Money was raised from wealthy townspeople, who had profited from the new trade and industries, as well as from kings and nobles. Master masons, who were both architects and engineers, designed the cathedrals.

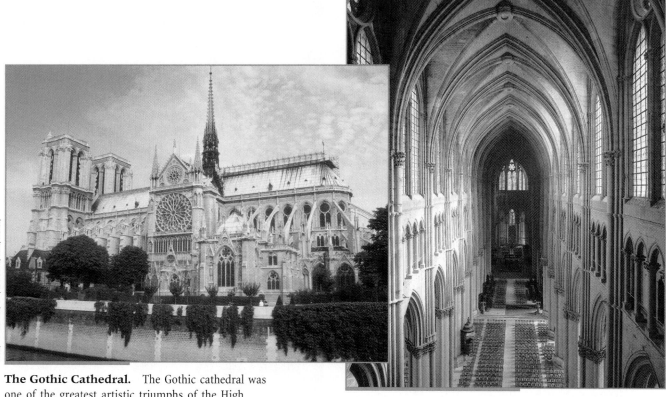

The Gothic Cathedral. The Gothic cathedral was one of the greatest artistic triumphs of the High Middle Ages. Shown here is the cathedral of Notre-Dame in Paris. Begun in 1163, it was not completed until the beginning of the fourteenth century.

Scala/Art Resource, NY (Note-Dame, Paris, France)

Interior of a Gothic Cathedral. The use of ribbed vaults and pointed arches gave the Gothic cathedral a feeling of upward movement. Moreover, due to the flying buttress, the cathedral could have thin walls with stained-glass windows that filled the interior with light. The flying buttress was a heavy pier of stone built onto the outside of the walls to bear the brunt of the weight of the church's vaulted ceiling.

© Art Archive/Dagli Orti

They drew up the plans and supervised the work of construction. Stonemasons and other craftspeople were paid a daily wage and provided the skilled labor to build the cathedrals. A Gothic cathedral symbolized the chief preoccupation of a medieval Christian community, its dedication to a spiritual ideal. As we have observed before, the largest buildings of an era reflect the values of its society. The Gothic cathedral, with its towers soaring toward heaven, gave witness to an age when a spiritual impulse still underlay most of existence.

CONCLUSION

The new European civilization that had emerged in the Early Middle Ages began to flourish in the High Middle Ages. Better growing conditions, an expansion of cultivated land, and technological and agricultural changes combined to enable Europe's food supply to increase significantly after 1000. This increase helped sustain a dramatic rise in population that was apparent in the expansion of towns and cities.

The High Middle Ages witnessed economic and social changes that some historians believe set European civilization on a path that lasted until the Industrial Revolution of the late eighteenth century created a new pattern. The revival of trade, the expansion of towns and cities, and the development of a money economy did not mean the end of a predominantly rural European society, but they did open the door to new ways to make a living and new opportunities for people to expand and enrich their lives. Eventually, they laid the foundations for the development of a mostly urban industrial society.

The High Middle Ages also gave birth to a cultural revival that led to a rediscovery of important aspects of the classical heritage, to new centers of learning in the universities, to the use of reason to systematize the study of theology, to the development of a vernacular literature that appealed to both knights and townspeople, and to a dramatic increase in the number and size of churches.

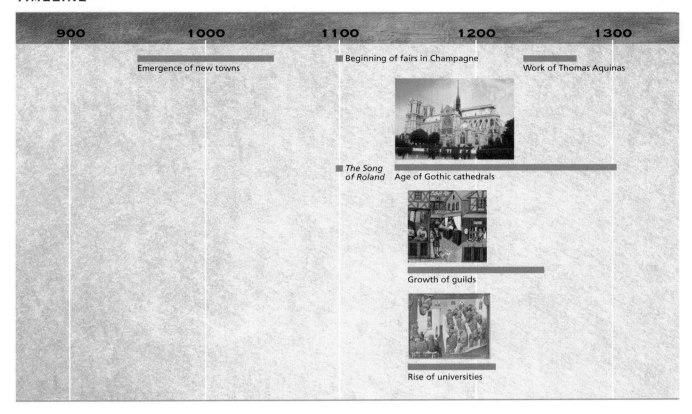

900	1000	1100	1200	1300

Emergence of new towns

Beginning of fairs in Champagne

Work of Thomas Aquinas

The Song of Roland

Age of Gothic cathedrals

Growth of guilds

Rise of universities

NOTES

1. Quoted in N. F. Cantor, ed., *The Medieval Reader* (New York, 1994), pp. 69–70.
2. Quoted in J. Gies and F. Gies, *Life in a Medieval Castle* (New York, 1974), p. 175.
3. Quoted in R. Delort, *Life in the Middle Ages,* trans. R. Allen (New York, 1972), p. 218.
4. Quoted in J. Gimpel, *The Medieval Machine* (Harmondsworth, England, 1977), p. 92.
5. Quoted in J. Mundy, *Europe in the High Middle Ages, 1150–1309* (New York, 1973), pp. 474–475.
6. Quoted in H. Waddell, *The Wandering Scholars* (New York, 1961), p. 222.
7. Quoted in J. W. Baldwin, *The Scholastic Cult of the Middle Ages, 1000–1300* (Lexington, Mass., 1971), p. 15.

SUGGESTIONS FOR FURTHER READING

For a good introduction to this period, see **W. C. Jordan, *Europe in the High Middle Ages*** (New York, 2003); **J. H. Mundy, *Europe in the High Middle Ages, 1150–1309,*** 3d ed. (New York, 1999); **M. Barber, *The Two Cities: Medieval Europe, 1050–1320*** (London, 1992); and **R. Bartlett, *The Making of Europe: Conquest, Colonization, and Cultural Change, 950–1350*** (Princeton, N.J., 1993). There is a good collection of essays on various facets of medieval history in **P. Linehan and J. L. Nelson,** eds., ***The Medieval World*** (London, 2001). On peasant life, see **R. Fossier, *Peasant Life in the Medieval West*** (New York, 1988).

Works on the function and activities of the nobility in the High Middle Ages include **S. Reynolds, *Kingdoms and Communities in Western Europe, 900–1300*** (Oxford, 1984); **R. W. Barber, *The Knight and Chivalry*** (Rochester, N.Y., 1995); and the classic work by **M. Bloch, *Feudal Society*** (London, 1961). Various aspects of the social history of the nobility can be found in **R. Barber** and **J. Barker, *Tournaments: Jousts, Chivalry, and Pageants in the Middle Ages*** (New York, 1989), on tournaments; **N. J. G. Pounds, *The Medieval Castle in England and Wales: A Social and Political History*** (New York, 1990); and **C. B. Bouchard, *Life and Society in the West: Antiquity and the Middle Ages*** (San Diego, Calif., 1988), ch. 6. On women, see **R. T. Morewedge,** ed., ***The Role of Women in the Middle Ages*** (Albany, N.Y., 1975), and **S. M. Stuard,** ed., ***Women in Medieval Society*** (Philadelphia, 1976).

On the revival of trade, see **R. S. Lopez, *The Commercial Revolution of the Middle Ages, 950–1350*** (Englewood Cliffs, N.J., 1971). Urban history is covered in **D. Nicholas, *The Growth of the Medieval City: From Late Antiquity to the Early Fourteenth Century*** (New York, 1997), and the classic work of **H. Pirenne, *Medieval Cities*** (Princeton, N.J., 1969). For a good collection of essays on urban culture, see **B. Hanawalt** and **K. I. Reyerson,** eds., ***City and Spectacle in Medieval Europe*** (Minneapolis, Minn., 1994).

A general work on medieval intellectual life is **M. L. Colish, *Medieval Foundations of the Western Intellectual Tradition, 400–1400*** (New Haven, Conn., 1997). See also the classic study by **F. Artz, *The Mind of the Middle Ages,*** 3d ed. (Chicago, 1980). The development of universities is covered in **S. Ferruolo, *The Origin of the University*** (Stanford, Calif., 1985); **A. B. Cobban, *The Medieval***

Universities (London, 1975); and the brief older work by **C. H. Haskins**, *The Rise of Universities* (Ithaca, N.Y., 1957). Various aspects of the intellectual and literary developments of the High Middle Ages are examined in **J. W. Baldwin**, *The Scholastic Culture of the Middle Ages, 1000–1300* (Lexington, Mass., 1971), and **H. Waddell**, *The Wandering Scholars* (New York, 1961). A good biography of Thomas Aquinas is **J. Weisheipl**, *Friar Thomas d'Aquino: His Life, His Thought and Work* (New York, 1974).

For a good introduction to the art and architecture of the Middle Ages, see **A. Shaver-Crandell**, *The Middle Ages,* in the Cambridge Introduction to Art Series (Cambridge, 1982). A good introduction to Romanesque style is **A. Petzold**, *Romanesque Art* (New York, 1995). On the Gothic movement, see **M. Camille**, *Gothic Art: Glorious Visions* (New York, 1996).

Thomson NOW! Enter *ThomsonNOW* using the access card that is available for *Western Civilization: A Brief History.* ThomsonNOW will help you understand this chapter with lesson plans generated for your needs. In addition, you can read the following documents, and many more, online:

Peter Abelard, *Story of My Misfortunes*
Thomas Aquinas, Part 1, Question 2, Article 3 of *Summa Theologica*

10

THE RISE OF KINGDOMS AND THE GROWTH OF CHURCH POWER

CHAPTER OUTLINE AND FOCUS QUESTIONS

The Emergence and Growth of European Kingdoms, 1000–1300

▢ What steps did the rulers of England and France take during the High Middle Ages to reverse the decentralizing tendencies of fief-holding?

▢ What were the major developments in Spain, the Holy Roman Empire, and northern and eastern Europe during the High Middle Ages?

The Recovery and Reform of the Catholic Church

▢ What was at issue in the Investiture Controversy, and what effect did the controversy have on the church and on Germany?

Christianity and Medieval Civilization

▢ What were the characteristics of the papal monarchy and the new religious orders of the High Middle Ages, and what role did women play in the religious life of the period?

The Crusades

▢ What were the reasons for the Crusades, and who or what benefited the most from the experience of the Crusades?

CRITICAL THINKING

▢ Why did centralized kingdoms develop in some parts of Europe and not in others?

A medieval abbot and his monks

© British Library/HIP/Art Resource, NY

*C*HE RECOVERY AND GROWTH of European civilization in the High Middle Ages also affected the state and the church. Both lords and vassals and the Catholic church recovered from the invasions and internal dissension of the Early Middle Ages. Although lords and vassals seemed forever mired in endless petty conflicts, some medieval kings began to exert a centralizing authority and inaugurated the process of developing new kinds of monarchical states. By the thirteenth century, European monarchs were solidifying their governmental institutions in pursuit of greater power.

The recovery of the Catholic church produced a reform movement that led to exalted claims of papal authority and subsequent conflict with state authorities. At the same time, vigorous papal leadership combined with new dimensions of religious life to make the Catholic church a forceful presence in every area of life. The role of the church in the new European civilization was quite evident in the career of a man named Samson, who became abbot or head of the great English abbey of Bury Saint Edmonds in 1182. According to Jocelyn of Brakeland, a monk who assisted him, Abbot Samson was a devout man who wore "undergarments of horsehair and a horsehair shirt." He loved virtue and "abhorred liars, drunkards and talkative folk." His primary concern was the spiritual well-being of his monastery, but he spent much of his time working on problems in the world beyond the abbey walls. Since the monastery had fallen into debt under his predecessors, Abbot Samson toiled tirelessly to recoup the abbey's fortunes by carefully supervising its manors. He also rounded up murderers to stand trial in Saint Edmunds and provided knights for the king's army. But his actions were not always tolerant or beneficial. He was instrumental in driving the Jews from the town of Saint Edmunds and was not above improving the abbey's possessions at the expense of his neighbors: "He built up the bank of the fish-pond at Babwell so high, for the service of a new mill, that by the keeping back the water there is not a man, rich or poor, but has lost his garden and his orchards." The abbot's worldly cares weighed heavily on him, but he had little choice if his abbey were to flourish and fulfill its spiritual and secular functions. But he did have regrets; as he remarked to Jocelyn: "If he could have returned to the circumstances he had enjoyed before he became a monk, he would never have become a monk or an abbot."[1]◆

The Emergence and Growth of European Kingdoms, 1000–1300

The domination of society by the nobility reached its apex in the High Middle Ages. During the same period, however, kings began the process of extending their power in more effective ways. Out of these growing monarchies would eventually come the European states that dominated much of later European history.

Kings possessed some sources of power that other lords did not. Usually, kings had greater opportunities to increase their lands through war and marriage alliances and then could use their new acquisitions to reward their followers and bind powerful nobles to them. In the High Middle Ages, kings found ways to strengthen governmental institutions and consequently to extend their powers. The growth of cities, the revival of commerce, and the emergence of a money economy enabled monarchs to hire soldiers and officials and to rely less on their vassals.

England in the High Middle Ages

In 1066, an army of heavily armed knights under William of Normandy landed on the coast of England and soundly defeated King Harold and the Anglo-Saxon foot soldiers at the Battle of Hastings on October 14. William (1066–1087) was crowned king of England at Christmastime in London and began the process of combining Anglo-Saxon and Norman institutions. Many of the Norman knights were given parcels of land that they held as fiefs from the new English king. William made all nobles swear an oath of loyalty to him and insisted that all people owed loyalty to the king rather than to their lords.

Gradually, fusion between the victorious Normans and the defeated Anglo-Saxons created a new England. Although the Norman ruling class spoke French, the intermarriage of the Norman-French with Anglo-Saxon nobility gradually blended Anglo-Saxon and French into a new English language. The Normans also took over existing Anglo-Saxon institutions, such as the office of sheriff. William took a census and more fully developed the system of taxation and royal courts begun by the Anglo-Saxon kings of the tenth and eleventh centuries. All in all, William of Normandy created a strong, centralized monarchy.

The Norman conquest of England had other repercussions as well. Because the new king of England was still the duke of Normandy, he was both a king (of England) and at the same time a vassal to a king (of France), but a vassal who was now far more powerful than his lord. This connection with France kept England heavily involved in Continental affairs throughout the High Middle Ages.

Bridgeman-Giraudon/Art Resource, NY (Musée de la Tapisserie, Bayeux, France)

Norman Conquest of England.
The Bayeux tapestry, which consists of woolen embroidery on a linen backing, was made by English needlewomen before 1082 for Bayeux Cathedral. It depicts scenes from the Norman invasion of England. This segment shows the Norman cavalry charging the shield wall of the Saxon infantry during the Battle of Hastings.

Henry II   In the twelfth century, the power of the English monarchy was greatly enlarged during the reign of Henry II (1154–1189), the founder of the Plantagenet dynasty. The new king was particularly successful in strengthening the power of the royal courts. Henry expanded the number of criminal cases tried in the king's court and also devised ways of taking property cases from local courts to the royal courts. Henry's goals were clear: expanding the jurisdiction of royal courts extended the king's power and, of course, brought revenues into his coffers. Moreover, because the royal courts were now found throughout England, a body of **common law** (law that was common to the whole kingdom) began to replace the local law codes, which differed from place to place.

Henry was less successful at imposing royal control over the church. The king claimed the right to punish clergymen in church courts, but Thomas à Becket, archbishop of Canterbury and therefore the highest-ranking English cleric, claimed that only church courts could try clerics. Attempts at compromise failed, and the angry king publicly expressed the desire to be rid of Becket: "Who will free me of this priest?" he screamed. Four knights took the challenge, went to Canterbury, and murdered the archbishop in the cathedral. Met with public outrage, Henry was forced to allow the right of appeal from English church courts to the papal court.

King John and Magna Carta   Many English nobles came to resent the continuing growth of the king's power and rose in rebellion during the reign of Henry's son, King John (1199–1216). At Runnymeade in 1215, John was forced to seal Magna Carta (the Great Charter). Magna Carta was, above all, a feudal document (see the box on p. 178). Feudal custom had always recognized that the relationship between king and vassals was based on mutual rights and obligations. Magna Carta gave written recognition to that fact and was used in subsequent years to strengthen the idea that the monarch's power was limited, not absolute.

Edward I and the Emergence of Parliament   During the reign of Edward I (1272–1307), an institution of great importance in the development of representative government—the English Parliament—emerged. Originally the word *parliament* was applied to meetings of the king's Great Council in which the greater barons and chief prelates of the church met with the king's judges and principal advisers to deal with judicial affairs. But out of a need for money, Edward in 1295 invited two knights from every county and two residents ("burgesses") from each town to meet with the Great Council to consent to new taxes. This was the first Parliament.

The English Parliament, then, came to be composed of two knights from every county and two burgesses from every town as well as the barons and eccelesiastical lords. Eventually, barons and church lords formed the House of Lords; knights and burgesses, the House of Commons. The Parliaments of Edward I granted taxes, discussed politics, passed laws, and handled judicial business.

By the end of the thirteenth century, the law of the realm was being determined not by the king alone but by the king in consultation with representatives of various groups that constituted the community.

The Growth of the French Kingdom

In 843, the Carolingian Empire had been divided into three major sections. The west Frankish lands formed the core of the eventual kingdom of France. In 987, after the death of the last Carolingian king, the west Frankish nobles chose Hugh Capet as the new king, thus establishing the Capetian dynasty of French kings. Although they carried the title of kings, the Capetians had little real power. They controlled as the royal domain (the lands of the king) only the lands around Paris known as the Île-de-France. As kings of France, the Capetians were formally the overlords of the great lords of France, such as the dukes of Normandy, Brittany, Burgundy, and Aquitaine (see Map 10.1). In reality, however, many of the dukes were considerably more powerful than the Capetian kings. It would take the Capetian dynasty hundreds of years to create a truly centralized monarchical authority in France.

The reign of King Philip II Augustus (1180–1223) was an important turning point. Philip II waged war against the Plantagenet rulers of England, who also ruled the French territories of Normandy, Maine, Anjou, and Aquitaine, and was successful in gaining control of most of these territories. Through these conquests, Philip quadrupled the income of the French monarchy and greatly enlarged its power. To administer justice and collect royal revenues in his new territories, Philip appointed new royal officials, thus inaugurating a French royal bureaucracy.

Capetian rulers after Philip II continued to add lands to the royal domain. Although Philip had used military force, other kings used both purchase and marriage to achieve the same end. Much of the thirteenth century was dominated by Louis IX (1226–1270), whom many consider the greatest of the medieval French kings. A deeply religious man, he was later canonized as a saint by the church, an unusual action. Louis was known for his attempts to bring justice to his people and ensure their rights. Sharing in the religious sentiments of his age, Louis played a major role in two of the later Crusades, but both were failures, and he met his death during an invasion of North Africa.

Philip IV and the Estates-General   One of Louis's successors, Philip IV the Fair (1285–1314), was particularly effective in strengthening the French monarchy. The machinery of government became even more specialized. French kings going back to the early Capetians had possessed a household staff for running their affairs. Over time, however, this household staff was enlarged and divided into three groups to form three major branches of royal administration: a council for advice, a chamber

MAGNA CARTA

*A*fter the dismal failure of King John to reconquer Normandy from the French king, some of the English barons rebelled against their king. At Runnymeade in 1215, King John agreed to seal Magna Carta, the Great Charter of liberties regulating the relationship between the king and his vassals. What made Magna Carta an important historical document was its more general clauses defining rights and liberties. These were later interpreted in broader terms to make them applicable to all the English people.

Magna Carta

John, by the Grace of God, king of England, lord of Ireland, duke of Normandy and Aquitaine, count of Anjou, to the archbishops, bishops, abbots, earls, barons, justiciars, foresters, sheriffs, reeves, servants, and all bailiffs and his faithful people greeting.

1. In the first place we have granted to God, and by this our present charter confirmed, for us and our heirs forever, that the English church shall be free, and shall hold its rights entire and its liberties uninjured.... We have granted moreover to all free men of our kingdom for us and our heirs forever all the liberties written below, to be had and holden by themselves and their heirs from us and our heirs.

2. If any of our earls or barons, or others holding from us in chief by military service shall have died, and when he had died his heir shall be of full age and owe relief, he shall have his inheritance by the ancient relief; that is to say, the heir or heirs of an earl for the whole barony of an earl a hundred pounds; the heir or heirs of a baron for a whole barony a hundred pounds; the heir or heirs of a knight, for a whole knight's fee, a hundred shillings at most; and who owes less let him give less according to the ancient custom of fiefs.

3. If moreover the heir of any one of such shall be under age, and shall be in wardship, when he comes of age he shall have his inheritance without relief and without a fine....

12. No scutage or aid shall be imposed in our kingdom except by the common council of our kingdom, except for the ransoming of our body, for the making of our oldest son a knight, and for once marrying our oldest daughter, and for these purposes it shall be only a reasonable aid....

13. And the city of London shall have all its ancient liberties and free customs, as well by land as by water. Moreover, we will and grant that all other cities and boroughs and villages and ports shall have all their liberties and free customs.

14. And for holding a common council of the kingdom concerning the assessment of an aid otherwise than in the three cases mentioned above, or concerning the assessment of a scutage we shall cause to be summoned the archbishops, bishops, abbots, earls, and greater barons by our letters under seal; and besides we shall cause to be summoned generally, by our sheriffs and bailiffs all those who hold from us in chief, for a certain day, that is at the end of forty days at least, and for a certain place; and in all the letters of that summons, we will express the cause of the summons, and when the summons has thus been given the business shall proceed on the appointed day, on the advice of those who shall be present, even if not all of those who were summoned have come....

39. No free man shall be taken or imprisoned or dispossessed, or outlawed, or banished, or in any way destroyed, nor will we go upon him, nor send upon him, except by the legal judgment of his peers or by the law of the land....

60. Moreover, all those customs and franchises mentioned above which we have conceded in our kingdom, and which are to be fulfilled, as far as pertains to us, in respect to our men; all men of our kingdom as well as clergy as laymen, shall observe as far as pertains to them, in respect to their men.

What are the major principles of Magna Carta as seen in this excerpt? Why has Magna Carta been considered such an important historical document?

---

of accounts for finances, and a *parlement* or royal court. By the beginning of the fourteenth century, the Capetians had established firm foundations for a royal bureaucracy.

Philip IV also brought a French parliament into being by summoning representatives of the three estates, or classes—the clergy (First Estate), the nobles (Second Estate), and the townspeople (Third Estate)—to meet with him. They did so in 1302, inaugurating the Estates-General, the first French parliament, although it had little real power. By the end of the thirteenth century, France was the largest, wealthiest, and best-governed monarchical state in Europe.

Christian Reconquest: The Spanish Kingdoms

Much of Spain had been part of the Islamic world since the eighth century. Muslim Spain had flourished in the Early Middle Ages. Córdoba became a major urban center with a population exceeding 300,000 people. Agriculture prospered, and Spain became known as well for excellent leather, wool, silk, and paper. Beginning in the tenth century, however, the most noticeable feature of Spanish history was the beginning of a Christian reconquest that lasted until the final expulsion of the Muslims at the end of the fifteenth century. The **Reconquista,** as the Spaniards

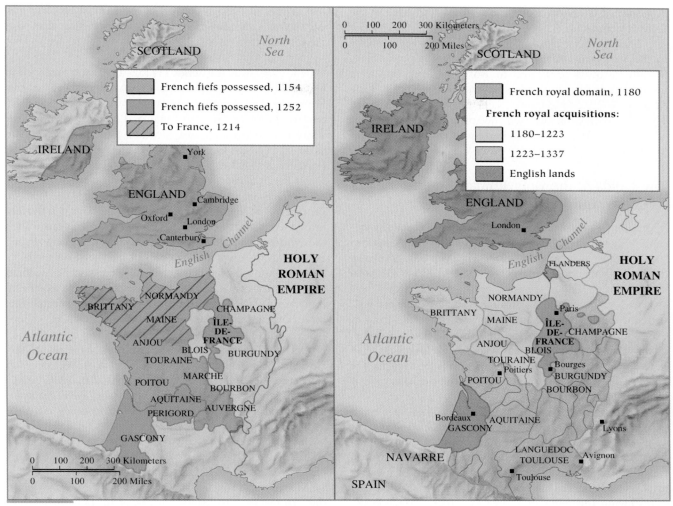

MAP 10.1 **England and France in the High Middle Ages: (*left*) England and Its French Holdings; (*right*) Growth of the French State.** King Philip II Augustus of France greatly expanded the power of the Capetian royal family through his victories over the Plantagenet monarchy of England, which enabled Philip to gain control over much of north-central France. **?** How might the existence of the English Channel have made it more difficult for England to rule its French possessions? ☞ **View an animated version of this map or related maps at** http://thomsonedu.com/history/spielvogel

called it, became over a period of time a sacred mission to many of the Christian rulers and inhabitants of the peninsula.

By the eleventh century, a number of small Christian kingdoms in northern Spain took the offensive against the Muslims. Rodrigo Díaz de Vivar, known as El Cid, was the most famous military adventurer of the time. Unlike the Christian warriors of France, El Cid fought under either Christian or Muslim rulers. He carved out his own kingdom of Valencia in 1094 but failed to create a dynasty when it was reconquered by the Muslims after his death.

By the end of the twelfth century, the northern half of Spain had been consolidated into the Christian kingdoms of Castile, Navarre, Aragon, and Portugal, which had emerged by 1179 as a separate kingdom (see Map 10.2).

The southern half of Spain remained under the control of the Muslims.

In the thirteenth century, Christian rulers took the offensive again in the reconquest of Muslim territory. Aragon and Castile had become the two strongest Spanish kingdoms, and Portugal had reached its modern boundaries. All three states made significant conquests of Muslim territory. Castile subdued most of Andalusia in the south, down to the Atlantic and the Mediterranean; at the same time, Aragon conquered Valencia. The crucial battle occurred in 1212 at Las Navas de Tolosa. Alfonso VIII of Castile (1155–1214) had amassed an army of sixty thousand and crushed the Muslim forces, leading to Christian victories over the next forty years. By the mid-thirteenth century, the Muslims remained only in the kingdom of Granada, along the southeastern edge of the Iberian peninsula.

The Spanish kingdoms followed no consistent policy in the treatment of the conquered Muslim population. Muslim farmers continued to work the land but were forced to pay very high rents in Aragon. In Castile, King Alfonso X (1252–1284), who called himself the "King of Three Religions," encouraged the continued development of a cosmopolitan culture shared by Christians, Jews, and Muslims.

The Lands of the Holy Roman Empire: Germany and Italy

In the tenth century, the powerful dukes of Saxony became kings of the lands of the eastern Frankish kingdom (or Germany, as it came to be known). The best known of the Saxon kings of Germany was Otto I (936–973), who intervened in Italian politics and for his efforts was crowned emperor of the Romans by the pope in 962, reviving a title that had not been used since the time of Charlemagne. Otto's creation of a new "Roman Empire" in the hands of the eastern Franks (or Germans, as they came to be called) added a tremendous burden to the kings of Germany, who now took on the onerous task of ruling Italy as well.

In the eleventh century, German kings created a strong monarchy and a powerful empire by leading armies into Italy. To strengthen their power, German kings had come to rely on their ability to control the church and select bishops and abbots, whom they could then use as royal administrators. But the struggle between church and state during the reign of Henry IV (1056–1106) weakened the king's ability to use church officials in this way. The German kings also tried to bolster their power by using their position as emperors to exploit the resources of Italy. But this tended to backfire; many a German king

lost armies in Italy in pursuit of a dream of empire, and no German dynasty demonstrates this better than the Hohenstaufens.

Frederick I Both Frederick I (1152–1190) and Frederick II (1212–1250), the two most famous members of the Hohenstaufen dynasty, tried to create a new kind of empire. Previous German kings had focused on building a strong German kingdom, to which Italy might be added as an appendage (see Map 10.3). Frederick I, known as Barbarossa (Redbeard) to the Italians, however, planned to get his chief revenues from Italy as the center of a "holy empire," as he called it (hence the name Holy Roman Empire). But his attempt to conquer northern Italy ran into severe difficulties. The pope opposed him, fearful that the emperor wanted to incorporate Rome and the Papal States into his empire. The cities of northern Italy, which had become used to their freedom, were also not willing to be Frederick's subjects. An alliance of these northern Italian cities, with the support of the papacy, defeated the forces of Emperor Frederick at Legnano in 1176.

Frederick II Frederick II was the most brilliant of the Hohenstaufen rulers. King of Sicily in 1198, king of Germany in 1212, and crowned emperor in 1220, Frederick II was a truly remarkable man who awed his contemporaries. Frederick had been raised in Sicily, with its diverse peoples, languages, and religions, and his court brought together a brilliant array of lawyers, poets, artists, and scientists. His main goal was to establish a strong centralized state in Italy dominated by his kingdom in Sicily. Frederick's major task was to gain control of northern Italy. In reaching to extend his power in Italy, he became involved in a deadly struggle with the popes, who realized that a single ruler of northern and southern Italy meant the end of papal secular power in central Italy. The northern Italian cities were also unwilling to give up their

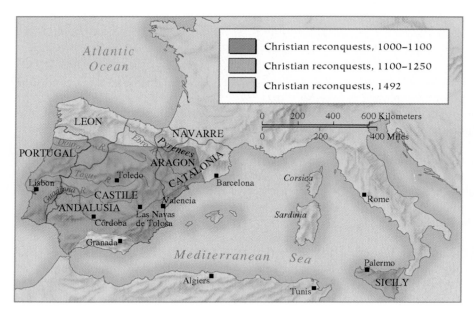

MAP 10.2 **Christian Reconquests in the Western Mediterranean.** Muslims seized most of Spain in the eighth century, near the end of the period of rapid Islamic expansion. In the eleventh century, small Christian kingdoms in the north began the *Reconquista,* finally conquering the last Moors near the end of the fifteenth century. ❓ How can you explain the roughly north-to-south conquest of the Muslim lands in Spain? 🔊 **View an animated version of this map or related maps at** http://thomsonedu.com/history/spielvogel

MAP 10.3 The Holy Roman Empire in the Twelfth Century. The Hohenstaufen rulers Frederick I and Frederick II sought to expand the Holy Roman Empire to include all of Italy. Frederick II had only fleeting success: after his death, several independent city-states arose in northern Italy, while at home, German nobles had virtually free reign within their domains. **?** Why did the territorial conquests of the Holy Roman Empire cause alarm in the papacy? **View an animated version of this map or related maps at** http://thomsonedu.com/history/spielvogel

freedom. Frederick waged a bitter struggle in northern Italy, winning many battles but ultimately losing the war.

Frederick's preoccupation with the creation of an empire in Italy left Germany in confusion and chaos until 1273, when the major German princes, serving as electors, chose an insignificant German noble, Rudolf of Habsburg, as the new German king. In choosing a weak king, the princes were ensuring that the German monarchy would remain impotent and incapable of reestablishing a centralized monarchical state. The failure of the Hohenstaufens had led to a situation where his exalted majesty, the German king and Holy Roman Emperor, had no real power over either Germany or Italy. Unlike France, England, and even Spain, neither Germany nor Italy created a unified national monarchy in the Middle Ages. Both became geographical designations for loose confederations of hundreds of petty states under the vague direction of king or emperor. In fact, neither Germany nor Italy would become united until the nineteenth century.

Following the death of Frederick II, Italy fell into political confusion. While the papacy remained in control of much of central Italy, the defeat of imperial power left the cities and towns of northern Italy independent of any other authority. Gradually, the larger ones began to emerge as strong city-states. Florence assumed the leadership of Tuscany, and Milan, under the guidance of the Visconti family, took control of the Lombard region.

With its great commercial wealth, the republic of Venice dominated the northeastern part of the peninsula.

New Kingdoms in Eastern Europe

In eastern Europe, Hungary, which had been a Christian state since 1000, remained relatively stable throughout the High Middle Ages, but the history of Poland and Russia was far more turbulent. In the thirteenth century, eastern Europe was beset by two groups of invaders, the Teutonic Knights from the west and the Mongols from the east.

In the eleventh century, a Polish kingdom existed as a separate state, but with no natural frontiers (see Map 10.4). Consequently, German settlers encroached on its territory on a regular basis, leading to considerable intermarriage between Slavs and Germans. During the thirteenth century, relations between the Germans and the Slavs of eastern Europe worsened due to the aggression of the Teutonic Knights. The Teutonic Knights had been founded near the end of the twelfth century to protect the Christian Holy Land. In the early thirteenth century, however, these Christian knights found greater opportunity to the east of Germany, where they attacked the pagan Slavs. East Prussia was given to the military order in 1226, and by the end of the thirteenth century, Prussia had become German and Christian as the pagan Slavs were forced to convert.

The Coronation of Frederick II. Shown here is the coronation of Frederick II of Germany as Holy Roman Emperor by Pope Honorius II in Rome on November 22, 1220. The pope agreed to do so after Frederick promised to lead a Crusade to the Holy Land, a promise that he took years to fulfill. This scene is taken from a fifteenth-century French manuscript on the monarchs of Europe.

MAP 10.4 Northern and Eastern Europe. Acceptance of Christianity gave many northern and eastern European kingdoms greater control over their subjects. Warfare was common in the region: dynastic struggles occurred in Scandinavia, and the Teutonic Knights, based in East Prussia, attacked the pagan Slavs. ❓ Which areas of northern and eastern Europe had large Slavic populations? (Look back at Map 8.4)

View an animated version of this map or related maps at http://thomsonedu.com/history/spielvogel

Central and eastern Europe had periodically been subject to invasions from fierce Asiatic nomads, including the Huns, Avars, Bulgars, and Magyars. In the thirteenth century, the Mongols exploded on the scene, causing far more disruption than earlier invaders.

Impact of the Mongol Empire

The Mongols rose to power in Asia with stunning speed. They were a pastoral people in the region of modern-day Outer Mongolia organized loosely in clans and tribes, often warring with each other. This changed when one leader, Temuchin, unified the Mongol tribes and gained the title of Genghis Khan (c. 1162–1227), which means "universal ruler." From that time on, Genghis Khan created a powerful military force and devoted himself to fighting. "Man's highest joy," Genghis Khan remarked, "is in victory: to conquer one's enemies, to pursue them, to deprive them of their possessions, to make their beloved weep, to ride on their horses, and to embrace their wives and daughters."[2] Genghis Khan was succeeded by equally competent sons and grandsons.

In the thirteenth century, the Mongols advanced eastward, eventually conquering China and Korea. One of Genghis Khan's grandsons, Khubilai Khan, completed the conquest of China and established a new Chinese dynasty of rulers known as the Yuan. In 1279, Khubilai Khan moved the capital of China northward to Khanbaliq ("city of the Khan"), which would later be known by the Chinese name Beijing.

The Mongol Empire

The Mongols also moved westward against the Islamic empire. Persia fell by 1233, and by 1258 they had conquered Baghdad and destroyed the Abbasid caliphate. Beginning in the 1230s, the Mongols had moved into Europe. They conquered Russia, advanced into Poland and Hungary, and destroyed a force of Poles and Teutonic Knights in Silesia in 1241. At that point, the Mongol hordes turned back because of internal fighting; western and southern Europe escaped their wrath. Overall, the Mongols had little impact in Europe, although their occupation of Russia had some residual effect.

The Development of Russia

The Kiev Rus state, which had become formally Christian in 987, prospered considerably afterward, reaching its high point in the first half of the eleventh century. Kievan society was dominated by a noble class of landowners known as the **boyars**. Kievan merchants maintained regular trade with Scandinavia to the north and the Islamic and Byzantine worlds to the south. But destructive civil wars and new invasions by Asiatic nomads caused the principality of Kiev to collapse, and the sack of Kiev by north Russian princes in 1169 brought an inglorious end to the first Russian state.

The fundamental civilizing and unifying force of early Russia was the Christian church. The Russian church imitated the liturgy and organization of the Byzantine Empire, whose Eastern Orthodox priests had converted the Kievan Rus to Christianity at the end of the tenth century. The Russian church became known for its rigid religious orthodoxy. Although Christianity provided a common bond between Russian and European civilization, Russia's religious development guaranteed an even closer affinity between Russian and Byzantine civilization.

In the thirteenth century, the Mongols conquered Russia and cut it off even more from western Europe. The Mongols were not numerous enough to settle the vast Russian lands but were content to rule directly an area along the lower Volga and north of the Caspian and Black Seas to Kiev and rule indirectly elsewhere. In the latter territories, Russian princes were required to pay tribute to the Mongol overlords.

One Russian prince soon emerged as more powerful than the others. Alexander Nevsky (c. 1220–1263), prince of Novgorod, defeated a German invading army in northwestern Russia in 1242. His cooperation with the Mongols won him their favor. The khan, leader of the western part of the Mongol empire, rewarded Alexander Nevsky with the title of grand-prince, enabling his descendants to become the princes of Moscow and eventually leaders of all Russia.

The Recovery and Reform of the Catholic Church

In the Early Middle Ages, the Catholic church had played a leading role in converting and civilizing first the Germanic invaders and later the Vikings and Magyars. Although

England	
Battle of Hastings	1066
William the Conqueror	1066–1087
Henry II, first of the Plantagenet dynasty	1154–1189
Murder of Thomas à Becket	1170
John	1199–1216
Magna Carta	1215
Edward I	1272–1307
The "greater Parliaments"	1295, 1297
France	
Hugh Capet, French king	987
Philip II Augustus	1180–1223
Louis IX	1226–1270
Philip IV	1285–1314
First Estates-General	1302
Spain	
El Cid in Valencia	1094–1099
Alfonso VIII of Castile	1155–1214
Establishment of Portugal	1179
Alfonso X of Castile	1252–1284
Germany, The Holy Roman Empire, and Italy	
Otto I	936–973
Henry IV	1056–1106
Frederick I Barbarossa	1152–1190
Lombard League defeats Frederick at Legnano	1176
Frederick II	1212–1250
Election of Rudolf of Habsburg as king of Germany	1273
Eastern Europe	
Alexander Nevsky, prince of Novgorod	c. 1220–1263
East Prussia given to the Teutonic Knights	1226
Mongol conquest of Russia	1230s

highly successful, this effort brought challenges that undermined the spiritual life of the church itself.

The Problems of Decline

Since the eighth century, the popes had reigned supreme over the affairs of the Catholic church. They had also come to exercise control over the territories in central Italy known as the Papal States; this kept popes involved in political matters, often at the expense of their spiritual obligations. At the same time, the church became increasingly entangled in the evolving lord-vassal relationships.

High officials of the church, such as bishops and abbots, came to hold their offices as fiefs from nobles. As vassals, they were obliged to carry out the usual duties, including military service. Of course, lords assumed the right to choose their vassals, even when those vassals included bishops and abbots. Because lords often selected their vassals from other noble families for political reasons, these bishops and abbots were often worldly figures who cared little about their spiritual responsibilities.

The monastic ideal had also suffered during the Early Middle Ages. Benedictine monasteries had sometimes been exemplary centers of Christian living and learning, but the invasions of Vikings, Magyars, and Muslims wreaked havoc with many monastic establishments. Discipline declined, and with it the monastic reputation for learning and holiness. At the same time, a growing number of monasteries fell under the control of local lords, as did much of the church. A number of people believed that the time for reform had come.

The Cluniac Reform Movement

Reform of the Catholic church began in Burgundy in eastern France in 910 when Duke William of Aquitaine founded the abbey of Cluny. The monastery began with a renewed dedication to the highest spiritual ideals of the Benedictine rule and was fortunate in possessing a series of abbots in the tenth century who maintained these ideals. Cluny was deliberately kept independent from secular control. As Duke William stipulated in his original charter, "It has pleased us also to insert in this document that, from this day, those same monks there congregated shall be subject neither to our yoke, nor to that of our relatives, nor to the sway of the royal might, nor to that of any earthly power."[3]

The Cluniac reform movement sparked an enthusiastic response, first in France and eventually in all of western and central Europe. New monasteries were founded on Cluniac ideals, and existing monasteries rededicated themselves by adopting the Cluniac program. The movement also began to reach beyond monasticism and into the papacy itself, which was in dire need of help.

Reform of the Papacy

By the eleventh century, church leaders realized the need to free the church from the interference of lords in the appointment of church officials. This issue of **lay investiture,** the practice by which secular rulers both chose and invested their nominees to church offices with the symbols of their office, was dramatically taken up by the greatest of the reform popes of the eleventh century, Gregory VII (1073–1085).

Elected pope in 1073, Gregory was convinced that he had been chosen by God to reform the church. In pursuit of those aims, Gregory claimed that he, as pope, was God's "vicar on earth" and that the pope's authority extended over all Christians, including rulers. Gregory sought the elimination of lay investiture. Only then could the church regain its freedom, by which Gregory meant the right to appoint its own clergy and run its own affairs. If rulers did not accept these "divine" commands, they could be deposed by the pope in his capacity as the vicar of Christ.

Gregory VII soon found himself in conflict with King Henry IV (1056–1106) of Germany over these claims. For many years, German kings had appointed high-ranking clerics, especially bishops, as their vassals in order to use them as administrators. Without them, the king could not hope to maintain his own power vis-à-vis the powerful German nobles. In 1075, Pope Gregory issued a decree forbidding important clerics from receiving their investiture from lay leaders: "We decree that no one of the clergy shall receive the investiture with a bishopric or abbey or church from the hand of an emperor or king or of any lay person."[4] Henry had no intention of obeying a decree that challenged the very heart of his administration.

The struggle between Henry IV and Gregory VII, which is known as the Investiture Controversy, was one of the great conflicts between church and state in the High Middle Ages. It dragged on until 1122, when a new German king and a new pope achieved a compromise in the Concordat of Worms. Under this agreement, a bishop in Germany was first elected by church officials. After election, the nominee paid homage to the king as his lord, who in turn invested him with the symbols of temporal office. A representative of the pope then invested the new bishop with the symbols of his spiritual office.

Christianity and Medieval Civilization

Christianity was an integral part of the fabric of medieval European society and the consciousness of Europe. Papal directives affected the actions of kings and princes alike, while Christian teaching and practices touched the economic, social, intellectual, cultural, and daily lives of all Europeans.

Growth of the Papal Monarchy

The popes of the twelfth century did not abandon the reform ideals of Gregory VII, but they were less dogmatic and more inclined to consolidate their power and build a strong administrative system. By the twelfth century, the Catholic church possessed a clearly organized hierarchical structure. The pope and **papal curia** (staffed by high church officials known as cardinals, the pope's major advisers and administrators) were at the center of the administrative structure. Below them were the bishops, since all of Christendom was divided into dioceses under their direction. Archbishops were in principle more powerful than the bishops, but at this time they were unable to exercise any real control over the internal affairs of the bishops' dioceses.

In the thirteenth century, the Catholic church reached the height of its political, intellectual, and secular power. The papal monarchy extended its sway over both ecclesiastical and temporal affairs, as was especially evident during the papacy of Pope Innocent III (1198–1216). At the beginning of his pontificate, in a letter to a priest, Innocent made a clear statement of his views on papal supremacy:

> As God, the creator of the universe, set two great lights in the firmament of heaven, the greater light to rule the day, and the lesser light to rule the night so He set two great dignities in the firmament of the universal church, . . . the greater to rule the day, that is, souls, and the lesser to rule the night, that is, bodies. These dignities are the papal authority and the royal power. And just as the moon gets her light from the sun, and is inferior to the sun . . . so the royal power gets the splendor of its dignity from the papal authority.[5]

Innocent's actions were those of a man who believed that he, as pope, was the supreme judge of European affairs. He forced King Philip Augustus of France to take back his wife and queen after Philip had tried to have the marriage annulled. The pope intervened in German affairs and installed his candidate as emperor. He compelled King John of England to accept the papal choice for the position of archbishop of Canterbury. To achieve his political ends, Innocent did not hesitate to use the spiritual weapons at his command, especially the **interdict**, which forbade priests to dispense the **sacraments** of the church in the hope that the people, deprived of the comforts of religion, would exert pressure against their ruler. Pope Innocent's interdict was so effective that it caused Philip to restore his wife to her rightful place as queen of France.

© Scala/Art Resource, NY

Pope Innocent III. Innocent III was an active and powerful pope during the High Middle Ages. He approved the creation of the Franciscan and Dominican religious orders and inaugurated the Fourth Crusade.

New Religious Orders and Spiritual Ideals

In the second half of the eleventh century and the first half of the twelfth, a wave of religious enthusiasm seized Europe, leading to a spectacular growth in the number of monasteries and the emergence of new monastic orders. Most important was the Cistercian order, founded in 1098 by a group of monks dissatisfied with the lack of strict discipline at their Benedictine monastery. Cistercian monasticism spread rapidly from southern France into the rest of Europe.

The Cistercians were strict. They ate a simple diet and possessed only a single robe each. All decorations were eliminated from their churches and monastic buildings. More time for prayer and manual labor was provided by shortening the number of hours spent at religious services. The Cistercians played a major role in developing a new, activist spiritual model for twelfth-century Europe. A Benedictine monk often spent hours in prayer to honor God. The Cistercian ideal had a different emphasis: "Arise, soldier of Christ, arise! Get up off the ground and return to the battle from which you have fled! Fight more boldly after your flight, and triumph in glory!"[6] These were the words of Saint Bernard of Clairvaux (1090–1153), who more than any other person embodied the new spiritual ideal of Cistercian monasticism (see the box on p. 186).

Women in Religious Orders Women were active participants in the spiritual movements of the age. The number of women joining religious houses increased perceptibly with the spread of the new orders of the twelfth century. In the High Middle Ages, most nuns were from the ranks of the landed aristocracy. Convents were convenient for families unable or unwilling to find husbands for their daughters and for aristocratic women who did not wish to marry. Female intellectuals found them a haven for their activities. Most of the learned women of the Middle Ages, especially in Germany, were nuns. One of the most distinguished was Hildegard of Bingen (1098–1179), who became abbess of a convent at Disibodenberg in western Germany.

Hildegard shared in the religious enthusiasm of the twelfth century. Soon after becoming abbess, she began to write an account of the mystical visions she had experienced for years. "A great flash of light from heaven pierced my brain and . . . in that instant my mind was imbued with the meaning of the sacred books,"[7] she wrote in a description typical of the world's mystical literature. Eventually she produced three books based on her visions. Hildegard gained considerable renown as a mystic and prophet, and popes, emperors, kings, dukes, and bishops eagerly sought her advice.

Living the Gospel Life In the thirteenth century, two new religious orders emerged that had a profound impact on the lives of ordinary people. The friars were particularly active in the cities, where, by their example, they strove to provide a more personal religious experience.

A MIRACLE OF SAINT BERNARD

Saint Bernard of Clairvaux has been called the most widely respected holy man of the twelfth century. He was an outstanding preacher, wholly dedicated to the service of God. His reputation reportedly influenced many young men to join the Cistercian order. He also inspired a myriad of stories dealing with his miracles.

A Miracle of Saint Bernard

A certain monk, departing from his monastery . . . threw off his habit, and returned to the world at the persuasion of the Devil. And he took a certain parish living; for he was a priest. Because sin is punished with sin, the deserter from his Order lapsed into the vice of lechery. He took a concubine to live with him, as in fact is done by many, and by her he had children.

But as God is merciful and does not wish anyone to perish, it happened that many years after, the blessed abbot [Saint Bernard] was passing through the village in which this same monk was living, and went to stay at his house. The renegade monk recognized him, and received him very reverently, and waited on him devoutly . . . but as yet the abbot did not recognize him.

On the morrow, the holy man said Matins and prepared to be off. But as he could not speak to the priest, since he had got up and gone to the church for Matins, he said to the priest's son "Go, give this message to your master." Now the boy had been born dumb. He obeyed the command and feeling in himself the power of him who had given it, he ran to his father and uttered the words of the Holy Father clearly and exactly. His father, on hearing his son's voice for the first time, wept for joy, and made him repeat the same words . . . and he asked what the abbot had done to him. "He did nothing to me," said the boy, "except to say 'Go and say this to your father.'"

At so evident a miracle the priest repented, and hastened after the holy man and fell at his feet saying, "My Lord and Father, I was your monk so-and-so, and at such-and-such a time I ran away from your monastery. I ask your Paternity to allow me to return with you to the monastery, for in your coming God has visited my heart." The saint replied unto him, "Wait for me here, and I will come back quickly when I have done my business, and I will take you with me." But the priest, fearing death (which he had not done before), answered, "Lord, I am afraid of dying before then." But the saint replied, "Know this for certain, that if you die in this condition, and in this resolve, you will find yourself a monk before God."

The saint [eventually] returned and heard that the priest had recently died and been buried. He ordered the tomb to be opened. And when they asked him what he wanted to do, he said, "I want to see if he is lying as a monk or a clerk in his tomb." "As a clerk," they said; "we buried him in his secular habit." But when they had dug up the earth, they found that he was not in the clothes in which they had buried him; but he appeared in all points, tonsure and habit, as a monk. And they all praised God.

What two miracles occur in this excerpt from the life of Saint Bernard? What does this document reveal about popular religious practices during the Middle Ages?

A Group of Nuns.   Although still viewed by the medieval church as inferior to men, women were as susceptible to the spiritual fervor of the twelfth century as men, and female monasticism grew accordingly. This manuscript illustration shows at left a group of nuns welcoming a novice (dressed in white) to their order. At the right a nun receives a sick person on a stretcher for the order's hospital care.

Like their founder, Saint Francis of Assisi (1182–1226), the Franciscan friars lived among the people, preaching repentance and aiding the poor. Their calls for a return to the simplicity and poverty of the early church, reinforced by their own example, were especially effective and made them very popular.

The Dominicans arose out of the desire of a Spanish priest, Dominic de Guzmán (1170–1221), to defend church teachings from heresy. The spiritual revival of the High Middle Ages had also led to the emergence of heretical movements, which became especially widespread in southern France. Unlike Francis, Dominic was an intellectual who was appalled by the growth of heresy within the church. He believed that a new religious order of men who lived lives of poverty but were learned and capable of preaching effectively would best be able to attack heresy.

Popular Religion in the High Middle Ages

We have witnessed the actions of popes, bishops, and monks. But what of ordinary clergy and laypeople? What were their religious hopes and fears? What were their spiritual aspirations?

The sacraments of the Catholic church ensured that the church was an integral part of people's lives, from birth to death. There were (and still are) seven sacraments, administered only by the clergy. Sacraments, such as baptism and the **Eucharist** (the Lord's Supper), were viewed as outward symbols of an inward grace (grace was God's freely given gift that enabled humans to be saved) and were considered imperative for a Christian's salvation. Therefore, the clergy were seen to have a key role in the attainment of salvation.

Other church practices were also important to ordinary people. Saints, it was believed, were men and women who, through their holiness, had achieved a special position in heaven, enabling them to act as intercessors before God. The saints' ability to protect poor souls enabled them to take on great importance at the popular level. Jesus' apostles were recognized throughout Europe as saints, but there were also numerous local saints who had special significance. New cults developed rapidly, particularly in the intense religious atmosphere of the eleventh and twelfth centuries. The English introduced Saint Nicholas, the patron saint of children, who remains instantly recognizable today through his identification with Santa Claus.

Of all the saints, the Virgin Mary occupied the foremost position in the High Middle Ages. Mary was viewed as the most important mediator with her son Jesus, the judge of all sinners. Moreover, from the eleventh century on, a fascination with Mary as Jesus' human mother became more evident. A sign of Mary's importance was the growing number of churches all over Europe that were dedicated to her in the twelfth and thirteenth centuries.

Emphasis on the role of the saints was closely tied to the use of **relics**, which also increased noticeably in the High Middle Ages. Relics were usually the bones of saints or objects intimately connected to saints that were considered worthy of veneration by the faithful. A twelfth-century English monk began his description of the abbey's relics by saying, "There is kept there a thing more precious than gold, . . . the right arm of St. Oswald. . . . This we have seen with our own eyes and have kissed, and have handled with our own hands. . . . There are kept here also part of his ribs and of the soil on which he fell."[8] The monk went on to list additional relics possessed by the abbey, which purported to include two pieces of Jesus' swaddling clothes, pieces of Jesus' manger, and part of the five loaves of bread with which Jesus fed five thousand people. Because the holiness of the saint was considered to be inherent in his relics, these objects were believed to be capable of healing people or producing other miracles.

Voices of Protest and Intolerance

The desire for more personal and deeper religious experience, which characterized the spiritual revival of the High Middle Ages, also led people in directions hostile to the institutional church. From the twelfth century on, heresy, or the holding of religious doctrines different from the orthodox teachings of the church as determined by church authorities, became a serious problem for the Catholic church. The best-known heresy of the twelfth and thirteenth centuries was Catharism. The Cathars (from the Greek word for "pure") were also called Albigensians, after the city of Albi, one of their strongholds in southern France. They believed in a dualist system in which good and evil were separate and distinct. The things of the spirit were good because they were created by God, the source of light; the things of the world were evil because they were created by Satan, the prince of darkness. Humans, too, were enmeshed in dualism. Their souls, which were good, were trapped in material bodies, which were evil. According to the Cathars, the Catholic church, itself a materialistic institution, had nothing to do with God and was essentially evil. There was no need to follow its teachings or recognize its authority. The Cathar movement gained valuable support from important nobles in southern France and northern Italy.

The spread of heresy in southern France alarmed the church authorities. Pope Innocent III appealed to the nobles of northern France for a **Crusade** (a military campaign in defense of Christianity) against the heretics. The Crusade against the Albigensians, which began in the summer of 1209 and lasted for almost two decades, was a bloody fight. Thousands of heretics (and innocents) were slaughtered, including entire populations of some towns. In Béziers, for example, seven thousand men, women, and children were massacred when they took refuge in the local church.

Southern France was devastated, but Catharism remained, which caused the Catholic church to devise a regular method for discovering and dealing with heretics. This led to the emergence of the Holy Office, as the papal Inquisition was called, a formal court whose job it was to

Expulsion of Albigensian Heretics. In 1209, Pope Innocent III authorized a Crusade against the heretical Albigensians. In this medieval illustration, French knights are shown expelling Albigensian heretics from the town of Carcassonne near Albi, an Albigensian stronghold in southern France.

CHRONOLOGY The Catholic Church in the High Middle Ages

Foundation of abbey of Cluny	910
Pope Gregory VII	1073–1085
Decree against lay investiture	1075
Pope Urban II	1088–1099
Founding of Cistercians	1098
Pope Innocent III	1198–1216
Start of Crusade against the Albigensians	1209
Fourth Lateran Council	1215

ferret out and try heretics. Anyone accused of heresy who refused to confess was considered guilty and was turned over to the secular authorities for execution. To the Christians of the thirteenth century, who believed that there was only one path to salvation, heresy was a crime against God and against humanity, and force was justified to save souls from damnation. The fanaticism and fear unleashed in the struggle against heretics were also used against others, especially the Jews.

Persecution of the Jews   The Jews were the only religious minority in medieval Europe that was allowed to practice a non-Christian religion. But the religious enthusiasm of the High Middle Ages produced an outburst of intolerance against the supposed enemies of Christianity. After Crusades were launched against the Muslims starting in 1096, European Christians took up the search for enemies at home, persecuting Jews in France and the Rhineland. Jews in Speyer, Worms, Mainz, and Cologne were all set upon by bands of Christian crusaders.

In the thirteenth century, in the supercharged atmosphere of fear created by the struggle with the heretics, Jews were persecuted more and more (see the box on p. 189). Friars urged action against these "murderers of Christ," contending that the Jews, having turned Jesus over to the Roman authorities, were responsible for his death, and organized the public burning of Jewish books. The Fourth Lateran Council in 1215 decreed that Jews must wear distinguishing marks, such as ribbons, yellow badges,

and special veils and cloaks, to differentiate themselves from Christians. The same council encouraged the development of Jewish ghettos, neighborhoods built behind walled enclosures to isolate Jews from Christians. The persecution and demonization of Jews stimulated a tradition of anti-Semitism that proved to be one of Christian Europe's most insidious contributions to the Western heritage.

European kings, who had portrayed themselves as protectors of the Jews, had so fleeced the Jewish communities of their money by the end of the thirteenth century that they no longer had reason to resist the mob fury. Edward I expelled all Jews from England in 1290. The French followed suit in 1306. As the policy of expulsion spread into central Europe, most northern European Jews were driven into Poland.

Intolerance and Homosexuality   The climate of intolerance that characterized thirteenth-century attitudes toward Muslims, heretics, and Jews was also evident toward homosexuals. Although the church had condemned homosexuality in the Early Middle Ages, it had not been overly concerned with homosexual behavior, an attitude also prevalent in the secular world. By the thirteenth century, these tolerant attitudes had altered drastically. Some historians connect this change to the century's climate of fear and intolerance against any group that deviated from the standards of the majority. A favorite approach of the critics was to identify homosexuals with other detested groups. Homosexuality was portrayed as a regular practice of Muslims and such notorious heretics as the Albigensians. Between 1250 and 1300, what had been tolerated in most of Europe became a criminal act deserving of death.

The legislation against homosexuality commonly referred to it as a "sin against nature." This is precisely the argument developed by Thomas Aquinas (see Chapter 9), who formed Catholic opinion on the subject for centuries to come. In his *Summa Theologica*, Aquinas argued that because the purpose of sex was procreation, it could only legitimately take place in ways that did not exclude this possibility. Hence homosexuality (like all other sexual

TREATMENT OF THE JEWS

*T*he development of new religious sensibilities in the High Middle Ages also had a negative side—the turning of Christians against their supposed enemies. Although the Crusades provide the most obvious example, Christians also turned on the "murderers of Christ," the Jews. As a result, Jews suffered increased persecution. These three documents show different sides of the picture. The first is Canon 68 of the decrees of the Fourth Lateran Council called by Pope Innocent III in 1215. The decree specifies the need for special dress, one of the ways Christians tried to separate Jews from their community. The second excerpt is a chronicler's account of the most absurd charge levied against the Jews—that they were guilty of the ritual murder of Christian children to obtain Christian blood for the Passover service. This charge led to the murder of many Jews. The third document, taken from a list of regulations issued by the city of Avignon, France, illustrates the contempt Christian society held for the Jews.

Canon 68

In some provinces a difference in dress distinguishes the Jews or Saracens [Muslims] from the Christians, but in certain others such a confusion has grown up that they cannot be distinguished by any difference. Thus it happens at times that through error Christians have relations with the women of Jews or Saracens, and Jews or Saracens with Christian women. Therefore, that they may not, under pretext of error of this sort, excuse themselves in the future for the excesses of such prohibited intercourse, we decree that such Jews and Saracens of both sexes in every Christian province and at all times shall be marked off in the eyes of the public from other peoples through the character of their dress....

Moreover, during the last three days before Easter and especially on Good Friday, they shall not go forth in public at all, for the reason that some of them on these very days, as we hear, do not blush to go forth better dressed and are not afraid to mock the Christians who maintain the memory of the most holy Passion by wearing signs of mourning.

The Jews and Ritual Murder of Christian Children

[The eight-year-old-boy] Harold, who is buried in the Church of St. Peter the Apostle, at Gloucester...is said to have been carried away secretly by Jews, in the opinion of many, on Feb. 21, and by them hidden till March 16. On that night, on the sixth of the preceding feast, the Jews of all England coming together as if to circumcise a certain boy, pretend deceitfully that they are about to celebrate the feast [Passover] appointed by law in such case, and deceiving the citizens of Gloucester with the fraud, they tortured the lad placed before them with immense tortures. It is true no Christian was present, or saw or heard the deed, nor have we found that anything was betrayed by any Jew. But a little while after when the whole convent of monks of Gloucester and almost all the citizens of that city, and innumerable persons coming to the spectacle, saw the wounds of the dead body, scars of fire, the thorns fixed on his head, and liquid wax poured into the eyes and face, and touched it with the diligent examination of their hands, those tortures were believed or guessed to have been inflicted on him in that manner. It was clear that they had made him a glorious martyr to Christ, being slain without sin, and having bound his feet with his own girdle, threw him into the river Severn.

The Regulations of Avignon, 1243

Likewise, we declare that Jews or whores shall not dare to touch with their hands either bread or fruit put out for sale, and that if they should do this they must buy what they have touched.

What do these documents reveal about Christian attitudes toward the Jews?

---

practices that could not result in pregnancy) was "contrary to nature" and a deviation from the natural order established by God. This argument and laws prohibiting homosexual activity on pain of death remained the norm in Europe until the twentieth century.

The Crusades

Another manifestation of the religious enthusiasm that seized Europe in the High Middle Ages was the series of Crusades mounted against the Muslims. These campaigns gave the revived papacy of the High Middle Ages yet another opportunity to demonstrate its influence over European society. The Crusades were a curious mix of God and warfare, two of the chief concerns of the Middle Ages.

Background to the Crusades

Although European civilization developed in relative isolation, it had never entirely lost contact with the lands and empires to the east. At the end of the eleventh century, that contact increased, in part because developments in the Islamic and Byzantine worlds prompted the first major attempt of the new European civilization to expand beyond Europe proper.

Islam and the Seljuk Turks By the mid-tenth century, the Islamic empire led by the Abbasid caliphate in Baghdad was in the process of disintegration. A Shi'ite dynasty known as the Fatimids managed to conquer Egypt and establish the new city of Cairo as their capital. In establishing a Shi'ite caliphate, they became rivals to the

Sunni caliphate of Baghdad, exacerbating the division in the Islamic world. Nevertheless, the Fatimid dynasty prospered and eventually surpassed the Abbasid caliphate as the dynamic center of the Islamic world. The Fatimids created a strong army by using nonnative peoples as mercenaries. One of these peoples, the Seljuk Turks, soon posed a threat to the Fatimids themselves.

The Seljuk Turks were a nomadic people from Central Asia who had been converted to Islam and flourished as military mercenaries for the Abbasid caliphate. Moving gradually into Persia and Armenia, they grew in number until by the eleventh century they were able to take over the eastern provinces of the Abbasid empire. In 1055, a Turkish leader captured Baghdad and assumed command of the Abbasid empire with the title of **sultan** ("holder of power"). By the second half of the eleventh century, the Seljuk Turks were exerting military pressure on Egypt and the Byzantine Empire. When the Byzantine emperor foolishly challenged the Turks, the latter routed the Byzantine army at Manzikert in 1071. In dire straits, the Byzantines turned to the west for help, setting in motion the papal pleas that led to the Crusades. To understand the complexities of the situation, however, we need to look first at the Byzantine Empire.

The Byzantine Empire   The Macedonian dynasty of the tenth and eleventh centuries had restored much of the power of the Byzantine Empire; its incompetent successors, however, reversed most of the gains. After the Macedonian dynasty was extinguished in 1056, the empire was beset by internal struggles for power between ambitious military leaders and aristocratic families who attempted to buy the support of the great landowners of Anatolia by allowing them greater control over their peasants.

The growing division between the Catholic church of the west and the Eastern Orthodox church of the Byzantine Empire also weakened the Byzantine state. The Eastern Orthodox church was unwilling to accept the pope's claim that he was the sole head of the church. This issue reached a climax when Pope Leo IX and the Patriarch Michael Cerularius, head of the Byzantine church, formally excommunicated each other in 1054, initiating a schism between the two great branches of Christianity that has not been healed to this day.

The Byzantine Empire faced external threats to its security as well. The greatest challenge came from the Seljuk Turks who had moved into Asia Minor, the heartland of the empire and its main source of food and manpower. After defeating Byzantine forces in 1071, the Turks advanced into Anatolia, where many peasants, already disgusted by their exploitation at the hands of Byzantine landowners, readily accepted Turkish control.

Another dynasty, however, soon breathed new life into the Byzantine Empire. The Comneni, under Alexius I Comnenus (1081–1118), were victorious on the Greek Adriatic coast against the Normans, defeated the Pechenegs in the Balkans, and stopped the Turks in Anatolia. Lacking the resources to undertake additional campaigns

against the Turks, Emperor Alexius I turned to the west for military assistance. It was the positive response of the west to the emperor's request that led to the Crusades.

The Early Crusades

The Crusades were conceived as a holy war against the infidel or unbelievers. The immediate impetus for the Crusades came when the Byzantine emperor Alexius I asked Pope Urban II (1088–1099) for help against the Seljuk Turks. The pope saw a golden opportunity to provide papal leadership for a great cause: to rally the warriors of Europe for the liberation of Jerusalem and the Holy Land from the Muslim infidel. At the Council of Clermont in southern France near the end of 1095, Urban challenged Christians to take up their weapons against the infidel and join in a holy war to recover the Holy Land. The pope promised remission of sins: "All who die by the way, whether by land or by sea, or in battle against the pagans, shall have immediate remission of sins. This I grant them through the power of God with which I am invested."[9]

The warriors of western Europe, particularly France, formed the first crusading armies. The knights who made up this first serious crusading host were motivated by religious fervor, but there were other attractions as well. Some sought adventure and welcomed a legitimate opportunity to pursue their favorite pastime—fighting. Others saw an opportunity to gain territory, riches, status, possibly a title, and even salvation—had the pope not offered a full remission of sins for those who participated in these "armed pilgrimages"? From the perspective of the pope and European monarchs, the Crusades offered a way to rid Europe of contentious young nobles who disturbed the peace and wasted lives and energy fighting each other. And merchants in many Italian cities relished the prospect of new trading opportunities in Muslim lands.

In the First Crusade, begun in 1096, three organized bands of noble warriors, most of them French, made their way to the east (see Map 10.5). This first crusading army probably numbered several thousand cavalry and as many as ten thousand foot soldiers. After the capture of Antioch in 1098, much of the crusading host proceeded down the coast of Palestine, evading the garrisoned coastal cities, and reached Jerusalem in June 1099. After a five-week siege, the Holy City was taken amid a horrible massacre of the inhabitants, men, women, and children (see the box on p. 192).

After further conquest of Palestinian lands, the crusaders ignored the wishes of the Byzantine emperor (who foolishly believed the crusaders were working on his behalf) and organized four Crusader States (Edessa, Antioch, Tripoli, and Jerusalem). Because the Crusader States were surrounded by Muslim enemies, they grew increasingly dependent on the Italian commercial cities for supplies from Europe. Some Italian cities, such as Genoa, Pisa, and especially Venice, became rich and powerful in the process.

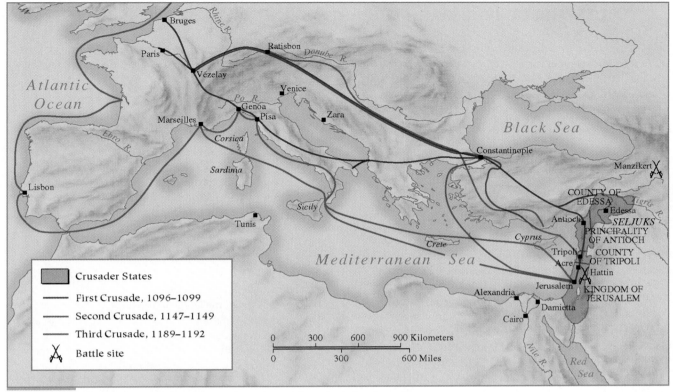

MAP 10.5   The Early Crusades. Pope Urban II launched the Crusades to recapture the Holy Land from the "enemies of God," a call met with great enthusiasm in Europe. The fighters of the First Crusade massacred the inhabitants of Jerusalem and established four Crusader States. ? In the Third Crusade, which countries sent crusaders by land and which by sea, and why would they choose these methods of travel? ● **View an animated version of this map or related maps at** http://thomsonedu.com/history/spielvogel

But it was not easy for the Crusader States to maintain themselves in the east. Already by the 1120s, the Muslims had begun to strike back. In 1144, Edessa became the first of the four Latin states to be recaptured. Its fall led to renewed calls for another Crusade, especially from the monastic firebrand Saint Bernard of Clairvaux, who exclaimed, "Now, on account of our sins, the sacrilegious enemies of the cross have begun to show their faces.... What are you doing, you servants of the cross? Will you throw to the dogs that which is most holy? Will you cast pearls before swine?"[10] Bernard aimed his message at knights and even managed to enlist two powerful rulers, King Louis VII of France and Emperor Conrad III of Germany. Their Second Crusade, however, proved a total failure.

The Third Crusade was a reaction to the fall of the Holy City of Jerusalem in 1187 to the Muslim forces under Saladin. Now all of Christendom was ablaze with calls for a new Crusade in the east. Three major monarchs agreed to lead new crusading forces in person: Emperor Frederick Barbarossa of Germany (1152–1190), Richard I the Lionhearted of England (1189–1199), and Philip II Augustus, king of France (1180–1223). Some of the crusaders finally arrived in the east by 1189 only to encounter problems. Frederick Barbarossa drowned while

swimming in a local river, and his army quickly fell apart. The English and French arrived by sea and met with success against the coastal cities, where they had the support of their fleets, but when they moved inland, they failed miserably. Eventually, after Philip went home, Richard negotiated a settlement whereby Saladin agreed to allow Christian pilgrims free access to Jerusalem.

The Crusades of the Thirteenth Century

After the death of Saladin in 1193, Pope Innocent III initiated a Fourth Crusade. On its way to the east, the crusading army became involved in a dispute over the succession to the Byzantine throne. The Venetian leaders of the Fourth Crusade saw an opportunity to neutralize their greatest commercial competitor, the Byzantine Empire. Diverted to Constantinople, the crusaders sacked that great capital city in 1204 and declared the new Latin Empire of Constantinople. Not until 1261 did a Byzantine army recapture Constantinople. The Byzantine Empire had been saved, but it was no longer a great Mediterranean power. The restored empire now consisted only of the city of Constantinople and its surrounding territory along with some lands in Asia Minor. Though reduced in size, the empire limped along for another 190

The Siege of Jerusalem: Christian and Muslim Perspectives

*D*uring the First Crusade, Christian knights laid siege to Jerusalem in June 1099. The first excerpt is taken from an account by Fulcher of Chartres, who accompanied the crusaders to the Holy Land. The second selection is by a Muslim writer, Ibn al-Athir, whose account of the First Crusade can be found in his history of the Muslim world.

Fulcher of Chartres, *Chronicle of the First Crusade*

Then the Franks entered the city magnificently at the noonday hour on Friday, the day of the week when Christ redeemed the whole world on the cross. With trumpets sounding and with everything in an uproar, exclaiming: "Help, God!" they vigorously pushed into the city, and straightway raised the banner on the top of the wall. All the heathen, completely terrified, changed their boldness to swift flight through the narrow streets of the quarters. The more quickly they fled, the more quickly they put to flight.

Count Raymond and his men, who were bravely assailing the city in another section, did not perceive this until they saw the Saracens [Muslims] jumping from the top of the wall. Seeing this, they joyfully ran to the city as quickly as they could, and helped the others pursue and kill the wicked enemy.

Then some, both Arabs and Ethiopians, fled into the Tower of David; others shut themselves in the Temple of the Lord and of Solomon, where in the halls a very great attack was made on them. Nowhere was there a place where the Saracens could escape swordsmen.

On the top of Solomon's Temple, to which they had climbed in fleeing, many were shot to death with arrows and cast down headlong from the roof. Within this Temple, about ten thousand were beheaded. If you had been there, your feet would have been stained up to the ankles with the blood of the slain. What more shall I tell? Not one of them was allowed to live. They did not spare the women and children.

Account of Ibn al-Athir

In fact Jerusalem was taken from the north on the morning of Friday 22 Sha'ban 492/15 July 1099. The population was put to the sword by the Franks, who pillaged the area for a week. A band of Muslims barricaded themselves into the Oratory of David and fought on for several days. They were granted their lives in return for surrendering. The Franks honored their word, and the group left by night for Ascalon. In the Masjid al-Aqsa the Franks slaughtered more than 70,000 people, among them a large number of Imams and Muslim scholars, devout and ascetic men who had left their homelands to live lives of pious seclusion in the Holy Place. The Franks stripped the Dome of the Rock of more than forty silver candelabra, each of them weighing 3,600 drams, and a great silver lamp weighing forty-four Syrian pounds, as well as a hundred and fifty smaller candelabra and more than twenty gold ones, and a great deal more booty. Refugees from Syria reached Baghdad in Ramadan, among them the qadi Abu sa'd al-Harawi. They told the Caliph's ministers a story that wrung their hearts and brought tears to their eyes. On Friday they went to the Cathedral Mosque and begged for help, weeping so that their hearers wept with them as they described the sufferings of the Muslims in that Holy City: the men killed, the women and children taken prisoner, the homes pillaged. Because of the terrible hardships they had suffered, they were allowed to break the fast.

How do these two accounts differ? What was the fate of the Muslims in Jerusalem?

---

years until its weakened condition finally enabled the Ottoman Turks to conquer it in 1453.

Despite the failures, the crusading ideal was not yet completely lost. In Germany in 1212, a youth known as Nicholas of Cologne announced that God had inspired him to lead a "Children's Crusade" to the Holy Land. Thousands of young people joined Nicholas and made their way down the Rhine and across the Alps to Italy, where the pope told them to go home. Most tried to do so. At about the same time, a group of about twenty thousand French children, also inspired by the desire to free the Holy Land from the Muslims, made their way to Marseilles, where two shipowners agreed to transport them to the Holy Land. Seven ships packed with hymn-singing youths soon left the port. Two of the ships sank in a storm near Sardinia; the other five sailed to North Africa, where the children were sold into slavery. Four more Crusades of adult warriors over the next half century were no more successful.

Effects of the Crusades

Whether the Crusades had much effect on European civilization is debatable. The crusaders made little long-term impact on the east, where the only visible remnants of their conquests were their castles. There may have been some broadening of perspective that comes from the exchange between two cultures, but the interaction of Christian Europe with the Muslim world was actually both more intense and more meaningful in Spain and Sicily than in the Holy Land.

Did the Crusades help stabilize European society by removing large numbers of young warriors who would have fought each other in Europe? Some historians think so and believe that western monarchs established their control more easily as a result. There is no doubt that the Italian seaports, especially Genoa, Pisa, and Venice, benefited economically from the Crusades, but even without them, Italian merchants would have pursued new trade contacts with the eastern world.

Pope Urban II's call for a Crusade at Clermont	1095
First Crusade	1096–1099
Fall of Edessa	1144
Second Crusade	1147–1149
Saladin's conquest of Jerusalem	1187
Third Crusade	1189–1192
Fourth Crusade—sack of Constantinople	1204
Latin Empire of Constantinople	1204–1261
Children's Crusade	1212
Fifth Crusade	1219–1221
Frederick II occupies Jerusalem (Sixth Crusade)	1228
First Crusade of Louis IX (Seventh Crusade)	1248–1254
Second Crusade of Louis IX (Eighth Crusade)	1270
Surrender of Acre and end of Christian presence in the Holy Land	1291

© Bettmann/CORBIS

The First Crusade.   Recruited from the noble class of western Europe, the first crusading army reached Constantinople by 1097. By 1098, the crusaders had taken Antioch. Working down of coast of Palestine, they captured Jerusalem in 1099. Along the way, the crusaders had an encounter with Muslim forces at Ascalon, as seen in this illustration from a glass painting on the Abbey of St. Denis in France.

The Crusades did have unfortunate side effects that would afflict European society for generations. The first widespread attacks on the Jews occurred during the Crusades. Some Christians argued that to undertake holy wars against infidel Muslims while the "murderers of Christ" ran free at home was unthinkable. The massacre of Jews became a regular feature of medieval European life.

CONCLUSION

The period from 1000 to 1300 was a dynamic time in the development of Western civilization. The nobles, whose warlike attitudes were rationalized by labeling themselves the defenders of Christian society, continued to dominate the medieval world politically, economically, and socially. But kings gradually began to expand their powers. Although the popes sometimes treated rulers condescendingly, by the thirteenth century, the monarchs were developing the machinery of government that would enable them to challenge exalted claims of papal power and assume political authority in Europe. The actions of these medieval monarchs laid the foundation for the European kingdoms that in one form or another have dominated the European political scene ever since.

The Catholic church shared in the challenge of new growth by reforming itself and striking out on a path toward greater papal power, both within the church and over European society. The High Middle Ages witnessed a spiritual renewal that led to numerous and even divergent paths: revived papal leadership, the development of centralized administrative machinery that buttressed papal authority, and new dimensions to the religious life of the clergy and laity. At the same time, this spiritual renewal also gave rise to the crusading "holy warrior" who killed for God.

The religious enthusiasm of the twelfth century continued well into the thirteenth as new orders of friars gave witness to spiritual growth and passion, but underneath lay seeds of discontent and change. Dissent from church teaching and practices grew, leading to a climate of fear and intolerance as the church responded with inquisitorial procedures to enforce conformity to its teachings. At the same time, papal claims of supremacy over secular authorities were increasingly challenged by the rising power of monarchical authorities, who, because of the growth of cities, the revival of trade, and the emergence of a money economy, were now able to hire soldiers and officials to carry out their wishes.

The High Middle Ages of the eleventh, twelfth, and thirteenth centuries had been a period of great innovation, evident in significant economic, social, political, religious, intellectual, and cultural changes. And yet by the end of the thirteenth century, certain tensions had begun to creep into European society. As we shall see in the next chapter, these tensions would soon bring a torrent of troubles.

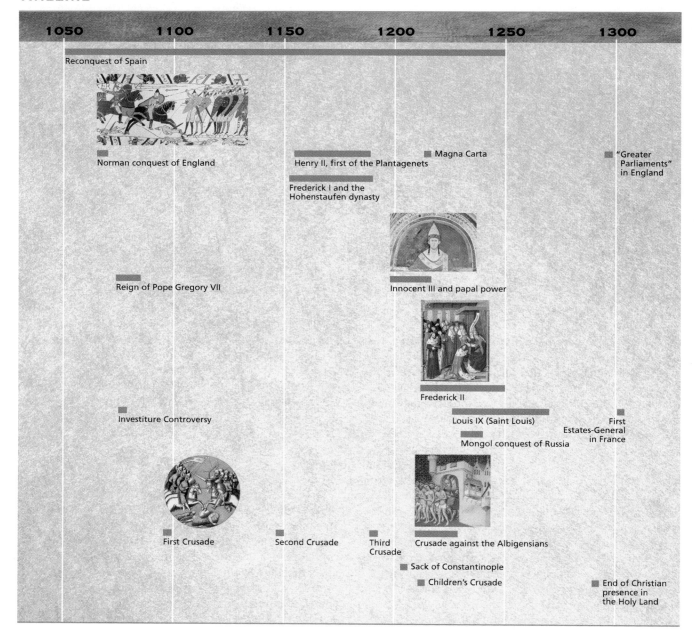

1050   **1100**   **1150**   **1200**   **1250**   **1300**

Reconquest of Spain

Norman conquest of England

Henry II, first of the Plantagenets

Magna Carta

"Greater Parliaments" in England

Frederick I and the Hohenstaufen dynasty

Reign of Pope Gregory VII

Innocent III and papal power

Frederick II

Investiture Controversy

Louis IX (Saint Louis)

First Estates-General in France

Mongol conquest of Russia

First Crusade

Second Crusade

Third Crusade

Crusade against the Albigensians

Sack of Constantinople

Children's Crusade

End of Christian presence in the Holy Land

NOTES

1. Quoted in N. F. Cantor, ed., *The Medieval Reader* (New York, 1994), pp. 42–47.
2. Quoted in J. K. Fairbank, E. O. Reischauer, and A. M. Craig, *East Asia: Tradition and Transformation* (Boston, 1973), p. 164.
3. E. F. Henderson, ed., *Selected Historical Documents of the Middle Ages* (London, 1892), p. 332.
4. Ibid., p. 365.
5. O. J. Thatcher and E. H. McNeal, eds., *A Source Book for Medieval History* (New York, 1905), p. 208.
6. Quoted in R. H. C. Davis, *A History of Medieval Europe from Constantine to Saint Louis*, 2d ed. (New York, 1988), p. 252.
7. Hildegard of Bingen, *The Book of Divine Works* (Santa Fe, N. M., 1987), 1:1.
8. Quoted in R. Brooke and C. N. L. Brooke, *Popular Religion in the Middle Ages* (London, 1984), p. 19.
9. Thatcher and McNeal, *Source Book for Medieval History*, p. 517.
10. Quoted in H. E. Mayer, *The Crusades*, trans. J. Gillingham (New York, 1972), pp. 99–100.

SUGGESTIONS FOR FURTHER READING

Works on the different medieval states are numerous. On England, see **R. Frame, *The Political Development of the British Isles, 1100–1400*** (Oxford, 1990). On France, see **J. Dunbabin, *France in the Making,***

843–1180 (Oxford, 1985), and **E. M. Hallam,** *Capetian France, 987–1328* (London, 1980), a well-done general account. On Spain, see **B. F. Reilly,** *The Medieval Spains* (Cambridge, 1993), and **M. R. Menocal,** *The Ornament of the World* (Boston, 2002). On Germany, see **A. Haverkamp,** *Medieval Germany* (Oxford, 1988); **H. Fuhrmann,** *Germany in the High Middle Ages, c. 1050–1250* (Cambridge, 1986), an excellent account; and **B. Arnold,** *Princes and Territories in Medieval Germany* (Cambridge, 1991). On Italy, see **P. Jones,** *The Italian City-State: From Commune to Signoria* (Oxford, 1997). On eastern Europe, see **N. Davies,** *God's Playground: A History of Poland* (Oxford, 1981); **J. Fennell,** *The Crisis of Medieval Russia, 1200–1304* (New York, 1983); and the books listed for Chapter 8.

For specialized studies in the political history of the thirteenth century, see **D. Abulafia,** *Frederick II: A Medieval Emperor* (London, 1987); **M. W. Labarge,** *St. Louis: The Life of Louis IX of France* (London, 1968); and **C. J. Halperin,** *Russia and the Golden Horde: The Mongol Impact on Medieval Russian History* (Bloomington, Ind., 1987).

For a good survey of religion in medieval Europe, see **B. Hamilton,** *Religion in the Medieval West* (London, 1986). On Europe during the time of the Investiture Controversy, see **U.-R. Blumenthal,** *The Investiture Controversy* (Philadelphia, 1988). For a general survey of church life, see **R. W. Southern,** *Western Society and the Church in the Middle Ages,* rev. ed. (New York, 1990).

On the papacy in the High Middle Ages, see the general surveys by **C. Morris,** *The Papal Monarchy* (Oxford, 1989), and **I. S. Robinson,** *The Papacy* (Cambridge, 1990). The papacy of Innocent III is covered in **J. E. Sayers,** *Innocent III, Leader of Europe, 1198–1216* (New York, 1994).

Good works on monasticism include **B. Bolton,** *The Medieval Reformation* (London, 1983), and **C. H. Lawrence,** *Medieval Monasticism* (London, 1984), a good general account. On the impact of the Franciscans and Dominicans, see **C. H. Lawrence,** *The Friars: The Impact of the Early Mendicant Movement on Western Society* (New York, 1994). On Saint Francis, see **A. House,** *Francis of Assisi: A Revolutionary Life* (London, 2001). For a good introduction to popular religion in the eleventh and twelfth centuries, see **R. Brooke** and **C. N. L. Brooke,** *Popular Religion in the Middle Ages* (London, 1984).

On dissent and heresy, see **M. Lambert,** *Medieval Heresy,* 2d ed. (New York, 1992), and **J. Strayer,** *The Albigensian Crusades,* 2d ed. (New York, 1992). On the Inquisition, see **B. Hamilton,** *The Medieval Inquisition* (New York, 1981). The persecution of Jews in the thirteenth century can be examined in **J. Cohen,** *The Friars and the Jews* (Oxford, 1985). The basic study on intolerance and homosexuality is **J. Boswell,** *Christianity, Social Tolerance, and Homosexuality* (Chicago, 1980).

Two good general surveys of the Crusades are **H. E. Mayer,** *The Crusades,* 2d ed. (New York, 1988), and **J. Riley-Smith,** *The Crusades: A Short History* (New Haven, Conn., 1987). Also see **J. Riley-Smith, ed.,** *The Oxford Illustrated History of the Crusades* (New York, 1995), and **A. Konstam,** *Historical Atlas of the Crusades* (New York, 2002). On the First Crusade, see **T. Asbridge,** *The First Crusade: A New History* (New York, 2003), The disastrous Fourth Crusade is examined in **J. Godfrey,** *1204: The Unholy Crusade* (Oxford, 1980). On the later Crusades, see **N. Housley,** *The Later Crusades, 1274–1580* (New York, 1992).

Thomson NOW! Enter *ThomsonNOW* using the access card that is available for *Western Civilization: A Brief History.* *ThomsonNOW* will help you understand this chapter with lesson plans generated for your needs. In addition, you can read the following documents, and many more, online:

Song of Roland
John of Salisbury, Book 5 of *Policraticus*

WESTERN CIVILIZATION RESOURCES

Visit the Web site for *Western Civilization: A Brief History* for resources specific to this book:

http://www.thomsonedu.com/history/spielvogel

For a variety of tools to help you succeed in this course, visit the Western Civilization Resource Center at

http://history.wadsworth.com/spielvogel

Included are quizzes, images, documents, interactive simulations, maps and timelines, movie explorations, and a wealth of other sources.

THE LATER MIDDLE AGES: CRISIS AND DISINTEGRATION IN THE FOURTEENTH CENTURY

CHAPTER OUTLINE AND FOCUS QUESTIONS

A Time of Troubles: Black Death and Social Crisis

☐ What was the Black Death, and what was its impact on European society?

War and Political Instability

☐ What major problems did European states face in the fourteenth century?

The Decline of the Church

☐ How and why did the authority and prestige of the papacy decline in the fourteenth century?

Cultural and Society in an Age of Adversity

☐ What were the major developments in art and literature in the fourteenth century?

☐ How did the adversities of the fourteenth century affect urban life and medical practices?

CRITICAL THINKING

☐ To what extent were climate and disease the key factors in producing economic, social, and political changes in the fourteenth century?

Mass burial of plague victims

Snark/Art Resource, NY (Bibliotheque Royale Albert I, Brussels)

S A RESULT of their conquests in the thirteenth and fourteenth centuries, the Mongols created a vast empire stretching from Russia in the west to China in the east. Mongol rule brought stability to the Eurasian trade routes; increased trade brought prosperity but also avenues for the spread of flea-infested rats that carried bubonic plague to both East Asia and Europe. In the mid-fourteenth century, one of the most destructive natural disasters in history erupted—the Black Death. One contemporary observer named Henry Knighton, a canon of Saint Mary-of-the-Meadow Abbey in Leicester, England, was simply over-whelmed by the magnitude of the catastrophe. Knighton began his account of the great plague with these words: "In this year [1348] and in the following one there was a general mortality of people throughout the whole world." Few were left untouched; the plague struck even isolated monasteries: "At Montpellier, there remained out of a hundred and forty friars only seven." Knighton was also stunned by the economic and social consequences of the Black Death. Prices dropped: "And the price of everything was cheap, because of the fear of death; there were very few who took any care for their wealth, or for anything else." Meanwhile, laborers were scarce, so their wages increased: "In the following autumn, one could not hire a reaper at a lower wage than eight pence with food, or a mower at less than twelve pence with food. Because of this, much grain rotted in the fields for lack of harvesting." So many people died that some towns were deserted and some villages disappeared altogether: "Many small villages and hamlets were completely deserted; there was not one house left in them, but all those who had lived in them were dead." Some people thought the end of the world was at hand.

Plague was not the only disaster in the fourteenth century, however. Signs of disintegration were everywhere: famine, economic depression, war, social upheaval, a rise in crime and violence, and a decline in the power of the universal Catholic church. Periods of disintegration, however, are often fertile grounds for change and new developments. Out of the dissolution of medieval civilization came a rebirth of culture that has come to be known as the Renaissance.✦

A Time of Troubles: Black Death and Social Crisis

For much of the thirteenth century, Europe had experienced good harvests and an expanding population. By century's end, however, a succession of disastrous changes had begun.

For one thing, there were noticeable changes in weather patterns as Europe entered a "little ice age." Shortened growing seasons and disastrous weather conditions, including heavy storms and constant rain, led to widespread famine and hunger. The great famine of 1315–1317 in northern Europe began an all-too-familiar pattern, as is evident in this scene described by a contemporary chronicler:

> We saw a larger number of both sexes, not only from nearby places but from as much as five leagues away, barefooted and maybe even, except for women, in a completely nude state, together with their priests coming in procession at the Church of the Holy Martyrs, their bones bulging out, devoutly carrying bodies of saints and other relics to be adorned hoping to get relief.[1]

Some historians have pointed out that famine could have led to chronic malnutrition, which in turn contributed to increased infant mortality, lower birthrates, and higher susceptibility to disease because malnourished people are less able to resist infection. This, they argue, helps explain the virulence of the great plague known as the Black Death.

The Black Death

The **Black Death** of the mid-fourteenth century was the most devastating natural disaster in European history, ravaging the population and causing economic, social, political, and cultural upheaval. Contemporary chroniclers lamented how parents abandoned their children; one

related the words: "Oh father, why have you abandoned me? . . . Mother, where have you gone?"[2] People were horrified by an evil force they could not understand and by the subsequent breakdown of all normal human relations.

Bubonic plague, the most common form of plague at the time, was spread by black rats infested with fleas who were host to the deadly bacterium *Yersinia pestis*. Symptoms of bubonic plague included high fever, aching joints, swelling of the lymph nodes, and dark blotches caused by bleeding beneath the skin. Bubonic plague was actually the least toxic form of plague but nevertheless killed 50 to 60 percent of its victims. In pneumonic plague, the bacterial infection spread to the lungs, resulting in severe coughing, bloody sputum, and the relatively easy spread of the bacillus from human to human by coughing.

Spread of the Plague The Black Death was the first major epidemic disease to strike Europe in seven centuries, an absence that helps explain medieval Europe's remarkable population growth. Having disappeared from Europe and the Middle East in the Middle Ages, bubonic plague continued to haunt parts of southwestern China, especially isolated rural territories. The arrival of Mongol troops in this area in the mid-thirteenth century became the means for the spread of the plague as flea-infested rats accompanied the Mongols into central and northwestern China and Central Asia. From there, trading caravans brought the plague to Caffa on the Black Sea in 1346.

The plague reached Europe in October 1347 when Genoese merchants brought it from Caffa to the island of Sicily off the coast of southern Italy. It quickly spread to southern Italy and southern France and Spain by the end of 1347 (see Map 11.1). Diffusion of the Black Death followed commercial trade routes. In 1348, the plague spread through France and the Low Countries and into Germany. By the end of that year, it had moved to England, ravaging it in 1349. By the end of 1349, the plague had reached Scandinavia. Eastern Europe and Russia were affected by 1351, although mortality rates were never as high there as they were in western and central Europe.

Mortality figures for the Black Death were incredibly high. Italy was especially hard hit. Its crowded cities suffered losses of 50 to 60 percent (see the box on p. 199). In northern France, farming villages suffered mortality rates of 30 percent, and cities such as Rouen experienced losses as high as 40 percent. In England and Germany, entire villages disappeared. In Germany, of approximately 170,000 inhabited locations, only 130,000 were left by the end of the fourteenth century.

It has been estimated that the European population declined by 25 to 50 percent between 1347 and 1351. If we accept the recent scholarly assessment of a European population of 75 million in the early fourteenth century, this means a death toll of 19 to 38 million people in four years. And the plague did not end in 1351. There were major outbreaks again in 1361–1362 and 1369 and then regular recurrences during the remainder of the fourteenth century

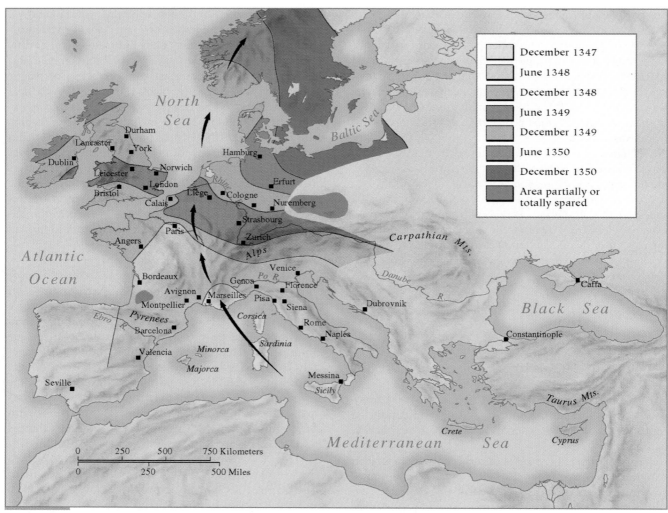

MAP 11.1 **Spread of the Black Death.** The plague entered Europe in Sicily in 1347 and within three years had killed between one-quarter and one-half of the population. Outbreaks continued into the early eighteenth century, and it took Europe two hundred years to return to the population level it had before the Black Death. **?** Is there a general pattern between distance from Sicily and the elapsed time before a region was infected with the plague? 🐚 **View an animated version of this map or related maps at** http://thomsonedu.com/history/spielvogel

and all of the fifteenth century. The European population did not start to recover until the end of the fifteenth century; not until the mid-sixteenth century did Europe return to thirteenth-century population levels.

Life and Death: Reactions to the Plague Attempts to explain the Black Death and mitigate its harshness led to extreme sorts of behavior. Many people believed that the plague had either been sent by God as a punishment for humans' sins or been caused by the devil. Some resorted to extreme asceticism to cleanse themselves of sin and gain God's forgiveness. Such was the flagellant movement, which became popular in 1348, especially in Germany. Groups of flagellants, both men and women, wandered from town to town, flogging each other with whips to win the forgiveness of a God whom they felt had sent the

plague to punish humans for their sinful ways. One contemporary chronicler described a flagellant procession:

> The penitents went about, coming first out of Germany. They were men who did public penance and scourged themselves with whips of hard knotted leather with little iron spikes. Some made themselves bleed very badly between the shoulder blades and some foolish women had cloths ready to catch the blood and smear it on their eyes, saying it was miraculous blood. While they were doing penance, they sang very mournful songs about the nativity and the passion of Our Lord. The object of this penance was to put a stop to the mortality, for in that time...at least a third of all the people in the world died.[3]

The flagellants attracted attention and caused mass hysteria wherever they went. The Catholic church, however, became alarmed when flagellant groups began to kill Jews and attack the clergy who opposed them. Pope

THE BLACK DEATH

he Black Death was the most terrifying natural calamity of the Middle Ages. It has been estimated that 25 to 50 percent of the population died as the plague spread throughout Europe between 1347 and 1351. This contemporary description of the great plague in Florence is taken from the preface to the *Decameron* by the fourteenth-century Italian writer Giovanni Boccaccio.

Giovanni Boccaccio, *Decameron*

In the year of Our Lord 1348 the deadly plague broke out in the great city of Florence, most beautiful of Italian cities. Whether through the operation of the heavenly bodies or because of our own iniquities which the just wrath of God sought to correct, the plague had arisen in the East some years before, causing the death of countless human beings. It spread without stop from one place to another, until, unfortunately, it swept over the West. Neither knowledge nor human foresight availed against it, though the city was cleansed of much filth by chosen officers in charge and sick persons were forbidden to enter it, while advice was broadcast for the preservation of health. Nor did humble supplications serve. Not once but many times they were ordained in the form of processions and other ways for the propitiation of God by the faithful, but, in spite of everything, toward the spring of the year the plague began to show its ravages....

It did not manifest itself as in the East, where if a man bled at the nose he had certain warning of inevitable death. At the onset of the disease both men and women were afflicted by a sort of swelling in the groin or under the armpits which sometimes attained the size of a common apple or egg. Some of these swellings were larger and some smaller, and were commonly called boils. From these two starting points the boils began in a little while to spread and appear generally all over the body. Afterwards, the manifestation of the disease changed into black or livid spots on the arms, thighs, and the whole person. In many these blotches were large and far apart, in others small and closely clustered. Like the boils, which had been and continued to be a certain indication of coming death, these blotches had the same meaning for everyone on whom they appeared.

Neither the advice of physicians nor the virtue of any medicine seemed to help or avail in the cure of these diseases. Indeed,... not only did few recover, but on the contrary almost everyone died within three days of the appearance of the signs—some sooner, some later.... The virulence of the plague was all the greater in that it was communicated by the sick to the well by contact, not unlike fire when dry or fatty things are brought near it. But the evil was still worse. Not only did conversation and familiarity with the diseased spread the malady and even cause death, but the mere touch of the clothes or any other object the sick had touched or used, seemed to spread the pestilence....

More wretched still were the circumstances of the common people and, for a great part, of the middle class, for, confined to their homes either by hope of safety or by poverty, and restricted to their own sections, they fell sick daily by thousands. There, devoid of help or care, they died almost without redemption. A great many breathed their last in the public streets, day and night; a large number perished in their homes, and it was only by the stench of their decaying bodies that they proclaimed their death to their neighbors. Everywhere the city was teeming with corpses....

So many bodies were brought to the churches every day that the consecrated ground did not suffice to hold them, particularly according to the ancient custom of giving each corpse its individual place. Huge trenches were dug in the crowded churchyards and the new dead were piled in them, layer upon layer, like merchandise in the hold of a ship. A little earth covered the corpses of each row, and the procedure continued until the trench was filled to the top.

According to Boccaccio, what was the cause of the plague, and what impact did it have on Florence and its inhabitants?

Clement VI condemned the flagellants in October 1349 and urged the public authorities to crush them. By the end of 1350, most of the flagellant movements had been destroyed.

An outbreak of virulent **anti-Semitism** also accompanied the Black Death. Jews were accused of causing the plague by poisoning town wells. Although Jews were persecuted in Spain, the worst **pogroms** against this helpless minority were carried out in Germany; more than sixty major Jewish communities in Germany had been exterminated by 1351. Many Jews fled eastward to Russia and especially to Poland, where the king offered them protection. Eastern Europe became home to large Jewish communities.

The prevalence of death because of the plague and its recurrences affected people in profound ways. Some survivors apparently came to treat life as something cheap and passing. Violence and violent death appeared to be more common after the plague than before. Post-plague Europe also demonstrated a morbid preoccupation with death. In their sermons, priests reminded parishioners that each night's sleep might be their last. Tombstones were decorated with macabre scenes of naked corpses in various stages of decomposition with snakes entwined in their bones and their innards filled with worms.

Economic Dislocation and Social Upheaval

The population collapse of the fourteenth century had dire economic and social consequences. Economic distress

The Flagellants. Reactions to the plague were extreme at times. Believing that asceticism could atone for humanity's sins and win God's forgiveness, flagellants wandered from town to town flogging themselves and each other with whips, as in this illustration.

brought social upheaval. Both peasants and noble landlords were affected. A serious labor shortage caused a dramatic rise in the price of labor. At Cuxham manor in England, for example, a farm laborer who had received 2 shillings a week in 1347 was paid 7 in 1349 and almost 11 by 1350. At the same time, the decline in population depressed the demand for agricultural produce, resulting in falling prices for output. Because landlords were having to pay more for labor at the same time that their income from rents was declining, they began to encounter economic hardship and lower standards of living. In England, aristocratic incomes dropped more than 20 percent between 1347 and 1353.

Landed aristocrats responded by seeking to lower the wage rate. The English Parliament passed the Statute of Laborers (1351), which attempted to limit wages to pre-plague levels and to forbid the mobility of peasants as well. Although such laws proved largely unworkable, they did keep wages from rising as high as they might have in a free market. Overall, the position of noble landlords continued to deteriorate during the late fourteenth and early fifteenth centuries. At the same time, the position of peasants improved, though not uniformly throughout Europe.

The decline in the number of peasants after the Black Death accelerated the process of converting labor services to rents, freeing peasants from the obligations of servile tenure and weakening the system of manorialism. But there were limits to how much the peasants could advance. They faced the same economic hurdles as the lords, while the latter also attempted to impose wage restrictions and

reinstate old forms of labor service. New governmental taxes also hurt. Peasant complaints became widespread and soon gave rise to rural revolts.

Peasant Revolts In 1358, a peasant revolt known as the *Jacquerie* broke out in northern France. The destruction of normal order by the Black Death and the subsequent economic dislocation were important factors in causing the revolt, but the ravages created by the Hundred Years' War (see "War and Political Instability" later in this chapter) also affected the French peasantry. Both the French and English forces followed a deliberate policy of laying waste to peasants' lands while bands of mercenaries lived off the land by taking peasants' produce as well.

Peasant anger was also exacerbated by growing class tensions. Many aristocrats looked on peasants with utter contempt. One French aristocrat said, "Should peasants eat meat? Rather should they chew grass on the heath with the horned cattle and go naked on all fours." The peasants reciprocated this contempt for their so-called social superiors.

The outburst of peasant anger led to savage confrontations. Castles were burned and nobles murdered. Such atrocities did not go unanswered, however. The *Jacquerie* failed when the privileged classes closed ranks, savagely massacred the rebels, and ended the revolt.

The English Peasants' Revolt of 1381 was the most prominent of all. It was a product not of desperation but of rising expectations. After the Black Death, the condition of the English peasants had improved as they enjoyed greater freedom and higher wages or lower rents. Aristocratic landlords had fought back with legislation to depress wages and an attempt to reimpose old feudal dues. The most immediate cause of the revolt, however, was the monarchy's attempt to raise revenues by imposing a poll tax, a flat charge on each adult member of the population. Peasants in eastern England, the wealthiest part of the country, refused to pay the tax and expelled the collectors forcibly from their villages.

This action produced a widespread rebellion of both peasants and townspeople led by a well-to-do peasant called Wat Tyler and a preacher named John Ball. The latter preached an effective message against the noble class, as recounted by the chronicler Froissart:

> Good people, things cannot go right in England and never will, until goods are held in common and there are no more peasants and gentlefolk, but we are all one and the same. In what way are those whom we call lords greater masters than ourselves? How have they deserved it? Why do they hold us in bondage? If we all spring from a single father and mother, Adam and Eve, how can they claim or prove that they are lords more than us, except by making us produce and grow the wealth which they spend.[4]

The revolt was initially successful as the rebels burned down the manor houses of aristocrats, lawyers, and government officers and murdered several important officials, including the archbishop of Canterbury. After the peasants marched on London, the young King Richard II

Peasant Rebellion. The fourteenth century witnessed a number of revolts of the peasantry against noble landowners. Although the revolts often met with initial success, they were soon crushed. This fifteenth-century illustration shows nobles during the French *Jacquerie* of 1358 massacring the rebels in the town of Meaux, in northern France.

(1377–1399) promised to grant the rebels' demands if they returned to their homes. They accepted the king's word and dispersed, but the king reneged and, with the assistance of the aristocrats, arrested hundreds of the rebels. The poll tax was eliminated, however.

Revolts in the Cities Revolts also erupted in the cities. Commercial and industrial activity suffered almost immediately from the Black Death. Florence's woolen industry, one of the giants, produced 70,000 to 80,000 pieces of cloth in 1338; in 1378, it was yielding only 24,000 pieces. Bourgeois merchants and manufacturers responded to a decline in trade and production by attempts to restrict competition and resist the demands of the lower classes.

In urban areas, where capitalist industrialists paid low wages and managed to prevent workers from forming organizations to help themselves, industrial revolts broke out throughout Europe. Most famous was the revolt of Florence's wool workers, the *ciompi*, in 1378. In the 1370s, the woolen industry was depressed, and wool workers saw their real wages decline when the coinage in which they were paid was debased. Their revolt won them some concessions from the municipal government, including the right to form guilds and be represented in the government. But their newly won rights were short-lived. A counterrevolution by government authorities brought an end to *ciompi* participation in the government by 1382.

Although the peasant and urban revolts sometimes resulted in short-term gains for the participants, the uprisings were relatively easily crushed and their gains quickly lost. Accustomed to ruling, the established classes easily combined and quashed dissent. Nevertheless, the rural and urban revolts of the fourteenth century ushered in an age of social conflict that characterized much of later European history.

War and Political Instability

Famine, plague, economic turmoil, social upheaval, and violence were not the only problems of the fourteenth century. War and political instability must also be added to the list. And of all the struggles of the period, the most famous and the most violent was the Hundred Years' War.

The Hundred Years' War

In the thirteenth century, the English king still held one small possession in France, known as the duchy of Gascony. As duke of Gascony, the English king pledged loyalty as a vassal to the French king. But when King Philip VI of France seized Gascony in 1337, the duke of Gascony—King Edward III of England—declared war on Philip. The attack on Gascony was a convenient excuse; Edward had already laid claim to the throne of France after the senior branch of the Capetian dynasty had become extinct in 1328 and a cousin of the Capetians, the duke of Valois, had become king as Philip VI.

The war began in a burst of knightly enthusiasm. Trained to be warriors, knights viewed the clash of battle as the ultimate opportunity to demonstrate their fighting abilities. But this struggle would change the nature of warfare, for as it dragged on, the outcomes of battles were increasingly determined not by knights but by peasant foot soldiers. The French army of 1337, with its heavily armed noble cavalry, resembled its twelfth- and thirteenth-century forebears. Considering themselves the fighting elite, the noble cavalry looked with contempt on foot soldiers and crossbowmen because they were peasants or other social inferiors. The English army, however, had evolved differently and had included peasants as paid foot soldiers. Armed with pikes, many of these foot soldiers had also adopted the longbow, invented by the Welsh. The longbow had greater striking power, longer range, and more rapid speed of fire than the crossbow. Although the English also used heavily armed cavalry, they relied even more on large numbers of foot soldiers.

Course of the War Edward III's early campaigns in France were indecisive and achieved little. In 1346, Edward was forced to fight at Crécy, just south of Flanders. The larger French army followed no battle plan but simply attacked the English lines in a disorderly fashion. The arrows of the English archers decimated the French cavalry. As the chronicler Froissart described it, "The English continued to shoot into the thickest part of the crowd, wasting none of their arrows. They impaled or wounded horses and riders, who fell to the ground in great distress, unable to get up again without the help of several men."[5] It was a stunning victory for the English.

The Battle of Crécy was not decisive, however. The English simply did not possess the resources to subjugate all France, and hostilities continued intermittently for another fifty years until a twenty-year truce was negotiated in 1396, seemingly bringing an end to this protracted series of struggles between the French and English.

In 1415, however, the English king, Henry V (1413–1422), renewed the war at a time when the French were enduring a civil war as the dukes of Burgundy and Orléans competed to control the weak French king, Charles VI. In the summer of 1413, Paris exploded with bloody encounters. Taking advantage of the chaos, Henry V invaded France in 1415. At the Battle of Agincourt (1415), the French suffered a disastrous defeat, and fifteen hundred French nobles died when the heavy, armor-plated French knights attempted to attack across a field turned to mud by heavy rain. Altogether, French losses were six thousand dead; the English lost only three hundred men. Henry went on to reconquer Normandy and forge an alliance with the duke of Burgundy, making the English masters of northern France (see Map 11.2).

The seemingly hopeless French cause fell into the hands of Charles the dauphin (heir to the throne), the son of Charles VI. The dauphin governed the southern two-thirds of French lands from Bourges. Charles was weak and timid and was unable to rally the French against the English, who in 1428 had turned south and were besieging the city of Orléans to gain access to the valley of the Loire. The French monarch was saved, quite unexpectedly, by a French peasant woman.

Joan of Arc Joan of Arc was born in 1412 to well-to-do peasants in the village of Domrémy in Champagne. Deeply religious, Joan experienced visions and came to believe

Joan of Arc. Pictured here in a suit of armor, Joan of Arc is holding aloft a banner that shows Jesus and two angels. This portrait dates from the late fifteenth century; there are no portraits of Joan made from life.

that her favorite saints had commanded her to free France and have the dauphin crowned king. In February 1429, Joan made her way to the dauphin's court, where her sincerity and simplicity persuaded Charles to allow her to accompany a French army to Orléans. Apparently inspired by the faith of the peasant girl, the French armies found new confidence in themselves and liberated Orléans, changing the course of the war. Within a few weeks, the entire Loire valley had been freed of the English. Joan had brought the war to a decisive turning point.

But she did not live to see the war concluded. Captured by the Burgundian allies of the English in 1430, Joan was turned over first to the English and then to the Inquisition on charges of witchcraft (see the box on p. 204). In the fifteenth century, spiritual visions were thought to be inspired either by God or the devil. Because Joan dressed in men's clothing, it was relatively easy to convince others that she was in league with the "prince of darkness." She was condemned to death as a heretic and burned at the stake in 1431. To the end, as the flames rose up around her, she declared "that her voices came from God and had not deceived her." Twenty-five years later, a new ecclesiastical court exonerated her of these charges,

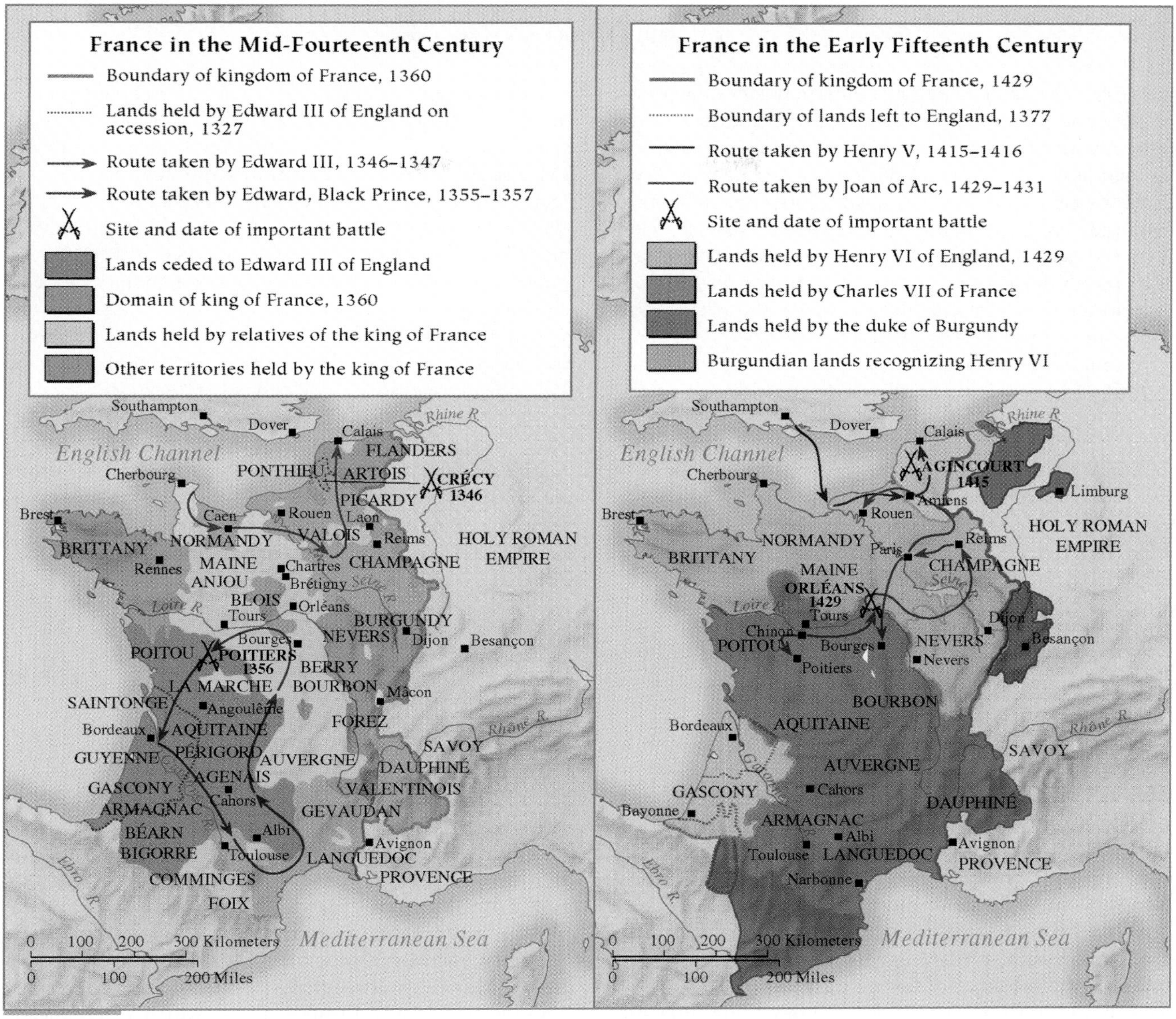
France in the Mid-Fourteenth Century
Boundary of kingdom of France, 1360
Lands held by Edward III of England on accession, 1327
Route taken by Edward III, 1346–1347
Route taken by Edward, Black Prince, 1355–1357
Site and date of important battle
Lands ceded to Edward III of England
Domain of king of France, 1360
Lands held by relatives of the king of France
Other territories held by the king of France
Southampton
Dover
Calais
Rhine R.
English Channel
FLANDERS
Cherbourg
PONTHIEU
ARTOIS
CRÉCY 1346
PICARDY
Brest
Caen
Rouen
Laon
BRITTANY
NORMANDY
VALOIS
Reims
HOLY ROMAN EMPIRE
Rennes
MAINE
ANJOU
Chartres
Brétigny
CHAMPAGNE
Seine R.
Loire R.
BLOIS
Tours
Orléans
BURGUNDY
NEVERS
Dijon
Besançon
POITOU
Bourges
POITIERS 1356
BERRY
LA MARCHE
BOURBON
Mâcon
SAINTONGE
Angoulême
FOREZ
Bordeaux
AQUITAINE
Rhône R.
GUYENNE
PÉRIGORD
AUVERGNE
SAVOY
AGENAIS
DAUPHINÉ
GASCONY
Cahors
VALENTINOIS
ARMAGNAC
GEVAUDAN
BÉARN
Albi
BIGORRE
Toulouse
Avignon
LANGUEDOC
Ebro R.
PROVENCE
COMMINGES
FOIX
Mediterranean Sea
0 100 200 300 Kilometers
0 100 200 Miles
France in the Early Fifteenth Century
Boundary of kingdom of France, 1429
Boundary of lands left to England, 1377
Route taken by Henry V, 1415–1416
Route taken by Joan of Arc, 1429–1431
Site and date of important battle
Lands held by Henry VI of England, 1429
Lands held by Charles VII of France
Lands held by the duke of Burgundy
Burgundian lands recognizing Henry VI
Southampton
Dover
Calais
Rhine R.
English Channel
AGINCOURT 1415
Cherbourg
Limburg
Amiens
Brest
Rouen
HOLY ROMAN EMPIRE
NORMANDY
Reims
BRITTANY
Paris
MAINE
CHAMPAGNE
ORLÉANS 1429
Seine R.
Loire R.
Tours
Dijon
Chinon
POITOU
Bourges
NEVERS
Besançon
Poitiers
Nevers
BOURBON
Bordeaux
AQUITAINE
Rhône R.
SAVOY
AUVERGNE
GASCONY
Cahors
DAUPHINÉ
Bayonne
ARMAGNAC
Albi
Toulouse
LANGUEDOC
Avignon
PROVENCE
Ebro R.
Narbonne
Mediterranean Sea
0 100 200 300 Kilometers
0 100 200 Miles

MAP 11.2 The Hundred Years' War. This long, exhausting struggle began in 1337 and dragged on until 1453. The English initially gained substantial French territory, but in the later phases of the war, France turned the tide, eventually expelling the English from all Continental lands except the port of Calais. ? What gains had the English made by 1429, and how do they correlate to proximity to England and the ocean? **View an animated version of this map or related maps at** http://thomsonedu.com/history/spielvogel

and five centuries later, in 1920, she was made a saint of the Roman Catholic church. Joan of Arc's accomplishments proved decisive.

End of the War Although the war dragged on for another two decades, defeats of English armies in Normandy and Aquitaine led to French victory. Important to the French success was the use of the cannon, a new weapon made possible by the invention of gunpowder. The Chinese had invented gunpowder in the eleventh century and devised a simple cannon by the thirteenth. The Mongols greatly improved this technology, developing more accurate cannons and cannonballs; both spread to the Middle East by the thirteenth century and to Europe by the fourteenth.

The death of England's best commanders and the instability of the English government under King Henry VI (1422–1461) also contributed to England's defeat. By 1453, the only part of France that was left in England's hands was the coastal town of Calais, which remained English for another century.

Political Instability

The fourteenth century was a period of adversity for the internal political stability of European governments.

THE TRIAL OF JOAN OF ARC

Feared by the English and Burgundians, Joan of Arc was put on trial on charges of witchcraft and heresy after her capture. She was condemned for heresy and burned at the stake on May 30, 1431. This excerpt is taken from the records of Joan's trial, which presented a dramatic confrontation between the judges, trained in the complexities of legal questioning, and a nineteen-year-old woman who relied only on the "voices" of saints who gave her advice. In this selection, Joan describes what these voices told her to do.

The Trial of Joan of Arc

Afterward, she declared that at the age of thirteen she had a voice from God to help her and guide her. And the first time she was much afraid. And this voice came toward noon, in summer, in her father's garden. . . . She heard the voice on her right, in the direction of the church; and she seldom heard it without a light. This light came from the same side as the voice, and generally there was a great light. . . .

Asked what instruction this voice gave her for the salvation of her soul: she said it taught her to be good and to go to church often. . . . She said that the voice told her to come, and she could no longer stay where she was; and the voice told her again that she should raise the siege of the city of Orléans. She said moreover that the voice told her that she, Joan, should go to Robert de Baudricourt, in the town of Vaucouleurs of which he was captain, and he would provide an escort for her. And the said Joan answered that she was a poor maid, knowing nothing of riding or fighting. She said she went to an uncle of hers, and told him she wanted to stay with him for some time; and she stayed there about eight days. And she told her uncle she must go to the said town of Vaucouleurs, and so her uncle took her.

Then she said that when she reached Vaucouleurs she easily recognized Robert de Baudricourt, although she had never seen him before; and she knew him through her voice, for the voice had told her it was he. . . . The said Robert twice refused to hear her and repulsed her; the third time he listened to her and gave her an escort. And the voice had told her that it would be so.

How would you explain Joan's "voices"? How would you defend Joan against her judges?

Although government bureaucracies grew ever larger, at the same time the question of who should control the bureaucracies led to internal conflict and instability. Like the lord and serf relationship, the lord and vassal relationship based on land and military service was being replaced by a contract based on money. Especially after the Black Death, money payments called **scutage** were increasingly substituted for military service. Monarchs welcomed this development because they could now hire professional soldiers, who tended to be more reliable anyway. As lord and vassal relationships became less personal and less important, new relationships based on political advantage began to be formed, creating new avenues for political influence—and for corruption as well. Especially noticeable, as the landed aristocrats suffered declining rents and social uncertainties with the new relationships, was the formation of factions of nobles who looked for opportunities to advance their power and wealth at the expense of other noble factions and of their monarchs. Others went to the royal courts, offering to serve the kings.

The kings had their own problems, however. By the mid-fifteenth century, reigning monarchs in many European countries were not the direct descendants of those ruling in 1300. The founders of these new dynasties had to struggle for position as factions of nobles vied to gain material advantages for themselves. At the end of the fourteenth century and beginning of the fifteenth, there were two claimants to the throne of France, and two aristocratic factions fought for control of England; in Germany, three princes struggled to be recognized as emperor.

Fourteenth-century monarchs, whether of old or new dynasties, faced financial problems as well. The shift to the use of mercenary soldiers left monarchs perennially short of cash. Traditional revenues, especially rents from property, increasingly proved insufficient to meet their needs. Monarchs attempted to generate new sources of revenues, especially through taxes, which often meant going through parliaments. This opened the door for parliamentary bodies to gain more power by asking for favors first. Although unsuccessful in most cases, the active role of parliaments added another element of uncertainty and confusion to fourteenth-century politics. Turning now to a survey of western and central European states, we can see how these disruptive factors worked.

Western Europe: England and France

In the fourteenth century, the lengthy reign of Edward III (1327–1377) was important for the evolution of English political institutions. Parliament increased in prominence and developed its basic structure and functions during Edward's reign. Due to his constant need for money to fight the Hundred Years' War, Edward came to rely on Parliament to levy new taxes. In return for regular grants, Edward made several concessions, including a commitment to levy no direct tax without Parliament's consent and to allow committees of Parliament to examine the

Outbreak of hostilities	1337
Battle of Crécy	1346
Truce	1396
War renewed by Henry V	1415
Battle of Agincourt	1415
French recovery under Joan of Arc	1429–1431
End of the war	1453

government accounts to ensure that the money was being spent properly. By the end of Edward's reign, Parliament had become an important component of the English governmental system.

During this same period, Parliament began to assume the organizational structure it has retained to this day. The Great Council of barons became the House of Lords and evolved into a body composed of the chief bishops and abbots of the realm and aristocratic peers whose position in Parliament was hereditary. The representatives of the shires and boroughs, who were considered less important than the lay and ecclesiastical lords, held collective meetings to decide policy and soon came to be regarded as the House of Commons. Together, the House of Lords and the House of Commons constituted Parliament. Although the House of Commons did little beyond approving measures proposed by the Lords, during Edward's reign the Commons did begin the practice of drawing up petitions, which, if accepted by the Lords and king, became law.

After Edward III's death, England began to experience the internal instability of aristocratic factionalism that was racking other European countries. After Richard II was deposed in 1399 and killed, the leader of the revolt of the barons, Henry of Lancaster, was made king. Although Henry IV (1399–1413) proved to be a competent ruler, factions of nobles rose to take advantage of the situation. England would soon be embroiled in a devastating series of civil wars known as the War of the Roses.

The Hundred Years' War left France prostrate. Depopulation, desolate farmlands, ruined commerce, and independent and unruly nobles made it difficult for the kings to assert their authority throughout the fourteenth century. The insanity of King Charles VI (1380–1422) especially opened the door to rival factions of French nobles aspiring to power and wealth. The dukes of Burgundy and Orléans competed to control Charles and the French monarchy. Their struggles created chaos for the French government and the French people. Many nobles supported the Orléanist faction; Paris and other towns favored the Burgundians. By the beginning of the fifteenth century, France seemed hopelessly mired in civil war.

The German Monarchy

England and France had developed strong national monarchies in the High Middle Ages. By the end of the fourteenth century, they seemed in danger of disintegrating due to dynastic problems and the pressures generated by the Hundred Years' War. In contrast, the Holy Roman Empire, whose core consisted of the lands of Germany, had already begun to fall apart in the High Middle Ages. Northern Italy, which the German emperors had tried to include in their medieval empire, had been free from any real imperial control since the end of the Hohenstaufen dynasty in the thirteenth century. In Germany itself, the failure of the Hohenstaufens ended any chance of centralized monarchical authority, and Germany became a land of hundreds of states that varied in size and power. These included princely states, such as the duchies of Bavaria and Saxony; free imperial city-states (self-governing cities directly under the control of the Holy Roman Emperor rather than a German territorial prince), such as Nuremberg; modest territories of petty imperial knights; and ecclesiastical states, such as the archbishopric of Cologne. In the ecclesiastical states, a high church official, such as a bishop, archbishop, or abbot, served in a dual capacity as an administrative official of the Catholic church and secular lord over the territories of the state. Although all of the rulers of these different states had some obligations to the German king and Holy Roman Emperor, more and more they acted independently.

The Holy Roman Empire in the Fourteenth Century

Because of its unique pattern of development in the High Middle Ages, the German monarchy had become established on an elective rather than hereditary basis. This principle of election was standardized in 1356 by the Golden Bull issued by Emperor Charles IV (1346–1378). This document stated that four lay princes and three ecclesiastical rulers would serve as electors with the legal power to elect the "king of the Romans and future emperor, to be ruler of the world and of the Christian people." "King of the Romans" was the official title of the German king; after his imperial coronation, he would also have the title of emperor.

In the fourteenth century, the electoral principle further ensured that kings of Germany were generally weak. Their ability to exercise effective power depended on the extent of their own family possessions. At the beginning of the fifteenth century, three emperors claimed the throne. Although the dispute was quickly settled, Germany entered the fifteenth century in a condition that verged on anarchy. Princes fought princes and leagues of cities. The emperors were virtually powerless to control any of them.

The States of Italy

By the fourteenth century, Italy, too, had failed to develop a centralized monarchical state. Papal opposition to the rule of the Hohenstaufen emperors in the thirteenth century had virtually guaranteed that. Moreover, southern Italy was divided into the kingdom of Naples, ruled by the house of Anjou, and Sicily, whose kings came from the Spanish house of Aragon. The center of the peninsula remained under the rather shaky control of the papacy. Lack of centralized authority had enabled numerous city-states in northern and central Italy to remain independent of any political authority.

In the course of the fourteenth century, two general tendencies can be discerned in Italy: the replacement of republican governments by tyrants and the expansion of the larger city-states at the expense of the less powerful ones. Nearly all the cities of northern Italy began their existence as free communes with republican governments. But in the fourteenth century, intense internal strife led city-states to resort to temporary expedients, allowing rule by one man with dictatorial powers. Limited rule, however, soon became long-term despotism, as tyrants proved willing to use force to maintain power. Eventually, such tyrants tried to legitimize their power by purchasing titles from the emperor (still nominally ruler of northern Italy as Holy Roman Emperor). In this fashion, the Visconti became the dukes of Milan and the d'Este the dukes of Ferrara.

The States of Italy in the Fourteenth Century

The other change of great significance was the development of regional entities as the larger states expanded at the expense of the smaller ones. By the beginning of the fifteenth century, three major states came to dominate northern Italy. In the fertile Po valley, where the chief trade routes from Italian coastal cities to the Alpine passes crossed, Milan was one of the richest city-states in Italy. Politically, it was also one of the most agitated until members of the Visconti family established themselves as hereditary dukes of Milan and extended their power over all of Lombardy. The republic of Florence dominated the region of Tuscany. In the course of the fourteenth century, a small but wealthy merchant oligarchy established control of the Florentine government, led the Florentines in a series of successful wars against their neighbors, and established Florence as a major territorial state in northern Italy. The other major northern Italian state was the maritime republic of Venice, which had grown rich from commercial activity in the eastern Mediterranean and northern Europe. Venice remained a stable political entity governed by a small oligarchy of merchant-aristocrats who had become extremely wealthy through their trading activities. Venice's commercial empire brought in enormous revenues and gave it the status of an international power. At the end of the fourteenth century, Venice embarked on the conquest of a territorial state in northern Italy to protect its food supply and its overland trade routes.

The Decline of the Church

The papacy of the Roman Catholic church reached the height of its power in the thirteenth century. Theories of papal supremacy included a doctrine of "fullness of power" as the spiritual head of Christendom and claims to universal temporal authority over all secular rulers. But the growing secular monarchies of Europe presented a challenge to papal claims of temporal supremacy that led the papacy into a conflict with these territorial states that it was unable to win. Papal defeat in turn led to other crises that brought into question and undermined not only the pope's temporal authority over all Christendom but his spiritual authority as well.

Boniface VIII and the Conflict with the State

The struggle between the papacy and the secular monarchies began during the pontificate of Pope Boniface VIII (1294–1303). One major issue appeared to be at stake between the pope and King Philip IV (1285–1314) of France. Looking for a source of new revenues, Philip expressed the right to tax the French clergy. Boniface VIII claimed that the clergy of any state could not pay taxes to their secular ruler without the pope's consent. Underlying this issue, however, was a basic conflict between the claims of the papacy to universal authority over both church and state, which necessitated complete control over the clergy, and the claims of the king that all subjects, including the clergy, were under the jurisdiction of the crown and subject to the king's authority on matters of taxation and justice. In short, the fundamental issue was the universal sovereignty of the papacy versus the royal sovereignty of the monarch.

Boniface VIII asserted his position in a series of papal bulls or letters, the most important of which was *Unam Sanctam*, issued in 1302. It was the strongest statement ever made by a pope on the supremacy of the spiritual authority over the temporal authority (see the box on

Pope Boniface VIII. The conflict between church and state in the Middle Ages reached its height in the struggle between Pope Boniface VIII and Philip IV of France. This fourteenth-century miniature depicts Boniface VIII presiding over a gathering of cardinals.

p. 208). When it became apparent that the pope had decided to act on his principles by excommunicating Philip IV of France, the latter sent a small contingent of French forces to capture Boniface and bring him back to France for trial. The pope was captured in Anagni, although Italian nobles from the surrounding countryside rescued him. The shock of this experience, however, soon led to the pope's death. Philip's strong-arm tactics had produced a clear victory for the national monarchy over the papacy, since no later pope dared renew the extravagant claims of Boniface VIII. To ensure his position and avoid any future papal threat, Philip IV brought enough pressure on the college of cardinals to achieve the election of a Frenchman, Clement V (1305–1314), as pope. Using the excuse of turbulence in the city of Rome, the new pope took up residence in Avignon, on the east bank of the Rhône River. Although Avignon was located in the Holy Roman Empire and was not a French possession, it lay just across the river from the possessions of King Philip IV and was French in culture.

The Papacy at Avignon (1305–1378)

The residency of the popes in Avignon for most of the fourteenth century led to a decline in papal prestige and growing antipapal sentiment. The city of Rome was the traditional capital of the universal church. The pope was the bishop of Rome, and his position was based on being the successor to the apostle Peter, the first bishop of Rome. It was unseemly that the head of the Catholic church should reside outside of Rome. In the 1330s, the popes began to construct a stately palace in Avignon, a clear indication that they intended to stay for some time.

Other factors also led to a decline in papal prestige during the Avignonese residency. Many contemporaries believed that the popes at Avignon were captives of the French monarchy. Although questionable, since Avignon did not belong to the French monarchy, it was easy to

believe in view of Avignon's proximity to French lands. Moreover, during the seventy-three years of the Avignonese papacy, of the 134 new cardinals created by the popes, 113 of them were French. At the same time, the popes attempted to find new sources of revenue to compensate for their loss of revenue from the Papal States and began to impose new taxes on the clergy. Furthermore, the splendor in which the pope and cardinals were living in Avignon led to a highly vocal criticism of both clergy and papacy in the fourteenth century. Avignon had become a powerful symbol of abuses within the church, and many people began to call for the pope's return to Rome. One of the most prominent calls came from Catherine of Siena (c. 1347–1380), whose saintly demeanor and claims of visions from God led the city of Florence to send her on a mission to Pope Gregory XI (1370–1378) in Avignon. She told the pope, "Because God has given you authority and because you have accepted it, you ought to use your virtue and power; if you do not wish to use it, it might be better for you to resign what you have accepted; it would give more honor to God and health to your soul."[6]

Avignon

The Great Schism

Catherine of Siena's admonition seemed to be heeded in 1377, when at long last Pope Gregory XI, perceiving the disastrous decline in papal prestige, returned to Rome. He died soon afterward, however, the following spring. When the college of cardinals met in conclave to elect a new pope, the citizens of Rome, fearful that the French majority would choose another Frenchman who would

BONIFACE VIII'S DEFENSE OF PAPAL SUPREMACY

*O*ne of the most remarkable documents of the four-teenth century was the exaggerated statement of papal supremacy issued by Pope Boniface VIII in 1302 in the heat of his conflict with the French king Philip IV. Ironically, this strongest statement ever made of papal supremacy was issued at a time when the rising power of the secular monarchies made it increasingly difficult for the premises to be accepted. Not long after issuing it, Boniface was taken prisoner by the French. Although freed by his fellow Italians, the humiliation of his defeat led to his death a short time later.

Pope Boniface VIII, *Unam Sanctam*

We are compelled, our faith urging us, to believe and to hold—and we do firmly believe and simply confess—that there is one holy catholic and apostolic church, outside of which there is neither salvation nor remission of sins.... In this church there is one Lord, one faith and one baptism.... Therefore, of this one and only church there is one body and one head ... Christ, namely, and the vicar of Christ, St. Peter, and the successor of Peter. For the Lord himself said to Peter, feed my sheep....

We are told by the word of the gospel that in this His fold there are two swords—a spiritual, namely, and a temporal.... Both swords, the spiritual and the material, there-fore, are in the power of the church; the one, indeed, to be wielded for the church, the other by the church; the one by the hand of the priest, the other by the hand of kings and knights, but at the will and sufferance of the priest. One sword, moreover, ought to be under the other, and the temporal authority to be subjected to the spiritual....

Therefore if the earthly power err it shall be judged by the spiritual power; but if the lesser spiritual power err, by the greater. But if the greatest, it can be judged by God alone, not by man, the apostle bearing witness. A spiritual man judges all things, but he himself is judged by no one. This authority, moreover, even though it is given to man and exercised through man, is not human but rather divine, being given by divine lips to Peter and founded on a rock for him and his successors through Christ himself whom he has confessed; the Lord himself saying to Peter: "Whatsoever you shall bind, etc." Whoever, therefore, resists this power thus ordained by God, resists the ordination of God....

Indeed, we declare, announce and define, that it is al-together necessary to salvation for every human creature to be subject to the Roman pontiff.

What claims does Boniface VIII make in Unam Sanctam? *To what extent are these claims a logical continuation of the development of the papacy in the Middle Ages? If you were a monarch, why would you object to this papal bull?*

---

return the papacy to Avignon, threatened that the car-dinals would not leave Rome alive unless a Roman or an Italian were elected pope. Indeed, the guards of the conclave warned the cardinals that they "ran the risk of being torn in pieces" if they did not choose an Italian. The terrified cardinals duly elected the Italian archbishop of Bari, who was subsequently crowned as Pope Urban VI (1378–1389) on Easter Sunday.

Following his election, Urban VI made clear his plans to reform the papal curia and even to swamp the college of cardinals with enough new Italian cardinals to elimi-nate the French majority. After many of the cardinals (the French ones) withdrew from Rome in late summer and were finally free of the Roman mob, they issued a man-ifesto, saying that they had been coerced by the mob and that Urban's election was therefore null and void. The dissenting cardinals thereupon chose one of their num-ber, a Frenchman, who took the title of Clement VII and promptly returned to Avignon. Since Urban remained in Rome, there were now two popes, initiating what has been called the **Great Schism** of the church.

Europe's loyalties soon became divided: France, Spain, Scotland, and southern Italy supported Clement, while England, Germany, Scandinavia, and most of Italy sup-ported Urban. These divisions generally followed political lines. Because the French supported the Avignonese, so

did their allies; their enemies, particularly England and its allies, supported the Roman pope.

The Great Schism badly damaged the faith of Christian believers. The pope was widely believed to be the leader of Christendom and, as Boniface VIII had pointed out, held the keys to the kingdom of heaven. Since both lines of popes denounced the other as the Antichrist, such a spectacle could not help but under-mine the institution that had become the very foundation of the church. The Great Schism introduced uncertainty into the daily lives of ordinary Christians.

The Conciliar Movement

As dissatisfaction with the papacy grew, so did the calls for a revolutionary approach to solving the church's in-stitutional problems. Final authority in spiritual matters must reside not with the popes, reformers claimed, but with a general church council representing all members. The Great Schism led large numbers of serious church-men to take up the theory of **conciliarism** in the belief that only a general council of the church could end the schism and bring reform to the church in its "head and members." In desperation, a group of cardinals from both lines of popes finally heeded these theoretical formula-tions and convened a general council. This Council of

Pisa, which met in 1409, deposed the two rival popes and elected a new one. The council's action proved disastrous when the two deposed popes refused to step down. There were now three popes, and the church seemed more hopelessly divided than ever.

Leadership in convening a new council now passed to the Holy Roman Emperor, Sigismund. As a result of his efforts, a new ecumenical church council met at Constance from 1414 to 1418. It had three major objectives: to end the schism, to eradicate heresy, and to reform the church in "head and members." The ending of the schism proved to be the Council of Constance's easiest task. After the three competing popes either resigned or were deposed, a new conclave elected a Roman cardinal, a member of a prominent Roman family, as Pope Martin V (1417–1431). The council was much less successful in dealing with the problems of heresy and reform.

Culture and Society in an Age of Adversity

In the midst of disaster, the fourteenth century proved creative in its own way. The rapid growth of vernacular literature and new inventions made an impact on European life at the same time that the effects of plague were felt in many areas of medieval towns and cities.

The Development of Vernacular Literature

Although Latin remained the language of the church liturgy and the official documents of both church and state, the fourteenth century witnessed a surge in literature written in vernacular languages, especially in Italy. By the late fifteenth century, vernacular literary forms had become so celebrated that they could compete with and would eventually replace works in Latin.

Dante Alighieri (1265–1321) came from an old Florentine noble family that had fallen on hard times. His masterpiece in the Italian vernacular was the *Divine Comedy,* written between 1313 and 1321. Cast in a typical medieval framework, the *Divine Comedy* is basically the story of the soul's progression to salvation, a fundamental medieval preoccupation. The lengthy poem was divided into three major sections corresponding to the realms of the afterworld: hell, purgatory, and heaven or paradise. In the "Inferno" (see the box on p. 210), Dante is led by his guide, the classical author Virgil, who is a symbol of human reason. But Virgil (or reason) can only lead the poet so far on his journey. At the end of "Purgatory," Beatrice (the true love of Dante's life), who represents revelation—which alone can explain the mysteries of heaven—becomes his guide into "Paradise." Here Beatrice presents Dante to Saint Bernard, a symbol of mystical contemplation. The saint turns Dante over to the Virgin Mary, since grace is necessary to achieve the final step of entering the presence of God, where one beholds "the love that moves the sun and the other stars."[7]

Geoffrey Chaucer (c. 1340–1400) brought a new level of sophistication to the English vernacular language in his famous work *The Canterbury Tales.* His beauty of expression and clear, forceful language were important in transforming his East Midland dialect into the chief ancestor of the modern English language. *The Canterbury Tales* is a collection of stories told by a group of twenty-nine pilgrims journeying from Southwark to the tomb of Saint Thomas at Canterbury. This format gave Chaucer the chance to portray an entire range of English society, from highborn to lowborn. The stories these pilgrims told to while away the time on the journey were just as varied as the storytellers themselves: knightly romances, fairy tales, saints' lives, sophisticated satires, and crude anecdotes.

One of the extraordinary vernacular writers of the age was Christine de Pizan (c. 1364–1430). Thanks to her father's position at the court of Charles V of France, she received a good education. Her husband died when she was only twenty-five (they had been married for ten years), leaving her with little income and three small children and her mother to support. Christine took the unusual step of becoming a writer to earn her living. Her poems were soon in demand, and by 1400 she had achieved financial security.

Christine de Pizan is best known, however, for her French prose works written in defense of women. In *The Book of the City of Ladies,* written in 1404, she denounced the many male writers who had argued that women by their very nature were prone to evil, unable to learn, and easily swayed and consequently needed to be controlled by men. With the help of Reason, Righteousness, and Justice, who appear to her in a vision, Christine refutes these antifeminist attacks. Women, she argues, are not evil by nature and could learn as well as men if they were permitted to attend the same schools: "Should I also tell you whether a woman's nature is clever and quick enough to learn speculative sciences as well as to discover them, and likewise the manual arts. I assure you that women are equally well-suited and skilled to carry them out and to put them to sophisticated use once they have learned them."[8] She ends the book by encouraging women to defend themselves against the attacks of men, who are incapable of understanding women.

DANTE'S VISION OF HELL

The *Divine Comedy* of Dante Alighieri is regarded as one of the greatest literary works of all time. Many people consider it the supreme summary of medieval thought. It combines allegory with a remarkable amount of contemporary history. Indeed, forty-three of the seventy-nine people consigned to hell in the "Inferno" were Florentines. This excerpt is taken from canto 18 of the "Inferno," in which Dante and Virgil visit the eighth circle of hell, which is divided into ten trenches containing those who had committed malicious frauds upon their fellow human beings.

Dante, "Inferno," *Divine Comedy*

We had already come to where the walk
crosses the second bank, from which it lifts
another arch, spanning from rock to rock.

Here we heard people whine in the next chasm,
and knock and thump themselves with open palms,
and blubber through their snouts as if in a spasm.

Steaming from that pit, a vapor rose
over the banks, crusting them with a slime
that sickened my eyes and hammered at my nose.

That chasm sinks so deep we could not sight
its bottom anywhere until we climbed
along the rock arch to its greatest height.

Once there, I peered down; and I saw long lines
of people in a river of excrement
that seemed the overflow of the world's latrines.

I saw among the felons of that pit
one wraith who might or might not have been tonsured—
one could not tell, he was so smeared with shit.

He bellowed: "You there, why do you stare at me
more than at all the others in this stew?"
And I to him: "Because if memory

serves me, I knew you when your hair was dry.
You are Alessio Interminelli da Lucca.
That's why I pick you from this filthy fry."

And he then, beating himself on his clown's head:
"Down to this have the flatteries I sold
the living sunk me here among the dead."

And my Guide prompted then: "Lean forward a bit
and look beyond him, there—do you see that one
scratching herself with dungy nails, the strumpet

who fidgets to her feet, then to a crouch?
It is the whore Thaïs who told her lover
when he sent to ask her, 'Do you thank me much?'

'Much? Nay, past all believing!' And with this
Let us turn from the sight of this abyss."

How does Dante's vision of hell reflect medieval religious thought? Why were there Florentines in hell?

Art and the Black Death

The fourteenth century produced an artistic outburst in new directions as well as a large body of morbid work influenced by the Black Death and the recurrence of the plague. The city of Florence witnessed the first dramatic break with medieval tradition in the work of Giotto (1266–1337), often considered a forerunner of Italian Renaissance painting. Although he worked throughout Italy, Giotto's most famous works were done in Padua and Florence. Coming out of the formal Byzantine school, Giotto transcended it with a new kind of realism, a desire to imitate nature that Renaissance artists later identified as the basic component of Classical art. Giotto's figures were solid and rounded, and placed realistically in relationship to each other and their background, they provided a sense of three-dimensional depth. The expressive faces and physically realistic bodies gave his sacred figures human qualities with which spectators could identify.

The Black Death had a visible impact on art. For one thing, it wiped out entire guilds of artists. At the same time, survivors, including the newly rich who patronized artists, were no longer so optimistic as before. Some were more guilty about enjoying life and more concerned about gaining salvation. Postplague art began to concentrate on pain and death. A fairly large number of artistic works came to be based on the *ars moriendi*, the art of dying.

Changes in Urban Life

One immediate by-product of the Black Death was a greater regulation of urban activities. Authorities tried to keep cities cleaner by enacting new ordinances against waste products in the streets. Viewed as unhealthy places, bathhouses were closed down, leading to a noticeable decline in cleanliness.

The effects of plague were also felt in other areas of medieval urban life. The basic unit of the late medieval urban environment was the nuclear family of husband, wife, and children. Especially in wealthier families, there might also be servants, apprentices, and other relatives, including widowed mothers and the husband's illegitimate children.

Before the Black Death, late marriages were common for urban couples. It was not unusual for husbands to be in their late thirties or forties and wives in their early

Giotto, *Lamentation.* The work of Giotto marked the first clear innovation in fourteenth-century painting, making him a forerunner of the early Renaissance. This fresco was part of a series done on the walls of the Arena chapel in Padua begun in 1305. Giotto painted thirty-eight scenes on three levels: the lives of Mary, the mother of Jesus, and her parents (top panel); the life and work of Jesus (middle panel); and his passion, crucifixion, and resurrection (bottom panel). Shown here from the bottom panel is the lamentation. A group of Jesus' followers, including his mother and Mary Magdalene, mourn over the body of Jesus before it is placed in its tomb. The solidity of Giotto's human figures gives them a three-dimensional quality. He also captured the grief and despair felt by the mourners.

twenties. The expense of beginning a household probably necessitated the delay in marriage. But the situation changed dramatically after the plague, reflecting new economic opportunities for the survivors and a reluctance to postpone living in the presence of so much death. The economic difficulties of the fourteenth century also had a tendency to strengthen the development of gender roles and to set new limits on employment opportunities for women. Based on the authority of Aristotle, Thomas Aquinas and other thirteenth-century scholastic theologians had advanced the belief that according to the natural order, men were active and domineering while women were passive and submissive. As more and more lawyers, doctors, and priests, who had been trained in universities where these notions were taught, entered society, these ideas of man's and woman's different natures became widely acceptable. Increasingly, women were expected to forgo any active functions in society and remain subject to direction from males. A fourteenth-century Parisian provost commented on glass cutters that "no master's widow who keeps working at his craft after her husband's death may take on apprentices, for the men of the craft do not believe that a woman can master it well enough to teach a child to master it, for the craft is a very delicate one."[9] Although this statement suggests that some women were in fact running businesses, it also reveals that they were viewed as incapable of undertaking all of men's activities. Based on a pattern of gender, Europeans created a division of labor roles between men and women that continued until the Industrial Revolution of the eighteenth and nineteenth centuries.

Inventions and New Patterns

Despite its problems, the fourteenth century witnessed a continuation of the technological innovations that had characterized the High Middle Ages. The most extraordinary of these inventions, and one that had a major impact on European cities, was the clock. The mechanical clock was invented at the end of the thirteenth century but not perfected until the fourteenth. The time-telling clock was actually a by-product of a larger astronomical clock. The best-designed one was constructed by Giovanni di Dondi in the mid-fourteenth century. Dondi's clock contained the signs of the zodiac but also struck on the hour. Because clocks were expensive, they were usually installed only in the towers of churches or municipal buildings. The first clock striking equal hours was in a church in Milan; in 1335, a chronicler described it as "a wonderful clock, with a very large clapper which strikes a bell twenty-four hours of the day and night and thus at the first hour of the night gives one sound, at the second two strikes . . . and so distinguishes one hour from another, which is of greatest use to men of every degree."[10]

Clocks introduced a wholly new conception of time into the lives of Europeans; they revolutionized how people thought about and used time. Throughout most of the Middle Ages, time was determined by natural rhythms (daybreak and nightfall) or church bells that were rung at more or less regular three-hour intervals, corresponding to the ecclesiastical offices of the church. Clocks made it possible to plan one's day and organize one's activities around the regular striking of bells. This brought a new regularity into the lives of workers and merchants, defining urban existence and enabling merchants and bankers to see the value of time in a new way.

Invented earlier by the Chinese, gunpowder also made its appearance in the West in the fourteenth century. The use of gunpowder eventually brought drastic changes to European warfare. Its primary use was in cannons, although early cannons were prone to blow up, making them as dangerous to the people firing them as to the enemy. Even as late as 1460, an attack on a castle using the "Lion," an enormous Flemish cannon, proved disastrous for the Scottish king James II when the "Lion" blew up, killing the king and a number of his retainers. Continued improvement in the construction of cannons, however, soon made them extremely valuable in reducing both castles and city walls.

Entertainment in the Middle Ages. Medieval people engaged in a variety of activities to be entertained. City dwellers enjoyed feast days and holidays, when minstrels and jugglers amused people with their arts and tricks. Castle life had its courtly feasts, featuring tournaments accompanied by banquets, music, and dancing. Games were popular at all levels of society; castle dwellers played backgammon, checkers, and chess. The illustration at the top, from a fifteenth-century fresco, shows a group of ladies and gentlemen playing cards.

Like children in all ages, medieval children joined with other children in playing a variety of games. A number of medieval writers on children saw play as a basic symbol of childhood itself. In this series of illustrations from medieval manuscripts, we see children engaged in riding hobbyhorses (undoubtedly popular in a society dependent on horses), catching butterflies and playing with a spinning top, and playing a game of blind man's bluff.

CONCLUSION

European civilization developed many of its fundamental features in the eleventh, twelfth, and thirteenth centuries. Territorial states, parliaments, capitalist trade and industry, banks, cities, and vernacular literatures were all products of that fertile period. During the same time, the Catholic church under the direction of the papacy reached its apogee. European society in the fourteenth century, however, was challenged by an overwhelming number of crises. Devastating plague, decline in trade and industry,

bank failures, peasant revolts pitting lower classes against the upper classes, seemingly constant warfare, aristocratic factional conflict that undermined political stability, the absence of the popes from Rome, and even the spectacle of two popes condemning each other as the Antichrist all seemed to overpower Europeans in this "calamitous century." Not surprisingly, much of the art of the period depicted the Four Horsemen of the Apocalypse described in the New Testament book of Revelation: Death, Famine,

Pestilence, and War. To some people, no doubt, the last days of the world seemed to be at hand.

The new European society, however, proved remarkably resilient. Periods of crisis usually give rise to new ideas and new practices. Intellectuals of the period saw themselves as standing on the threshold of a new age and a rebirth of the best features of classical civilization, an era widely referred to as the Renaissance.

TIMELINE

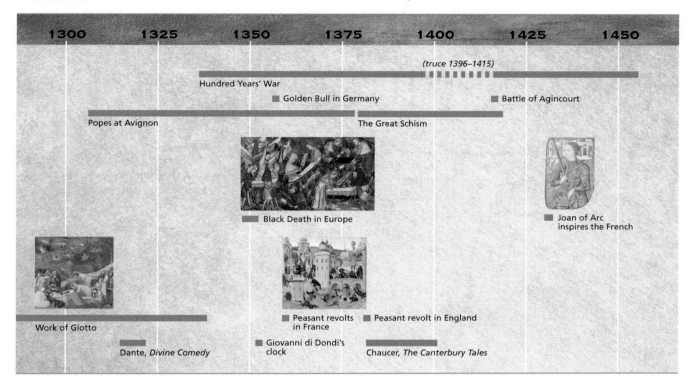

| 1300 | 1325 | 1350 | 1375 | 1400 | 1425 | 1450 |

(truce 1396–1415)

Hundred Years' War

Golden Bull in Germany

Battle of Agincourt

Popes at Avignon

The Great Schism

Black Death in Europe

Joan of Arc inspires the French

Work of Giotto

Peasant revolts in France

Peasant revolt in England

Dante, *Divine Comedy*

Giovanni di Dondi's clock

Chaucer, *The Canterbury Tales*

NOTES

1. Quoted in H. S. Lucas, "The Great European Famine of 1315, 1316, and 1317," *Speculum* 5 (1930): 359.
2. Quoted in D. Herlihy, *The Black Death and the Transformation of the West*, ed. S. K. Cohn Jr. (Cambridge, Mass., 1997), p. 9.
3. J. Froissart, *Chronicles*, ed. and trans. G. Brereton (Harmondsworth, England, 1968), p. 111.
4. Ibid. p. 212.
5. Ibid. p. 89.
6. Quoted in R. Coogan, *Babylon on the Rhône: A Translation of Letters by Dante, Petrarch, and Catherine of Siena* (Washington, D.C., 1983), p. 115.
7. Dante, *Divine Comedy*, trans. D. Sayers (New York, 1962), "Paradise," canto 33, line 145.
8. Christine de Pizan, *The Book of the City of Ladies*, trans. E. J. Richards (New York, 1982), pp. 83–84.
9. Quoted in S. Stuard, "Dominion of Gender: Women's Fortunes in the High Middle Ages," in R. Bridenthal, C. Koonz, and S. Stuard, eds., *Becoming Visible: Women in European History*, 2d ed. (Boston, 1987), p. 169.
10. Quoted in J. Gimpel, *The Medieval Machine* (New York, 1976), p. 168.

SUGGESTIONS FOR FURTHER READING

For a general introduction to the fourteenth century, see **D. P. Waley**, *Later Medieval Europe,* 2d ed. (London, 1985), and **G. Holmes**, *Europe: Hierarchy and Revolt, 1320–1450* (New York, 1975).

On the Black Death, see **P. Ziegler**, *The Black Death* (New York, 1969); **D. Herlihy**, *The Black Death and the Transformation of the West,* ed. **S. K. Cohn Jr.** (Cambridge, Mass., 1997); and the well-written popular history by **J. Kelly**, *The Great Mortality* (New York, 2005).

Good accounts of the Hundred Years' War include **A. Curry**, *The Hundred Years' War* (New York, 1993), and **R. H. Neillands**, *The Hundred Years' War* (New York, 1990). On Joan of Arc, see **M. Warner**, *Joan of Arc: The Image of Female Heroism* (New York, 1981). On the political history of the period, see **B. Guenée**, *States and Rulers in Later Medieval Europe,* trans. **J. Vale** (Oxford, 1985).

A good general study of the church in the fourteenth century can be found in **F. P. Oakley**, *The Western Church in the Later Middle Ages* (Ithaca, N.Y., 1980). See also **J. H. Lynch**, *The Medieval Church: A Brief History* (New York, 1992). On the Avignonese papacy, see **Y. Renouard**, *The Avignon Papacy, 1305–1403* (London, 1970). On late medieval religious practices, see **R. N. Swanson**, *Religion and Devotion in Europe, c. 1215–1515* (Cambridge, 1995).

A classic work on the life and thought of the Late Middle Ages is **J. Huizinga**, *The Autumn of the Middle Ages,* trans. **R. J. Payton** and **U. Mammitzsch** (Chicago, 1996). On the impact of the plague on culture, see the brilliant study by **M. Meiss**, *Painting in Florence and Siena After the Black Death* (New York, 1964). On Dante, see **J. Freccero**, *Dante and the Poetics of Conversion* (Cambridge, Mass., 1986). On Chaucer, see **G. Kane**, *Chaucer* (New York, 1984). The best work on Christine de Pizan is by **C. C. Willard**, *Christine de Pizan: Her Life and Works* (New York, 1984).

A wealth of material on everyday life is provided in the second volume of *A History of Private Life,* ed. **G. Duby**, *Revelations of the Medieval World* (Cambridge, Mass., 1988). On women in the Later Middle Ages, see **S. Shahar**, *The Fourth Estate: A History of Women in the Middle Ages,* trans. **C. Galai** (London, 1983), and **D. Herlihy**, *Women, Family, and Society: Historical Essays, 1978–1991* (Providence, R.I., 1995). Poor people are discussed in **M. Mollat**, *The Poor in the Middle Ages* (New Haven, Conn., 1986). The

importance of inventions is discussed in **J. Gimpel**, *The Medieval Machine* (New York, 1976). Another valuable discussion of medieval technology can be found in **J. Le Goff**, *Time, Work, and Culture in the Middle Ages* (Chicago, 1980).

Thomson NOW! Enter *ThomsonNOW* using the access card that is available for *Western Civilization: A Brief History*. *ThomsonNOW* will help you understand this chapter with lesson plans generated for your needs. In addition, you can read the following documents, and many more, online:

> Jean Froissart, *The Battle of Crécy, The Burghers of Calais,* and *The Battle of Poitiers*

WESTERN CIVILIZATION RESOURCES

Visit the Web site for *Western Civilization: A Brief History* for resources specific to this book:
    http://www.thomsonedu.com/history/spielvogel
For a variety of tools to help you succeed in this course, visit the Western Civilization Resource Center at
    http://history.wadsworth.com/spielvogel
Included are quizzes, images, documents, interactive simulations, maps and timelines, movie explorations, and a wealth of other sources.

12

RECOVERY AND REBIRTH: THE RENAISSANCE

Michelangelo's Creation of Adam *on the Sistine Chapel ceiling*

© Vatican Museums and Galleries, Vatican City, Vatican State/Bridgeman Art Library

CHAPTER OUTLINE AND FOCUS QUESTIONS

Meaning and Characteristics of the Italian Renaissance

☐ What characteristics distinguish the Renaissance from the Middle Ages?

The Making of Renaissance Society

☐ What major social changes occurred in the Renaissance?

The Italian States in the Renaissance

☐ How did Machiavelli's works reflect the political realities of Renaissance Italy?

The Intellectual Renaissance in Italy

☐ What were the chief characteristics of humanism?

The Artistic Renaissance

☐ What were the chief characteristics of Renaissance art, and how did it differ in Italy and northern Europe?

The European State in the Renaissance

☐ Why do historians sometimes refer to the monarchies of the late fifteenth century as "new monarchies" or "Renaissance states"?

The Church in the Renaissance

☐ What were the policies of the Renaissance popes, and what impact did those policies have on the Catholic church?

CRITICAL THINKING

☐ How did Renaissance art and the humanist movement reflect the political, economic, and social developments of the period?

ERE THE FOURTEENTH and fifteenth centuries a continuation of the Middle Ages or the beginning of a new era? The answer is that both positions are true. Although the disintegrative patterns of the fourteenth century continued into the fifteenth, at the same time there were elements of recovery that made the fifteenth century a period of significant political, economic, artistic, and intellectual change. The humanists or intellectuals of the age considered their period (from the mid-fourteenth to the mid-sixteenth century) an age of rebirth, believing that they had restored arts and letters to new glory after they had been "neglected" or "dead" for centuries. The humanists also saw their age as one of accomplished individuals who dominated the landscape of their time. Michelangelo, the great Italian artist of the early sixteenth century, and Pope Julius II, the "warrior pope," were two such titans. The artist's temperament and the pope's temper led to many lengthy and often loud quarrels between the two. Among other commissions, the pope had hired Michelangelo to paint the ceiling of the Sistine Chapel in Rome, a daunting task for a man long accustomed to being a sculptor. Michelangelo undertook the project but refused for a long time to allow anyone, including the pope, to see his work. Julius grew anxious, pestering Michelangelo on a regular basis about when the ceiling would be finished. Exasperated by the pope's requests, Michelangelo once replied, according to Giorgio Vasari, his contemporary biographer, that the ceiling would be completed "when it satisfies me as an artist." The pope responded, "And we want you to satisfy us and finish it soon," and then threatened that if Michelangelo did not "finish the ceiling quickly [the pope] would have him thrown down from the scaffolding." Fearing the pope's anger, Michelangelo "lost no time in doing all that was wanted" and quickly completed the ceiling, one of the great masterpieces of Western art.

The humanists' view of their age as a rebirth of the classical civilization of the Greeks and Romans ultimately led historians to use the French word *Renaissance* to identify this age. Although recent historians have emphasized the many elements of continuity between the Middle Ages and the Renaissance, the latter age was also distinguished by its own unique characteristics.◆

Meaning and Characteristics of the Italian Renaissance

Renaissance means "rebirth." Many people who lived in Italy between 1350 and 1550 believed that they were witnessing a rebirth of antiquity or Greco-Roman civilization, marking a new age. To them, the thousand or so years between the end of the Roman Empire and their own era was a middle period (the "Middle Ages"), characterized by darkness because of its lack of classical culture. Historians of the nineteenth century later used similar terminology to describe this period in Italy. The Swiss historian and art critic Jacob Burckhardt created the modern concept of the **Renaissance** in his celebrated work *Civilization of the Renaissance in Italy*, published in 1860. He portrayed Italy in the fourteenth and fifteenth centuries as the birthplace of the modern world and saw the revival of antiquity, the "perfecting of the individual," and secularism ("worldliness of the Italians") as its distinguishing features. Burckhardt established the framework for all modern interpretations of the period. Although contemporary scholars do not believe that the Renaissance represents a sudden or dramatic cultural break with the Middle Ages (as Burckhardt argued)—there was, after all, much continuity between the two periods in economic, political, and social life—the Renaissance can still be viewed as a distinct period of European history that manifested itself first in Italy and then spread to the rest of Europe. What, then, are the characteristics of the Italian Renaissance?

Renaissance Italy was largely an urban society. The city-states, especially those of northern Italy, became the centers of Italian political, economic, and social life. In this new urban society, a secular spirit emerged as increasing wealth created new possibilities for the enjoyment of worldly things (see the box on p. 217).

Above all, the Renaissance was an age of recovery from the "calamitous fourteenth century." Italy and the rest of Europe began a slow process of recuperation from the effects of the Black Death, political disorder, and economic recession. Recovery was accompanied by a rediscovery of the culture of classical antiquity. Increasingly aware of their own historical past, Italian intellectuals became intensely interested in the Greco-Roman culture of the ancient Mediterranean world. This revival of classical antiquity (the Middle Ages had in fact preserved much of ancient Latin culture) affected politics and art and led to new attempts to reconcile the pagan philosophy of antiquity with Christian thought, as well as new ways of viewing human beings.

A revived emphasis on individual ability became characteristic of the Italian Renaissance. As the fifteenth-century Florentine architect Leon Battista Alberti expressed it, "Men can do all things if they will."[1] A high regard for human dignity and worth and a realization of individual potentiality created a new social ideal of the well-rounded personality or universal person (*l'uomo universale*) who was capable of achievements in many areas of life.

These general features of the Italian Renaissance were not characteristic of all Italians but were primarily the preserve of the wealthy upper classes, who constituted a small percentage of the total population. The achievements of the Italian Renaissance were thus the product of an elite, rather than a mass, movement. Nevertheless, indirectly it did have some impact on ordinary people, especially in the cities, where so many of the intellectual and artistic accomplishments of the period were most apparent.

The Making of Renaissance Society

After the severe economic reversals and social upheavals of the second half of the fourteenth century, the European economy gradually recovered during the fifteenth century as manufacturing and trade increased in volume.

Economic Recovery

By the fourteenth century, Italian merchants were carrying on a flourishing commerce throughout the Mediterranean and had also expanded their lines of trade north along the Atlantic seaboard. The great galleys of the Venetian Flanders Fleet maintained a direct sea route from Venice to England and the Netherlands, where Italian merchants came into contact with the increasingly powerful Hanseatic League of merchants. Hard hit by the plague, the Italians lost their commercial preeminence while the Hanseatic League continued to prosper.

Expansion of Trade   As early as the thirteenth century, a number of north German coastal towns had formed a commercial and military league known as the Hansa or Hanseatic League. By 1500, more than eighty cities belonged to the League, which established settlements and commercial bases in northern Europe and England. For

A RENAISSANCE BANQUET

As in Greek and Roman society, the Renaissance banquet was an occasion for good food, interesting conversation, music, and dancing. In Renaissance society, it was also a symbol of status and an opportunity to impress people with the power and wealth of one's family. Banquets were held to celebrate public and religious festivals, official visits, anniversaries, and weddings. The following menu lists the foods served at a grand banquet given by Pope Pius V in the sixteenth century.

A Sixteenth-Century Banquet

First Course: Cold Delicacies from the Sideboard

Pieces of marzipan and marzipan balls
Neapolitan spice cakes
Malaga wine and Pisan biscuits
Fresh grapes
Prosciutto cooked in wine, served with capers and grape pulp
Salted pork tongues cooked in wine, sliced
Spit-roasted songbirds, cold, with their tongues sliced over them
Sweet mustard

Second Course: Hot Foods from the Kitchen, Roasts

Fried veal sweetbreads and liver
Spit-roasted skylarks with lemon sauce
Spit-roasted quails with sliced eggplants
Stuffed spit-roasted pigeons with capers sprinkled over them
Spit-roasted rabbits, with sauce and crushed pine nuts
Partridges larded and spit-roasted, served with lemon
Heavily seasoned poultry with lemon slices
Slices of veal, spit-roasted with a sauce made from the juices
Leg of goat spit-roasted with a sauce made from the juices
Soup of almond paste, with the flesh of three pigeons to each serving

Third Course: Hot Foods from the Kitchen, Boiled Meats and Stews

Stuffed fat geese, boiled Lombard style and covered with sliced almonds
Stuffed breast of veal, boiled, garnished with flowers
Very young calf, boiled, garnished with parsley
Almonds in garlic sauce
Turkish-style rice with milk, sprinkled with cinnamon
Stewed pigeons with mortadella sausage and whole onions
Cabbage soup with sausages
Poultry pie, two chickens to each pie
Fricasseed breast of goat dressed with fried onions
Pies filled with custard cream
Boiled calves' feet with cheese and egg

Fourth Course: Delicacies from the Sideboard

Bean tarts
Quince pastries
Pear tarts, the pears wrapped in marzipan
Parmesan cheese and Riviera cheese
Fresh almonds on vine leaves
Chestnuts roasted over the coals and served with salt and pepper
Milk curds
Ring-shaped cakes
Wafers made from ground grain

What kinds of people would be present at a banquet where the foods listed on this menu would be served?

---

almost two hundred years, the Hansa had a monopoly on northern European trade in timber, fish, grain, metals, honey, and wines. Its southern outlet in Flanders, the city of Bruges, became the economic crossroads of Europe in the fourteenth century because it served as the meeting place between Hanseatic merchants and the Flanders Fleet of Venice. In the fifteenth century, however, the Hanseatic League proved increasingly unable to compete with the developing larger territorial states.

Overall, trade recovered dramatically from the economic contraction of the fourteenth century. The Italians and especially the Venetians continued to maintain a wealthy commercial empire. Not until the sixteenth century, when overseas discoveries gave new importance to the states facing the Atlantic, did the petty Italian city-states begin to suffer from the competitive advantages of the ever-growing and more powerful national territorial states.

Industries Old and New The economic depression of the fourteenth century also affected patterns of manufacturing. The woolen industries of Flanders and the northern Italian cities had been particularly devastated. By the beginning of the fifteenth century, however, the Florentine woolen industry began to recover. At the same time, the Italian cities began to develop and expand luxury industries, including lace and silk, glassware, and handworked items in metal and precious stones.

Other new industries, especially printing, mining, and metallurgy, began to rival the textile industry in importance in the fifteenth century. New machinery and techniques for digging deeper mines and for separating metals from ore and purifying them were developed, and **entrepreneurs** quickly developed large mining operations to produce copper, iron, and silver. Especially valuable were the rich mineral deposits in central Europe. Expanding iron production and new skills in metalworking in turn contributed to the development of firearms that were more effective than the crude weapons of the fourteenth century.

Banking and the Medici The city of Florence regained its preeminence in banking in the fifteenth century, due primarily to the Medici family. In its best days (in the fifteenth century), the house of Medici was the greatest banking house in Europe, with branches in Venice, Milan, Rome, Avignon, Bruges, London, and Lyons. Moreover, the family had controlling interests in industrial enterprises for wool, silk, and the mining of alum, which was used to dye textiles. Despite its great success, the Medici bank suffered a sudden decline at the end of the fifteenth century due to poor leadership and a series of bad loans, especially to rulers. In 1494, when the French expelled the Medici from Florence and confiscated their property, the entire financial edifice collapsed.

Social Changes in the Renaissance

The Renaissance inherited its social structure from the Middle Ages. Society remained fundamentally divided into three **estates:** the First Estate, the clergy, whose preeminence was grounded in the belief that people should be guided to spiritual ends; the Second Estate, the nobility, whose privileges were based on the principle that the nobles provided security and justice for society; and the Third Estate, the peasants and inhabitants of the towns and cities. This social order experienced certain adaptations in the Renaissance, which we can see by examining the Second and Third Estates (the clergy will be examined in Chapter 13).

The Nobility Throughout much of Europe, the landholding nobles faced declining real incomes during the greater part of the fourteenth and fifteenth centuries. But many members of the old nobility survived, and new blood infused its ranks. A reconstruction of the aristocracy was well under way by 1500. As a result of this reconstruction, the nobles, old and new, who constituted between 2 and 3 percent of the population in most countries, managed to dominate society as they had done in the Middle Ages, serving as military officers and holding important political posts as well as advising the king.

By 1500, the noble or aristocrat was expected to evince certain ideals. These ideals were best expressed in *The Book of the Courtier* by the Italian Baldassare Castiglione (1478–1529). Published in 1528, Castiglione's work soon became popular throughout Europe, and it remained a basic handbook for European aristocrats well into the twentieth century.

In his book, Castiglione described the three basic attributes of the perfect courtier. First, nobles should possess fundamental native endowments, such as impeccable character, grace, talents, and noble birth. The perfect courtier must also cultivate certain achievements. Primarily, he should participate in military and bodily exercises because the principal profession of a courtier was arms. But unlike the medieval knight, the Renaissance courtier was also expected to have a classical education and adorn his life with the arts by playing a musical instrument, drawing, and painting. In Castiglione's hands, the Renaissance ideal of the well-developed personality became a social ideal of the aristocracy. Finally, the aristocrat was expected to follow a certain standard of conduct. Nobles were to make a good impression; while being modest, they should not hide their accomplishments but show them with grace.

What was the purpose of these courtly standards? Castiglione said:

> I think that the aim of the perfect Courtier . . . is so to win for himself, by means of the accomplishments ascribed to him by these gentlemen, the favor and mind of the prince whom he serves that he may be able to tell him, and always will tell him, the truth about everything he needs to know, without fear or risk of displeasing him; and that when he sees the mind of his prince inclined to a wrong action, he may dare to oppose him . . . so as to dissuade him of every evil intent and bring him to the path of virtue.[2]

The aim of the perfect noble, then, was to serve his prince in an effective and honest way. Nobles would adhere to these principles for hundreds of years while they continued to dominate European life socially and politically.

Peasants and Townspeople Peasants made up the overwhelming mass of the Third Estate, and except in the highly urbanized areas of northern Italy and Flanders, they continued to constitute as much as 85 to 90 percent of the total European population. The most noticeable trend produced by the economic crisis of the fourteenth century was the decline of the manorial system and the continuing elimination of serfdom. The contraction of the peasantry after the Black Death simply accelerated the process of converting servile labor dues into rents paid in money. By the end of the fifteenth century, primarily in western Europe, serfdom was declining, and more and more peasants were becoming legally free.

The remainder of the Third Estate centered around the inhabitants of towns and cities, originally the merchants and artisans who formed the bourgeoisie. The Renaissance town or city of the fifteenth century actually possessed a multitude of townspeople widely separated socially and economically.

At the top of urban society were the patricians, whose wealth from capitalistic enterprises in trade, industry, and banking enabled them to dominate their urban communities economically, socially, and politically. Below them were the petty burghers, the shopkeepers, artisans, guildmasters, and guildsmen who were largely concerned with providing goods and services for local consumption. Below these two groups were the propertyless workers earning pitiful wages and the unemployed, living squalid and miserable lives; these people constituted as much as 30 to 40 percent of the urban population. Everywhere in Europe in the late fourteenth and fifteenth centuries, urban poverty had increased dramatically. One rich merchant of Florence wrote:

MARRIAGE NEGOTIATIONS

*M*arriages were so important in maintaining families in Renaissance Italy that much energy was put into arranging them. Parents made the choices for their children, most often for considerations that had little to do with the modern notion of love. This selection is taken from the letters of a Florentine matron of the illustrious Strozzi family to her son Filippo in Naples. The family's considerations were complicated by the fact that the son was in exile.

Alessandra Strozzi to Her Son Filippo in Naples

[April 20, 1464]...Concerning the matter of a wife [for Filippo], it appears to me that if Francesco di Messer Tanagli wishes to give his daughter, that it would be a fine marriage....Now I will speak with Marco [Parenti, Alessandra's son-in-law], to see if there are other prospects that would be better, and if there are none, then we will learn if he wishes to give her [in marriage]....Francesco Tanagli has a good reputation, and he has held office, not the highest, but still he has been in office. You may ask: "Why should he give her to someone in exile?" There are three reasons. First, there aren't many young men of good family who have both virtue and property. Secondly, she has only a small dowry, 1,000 florins, which is the dowry of an artisan [although not a small sum, either—senior officials in the government bureaucracy earned 300 florins a year]....Third, I believe that he will give her away, because he has a large family and he will need help to settle them....

[July 26, 1465]...Francesco is a good friend of Marco and he trusts him. On [Saint] Jacopo's day, he spoke to him discreetly and persuasively, saying that for several months he had heard that we were interested in the girl and...that when we had made up our minds, she will come to us willingly. [He said that] you were a worthy man, and that his family had always made good marriages, but that he had only a small dowry to give her, and so he would prefer to send her outside of Florence to someone of worth, rather than to give her to someone here, from among those who were available, with little money....We have information that she is affable and competent. She is responsible for a large family (there are twelve children, six boys and six girls), and the mother is always pregnant and isn't very competent....

[August 31, 1465]...I have recently received some very favorable information [about the Tanagli girl] from two individuals....They are in agreement that whoever gets her will be content....Concerning her beauty, they told me what I had already seen, that she is attractive and well-proportioned. Her face is long, but I couldn't look directly into her face, since she appeared to be aware that I was examining her...and so she turned away from me like the wind....She reads quite well...and she can dance and sing....

So yesterday I sent for Marco and told him what I had learned. And we talked about the matter for a while, and decided that he should say something to the father and give him a little hope, but not so much that we couldn't withdraw, and find out from him the amount of the dowry.... May God help us to choose what will contribute to our tranquility and to the consolation of us all.

[September 13, 1465]...Marco came to me and said that he had met with Francesco Tanagli, who had spoken very coldly, so that I understand that he had changed his mind....

[Filippo Strozzi eventually married Fiametta di Donato Adimari in 1466.]

What were the most important considerations in marriage negotiations? Why were they so important?

Those that are lazy and indolent in a way that does harm to the city, and who can offer no just reason for their condition, should either be forced to work or expelled from the Commune. The city would thus rid itself of that most harmful part of the poorest class....If the lowest order of society earn enough food to keep them going from day to day, then they have enough.[3]

But even this large group was not at the bottom of the social scale; beneath it stood a significantly large group of slaves, especially in the cities of Italy.

Family and Marriage in Renaissance Italy

The family bond was a source of great security in the urban world of Renaissance Italy. To maintain the family, careful attention was given to marriages that were arranged by parents, often to strengthen business or family ties. Details were worked out well in advance, sometimes when children were only five or six, and reinforced by a legally binding marriage contract (see the box above). The important aspect of the contract was the size of the dowry, a sum of money presented by the wife's family upon marriage. The dowry could involve large sums of money and was expected of all families.

The father-husband was the center of the Italian family. He gave it his name, was responsible for it in all legal matters, managed all finances (his wife had no share in his wealth), and made the crucial decisions in his children's lives. A father's authority over his children was absolute until he died or formally freed his children. The age of emancipation varied from early teens to late twenties.

The wife managed the household, a position that gave women a certain degree of autonomy in their daily lives. Most wives, however, also knew that their primary function was to bear children. Upper-class wives were frequently pregnant; Alessandra Strozzi of Florence, for example, who had been married at the age of sixteen, bore eight children in ten years.

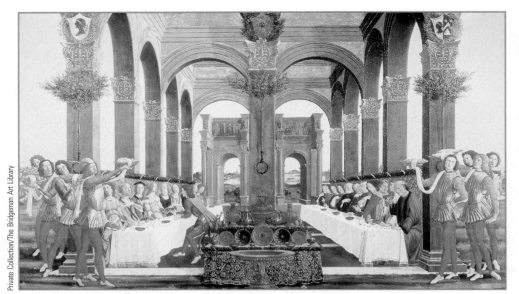

Wedding Banquet. Parents arranged marriages in Renaissance Italy to strengthen business or family ties. A legally binding marriage contract was considered a necessary part of the marital arrangements. So was a wedding feast. This painting by Botticelli shows the wedding banquet in Florence that celebrated the marriage of Nastagio degli Onesti and the daughter of Paulo Traversaro.

For women in the Renaissance, childbirth was a fearful occasion. Not only was it painful, but it could be deadly; possibly as many as 10 percent of mothers died in childbirth. In his memoirs, the Florentine merchant Gregorio Dati recalled that three of his four wives died in childbirth. His third wife, after delivering eleven children in fifteen years, "died in childbirth after lengthy suffering, which she bore with remarkable strength and patience."[4] Nor did the tragedies end with childbirth. Surviving mothers often faced the death of their children. In Florence in the fifteenth century, for example, almost half of the children born to merchant families died before the age of twenty. Given these mortality rates, many upper-class families sought to have as many children as possible in order to ensure a surviving male heir to the family fortune. This concern is evident in the Florentine humanist Leon Battista Alberti's treatise *On the Family*, when one of the characters remarks, "How many families do we see today in decadence and ruin! . . . Of all these families not only the magnificence and greatness but the very men, not only the men but the very names are shrunk away and gone. Their memory . . . is wiped out and obliterated."[5]

The Italian States in the Renaissance

By the fifteenth century, five major powers dominated the Italian peninsula: the duchy of Milan, Venice, Florence, the Papal States, and the kingdom of Naples (see Map 12.1). Northern Italy was divided between Milan and Venice. After the death of the last Visconti ruler of Milan in 1447, Francesco Sforza, one of the leading ***condottieri*** (a *condottiere* was the leader of a mercenary band) of the time, turned on his Milanese employers, conquered the city, and became its new duke. Both the Visconti and Sforza rulers worked to create a highly centralized territorial

state. They were especially successful in devising systems of taxation that generated enormous revenues for the government. The maritime republic of Venice remained an extremely stable political entity governed by a small oligarchy of merchant-aristocrats. Its commercial empire brought in enormous revenues and gave it the status of an international power.

The republic of Florence dominated the region of Tuscany. In 1434, Cosimo de'Medici (1434–1464) took control of the ruling oligarchy. Although the wealthy Medici family maintained republican forms of government for appearance's sake, it ran the government from behind the scenes. Through lavish patronage and careful courting of political allies, Cosimo and later his grandson Lorenzo the Magnificent (1469–1492) were successful in dominating the city at a time when Florence was the center of the cultural Renaissance.

The Papal States lay in central Italy. Nominally under the control of the popes, papal residence in Avignon and the Great Schism had enabled individual cities and territories, such as Urbino and Ferrara, to become independent of papal authority. The popes of the fifteenth century directed much of their energy toward reestablishing their control over the Papal States. The kingdom of Naples, which encompassed most of southern Italy and usually the island of Sicily, remained a backward monarchy that shared little in the cultural glories of the Renaissance.

A number of independent city-states under the control of powerful ruling families also became brilliant centers of Renaissance culture in the fifteenth century. Perhaps most famous was Urbino, ruled by the Montefeltro dynasty. Federigo da Montefeltro, who ruled Urbino from 1444 to 1482, received a classical education. He had also learned the skills of fighting, since the Montefeltro family compensated for the poverty of Urbino by hiring themselves out as *condottieri*. Federigo was not only a good ruler but also a rather unusual *condottiere* by fifteenth-century standards.

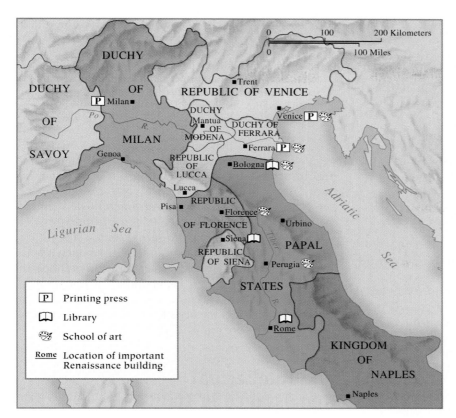

MAP 12.1 **Renaissance Italy.** Italy in the late fourteenth century was a land of five major states and numerous independent city-states. Increased prosperity and a supportive intellectual climate helped create the atmosphere for the middle and upper classes to "rediscover" Greco-Roman culture. Modern diplomacy was also a product of Renaissance Italy. **?** Could the presence of several other powers within easy marching distance make a ruler recognize the importance of diplomacy? **View an animated version of this map or related maps at** http://thomsonedu.com/history/spielvogel

Although not a brilliant general, he was reliable and honest. At the same time, Duke Federigo was one of the greatest patrons of Renaissance culture. Under his direction, Urbino became a well-known cultural and intellectual center.

A noticeable feature of these smaller Italian courts was the important role played by women. The most famous of the Italian ruling women was Isabella d'Este (1474–1539), daughter of the duke of Ferrara, who married Francesco Gonzaga, marquis of Mantua. Their court was another important center of art and learning in the Renaissance. Educated at the brilliant court of Ferrara, Isabella was known for her intelligence and political wisdom. Called the "first lady of the world," she attracted artists and intellectuals to the Mantuan court and was responsible for amassing one of the finest libraries in all of Italy. Her numerous letters to friends, family, princes, and artists all over Europe disclose her political acumen as well as a good sense of humor. Both before and after the death of her husband Francesco, she effectively ruled Mantua.

The growth of powerful monarchical states led to trouble for the Italians and brought an end to the independence of the Italian states. Attracted by the riches of Italy, the French king Charles VIII (1483–1498) led an army of thirty thousand men into Italy in 1494 and occupied the kingdom of Naples. Other Italian states turned for help to the Spanish, who gladly complied. For the next thirty years, the French and Spanish competed to dominate Italy, which was merely a pawn for the two great powers, a convenient arena for fighting battles. The terrible sack of Rome in 1527 by the armies of the Spanish king Charles I brought a temporary end to the Italian wars. From then on, the Spaniards dominated Italy; the Renaissance in Italy was at an end.

Machiavelli and the New Statecraft

No one gave better expression to the Renaissance preoccupation with political power than Niccolò Machiavelli (1469–1527). Although he ably served as a diplomat for Florence, he was eventually forced into exile. Embittered by this and compelled by the great love of his life—politics— he wrote *The Prince*, one of the most influential works on political power in the Western world.

Machiavelli's major concerns in *The Prince* were the acquisition, maintenance, and expansion of political power as the means to restore and maintain order in his time. In the Middle Ages, many political theorists stressed the ethical side of a prince's activity—how a ruler ought to behave based on Christian moral principles. Machiavelli bluntly contradicted this approach:

My hope is to write a book that will be useful, at least to those who read it intelligently, and so I thought it sensible to go straight to a discussion of how things are in real life and not waste time with a discussion of an imaginary world . . . for the gap between how people actually behave and how they ought to behave is so great that anyone who ignores everyday reality in order to live up to an ideal will soon discover he had been taught how to destroy himself, not how to preserve himself.[6]

Machiavelli considered his approach far more realistic than that of his medieval forebears.

From Machiavelli's point of view, a prince's attitude toward power must be based on an understanding of human nature, which he perceived as basically self-centered. He said, "Of men one can, in general, say this: They are ungrateful, fickle, deceptive and deceiving, avoiders of danger, eager to gain." Political activity, therefore, could not be restricted by moral considerations. The prince acts on behalf of the state and for the sake of the state must be willing to let his conscience sleep. As Machiavelli put it:

Niccolò Machiavelli. In *The Prince*, Machiavelli gave concrete expression to the Renaissance preoccupation with political power. This slender volume remains one of the most famous Western treatises on politics. Machiavelli is seen here in a portrait by Santi di Tito.

You need to understand this: A ruler, and particularly a ruler who is new to power, cannot conform to all those rules that men who are thought good are expected to respect, for he is often obliged, in order to hold on to power, to break his word, to be uncharitable, inhumane, and irreligious. So he must be mentally prepared to act as circumstances and changes in fortune require. As I have said, he should do what is right if he can; but he must be prepared to do wrong if necessary.[7]

In Cesare Borgia, the son of Pope Alexander VI (popes were supposed to be celibate), who used ruthless measures to achieve his goal of carving out a new state in central Italy, Machiavelli found a good example of the new Italian ruler. As he said, "So anyone who decides that the policy to follow when one has newly acquired power is to destroy one's enemies, to secure some allies, to win wars, whether by force or by fraud, to make oneself both loved and feared by one's subjects,...cannot hope to find, in the recent past, a better model to imitate than Cesare Borgia."[8] Machiavelli was among the first to abandon morality as the basis for the analysis of political activity (see the box on p. 223).

The Intellectual Renaissance in Italy

Individualism and **secularism**—two characteristics of the Italian Renaissance—were most noticeable in the intellectual and artistic realms. Italian culture had matured by the fourteenth century. For the next two centuries, Italy was the cultural leader of Europe. This new Italian culture was primarily the product of a relatively wealthy, urban lay society. The most important literary movement associated with the Renaissance is **humanism.**

Italian Renaissance Humanism

Renaissance humanism was an intellectual movement based on the study of the classical literary works of Greece and Rome. Humanists studied the liberal arts—grammar, rhetoric, poetry, moral philosophy or ethics, and history—all based on the writings of ancient Greek and Roman authors. These are the subjects we call the humanities.

Petrarch (1304–1374), often called the father of Italian Renaissance humanism, did more than any other individual in the fourteenth century to foster development of the movement. Petrarch sought to find forgotten Latin manuscripts and set in motion a search of monastic libraries throughout Europe. In his preoccupation with the classics and their secular content, Petrarch doubted at times whether he was sufficiently attentive to spiritual ideals. His qualms, however, did not prevent him from inaugurating the humanist emphasis on the use of pure classical Latin, making it fashionable for humanists to use Cicero as a model for prose and Virgil for poetry. Petrarch said, "Christ is my God; Cicero is the prince of the language."

MACHIAVELLI: "IS IT BETTER TO BE LOVED THAN FEARED?"

*I*n 1513, Niccolò Machiavelli wrote a short treatise on political power that, justly or unjustly, has given him a reputation as a political opportunist. In this passage from Chapter 17 of *The Prince*, Machiavelli analyzes whether it is better for a ruler to be loved than feared.

Machiavelli, *The Prince*

This leads us to a question that is in dispute: Is it better to be loved than feared, or vice versa? My reply is one ought to be both loved and feared; but, since it is difficult to accomplish both at the same time, I maintain it is much safer to be feared than loved, if you have to do without one of the two. For of men one can, in general, say this: They are ungrateful, fickle, deceptive and deceiving, avoiders of danger, eager to gain. As long as you serve their interests, they are devoted to you. They promise you their blood, their possessions, their lives, and their children, as I said before, so long as you seem to have no need of them. But as soon as you need help, they turn against you. Any ruler who relies simply on their promises and makes no other preparations, will be destroyed. For you will find that those whose support you buy, who do not rally to you because they admire your strength of character and nobility of soul, these are people you pay for, but they are never yours, and in the end you cannot get the benefit of your investment. Men are less nervous of offending someone who makes himself lovable, than someone who makes himself frightening. For love attaches men by ties of obligation, which, since men are wicked, they break whenever their interests are at stake. But fear restrains men because they are afraid of punishment, and this fear never leaves them. Still, a ruler should make himself feared in such a way that, if he does not inspire love, at least he does not provoke hatred. For it is perfectly possible to be feared and not hated. You will only be hated if you seize the property or the women of your subjects and citizens. Whenever you have to kill someone, make sure that you have a suitable excuse and an obvious reason; but, above all else, keep your hands off other people's property; for men are quicker to forget the death of their father than the loss of their inheritance. Moreover, there are always reasons why you might want to seize people's property; and he who begins to live by plundering others will always find an excuse for seizing other people's possessions; but there are fewer reasons for killing people, and one killing need not lead to another.

When a ruler is at the head of his army and has a vast number of soldiers under his command, then it is absolutely essential to be prepared to be thought cruel; for it is impossible to keep an army united and ready for action without acquiring a reputation for cruelty.

Why does Machiavelli think it is better for a ruler to be loved than feared? How do his theories make his politics modern, and how do they differ from medieval and Roman notions of good rulership?

In Florence, the humanist movement took a new direction at the beginning of the fifteenth century when it became closely tied to Florentine civic spirit and pride, giving rise to what has been labeled **civic humanism**. Fourteenth-century humanists such as Petrarch had described the intellectual life as one of solitude. They rejected family and a life of action in the community. In the busy civic world of Florence, however, intellectuals began to take a new view of their role as intellectuals. The classical Roman statesman and intellectual Cicero became their model. Leonardo Bruni (1370–1444), a humanist, Florentine patriot, and chancellor of the city, wrote a biography of Cicero titled the *New Cicero*, in which he waxed enthusiastic about the fusion of political action and literary creation in Cicero's life. From Bruni's time on, Cicero served as the inspiration for the Renaissance ideal that it was the duty of an intellectual to live an active life for one's state. An individual only "grows to maturity—both intellectually and morally—through participation" in the life of the state. Civic humanism reflected the values of the urban society of the Italian Renaissance. Humanists came to believe that their study of the humanities should be put to the service of the state. It is no accident that humanists served the state as chancellors, councillors, and advisers.

Also evident in the humanism of the first half of the fifteenth century was a growing interest in classical Greek civilization. Bruni was one of the first Italian humanists to gain a thorough knowledge of Greek. He became an enthusiastic pupil of the Byzantine scholar Manuel Chrysoloras, who taught in Florence from 1396 to 1400. Humanists eagerly perused the works of Plato as well as Greek poets, dramatists, historians, and orators, such as Thucydides, Euripides, and Sophocles, all of whom had been neglected by the scholastics of the High Middle Ages.

Humanism and Philosophy   In the second half of the fifteenth century, a dramatic upsurge of interest in the works of Plato occurred. Cosimo de'Medici, the de facto ruler of Florence, encouraged this development by commissioning a translation of Plato's dialogues by Marsilio Ficino (1433–1499), who dedicated his life to the translation of Plato and the exposition of the Platonic philosophy known as **Neoplatonism.**

In two major works, Ficino undertook the synthesis of Christianity and Platonism into a single system. His Neoplatonism was based on two primary ideas, the Neoplatonic hierarchy of substances and a theory of spiritual love. The former postulated a hierarchy of substances, or great chain of being, from the lowest form of physical matter (plants) to the purest spirit (God), in which humans occupied a central or middle position. They were the link between the material world (through the body) and the spiritual world (through the soul), and their highest duty was to ascend toward that union with God that was the true end of human existence. Ficino's theory of spiritual or Platonic love maintained that just as all people are bound together in their common humanity by love, so too are all parts of the universe held together by bonds of sympathetic love.

Renaissance Hermeticism **Hermeticism** was another product of the Florentine intellectual environment of the late fifteenth century. At the request of Cosimo de' Medici, Ficino translated into Latin a Greek work titled *Corpus Hermeticum*. The Hermetic manuscripts offered Renaissance intellectuals a new view of humankind. They believed that humans had been created as divine beings endowed with divine creative power but had freely chosen to enter the material world (nature). Humans could recover their divinity, however, through a regenerative experience or purification of the soul. Thus regenerated, they became true sages or magi, as the Renaissance called them, who had knowledge of God and of truth. In regaining their original divinity, they reacquired an intimate knowledge of nature and the ability to employ the powers of nature for beneficial purposes.

In Italy, the most prominent magi in the late fifteenth century were Ficino and his friend and pupil Giovanni Pico della Mirandola (1463–1494). Pico produced one of the most famous treatises of the Renaissance, *Oration on the Dignity of Man*. Pico combed diligently through the writings of many philosophers of different backgrounds for the common "nuggets of universal truth" that he believed were all part of God's revelation to humanity. In the *Oration*, Pico offered a ringing statement of unlimited human potential: "To him it is granted to have whatever he chooses, to be whatever he wills."[9] Like Ficino, Pico took an avid interest in Hermetic philosophy, accepting it as the "science of the Divine," which "embraces the deepest contemplation of the most secret things, and at last the knowledge of all nature."[10]

Education in the Renaissance

The humanist movement had a profound effect on education. Renaissance humanists believed that human beings could be dramatically changed by education, and as a result, they wrote treatises on education and opened schools based on their ideas. At the core of humanist schools were the "liberal studies." Humanists believed that the "liberal studies" (what we call the liberal arts) were the key to true freedom, enabling individuals to reach their full potential. The liberal studies included history, moral philosophy, eloquence (rhetoric), letters (grammar and logic), poetry, mathematics, astronomy, and music. The purpose of a liberal education was thus to produce individuals who followed a path of virtue and wisdom and possessed the rhetorical skills by which they could persuade others to do the same. Following the Greek precept of a sound mind in a sound body, humanist educators also stressed physical education. Pupils were taught the skills of javelin throwing, archery, and dancing and encouraged to run, wrestle, hunt, and swim.

The purpose of these humanist schools was to educate an elite, the ruling classes of their communities. Largely absent from such schools were females. The few female students who did attend humanist schools studied the classics and were encouraged to know some history and to ride, dance, sing, play the lute, and appreciate poetry. But they were told not to learn mathematics and rhetoric. Religion and morals were thought to hold first place in the education of Christian ladies and help prepare them for their roles as mothers and wives.

Nevertheless, some women in Italy who were educated in the humanist fashion went on to establish their own literary careers. Isotta Nogarola, born to a noble family in Verona, mastered Latin and wrote numerous letters and treatises that brought her praise from male Italian intellectuals. Laura Cereta was educated in Latin by her father, a physician from Brescia. Laura defended the ability of women to pursue scholarly pursuits (see the box on p. 225).

Humanist education was thought to be a practical preparation for life. Its aim was the creation not of a great scholar but of a complete citizen. As one humanist said, "Not everyone is obliged to excel in philosophy, medicine, or the law, nor are all equally favored by nature; but all are destined to live in society and to practice virtue."[11] Humanist schools provided the model for the basic education of the European ruling classes until the twentieth century.

The Impact of Printing

The Renaissance period witnessed the development of printing, one of the most important technological innovations of Western civilization. The art of printing had an immediate impact on European intellectual life and thought. Printing from hand-carved wooden blocks had been done in the West since the twelfth century and in China even before that. What was new to Europe in the fifteenth century was repeatable printing with movable metal type. The development of printing from movable type was a gradual process that culminated between 1445 and 1450; Johannes Gutenberg of Mainz played an important role in bringing the process to completion. Gutenberg's Bible, completed in 1455 or 1456, was the first true book in the West produced with movable type.

The new printing capability spread rapidly throughout Europe in the second half of the fifteenth century. By 1500, there were more than a thousand printers in Europe who had published almost forty thousand titles (between eight and ten million copies). Probably 50 percent of these books were religious—Bibles, books of devotion, and sermons. Next in importance were the Latin and Greek classics,

A Woman's Defense of Learning

As a young woman, Laura Cereta was proud of her learning but condemned by a male world that found it unseemly for women to be scholars. One monk said to her father, "She gives herself to things unworthy of her—namely, the classics." Before being silenced, Laura Cereta wrote a series of letters, including one to a male critic who had argued that her work was so good it could not have been written by a woman.

Laura Cereta, *Defense of the Liberal Instruction of Women*

My ears are wearied by your carping. You brashly and publicly not merely wonder but indeed lament that I am said to possess as fine a mind as nature ever bestowed upon the most learned man. You seem to think that so learned a woman has scarcely before been seen in the world. You are wrong on both counts. . . .

I would have been silent. . . . But I cannot tolerate your having attacked my entire sex. For this reason my thirsty soul seeks revenge, my sleeping pen is aroused to literary struggle, raging anger stirs mental passions long chained by silence. With just cause I am moved to demonstrate how great a reputation for learning and virtue women have won by their inborn excellence, manifested in every age as knowledge. . . .

Only the question of the rarity of outstanding women remains to be addressed. The explanation is clear: women have been able by nature to be exceptional, but have chosen lesser goals. For some women are concerned with parting their hair correctly, adorning themselves with lovely dresses, or decorating their fingers with pearls and other gems. Others delight in mouthing carefully composed phrases, indulging in dancing, or managing spoiled puppies. Still others wish to gaze at lavish banquet tables, to rest in sleep, or, standing at mirrors, to smear their lovely faces. But those in whom a deeper integrity yearns for virtue, restrain from the start their youthful souls, reflect on higher things, harden the body with sobriety and trials, and curb their tongues, open their ears, compose their thoughts in wakeful hours, their minds in contemplation, to letters bonded to righteousness. For knowledge is not given as a gift, but [is gained] with diligence. The free mind, not shirking effort, always soars zealously toward the good, and the desire to know grows ever more wide and deep. It is because of no special holiness, therefore, that we [women] are rewarded by God the Giver with the gift of exceptional talent. Nature has generously lavished its gifts upon all people, opening to all the doors of choice through which reason sends envoys to the will, from which they learn and convey its desires. The will must choose to exercise the gift of reason. . . .

I have been praised too much; showing your contempt for women, you pretend that I alone am admirable because of the good fortune of my intellect. . . . Do you suppose, O most contemptible man on earth, that I think myself sprung [like Athena] from the head of Jove? I am a school girl, possessed of the sleeping embers of an ordinary mind. Indeed I am too hurt, and my mind, offended, too swayed by passions, sighs, tormenting itself, conscious of the obligation to defend my sex. For absolutely everything—that which is within us and that which is without—is made weak by association with my sex.

_____

What was Laura Cereta's attitude toward the man who had criticized her for her intellect? Why were Renaissance women not taken seriously in their desire for educational opportunities?

---

medieval grammars, legal handbooks, works on philosophy, and an ever-growing number of popular romances.

Printing became one of the largest industries in Europe, and its effects were soon felt in many areas of European life. The printing of books encouraged the development of scholarly research and the desire to attain knowledge. Moreover, printing facilitated cooperation among scholars and helped produce standardized and definitive texts. Printing also stimulated the development of an ever-expanding lay reading public, a development that had an enormous impact on European society. Indeed, the new religious ideas of the Reformation would never have spread as rapidly as they did in the sixteenth century without the printing press.

The Artistic Renaissance

Leonardo da Vinci, one of the great Italian Renaissance artists, once explained, "The painter will produce pictures of small merit if he takes for his standard the pictures of others, but if he will study from natural objects he will bear good fruit. . . . Those who take for their standard any one but nature . . . weary themselves in vain."[12] Renaissance artists considered the imitation of nature their primary goal. Their search for naturalism became an end in itself: to persuade onlookers of the reality of the object or event they were portraying. At the same time, the new artistic standards reflected a new attitude of mind as well, one in which human beings became the focus of attention, the "center and measure of all things," as one artist proclaimed.

Early Renaissance Art

The frescoes by Masaccio (1401–1428) in the Brancacci chapel in Florence have long been regarded as the first masterpieces of Early Renaissance art. In his use of monumental figures, the demonstration of a more realistic relationship

Masaccio, *Tribute Money*.   With the frescoes of Masaccio, regarded by many as the first great works of Early Renaissance art, a new realistic style of painting was born. *Tribute Money* was one of a series of frescoes that Masaccio painted in the Brancacci Chapel of the Church of Santa Maria del Carmine in Florence. In *Tribute Money*, Masaccio illustrated the biblical story of Jesus' confrontation by a tax collector at the entrance to the town of Capernaum (seen at center). Jesus sent Peter to collect a coin from the mouth of a fish from Lake Galilee (seen at left); Peter then paid the tax collector (seen at right). In illustrating this story from the Bible, Masaccio used a rational system of perspective to create a realistic relationship between the figures and their background; the figures themselves are realistic. As one Renaissance observer said, "The works made before Masaccio's day can be said to be painted, while his are living, real, and natural."

between figures and landscape, and the visual representation of the laws of perspective, a new realistic style of painting was born. Onlookers became aware of a world of reality that appeared to be a continuation of their own world.

This new or Renaissance style was absorbed and modified by other Florentine painters in the fifteenth century. Especially important was the development of an experimental trend that took two directions. One emphasized the mathematical side of painting, the working out of the laws of perspective and the organization of outdoor space and light by geometry and perspective. The other aspect of the experimental trend involved the investigation of movement and anatomical structure. Indeed, the realistic portrayal of the human nude became one of the foremost preoccupations of Italian Renaissance art. The fifteenth century, then, was a period of experimentation and technical mastery.

The revolutionary achievements of Florentine painters in the fifteenth century were matched by equally stunning advances in sculpture and architecture. Donato di Donatello (1386–1466) spent time in Rome, studying and copying the statues of antiquity. His subsequent work in Florence reveals how well he had mastered the essence of what he saw. Among his numerous works was a statue of David that was the first known life-size freestanding bronze nude in European art since antiquity. Like Donatello's other statues, *David* radiated a simplicity and strength that reflected the dignity of humanity.

Filippo Brunelleschi (1377–1446) was a friend of Donatello's who accompanied him to Rome. Brunelleschi drew much inspiration from the architectural monuments of Roman antiquity, and when he returned to Florence, the Medici commissioned him to design the church of San Lorenzo. Inspired by Roman models, Brunelleschi created a church interior very different from that of the great medieval cathedrals. San Lorenzo's Classical columns, rounded arches, and coffered ceiling created an environment that did not overwhelm the worshiper, materially or psychologically, as Gothic cathedrals did; instead, it comforted in that it was a space created to fit human, not divine, measurements.

The Artistic High Renaissance

By the end of the fifteenth century, Italian painters, sculptors, and architects had created a new artistic environment. Many artists had mastered the new techniques for a scientific observation of the world around them and were now ready to move into individualistic forms of creative expression. This final stage of Renaissance art, which flourished between 1480 and 1520, is called the High Renaissance. The High Renaissance was marked by the increasing importance of Rome as a new cultural center.

The High Renaissance was dominated by the work of three artistic giants: Leonardo da Vinci (1452–1519), Raphael (1483–1520), and Michelangelo (1475–1564).

Filippo Brunelleschi, Interior of San Lorenzo. Cosimo de' Medici contributed massive amounts of money to the rebuilding of the Church of San Lorenzo. As seen in this view of the nave and choir of the church, Brunelleschi's architectural designs were based on the basilica plan borrowed by early Christians from pagan Rome. San Lorenzo's simplicity, evident in its rows of slender Corinthian columns, created a human-centered space.

Donatello, *David*. Donatello's *David* first stood in the courtyard of the Medici Palace. On its base was an inscription praising Florentine heroism and virtue, leading art historians to assume that the statue was meant to commemorate the victory of Florence over Milan in 1428. David's pose and appearance are reminiscent of the nude statues of antiquity.

Leonardo represents a transitional figure in the shift to High Renaissance principles. He stressed the need to advance beyond such realism and initiated the High Renaissance's preoccupation with the idealization of nature, or the attempt to generalize from realistic portrayal to an ideal form. Leonardo's *Last Supper,* painted in Milan, is a brilliant summary of fifteenth-century trends in its organization of space and use of perspective to depict subjects three dimensionally. But it is also more. The figure of Philip is idealized, and there are profound psychological dimensions to the work. Jesus' words—"One of you shall betray me"—are experienced directly as each of the apostles reveals his personality and his relationship to the Savior. Through gestures and movement, Leonardo hoped to reveal a person's inner life.

Raphael blossomed as a painter at an early age; at twenty-five, he was already regarded as one of Italy's best painters. Raphael was acclaimed for his numerous madonnas (portraits of the Virgin Mary), in which he attempted to achieve an ideal of beauty far surpassing human standards. He is well known for his frescoes in the Vatican Palace; his *School of Athens* reveals a world of balance, harmony, and order—the underlying principles of the art of classical Greece and Rome.

Michelangelo, an accomplished painter, sculptor, and architect, was another giant of the High Renaissance. Fiercely driven by his desire to create, he worked with great passion and energy on a remarkable number of projects. Michelangelo was influenced by Neoplatonism, especially evident in his figures on the ceiling of the Sistine Chapel in Rome. In 1508, Pope Julius II had called Michelangelo to Rome and commissioned him to decorate the chapel ceiling. This colossal project was not completed until 1512. Michelangelo attempted to tell the story of the Fall of Man by depicting nine scenes from the biblical book of Genesis. In his *Creation of Adam* (reproduced at the start of this chapter), the well-proportioned figure of Adam awaits the divine spark. Adam, like the other muscular figures on the ceiling, reveals an ideal type of human being with perfect proportions. In good Neoplatonic fashion, the beauty of these figures is meant to be a reflection of divine beauty; the more beautiful the body, the more God-like the figure.

Scala/Art Resource, NY (S. Maria delle Grazie, Milan)

Leonardo da Vinci, *The Last Supper.* Leonardo da Vinci was the impetus behind the High Renaissance concern for the idealization of nature, moving from a realistic portrayal of the human figure to an idealized form. Evident in Leonardo's *Last Supper* is his effort to depict a person's character and inner nature by the use of gesture and movement. Unfortunately, Leonardo used an experimental technique in this fresco, which soon led to its physical deterioration.

Erich Lessing/Art Resource, NY (Vatican Palace)

Raphael, *School of Athens.* Raphael arrived in Rome in 1508 and began to paint a series of frescoes commissioned by Pope Julius II for the papal apartments at the Vatican. In *School of Athens*, painted in 1510 or 1511, Raphael created an imaginary gathering of ancient philosophers. In the center stand Plato and Aristotle. At the left is Pythagoras, showing his system of proportions on a slate. At the right is Ptolemy, holding a celestial globe.

Michelangelo, *David.* This statue of David exalts the beauty of the human body and is a fitting symbol of the Italian Renaissance's affirmation of human power. Completed in 1504, *David* was moved by Florentine authorities to a special location in front of the Palazzo Vecchio, the seat of the Florentine government.

Jan van Eyck, *Giovanni Arnolfini and His Bride.* Northern painters took great care in depicting each object and became masters at rendering details. This emphasis on a realistic portrayal is clearly evident in this oil painting, said to be a portrait of Giovanni Arnolfini, an Italian merchant who had settled in Bruges, and his wife, Giovanna Cenami.

Another manifestation of Michelangelo's search for ideal beauty was his *David,* a colossal marble statue commissioned by the Florentine government in 1501 and completed in 1504. Michelangelo maintained that the form of a statue already resided in the uncarved piece of stone: "I only take away the surplus; the statue is already there."[13] Out of a piece of marble that had remained unused for fifty years, Michelangelo created a 14-foot-high figure, the largest sculpture in Italy since Roman times. An awe-inspiring hero, Michelangelo's *David* proudly proclaims the beauty of the human body and the glory of human beings.

The Northern Artistic Renaissance

In trying to provide an exact portrayal of their world, the artists of the north (especially the Low Countries) and Italy took different approaches. In Italy, the human form became the primary vehicle of expression as Italian artists sought to master the technical skills that allowed them to portray humans in realistic settings. The large wall spaces of Italian churches had given rise to the art of fresco painting, but in the north, the prevalence of Gothic cathedrals with their stained-glass windows resulted in more emphasis on illuminated manuscripts and wooden panel painting for altarpieces. The space available in these works was limited, and great care was required to depict each object, leading northern painters to become masters at rendering details.

The most influential northern school of art in the fifteenth century was centered in Flanders. Jan van Eyck (c. 1380–1441) was among the first to use oil paint, a medium that enabled the artist to use a varied range of colors and make changes to create fine details. In the famous *Giovanni Arnolfini and His Bride,* van Eyck's attention to detail is staggering in the precise portraits, a glittering chandelier, and a mirror reflecting the objects in the room. Although each detail was rendered as observed, it is evident that van Eyck's comprehension of perspective was still uncertain. His work is truly indicative of northern Renaissance painters, who, in their effort to imitate nature, did so not by mastery of the laws of perspective and proportion but by empirical observation of visual reality and the accurate portrayal of details. Moreover, northern painters placed great emphasis on the emotional intensity of religious feeling and created great works of devotional art, especially in their altarpieces. By the end of the fifteenth century, however, artists from the north began to study in Italy and were visually influenced by what artists were doing there.

One northern artist of this later period who was greatly influenced by the Italians was Albrecht Dürer (1471–1528) from Nuremberg. Dürer made two trips to Italy and absorbed most of what the Italians could teach, as is evident in his mastery of the laws of perspective and Renaissance theories of proportion. He wrote detailed treatises on both subjects. At the same time, as in his famous *Adoration of the Magi*, Dürer did not reject the use of minute details characteristic of northern artists. He did try, however, to integrate those details more harmoniously into his works and, like the Italian artists of the High Renaissance, tried to achieve a standard of ideal beauty by a careful examination of the human form.

The European State in the Renaissance

In the first half of the fifteenth century, European states continued the disintegrative patterns of the previous century. In the second half of the century, however, recovery set in, and attempts were made to reestablish the centralized power of monarchical governments. To characterize the results, some historians have used the label "Renaissance states"; others have spoken of the "new monarchies," especially those of France, England, and Spain at the end of the fifteenth century. Whereas monarchs succeeded to varying degrees at extending their political authority in western Europe, rulers in central and eastern Europe were often weak and unable to impose their will.

The Renaissance State in Western Europe

Although the Hundred Years' War (1337–1453; see Chapter 11) had made it difficult for French kings to assert their authority, the war had also developed a strong degree of French national feeling toward a common enemy that the kings could use to reestablish monarchical power. The process of developing a French territorial state was greatly advanced by King Louis XI (1461–1483), known as the Spider because of his devious ways. Louis strengthened the use of the *taille*—an annual direct tax, usually on land or property—as a tax imposed by royal authority, giving him a regular and reliable source of income. Louis repressed the French nobility and brought

Albrecht Dürer, ***Adoration of the Magi.*** By the end of the fifteenth century, northern artists began studying in Italy and adopting many of the techniques used by Italian painters. As is evident in this painting, which was the central panel for an altarpiece done for Frederick the Wise in 1504, Albrecht Dürer masterfully incorporated the laws of perspective and the ideals of proportion into his works. At the same time, he did not abandon the preoccupation with detail typical of northern artists.

the provinces of Anjou, Maine, Bar, and Provence under royal control.

England The Hundred Years' War also strongly affected the other protagonist in that conflict, England. The cost of the war in its final years and the losses in manpower strained the English economy. Moreover, the end of the war brought even greater domestic turmoil to England when the War of the Roses broke out in the 1450s. This civil war pitted the ducal house of Lancaster, whose symbol was a red rose, against the ducal house of York, whose symbol was a white rose. Many aristocratic families of England were drawn into the conflict. Finally, in 1485, Henry Tudor, duke of Richmond, defeated the last Yorkist king, Richard III (1483–1485), at Bosworth Field and established a new dynasty.

As the first Tudor king, Henry VII (1485–1509) worked to reduce internal dissension and establish a strong monarchical government. The new king was particularly successful in obtaining sufficient income from the traditional financial resources of the English monarch, such as the crown lands, judicial fees and fines, and customs duties. By using diplomacy to avoid wars, which are always expensive, the king avoided having to call Parliament on any regular basis to grant him funds. By not overburdening the landed gentry and middle class with taxes, Henry won their favor, and they provided much support for his monarchy. Henry's policies gave England

MAP 12.2 **Europe in the Second Half of the Fifteenth Century.** By the second half of the fifteenth century, states in western Europe, particularly France, Spain, and England, had begun the process of modern state building. With varying success, they reined in the power of the church and nobles, increased the ability to levy taxes, and established effective government bureaucracies. ❓ What aspects of Europe's political boundaries help explain why France and the Holy Roman Empire were often at war with each other? 🖱 **View an animated version of this map or related maps at** http://thomsonedu.com/history/spielvogel

a stable and prosperous government and enhanced the status of the monarchy.

Spain Spain, too, experienced the growth of a strong national monarchy by the end of the fifteenth century. During the Middle Ages, several independent Christian kingdoms had emerged in the course of the long reconquest of the Iberian peninsula from the Muslims (see Map 12.2). Aragon and Castile were the strongest Spanish kingdoms; in the west was the independent monarchy of Portugal; in the north, the small kingdom of Navarre; and in the south, the Muslim kingdom of Granada.

A major step toward the unification of Spain was taken with the marriage of Isabella of Castile (1474–1504) and Ferdinand of Aragon (1479–1516) in 1469. This was a dynastic union of two rulers, not a political union. Both kingdoms maintained their own parliaments (Cortes), courts, laws, coinage, speech, customs, and political organs.

Nevertheless, the two rulers worked to strengthen royal control of government, especially in Castile. The royal council, which was supposed to supervise local administration and oversee the implementation of government policies, was stripped of aristocrats and filled primarily with middle-class lawyers. Trained in the principles of Roman law, these officials operated on the belief that the monarchy embodied the power of the state.

Ferdinand and Isabella reorganized the military forces of Spain, seeking to replace the undisciplined feudal levies they had inherited with a more professional royal army. The development of a strong infantry force as the heart of the new Spanish army made it the best in Europe by the sixteenth century, and Spain emerged as an important power in European affairs.

Ferdinand and Isabella also pursued a policy of strict religious uniformity. Spain possessed two large religious minorities, Jews and Muslims, both of whom had been largely tolerated in medieval Spain. Increased persecution in the fourteenth century, however, led the majority of Spanish Jews to convert to Christianity. But complaints about the sincerity of these Jewish converts prompted Ferdinand and Isabella to ask the pope to introduce the Inquisition into Spain in 1478. Under royal control, the Inquisition worked with cruel efficiency to guarantee the orthodoxy of the converts but had no authority over practicing Jews. Consequently, in 1492, flush with the success of the conquest of Muslim Granada, Ferdinand and Isabella took the drastic step of expelling all professed Jews from Spain. It is estimated that 150,000 out of possibly 200,000 Jews fled. Muslims, too, were then "encouraged" to convert to Christianity, and in 1502, Isabella issued a decree expelling all professed Muslims from her kingdom. To a very large degree, the "most Catholic" monarchs had achieved their goal of absolute religious orthodoxy as a basic ingredient of the Spanish state. To be Spanish was to be Catholic, a policy of uniformity enforced by the Inquisition.

Central Europe: The Holy Roman Empire

After 1438, the position of Holy Roman Emperor was in the hands of the Habsburg dynasty. Having gradually acquired a number of possessions along the Danube, known collectively as Austria, the house of Habsburg had become one of the wealthiest landholders in the empire and by the mid-fifteenth century began to play an important role in European affairs. Much of the Habsburg success in the fifteenth century was due not to military victories but to a well-executed policy of dynastic marriages.

Much was expected of the flamboyant Maximilian I (1493–1519) when he became emperor. Through the Reichstag, the imperial diet or parliament, Maximilian attempted to centralize the administration by creating new institutions common to the entire empire. Opposition from the German princes doomed these efforts, however. Maximilian's only real success lay in his marriage alliances, which led to a grandson, Charles V, inheriting the traditional lands of the Habsburg, Burgundian, and Spanish monarchical lines at the beginning of the sixteenth century, making him the leading monarch of his age (see Chapter 13).

The Struggle for Strong Monarchy in Eastern Europe

In eastern Europe, rulers struggled to achieve the centralization of their territorial states but faced serious obstacles. Although the population was mostly Slavic, there were islands of other ethnic groups that caused difficulties. Religious differences also troubled the area, as Roman Catholics, Greek Orthodox Christians, and pagans confronted each other.

Much of Polish history revolved around a bitter struggle between the crown and the landed nobility until the end of the fifteenth century, when the preoccupation of the Polish monarchy with problems in Bohemia and Hungary as well as war with the Russians and Turks enabled the aristocrats to reestablish their power. Through their control of the Sejm or national parliament, the magnates reduced the peasantry to serfdom by 1511 and established the right to elect their kings. The Polish kings proved unable to establish a strong royal authority.

Since the conversion of Hungary to Roman Catholicism by German missionaries, its history had been closely tied to that of central and western Europe. The church became a large and prosperous institution. Wealthy bishops, along with great territorial lords, became powerful, independent political figures. For a brief while, Hungary developed into an important European state, the dominant power in eastern Europe. King Matthias Corvinus (1458–1490) broke the power of the wealthy lords and created a well-organized central administration. After his death, Hungary returned to weak rule, however, and the work of Corvinus was largely undone.

Since the thirteenth century, Russia had been under the domination of the Mongols. Gradually, the princes of Moscow rose to prominence by using their close relationship to the Mongol khans to increase their wealth and expand their possessions. In the reign of the great prince Ivan III (1462–1505), a new Russian state was born. Ivan III annexed other Russian principalities and took advantage of dissension among the Mongols to throw off their yoke by 1480.

The Ottoman Turks and the End of the Byzantine Empire

Eastern Europe was increasingly threatened by the steadily advancing Ottoman Turks. The Byzantine Empire had served as a buffer between the Muslim Middle East and the Latin West for centuries, but it was severely weakened by the sack of Constantinople in 1204 and its occupation by the West. Although the Paleologus dynasty (1260–1453) had tried to reestablish Byzantine power in the Balkans, the threat from the Turks finally doomed the long-lasting empire.

Beginning in northeastern Asia Minor in the thirteenth century, the Ottoman Turks spread rapidly, seizing the lands of the Seljuk Turks and the Byzantine Empire. In 1345, they bypassed Constantinople and moved into the Balkans. Under Sultan Murad, Ottoman forces moved through Bulgaria and into the lands of the Serbians, who provided a strong center of opposition under King Lazar. But in 1389, at the Battle of Kosovo, Ottoman forces defeated the Serbs; both King Lazar and Sultan Murad perished in the battle. Kosovo became a battlefield long revered and remembered by the Serbs. Not until 1480 were Bosnia, Albania, and the rest of Serbia added to the Ottoman Empire in the Balkans.

In the meantime, in 1453, the Ottomans also completed the demise of the Byzantine Empire. With eighty thousand troops ranged against only seven thousand defenders, Sultan Mehmet II laid siege to Constantinople. In their attack on the city, the Turks made use of massive cannons with 26-foot barrels that could launch stone balls

France	
Louis XI the Spider	1461–1483
England	
War of the Roses	1450s–1485
Richard III	1483–1485
Henry VII	1485–1509
Spain	
Isabella of Castile	1474–1504
Ferdinand of Aragon	1479–1516
Marriage of Ferdinand and Isabella	1469
Introduction of Inquisition	1478
Expulsion of Jews	1492
Expulsion of Muslims	1502
Holy Roman Empire	
Maximilian I	1493–1519
Eastern Europe	
Hungary: Matthias Corvinus	1458–1490
Russia: Ivan III	1462–1505
Fall of Constantinople and Byzantine Empire	1453

weighing up to 1,200 pounds each. Finally, the walls were breached; the Byzantine emperor died in the final battle. Mehmet II, standing before the palace of the emperor, paused to reflect on the passing nature of human glory.

After consolidating their power, the Turks prepared to exert renewed pressure on the West, both in the Mediterranean and up the Danube valley toward Vienna. By the end of the fifteenth century, they were threatening Hungary, Austria, Bohemia, and Poland.

The Church in the Renaissance

As a result of the efforts of the Council of Constance, the Great Schism of the Catholic church had finally been brought to an end in 1417. Ending the schism proved to be the council's easiest task; it was much less successful in dealing with the problems of heresy and reform.

The Problems of Heresy and Reform

Heresy was not a new problem, and in the thirteenth century, the church had developed inquisitorial machinery to deal with it. But two widespread movements in the fourteenth and early fifteenth centuries—Lollardy and Hussitism—posed new threats to the church.

Wyclif and Lollardy English Lollardy was a product of the Oxford theologian John Wyclif (c. 1328–1384), whose disgust with clerical corruption led him to a far-ranging attack on papal authority and medieval Christian beliefs and practices. Wyclif alleged that there was no basis in Scripture for papal claims of temporal authority and advocated that the popes be stripped of their authority and their property. Believing that the Bible should be a Christian's sole authority, Wyclif urged that it be made available in the vernacular languages so that every Christian could read it. Rejecting all practices not mentioned in Scripture, Wyclif condemned pilgrimages and the veneration of saints. Wyclif attracted a number of followers who came to be known as Lollards.

Hus and the Hussites A marriage between the royal families of England and Bohemia enabled Lollard ideas to spread to Bohemia, where they reinforced the ideas of a group of Czech reformers led by the chancellor of the university at Prague, John Hus (1374–1415). In his call for reform, Hus urged the elimination of the worldliness and corruption of the clergy and attacked the excessive power of the papacy within the Catholic church. Hus's objections fell on receptive ears, for the Catholic church, as one of the largest landowners in Bohemia, was already widely criticized. Moreover, many clergymen were German, and the native Czechs' strong resentment of the Germans who dominated Bohemia also contributed to Hus's movement.

The Council of Constance attempted to deal with the growing problem of heresy by summoning Hus to the council. Granted safe conduct by Emperor Sigismund, Hus went in the hope of a free hearing of his ideas. Instead he was arrested, condemned as a heretic, and burned at the stake in 1415. This action turned the unrest in Bohemia into revolutionary upheaval, and the resulting Hussite wars racked the Holy Roman Empire until a truce was arranged in 1436.

Reform of the Church The reform of the church was even less successful than the attempt to eradicate heresy. The Council of Constance passed two reform decrees. One stated that a general council of the church received its authority from God; hence every Christian, including the pope, was subject to its authority. The other decree provided for the regular holding of general councils to ensure that church reform would continue. Decrees alone, however, proved insufficient to reform the church. Councils could issue decrees, but popes had to execute them, and popes would not cooperate with councils that diminished their absolute authority. Beginning already in 1417, successive popes worked steadfastly for the next thirty years to defeat the conciliar movement (see Chapter 11).

By the mid-fifteenth century, the popes had reasserted their supremacy over the Catholic church. No longer, however, did they have any possibility of asserting supremacy over temporal governments as the medieval papacy had. Although the papal monarchy had been maintained, it had lost much moral prestige. In the fifteenth century, the Renaissance papacy contributed to an even further decline in the moral leadership of the popes.

The Renaissance Papacy

The Renaissance papacy refers to the line of popes from the end of the Great Schism in 1417 to the beginning of the Reformation in the early sixteenth century. The primary concern of the papacy is governing the Catholic church as its spiritual leader. But as heads of the church, popes had temporal preoccupations as well, and the story of the Renaissance papacy is really an account of how the latter came to overshadow the popes' spiritual functions.

The manner in which Renaissance popes pursued their interests in the Papal States and Italian politics, especially their use of intrigue and even bloodshed, seemed shocking. Of all the Renaissance popes, Julius II (1503–1513) was most involved in war and politics. The fiery "warrior pope" personally led armies against his enemies, much to the disgust of pious Christians, who viewed the pope as a spiritual leader. As one intellectual wrote at the beginning of the sixteenth century: "How, O bishop standing in the room of the Apostles [the pope], dare you teach the people the things that pertain to war?"

To further their territorial aims in the Papal States, the popes needed loyal servants. Because they were not hereditary monarchs, popes could not build dynasties over several generations and came to rely on the practice of **nepotism** to promote their families' interests. Pope Sixtus IV (1471–1484), for example, made five of his nephews (the word *nepotism* is in fact derived from the Greek *nepos,* meaning "nephew") cardinals and gave them an abundance of church offices to build up their finances. The infamous Borgia pope, Alexander VI (1492–1503), known for his debauchery and sensuality, raised one son, one nephew, and the brother of one mistress to the cardinalate. Alexander scandalized the church by encouraging his son Cesare to carve a state out of the territories of the Papal States in central Italy.

The Renaissance popes were great patrons of Renaissance culture, and their efforts made Rome a cultural leader at the beginning of the sixteenth century. The warrior pope Julius II endeavored to add to the splendor of his pontificate by tearing down an old church and beginning construction of what was to be the greatest building in Christendom, Saint Peter's basilica. Julius's successor, Leo X (1513–1521), was also a patron of Renaissance culture. A member of the Medici family, he

Scala/Art Resource, NY (Uffizi, Florence)

A Renaissance Pope: Leo X. The Renaissance popes allowed secular concerns to overshadow their spiritual duties. Shown here is the Medici pope Leo X. Raphael portrays the pope as a collector of books, looking up after examining an illuminated manuscript with a magnifying glass. At the left is the pope's cousin Guilio, a cardinal. Standing behind the pope is Luigi de'Rossi, another relative who had also been made a cardinal.

was made a cardinal at the age of thirteen and acquired a refined taste in art, manners, and social life among the Florentine elite. He became pope at the age of thirty-seven, supposedly remarking to the Venetian ambassador, "Let us enjoy the papacy, since God has given it to us." Raphael was commissioned to do paintings, and the construction of Saint Peter's was accelerated as Rome became the literary and artistic center of the Renaissance.

CONCLUSION

The Renaissance was a period of transition that witnessed a continuation of the economic, political, and social trends that had begun in the High Middle Ages. It was also a movement in which intellectuals and artists proclaimed a new vision of humankind and raised fundamental questions about the value and importance of the individual. Of course, intellectuals and artists wrote and painted for the upper classes, and the brilliant intellectual, cultural, and artistic accomplishments of the Renaissance were really products of and for the elite. The ideas of the Renaissance did not have a broad base among the masses of the people. As Lorenzo the Magnificent, ruler of Florence, once commented, "Only men of noble birth can obtain perfection. The poor, who work with their hands and have no time to cultivate their minds, are incapable of it."

The Renaissance did, however, raise new questions about medieval traditions. In criticizing current religious practices, the humanists raised fundamental issues about the Catholic church, which was still an influential institution. As we shall see in the next chapter, the intellectual revolution of the fifteenth century gave way to a religious renaissance that touched the lives of people, including the masses, in new and profound ways. After the Reformation, Europe would never again be the unified Christian commonwealth it once believed it was.

TIMELINE

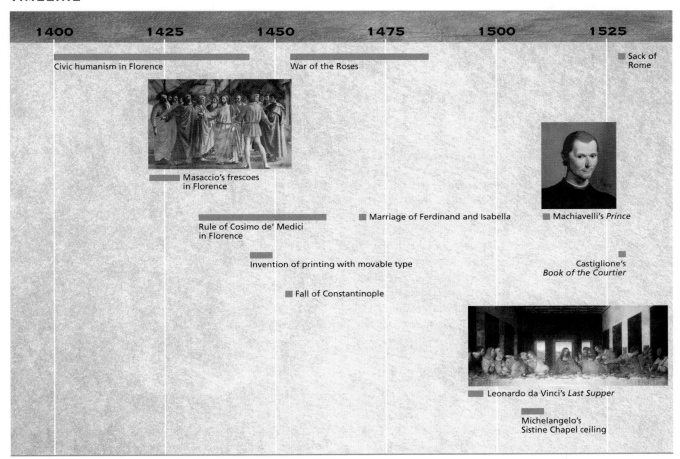

| 1400 | 1425 | 1450 | 1475 | 1500 | 1525 |

Civic humanism in Florence

War of the Roses

Sack of Rome

Masaccio's frescoes in Florence

Rule of Cosimo de' Medici in Florence

Marriage of Ferdinand and Isabella

Machiavelli's *Prince*

Invention of printing with movable type

Castiglione's *Book of the Courtier*

Fall of Constantinople

Leonardo da Vinci's *Last Supper*

Michelangelo's Sistine Chapel ceiling

NOTES

1. Quoted in J. Burckhardt, *The Civilization of the Renaissance in Italy*, trans. S. G. C. Middlemore (London, 1960), p. 81.
2. B. Castiglione, *The Book of the Courtier*, trans. C. S. Singleton (Garden City, N.Y., 1959), pp. 288–289.
3. Quoted in D. L. Jensen, *Renaissance Europe* (Lexington, Mass., 1981), p. 94.
4. G. Brucker, ed., *Two Memoirs of Renaissance Florence* (New York, 1967), p. 132.
5. Quoted in M. L. King, *Women of the Renaissance* (Chicago, 1991), p. 3.
6. N. Machiavelli, *The Prince*, trans. D. Wootton (Indianapolis, 1995), p. 48.
7. Ibid., p. 55.
8. Ibid., p. 27.
9. G. Pico della Mirandola, *Oration on the Dignity of Man*, in E. Cassirer, P. O. Kristeller, and J. H. Randall Jr., eds., *The Renaissance Philosophy of Man* (Chicago, 1948), p. 225.
10. Ibid., pp. 247–249.
11. Quoted in I. Origo, *The Light of the Past* (New York, 1959), p. 136.
12. Quoted in E. G. Holt, ed., *A Documentary History of Art* (Garden City, N.Y., 1959), vol. 1, p. 286.
13. Quoted in R. M. Letts, *The Cambridge Introduction to Art: The Renaissance* (Cambridge, 1981), p. 86.

SUGGESTIONS FOR FURTHER READING

The classic study of the Italian Renaissance is **J. Burckhardt**, *The Civilization of the Renaissance in Italy*, trans. S.G.C. Middlemore (London, 1960), first published in 1860. General works on the Renaissance in Europe include **D. L. Jensen**, *Renaissance Europe* (Lexington, Mass., 1981); **P. Burke**, *The European Renaissance: Centres and Peripheries* (Oxford, 1998); **J. Hale**, *The Civilization of Europe in the Renaissance* (New York, 1994); and the classic work by **M. P. Gilmore**, *The World of Humanism, 1453–1517* (New York, 1962). Although many of its interpretations are outdated, **W. Ferguson**, *Europe in Transition, 1300–1520* (Boston, 1962), contains a wealth of information. The brief study by **P. Burke**, *The Renaissance*, 2d ed. (New York, 1997), is a good summary of modern literature on the Renaissance. For beautifully illustrated introductions to the Renaissance, see **G. Holmes**, *Renaissance* (New York, 1996), and **M. Aston**, ed., *The Panorama of the Renaissance* (New York, 1996).

Brief but basic works on Renaissance economic matters are **H. A. Miskimin**, *The Economy of Early Renaissance Europe, 1300–1460* (New York, 1975) and *The Economy of Later Renaissance Europe, 1460–1600* (New York, 1978). For a reinterpretation of economic matters, see **L. Jardine**, *Worldly Goods* (New York, 1996). On family and marriage, see **D. Herlihy**, *The Family in Renaissance Italy* (Saint Louis, Mo., 1974), and **C. Klapisch-Zuber**, *Women, Family, and Ritual in Renaissance Italy* (Chicago, 1985). On women, see **M. L. King**, *Women of the Renaissance* (Chicago, 1991), and **N. Z. Davis** and **A. Farge**, eds., *A History of Women: Renaissance and Enlightenment Paradoxes* (Cambridge, Mass., 1993).

The best overall study of the Italian city-states is **L. Martines**, *Power and Imagination: City-States in Renaissance Italy* (New York, 1979); **D. Hay** and **J. Law**, *Italy in the Age of the Renaissance* (London, 1989), is also a good survey. There is an enormous literature on Renaissance Florence. The best introduction is **G. Brucker**, *Florence: The Golden Age, 1138–1737* (Berkeley, Calif., 1988). Machiavelli's life can be examined in **Q. Skinner**, *Machiavelli* (Oxford, 1981).

Brief introductions to Renaissance humanism can be found in **D. R. Kelley**, *Renaissance Humanism* (Boston, 1991); **C. G. Nauert Jr.**, *Humanism and the Culture of Renaissance Europe* (Cambridge, 1995); and **F. B. Artz**, *Renaissance Humanism, 1300–1550* (Oberlin, Ohio, 1966). The impact of printing is exhaustively examined in **E. Eisenstein**, *The Printing Press as an Agent of Change*, 2 vols. (New York, 1978).

For brief introductions to Renaissance art, see **R. M. Letts**, *The Cambridge Introduction to Art: The Renaissance* (Cambridge, 1981), and **B. Cole** and **A. Gealt**, *Art of the Western World* (New York, 1989), ch. 6–8. Good surveys of Renaissance art include **F. Hartt**, *History of Italian Renaissance Art*, 4th ed. (Englewood Cliffs, N.J., 1994);

S. Elliott, *Italian Renaissance Painting*, 2d ed. (London, 1993); **R. Turner**, *Renaissance Florence: The Invention of a New Art* (New York, 1997); **P. F. Brown**, *Art and Life in Renaissance Venice* (Upper Saddle River, N.J., 1997); and **L. Murray**, *The High Renaissance* (New York, 1967). For a lively account of the painting of the Sistine Chapel ceiling, see **R. King**, *Michelangelo and the Pope's Ceiling* (New York, 2002).

For a general work on the political development of Europe in the Renaissance, see **J. H. Shennan**, *The Origins of the Modern European State, 1450–1725* (London, 1974). On France, see **R. J. Knecht**, *The Rise and Fall of Renaissance France, 1483–1610,* 2d ed. (Oxford, 2001). Early Renaissance England is examined in **J. R. Lander**, *Crown and Nobility, 1450–1509* (London, 1976). Good coverage of Renaissance Spain can be found in **J. N. Hillgarth**, *The Spanish Kingdoms, 1250–1516,* vol. 2, *Castilian Hegemony, 1410–1516* (New York, 1978). Two good works on eastern Europe include **P. W. Knoll**, *The Rise of the Polish Monarchy* (Chicago, 1972), and **C. A. Macartney**, *Hungary: A Short History* (Edinburgh, 1962). On the Ottomans and their expansion, see **H. Inalcik**, *The Ottoman Empire: The Classical Age, 1300–1600* (London, 1973).

Aspects of the Renaissance papacy can be examined in **E. Lee**, *Sixtus IV and Men of Letters* (Rome, 1978), and **M. Mallett**, *The Borgias* (New York, 1969). On Rome, see especially **P. Partner**, *Renaissance Rome, 1500–1559: A Portrait of a Society* (Berkeley, Calif., 1976).

Thomson NOW! Enter *ThomsonNOW* using the access card that is available for *Western Civilization: A Brief History*. *ThomsonNOW* will help you understand this chapter with lesson plans generated for your needs. In addition, you can read the following documents, and many more, online:

Giovanni Villani, selections from Books 8 and 9 of *Chronicle*
Two Tractates from Vittorino da Feltre and other Humanist Educators
Giorgio Vasari, Excerpts from *Life of Michelangelo* and *Life of da Vinci*

WESTERN CIVILIZATION RESOURCES

Visit the Web site for *Western Civilization: A Brief History* for resources specific to this book:

http://www.thomsonedu.com/history/spielvogel

For a variety of tools to help you succeed in this course, visit the Western Civilization Resource Center at

http://history.wadsworth.com/spielvogel

Included are quizzes, images, documents, interactive simulations, maps and timelines, movie explorations, and a wealth of other sources.

REFORMATION AND RELIGIOUS WARFARE IN THE SIXTEENTH CENTURY

CHAPTER OUTLINE AND FOCUS QUESTIONS

Prelude to Reformation

☐ Who were the Christian humanists, and how did they differ from the Protestant reformers?

Martin Luther and the Reformation in Germany

☐ What were Martin Luther's main disagreements with the Roman Catholic church, and why did the movement he began spread so quickly across Europe?

The Spread of the Protestant Reformation

☐ What were the chief tenets of Zwinglianism, Anabaptism, Anglicanism, and Calvinism?

The Social Impact of the Protestant Reformation

☐ What impact did the Protestant Reformation have on the society of the sixteenth century?

The Catholic Reformation

☐ What measures did the Roman Catholic church take to reform itself and to combat Protestantism in the sixteenth century?

Politics and the Wars of Religion in the Sixteenth Century

☐ What role did religion play in the European wars of the sixteenth century?

CRITICAL THINKING

☐ What were the main tenets of the major Protestant groups, and how did they differ from each other and from Catholicism? What were the results of these differences?

A sixteenth-century engraving of Martin Luther in front of Charles V at the Diet of Worms

Bibliotheque Nationale, Paris/The Bridgeman Art Library

*O*N APRIL 18, 1520, a lowly monk stood before the emperor and princes of the Holy Roman Empire in the city of Worms. He had been called before this august gathering to answer charges of heresy, charges that could threaten his very life. The monk was confronted with a pile of his books and asked if he wished to defend them all or reject a part. Courageously, Martin Luther defended them all and asked to be shown where any part was in error on the basis of "Scripture and plain reason." The emperor was outraged by Luther's response and made his own position clear the next day: "Not only I, but you of this noble German nation, would be forever disgraced if by our negligence not only heresy but the very suspicion of heresy were to survive. After having heard yesterday the obstinate defense of Luther, I regret that I have so long delayed in proceeding against him and his false teaching. I will have no more to do with him." Luther's appearance at Worms set the stage for a serious challenge to the authority of the Catholic church. This was by no means the first crisis in the church's fifteen-hundred-year history, but its consequences were more far-reaching than anyone at Worms in 1520 could have imagined.

Throughout the Middle Ages, the Catholic church continued to assert its primacy of position. It had overcome defiance of its temporal authority by emperors while challenges to its doctrines had been crushed by the Inquisition and combated by new religious orders that carried its message of salvation to all the towns and villages of medieval Europe. The growth of the papacy had paralleled the growth of the church, but by the end of the Middle Ages, challenges to papal authority from the rising power of monarchical states had resulted in a loss of papal temporal authority. An even greater threat to papal authority and church unity arose in the sixteenth century when the unity of Christendom was shattered by the Reformation.

The movement begun by Martin Luther when he made his dramatic stand quickly spread across Europe, a clear indication of dissatisfaction with Catholic practices. Within a short time, new religious practices, doctrines, and organizations, including Zwinglianism, Calvinism, Anabaptism, and Anglicanism, were attracting adherents all over Europe. Seemingly helpless to stop the new Protestant churches, the Catholic church too underwent a religious renaissance and managed to revive its fortunes by the mid-sixteenth century. All too soon, the religious divisions between Protestants and Catholics became instrumental in triggering a series of religious wars that dominated the history of western Europe in the second half of the sixteenth century.◆

Prelude to Reformation

Martin Luther's reform movement was not the first in sixteenth-century Europe. During the second half of the fifteenth century, the new classical learning that was part of Italian Renaissance humanism spread to northern Europe and spawned a movement called **Christian** or **northern Renaissance humanism**, whose major goal was the reform of Christendom.

Christian or Northern Renaissance Humanism

The most important characteristic of northern Renaissance humanism was its reform program. Convinced of the ability of human beings to reason and improve themselves, the northern humanists thought that through education in the sources of classical, and especially Christian, antiquity, they could instill a true inner piety or an inward religious feeling that would bring about a reform of the church and society. For this reason, Christian humanists supported schools, brought out new editions of the classics, and prepared new editions of the Bible and writings of such church fathers as Augustine, Ambrose, and Jerome. In the preface to his edition of the Greek New Testament, the famous humanist Erasmus wrote:

Indeed, I disagree very much with those who are unwilling that Holy Scripture, translated into the vulgar tongue, be read by

the uneducated, as if Christ taught such intricate doctrines that they could scarcely be understood by very few theologians, or as if the strength of the Christian religion consisted in men's ignorance of it. . . . I would that even the lowliest women read the Gospels and the Pauline Epistles. And I would that they were translated into all languages so that they could be read and understood not only by Scots and Irish but also by Turks and Saracens [Arabs].[1]

Like later intellectuals, Christian humanists believed that to change society, they must first change the human beings who compose it.

Erasmus The most influential of all the Christian humanists was the Dutch-born scholar Desiderius Erasmus (1466–1536). After withdrawing from a monastery, he wandered to France, England, Italy, Germany, and Switzerland, conversing everywhere in the classical Latin that might be called his mother tongue. The *Handbook of the Christian Knight*, published in 1503, reflected his preoccupation with religion. He called his conception of religion "the philosophy of Christ," by which he meant that Christianity should be a guiding philosophy for the direction of daily life rather than the system of dogmatic beliefs and practices that the medieval church seemed to stress. In other words, he emphasized inner piety and deemphasized the external forms of religion (such as the sacraments, pilgrimages, fasts, veneration of saints, and relics). To return to the simplicity of the early church, people needed to understand the original meaning of the Scriptures and early church fathers.

To Erasmus, the reform of the church meant spreading an understanding of the philosophy of Jesus, providing enlightened education in the sources of early Christianity, and making commonsense criticism of the abuses in the church. This critical approach is especially evident in *The Praise of Folly*, written in 1511, in which Erasmus was able to engage in a humorous yet effective criticism of the most corrupt practices of his own society. He was especially harsh on the abuses within the ranks of the clergy:

Many of [the monks] work so hard at protocol and at traditional fastidiousness that they think one heaven hardly a suitable reward for their labors; never recalling, however, that the time will come when Christ will demand a reckoning of that which he had prescribed, namely charity, and that he will hold their deeds of little account. One monk will then exhibit his belly filled with every kind of fish; another will profess a knowledge of over a hundred hymns. Still another will reveal a countless number of fasts that he has made, and will account for his large belly by explaining that his fasts have always been broken by a single large meal.[2]

Erasmus' program did not achieve the reform of the church that he so desired. His moderation and his emphasis on education were quickly overwhelmed by the passions of the Reformation. Undoubtedly, though, his work helped prepare the way for the Reformation; as contemporaries proclaimed, "Erasmus laid the egg that Luther hatched." Yet Erasmus eventually disapproved of

Erasmus. Desiderius Erasmus was the most influential of the northern Renaissance humanists. He sought to restore Christianity to the early simplicity found in the teachings of Jesus. This portrait of Erasmus was painted in 1523 by Hans Holbein the Younger, who had formed a friendship with the great humanist while they were in Basel.

who were sometimes not appropriately qualified. Complaints about the ignorance and ineptness of parish priests became widespread in the fifteenth century.

While the leaders of the church were failing to meet their responsibilities, ordinary people were clamoring for meaningful religious expression and certainty of salvation. As a result, the salvation process became almost mechanical. As more and more people sought salvation through the veneration of relics, collections of such objects grew. Frederick the Wise, elector of Saxony and Luther's prince, had amassed over five thousand relics to which were attached **indulgences** (remissions of the penalties for sin) that could reduce one's time in purgatory by nearly two million years. Other people sought salvation in the popular mystical movement known as the Modern Devotion. The Modern Devotion downplayed religious dogma and stressed the need to follow the teachings of Jesus. Thomas à Kempis, author of *The Imitation of Christ*, wrote that "truly, at the day of judgment we shall not be examined by what we have read, but what we have done; not how well we have spoken, but how religiously we have lived."

What is striking about the revival of religious piety in the fifteenth century was its adherence to the orthodox beliefs and practices of the Catholic church. The agitation for certainty of salvation and spiritual peace was done within the framework of the "holy mother Church." But as the devout experienced the clergy's inability to live up to their expectations, disillusionment grew. The intensification of religious feeling, especially in the second half of the fifteenth century, resonated little among the worldly-wise clergy, and this divergence may explain the tremendous and immediate impact of Luther's ideas.

Luther and the Protestant reformers. He had no intention of destroying the unity of the medieval Christian church; instead, his whole program was based on reform within the church.

Church and Religion on the Eve of the Reformation

Corruption in the Catholic church was another factor that spurred people to want reform. No doubt the failure of the Renaissance popes to provide spiritual leadership had affected the spiritual life of all Christendom. The papal court's preoccupation with finances had an especially strong impact on the clergy. So did the economic changes of the fourteenth and fifteenth centuries. The highest positions among the clergy were increasingly held by either nobles or wealthy members of the bourgeoisie. Moreover, to increase their revenues, high church officials (such as bishops, archbishops, and cardinals) took over more than one church office. This **pluralism** (the holding of multiple church offices) begat absenteeism: church officeholders ignored their duties and hired underlings

Martin Luther and the Reformation in Germany

The Protestant Reformation began with a typical medieval question: What must I do to be saved? Martin Luther, a deeply religious man, found an answer that did not fit within the traditional teachings of the late medieval church. Ultimately, he split with that church, destroying the religious unity of western Christendom.

The Early Luther

Martin Luther was born in Germany on November 10, 1483. His father wanted him to become a lawyer, so Luther enrolled at the University of Erfurt. In 1505, after becoming a master in the liberal arts, the young man began to study law. But Luther was not content, not in small part due to his long-standing religious inclinations. That summer, while returning to Erfurt after a brief visit home, he was caught in a ferocious thunderstorm and vowed that if he survived unscathed, he would become a monk. He then entered the monastic order of the

Augustinian Hermits in Erfurt, much to his father's disgust. In the monastery, Luther focused on his major concern, the assurance of salvation. The traditional beliefs and practices of the church seemed unable to relieve his obsession with this question. Luther threw himself into his monastic routine with a vengeance:

> I was indeed a good monk and kept my order so strictly that I could say that if ever a monk could get to heaven through monastic discipline, I was that monk. . . . And yet my conscience would not give me certainty, but I always doubted and said, "You didn't do that right. You weren't contrite enough. You left that out of your confession." The more I tried to remedy an uncertain, weak and troubled conscience with human traditions, the more I daily found it more uncertain, weaker and more troubled.[3]

Despite his herculean efforts, Luther achieved no certainty of salvation.

To help overcome his difficulties, his superiors recommended that he study theology. Luther received his doctorate in 1512 and then became a professor in the theological faculty at the University of Wittenberg, lecturing on the Bible. Sometime between 1513 and 1516, through his study of the Bible, he arrived at an answer to his problem.

Catholic doctrine had emphasized that both faith and good works were required of a Christian to achieve personal salvation. In Luther's eyes, human beings, weak and powerless in the sight of an almighty God, could never do enough good works to merit salvation. Through his study of the Bible, especially his work on Paul's Epistle to the Romans, Luther rediscovered another way of viewing this problem. To Luther, humans are saved not through their good works but through faith in the promises of God, made possible by the sacrifice of Jesus on the cross. The doctrine of salvation or justification by grace through faith alone became the primary doctrine of the Protestant Reformation (**justification** is the act by which a person is made deserving of salvation). Because Luther had arrived at this doctrine from his study of the Bible, the Bible became for him, as for all other Protestants, the chief guide to religious truth. Justification by faith and the Bible as the sole authority in religious affairs were the twin pillars of the Protestant Reformation.

The Indulgence Controversy   Luther did not see himself as either an innovator or a heretic, but his involvement in the indulgence controversy propelled him into an open confrontation with church officials and forced him to see the theological implications of justification by faith alone. Luther was greatly distressed by the widespread selling of indulgences, certain that people were guaranteeing their eternal damnation by relying on these pieces of paper to assure themselves of salvation. Johann Tetzel, a rambunctious Dominican, hawked the indulgences with the slogan "As soon as the coin in the coffer [money box] rings, the soul from purgatory springs."

Greatly angered, Luther issued a stunning indictment of the abuses in the sale of indulgences, known as the Ninety-Five Theses (see the box on p. 241). It is doubtful that Luther intended to break with the church over the issue of indulgences. If the pope had clarified the use of indulgences, as Luther wished, Luther would probably have been satisfied. But Pope Leo X did not take the issue seriously and is even reported to have said that Luther was simply "some drunken German who will amend his ways when he sobers up." A German translation of the Ninety-Five Theses was quickly printed in thousands of copies and received sympathetically in a Germany that had a long tradition of dissatisfaction with papal policies and power.

The Quickening Rebellion   In three pamphlets published in 1520, Luther moved toward a more definite break with the Catholic church. *Address to the Nobility of the German Nation* was a political tract written in German in which Luther called on the German princes to overthrow the papacy in Germany and establish a reformed German church. *The Babylonian Captivity of the Church* attacked the sacramental system as the means by which the pope and church had held the real meaning of the Gospel captive for a thousand years. He called for the reform of monasticism and for the clergy to marry. While virginity is good, Luther argued, marriage is better, and freedom of choice is best. *On the Freedom of a Christian Man* was a short treatise on the doctrine of salvation. It is faith alone, not good works, that justifies, frees, and brings salvation through Jesus. Being saved and freed by his faith in Jesus, however, does not free the Christian from doing good works. Rather he performs good works out of gratitude to God: "Good works do not make a good man, but a good man does good works."[4]

Unable to accept Luther's forcefully worded dissent from traditional Catholic teachings, the church excommunicated him in January 1521. He was also summoned to appear before the imperial diet (Reichstag) of the Holy Roman Empire in Worms, convened by the newly elected Emperor Charles V (1519–1556). Expected to recant the heretical doctrines he had espoused, Luther refused and made the famous reply that became the battle cry of the Reformation:

> Since then Your Majesty and your lordships desire a simple reply, I will answer without horns and without teeth. Unless I am convicted by Scripture and plain reason—I do not accept the authority of popes and councils, for they have contradicted each other—my conscience is captive to the Word of God. I cannot and I will not recant anything, for to go against conscience is neither right nor safe. Here I stand, I cannot do otherwise. God help me. Amen.[5]

The young Emperor Charles was outraged at Luther's audacity and gave his opinion that "a single friar who goes counter to all Christianity for a thousand years must be wrong." By the Edict of Worms, Martin Luther was made an outlaw within the empire. His works were to be

LUTHER AND THE NINETY-FIVE THESES

To most historians, the publication of Luther's Ninety-Five Theses marks the beginning of the Reformation. To Luther, they were simply a response to what he considered the blatant abuse of Johann Tetzel's selling of indulgences. Although written in Latin, the theses were soon translated into German and disseminated widely across Germany.

Martin Luther, *Selections from the Ninety-Five Theses*

5. The Pope has neither the will nor the power to remit any penalties beyond those he has imposed either at his own discretion or by canon law.

21. Hence those preachers of Indulgences are wrong when they say that a man is absolved and saved from every penalty by the Pope's Indulgences.

27. It is mere human talk to preach that the soul flies out [of purgatory] immediately the money clinks in the collection-box.

28. It is certainly possible that when the money clinks in the collection-box greed and avarice can increase; but the intercession of the Church depends on the will of God alone.

50. Christians should be taught that, if the Pope knew the exactions of the preachers of Indulgences, he would rather have the basilica of St. Peter reduced to ashes than built with the skin, flesh and bones of his sheep.

81. This wanton preaching of pardons makes it difficult even for learned men to redeem respect due to the Pope from the slanders or at least the shrewd questionings of the laity.

82. For example: "Why does not the Pope empty purgatory for the sake of most holy love and the supreme need of souls? This would be the most righteous of reasons, if he can redeem innumerable souls for sordid money with which to build a basilica, the most trivial of reasons."

86. Again: "Since the Pope's wealth is larger than that of the crassest Crassi of our time, why does he not build this one basilica of St. Peter with his own money, rather than with that of the faithful poor?"

90. To suppress these most conscientious questionings of the laity by authority only, instead of refuting them by reason, is to expose the Church and the Pope to the ridicule of their enemies, and to make Christian people unhappy.

94. Christians should be exhorted to seek earnestly to follow Christ, their Head, through penalties, deaths, and hells.

95. And let them thus be more confident of entering heaven through many tribulations rather than through a false assurance of peace.

What are the major ideas of Luther's Ninety-Five Theses? Why did they have such a strong appeal in Germany?

---

burned and Luther himself captured and delivered to the emperor.

The Development of Lutheranism

Between 1521 and 1525, Luther's religious movement became a revolution. Lutheranism had much appeal and spread rapidly. The preaching of evangelical sermons, based on a return to the original message of the Bible, found favor throughout Germany. Also useful to the spread of the Reformation were pamphlets illustrated with vivid woodcuts portraying the pope as a hideous Antichrist and titled with catchy phrases such as "I Wonder Why There Is No Money in the Land" (which, of course, was an attack on papal greed).

Luther was able to gain the support of his prince, the elector of Saxony, as well as other German rulers among the more than three hundred states that made up the Holy Roman Empire. Lutheranism spread to both princely and ecclesiastical states in northern and central Germany as well as to two-thirds of the free imperial cities, especially those of southern Germany, where prosperous burghers, for both religious and secular reasons, became committed to Luther's cause. At its outset, the Reformation in Germany was largely an urban phenomenon.

A series of crises in the mid-1520s made it apparent, however, that spreading the word of God was not as easy as Luther had originally envisioned—the usual plight of most reformers. Luther experienced dissent within his own ranks in Wittenberg as well as defection from many Christian humanists who feared that Luther's movement threatened the unity of Christendom. The Peasants' War constituted Luther's greatest challenge, however. In June 1524, peasants in Germany rose in revolt against their lords and looked to Luther for support. But Luther, who knew how much his reformation of the church depended on the full support of the German princes and magistrates, supported the rulers. To Luther, the state and its rulers were ordained by God and given the authority to maintain the peace and order necessary for the spread of the Gospel. It was the duty of princes to suppress all revolt. By May 1525, the German princes had ruthlessly suppressed the peasant hordes. By this time, Luther found himself ever more dependent on state authorities for the growth and maintenance of his reformed church.

Church and State

Justification by faith was the starting point for most of Protestantism's major doctrines. Since Luther downplayed

Woodcut: Luther Versus the Pope. In the 1520s, after Luther's return to Wittenberg, his teachings began to spread rapidly, ending ultimately in a reform movement supported by state authorities. Pamphlets containing picturesque woodcuts were important in the spread of Luther's ideas. In the woodcut shown here, the crucified Jesus attends Luther's service on the left, while on the right the pope is at a table selling indulgences.

the role of good works in salvation, the sacraments also had to be redefined. No longer were they merit-earning works; they were now divinely established signs signifying the promise of salvation. Luther kept only two of the Catholic church's seven sacraments: baptism and the Lord's Supper. Baptism signified rebirth through grace. Regarding the Lord's Supper or the Eucharist, Luther denied the Catholic doctrine of **transubstantiation,** which taught that the substance of the bread and wine consumed in the rite is miraculously transformed into the body and blood of Jesus. Yet he continued to insist on the real presence of Jesus' body and blood in the bread and wine given as a testament to God's forgiveness of sin.

Luther took an active role in establishing a reformed church. Since the Catholic ecclesiastical hierarchy had been scrapped, Luther came to rely increasingly on the princes or state authorities to organize and guide the new Lutheran reformed churches. The Lutheran churches in Germany (and later in Scandinavia) quickly became territorial or state churches in which the state supervised and disciplined church members. As part of the development of these state-dominated churches, Luther also instituted new religious services to replace the Mass. These featured a worship service consisting of a German liturgy that focused on Bible reading, preaching the word of God, and song. Following his own denunciation of clerical celibacy, Luther married a former nun, Katherina von Bora, in 1525. His union provided a model of married and family life for the new Protestant minister.

Germany and the Reformation: Religion and Politics

From its very beginning, the fate of Luther's movement was closely tied to political affairs. In 1519, Charles I, king of Spain and the grandson of the Emperor Maximilian, was elected Holy Roman Emperor as Charles V (1519–1556). Charles V ruled over an immense empire, consisting of Spain and its overseas possessions, the traditional Austrian Habsburg lands, Bohemia, Hungary, the Low Countries, and the kingdom of Naples in southern Italy (see Map 13.1). The extent of his possessions was reflected in the languages he used: "I speak Spanish to God, Italian to women, French to men, and German to my horse." Politically, Charles wanted to maintain his

242   CHAPTER 13

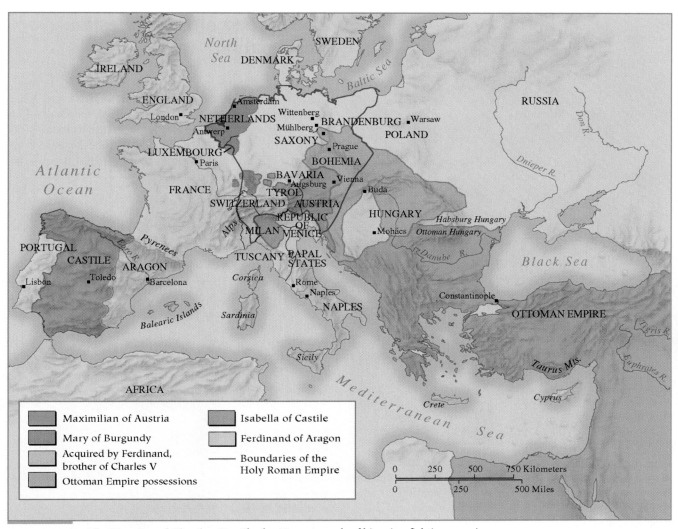

MAP 13.1 **The Empire of Charles V.** Charles V spent much of his reign fighting wars in Italy, against France and the Ottoman Empire, and within the borders of the Holy Roman Empire. He failed in his main goal to secure Europe for Catholicism: the 1555 Peace of Augsburg recognized the equality of Catholicism and Lutheranism and let each German prince choose his realm's religion. **?** Why would France feel threatened by the empire of Charles V? **View an animated version of this map or related maps at** http://thomsonedu.com/history/spielvogel

dynasty's control over his enormous empire; religiously, he hoped to preserve the unity of the Catholic faith throughout his empire. Despite his strengths, Charles spent a lifetime in futile pursuit of his goals. Four major problems—the French, the papacy, the Turks, and Germany's internal situation—cost him both his dream and his health.

The chief political concern of Charles V was his rivalry with the Valois king of France, Francis I (1515–1547). Encircled by the possessions of the Habsburg empire, Francis became embroiled in conflict with Charles over disputed territories in southern France, the Netherlands, the Rhineland, northern Spain, and Italy. These conflicts, known as the Habsburg-Valois Wars,

were fought intermittently for more than two decades (1521–1544).

At the same time, Charles faced opposition from Pope Clement VII (1523–1534), who, guided by political considerations, joined the side of Francis I. The advance of the Ottoman Turks into the eastern part of Charles's empire forced the emperor to divert forces there as well. Under Suleiman the Magnificent (1520–1566), the Ottoman Turks overran most of Hungary, moved into Austria, and advanced as far as Vienna, where they were finally repulsed in 1529.

Finally, the internal political situation in the Holy Roman Empire was also not in Charles's favor. Germany was a land of several hundred territorial states—princely

Charles V. Charles V sought to create religious unity throughout his vast empire by keeping all his subjects within the bounds of the Catholic church. Due to his conflict with Francis I as well as his difficulties with the Turks, the papacy, and the German princes, Charles was never able to check the spread of Lutheranism. This is a portrait of Charles V by the Venetian painter Titian.

states, ecclesiastical principalities, and free imperial cities. Although all owed loyalty to the emperor, Germany's medieval development had enabled these states to become quite independent of imperial authority. They had no desire to have a strong emperor. By the time Charles V was able to bring military forces to Germany in 1546, Lutheranism had become well established and the Lutheran princes were well organized. Unable to impose his will on Germany, Charles was forced to negotiate a truce. An end to religious warfare in Germany came in 1555 with the Peace of Augsburg, which marked an important turning point in the history of the Reformation. The division of Christianity was formally acknowledged, with Lutheranism granted equal legal standing with Catholicism. Moreover, the peace settlement accepted the right of each German ruler to determine the religion of his subjects. Charles's hope for a united empire had been completely dashed, and the ideal of medieval Christian unity was irretrievably lost. The rapid proliferation of new Protestant groups served to underscore the new reality.

The Spread of the Protestant Reformation

For both Catholics and Protestant reformers, Luther's heresy also raised the question of how to determine what constituted the correct interpretation of the Bible. The inability to agree on this issue led not only to theological confrontations but also to bloody warfare because each Christian group was unwilling to admit that it could be wrong.

The Zwinglian Reformation

In the sixteenth century, the Swiss Confederation was a loose association of thirteen self-governing states called cantons. Theoretically part of the Holy Roman Empire, they had become virtually independent in 1499. The six forest cantons were democratic republics, while the seven urban cantons, which included Zürich, Bern, and Basel, were governed primarily by city councils controlled by narrow oligarchies of wealthy citizens.

Zwingli's Zürich

Ulrich Zwingli (1484–1531) was ordained a priest in 1506 and accepted an appointment as a cathedral priest in the Great Minster of Zürich in 1518. Zwingli's preaching of the Gospel caused such unrest that the city council in 1523 held a public disputation or debate in the town hall. Zwingli's party was accorded the victory, and the council declared that "Mayor, Council and Great Council of Zürich, in order to do away with disturbance and discord, have upon due deliberation and consultation decided and resolved that Master Zwingli should continue as heretofore to proclaim the Gospel and the pure sacred Scriptures."[6] Over the next two years, evangelical reforms were promulgated in Zürich by a city council strongly influenced by Zwingli. Relics and images were abolished; all paintings and decorations were removed from the churches and replaced by whitewashed walls. The Mass was replaced by a new liturgy consisting of Scripture reading, prayer, and sermons. Monasticism, pilgrimages, the veneration of saints, clerical celibacy, and the pope's authority were all abolished as remnants of papal Christianity.

A Reformation Debate: The Marburg Colloquy

Debates played a crucial role in the Reformation period. They were a primary instrument in introducing the Reformation into innumerable cities as well as a means of resolving differences among the like-minded Protestant groups. This selection contains an excerpt from the vivacious and often brutal debate between Luther and Zwingli over the sacrament of the Lord's Supper, held at Marburg in 1529. The two protagonists failed to reach agreement.

The Marburg Colloquy, 1529

HESSIAN CHANCELLOR FEIGE: My gracious prince and lord [Landgrave Philip of Hesse] has summoned you for the express and urgent purpose of settling the dispute over the sacrament of the Lord's Supper. . . . And let everyone on both sides present his arguments in a spirit of moderation, as becomes such matters. . . . Now then, Doctor Luther, you may proceed.

LUTHER: Noble prince, gracious lord! Undoubtedly the colloquy is well intentioned. . . . Although I have no intention of changing my mind, which is firmly made up, I will nevertheless present the grounds of my belief and show where the others are in error. . . . Your basic contentions are these: In the last analysis you wish to prove that a body cannot be in two places at once, and you produce arguments about the unlimited body which are based on natural reason. I do not question how Christ can be God and man and how the two natures can be joined. For God is more powerful than all our ideas, and we must submit to his word.

Prove that Christ's body is not there where the Scripture says, "This is my body!" Rational proofs I will not listen to. . . . God is beyond all mathematics and the words of God are to be revered and carried out in awe. It is God who commands, "Take, eat, this is my body." I request, therefore, valid scriptural proof to the contrary.

Luther writes on the table in chalk, "This is my body," and covers the words with a velvet cloth.

OECOLAMPADIUS [leader of the reform movement in Basel and a Zwinglian partisan]: The sixth chapter of John clarifies the other scriptural passages. Christ is not speaking there about a local presence. "The flesh is of no avail," he says [John 6:63]. It is not my intention to employ rational, or geometrical, arguments—neither am I denying the power of God—but as long as I have the complete faith I will speak from that. For Christ is risen; he sits at the right hand of God; and so he cannot be present in the bread. Our view is neither new nor sacrilegious, but is based on faith and Scripture. . . .

ZWINGLI: I insist that the words of the Lord's Supper must be figurative. This is ever apparent, and even required by the article of faith: "taken up into heaven, seated at the right hand of the Father." Otherwise, it would be absurd to look for him in the Lord's Supper at the same time that Christ is telling us that he is in heaven. One and the same body cannot possibly be in different places. . . . I stand by this passage in the sixth chapter of John, verse 63, and shall not be shaken from it. You'll have to sing another tune.

LUTHER: You're being obnoxious.

ZWINGLI: (*excitedly*) Don't you believe that Christ was attempting in John 6 to help those who did not understand?

LUTHER: You're trying to dominate things! You insist on passing judgment! Leave that to someone else! . . . It is your point that must be proved, not mine. But let us stop this sort of thing. It serves no purpose.

ZWINGLI: It certainly does! It is for you to prove that the passage in John 6 speaks of a physical repast.

LUTHER: You express yourself poorly and make about as much progress as a cane standing in a corner. You're going nowhere.

ZWINGLI: No, no, no! This is the passage that will break your neck!

LUTHER: Don't be so sure of yourself. Necks don't break this way. You're in Hesse, not Switzerland. . . .

Based on this example, why do you think Reformation debates led to further hostility rather than compromise and unity?

As his movement began to spread to other cities in Switzerland, Zwingli sought an alliance with Martin Luther and the German reformers. Protestant political leaders attempted to promote an alliance of the Swiss and German reformed churches by persuading the leaders of both groups to attend a colloquy (conference) at Marburg to resolve their differences. Although both the German and Swiss reformers realized the need for unity to defend against the opposition of Catholic authorities, they were unable to agree on the interpretation of the Lord's Supper (see the box above). Zwingli believed that the scriptural words "This is my body" and "This is my blood" should be taken symbolically, not literally. To Zwingli, the Lord's Supper was only a meal of remembrance, and he refused to accept Luther's insistence on the real presence of the body and blood of Jesus. The Marburg Colloquy produced no agreement.

In October 1531, war erupted between the Swiss Protestant and Catholic cantons. Zürich's army was routed, and Zwingli was found wounded on the battlefield. His enemies killed him, cut up his body, burned it, and scattered the ashes. This Swiss civil war of 1531 provided an early indication of what religious passions would lead to in the sixteenth century. Unable to find peaceful ways to agree on the meaning of the Gospel, the disciples of Christianity resorted to violence and decision by force. When informed of Zwingli's death, Martin Luther, who had not forgotten the confrontation at Marburg, is supposed to have remarked that Zwingli "got what he deserved."

The Radical Reformation: The Anabaptists

Although many reformers were ready to allow the state to play an important, if not dominant, role in church affairs, some people rejected this kind of magisterial reformation and favored a far more radical reform movement. Collectively called the Anabaptists, these radicals were actually members of a large variety of groups who had certain characteristics in common.

To the Anabaptists, the true Christian church was a voluntary association of believers who had undergone spiritual rebirth and had then been baptized into the church. Anabaptists advocated adult rather than infant baptism. No one, they believed, should be forced to accept the truth of the Bible. They also tried to return literally to the practices and spirit of early Christianity. Adhering to the accounts of early Christian communities in the New Testament, they followed a strict sort of democracy in which all believers were considered equal. Each church chose its own minister, who might be any member of the community because all Christians were considered priests (though women were often excluded). Those chosen as ministers had the duty to lead services, which were very simple and contained nothing not found in the early church. Like early Christians, Anabaptists, who called themselves "Christians" or "Saints," accepted that they would have to suffer for their faith. Anabaptists rejected theological speculation in favor of simple Christian living according to what they believed was the pure word of God. The Lord's Supper was interpreted as a remembrance, a meal of fellowship celebrated in the evening in private houses according to Jesus' example.

Unlike the Catholics and other Protestants, most Anabaptists believed in the complete separation of church and state. Not only was government to be excluded from the realm of religion, but it was not even supposed to exercise political jurisdiction over true Christians. Human law had no power over those whom God had saved. Anabaptists refused to hold political office or bear arms because many took the commandment "Thou shall not kill" literally, although some Anabaptist groups did resort to violence. Their political beliefs as much as their religious beliefs caused the Anabaptists to be regarded as dangerous radicals who threatened the fabric of sixteenth-century society. Indeed, the chief thing Protestants and Catholics could agree on was the need to stamp out the Anabaptists.

One early group of Anabaptists known as the Swiss Brethren arose in Zürich. Their ideas frightened Zwingli,

and they were soon expelled from the city. As their teachings spread through southern Germany, the Austrian Habsburg lands, and Switzerland, Anabaptists suffered ruthless persecution, especially after the Peasants' War of 1524–1525, when the upper classes resorted to repression. Virtually eliminated in Germany, Anabaptist survivors emerged in Moravia, Poland, and the Netherlands.

Menno Simons (1496–1561) was the most responsible for rejuvenating Dutch Anabaptism. A popular leader, Menno dedicated his life to the spread of a peaceful, evangelical Anabaptism that stressed separation from the world in order to live a truly Jesus-like life. The Mennonites, as his followers were called, spread from the Netherlands into northwestern Germany and eventually into Poland and Lithuania as well as the New World. Remnant communities of both Mennonites and Amish, who are also descended from the Anabaptists, can still be found in the United States and Canada today.

The Reformation in England

The English Reformation was initiated by King Henry VIII (1509–1547), who wanted to divorce his first wife, Catherine of Aragon, because she had failed to produce a male heir. Furthermore, Henry had fallen in love with Anne Boleyn, a lady-in-waiting to Queen Catherine. Anne's discontent with being merely the king's mistress and the king's desire to have a legitimate male heir made their marriage imperative, but the king's first marriage stood in the way.

Normally, church authorities might have been willing to grant the king an annulment of his marriage, but Pope Clement VII was dependent on the Holy Roman Emperor, Charles V, who happened to be Catherine's nephew. Impatient with the pope's inaction, Henry sought to obtain an annulment of his marriage in England's own ecclesiastical courts. As archbishop of Canterbury and head of the highest ecclesiastical court in England, Thomas Cranmer held official hearings on the king's case and ruled in May 1533 that the king's marriage to Catherine was "null and absolutely void." He then validated Henry's secret marriage to Anne, who had become pregnant. At the beginning of June, Anne was crowned queen. Three months later, a child was born. Much to the king's disappointment, the baby was a girl, the future Queen Elizabeth.

In 1534, at Henry's request, Parliament moved to finalize the Church of England's break with Rome. The Act of Supremacy of 1534 declared that the king was "taken, accepted, and reputed the only supreme head on earth of the Church of England," a position that gave him control of doctrine, clerical appointments, and discipline.

Although Henry VIII had broken with the papacy, little changed in matters of doctrine, theology, and ceremony. Some of his supporters, such as Archbishop Cranmer, sought a religious reformation as well as an administrative one, but Henry was unyielding. When

Henry died in 1547, he was succeeded by his son, the underage and sickly Edward VI (1547–1553). During Edward's reign, Cranmer and others inclined toward Protestant doctrines were able to move the Church of England (also known as the Anglican church) in more of a Protestant direction. New acts of Parliament instituted the right of the clergy to marry, the elimination of religious images, and the creation of a revised Protestant liturgy that was elaborated in a new prayer book known as the Book of Common Prayer. These rapid changes in doctrine and liturgy aroused much opposition and prepared the way for the reaction that occurred when Mary, Henry's first daughter by Catherine of Aragon, came to the throne.

Mary (1553–1558) was a Catholic who intended to restore England to Roman Catholicism. But her restoration of Catholicism aroused much opposition. There was widespread antipathy to Mary's unfortunate marriage to Philip II, the son of Charles V and future king of Spain. Philip was strongly disliked in England, and Mary's foreign policy of alliance with Spain simply aroused further hostility. The burning of more than three hundred Protestant heretics aroused further ire against "Bloody Mary." As a result of her policies, Mary managed to achieve the opposite of what she had intended: England was more Protestant by the end of her reign than it had been at the beginning.

John Calvin and the Development of Calvinism

Of the second generation of Protestant reformers, one stands out as the premier systematic theologian and organizer of the Protestant movement—John Calvin (1509–1564). Calvin was educated in his native France, but after his conversion to Protestantism, he was forced to flee to the safety of Switzerland. In 1536, he published the first edition of the *Institutes of the Christian Religion,* a masterful synthesis of Protestant thought that immediately secured Calvin's reputation as one of the new leaders of Protestantism.

Calvin's Ideas On most important doctrines, Calvin stood very close to Luther. He adhered to the doctrine of justification by faith alone to explain how humans achieved salvation. But Calvin also placed much emphasis on the absolute sovereignty of God or the "power, grace, and glory of God." One of the ideas derived from his emphasis on the absolute sovereignty of God—**predestination**—gave a unique cast to Calvin's teachings. This "eternal decree," as Calvin called it, meant that God had predestined some people to be saved (the elect) and others to be damned (the reprobate). According to Calvin, "He has once for all determined, both whom he would admit to salvation, and whom he would condemn to destruction."[7] Although Calvin stressed that there could be no absolute certainty of salvation, some of his followers did not always make this distinction. The

John Calvin. After a conversion experience, John Calvin abandoned his life as a humanist and became a reformer. In 1536, Calvin began working to reform the city of Geneva, where he remained until his death in 1564. This sixteenth-century portrait of Calvin pictures him near the end of his life.

practical psychological effect of predestination was to give some later Calvinists an unshakable conviction that they were doing God's work on earth. Thus Calvinism became a dynamic and activist faith. It is no accident that Calvinism became the militant international form of Protestantism.

To Calvin, the church was a divine institution responsible for preaching the word of God and administering the sacraments. Calvin kept the same two sacraments as other Protestant reformers, baptism and the Lord's Supper. Calvin believed in the real presence of Jesus in the sacrament of the Lord's Supper, but only in a spiritual sense. Jesus' body is at the right hand of God and thus cannot be in the sacrament, but to the believer, Jesus is spiritually present in the Lord's Supper.

In 1536, Calvin began working to reform the city of Geneva. He established a church government that used both clergy and laymen in the service of the church. The Consistory, a special body for enforcing moral discipline,

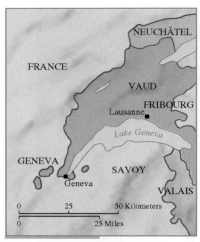

Calvin's Geneva

was set up as a court to oversee the moral life and doctrinal purity of Genevans. The Consistory had the right to punish people who deviated from the church's teachings and moral principles.

Calvin's success in Geneva enabled the city to become a vibrant center of Protestantism. John Knox, the Calvinist reformer of Scotland, called Geneva "the most perfect school of Christ on earth." Following Calvin's lead, missionaries trained in Geneva were sent to all parts of Europe. Calvinism became established in France, the Netherlands, Scotland, and central and eastern Europe. By the mid-sixteenth century, Calvinism had replaced Lutheranism as the militant international form of Protestantism, and Calvin's Geneva stood as the fortress of the Reformation.

The Social Impact of the Protestant Reformation

Because Christianity was such an integral part of European life, it was inevitable that the Reformation would have an impact on the family and popular religious practices.

The Family

For centuries, Catholicism had praised the family and sanctified its existence by making marriage a sacrament. But the Catholic church's high regard for abstinence from sex as the surest way to holiness made the celibate state of the clergy preferable to marriage. Nevertheless, because not all men could remain chaste, marriage offered the best means to control sexual urges and give them a purpose, the procreation of children. To some extent, this attitude persisted among the Protestant reformers; Luther, for example, argued that sex in marriage allowed one to "make use of this sex in order to avoid sin," and Calvin advised that every man should "abstain from marriage only so long as he is fit to observe celibacy." If "his power to tame lust fails him," then he must marry.

But the Reformation did bring some change to the conception of the family. Both Catholic and Protestant clergy preached sermons advocating a more positive side to family relationships. The Protestants were especially important in developing this new view of the family. Because Protestantism had eliminated any idea of special holiness for celibacy, abolishing both monasticism and a

celibate clergy, the family could be placed at the center of human life, and a new stress on "mutual love between man and wife" could be extolled. But were doctrine and reality the same? For more radical religious groups, at times they were. One Anabaptist wrote to his wife before his execution: "My faithful helper, my loyal friend. I praise God that he gave you to me, you who have sustained me in all my trial."[8] But more often reality reflected the traditional roles of husband as the ruler and wife as the obedient servant whose chief duty was to please her husband. Luther stated it clearly:

> The rule remains with the husband, and the wife is compelled to obey him by God's command. He rules the home and the state, wages war, defends his possessions, tills the soil, builds, plants, etc. The woman on the other hand is like a nail driven into the wall . . . so the wife should stay at home and look after the affairs of the household, as one who has been deprived of the ability of administering those affairs that are outside and that concern the state. She does not go beyond her most personal duties.[9]

Obedience to her husband was not a woman's only role; her other important duty was to bear children. To Calvin and Luther, this function of women was part of the divine plan. God punishes women for the sins of Eve by the burdens of procreation and feeding and nurturing their children, but "it is a gladsome punishment if you consider the hope of eternal life and the honor of motherhood which had been left to her."[10] Although the Protestant reformers sanctified this role of woman as mother and wife, viewing it as a holy vocation, Protestantism also left few alternatives for women. Because monasticism had been destroyed, that career avenue was no longer available; for most Protestant women, family life was their only destiny. At the same time, by emphasizing the father as "ruler" and hence the center of household religion, Protestantism even removed the woman from her traditional role as controller of religion in the home. Overall, the Protestant Reformation did not noticeably transform women's subordinate place in society.

Religious Practices and Popular Culture

The attacks of Protestant reformers on the Catholic church led to radical changes in religious practices. The Protestant Reformation abolished or severely curtailed such customary practices as indulgences, the veneration of relics and saints, pilgrimages, monasticism, and clerical celibacy. The elimination of saints put an end to the numerous celebrations of religious holy days and changed a community's sense of time. Thus in Protestant communities, religious ceremonies and imagery, such as processions and statues, tended to be replaced with individual private prayer, family worship, and collective prayer and worship at the same time each week on Sunday.

In addition to abolishing saints' days and religious carnivals, some Protestant reformers even tried to eliminate customary forms of entertainment. Puritans (as

English Calvinists were known), for example, attempted to ban drinking in taverns, dramatic performances, and dancing. Dutch Calvinists denounced the tradition of giving small presents to children on the feast of Saint Nicholas in December. Many of these Protestant attacks on popular culture were unsuccessful, however. The importance of taverns in English social life made it impossible to eradicate them, and celebrations at Christmastime persisted in the Dutch Netherlands.

The Catholic Reformation

By the mid-sixteenth century, Lutheranism had become established in Germany and Scandinavia and Calvinism in parts of Switzerland, France, the Netherlands, and eastern Europe (see Map 13.2). In England, the split from

Rome had resulted in the creation of a national church. The situation in Europe did not look particularly favorable for the Roman Catholic church. But even at the beginning of the sixteenth century, constructive, positive forces were at work for reform within the Catholic church, and in a few decades, these efforts were being directed by a revived and reformed papacy, giving rise to a Catholic Reformation. Historians focus on three chief pillars of the Catholic Reformation: the development of the Jesuits, the creation of a reformed and revived papacy, and the Council of Trent.

The Society of Jesus

The Society of Jesus, members of which are known as Jesuits, was founded by a Spanish nobleman, Ignatius of

MAP 13.2 **Catholics and Protestants in Europe by 1560.** The Reformation continued to evolve beyond the basic split of the Lutherans from the Catholics. Several Protestant sects broke away from the teachings of Martin Luther, each with a separate creed and different ways of worship. In England, Henry VIII broke with the Catholic church for political and dynastic reasons. ❓ Which areas of Europe were solidly Catholic, which were solidly Lutheran, and which were neither? 🔊 **View an animated version of this map or related maps at** http://thomsonedu.com/history/spielvogel

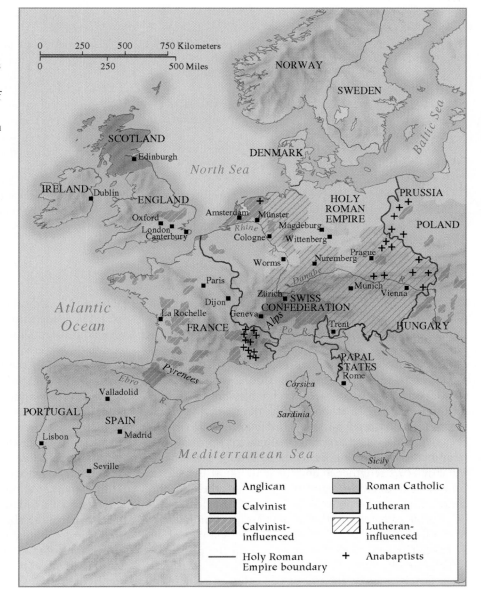

LOYOLA AND OBEDIENCE TO "OUR HOLY MOTHER, THE HIERARCHICAL CHURCH"

*I*n his *Spiritual Exercises,* Ignatius of Loyola developed a systematic program for "the conquest of self and the regulation of one's life" for service to the hierarchical Catholic church. Ignatius' supreme goal was the commitment of the Christian to active service in the Church of Christ (the Catholic church). In the final section of *The Spiritual Exercises,* Loyola explained the nature of that commitment in a series of "rules for thinking with the church."

Ignatius of Loyola, "Rules for Thinking with the Church"

The following rules should be observed to foster the true attitude of mind we ought to have in the Church militant.

1. We must put aside all judgment of our own, and keep the mind ever ready and prompt to obey in all things the true Spouse of Jesus Christ, our holy Mother, the hierarchical Church.
2. We should praise sacramental confession, the yearly reception of the Most Blessed Sacrament [the Lord's Supper], and praise more highly monthly reception, and still more weekly Communion. . . .
3. We ought to praise the frequent hearing of Mass, the singing of hymns, psalmody, and long prayers whether in the church or outside. . . .
4. We must praise highly religious life, virginity, and continency; and matrimony ought not be praised as much as any of these. . . .
6. We should show our esteem for the relics of the saints by venerating them and praying to the saints. We should praise visits to the Station Churches, pilgrimages,

indulgences, jubilees, the lighting of candles in churches. . . .

8. We ought to praise not only the building and adornment of churches, but also images and veneration of them according to the subject they represent.
9. Finally, we must praise all the commandments of the Church, and be on the alert to find reasons to defend them, and by no means in order to criticize them.
10. We should be more ready to approve and praise the orders, recommendations, and way of acting of our superiors than to find fault with them. Though some of the orders, etc., may not have been praiseworthy, yet to speak against them, either when preaching in public or in speaking before the people, would rather be the cause of murmuring and scandal than of profit. As a consequence, the people would become angry with their superiors, whether secular or spiritual. But while it does harm in the absence of our superiors to speak evil of them before the people, it may be profitable to discuss their bad conduct with those who can apply a remedy.
13. If we wish to proceed securely in all things, we must hold fast to the following principle: What seems to me white, I will believe black if the hierarchical Church so defines. For I must be convinced that in Christ our Lord, the bridegroom, and in His spouse the Church, only one Spirit holds sway, which governs and rules for the salvation of souls.

What are the fundamental assumptions that inform Loyola's rules for thinking with the church? What do these assumptions tell you about the nature of the Catholic reform movement?

Loyola (1491–1556), whose injuries in battle cut short his military career. Loyola experienced a spiritual torment similar to Luther's, but unlike Luther, he resolved his problems not by a new doctrine but by a decision to submit to the will of the church. Unable to be a real soldier, he vowed to be a soldier of God. Over a period of twelve years, Loyola prepared for his lifework by prayer, pilgrimages, going to school, and working out a spiritual program in his brief but powerful book, *The Spiritual Exercises.* This was a training manual for spiritual development emphasizing exercises by which the human will could be strengthened and made to follow the will of God as manifested through his instrument, the Catholic church (see the box above).

Loyola gathered together a small group of individuals who were recognized as a religious order by a papal bull in 1540. The new order was grounded on the principles of absolute obedience to the papacy, a strict hierarchical order for the society, the use of education to achieve its

goals, and a dedication to engage in "conflict for God." Executive leadership was put in the hands of a general, who nominated all important positions in the order and was to be revered as the absolute head of the order. Loyola served as the first general of the order until his death in 1556. A special vow of absolute obedience to the pope made the Jesuits an important instrument for papal policy.

The Jesuits were active on behalf of the Catholic faith. They established well-disciplined schools, believing that the thorough education of young people was crucial to combat the advance of Protestantism. Another prominent Jesuit activity was the propagation of the Catholic faith among non-Christians. Francis Xavier (1506–1552), one of the original members of the Society of Jesus, carried the message of Catholic Christianity to the East. After converting tens of thousands in India, he traveled to Malacca and the Moluccas before reaching Japan in 1549. He spoke highly of the Japanese: "They are a people of excellent

Ignatius of Loyola. The Jesuits became the most important new religious order of the Catholic Reformation. Shown here in a sixteenth-century painting by an unknown artist is Ignatius of Loyola, founder of the Society of Jesus. Loyola is seen kneeling before Pope Paul III, who officially recognized the Jesuits in 1540.

morals—good in general and not malicious."[11] Thousands of Japanese, especially in the southernmost islands, became Christians. In 1552, Xavier set out for China but died of fever before he reached the mainland.

Although conversion efforts in Japan proved short-lived, Jesuit activity in China, especially that of the Italian Matteo Ricci (1552–1610), was more long-lasting. Recognizing the Chinese pride in their own culture, the Jesuits attempted to draw parallels between Christian and Confucian concepts and to show the similarities between Christian morality and Confucian ethics. For their part, the missionaries were impressed with many aspects of Chinese civilization, and reports of their experiences heightened European curiosity about this great society on the other side of the world.

The Jesuits were also determined to carry the Catholic banner and fight Protestantism. Jesuit missionaries succeeded in restoring Catholicism to parts of Germany and eastern Europe. Poland was largely won back for the Catholic church through Jesuit efforts.

A Revived Papacy

A reformed papacy was another important factor in the development of the Catholic Reformation. The pontificate of Pope Paul III (1534–1549) proved significant. Raised in the lap of luxury, Paul III continued Renaissance papal practices by appointing his nephews as cardinals, involving himself in politics, and patronizing arts and letters on a lavish scale. Nevertheless, he perceived the need for change and expressed it decisively. Advocates of reform,

such as Gasparo Contarini and Gian Pietro Caraffa, were made cardinals. In 1535, Paul took the audacious step of appointing a commission to study the church's condition. The Reform Commission's report in 1537 blamed the church's problems on the corrupt policies of popes and cardinals. It was also Paul III who formally recognized the Jesuits and began the Council of Trent.

A decisive turning point in the direction of the Catholic Reformation and the nature of papal reform came in the 1540s. In 1541, a colloquy had been held at Regensburg in a final attempt to settle the religious division peacefully. Here Catholic moderates, such as Cardinal Contarini, who favored concessions to Protestants in the hope of restoring Christian unity, reached a compromise with Protestant moderates on a number of doctrinal issues. When Contarini returned to Rome with these proposals, Cardinal Caraffa and other hard-liners, who regarded all compromise with Protestant innovations as heresy, accused him of selling out to the heretics. It soon became apparent that the conservative reformers were in the ascendancy when Caraffa was able to persuade Paul III to establish the Roman Inquisition or Holy Office in 1542 to ferret out doctrinal errors. There was to be no compromise with Protestantism.

When Cardinal Caraffa was chosen pope as Paul IV (1555–1559), he so increased the power of the Inquisition that even liberal cardinals were silenced. This "first true pope of the Catholic Counter-Reformation," as he has been called, also created the Index of Forbidden Books, a list of books that Catholics were not allowed to read. It included all the works of Protestant theologians.

Any hope of restoring Christian unity by compromise was fading fast. The activities of the Council of Trent, the third major pillar of the Catholic Reformation, made compromise virtually impossible.

The Council of Trent

In March 1545, a group of cardinals, archbishops, bishops, abbots, and theologians met in the city of Trent on the border between Germany and Italy and initiated the Council of Trent, which met intermittently from 1545 to 1563 in three major sessions. Moderate Catholic reformers hoped that compromises would be made in formulating doctrinal definitions that would encourage Protestants to return to the church. Conservatives, however, favored an uncompromising restatement of Catholic doctrines in strict opposition to Protestant positions. The latter group won, although not without a struggle.

The final doctrinal decrees of the Council of Trent reaffirmed traditional Catholic teachings in opposition to Protestant beliefs. Scripture and tradition were affirmed as equal authorities in religious matters; only the church could interpret Scripture. Both faith and good works were declared necessary for salvation. The seven sacraments, the Catholic doctrine of transubstantiation (rejected by the Protestant reformers), and clerical celibacy were all upheld. Belief in purgatory and in the efficacy of indulgences was strengthened, although the hawking of indulgences was prohibited.

After the Council of Trent, the Roman Catholic church possessed a clear body of doctrine and a unified church under the acknowledged supremacy of the popes who had triumphed over bishops and councils. The Roman Catholic church had become one Christian denomination among many with an organizational framework and doctrinal pattern that would not be significantly altered until the Second Vatican Council four hundred years later. With a new spirit of confidence, the Catholic church entered a militant phase, as well prepared as the Calvinists to do battle for the Lord. An era of religious warfare was about to unfold.

Politics and the Wars of Religion in the Sixteenth Century

By the middle of the sixteenth century, Calvinism and Catholicism had become militant religions dedicated to spreading the word of God as they interpreted it. Although this religious struggle for the minds and hearts of Europeans is at the core of the religious wars of the sixteenth century, economic, social, and political forces also played important roles in these conflicts. Of the sixteenth-century religious wars, none were more momentous or more shattering than the French civil wars known as the French Wars of Religion.

The French Wars of Religion (1562–1598)

Religion was the engine that drove the French civil wars of the sixteenth century. The growth of Calvinism led to persecution by the French kings but did little to stop the spread of Calvinism. **Huguenots,** as the French Calvinists were called, came from all layers of society: artisans and shopkeepers hurt by rising prices and a rigid guild system, merchants and lawyers in provincial towns whose local privileges were tenuous, and members of the nobility. Possibly 40 to 50 percent of the French nobility became Huguenots, including the house of Bourbon, which stood next to the Valois dynasty in the royal line of succession and ruled the southern French kingdom of Navarre. The conversion of so many nobles made the Huguenots a potentially dangerous political threat to monarchical power. Though the Calvinists constituted only about 7 percent of the population, they were a strong-willed and well-organized minority.

The Catholic majority greatly outnumbered the Calvinist minority. The Valois monarchy was staunchly Catholic, and its control of the Catholic church gave it little incentive to look favorably on Protestantism. At the same time, an extreme Catholic party—known as the Ultra-Catholics—favored strict opposition to the Huguenots and were led by the Guise family. They received support abroad from the papacy and Jesuits who favored their uncompromising Catholic position.

But religion was not the only factor that contributed to the French civil wars. Towns and provinces, which had long resisted the growing power of monarchical centralization, were only too willing to join a revolt against the monarchy. This was also true of the nobility, and the fact that so many of them were Calvinists created an important base of opposition to the crown. The French Wars of Religion, then, presented a major constitutional crisis for France and temporarily halted the development of the French centralized state. The claim to a person's loyalties by the ruling dynasty was temporarily superseded by loyalty to one's religious beliefs. For thirty years, battles raged in France between Catholic and Calvinist parties, who obviously considered the unity of France less important than religious truth. But there also emerged in France a group known as the *politiques* who placed politics before religion and believed that no religious truth was worth the ravages of civil war. The *politiques* ultimately prevailed, but not until both sides had become exhausted by bloodshed.

Finally, in 1589, Henry of Navarre, the political leader of the Huguenots and a member of the Bourbon dynasty, succeeded to the throne as Henry IV (1589–1610). Realizing, however, that he would never be accepted by Catholic France, Henry took the logical way out and converted to Catholicism. With his coronation in 1594, the Wars of Religion came to an end. The Edict of Nantes in 1598 solved the religious problem by acknowledging Catholicism as the official religion of France while guaranteeing the Huguenots the right to worship and to enjoy all political privileges, including the holding of public offices.

Philip II and Militant Catholicism

The greatest advocate of militant Catholicism in the second half of the sixteenth century was King Philip II of Spain (1556–1598), the son and heir of Charles V. Philip's reign ushered in an age of Spanish greatness, both politically and culturally. Philip's first major goal was to consolidate and secure the lands he had inherited from his father. These included Spain, the Netherlands, and possessions in Italy and the New World. For Philip, this meant strict conformity to Catholicism and the establishment of strong monarchical authority. Establishing this authority was not an easy task because Philip had inherited a governmental structure in which each of the various states and territories of his empire stood in an individual relationship to the king.

Crucial to an understanding of Philip II is the importance of Catholicism to the Spanish people and their ruler. Driven by a heritage of crusading fervor, the Spanish had little difficulty seeing themselves as a nation divinely chosen to save Catholic Christianity from the Protestant heretics. Philip II, the "Most Catholic King," became the champion of Catholicism throughout Europe, a role that led him to spectacular victories and equally spectacular defeats. Spain's leadership of a "holy league" against Turkish encroachments in the Mediterranean resulted in a stunning victory over the Turkish fleet in the Battle of Lepanto in 1571. But Philip's attempt to crush the revolt in the Netherlands and his tortured policy with England's Queen Elizabeth led to his greatest misfortunes.

Revolt of the Netherlands

As one of the richest parts of Philip's empire, the Spanish Netherlands was of great importance to the "Most Catholic King." Philip's attempt to strengthen his control in the Netherlands, which consisted of seventeen provinces (modern Netherlands, Belgium, and Luxembourg), soon led to a revolt. The nobles, who stood to lose the most politically if their jealously guarded privileges and freedoms were weakened, strongly opposed Philip's efforts. Resentment against Philip was also aroused by his use of taxes collected in the Netherlands to further Spanish interests. Finally, religion became a major catalyst for rebellion when Philip attempted to crush Calvinism. Violence erupted in 1566 when Calvinists—many of them nobles—began to smash statues and stained-glass windows in Catholic churches. Philip responded by sending the duke of Alva with ten thousand veteran Spanish and Italian troops to crush the rebellion.

But the revolt became organized, especially in the seven northern provinces, where the Dutch, under the

CHRONOLOGY	Wars of Religion in the Sixteenth Century	
The French Wars of Religion		1562–1598
Coronation of Henry IV		1594
Edict of Nantes		1598
Outbreak of revolt in the Netherlands		1566
Battle of Lepanto		1571
Spanish armada		1588
Twelve-year truce (Spain and the Netherlands)		1609
Independence of the United Provinces		1648

leadership of William of Nassau, the prince of Orange, offered growing resistance. The struggle dragged on for decades until 1609, when a twelve-year truce ended the war, virtually recognizing the independence of the northern provinces. These seven northern provinces, which began to call themselves the United Provinces of the Netherlands in 1581, soon emerged as the Dutch Republic, although the Spanish did not formally recognize them as independent until 1648. The ten southern provinces remained a Spanish possession.

The Netherlands

The England of Elizabeth

After the death of Queen Mary in 1558, her half-sister Elizabeth, the daughter of Henry VIII and Anne Boleyn, ascended the throne of England. During Elizabeth's reign, England rose to prominence as the relatively small island kingdom became the leader of the Protestant nations of Europe and laid the foundations for a world empire.

Intelligent, cautious, and self-confident, Elizabeth moved quickly to solve the difficult religious problem she inherited from her half-sister. Elizabeth's religious policy was based on moderation and compromise (see the box on p. 254). The Catholic laws of Mary's reign were repealed, and the new Act of Supremacy designated Elizabeth as "the only supreme governor" of both church and state. The church service used during the reign of Edward VI was revised to make it more acceptable to Catholics. The Church of England under Elizabeth was basically Protestant, but of a moderate sort that kept most people satisfied.

Caution, moderation, and expediency also dictated Elizabeth's foreign policy. Fearful of other countries' motives, Elizabeth realized that war could be disastrous for her island kingdom and her own rule. While encouraging

QUEEN ELIZABETH ADDRESSES PARLIAMENT (1601)

*Q*ueen Elizabeth I ruled England from 1558 to 1603 with a consummate skill that contemporaries considered unusual in a woman. Though shrewd and paternalistic, Elizabeth, like other sixteenth-century monarchs, depended for her power on the favor of her people. This selection is taken from her speech to Parliament in 1601, when she had been forced to retreat on the issue of monopolies after vehement protest by members of Parliament. Although the speech was designed to make peace with Parliament, some historians also feel that it was a sincere expression of the rapport that existed between the queen and her subjects.

Queen Elizabeth I, "The Golden Speech"

I do assure you there is no prince that loves his subjects better, or whose love can countervail our love. There is no jewel, be it of never so rich a price, which I set before this jewel: I mean your love. For I do esteem it more than any treasure of riches. . . . And, though God has raised me high, yet this I count the glory of my crown, that I have reigned with your loves. This makes me that I do not so much rejoice that God has made me to be a Queen, as to be a Queen over so thankful a people. . . .

Of myself I must say this: I never was any greedy, scraping grasper, nor a strait, fast-holding Prince, nor yet a waster. My heart was never set on any worldly goods, but only for my subjects' good. What you bestow on me, I will not hoard it up, but receive it to bestow on you again. Yea, mine own properties I account yours, to be expended for your good. . . .

I have ever used to set the Last-Judgment Day before mine eyes, and so to rule as I shall be judged to answer before a higher judge, to whose judgment seat I do appeal, that never thought was cherished in my heart that tended not unto my people's good. And now, if my kingly bounties have been abused, and my grants turned to the hurt of my people, contrary to my will and meaning, and if any in authority under me neglected or perverted what I have committed to them, I hope God will not lay their [crimes] and offenses to my charge; who, though there were danger in repealing our grants, yet what danger would I not rather incur for your good, than I would suffer them still to continue?

There will never Queen sit in my seat with more zeal to my country, care for my subjects, and that will sooner with willingness venture her life for your good and safety, than myself. For it is my desire to live nor reign no longer than my life and reign shall be for your good. And though you have had and may have many princes more mighty and wise sitting in this seat, yet you never had nor shall have any that will be more careful and loving.

What are the arguments that Elizabeth makes in her speech to Parliament? How does this speech reveal Elizabeth's intelligence as a ruler?

English piracy and providing clandestine aid to French Huguenots and Dutch Calvinists to weaken France and Spain, Elizabeth pretended complete aloofness and avoided alliances that would force her into war with any major power. Gradually, however, Elizabeth was drawn into conflict with Spain. After years of resisting the idea of invading England as too impractical, Philip II of Spain was finally persuaded to do so by advisers who assured him that the people of England would rise against their queen when the Spaniards arrived. A successful invasion of England would mean the overthrow of heresy and the return of England to Catholicism, surely an act in accordance with the will of God. Philip therefore ordered preparations for an armada (fleet of warships) to spearhead the invasion of England in 1588.

The armada proved a disaster. The Spanish fleet that finally set sail had neither the ships nor the troops that Philip had planned to send. A conversation between a papal emissary and an officer of the Spanish fleet before the armada departed reveals the fundamental flaw:

"And if you meet the English armada in the Channel, do you expect to win the battle?"

"Of course," replied the Spaniard.

"How can you be so sure?" [asked the emissary.]

"It's very simple. It is well known that we fight in God's cause. So, when we meet the English, God will surely arrange matters so that we can grapple and board them, either by sending some strange streak of weather, or, more likely, just by depriving the English of their wits. If we can come to close quarters, Spanish valor and Spanish steel (and the great masses of soldiers we shall have on board) will make our victory certain. But unless God helps us by a miracle the English, who have faster and handier ships than ours, and many more long-range guns, and who know their advantage just as well as we do, will never close with us at all, but stand aloof and knock us to pieces with their culverins, without our being able to do them any serious hurt. So," concluded the captain, and one fancies a grim smile, "we are sailing against England in the confident hope of a miracle."[12]

The hoped-for miracle never materialized. The Spanish fleet, battered by a number of encounters with the

Procession of Queen Elizabeth I.
Intelligent and learned, Elizabeth was familiar with Latin and Greek and spoke several European languages. Served by able administrators, she ruled for nearly forty-five years and generally avoided open military action against any major power. Her participation in the revolt of the Netherlands, however, brought England into conflict with Spain. This picture, painted near the end of her reign, shows the queen on a ceremonial procession.

English, sailed back to Spain by a northward route around Scotland and Ireland along which it was further battered by storms. Although the English and Spanish would continue their war for another sixteen years, the defeat of the Spanish armada guaranteed for the time being that England would remain a Protestant country. Although Spain made up for its losses within a year and a half, the defeat was a psychological blow to the Spaniards.

TIMELINE

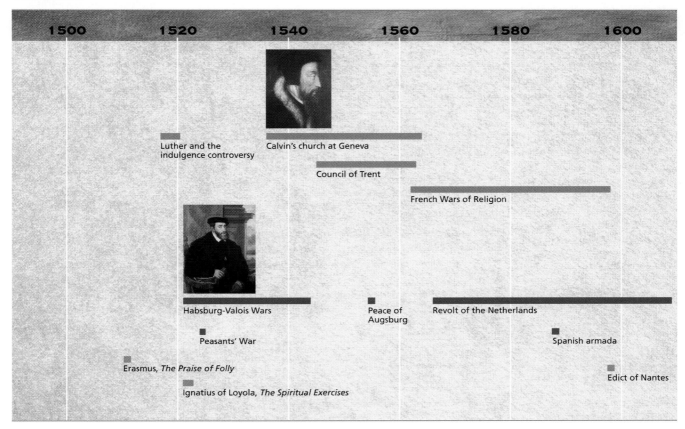

| 1500 | 1520 | 1540 | 1560 | 1580 | 1600 |

Luther and the indulgence controversy

Calvin's church at Geneva

Council of Trent

French Wars of Religion

Habsburg-Valois Wars

Peace of Augsburg

Revolt of the Netherlands

Peasants' War

Spanish armada

Erasmus, *The Praise of Folly*

Edict of Nantes

Ignatius of Loyola, *The Spiritual Exercises*

When the Augustinian monk Martin Luther burst onto the scene with a series of theses on indulgences, few people suspected that his observations would eventually split all of Europe along religious lines. But the yearning for reform of the church and meaningful religious experience caused a seemingly simple dispute to escalate into a powerful movement.

Although Luther felt that his revival of Christianity based on his interpretation of the Bible should be acceptable to all, others soon appeared who also read the Bible but interpreted it in different ways. Protestantism fragmented into different sects, which, though united in their dislike of Catholicism, were themselves divided over the interpretation of the sacraments and religious practices. As reform ideas spread, religion and politics became ever more intertwined.

By 1555, Lutheranism had lost much of its momentum; its energy was largely replaced by the new Protestant form of Calvinism, which had a clarity of doctrine and a fervor that made it attractive to a whole new generation of Europeans. Although Calvinism's militancy enabled it to expand across Europe, Catholicism was also experiencing its own revival and emerged as a militant faith, prepared to do combat for the souls of the faithful. An age of religious passion was followed by an age of religious warfare.

That people who were disciples of the Apostle of Peace would kill each other—often in brutal and painful fashion—aroused skepticism about Christianity itself. As one German writer put it, "Lutheran, popish, and Calvinistic, we've got all these beliefs here; but there is some doubt about where Christianity has got."[13] It is surely no accident that the search for a stable, secular order of politics and for order in the universe through natural laws soon came to play important roles. Before we look at this search for order in the seventeenth century, however, we need first to look at the adventures that plunged Europe into its new role in the world.

NOTES

1. D. Erasmus, *The Paraclesis,* in J. Olin, ed., *Christian Humanism and the Reformation: Selected Writings of Erasmus,* 3d ed. (New York, 1987), p. 101.
2. J. P. Dolan, ed., *The Essential Erasmus* (New York, 1964), p. 149.
3. Quoted in A. E. McGrath, *Reformation Thought: An Introduction* (Oxford, 1988), p. 72.
4. Quoted in E. G. Rupp and B. Drewery, eds., *Martin Luther* (New York, 1970), p. 50.
5. Quoted in R. Bainton, *Here I Stand: A Life of Martin Luther* (New York, 1950), p. 144.
6. Quoted in D. L. Jensen, *Reformation Europe* (Lexington, Mass., 1981), p. 83.
7. J. Calvin, *Institutes of the Christian Religion,* trans. J. Allen (Philadelphia, 1936), vol. 1, p. 228; vol. 2, p. 181.
8. Quoted in R. Bainton, *Women of the Reformation in Germany and Italy* (Boston, 1971), p. 154.
9. Quoted in B. S. Anderson and J. P. Zinsser, *A History of Their Own: Women in Europe from Prehistory to the Present* (New York, 1988), vol. 1, p. 259.
10. Quoted in J. A. Phillips, *Eve: The History of an Idea* (New York, 1984), p. 105.
11. Quoted in J. O'Malley, *The First Jesuits* (Cambridge, Mass., 1993), p. 76.
12. Quoted in G. Mattingly, *The Armada* (Boston, 1959), pp. 216–217.
13. Quoted in T. Schieder, *Handbuch der Europäischen Geschichte* (Stuttgart, 1979), vol. 3, p. 579.

SUGGESTIONS FOR FURTHER READING

Basic surveys of the Reformation period include **H. J. Grimm, *The Reformation Era, 1500–1650,*** 2d ed. (New York, 1973); **C. Lindberg,** *The European Reformations* (Cambridge, Mass., 1996); **D. L. Jensen, *Reformation Europe*** (Lexington, Mass., 1981); **G. R. Elton** *Reformation Europe, 1517–1559* (Cleveland, Ohio, 1963); **J. D. Tracy, *Europe's Reformations, 1450–1650*** (Oxford, 1999); **D. MacCulloch, *The Reformation*** (New York, 2003); and **E. Cameron, *The European Reformation*** (New York, 1991). The significance of the Protestant Reformation is examined in **S. Ozment, *Protestants: The Birth of a Revolution*** (New York, 1992). A brief but very useful introduction to the theology of the Reformation can be found in **A. McGrath, *Reformation Thought: An Introduction,*** 3d rev. ed. (Oxford, 1999).

The development of humanism outside Italy is examined in **C. G. Nauert Jr., *Humanism and the Culture of Renaissance Europe*** (Cambridge, 1995). On Erasmus, see **J. McConica, *Erasmus*** (Oxford, 1991).

The classic account of Martin Luther's life is **R. Bainton, *Here I Stand: A Life of Martin Luther*** (New York, 1950). More recent works include **H. A. Oberman, *Luther*** (New York, 1992), and **J. M. Kittelson, *Luther the Reformer: The Story of the Man and His Career*** (Minneapolis, 1986). See also the brief biography by **M. Marty, *Martin Luther*** (New York, 2004). On the Peasants' War, see especially **P. Blickle, *The Revolution of 1525: The German Peasants' War from a New Perspective*** (Baltimore, 1981). On the role of Charles V, see **W. Maltby, *The Reign of Charles V*** (New York, 2002).

The best account of Ulrich Zwingli is **G. R. Potter, *Zwingli*** (Cambridge, 1976), although **W. P. Stephens's *Zwingli*** (Oxford, 1994) is an important study of the man's ideas. The most comprehensive account of the various groups and individuals who are called Anabaptists is **G. H. Williams, *The Radical Reformation,*** 2d ed. (Kirksville, Mo., 1992).

Two worthwhile surveys of the English Reformation are **A. G. Dickens, *The English Reformation,*** 2d ed. (New York, 1989), and **G. R. Elton, *Reform and Reformation: England, 1509–1558*** (Cambridge, Mass., 1977). On John Calvin, see **A. McGrath, *A Life of John Calvin: A Study in the Shaping of Western Culture*** (Cambridge,

Mass., 1990), and **W. J. Bouwsma,** *John Calvin* (New York, 1988). On the impact of the Reformation on the family, see **J. F. Harrington, *Reordering Marriage and Society in Reformation Germany*** (New York, 1995). **M. E. Wiesner's *Working Women in Renaissance Germany*** (New Brunswick, N.J., 1986) covers primarily the sixteenth century.

Good introductions to the Catholic Reformation can be found in **M. R. O'Connell, *The Counter-Reformation, 1559–1610*** (New York, 1974), and **R. P. Hsia, *The World of Catholic Renewal, 1540–1770*** (Cambridge, 1998). For new perspectives, see **R. Bireley, *The Refashioning of Catholicism, 1450–1700*** (Washington, D.C., 1999), and **J. O'Malley, *Trent and All That: Renaming Catholicism in the Early Modern Era*** (Cambridge, Mass., 2002). On Loyola, see **P. Caravan, *Ignatius Loyola: A Biography of the Founder of the Jesuits*** (San Francisco, 1990). **J. O'Malley, *The First Jesuits*** (Cambridge, Mass., 1995), offers a clear discussion of the founding of the Jesuits.

For good introductions to the French Wars of Religion, see **M. P. Holt, *The French Wars of Religion, 1562–1629*** (Cambridge, 1995), and **R. J. Knecht, *The French Wars of Religion, 1559–1598,*** 2d ed. (New York, 1996). A good history of Spain in the sixteenth century is **J. Lynch, *Spain, 1516–1598: From Nation-State to World Empire*** (Cambridge, Mass., 1994). On Philip II, see **G. Parker, *Philip II,*** 3d ed. (Chicago, 1995). Elizabeth's reign can be examined in two good biographies: **C. Haigh, *Elizabeth I,*** 2d ed. (New York, 1998), and **W. T. MacCaffrey, *Elizabeth I*** (London, 1993). The classic work on

the Spanish armada is the beautifully written book *The Armada* by **G. Mattingly** (Boston, 1959).

Thomson NOW! Enter *ThomsonNOW* using the access card that is available for *Western Civilization: A Brief History*. *ThomsonNOW* will help you understand this chapter with lesson plans generated for your needs. In addition, you can read the following documents, and many more, online:

Martin Luther, *Letter to the German Nobility, On Christian Liberty* and *Twelve Articles*
John Calvin, *Institutes of the Christian Religion*
Pope Paul III, Canons on Justification
King Henry IV, Edict of Nantes

WESTERN CIVILIZATION RESOURCES

Visit the Web site for *Western Civilization: A Brief History* for resources specific to this book:

http://www.thomsonedu.com/history/spielvogel

For a variety of tools to help you succeed in this course, visit the Western Civilization Resource Center at

http://history.wadsworth.com/spielvogel

Included are quizzes, images, documents, interactive simulations, maps and timelines, movie explorations, and a wealth of other sources.

EUROPE AND THE WORLD: NEW ENCOUNTERS, 1500–1800

CHAPTER OUTLINE AND FOCUS QUESTIONS

On the Brink of a New World

☐ Why did Europeans begin to embark on voyages of discovery and expansion at the end of the fifteenth century?

New Horizons: The Portuguese and Spanish Empires

☐ How did Portugal and Spain acquire their overseas empires, and how did their empires differ?

New Rivals on the World Stage

☐ How did the arrival of the Dutch, British, and French on the world scene in the seventeenth and eighteenth centuries affect Africa, India, Southeast Asia, China, and Japan?

Toward a World Economy

☐ What was mercantilism, and what was its relationship to colonial empires?

The Impact of European Expansion

☐ How did European expansion affect both the conquerors and the conquered?

CRITICAL THINKING

☐ What was the relationship between European overseas expansion and political, economic, and social developments in Europe?

A late-sixteenth-century map of the Americas featuring Columbus, Vespucci, Magellan, and Pizarro

WHILE MANY EUROPEANS were occupied with the problems of dynastic expansion and religious reform, others were taking voyages that propelled Europeans far beyond the medieval walls in which they had been enclosed for almost a thousand years. One of these adventurers was the Portuguese explorer Ferdinand Magellan. Convinced that he could find a sea passage to Asia through America, Magellan persuaded the king of Spain to finance an exploratory voyage. On August 10, 1519, Magellan set sail on the Atlantic with five ships and a Spanish crew of 277 men. After a stormy and difficult crossing of the ocean, Magellan's fleet moved down the coast of South America, searching for the strait that would take him through. His Spanish ship captains thought he was crazy: "The fool is obsessed with his search for a strait," one remarked. "On the flame of his ambition he will crucify us all." At last, in October 1520, he found it, passing through a narrow waterway (later named the Strait of Magellan) and emerging into an unknown ocean that he called the Pacific Sea. Magellan reckoned that it would then be a short distance to the Spice Islands of the East, but he was badly mistaken. Week after week, he and his crew sailed on across the Pacific as their food supplies dwindled. According to one account, "When their last biscuit had gone, they scraped the maggots out of the casks, mashed them and served them as gruel. They made cakes out of sawdust soaked with the urine of rats—the rats themselves, as delicacies, had long since been hunted to extinction." At last they reached the Philippines (named after King Philip II of Spain), where Magellan met his death at the hands of the natives. Although only one of his original fleet of five ships survived and returned to Spain, Magellan is still remembered as the first person to circumnavigate the world.

At the beginning of the sixteenth century, European adventurers like Magellan had begun launching small fleets into the vast reaches of the Atlantic Ocean. They were hardly aware that they were beginning a new era, not only for Europe, but for the peoples of Asia, Africa, and the Americas as well. Nevertheless, the voyages of these Europeans marked the beginning of a process that led to radical changes in the political, economic, and cultural life of the entire world.

Between 1500 and 1800, European power engulfed the globe. In the Americas, Europeans established colonies that spread their laws, religions, and cultures. In the island regions of Southeast Asia, Europeans firmly implanted their rule. In Africa and other parts of Asia, their trading activities dramatically affected the lifeways of the local peoples.◆

On the Brink of a New World

Never has the dynamic and at times ruthless energy of Western civilization been more apparent than during its sixteenth-century expansion into the rest of the world. By then the Atlantic seaboard had become the center of a commercial activity that raised Portugal and Spain and later the Dutch Republic, England, and France to prominence. Global expansion was a crucial factor in Europe's transition from the agrarian economy of the Middle Ages to a commercial and industrial capitalistic system that survives to this day. Expansion also led Europeans into new and lasting contacts with non-European peoples that inaugurated a new interactive age of world history in the sixteenth century.

The Motives for Expansion

Europeans had long been attracted to lands outside of Europe. Indeed, a large body of fantasy literature about "other worlds" blossomed in the Middle Ages. In *The Travels of John Mandeville* in the fourteenth century, the author spoke of lands (which he had never seen) filled with precious stones and gold. Other lands were more frightening, "where the folk be great giants of twenty-eight foot long, or thirty foot long. . . . And they eat more gladly man's flesh than any other flesh," as well as lands farther north full of "cruel and evil women. And they have precious stones in their eyes. And they be of that kind that if they behold any

man with wrath they slay him at once with the beholding."[1] Other writers spoke of mysterious Christian kingdoms: the magical kingdom of Prester John in Africa and a Christian community in southern India that was supposedly founded by Thomas, the apostle of Jesus.

Although Muslim control of Central Asia cut Europe off from the countries farther east, the Mongol conquests in the thirteenth century had reopened the doors. The most famous medieval travelers to the East were the Polos of Venice. Niccolò and Maffeo, merchants from Venice, accompanied by Niccolò's son Marco, undertook the lengthy journey to the court of the great Mongol ruler Khubilai Khan (1259–1294) in 1271. An account of Marco's experiences, the *Travels*, proved to be the most informative of all the descriptions of Asia by medieval European travelers. Others followed the Polos, but in the fourteenth century, the conquests of the Ottoman Turks and then the breakup of the Mongol Empire reduced Western traffic to the East. With the closing of the overland routes, a number of people in Europe became interested in the possibility of reaching Asia by sea to gain access to the spices and other precious resources of the region. Christopher Columbus had a copy of Marco Polo's *Travels* in his possession when he began to envision his epoch-making voyage across the Atlantic Ocean.

An economic motive thus loomed large in Renaissance European expansion. Merchants, adventurers, and government officials had high hopes of finding precious metals and new areas of trade. Many European explorers and conquerors did not hesitate to express their desire for material gain. One Spanish conquistador explained that he and his kind went to the New World to "serve God and His Majesty, to give light to those who were in darkness, and to grow rich, as all men desire to do."[2]

This statement expresses another major reason for the overseas voyages—religious zeal. Hernán Cortés, the conqueror of Mexico, asked his Spanish rulers if it was not their duty to ensure that the native Mexicans "are introduced into and instructed in their holy Catholic faith."[3] Spiritual and secular affairs were closely intertwined in the sixteenth century. No doubt grandeur and glory, as well as plain intellectual curiosity and the spirit of adventure, also played some role in the European expansion.

The Means for Expansion

If "God, glory, and gold" were the motives, what made the voyages possible? First of all, the expansion of Europe was connected to the growth of centralized monarchies during the Renaissance. By the second half of the fifteenth century, European monarchies had increased both their authority and their resources and were in a position to turn their energies beyond their borders. At the same time, by the end of the fifteenth century, European states had achieved a level of wealth and technology that enabled them to undertake a regular series of voyages beyond Europe. Europeans had developed remarkably seaworthy ships and reliable navigational aids, such as the compass and astrolabe (an instrument used to determine the position of heavenly bodies).

One of the most important world maps available to Europeans at the end of the fifteenth century was that of Ptolemy, an astronomer of the second century A.D. Ptolemy's work, the *Geography*, had been known to Arab geographers as early as the eighth century, but it was not until the fifteenth century that a Latin translation was made. Printed editions of Ptolemy's *Geography*, which contained his world map, became available in 1477. Ptolemy's map showed the world as spherical with three major landmasses—Europe, Asia, and Africa—and only two oceans. In addition to showing the oceans as considerably smaller than the landmasses, Ptolemy had also dramatically underestimated the circumference of the earth, which led Columbus and other adventurers to believe that it would be feasible to sail west from Europe to Asia.

New Horizons: The Portuguese and Spanish Empires

Portugal took the lead in the European age of expansion when it began to explore the coast of Africa under the sponsorship of Prince Henry the Navigator (1394–1460). His motives were a blend of seeking a Christian kingdom as an ally against the Muslims, acquiring trade opportunities for Portugal, and extending Christianity.

The Development of a Portuguese Maritime Empire

In 1419, Portuguese fleets began probing southward along the western coast of Africa. After Prince Henry's death in 1460, exploration slowed, but Portuguese ships gradually crept down the African coast until Bartholomeu Dias finally rounded the Cape of Good Hope at the southern tip of Africa in 1488 (see Map 14.1). Ten years later, a fleet under the command of Vasco da Gama rounded the cape and stopped at several ports controlled by Muslim merchants along the coast of East Africa. Da Gama's fleet then crossed the Arabian Sea and reached the port of Calicut on the southwestern coast of India on May 18, 1498. Upon his arrival, da Gama announced to his surprised hosts that he had come in search of "Christians and spices." He did not find the first, but he did find the second. Although he lost two ships en route, da Gama's remaining vessels returned to Europe with their holds filled with ginger and cinnamon, a cargo that earned the investors a profit of several thousand percent. Da Gama's successful voyage marked the beginning of an all-water trade route to India. By 1501, annual Portuguese fleets to India were making serious inroads into the Mediterranean trade of the Venetians and Turks.

Under the direction of officials known as viceroys, Portugal now created an overseas empire. Most important of the viceroys was Alfonso d'Albuquerque (c. 1462–1515), a tough nobleman who took the lead in establishing a ring of commercial-military bases centered at Goa, just north of the Malabar Coast of India. The Portuguese also reached beyond India by taking the island of Macao at the mouth of the Pearl River in China. The Portuguese empire remained a limited one of enclaves or trading posts on the coasts of India and China. The Portuguese did not have the power, the people, or the desire to colonize the Asian regions.

Why were the Portuguese so successful? Basically, it was a matter of guns and seamanship. By the end of the

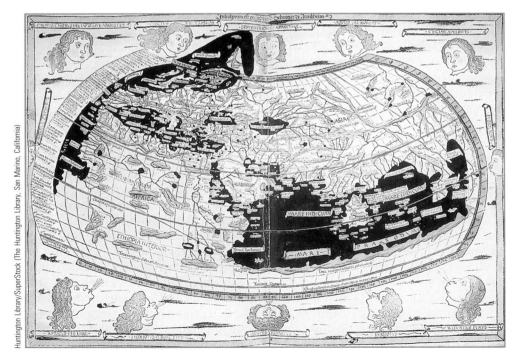

Ptolemy's World Map. Contained in the Latin translation of Ptolemy's *Geography* was this world map, which did not become available to Europeans until the late 1400s. Scholars quickly accepted it as the most accurate map of its time. The twelve "wind-faces," meant to show wind currents around the earth, were a fifteenth-century addition to the ancient map.

Huntington Library/SuperStock (The Huntington Library, San Marino, California)

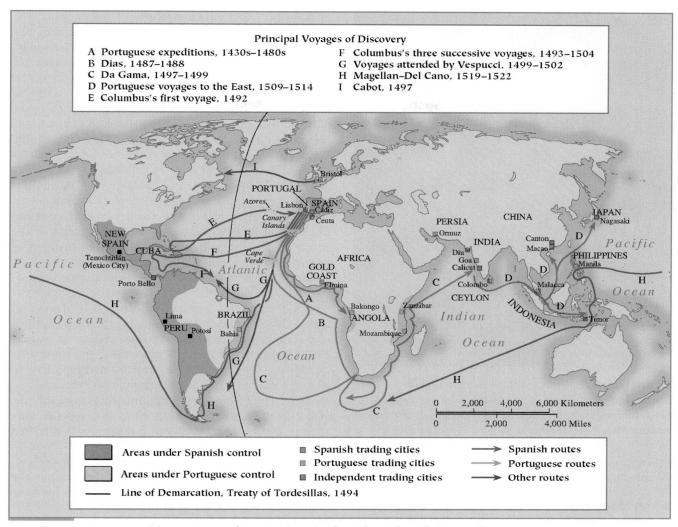

Principal Voyages of Discovery

A Portuguese expeditions, 1430s–1480s
B Dias, 1487–1488
C Da Gama, 1497–1499
D Portuguese voyages to the East, 1509–1514
E Columbus's first voyage, 1492
F Columbus's three successive voyages, 1493–1504
G Voyages attended by Vespucci, 1499–1502
H Magellan–Del Cano, 1519–1522
I Cabot, 1497

Areas under Spanish control
Areas under Portuguese control
Line of Demarcation, Treaty of Tordesillas, 1494
Spanish trading cities
Portuguese trading cities
Independent trading cities
Spanish routes
Portuguese routes
Other routes

MAP 14.1 **European Discoveries and Possessions in the Fifteenth and Sixteenth Centuries.** Desire for wealth was the main motivation of the early explorers, although spreading Christianity was also an important factor. Portugal under Prince Henry the Navigator initiated the first voyages in the early fifteenth century; Spain's explorations began at the century's end. ❓ Which regions of the globe were primarily explored by Portugal, and which were the main focus of Spain's voyages? 🕮 View an animated version of this map or related maps at http:// thomsonedu.com/history/spielvogel

sixteenth century, Portuguese fleets were heavily armed and able not only to intimidate but also to inflict severe defeats if necessary on local naval and land forces. The Portuguese did not possess a monopoly on the use of firearms and explosives, but their effective use of naval technology, heavy guns, and tactics gave them military superiority over lightly armed rivals that they were able to exploit until the arrival of other European forces—the English, Dutch, and French—in the seventeenth century.

Voyages to the New World

While the Portuguese were seeking access to the spice trade of the Indies by sailing eastward through the Indian Ocean, the Spanish were attempting to reach the same destination by sailing westward across the Atlantic. Although the Spanish came to overseas discovery and exploration after the initial efforts of Henry the Navigator, their greater resources enabled them to establish a far grander overseas empire quite different from that of the Portuguese.

An important figure in the history of Spanish exploration was an Italian known as Christopher Columbus (1451–1506). Europeans were aware that the world was round but had little understanding of its circumference or the size of the continent of Asia. Convinced that the earth was smaller and Asia larger than people thought, Columbus believed that Asia could be reached by sailing directly west instead of traveling around Africa. Rebuffed by the Portuguese, he persuaded Queen Isabella of Spain to finance his exploratory expedition.

Christopher Columbus. Columbus was an Italian explorer who worked for the queen of Spain. He has become a symbol for two entirely different perspectives. To some, he was a great and heroic explorer who discovered the New World; to others, especially in Latin America, he was responsible for beginning a process of invasion that led to the destruction of an entire way of life. Because Columbus was never painted in his lifetime, the numerous portraits of him are mostly fanciful rather than accurate. The portrait shown here was probably done by the Italian painter Ridolfo Ghirlandaio.

With three ships, the *Santa María*, the *Niña*, and the *Pinta*, and a crew of ninety men, Columbus set sail on August 3, 1492. On October 12, he reached the Bahamas and then went on to explore the coastline of Cuba and the northern shores of Hispaniola (present-day Haiti and the Dominican Republic). Columbus believed that he had reached Asia, and in his reports to Queen Isabella and King Ferdinand upon his return to Spain, he assured them not only that he would eventually find gold but also that they had a golden opportunity to convert the natives—whom Columbus persisted in calling "Indians"—to Christianity. In three subsequent voyages (1493, 1498, 1502), Columbus sought in vain to find a route to the Asian mainland. In his four voyages, Columbus landed on all the major islands of the Caribbean and the mainland of Central America, still convinced that he had reached the Indies in Asia.

Although Columbus clung to his belief until his death, other explorers soon realized that he had discovered a new frontier altogether. State-sponsored explorers joined the race to the New World. A Venetian seaman, John Cabot, explored the New England coastline of the Americas

under a license from King Henry VII of England. The continent of South America was discovered accidentally by the Portuguese sea captain Pedro Cabral in 1500. Amerigo Vespucci, a Florentine, accompanied several voyages and wrote a series of letters describing the geography of the New World. The publication of these letters led to the use of the name "America" (after Amerigo) for the new lands.

The first two decades of the sixteenth century witnessed numerous overseas voyages that explored the eastern coasts of both North and South America. Perhaps the most dramatic of all these expeditions was the journey of Ferdinand Magellan (1480–1521) in 1519. After passing through the strait named after him at the southern tip of South America, he sailed across the Pacific Ocean and reached the Philippines, where he met his death at the hands of the natives. Although only one of his original fleet of five ships survived and returned to Spain, Magellan's name is still associated with the first known circumnavigation of the earth.

The Europeans referred to the newly discovered territories as the New World, even though they contained flourishing civilizations populated by millions of people. But America was indeed new to the Europeans, who quickly saw opportunities for conquest and exploitation. The Spanish, in particular, were interested because the 1494 Treaty of Tordesillas had somewhat arbitrarily divided up the newly discovered world into separate Portuguese and Spanish spheres of influence, and it turned out that most of South America fell within the Spanish sphere. Hereafter the route east around the Cape of Good Hope was to be reserved for the Portuguese while the route across the Atlantic (except for the eastern hump of South America) was assigned to Spain.

The Spanish Empire in the New World

The Spanish **conquistadors** were hardy individuals motivated by a typical sixteenth-century blend of glory, greed, and religious zeal. Although authorized by the Castilian crown, these groups were financed and outfitted privately, not by the government. Their superior weapons, organizational skills, and determination brought the conquistadors incredible success. They also benefited from rivalries among the native peoples and the decimation of the native peoples by European diseases.

Early Civilizations in Mesoamerica Before the Spaniards arrived in the New World, Mesoamerica (modern Mexico and Central America) had already hosted a number of flourishing civilizations. Beginning around A.D. 300, a people known as the Maya had developed on the Yucatán peninsula one of the most sophisticated civilizations in the Americas. The Maya built splendid temples and pyramids, were accomplished artists, and devised a sophisticated calendar, as accurate as any in existence in the world at that time. The Maya were an agrarian people who cleared the dense rain forests, farmed, and created a

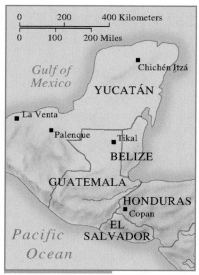

Lands of the Maya

patchwork of city-states. Mayan civilization came to include much of Central America and southern Mexico. For a number of reasons, Mayan civilization began to decline around 800 and collapsed within a century.

Sometime during the early twelfth century A.D., a people known as the Aztecs began a long migration that brought them to the Valley of Mexico. They established their capital at Tenochtitlán, on an island in the middle of Lake Texcoco (now the location of Mexico City). For the next hundred years, the Aztecs built their city, constructing temples, other public buildings, houses, and causeways of stone across Lake Texcoco to the north, south, and west, linking the many islands to the mainland.

The Aztecs were outstanding warriors, and while they were building their capital city, they also set out to bring the surrounding area under their control. By the early fifteenth century, they had become the leading city-state in the lake region. During the remainder of that century, the Aztecs consolidated their rule over much of what is modern Mexico, from the Atlantic to the Pacific Oceans and as far south as the Guatemalan border. The new kingdom was not a centralized state but a collection of semi-independent territories governed by local lords.

The Spanish Conquest of the Aztec Empire In 1519, a Spanish expedition under the command of Hernán Cortés (1485–1547) landed at Veracruz, on the Gulf of Mexico. He marched to the city of Tenochtitlán (see the box on p. 264) at the head of a small contingent of troops (550 soldiers and 16 horses); as he went, he made alliances with city-states that had tired of the oppressive rule of the Aztecs. Especially important was Tlaxcala, a state that the Aztecs had not been able to conquer. In November, Cortés arrived at Tenochtitlán, where he received a friendly welcome from the Aztec monarch Moctezuma (often called Montezuma). At first, Moctezuma believed that his visitor was a representative of Quetzalcoatl, the god who had departed from his homeland centuries before and had promised that he would return.

But the Spaniards quickly wore out their welcome. The took Moctezuma hostage and proceeded to pillage the city. In the fall of 1520, one year after Cortés had arrived, the local population revolted and drove the invaders from the city. Many of the Spaniards were killed, but the Aztecs soon experienced new disasters. As one Aztec related, "At about the time that the Spaniards had fled from Mexico, there came a great sickness, a pestilence, the smallpox." With no natural immunity to the diseases of Europeans, many Aztecs fell sick and died. Meanwhile, Cortés received fresh soldiers from his new allies; the state of Tlaxcala alone provided fifty thousand warriors. After four months, the city capitulated. And then the destruction began. The pyramids, temples, and palaces were leveled, and the stones were used to build Spanish government buildings and churches. The rivers and canals were filled in. The mighty Aztec Empire on mainland Mexico was no more. Between 1531 and 1550, the Spanish gained control of northern Mexico.

The Inca and the Spanish In the late fourteenth century, the Inca were a small community in the area of Cuzco, a city located at an altitude of 10,000 feet in the mountains of southern Peru. In the 1440s, however, under the leadership of their powerful ruler Pachakuti,

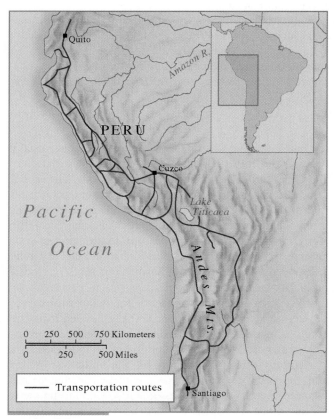

Lands of the Inca

The Aztec Empire

THE SPANISH CONQUISTADOR: CORTÉS AND THE CONQUEST OF MEXICO

*H*ernán Cortés was a minor Spanish nobleman who came to the New World in 1504 to seek his fortune. Contrary to his superior's orders, Cortés waged an independent campaign of conquest and overthrew the Aztec empire of Mexico (1519–1521). Cortés wrote a series of five reports to Emperor Charles V to justify his action. The second report includes a description of Tenochtitlán, the capital of the Aztec Empire. The Spanish conquistador and his men were obviously impressed by this city, awesome in its architecture yet built by people who lacked European technology, such as wheeled vehicles and tools of hard metal.

Cortés's Description of Tenochtitlán

The great city Tenochtitlán is built in the midst of this salt lake, and it is two leagues [about 6 miles] from the heart of the city to any point on the mainland. Four causeways lead to it, all made by hand and some twelve feet wide. The city itself is as large as Seville or Córdoba. The principal streets are very broad and straight, the majority of them being of beaten earth, but a few and at least half the smaller thoroughfares are waterways along which they pass in their canoes. Moreover, even the principal streets have openings at regular distances so that the water can freely pass from one to another, and these openings which are very broad are spanned by great bridges of huge beams, very stoutly put together, so firm indeed that over many of them ten horsemen can ride at once. . . .

The city has many open squares in which markets are continuously held and the general business of buying and selling proceeds. One square in particular is twice as big as that of Salamanca and completely surrounded by arcades where there are daily more than sixty thousand folk buying and selling. Every kind of merchandise such as may be met with in every land is for sale there, whether of food and victuals, or ornaments of gold and silver, or lead, brass, copper, tin, precious stones, bones, shells, snails and feathers; limestone for building is likewise sold there, stone both rough and polished, bricks burnt and unburnt, wood of all kinds and in all stages of preparation. . . . There is a street of herb-sellers where there are all manner of roots and medicinal plants that are found in the land. There are houses as it were of apothecaries where they sell medicines made from these herbs, both for drinking and for use as ointments and salves. . . .

Finally, to avoid [excess] in telling all the wonders of this city, I will simply say that the manner of living among the people is very similar to that in Spain, and considering that this is a barbarous nation shut off from a knowledge of the true God or communication with enlightened nations, one may well marvel at the orderliness and good government which is everywhere maintained.

The actual service of Moctezuma and those things which call for admiration by the greatness and state would take so long to describe that I assure your Majesty I do not know where to begin with any hope of ending. For as I have already said, what could there be more astonishing than that a barbarous monarch such as he should have reproductions made in gold, silver, precious stones, and feathers of all things to be found in his land, and so perfectly reproduced that there is no goldsmith or silversmith in the world who could better them.

What does Cortés focus on in his description of this Aztec city? Why do you think he felt justified in overthrowing the Aztec Empire?

---

the Inca launched a campaign of conquest that eventually brought the entire region under their control.

Pachakuti created a highly centralized state. The capital of Cuzco was transformed from a city of mud and thatch into an imposing city of stone. Under Pachakuti and his immediate successors, Topa Inca and Huayna Inca (the word *Inca* means "ruler"), the boundaries of the Inca Empire were extended as far as Ecuador, central Chile, and the edge of the Amazon basin. The empire included perhaps twelve million people.

The Inca were great builders. One major project was a system of 24,800 miles of roads that extended from the border of modern-day Colombia to a point south of modern-day Santiago, Chile. Two major roadways extended in a north-south direction, one through the Andes Mountains and the other along the coast, with connecting routes between them. Various types of bridges, including some of the finest examples of suspension bridges in premodern times, were built over ravines and waterways.

The Inca Empire was still flourishing when the first Spanish expeditions arrived in the area. In December 1530, Francisco Pizarro (c. 1475–1541) landed on the Pacific coast of South America with a band of about 180 men, but like Cortés, he had steel weapons, gunpowder, and horses, none of which were familiar to his hosts. Pizarro was also lucky because the Inca Empire had already succumbed to an epidemic of smallpox. Like the Aztecs, the Inca had no immunities to European diseases, and all too soon, smallpox was devastating entire villages. In another stroke of good fortune for Pizarro, even the Incan emperor was a victim. Upon the emperor's death, two sons claimed the throne, leading to a civil war. Pizarro took advantage of the situation by seizing Atahualpa, whose forces had just defeated his brother's. Armed only with stones, arrows, and light spears, Incan soldiers provided little challenge to the charging horses of the Spanish, let alone their guns and cannons. After executing Atahualpa, Pizarro and his soldiers, aided by their Incan allies, marched

Bartholomeu Dias sails around the tip of Africa	1488
Voyages of Columbus	1492–1502
Treaty of Tordesillas	1494
Vasco da Gama lands at Calicut in India	1498
Portuguese ships land in southern China	1514
Magellan's voyage around the world	1519–1522
Spanish conquest of Mexico	1519–1522
Pizarro's conquest of the Inca	1530–1535

on Cuzco and captured the Incan capital. By 1535, Pizarro had established a capital at Lima for a new colony of the Spanish Empire.

Administration of the Spanish Empire Spanish policy toward the native peoples of the New World was a combination of confusion, misguided paternalism, and cruel exploitation. Whereas the conquistadors made decisions based on expediency and their own interests, Queen Isabella declared the natives to be subjects of Castile and instituted the Spanish *encomienda,* a system that permitted the conquering Spaniards to collect tribute from the natives and use them as laborers. In return, the holders of an *encomienda* were supposed to protect the Indians, pay them wages, and supervise their spiritual needs. In practice, this meant that the settlers were free to implement the paternalistic system of the government as they pleased. Three thousand miles from Spain, Spanish settlers largely ignored their government and brutally used the Indians to pursue their own economic interests. Indians were put to work on plantations and in the lucrative gold and silver mines. Forced labor, starvation, and especially disease took a fearful toll of Indian lives. The natives were ravaged by the smallpox, measles, and typhus that came with the explorers and the conquistadors—perhaps 30 to 40 percent of them died. Hispaniola was badly devastated: of an initial population of 100,000 when Columbus arrived in 1493, only 300 natives survived by 1570.

In the New World, the Spanish developed an administrative system based on viceroys. Spanish possessions were initially divided into two major administrative units: New Spain (Mexico, Central America, and the Caribbean islands), with its center at Mexico City, and Peru (western South America), governed by a viceroy in Lima. Each viceroy served as the king's chief civil and military officer.

By papal agreement, the Catholic monarchs of Spain were given extensive rights over ecclesiastical affairs in the New World. They could appoint all bishops and clergy, build churches, collect fees, and supervise the affairs of the various religious orders that sought to Christianize the heathen. Catholic missionaries—especially the Dominicans, Franciscans, and Jesuits—fanned out across the Spanish Empire, where they converted and baptized hundreds of thousands of Indians in the early years of the conquest. Soon after the missionaries came the establishment of dioceses, parishes, cathedrals, schools, and hospitals—all the trappings of civilized European society.

New Rivals on the World Stage

Portugal and Spain had been the first Atlantic nations to take advantage of the Age of Exploration, starting in the late fifteenth century, and both had become great colonial powers. In the seventeenth century, however, their European neighbors to the north—first the Dutch and then the French and British—moved to replace the Portuguese and Spanish and create their own colonial empires. The new rivals and their rivalry soon had an impact on much of the rest of the world—in Africa, Asia, and the Americas.

Africa: The Slave Trade

Although the primary objective of the Portuguese in sailing around Africa was to find a sea route to the Spice Islands, they soon discovered that profits could be made in Africa itself. So did other Europeans who also realized the financial benefits of trade in slaves.

Of course, traffic in slaves was not new, and at first, the Portuguese simply replaced European slaves with African ones. During the second half of the fifteenth century, about a thousand slaves were taken to Portugal each year. Most wound up serving as domestic servants for affluent families in Europe. But the discovery of the Americas in the 1490s and the planting of sugarcane in South America and on the islands of the Caribbean changed the situation drastically.

Cane sugar had first been introduced to Europeans from the Middle East during the Crusades. During the sixteenth century, sugarcane plantations were set up along the eastern coast of Brazil and on several islands in the Caribbean. Because the growing of cane sugar demands both skill and large quantities of labor, the new plantations required more workers than could be provided by the small native population in the New World, decimated by diseases imported from the Old World. Since the climate and soil of much of West Africa were not conducive to the cultivation of sugar, African slaves began to be shipped to Brazil and the Caribbean to work on the plantations. The first were sent from Portugal, but in 1518, a Spanish ship carried the first boatload of African slaves directly from Africa to the New World.

Growth in the Slave Trade During the next two centuries, the trade in slaves grew dramatically and became part of the **triangular trade** that characterized the new Atlantic economy connecting Europe, Africa, and the American continents (see Map 14.2). European merchant ships (primarily those of Britain, France, Spain, Portugal, and the Dutch Republic) carried European manufactured

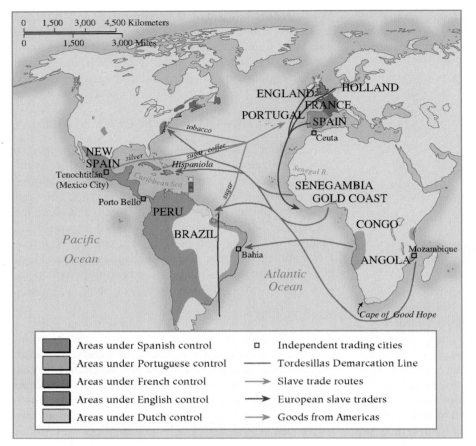

MAP 14.2 **Triangular Trade in the Atlantic Economy.** As the trade in slaves grew, it became a part of the triangular trade route that characterized the Atlantic economy, involving the exchange of goods and slaves between the western coast of Europe, the slave depots on the African coast, and the ports of North and South America. ❓ What were the important source regions for slaves, and where were most of the slaves taken? 🔊 **View an animated version of this map or related maps at** http://thomsonedu.com/history/spielvogel

Map legend:

- Areas under Spanish control
- Areas under Portuguese control
- Areas under French control
- Areas under English control
- Areas under Dutch control
- □ Independent trading cities
- —— Tordesillas Demarcation Line
- → Slave trade routes
- → European slave traders
- → Goods from Americas

goods, such as guns, gin, and cloth, to Africa, where they were traded for cargoes of slaves. The slaves were then shipped to the Americas and sold. European merchants then bought tobacco, molasses, sugar, rum, coffee, and raw cotton and shipped them back to Europe to be sold in European markets.

An estimated 275,000 enslaved Africans were exported to other countries during the sixteenth century, with two thousand going annually to the Americas alone. In the seventeenth century, the total climbed to over a million and jumped to six million in the eighteenth century, when the trade spread from West and Central Africa to East Africa. Altogether as many as ten million African slaves were transported to the Americas between the early sixteenth and nineteenth centuries.

One reason for the astonishing numbers of slaves, of course, was the high death rate. The arduous journey of slaves from Africa to the Americas became known as the **Middle Passage,** the middle leg of the triangular trade route. African slaves were closely packed into cargo ships,

The Sale of Slaves. The slave trade was one of the most profitable commercial enterprises of the eighteenth century. This painting shows a Western slave merchant negotiating with a local African leader over slaves at Gorée, Senegal, in West Africa in the late eighteenth century.

300 to 450 per ship, and chained in holds without sanitary facilities or enough space to stand up; there they remained during the voyage to America, which took at least 100 days (see the box on p. 268). Mortality rates averaged 10 percent; longer journeys due to storms or adverse winds resulted in even higher death rates. The Africans who survived the journey were subject to high death rates from diseases to which they had little or no immunity.

Before the coming of Europeans in the fifteenth century, most slaves in Africa were prisoners of war. When Europeans first began to take part in the slave trade, they bought slaves from local African merchants at slave markets in return for gold, guns, or other European goods such as textiles or copper or iron utensils.

Local slave traders originally obtained their supply from regions nearby, but as demand increased, they had to move farther inland to find their victims. In a few cases, local rulers became concerned about the impact of the slave trade on the well-being of their societies. In a letter to the king of Portugal in 1526, King Affonso of Congo (Bakongo) complained, "So great, Sire, is the corruption and licentiousness that our country is being completely depopulated."[4] Protests from Africans were generally ignored by Europeans as well as by other Africans.

Effects of the Slave Trade   The effects of the slave trade varied from area to area. Of course, it had tragic effects on the lives of the slaves and their families. There was also an economic price as the importation of cheap manufactured goods from Europe undermined local cottage industries and forced countless families into poverty. The slave trade also led to the depopulation of some areas and deprived many African communities of their youngest and strongest men and women.

The political effects of the slave trade were devastating. The need to maintain a constant supply of slaves led to increased warfare and violence as African chiefs and their followers, armed with guns acquired from the proceeds of the trade in slaves, increased their raids and wars on neighboring peoples. A few Europeans lamented what they were doing to traditional African societies. One Dutch slave trader remarked, "From us they have learned strife, quarrelling, drunkenness, trickery, theft, unbridled desire for what is not one's own, misdeeds unknown to them before, and the accursed lust for gold."[5] But the slave trade continued unabated.

Despite a rising chorus of humanitarian sentiments from European intellectuals, the use of black slaves remained largely acceptable to Western society. Europeans continued to view blacks as inferior beings fit primarily for slave labor. Not until the Society of Friends, known as the Quakers, began to criticize slavery in the 1770s and exclude from their church any member adhering to slave trafficking did European sentiment against slavery begin to build. Even then, it was not until the radical stage of the French Revolution in the 1790s that the French abolished slavery. The British followed suit in 1807. Despite the elimination of the African source, slavery continued in the newly formed United States until the 1860s.

The West in Southeast Asia

Portugal's efforts to dominate the trade of Southeast Asia were never totally successful. The Portuguese lacked both the numbers and the wealth to overcome local resistance and colonize the Asian regions. Portugal's empire was simply too large and Portugal too small to maintain it. By the end of the sixteenth century, new European rivals had entered the fray.

One of them was Spain. The Spanish had established themselves in the region when Magellan had landed in the Philippines. Although he was killed there, the Spanish were able to gain control over the Philippines, which eventually became a major Spanish base in the trade across the Pacific. Spanish ships carried silk and other luxury goods to Mexico in return for silver from the mines of Mexico.

The primary threat to the Portuguese Empire in Southeast Asia, however, came with the arrival of the Dutch and the English, who were better financed than the Portuguese. The shift in power began in the early seventeenth century when the Dutch seized a Portuguese fort in the Moluccas and then gradually pushed the Portuguese out of the spice trade. During the next fifty years, the Dutch occupied most of the Portuguese coastal forts along the trade routes throughout the Indian Ocean, including the island of Ceylon (today's Sri Lanka) and Malacca. The aggressive Dutch drove the English traders out of the spice market as well.

The Dutch also began to consolidate their political and military control over the entire area. On the island of Java, where they had established a fort at Batavia (modern Jakarta) in 1619, the Dutch found that it was necessary to bring the inland regions under their control to protect their position. On Java and the neighboring island of Sumatra, the Dutch East India Company established pepper plantations, which soon became the source of massive profits for Dutch merchants in Amsterdam. By the end of the eighteenth century, the Dutch had

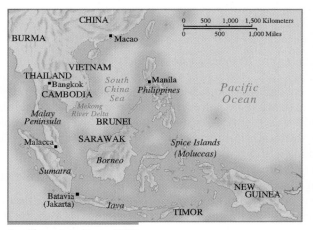

Southeast Asia, c. 1700

THE ATLANTIC SLAVE TRADE

*O*ne of the most odious practices of early modern Western society was the Atlantic slave trade, which reached its height in the eighteenth century. Blacks were transported in densely packed cargo ships from the western coast of Africa to the Americas to work as slaves in the plantation economy. This excerpt presents a criticism of the slave trade from an anonymous French writer.

Diary of a Citizen

As soon as the ships have lowered their anchors off the coast of Guinea, the price at which the captains have decided to buy the captives is announced to the Negroes who buy prisoners from various princes and sell them to Europeans. Presents are sent to the sovereign who rules over that particular part of the coast, and permission to trade is given. Immediately the slaves are brought by inhuman brokers like so many victims dragged to a sacrifice. White men who covet that portion of the human race receive them in a little house they have erected on the shore, where they have entrenched themselves with two pieces of cannon and twenty guards. As soon as the bargain is concluded, the Negro is put in chains and led aboard the vessel, where he meets his fellow sufferers. . . .

The vessel sets sail for the Antilles, and the Negroes are chained in a hold of the ship, a kind of lugubrious prison where the light of day does not penetrate, but into which the air is introduced by means of a pump. Twice a day some disgusting food is distributed to them. Their consuming sorrow and the sad state to which they are reduced would make them commit suicide if they were not deprived of all the means for an attempt upon their lives. Without any kind of clothing it would be difficult to conceal from the watchful eyes of the sailors in charge any instrument apt to alleviate their despair. The fear of a revolt, such as sometimes happens on the voyage from Guinea, is the basis of a common concern and produces as many guards as there are men in the crew. The slightest noise or a secret conversation among two Negroes is punished with utmost severity. All in all, the voyage is made in a continuous state of alarm on the part of the white men, who fear a revolt, and in a cruel state of uncertainty on the part of the Negroes, who do not know the fate awaiting them.

When the vessel arrives at a port in the Antilles, they are taken to a warehouse where they are displayed, like any merchandise, to the eyes of buyers. The plantation owner pays according to the age, strength, and health of the Negro he is buying. He has him taken to his plantation, and there he is delivered to an overseer who then and there becomes his tormentor. In order to domesticate him, the Negro is granted a few days of rest in his new place, but soon he is given a hoe and a sickle and made to join a work gang. Then he ceases to wonder about his fate; he understands that only labor is demanded of him. But he does not know yet how excessive this labor will be. As a matter of fact, his work begins at dawn and does not end before nightfall; it is interrupted for only two hours at dinnertime. The food a full-grown Negro is given each week consists of two pounds of salt beef or cod and two pots of tapioca meal.

What does this account reveal about the nature of slave trade practices and white attitudes toward blacks in the eighteenth century?

---

succeeded in bringing almost the entire Indonesian archipelago under their control.

The arrival of the Europeans had less impact on mainland Southeast Asia, where strong monarchies in Burma, Siam (modern Thailand), and Vietnam resisted foreign encroachment. In the sixteenth century, the Portuguese established limited trade relations with several mainland states, including Siam, Burma, Vietnam, and the remnants of the old Angkor kingdom in Cambodia. By the early seventeenth century, other nations had followed and had begun to compete actively for trade and missionary privileges. In general, however, these states were able to unite and drive the Europeans out.

In Vietnam, the arrival of Western merchants and missionaries coincided with a period of internal conflict among ruling groups in the country. After their arrival in the mid-seventeenth century, the European powers began to take sides in local politics, with the Portuguese and the Dutch supporting rival factions. The Europeans also set up trading posts for their merchants, but by the end of the seventeenth century, when it became clear that economic opportunities were limited, most of them were abandoned. French missionaries attempted to remain, but their efforts were blocked by the authorities, who viewed converts to Catholicism as a threat to the prestige of the Vietnamese emperor (see the box on p. 270).

The French and British in India

When a Portuguese fleet arrived at the port of Calicut in the spring of 1498, the Indian subcontinent was divided into a number of Hindu and Muslim kingdoms. But it was on the verge of a new era of unity that would be brought about by a foreign dynasty called the Mughals. The founders of the Mughal Empire were not natives of India but came from the mountainous region north of the Ganges River valley. The founder of the dynasty, Babur, had an illustrious background. His father was descended from the great Asian conqueror Tamerlane; his mother, from the Mongol conqueror Genghis Khan. It was

Europe in Asia. As Europeans began to move into parts of Asia, they reproduced many of the physical surroundings of their homeland in the port cities they built there. This is evident in comparing these two scenes. Below is a seventeenth-century view of Batavia, which the Dutch built as their headquarters on the northern coast of Java in 1619. The scene at the right is from a sixteenth-century engraving of Amsterdam. This Dutch city had become the financial and commercial capital of Europe. It was also the chief port for the ships of the Dutch East India Company, which brought the spices of the East to Europe.

Akbar, Babur's grandson, however, who brought Mughal rule to most of India, creating the greatest Indian empire since the Mauryan dynasty nearly two thousand years earlier.

The Impact of the Western Powers As we have seen, the first Europeans to arrive in India were the Portuguese. At first, Portugal dominated regional trade in the Indian Ocean, but at the end of the sixteenth century, the British and the Dutch arrived on the scene. Soon both powers were competing with Portugal, and with each other, for trading privileges in the region.

During the first half of the seventeenth century, the British presence in India steadily increased. By 1650, British trading posts had been established at Surat (a thriving port along the northwestern coast of India), Fort William (later the great city of Calcutta) near the Bay of Bengal, and Madras on the southeastern coast. From Madras, British ships carried Indian-made cotton goods to the East Indies, where they were bartered for spices, which were shipped back to Britain.

British success in India attracted rivals, including the Dutch and the French. The Dutch abandoned their interests

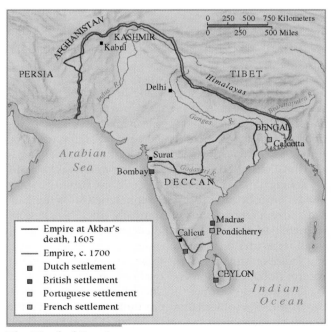

The Mughal Empire

WEST MEETS EAST: AN EXCHANGE OF ROYAL LETTERS

*E*conomic gain was not the only motivation of Western rulers who wished to establish a European presence in the East. In 1681, King Louis XIV of France wrote a letter to the king of Tonkin (the Trinh family head, then acting as viceroy to the Vietnamese emperor) asking permission for Christian missionaries to proselytize in Vietnam. The king of Tonkin politely declined the request.

A Letter to the King of Tonkin

Most high, most excellent, most mighty and most magnanimous Prince, our very dear and good friend, may it please God to increase your greatness with a happy end!

We hear from our subjects who were in your Realm what protection you accorded them. We appreciate this all the more since we have for you all the esteem that one can have for a prince as illustrious through his military valor as he is commendable for the justice which he exercises in his Realm. . . . Since the war which we have had for several years, in which all of Europe had banded together against us, prevented our vessels from going to the Indies, at the present time, when we are at peace after having gained many victories and expanded our Realm through the conquest of several important places, we have immediately given orders to the Royal Company to establish itself in your kingdom as soon as possible. . . . We have given orders to have brought to you some presents which we believe might be agreeable to you. But the one thing in the world which we desire most, both for you and for your Realm, would be to obtain for your subjects who have already embraced the law of the only true God of heaven and earth, the freedom to profess it, since this law is the highest, the noblest, the most sacred and especially the most suitable to have kings reign absolutely over the people.

We are even quite convinced that, if you knew the truths and the maxims which it teaches, you would give first of all to your subjects the glorious example of embracing it. We wish you this incomparable blessing together with a long and happy reign, and we pray God that it may please Him to augment your greatness with the happiest of endings.

Written at Saint-Germain-en-Laye, the 10th day of January; 1681.

Your very dear and good friend,
Louis

Answer from the King of Tonkin to Louis XIV

The King of Tonkin sends to the King of France a letter to express to him his best sentiments. . . . Your communication, which comes from a country which is a thousand leagues away, and which proceeds from the heart as a testimony of your sincerity, merits repeated consideration and infinite praise. Politeness toward strangers is nothing unusual in our country. There is not a stranger who is not well received by us. How then could we refuse a man from France, which is the most celebrated among the kingdoms of the world and which for love of us wishes to frequent us and bring us merchandise? These feelings of fidelity and justice are truly worthy to be applauded. As regards your wish that we should cooperate in propagating your religion, we do not dare to permit it, for there is an ancient custom, introduced by edicts, which formally forbids it. Now, edicts are promulgated only to be carried out faithfully; without fidelity nothing is stable. How could we disdain a well-established custom to satisfy a private friendship? . . . This then is my letter. We send you herewith a modest gift which we offer you with a glad heart.

This letter was written at the beginning of winter and on a beautiful day.

What are the underlying beliefs and approaches of these two rulers? How are they alike? How are they different?

---

to concentrate on the spice trade in the middle of the seventeenth century, but the French were more persistent and established their own forts on the east coast. For a brief period, the French competed successfully with the British, even capturing the British fort at Madras.

But the British were saved by the military genius of Sir Robert Clive (1725–1774), an aggressive British empire-builder who became the chief representative of the East India Company in India. Eventually, the French were restricted to the fort at Pondicherry and a handful of small territories on the southeastern coast.

In the meantime, Clive began to consolidate British control in Bengal, where the local ruler had attacked Fort William and imprisoned the local British population in the "Black Hole of Calcutta" (an underground prison for holding the prisoners, many of whom died in captivity). In 1757, a small British force numbering about three thousand defeated a Mughal-led army more than ten times its size in the Battle of Plassey. As part of the spoils of victory, the British East India Company received from the now-decrepit Mughal court the authority to collect taxes from lands in the area surrounding Calcutta. During the Seven Years' War (1756–1763), the British forced the French to withdraw completely from India (see Chapter 18).

China

In 1514, a Portuguese fleet dropped anchor off the coast of China. At the time, the Chinese thought little of the event. China appeared to be at the height of its power as the most magnificent civilization on the face of the earth. Its empire stretched from the steppes of Central Asia to the China Sea, from the Gobi Desert to the tropical rain forests of Southeast Asia. From the lofty perspective of the imperial throne in Beijing, the Europeans could only be seen as an unusual form of barbarian. To the Chinese ruler, the rulers of all other countries were simply "younger brothers" of the Chinese emperor, who was viewed as the Son of Heaven.

By the time the Portuguese fleet arrived off the coast of China, the Ming dynasty, which ruled from 1369 to 1644, had already begun a new era of greatness in Chinese history. Under a series of strong rulers, China extended its rule into Mongolia and Central Asia. The Ming even briefly reconquered Vietnam. Along the northern frontier, they strengthened the Great Wall and made peace with the nomadic tribesmen who had troubled China for centuries.

But the days of the Ming dynasty were numbered. After a period of prosperity and growth, the Ming gradually began to decline. During the late sixteenth century, a series of weak rulers led to a period of government corruption. As always, internal problems went hand in hand with unrest along the northern frontier. The Ming had tried to come to terms with the frontier tribes by making alliances with them. One of the alliances was with the Manchus, who lived northeast of the Great Wall in the area known today as Manchuria. In 1644, the Manchus overthrew the last Ming emperor and declared the creation of a new dynasty with the reign title of the Qing (Ch'ing,"Pure"). The Qing were blessed with a series of strong early rulers who pacified the country, corrected the most serious social and economic ills, and restored peace and prosperity. Two Qing monarchs, Kangxi and Qianlong, ruled China for well over a century, from the middle of the seventeenth century to the end of the eighteenth. They were responsible for much of the greatness of Manchu China.

The Qing Empire

Western Inroads Although China was at the height of its power and glory in the mid-eighteenth century, the first signs of the internal decay of the Manchu dynasty were beginning to appear. Unfortunately for China, the decline of the Qing dynasty occurred just as Europe was increasing pressure for more trade. The first conflict had come from the north, where Russian traders sought skins and furs. Formal diplomatic relations between China and Russia were established in 1689 and provided for regular trade between the two countries.

Dealing with the foreigners who arrived by sea was more difficult. By the end of the seventeenth century, the

English had replaced the Portuguese as the dominant force in European trade. Operating through the East India Company, which served as both a trading unit and the administrator of English territories in Asia, the English established their first trading post at Canton in 1699. Over the next decades, trade with China, notably the export of tea and silk to England, increased rapidly. To limit contacts between Europeans and Chinese, the Qing government confined all European traders to a small island just outside the city walls of Canton and permitted them to reside there only from October through March.

By the end of the eighteenth century, some British traders had begun to demand access to other cities along the Chinese coast and insist that the country be opened to British manufactured goods. In 1793, a British mission under Lord Macartney visited Beijing to press for liberalization of trade restrictions. But Emperor Qianlong expressed no interest in British products. The Chinese would later pay for their rejection of the British request (see Chapter 24).

Japan

At the end of the fifteenth century, Japan was at a point of near anarchy, but in the course of the sixteenth century, a number of powerful individuals achieved the unification of Japan. One of them, Tokugawa Ieyasu (1543–1616), took the title of *shogun* ("general") in 1603, an act that initiated the most powerful and longest-lasting of all the Japanese shogunates. The Tokugawa rulers completed the restoration of central authority and remained in power until 1868.

Opening to the West Portuguese traders had landed on the islands of Japan in 1543, and in a few years, Portuguese ships began stopping at Japanese ports on a regular basis to take part in the regional trade between Japan, China, and Southeast Asia. The first Jesuit missionary, Francis Xavier, arrived in 1549 and had some success in converting the local population to Christianity.

Initially, the visitors were welcomed. The curious Japanese were fascinated by tobacco, clocks, eyeglasses, and other European goods, and local nobles were interested in purchasing all types of European weapons and armaments. Japanese rulers found the new firearms especially helpful in defeating their enemies and unifying the islands.

The success of Catholic missionaries, however, created a strong reaction against the presence of Westerners. When missionaries began to interfere in local politics, Tokugawa Ieyasu, newly come to power, expelled them all and sanctioned the persecution of Japanese Christians.

European merchants were the next to go. The government closed the two major foreign trading posts on the island of Hirado and at Nagasaki. Only a small Dutch community in Nagasaki was allowed to remain in Japan. The Dutch, unlike the Spanish and Portuguese, had not allowed missionary activities to interfere with their trade

Arnaudet/Réunion des Musées Nationaux/Art Resource, NY (Musee des Arts Asiatiques-Guimet, Paris)

Arrival of the Portuguese at Nagasaki.   Portuguese traders landed accidentally in Japan in 1543. In a few years, they arrived regularly, taking part in a regional trade network between Japan, China, and Southeast Asia. In these panels, done in black lacquer and gold leaf, we see a late-sixteenth-century Japanese interpretation of the first Portuguese landing at Nagasaki.

interests. But the conditions for staying were strict. Dutch ships were allowed to dock at Nagasaki harbor once a year and could remain for only two to three months.

The Americas

In the sixteenth century, Spain and Portugal had established large colonial empires in the Americas. Portugal continued to profit from its empire in Brazil. The Spanish also maintained an enormous South American empire, but Spain's importance as a commercial power declined rapidly in the seventeenth century because of a drop in the output of the silver mines and the poverty of the Spanish monarchy. By the start of the seventeenth century, both Portugal and Spain found themselves facing new challenges to their American empires from the Dutch, British, and French, who increasingly sought to create their own colonial empires in the New World.

The West Indies   Both the French and British colonial empires in the New World included large parts of the West Indies. The British held Barbados, Jamaica, and Bermuda, and the French possessed Saint-Domingue, Martinique, and Guadeloupe. On these tropical islands, both the British and the French had developed plantation

economies, worked by African slaves, that produced tobacco, cotton, coffee, and sugar, all products increasingly in demand in Europe.

The "sugar factories," as the sugar plantations in the Caribbean were called, played an especially prominent role. By the 1780s, Jamaica, one of Britain's most important colonies, was producing 50,000 tons of sugar annually with the slave labor of 200,000 blacks. The French colony of Saint-Domingue (later known as Haiti) had 500,000 slaves working on three thousand plantations at the same time. This colony produced 100,000 tons of sugar a year, but at the expense of a high death rate from the brutal treatment of the slaves.

British North America   The Dutch were among the first to establish settlements on the North American continent after Henry Hudson, an English explorer hired by the Dutch, discovered in 1609 the river that bears his name. Within a few years, the Dutch had established the mainland colony of New Netherlands, which stretched from the mouth of the Hudson River as far north as Albany, New York. After 1650, competition from the English and French and years of warfare with those rivals led to the decline of the Dutch commercial empire. In 1664, the English

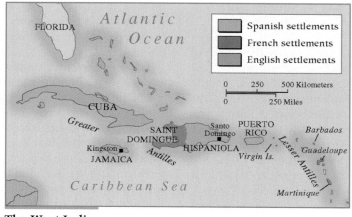

The West Indies

Portuguese traders land in Japan	1543
British East India Company formed	1600
Dutch East India Company formed	1602
English settlement at Jamestown	1607
Dutch fort established at Batavia	1619
Dutch seize Malacca from the Portuguese	1641
English seize New Netherlands	1664
English establish trading post at Canton	1699
Battle of Plassey	1757
French cede Canada to the British	1763
British mission to China	1793

seized the colony of New Netherlands and renamed it New York.

In the meantime, the British had begun to establish their own colonies in North America. The first permanent English settlement in America was Jamestown, founded in 1607 in modern Virginia. It barely survived, making it clear that the colonizing of American lands was not necessarily conducive to quick profits. But the desire to practice one's own religion, combined with economic interests, could lead to successful colonization, as the Massachusetts Bay Company demonstrated. The Massachusetts colony had four thousand settlers in its early years but by 1660 had swelled to forty thousand. By the end of the seventeenth century, the English had established control over most of the eastern seaboard of the present United States.

British North America came to consist of thirteen colonies. They were thickly populated, containing about 1.5 million people by 1750, and prosperous. Ostensibly run by the British Board of Trade, the Royal Council, and Parliament, these thirteen colonies had legislatures that tended to act independently. Merchants in such port cities as Boston, Philadelphia, New York, and Charleston resented and resisted regulation from the British government.

French North America   The French also established a colonial empire in North America. In 1663, Canada was made the property of the French crown and administered by a French governor like a French province.

French North America was run autocratically as a vast trading area, where valuable furs, leather, fish, and timber were acquired. However, the inability of the French government to get people to emigrate to its Canadian possessions left them thinly populated. By 1750, there were about fifteen thousand French Canadians, most of whom were hunters, trappers, missionaries, and explorers. The French failed to provide adequate men or money, allowing their Continental wars to take precedence over the conquest of the North American continent.

Toward a World Economy

During the High Middle Ages, Europeans had engaged in a commercial revolution that created new opportunities for townspeople in a basically agrarian economy. Although this commercial thrust was slowed by the crises of the fourteenth century, Europe's discovery of the world outside in the fifteenth century led to an even greater burst of commercial activity and the inception of a world market.

Economic Conditions in the Sixteenth Century

Inflation was a major economic problem in the sixteenth and early seventeenth centuries. This so-called **price revolution** was a Europe-wide phenomenon, although different areas were affected at different times. Foodstuffs were most subject to price increases. But wages failed to keep up with price increases. Wage earners, especially agricultural laborers and salaried workers in urban areas, saw their standard of living drop. At the same time, landed aristocrats, who could raise rents, managed to prosper. Commercial and industrial entrepreneurs also benefited from the price revolution because of rising prices, expanding markets, and relatively cheaper labor costs. Some historians regard this profit inflation as a valuable stimulus to investment and the growth of capitalism, laying the groundwork for the economic expansion and prosperity of the sixteenth century. Governments were likewise affected by inflation. They borrowed heavily from bankers and imposed new tax burdens on their subjects, often stirring additional discontent.

The Growth of Commercial Capitalism

The flourishing European trade of the sixteenth century revolved around three major areas: the Mediterranean in the south, the Low Countries and the Baltic region in the north, and central Europe, whose inland trade depended on the Rhine and Danube Rivers. As overseas trade expanded, however, the Atlantic seaboard began to play a more important role, linking all three trading areas together and making Europe into a more integrated market that was all the more vulnerable to price shifts.

The commercial expansion of the sixteenth and seventeenth centuries was made easier by new forms of commercial organization, especially the **joint-stock company.** Individuals bought shares in a company and received dividends on their investment while a board of directors ran the company and made the important business decisions. The return on investments could be spectacular. During its first ten years, investors received 30 percent on their money from the Dutch East India Company, which opened the Spice Islands and Southeast Asia to Dutch activity. The joint-stock company made it easier to raise large amounts of capital for world trading ventures.

Traditional family banking firms were no longer able to supply the numerous services needed for the commercial capitalism of the seventeenth century, and new institutions arose to take their place. In 1609, the city of Amsterdam created the Bank of Amsterdam as both a deposit and a transfer institution and the Amsterdam Bourse, or Exchange, where the trading of stocks replaced the exchange of goods. By the first half of the seventeenth century, the Amsterdam Exchange had emerged as the hub of the European business world, just as Amsterdam had replaced Antwerp as the greatest commercial and banking center of Europe.

Despite the growth of commercial capitalism, most of the European economy still depended on an agricultural system that had experienced few changes since the thirteenth century. At least 80 percent of Europeans still worked on the land. Almost all of the peasants of western Europe were free of serfdom, although many still owed a variety of feudal dues to the nobility. Despite the expanding markets and rising prices, European peasants saw little or no improvement in their lot as they faced increased rents and fees and higher taxes imposed by the state.

Mercantilism

Mercantilism is the name historians use to identify a set of economic tendencies that came to dominate economic practices in the seventeenth century. Fundamental to mercantilism was the belief that the total volume of trade was unchangeable. Since one nation could expand its trade and hence its prosperity only at the expense of others, to mercantilists, economic activity was war carried on by peaceful means.

According to the mercantilists, the prosperity of a nation depended on a plentiful supply of bullion, or gold and silver. For this reason, it was desirable to achieve a favorable balance of trade in which goods exported were of greater value than those imported, promoting an influx of gold and silver payments that would increase the quantity of bullion. Furthermore, to encourage exports, governments should stimulate and protect export industries and trade by granting trade monopolies, encouraging investment in new industries through subsidies, importing foreign artisans, and improving transportation systems by building roads, bridges, and canals. By placing high tariffs on foreign goods, they could be kept out of the country and prevented from competing with domestic industries. Colonies were also deemed valuable as sources of raw materials and markets for finished goods.

Mercantilism focused on the role of the state, believing that state intervention in some aspects of the economy was desirable for the sake of the national good. Government regulations to ensure the superiority of export goods, the construction of roads and canals, and the granting of subsidies to create trade companies were all predicated on government involvement in economic affairs.

Overseas Trade and Colonies: Movement Toward Globalization

Mercantilist theory on the role of colonies was matched in practice by Europe's overseas expansion. With the development of colonies and trading posts in the Americas and the East, Europeans embarked on an adventure in international commerce in the seventeenth century. Although some historians speak of a nascent world economy, we should remember that local, regional, and intra-European trade still predominated. About one-tenth of English and Dutch exports were shipped across the Atlantic; slightly more went to the East. What made the transoceanic trade rewarding, however, was not the volume but the value of its goods. Dutch, English, and French merchants were bringing back products that were still consumed largely by the wealthy but were beginning to make their way into the lives of artisans and merchants. Pepper and spices from the Indies, West Indian and Brazilian sugar, and Asian coffee and tea were becoming more readily available to European consumers.

Trade within Europe remained strong throughout the eighteenth century, although this trade increased only slightly while overseas trade boomed. From 1716 to 1789, total French exports quadrupled; intra-European trade, which constituted 75 percent of these exports in 1716, accounted for only 50 percent of the total in 1789. This increase in overseas trade has led some historians to proclaim the emergence of a truly global economy in the eighteenth century. Trade patterns now interlocked Europe, Africa, the East, and the Americas.

The Impact of European Expansion

Between 1500 and 1800, the Atlantic nations of Europe moved into all parts of the world. The first had been Spain and Portugal, the two great colonial powers of the sixteenth century, followed by the Dutch, who built their colonial empire in the seventeenth century as Portugal and Spain declined. The Dutch were soon challenged by the British and French, who outstripped the others in the eighteenth century while becoming involved in a bitter rivalry. By the end of the eighteenth century, it appeared that Great Britain would become the great European imperial power. European expansion made a great impact on both the conquerors and the conquered.

The Conquered

The native American civilizations, which had their own unique qualities and a degree of sophistication not much appreciated by Europeans, were virtually destroyed. In addition to enormous losses of population from European diseases, ancient social and political structures were ripped up and replaced by European institutions, religion, language, and culture. In Africa, European involvement in the slave trade had devastating effects, especially in coastal areas. The Portuguese trading posts in the East had little impact on native Asian civilizations, although Dutch control of the Indonesian archipelago was more intrusive. China and Japan were still little affected by Westerners, although India was subject to ever-growing British encroachment.

In Central and South America, a new civilization arose that we have come to call Latin America. It was a multiracial society. Spanish and Portuguese settlers who arrived in the Western Hemisphere were few in number compared to the native Indians; many of the newcomers were males who not only used female natives for their sexual pleasure but married them as well. Already by 1501, Spanish rulers had authorized intermarriage between Europeans and native American Indians, whose offspring became known as mestizos. Another group of people brought to Latin America were the Africans. Over a period of three centuries, possibly as many as eight million slaves were brought to Spanish and Portuguese America to work the plantations. Africans also contributed to Latin America's multiracial character. Mulattoes—the offspring of Africans and whites—joined mestizos and descendants of whites, Africans, and native Indians to produce a unique society in Latin America. Unlike Europe or British North America, Latin America developed a multihued society with less rigid attitudes about race.

The ecology of conquered areas was also affected by the European presence. Europeans brought horses and cattle to the Americas. Horses revolutionized the life of the Plains Indians. Europeans brought new crops, such as wheat and cane sugar, to be cultivated on large plantations by native or imported slave labor. In their trips to other parts of the world, Europeans also carried New World plants with them. Thus Europeans introduced sweet potatoes and maize (Indian corn) to Africa in the sixteenth century.

Catholic Missionaries   Although there were some Protestant missionaries in the world outside Europe, Catholic missionaries were far more active in spreading Christianity. From the beginning of their conquest of the New World, Spanish and Portuguese rulers were determined to Christianize the native peoples. This policy gave the Catholic church an important role to play in the New World, one that added considerably to church power. Catholic missionaries—especially the Dominicans, Franciscans, and Jesuits—fanned out to different parts of the Spanish Empire.

To facilitate their efforts, missionaries brought Indians together into villages, where the natives could be converted, taught trades, and encouraged to grow crops. These missions enabled the missionaries to control the lives of the Indians and helped ensure that they would remain docile members of the empire (see the box on p. 276). Basically, missions benefited the missionaries more than the Indians. In frontier districts such as California and Texas, missions also served as military barriers to foreign encroachment.

The Catholic church constructed hospitals, orphanages, and schools. Monastic schools instructed Indian students in the rudiments of reading, writing, and arithmetic. The Catholic church also provided outlets for women other than marriage. Nunneries were places of prayer and quiet contemplation, but women in religious orders, many of them of aristocratic background, often lived well and worked outside their establishments by running schools and hospitals. Indeed, one of these nuns, Sor Juana Inés de la Cruz (1651–1695), was one of seventeenth-century Latin America's best-known literary figures. She wrote poetry and prose and urged that women be educated.

Christian missionaries had also made the long voyage to China on European merchant ships. The Jesuits were among the most active and the most effective. Many of the early Jesuit missionaries to China were highly educated men who were familiar with European philosophical and scientific developments. They brought along clocks and various other instruments that impressed Chinese officials and made them more open to Western ideas.

The Jesuits used this openness to promote Christianity. To make it easier for the Chinese to accept Christianity, the Jesuits pointed to similarities between Christian morality and Confucian ethics. The efforts of the Christian missionaries reached their height in the early eighteenth century. Several hundred Chinese officials became Catholics, as did an estimated 300,000 ordinary Chinese. But ultimately the Christian effort was undermined by squabbling among the religious orders themselves. To make it easier for the Chinese to convert, the Jesuits had allowed the new Catholics to continue the practice of ancestor worship. Jealous Dominicans and Franciscans complained to the pope, who condemned the practice. Soon Chinese authorities began to suppress Christian activities throughout China.

The Jesuits also had some success in Japan, where they converted a number of local nobles. By the end of the sixteenth century, thousands of Japanese on the southernmost islands of Kyushu and Shikoku had become Christians. But the Jesuit practice of destroying local idols and shrines and turning some temples into Christian schools or churches caused a severe reaction. When a new group of Spanish Franciscans continued the same policies, the government ordered the execution of nine missionaries and a number of their Japanese converts.

The Conquerors

For some Europeans, expansion abroad brought hopes for land, riches, and social advancement. One Spaniard commented in 1572 that many "poor young men" left Spain for Mexico, where they might hope to acquire landed estates and call themselves "gentlemen." Although some wives accompanied their husbands abroad, many ordinary European women found new opportunities for marriage in the New World because of the lack of white women. Indeed, as one commentator bluntly put it, even "a whore, if handsome, [can] make a wife for some rich planter."[6] In the violence-prone world of early Spanish America, a number of women also found themselves rich after their husbands were killed unexpectedly. In one area of Central America, women owned about 25 percent of the landed estates by 1700.

THE MISSION

In 1609, two Jesuit priests embarked on a missionary calling with the Guaraní Indians in eastern Paraguay. Eventually, the Jesuits established more than thirty missions in the region. This description of a Jesuit mission in Paraguay was written by Félix de Azara, a Spanish soldier and scientist.

Félix de Azara, *Description and History of Paraguay and Rio de la Plata*

Having spoken of the towns founded by the Jesuit fathers, and of the manner in which they were founded, I shall discuss the government which they established in them...In each town resided two priests, a curate and a subcurate, who had certain assigned functions. The subcurate was charged with all the spiritual tasks, and the curate with every kind of temporal responsibility....

The curate allowed no one to work for personal gain; he compelled everyone, without distinction of age or sex, to work for the community, and he himself saw to it that all were equally fed and dressed. For this purpose the curates placed in storehouses all the fruits of agriculture and the products of industry, selling in the Spanish towns their surplus of cotton, cloth, tobacco, vegetables, skins, and wood, transporting them in their own boats down the nearest rivers, and returning with implements and whatever else was required.

From the foregoing one may infer that the curate disposed of the surplus funds of the Indian towns, and that no Indian could aspire to own private property. This deprived them of any incentive to use reason or talent, since the most industrious, able, and worthy person had the same food, clothing, and pleasures as the most wicked, dull, and indolent. It also follows that although this form of government was well designed to enrich the communities it also caused the Indian to work at a languid pace, since the wealth of his community was of no concern to him.

It must be said that although the Jesuit fathers were supreme in all respects, they employed their authority with a mildness and a restraint that command admiration. They supplied everyone with abundant food and clothing. They compelled the men to work only half a day, and did not drive them to produce more. Even their labor was given a festive air, for they went in procession to the fields, to the sound of music...and the music did not cease until they had returned in the same way they had set out. They gave them many holidays, dances, and tournaments, dressing the actors and the members of the municipal councils in gold or silver tissue and the most costly European garments, but they permitted the women to act only as spectators.

They likewise forbade the women to sew; this occupation was restricted to the musicians, sacristans, and acolytes. But they made them spin cotton; and the cloth that the Indians wove, after satisfying their own needs, they sold together with the surplus cotton in the Spanish towns, as they did with the tobacco, vegetables, wood, and skins. The curate and his companion, or subcurate, had their own plain dwellings, and they never left them except to take the air in the great enclosed yard of their college. They never walked through the streets of the town or entered the house of any Indian or let themselves be seen by any woman—or indeed, by any man, except for those indispensable few through whom they issued their orders.

How were the missions organized to enable missionaries to control many aspects of the Indian's lives? Why was this deemed necessary?

European expansion also had other economic effects on the conquerors. Wherever they went in the New World, Europeans sought to find sources of gold and silver. One Aztec commented that the Spanish conquerors "longed and lusted for gold. Their bodies swelled with greed, and their hunger was ravenous; they hungered like pigs for that gold."[7] Rich silver deposits were found and exploited in Mexico and southern Peru (modern Bolivia). When the mines at Potosí in Peru were opened in 1545, the value of precious metals imported into Europe quadrupled. Between 1503 and 1650, nearly 18,000 tons of silver and more than 200 tons of gold entered the port of Seville, setting off a price revolution in the Spanish economy.

But gold and silver were only two of the products that became part of the exchange between the New World and the Old. Historians refer to the reciprocal importation and exportation of plants and animals between Europe and the Americas as the **Columbian Exchange.** While Europeans were bringing horses, cattle, and wheat to the New World, they were taking new agricultural products such as potatoes, chocolate, corn, tomatoes, and tobacco back to Europe. Potatoes became especially popular as a basic dietary staple in some areas of Europe. High in carbohydrates and rich in vitamins A and C, potatoes could be easily stored for winter use and soon enabled more people to survive on smaller plots of land. This improvement in nutrition was soon reflected in a rapid increase in population.

The European lifestyle was greatly affected by new products from abroad. In addition to new foods, new drinks also appeared in Europe. Chocolate, which had been brought to Spain from Aztec Mexico, became a common drink by 1700. The first coffee and tea houses opened in London in the 1650s and spread rapidly to other parts of Europe. In the eighteenth century, a craze for Chinese furniture and porcelain spread among the upper classes. Chinese ideas would also make an impact on intellectual attitudes (see Chapter 17).

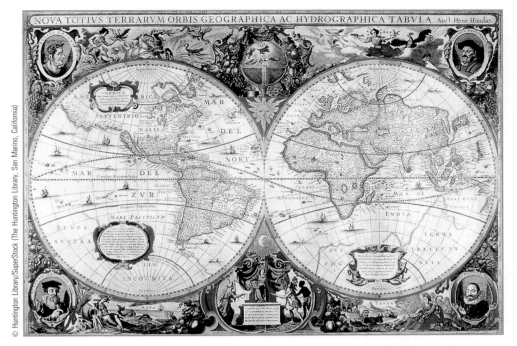

A Seventeenth-Century World Map. This beautiful map was prepared in 1630 by Henricus Hondius. The portraits in the corners are of Caesar, the Roman statesman; Ptolemy, the second-century astronomer; Mercator, the Flemish cartographer whose map projection Hondius followed; and Hondius himself. Comparing this map to the one of Ptolemy on page 260, you can see how much Europeans had learned about the shape of the world by the seventeenth century.

European expansion, which was in part a product of European rivalries, also deepened those rivalries and increased the tensions among European states. Bitter conflicts arose over the cargoes coming from the New World and Asia. The Anglo-Dutch trade wars and the British-French rivalry over India and North America became part of a new pattern of worldwide warfare in the eighteenth century (see Chapter 18). Bitter rivalries also led to state-sponsored piracy in which governments authorized private captains to attack enemy shipping and keep part of the proceeds for themselves.

In the course of their expansion, Europeans also came to have a new view of the world. When the travels began in the fifteenth century, Europeans were dependent on maps that were often fanciful and inaccurate. Their explorations helped them create new maps that gave a more realistic portrayal of the world, as well as new techniques called map projections that allowed them to represent the round surface of a sphere on a flat piece of paper. The most famous of these is the Mercator projection, the work of a Flemish cartographer, Gerardus Mercator (1512–1594). Mercator's is what mapmakers call a conformal projection, which tries to show the true shape of landmasses, but only of a limited area. On the Mercator projection, the shapes of lands near the equator are quite accurate, but the farther away from the equator they lie, the more exaggerated their size becomes. Nevertheless, the Mercator projection was valuable to ship captains. Every straight line on a Mercator projection is a line of true direction, whether north, south, east, or west. For four centuries, ship captains were very grateful to Mercator.

The psychological impact of colonization on the colonizers is awkward to evaluate but hard to deny. Europeans were initially startled by the discovery of new peoples in the Americas. Some deemed them inhuman and thus fit to be exploited for labor. Others, however, found them to be refreshingly natural and not yet touched by European corruption. But even most members of the latter group believed that the Indians should be converted—if not forcefully, at least peacefully—to Christianity. Overall, the relatively easy European success in dominating native peoples (in Africa and America) reinforced Christian Europe's belief in the inherent superiority of European civilization and religion. The Scientific Revolution of the seventeenth century (see Chapter 16), the Enlightenment of the eighteenth (see Chapter 17), and the imperialism of the nineteenth (see Chapter 24) would all bolster this Eurocentric perspective, which has pervaded Western civilization's relationship with the rest of the world.

CONCLUSION

At the end of the fifteenth century, Europeans sailed out into the world in all directions. Beginning with the handful of Portuguese ships that ventured southward along the West African coast in the mid-fifteenth century, the process accelerated with the epochal voyages of Christopher Columbus to the Americas and Vasco da Gama to the Indian Ocean in the 1490s. Soon a number of other European states had joined in the adventure, and by the end of the eighteenth century, they had created a global trade network dominated by Western ships and Western power.

In less than three hundred years, the European Age of Exploration changed the shape of the world. In some areas, such as the Americas and the Spice Islands, it led to the destruction of indigenous civilizations and the establishment of European colonies. In others, as in Africa, India, and mainland Southeast Asia, it left native regimes intact but had a strong impact on local societies and regional trade patterns.

At the time, many European observers viewed the process in a favorable light. It not only expanded wealth through world trade and exchanged crops and discoveries between the Old World and the New, they believed, but it also introduced "heathen peoples" to the message of Jesus Christ. The conquest of the Americas and expansion into the rest of the world brought out most of the worst and some of the best aspects of European civilization. The greedy plundering of resources and the brutal repression and enslavement were hardly balanced by attempts to create new institutions, convert the natives to Christianity, and foster the rights of the indigenous peoples. In any case, Europeans had begun to change the face of the world and increasingly saw their culture, with its religion, languages, and technology, as a coherent force to be exported to all corners of the earth.

TIMELINE

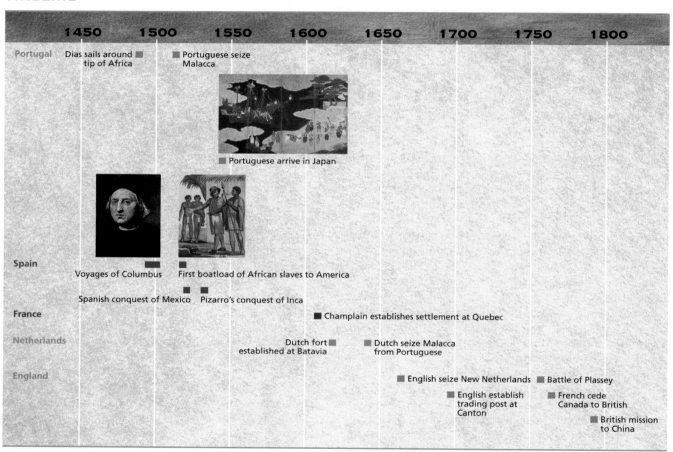

	1450	1500	1550	1600	1650	1700	1750	1800

Portugal — Dias sails around tip of Africa · Portuguese seize Malacca · Portuguese arrive in Japan

Spain — Voyages of Columbus · First boatload of African slaves to America · Spanish conquest of Mexico · Pizarro's conquest of Inca

France — Champlain establishes settlement at Quebec

Netherlands — Dutch fort established at Batavia · Dutch seize Malacca from Portuguese

England — English seize New Netherlands · Battle of Plassey · English establish trading post at Canton · French cede Canada to British · British mission to China

NOTES

1. Quoted in J. R. Hale, *Renaissance Exploration* (New York, 1968), p. 32.
2. Quoted in J. H. Parry, *The Age of Reconnaissance: Discovery, Exploration, and Settlement, 1450 to 1640* (New York, 1963), p. 33.
3. Quoted in R. B. Reed, "The Expansion of Europe," in R. De Molen, ed., *The Meaning of the Renaissance and Reformation* (Boston, 1974), p. 308.
4. Quoted in B. Davidson, *Africa in History: Themes and Outlines*, rev. ed. (New York, 1991), p. 213.
5. Quoted in ibid., p. 198
6. Quoted in G.V. Scammell, *The First Imperial Age: European Overseas Expansion, c. 1400–1715* (London, 1989), p. 62.
7. M. Leon-Portilla, ed., *The Broken Spears: The Aztec Account of the Conquest of Mexico* (Boston, 1969), p. 51.

SUGGESTIONS FOR FURTHER READING

The best general accounts of European discovery and expansion are **G. V. Scammell**, *The First Imperial Age: European Overseas Expansion, c. 1400–1715* (London, 1989); **J. H. Parry**, *The Age of Reconnaissance: Discovery, Exploration, and Settlement, 1450 to 1650* (New York, 1963); and **B. Penrose**, *Travel and Discovery in the Renaissance, 1420–1620* (New York, 1962). On the medieval background to European expansion, see **J.R.S. Phillips**, *The Medieval Expansion of Europe* (New York, 1988). On European perceptions of the world outside Europe, see **M. Campbell**, *The Witness and the Other World: Exotic European Travel Writing, 400–1600* (Ithaca, N.Y., 1991). On the technological aspects, see **R. C. Smith**, *Vanguard of Empire: Ships of Exploration in the Age of Columbus* (Oxford, 1993).

On Portuguese expansion, see **S. Subrahmanyam**, *The Portuguese Empire in Asia, 1500–1700: A Political and Economic History* (New York, 1993). On Columbus, see **F. Fernandez-Armesto**, *Columbus* (New York, 1991), and **W. D. Phillips and C. R. Phillips**, *The Worlds of Christopher Columbus* (Cambridge, 1992). On the Spanish Empire in the New World, see **J. H. Parry**, *The Spanish Seaborne Empire* (New York, 1966). For a theoretical discussion of violence and gender in America, see **R. Trexler**, *Sex and Conquest: Gendered Violence, Political Order, and the European Conquest of the Americas* (Ithaca, N.Y., 1995). On the conquistadors, see the beautifully illustrated work by **M. Wood**, *Conquistadors* (Berkeley, Calif., 2000). On the destructive nature of the Spanish conquest of the Americas, see **D. E. Standard**, *American Holocaust: Columbus and the Conquest of the New World* (New York, 1993). For a revisionist view of the Spanish conquest of the Americas, see **M. Restall**, *Seven Myths of the Spanish Conquest* (Oxford, 2003).

The subject of mercantile empires and worldwide trade is covered in **J. D. Tracy**, *The Rise of Merchant Empires: Long-Distance Trade in the Early Modern World, 1350–1750* (Cambridge, 1990), and **T. Benjamin, T. Hall**, and **D. Rutherford**, eds., *The Atlantic World in the Age of Empire* (New York, 2001). See also **A. Pagden**, *Lords of All the Worlds: Ideologies of Empire in Spain, Britain and France, c. 1500–c. 1850* (New Haven, Conn., 1995). On the African slave trade, see **H. Thomas**, *The Slave Trade: The Story of the Atlantic Slave Trade, 1440–1870* (New York, 1997), and the collection of articles in **D. Northrup**, ed., *The Atlantic Slave Trade* (Lexington, Mass., 1994). The effects of European trade in Southeast Asia are discussed in **A. Reid**, *Southeast Asia in the Age of Commerce, 1450–1680* (New Haven, Conn., 1989). See also **K. N. Chaudhuri**, *Trade and Civilization in the Indian Ocean: An Economic History from the Rise of Islam to 1750* (Cambridge, 1985).

On the economic dimensions of expansion, there are the three volumes by **F. Braudel**, *Civilization and Capitalism in the 15th to 18th Century: The Structures of Everyday Life* (London, 1981), *The Wheels of Commerce* (London, 1982), and *The Perspective of the World* (London, 1984). On mercantilism, see **L. Magnusson**, *Mercantilism: The Shaping of an Economic Language* (New York, 1994). On the concept of a world economy, see **A. K. Smith**, *Creating a World Economy: Merchant Capital, Colonialism, and World Trade, 1400–1825* (Boulder, Colo., 1991).

The impact of expansion on European consciousness is explored in **A. Pagden**, *European Encounters with the New World: From Renaissance to Romanticism* (New Haven, Conn., 1993). The human and ecological effects of the interaction of New World and Old World cultures are examined thoughtfully in **A. W. Crosby**, *The Columbian Exchange: Biological and Cultural Consequences of 1492* (Westport, Conn., 1972) and *Ecological Imperialism: The Biological Expansion of Europe* (New York, 1986). For a general view of the interaction of cultures, see **J. Diamond**, *Guns, Germs, and Steel* (New York, 1997). The native American female experience with the European encounter is presented in **R. Gutierrez**, *When Jesus Came the Corn Mother Went Away: Marriage, Sexuality, and Power in New Mexico, 1500–1846* (Stanford, Calif., 1991).

Thomson NOW! Enter *ThomsonNOW* using the access card that is available for *Western Civilization: A Brief History*. *ThomsonNOW* will help you understand this chapter with lesson plans generated for your needs. In addition, you can read the following documents, and many more, online:

Marco Polo, Prologue to *Travels*
Prince Henry the Navigator, *Chronicle of the Discovery and Conquest of Guinea,* chapters 7–9
Nicolò Conti (as told to Bracciolini), *Travels of Nicolò Conti in the East*
Francesco Pegolotti, *Cathay and the Way Thither*

WESTERN CIVILIZATION RESOURCES

Visit the Web site for *Western Civilization: A Brief History* for resources specific to this book:

http://www.thomsonedu.com/history/spielvogel

For a variety of tools to help you succeed in this course, visit the Western Civilization Resource Center at

http://history.wadsworth.com/spielvogel

Included are quizzes, images, documents, interactive simulations, maps and timelines, movie explorations, and a wealth of other sources.

15

STATE BUILDING AND THE SEARCH FOR ORDER IN THE SEVENTEENTH CENTURY

CHAPTER OUTLINE AND FOCUS QUESTIONS

Social Crises, War, and Rebellions

☐ What economic, social, and political crises did Europe experience in the first half of the seventeenth century?

The Practice of Absolutism: Western Europe

☐ What was absolutism in theory, and how did its actual practice in France measure up against the theory?

Absolutism in Central and Eastern Europe

☐ What developments enabled Brandenburg-Prussia, Austria, and Russia to emerge as major powers in the seventeenth century?

Limited Monarchy: The Dutch Republic and England

☐ What were the main issues in the struggle between king and Parliament in seventeenth-century England, and how were they resolved?

The Flourishing of European Culture

☐ What were the main features of art and literature in the sixteenth and seventeenth centuries?

CRITICAL THINKING

☐ How did the artistic and literary achievements of this era reflect the political and economic developments of the period?

Hyacinth Rigaud's portrait of Louis XIV captures the king's sense of royal grandeur

Hervé Lewandowski/Réunion des Musées Nationaux/Art Resource, NY (Louvre, Paris)

*B*Y THE END of the sixteenth century, Europe was beginning to experience some decline in religious passions and a growing secularization that affected both the political and intellectual worlds (the intellectual effect will be discussed in Chapter 16). Some historians like to speak of the seventeenth century as a turning point in the evolution of the modern state system in Europe. The ideal of a united Christian Europe gave way to the practical realities of a system of secular entities in which matters of state took precedence over the salvation of subjects' souls. By the seventeenth century, the credibility of Christianity had been so weakened through religious wars that more and more Europeans came to think of politics in secular terms.

One of the responses to the religious wars and other crises of the time was a yearning for order. As the internal social and political rebellions and revolts died down, it became apparent that the privileged classes of society—the aristocrats—remained in control, although important differences in political forms existed in the various states. In many places, the extension of monarchical power was viewed as a stabilizing force. This development, which historians have called absolutism or absolute monarchy, was most evident in France during the flamboyant reign of Louis XIV, widely regarded as the perfect embodiment of an absolute monarch. In his memoirs, the duc de Saint-Simon, who had firsthand experience of French court life, said that Louis was "the very figure of a hero, so imbued with a natural but most imposing majesty that it appeared even in his most insignificant gestures and movements." The king's natural grace gave him a special charm as well: "He was as dignified and majestic in his dressing gown as when dressed in robes of state, or on horseback at the head of his troops." His life was orderly: "Nothing could be regulated with greater exactitude than were his days and hours." His self-control was impeccable: "He did not lose control of himself ten times in his whole life, and then only with inferior persons." But even absolute monarchs had imperfections, and Saint-Simon had the courage to point them out: "Louis XIV's vanity was without limit or restraint," which led to his "distaste for all merit, intelligence, education, and, most of all, for all independence of character and sentiment in others," as well as his "mistakes of judgment in matters of importance."

But absolutism was not the only response to the search for order in the seventeenth century. Other states, such as England, reacted differently to domestic crisis, and another very different system emerged where monarchs were limited by the power of their representative assemblies. Absolute and limited monarchy were the two poles of seventeenth-century state building.◆

Social Crises, War, and Rebellions

The inflation-fueled prosperity of the sixteenth century showed signs of slackening in the seventeenth. Economic contraction was evident in some parts of Europe by the 1620s. In the 1630s and 1640s, as imports of silver from the Americas declined, economic recession intensified, especially in the Mediterranean area. Italy, the industrial and financial center of Europe in the Renaissance, was becoming an economic backwater. Spain's economy was also seriously failing by the 1640s.

Population trends of the sixteenth and seventeenth centuries also testify to Europe's worsening conditions. The sixteenth century was a period of expanding population, possibly related to a warmer climate and increased food supplies. It has been estimated that the population of Europe increased from 60 million in 1500 to 85 million by 1600, the first major recovery since the devastation of the Black Death in the mid-fourteenth century. However, records also indicate a leveling off of the population by 1620 and even a decline by 1650, especially in central and southern parts of the Continent. Europe's longtime adversaries—war, famine, and plague—continued to affect population levels, and another "little ice age" midway through the sixteenth century, when average temperatures fell, affected harvests and gave rise to famines. These problems created social tensions that came to a boil in the witchcraft craze.

The Witchcraft Craze

Hysteria over witchcraft affected the lives of many Europeans in the sixteenth and seventeenth centuries. Witchcraft trials were held in England, Scotland, Switzerland, Germany, some parts of France and the Low Countries, and even New England in America.

Witchcraft was not a new phenomenon. Its practice had been part of traditional village culture for centuries, but it came to be viewed as both sinister and dangerous when the medieval church began to connect witches to the activities of the devil, thereby transforming witchcraft into a heresy that had to be extirpated. After the creation of the Inquisition in the thirteenth century, people were accused of a variety of witchcraft practices and, following the biblical injunction "Thou shalt not suffer a witch to live," were turned over to secular authorities for burning at the stake or, in England, hanging.

The Spread of Witchcraft What distinguished witchcraft in the sixteenth and seventeenth centuries from these previous developments was the increased number of trials and executions of presumed witches. Perhaps more than a hundred thousand people were prosecuted throughout Europe on charges of witchcraft. Although larger cities were affected first, the trials spread to smaller towns and rural areas as the hysteria persisted well into the seventeenth century (see the box on p. 282).

The accused witches usually confessed to a number of practices, most often after intense torture. Many said that they had sworn allegiance to the devil and attended sabbats, nocturnal gatherings where they feasted, danced, and even copulated with the devil in sexual orgies. More common, however, were admissions of using evil incantations and special ointments and powders to wreak havoc on neighbors by killing their livestock, injuring their children, or raising storms to destroy their crops.

A number of contributing factors have been suggested to explain why the witchcraft frenzy became so widespread in the sixteenth and seventeenth centuries. Religious uncertainties clearly played some part. Many witchcraft trials occurred in areas where Protestantism had been recently victorious or in regions, such as southwestern Germany, where controversies between Protestants and Catholics still raged. As religious passions became inflamed, accusations of being in league with the devil became common on both sides. Recently, however, historians have emphasized the importance of social conditions, especially the problems of a society in turmoil, in explaining the witchcraft hysteria. At a time when the old communal values that stressed working together for the good of the community were disintegrating, property owners became more fearful of the growing numbers of poor among them and transformed them psychologically into agents of the devil. Old women were particularly susceptible to suspicion. When problems arose—and there were many in this crisis-laden period—these people were the most likely scapegoats.

A WITCHCRAFT TRIAL IN FRANCE

Persecutions for witchcraft reached their high point in the sixteenth and seventeenth centuries when tens of thousands of people were brought to trial. In this excerpt from the minutes of a trial in France in 1652, we can see why the accused witch stood little chance of exonerating herself.

The Trial of Suzanne Gaudry

28 May, 1652 . . . . Interrogation of Suzanne Gaudry, prisoner at the court of Rieux. . . . [During interrogations on May 28 and May 29, the prisoner confessed to a number of activities involving the devil.]

Deliberation of the Court—June 3, 1652

The undersigned advocates of the Court have seen these interrogations and answers. They say that the afore-mentioned Suzanne Gaudry confesses that she is a witch, that she had given herself to the devil, that she had re-nounced God, Lent, and baptism, that she has been marked on the shoulder, that she has cohabited with the devil and that she has been to the dances, confessing only to have cast a spell upon and caused to die a beast of Philippe Cornié. . . .

Third Interrogation—June 27

The prisoner being led into the chamber, she was examined to know if things were not as she had said and confessed at the beginning of her imprisonment.

—Answers no, and that what she has said was done so by force.

Pressed to say the truth, that otherwise she would be subjected to torture, having pointed out to her that her aunt was burned for this same subject.

—Answers that she is not a witch. . . .

She was placed in the hands of the officer in charge of torture, throwing herself on her knees, struggling to cry, uttering several exclamations, without being able, never-theless, to shed a tear. Saying at every moment that she is not a witch.

The Torture

On this same day, being at the place of torture.

This prisoner, before being strapped down, was admon-ished to maintain herself in her first confessions and to re-nounce her lover.

—Says that she denies everything she has said, and that she has no lover. Feeling herself being strapped down, says

that she is not a witch, while struggling to cry . . . and upon being asked why she confessed to being one, said that she was forced to say it.

Told that she was not forced, that on the contrary she declared herself to be a witch without any threat.

—Says that she confessed it and that she is not a witch, and being a little stretched [on the rack] screams ceaselessly that she is not a witch. . . .

Asked if she did not confess that she had been a witch for twenty-six years.

—Says that she said it, that she retracts it, crying that she is not a witch.

Asked if she did not make Philippe Cornié's horse die, as she confessed.

—Answers no, crying Jesus-Maria, that she is not a witch.

The mark having been probed by the officer, in the presence of Doctor Bouchain, it was adjudged by the afore-said doctor and officer truly to be the mark of the devil.

Being more tightly stretched upon the torture-rack, urged to maintain her confessions.

—Said that it was true that she is a witch and that she would maintain what she had said.

Asked how long she has been in subjugation to the devil.

—Answers that it was twenty years ago that the devil appeared to her, being in her lodgings in the form of a man dressed in a little cow-hide and black breeches. . . .

Verdict

July 9, 1652. In the light of the interrogations, answers and investigations made into the charge against Suzanne Gaudry, . . . seeing by her own confessions that she is said to have made a pact with the devil, received the mark from him, . . . and that following this, she had renounced God, Lent, and baptism and had let herself be known carnally by him, in which she received satisfaction. Also, seeing that she is said to have been a part of nocturnal carols and dances.

For expiation of which the advice of the undersigned is that the office of Rieux can legitimately condemn the aforesaid Suzanne Gaudry to death, tying her to a gallows, and strangling her to death, then burning her body and burying it here in the environs of the woods.

Why were women, particularly older women, especially vulnerable to accusations of witchcraft? What "proofs" are offered here that Suzanne Gaudry had consorted with the devil? What does this account tell us about the spread of witchcraft persecutions in the seventeenth century?

That women should be the chief victims of witchcraft trials was hardly accidental. Nicholas Rémy, a witchcraft judge in France in the 1590s, found it "not unreasonable that this scum of humanity, i.e., witches, should be drawn chiefly from the feminine sex."[1] To another judge, it came as no surprise that witches would confess to sexual ex-periences with Satan: "The Devil uses them so, because he knows that women love carnal pleasures, and he means to bind them to his allegiance by such agreeable provocations."[2] Of course, not only witch hunters held such low estimates of women. Most theologians, lawyers, and philosophers in early modern Europe maintained a belief in the natural inferiority of women, making it seem plausible that women would be more susceptible to witchcraft.

Decline By the mid-seventeenth century, the witchcraft hysteria began to subside. The destruction of the religious wars had at least forced people to accept a grudging toleration, tempering religious passions. Moreover, as governments began to stabilize after the period of crisis, fewer magistrates were willing to accept the unsettling and divisive conditions generated by the trials of witches. Finally, by the turn of the eighteenth century, more and more people were questioning their old attitudes toward religion and found it contrary to reason to believe in a world haunted by evil spirits.

The Thirty Years' War

Although many Europeans responded to the upheavals of the second half of the sixteenth century with a desire for peace and order, the first fifty years of the seventeenth century continued to be plagued by crises. A devastating war that affected much of Europe and rebellions seemingly everywhere protracted an atmosphere of disorder and violence.

Religion, especially the struggle between militant Catholicism and militant Calvinism, played an important role in the outbreak of the Thirty Years' War (1618–1648), often called the "last of the religious wars." As the war progressed, however, it became increasingly clear that secular, dynastic-nationalist considerations were far more important.

The Thirty Years' War began in the Germanic lands of the Holy Roman Empire as a struggle between Catholic forces, led by the Habsburg Holy Roman Emperors, and Protestant—primarily Calvinist—nobles in Bohemia who rebelled against Habsburg authority. What began as a struggle over religious issues soon became a wider conflict determined by political motivations as both minor and major European powers—Denmark, Sweden, France, and Spain—made the war a Europe-wide struggle (see Map 15.1). The struggle for European leadership between the Bourbon dynasty of France and the Habsburg dynasties of Spain and the Holy Roman Empire was an especially important factor. Nevertheless, most of the battles were fought on German soil, with devastating results for the German people.

The war in Germany was officially ended by the Peace of Westphalia in 1648, which ensured that all German states, including the Calvinist ones, were free to determine their own religion. The major contenders gained new territories, and one of them, France, emerged as the dominant nation in Europe. The more than three hundred states that made up the Holy Roman Empire were virtually recognized as independent, since each received the power to conduct its own foreign policy. The Habsburg emperor had been reduced to a figurehead. The Peace of Westphalia also made it clear that religion and politics were now separate in the Holy Roman Empire. Political motives became the guiding forces in public affairs as religion moved closer to becoming primarily a matter of personal conviction and individual choice.

The economic and social effects of the Thirty Years' War on Germany are still debated. An older view pictured a ruined German economy and a decline in German population from 21 to 13 million between 1600 and 1650, but more recent opinions have estimated that Germany's population grew from 16 to 17 million while a redistribution of economic activity rather than an overall decline took place. Both views contain some truth. Some areas of Germany were completely devastated while others remained relatively untouched and even experienced economic growth.

Rebellions

Before, during, and after the Thirty Years' War, a series of rebellions and civil wars stemming from the discontent of both nobles and commoners rocked the domestic stability of many European governments. To strengthen their power, monarchs attempted to extend their authority at the expense of traditional powerful elements who resisted the rulers' efforts. At the same time, to fight their battles, governments increased taxes and caused such hardships that common people also rose in opposition.

Between 1590 and 1640, peasant and lower-class revolts occurred in central and southern France, Austria, and Hungary. Portugal and Catalonia rebelled against the Spanish government in 1640. Russia, too, was rocked by urban uprisings in 1641, 1645, and 1648. Nobles rebelled in France from 1648 to 1652 to halt the growth of royal power. The northern states of Sweden, Denmark, and the United Provinces were also not immune from upheavals involving clergy, nobles, and mercantile groups. Even relatively stable Switzerland had a peasant rebellion in 1656. The most famous and widest-ranging struggle, however, was the civil war and rebellion in England, commonly known as the English Revolution (discussed later in this chapter).

The Practice of Absolutism: Western Europe

Absolute monarchy or **absolutism** meant that the sovereign power or ultimate authority in the state rested in the hands of a king who claimed to rule by divine right—that kings received their power from God and were responsible to no one (including parliaments) except God. But what did sovereignty mean? The late-sixteenth-century political theorist Jean Bodin believed that sovereign power consisted of the authority to make laws, tax, mete out justice, control the state's administrative system,

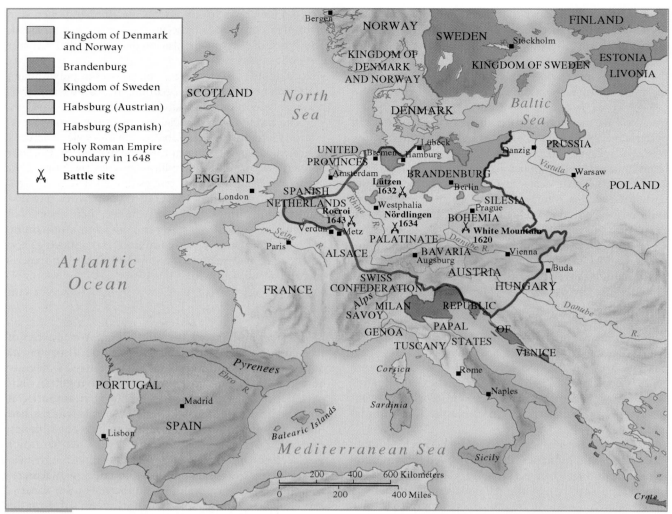

MAP 15.1 **The Thirty Years' War.** The conflict began in the German states as Europe's major powers backed either the northern Protestant Union or the southern Catholic League. As the war progressed, religion receded in importance, replaced by a dynastic struggle between the French Bourbons and the Spanish and Austrian Habsburgs. ⁇ Compare this map with Map 13.2. Which countries engaged in the war were predominantly Protestant, which were predominantly Catholic, and which were mixed? 🔊 **View an animated version of this map or related maps at** http://thomsonedu.com/history/spielvogel

and determine foreign policy. These powers made a ruler sovereign.

France: Foundations of Absolutism

France during the reign of Louis XIV (1643–1715) has traditionally been regarded as the best example of the practice of absolute monarchy in the seventeenth century. French culture, language, and manners reached into all levels of European society. French diplomacy and wars shaped the political affairs of western and central Europe. Of course, the stability of Louis's reign was magnified by the instability that had preceded it.

The fifty years of French history before Louis XIV came to power were a time in which royal and ministerial governments struggled to avoid the breakdown of the

state. The situation was especially complicated by the fact that in 1610 and 1643, when Louis XIII and Louis XIV, respectively, succeeded to the throne, they were only boys, leaving the government dependent on royal ministers. Two especially competent ministers played crucial roles in maintaining monarchical authority.

Cardinal Richelieu, Louis XIII's chief minister from 1624 to 1642, initiated policies that eventually strengthened the power of the monarchy. By eliminating the political and military rights of the Huguenots while preserving their religious ones, Richelieu transformed the Huguenots into more reliable subjects. Richelieu acted more cautiously in "humbling the pride of the great men," the important French nobility. He understood the influential role played by the nobles in the French state. The dangerous ones were those who asserted their territorial independence when they were excluded from participating in the central government. Proceeding slowly but determinedly, Richelieu developed an efficient network of spies to uncover noble plots and then crushed the conspiracies and executed the conspirators, thereby eliminating a major threat to royal authority.

When Louis XIV succeeded to the throne in 1643 at the age of four, Cardinal Mazarin, the trained successor of Cardinal Richelieu, dominated the government. An Italian who had come to France as a papal legate and then became naturalized, Mazarin attempted to carry on Richelieu's policies. The most important event during Mazarin's rule was the Fronde, a revolt led primarily by nobles who wished to curb the centralized administrative power being built up at the expense of the provincial nobility. The Fronde was crushed by 1652, and with its end, a vast number of French people concluded that the best hope for stability in France lay in the crown. When Mazarin died in 1661, the greatest of the seventeenth-century monarchs, Louis XIV, took over supreme power.

The Reign of Louis XIV (1643–1715)

The day after Cardinal Mazarin's death, Louis XIV, at the age of twenty-three, expressed his determination to be a real king and the sole ruler of France:

> Up to this moment I have been pleased to entrust the government of my affairs to the late Cardinal. It is now time that I govern them myself. You [secretaries and ministers of state] will assist me with your counsels when I ask for them. I request and order you to seal no orders except by my command. . . . I order you not to sign anything, not even a passport . . . without my command; to render account to me personally each day and to favor no one.[3]

His mother, who was well aware of Louis's proclivity for fun and games and getting into the beds of the maids in the royal palace, laughed aloud at these words. But Louis was quite serious.

Louis proved willing to pay the price of being a strong ruler. He established a conscientious routine from which he seldom deviated. Eager for glory (in the French sense of achieving what was expected of a person who held an important position), Louis created a grand and majestic spectacle at the court of Versailles. Consequently, Louis and his court came to set the standard for monarchies and aristocracies all over Europe.

Although Louis may have believed in the theory of absolute monarchy and consciously fostered the myth of himself as the Sun King, the source of light for all of his people, historians are quick to point out that the realities fell far short of the aspirations. Despite the centralizing efforts of Cardinals Richelieu and Mazarin, seventeenth-century France still possessed a bewildering system of overlapping authorities. Provinces had their own regional courts, their own local Estates, their own sets of laws. Members of the high nobility, with their huge estates, and

clients among the lesser nobility still exercised much authority. Both towns and provinces possessed privileges and powers seemingly from time immemorial that they would not easily relinquish.

Administration of the Government   One of the keys to Louis's power was that he was able to restructure the central policy-making machinery of government because it was part of his own court and household. The royal court located at Versailles was an elaborate structure that served three purposes simultaneously: it was the personal household of the king, the location of central governmental machinery, and the place where powerful subjects came to find favors and offices for themselves and their clients, as well as the main arena where rival aristocratic factions jostled for power. The greatest danger to Louis's personal rule came from the very high nobles and "princes of the blood" (royal princes) who considered it their natural function to assert the policy-making role of royal ministers. Louis eliminated this threat by removing them from the royal council, the chief administrative body of the king and overseer of the central machinery of government, and enticing them to his court, where he could keep them preoccupied with court life and out of politics. In place of the high nobility and royal princes, Louis relied for his ministers on other nobles. His ministers were expected to be subservient; said Louis, "I had no intention of sharing my authority with them."

Louis's domination of his ministers and secretaries gave him control of the central policy-making machinery of government and thus authority over the traditional areas of monarchical power: the formulation of foreign policy, the making of war and peace, the assertion of the secular power of the crown against any religious authority, and the ability to levy taxes to fulfill these functions. However, Louis had considerably less success with the internal administration of the kingdom. The traditional groups and institutions of French society—the nobles, officials, town councils, guilds, and representative Estates in some provinces—were simply too powerful for the king to control. As a result, the actual governing of the provinces and the people was accomplished largely by careful bribery of important people to ensure that the king's policies were carried out.

Religious Policy   The maintenance of religious harmony had long been considered an area of monarchical power. The desire to keep it led Louis to pursue an anti-Protestant policy, aimed at converting the Huguenots to Catholicism. In October 1685, Louis issued the Edict of Fontainebleau. In addition to revoking the Edict of Nantes, the new edict provided for the destruction of the Huguenots' churches and the closing of their schools.

Financial Issues   The cost of building palaces, maintaining his court, and pursuing his wars made finances a crucial issue for Louis XIV. He was most fortunate in

The Palace of Versailles as Depicted in an Eighteenth-Century Engraving.
Louis XIV spent untold sums of money on the construction of a new royal residence at Versailles.
The enormous palace (it was more than a quarter of a mile long) also housed the members of the
king's government and served as home for thousands of French nobles. As the largest royal
residence in Europe, Versailles impressed foreigners and became a source of envy for other rulers.

having the services of Jean-Baptiste Colbert (1619–1683)
as controller-general of finances. Colbert was an avid
practitioner of mercantilism. To decrease the need for
imports and increase exports, he founded new luxury
industries and granted special privileges, including tax
exemptions, loans, and subsidies, to individuals who established new industries. To improve communications
and the transportation of goods internally, he built roads
and canals. To decrease imports directly, Colbert raised
tariffs on foreign manufactured goods and created a
merchant marine to carry French goods.

The Wars of Louis XIV Both the increase in royal
power that Louis pursued and his desire for military
glory led the king to develop a professional army numbering 100,000 men in peacetime and 400,000 in time of
war. Louis made war an almost incessant activity of his
reign. To achieve the prestige and military glory befitting
the Sun King as well as to ensure the domination of his
Bourbon dynasty over European affairs, Louis waged four
wars between 1667 and 1713. His ambitions roused much
of Europe to form coalitions to prevent destruction of the
European balance of power that Bourbon hegemony
would cause. Although Louis added some territory to
France's northeastern frontier and established a member
of his own Bourbon dynasty on the throne of Spain, he
also left France impoverished and surrounded by enemies.

The Decline of Spain

At the beginning of the seventeenth century, Spain possessed the most populous empire in the world, controlling

almost all of South America and a number of settlements in Asia and Africa. To most Europeans, Spain still seemed the greatest power of the age, but the reality was quite different. The treasury was empty; Philip II went bankrupt in 1596 from excessive expenditures on war, and his successor did the same in 1607 by spending a fortune on his court. The armed forces were obsolescent, the government was inefficient, and the commercial class was weak in the midst of a suppressed peasantry, a luxury-loving class of nobles, and an oversupply of priests and monks.

During the reign of Philip III (1598–1621), many of Spain's weaknesses became all too apparent. Interested only in court luxury or miracle-working relics, Philip III allowed his first minister, the greedy duke of Lerma, to run the country. The aristocratic Lerma's primary interest was accumulating power and wealth for himself and his family. As important offices were filled with his relatives, crucial problems went unsolved.

At first, the reign of Philip IV (1621–1665) seemed to offer hope for a revival of Spain's energies, especially in the capable hands of his chief minister, Gaspar de Guzman, the count of Olivares. This clever, dedicated, and power-hungry statesman worked to revive the interests of the monarchy. A flurry of domestic reform decrees, aimed at curtailing the power of the church and the landed aristocracy, was soon followed by a political reform program whose purpose was to further centralize the government of all Spain and its possessions in monarchical hands. All of these efforts met with little real success, however, because both the number (estimated at one-fifth of the population) and power of the Spanish aristocrats made them too strong to curtail in any significant fashion.

At the same time, most of the efforts of Olivares and Philip were undermined by their desire to pursue Spain's imperial glory and by a series of internal revolts. Spain's involvement in the Thirty Years' War led to a series of frightfully expensive military campaigns that provoked internal revolts and years of civil war. Unfortunately for Spain, the campaigns also failed to produce victory. As

Olivares wrote to King Philip IV, "God wants us to make peace; for He is depriving us visibly and absolutely of all the means of war."[4]

The defeats in Europe and the internal revolts of the 1640s ended any illusions about Spain's greatness. The actual extent of its economic difficulties is still debated, but there is no question about its foreign losses. Dutch independence was formally recognized by the Peace of Westphalia in 1648, and the Peace of the Pyrenees with France in 1659 meant the surrender of some border regions to France.

Absolutism in Central and Eastern Europe

During the seventeenth century, a development of great importance for the modern Western world took place in central and eastern Europe, the appearance of three new powers: Prussia, Austria, and Russia.

The German States

The Peace of Westphalia, which officially ended the Thirty Years' War in 1648, left each of the more than three hundred German states comprising the Holy Roman Empire virtually autonomous and sovereign. Of these states, two emerged in the seventeenth and eighteenth centuries as great European powers.

The Rise of Brandenburg-Prussia The development of Brandenburg as a state was largely the story of the Hohenzollern dynasty. By the seventeenth century, the dominions of the house of Hohenzollern, now called Brandenburg-Prussia, consisted of three disconnected masses in western, central, and eastern Germany (see Map 15.2).

The foundation for the Prussian state was laid by Frederick William the Great Elector (1640–1688). Realizing that Brandenburg-Prussia was a small, open territory with no natural frontiers for defense, Frederick William built an army of forty thousand men, making it the fourth largest in Europe. To sustain the army, Frederick William established the General War Commissariat to levy taxes to support the army and oversee its growth. The Commissariat soon evolved into an agency for civil government as well. Directly responsible to the elector, the new bureaucratic machine became his chief instrument to govern the state. Many of its officials were members of the Prussian landed aristocracy, the Junkers, who also served as officers in the all-important army.

Frederick William was succeeded by his son Frederick III (1688–1713), who made one significant contribution to the development of Prussia. In return for his commitment to aid the Holy Roman Emperor in a war against Spain, he received the title of King-in-Prussia in

MAP 15.2 The Growth of Brandenberg-Prussia. Frederick William the Great Elector laid the foundation for a powerful state when he increased the size and efficiency of the army, raised taxes and created an efficient bureaucracy to collect them, and gained the support of the landed aristocracy. Later rulers added more territory. **?** Why was the acquisition of Pomerania and West Prussia important for the continued rise in power of Brandenburg-Prussia? **View an animated version of this map or related maps at** http://thomsonedu.com/history/spielvogel

1701. Elector Frederick III was transformed into King Frederick I, and Brandenburg-Prussia became simply Prussia. In the eighteenth century, Prussia emerged as a great power on the European stage.

The Emergence of Austria

The Austrian Habsburgs had long played a significant role in European politics as Holy Roman Emperors. By the end of the Thirty Years' War, the Habsburg hopes of forging an empire in Germany had been dashed. In the seventeenth century, the house of Austria assembled a new empire in eastern and southeastern Europe.

The nucleus of the new Austrian Empire remained the traditional Austrian hereditary possessions: Lower and Upper Austria, Carinthia, Carniola, Styria, and Tyrol (see Map 15.3). To these had been added the kingdom of Bohemia and parts of northwestern Hungary in the sixteenth century. In the seventeenth century, Leopold I (1658–1705) encouraged the eastward movement of the Austrian Empire, but he was sorely challenged by the revival of Ottoman power. The Ottomans eventually pushed westward and laid siege to Vienna in 1683. A European army, led by the Austrians, counterattacked and decisively defeated the Ottomans in 1687. Austria took control of Hungary, Transylvania, Croatia, and Slovenia, thus establishing an Austrian Empire in southeastern Europe. By the beginning of the eighteenth century, the house of Austria had acquired an empire of considerable size.

Yet Austria never became a highly centralized, absolutist state, primarily because it contained so many different national groups. The empire remained a collection of territories held together by a personal union. The Habsburg emperor was archduke of Austria, king of Bohemia, and king of Hungary. Each of these areas, however, had its own laws, Estates-General, and political life.

Russia: From Fledgling Principality to Major Power

A new Russian state had emerged in the fifteenth century under the leadership of the principality of Moscow and its grand dukes. In the sixteenth century, Ivan IV the Terrible (1533–1584) was the first ruler to take the title of tsar (the Russian word for "Caesar"). Ivan expanded the territories of Russia eastward and also extended the autocracy of the tsar by crushing the power of the Russian nobility, known as the boyars. Ivan's dynasty came to an end in 1598 and was followed by a resurgence of aristocratic power in a period of anarchy known as the Time of Troubles. It did not end until the Zemsky Sobor, or national assembly, chose Michael Romanov in 1613 as the new tsar, beginning a dynasty that lasted until 1917.

In the seventeenth century, Muscovite society was highly stratified. At the top was the tsar, who claimed to be a divinely ordained autocratic ruler. Russian society was dominated by an upper class of landed aristocrats who, in the course of the seventeenth century, managed to bind their peasants to the land. Townspeople were also controlled. Many merchants were not allowed to move from their cities without government permission or to sell their businesses to anyone outside their class. In the seventeenth century, merchant and peasant revolts as well as a schism in the Russian Orthodox church created very unsettled conditions. In the midst of these political and religious upheavals, Russia was experiencing more frequent contacts with the West, and Western ideas were beginning to penetrate a few Russian circles. At the end of the seventeenth century, Peter the Great noticeably accelerated this westernizing process.

The Reign of Peter the Great (1689–1725) Peter the Great was an unusual character. A strong man towering

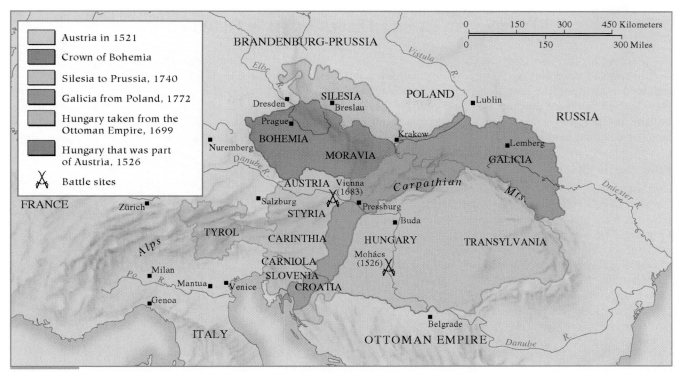

MAP 15.3 **The Growth of the Austrian Empire.** The Habsburgs had hoped to establish an empire of Germans, but the results of the Thirty Years' War crushed that dream. So Austria expanded to the east and the south, primarily at the expense of the Ottoman Empire, and also gained the Spanish Netherlands and former Spanish territories in Italy. **?** In which areas did the Austrian Empire have access to the Mediterranean Sea, and why would that potentially be important? **👁** **View an animated version of this map or related maps at** http://thomsonedu.com/history/ spielvogel

6 feet 9 inches tall, Peter enjoyed low humor—belching contests and crude jokes—and vicious punishments— flogging, impalings, and roastings (see the box on p. 290). He got a firsthand view of the West when he made a trip there in 1697–1698 and returned home determined to Europeanize Russia. He was especially eager to borrow European technology, convinced it would give him the military muscle he needed to make Russia a great power.

As could be expected, one of his first priorities was the reorganization of the armed forces. Employing both Russians and Europeans as officers, he conscripted peasants for twenty-five-year stints of service to build a standing army of 210,000 men. Peter has also been given credit for forming the first Russian navy.

Peter reorganized the central government, partly along Western lines. To impose the rule of the central government more effectively throughout the land, he divided Russia into eight provinces and later, in 1719, into fifty. Although he hoped to create a "police state," by which he meant a well-ordered community governed in accordance with law, few of his bureaucrats shared his concept of honest service and duty to the state. Peter hoped for a sense of civic duty, but his own forceful personality created an atmosphere of fear that prevented it.

Peter also sought to gain state control of the Russian Orthodox church. In 1721, he abolished the position of patriarch and created a body called the Holy Synod to make decisions for the church. At its head stood a **procurator**, a layman who represented the interests of the tsar and assured Peter of effective domination of the church.

Immediately upon returning from his trip to the West in 1698, Peter began to introduce Western customs, practices, and manners into Russia. He ordered the preparation of the first Russian book of etiquette to teach Western manners. Among other things, it pointed out that it was not polite to spit on the floor or scratch oneself at dinner. Because Westerners did not wear beards or the traditional long-skirted coat, Russian beards had to be shaved and coats shortened, a reform Peter personally enforced at court by shaving off his nobles' beards and cutting their coats at the knees with his own hands. Outside the court, the edicts were enforced by barbers and tailors planted at town gates with orders to cut the beards and cloaks of all who entered or left.

One group of Russians benefited greatly from Peter's cultural reforms—women. Having watched women mixing freely with men in Western courts, Peter shattered the

PETER THE GREAT DEALS WITH A REBELLION

During his first visit to the West in 1697–1698, Peter received word that the Streltsy, an elite military unit stationed in Moscow, had revolted against his authority. Peter hurried home and crushed the revolt in a very savage fashion. This selection is taken from an Austrian account of how Peter dealt with the rebels.

Peter and the Streltsy

How sharp was the pain, how great the indignation, to which the tsar's Majesty was mightily moved, when he knew of the rebellion of the Streltsy, betraying openly a mind panting for vengeance! He was still tarrying at Vienna, quite full of the desire of setting out for Italy; but, fervid as was his curiosity of rambling abroad, it was, nevertheless, speedily extinguished on the announcement of the troubles that had broken out in the bowels of his realm. Going immediately to Lefort . . . , he thus indignantly broke out: "Tell me, Francis, how I can reach Moscow by the shortest way, in a brief space, so that I may wreak vengeance on this great perfidy of my people, with punishments worthy of their abominable crime. Not one of them shall escape with impunity. Around my royal city, which, with their impious efforts, they planned to destroy, I will have gibbets and gallows set upon the walls and ramparts, and each and every one of them will I put to a direful death." Nor did he long delay the plan for his justly excited wrath; he took the quick post, as his ambassador suggested, and in four weeks' time he had got over about three hundred miles without accident, and arrived the 4th of September, 1698,–a monarch for the well deposed, but an avenger for the wicked.

His first anxiety after his arrival was about the rebellion—in what it consisted, what the insurgents meant, who dared to instigate such a crime. And as nobody could answer accurately upon all points, and some pleaded their own ignorance, others the obstinacy of the Streltsy, he began to have suspicions of everybody's loyalty. . . . No day, holy or profane, were the inquisitors idle; every day was deemed fit and lawful for torturing. There was as many scourges as there were accused, and every inquisitor was a butcher. . . . The whole month of October was spent on lacerating the backs of culprits with the knout and with flames; no day were those that were left alive exempt from scourging or scorching; or else they were broken upon the wheel, or driven to the gibbet, or slain with the ax. . . .

To prove to all people how holy and inviolable are those walls of the city which the Streltsy rashly meditated scaling in a sudden assault, beams were run out from all the embrasures in the walls near the gates, in each of which two rebels were hanged. This day beheld about two hundred and fifty die that death. There are few cities fortified with as many palisades as Moscow has given gibbets to her guardian Streltsy.

How did Peter the Great deal with the revolt of the Streltsy? What does his approach to this problem tell us about the tsar?

---

seclusion of upper-class Russian women and demanded that they remove the traditional veils that covered their faces. Peter also decreed that social gatherings be held three times a week in the large houses of Saint Petersburg where men and women could mix for conversation, card games, and dancing, which Peter had learned in the West. The tsar also now insisted that women could marry of their own free will.

The object of Peter's domestic reforms was to make Russia into a great state and military power. His primary goal was to "open a window to the West," which required an ice-free port easily accessible to Europe. This could be achieved only on the Baltic, but at that time the Baltic coast was controlled by Sweden, the most important power in northern Europe. Desirous of these lands, Peter attacked Sweden in the summer of 1700, believing that its young king, Charles XII, could easily be defeated. Charles, however, proved to be a brilliant general and, with a well-disciplined force of only eight thousand men, routed the Russian army of forty thousand at the Battle of Narva (1700). The Great Northern War (1701–1721) soon ensued.

Peter fought back. He reorganized his army along Western lines and at the Battle of Poltava in July 1709 decisively defeated Charles's army. Although the war dragged on for another twelve years, the Peace of Nystadt in 1721 gave formal recognition to what Peter had already achieved: the acquisition of Estonia, Livonia, and Karelia (see Map 15.4). Sweden became a second-rate power, and Russia was now the great European state Peter had envisioned. Already in 1703, Peter had begun the construction of a new city on the Baltic, Saint Petersburg, his window to the West and a symbol that Russia was looking toward Europe. Peter realized his dream: by the time of his death in 1725, Russia had become a great military power and an important actor on the European stage.

The Ottoman Empire

After their conquest of Constantinople in 1453, the Ottoman Turks tried but failed to complete their conquest of the Balkans, where they had been established since the fourteenth century (see Map 15.3). The reign of Sultan Suleiman I the Magnificent (1520–1566), however, brought the Ottomans back to Europe's attention. Advancing up the Danube, the Ottomans seized Belgrade in

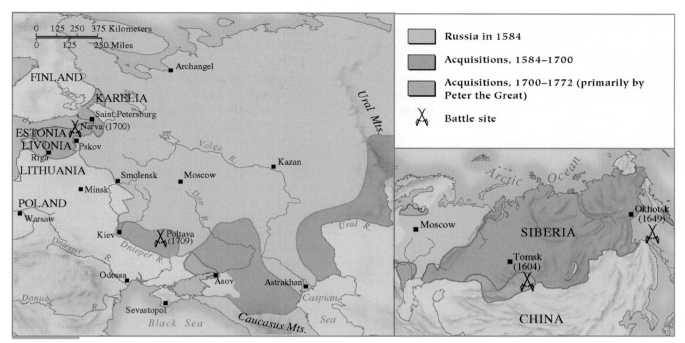

MAP 15.4 **Russia: From Principality to Nation-State.** Russia had swelled in size since its emergence in the fifteenth century. However, Peter the Great modernized the country, instituting bureaucratic and taxation reforms and building up the military. He won territory on the Baltic from Sweden, giving Russia a port at Saint Petersburg. ? Why would the westward expansion of Russia during Peter's reign affect the international balance of power in Europe?

View an animated version of this map or related maps at http://thomsonedu.com/history/spielvogel

1521 and Hungary by 1526, although their attempts to conquer Vienna in 1529 were repulsed. At the same time, the Ottomans extended their power into the western Mediterranean, threatening to turn it into an Ottoman lake until a large Ottoman fleet was destroyed by the Spanish at Lepanto (in modern-day Greece) in 1571. Despite the defeat, the Ottomans continued to hold nominal control over the southern shores along the Mediterranean.

Although Europeans frequently spoke of new Christian crusades against the "infidel" Ottomans, by the beginning of the seventeenth century, their empire was being treated like any other European power by European rulers seeking alliances and trade concessions. In the first half of the century, the Ottoman Empire was a "sleeping giant." Occupied by domestic bloodletting and severely threatened by a challenge from Persia, the Ottomans were content with the status quo in eastern Europe. But under a new line of grand viziers in the second half of the seventeenth century, the Ottoman Empire again took the offensive. By 1683, the Ottomans had marched through the Hungarian plain and laid siege to Vienna. Repulsed by a mixed army of Austrians, Poles, Bavarians, and Saxons, the Ottomans retreated and were pushed out of Hungary by a new European coalition. Although they retained the core of their empire, the Ottoman Turks would never again be a threat to Europe.

The Limits of Absolutism

In recent decades, historical studies of local institutions have challenged the traditional picture of absolute monarchs. It is misleading to think that these rulers actually controlled the lives of their subjects. In 1700, government for most people still meant the local institutions that affected their lives: local courts, local tax collectors, and local organizers of armed forces. Kings and ministers might determine policies and issue guidelines, but they still had to function through local agents and had no guarantee that their wishes would be carried out. A mass of urban and provincial privileges, liberties, and exemptions (including from taxation) and a whole host of corporate bodies and interest groups—provincial and national Estates, clerical officials, officeholders who had bought or inherited their positions, and provincial nobles—limited what monarchs could achieve. The most successful rulers were not those who tried to destroy the old system but rather those like Louis XIV who knew how to use the old system to their advantage. Above all other considerations stood the landholding nobility. Everywhere in the seventeenth century, the landed aristocracy played an important role in the European monarchical system. As military officers, judges, officeholders, and landowners in control of vast, untaxed estates, their power remained immense. In some places, their

Brandenburg-Prussia	
Frederick William the Great Elector	1640–1688
Elector Frederick III (King Frederick I)	1688–1713
Austrian Empire	
Leopold I	1658–1705
Ottoman siege of Vienna	1683
Russia	
Ivan IV the Terrible	1533–1584
Time of Troubles	1598–1613
Michael Romanov	1613–1645
Peter the Great	1689–1725
First trip to the West	1697–1698
Great Northern War	1701–1721
Founding of Saint Petersburg	1703
Battle of Poltava	1709
Holy Synod	1721
Ottoman Empire	
Suleiman I the Magnificent	1520–1566
Battle of Lepanto	1571
Ottoman defeat at Vienna	1683

strength even put severe limits on how effectively monarchs could rule.

Limited Monarchy: The Dutch Republic and England

Almost everywhere in Europe in the seventeenth century, kings and their ministers were in control of central governments. But not all European states followed the pattern of absolute monarchy. In western Europe, two great states—the Dutch Republic and England—successfully resisted the power of hereditary monarchs.

The Golden Age of the Dutch Republic

The seventeenth century has often been called the golden age of the Dutch Republic as the United Provinces held center stage as one of Europe's great powers. Like France and England, the United Provinces was an Atlantic power, underlining the importance of that shift of political and economic power in the seventeenth century from the Mediterranean Sea to the countries on the Atlantic seaboard. As a result of the sixteenth-century revolt of the Netherlands, the seven northern provinces, which began to call themselves the United Provinces of the Netherlands in 1581, became the core of the modern

Dutch state. The new state was officially recognized by the Peace of Westphalia in 1648.

With independence came internal dissension. There were two chief centers of political power in the new state. Each province had an official known as a stadholder who was responsible for leading the army and maintaining order. Beginning with William of Orange and his heirs, the house of Orange occupied the stadholderate in most provinces and favored the development of a centralized government with themselves as hereditary monarchs. The States General, an assembly of representatives from every province, opposed the Orangist ambitions and advocated a decentralized or republican form of government. For much of the seventeenth century, the republican forces were in control. But in 1672, burdened with war against both France and England, the United Provinces allowed William III (1672–1702) of the house of Orange to establish a monarchical regime. However, his death in 1702 without direct heirs enabled the republican forces to gain control once more. The Dutch Republic would not be seriously threatened again by the monarchical forces.

Underlying Dutch prominence in the seventeenth century was its economic prosperity, fueled by the role of the Dutch as carriers of European trade. But war proved disastrous to the Dutch Republic. Wars with France and England placed heavy burdens on Dutch finances and manpower. English shipping began to challenge what had been Dutch commercial supremacy, and by 1715, the Dutch were experiencing a serious economic decline.

England and the Emergence of Constitutional Monarchy

One of the most prominent examples of resistance to absolute monarchy came in seventeenth-century England, where king and Parliament struggled to determine the role each should play in governing the nation.

Revolution and Civil War With the death of Queen Elizabeth in 1603, the Tudor dynasty became extinct, and the Stuart line of rulers was inaugurated with the accession to the throne of Elizabeth's cousin, King James VI of Scotland, who became James I (1603–1625) of England. James espoused the divine right of kings, a viewpoint that alienated Parliament, which had grown accustomed under the Tudors to act on the premise that monarch and Parliament together ruled England as a "balanced polity." Parliament expressed its displeasure with James's claims by refusing his requests for additional monies he needed to meet the increased cost of government. Parliament's power of the purse proved to be its trump card in its relationship with the king.

Some members of Parliament were also alienated by James's religious policy. The **Puritans**—Protestants within the Anglican church inspired by Calvinist theology—wanted James to eliminate the episcopal system of church organization used in the Church of England (in which the

Cleanliness Is Next to Godliness. During the Golden Age of the Dutch Republic, Dutch burghers held to very strict standards of cleanliness. Household manuals, such as *The Experienced and Knowledgeable Hollands Householder*, provided detailed outlines of the cleaning tasks that should be performed each day of the week. This emphasis on cleanliness is evident in this work by Pieter de Hooch, who specialized in painting pictures of Dutch interiors. In *The Mother*, de Hooch portrays a tranquil scene of a mother with her infant and small daughter. The spotless, polished floors reflect the sunlight streaming in through the open door. The rooms are both clean and in good order.

bishop or *episcopos* played the major administrative role) in favor of a Presbyterian model (used in Scotland and patterned after Calvin's church organization in Geneva, where ministers and elders—also called presbyters—played an important governing role). James refused because he realized that the Anglican church, with its bishops appointed by the crown, was a major supporter of monarchical authority. But the Puritans were not easily cowed and added to the rising chorus of opposition to the king. Many of England's **gentry,** mostly well-to-do landowners below the level of the nobility, had become Puritans, and these Puritan gentry formed an important and substantial part of the House of Commons, the lower house of Parliament. It was not wise to alienate them.

The conflict that began during the reign of James came to a head during the reign of his son, Charles I (1625–1649). In 1628, Parliament passed a petition of right that the king was supposed to accept before being granted any tax revenues. This petition prohibited levying taxes without Parliament's consent, arbitrary imprisonment, the quartering of soldiers in private houses, and the declaration of martial law in peacetime. Although he initially accepted it, Charles later reneged on the agreement because of its limitations on royal power. In 1629,

Charles decided that because he could not work with Parliament, he would not summon it to meet. From 1629 to 1640, Charles pursued a course of "personal rule," which forced him to find ways to collect taxes without Parliament's cooperation. These expedients aroused opposition from middle-class merchants and landed gentry who believed that the king was attempting to tax without Parliament's consent.

The king's religious policy also proved disastrous. His attempt to impose more ritual on the Anglican church struck the Puritans as a return to Catholic popery. Charles's efforts to force them to conform to his religious policies infuriated the Puritans, thousands of whom abandoned England for the "howling wildernesses" of America.

Grievances mounted until England finally slipped into a civil war (1642–1648) that was won by the parliamentary forces. Most important to Parliament's success was the creation of the New Model Army, one of whose leaders was Oliver Cromwell, the only real military genius of the war. The New Model Army was composed primarily of more extreme Puritans known as the Independents, who, in typical Calvinist fashion, believed they were doing battle for the Lord. As Cromwell wrote in one of his military reports, "Sir, this is none other but the hand of God; and to Him alone belongs the glory."

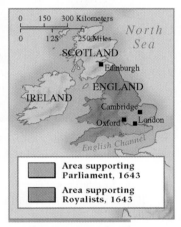

Civil War in England

Between 1648 and 1660, England faced a trying situation. After the execution of Charles I on January 30, 1649, Parliament abolished the monarchy and the House of Lords and proclaimed England a republic or commonwealth. But Cromwell and his army, unable to work effectively with Parliament, dispersed it by force. As the members of Parliament departed in April 1653, Cromwell shouted after them, "It's you that have forced me to do this, for I have sought the Lord night and day that He would slay me rather than put upon me the doing of this work." With the certainty of one who is convinced he is right, Cromwell had destroyed both king and Parliament.

Finally, Cromwell dissolved Parliament and divided the country into eleven regions, each ruled by a major general who served virtually as a military governor. Unable to establish a constitutional basis for a working government, Cromwell had resorted to military force to maintain the rule of the Independents.

Oliver Cromwell died in 1658. After floundering for eighteen months, the military establishment decided that arbitrary rule by the army was no longer feasible and reestablished the monarchy in the person of Charles II

Oliver Cromwell. Oliver Cromwell was a dedicated Puritan who formed the New Model Army and defeated the forces supporting King Charles I. Unable to work with Parliament, he came to rely on military force to rule England. Cromwell is pictured here in 1649, on the eve of his military campaign in Ireland.

CHRONOLOGY **Limited Monarchy and Republics**

United Provinces of the Netherlands	
Official recognition	1648
House of Orange: William III	1672–1702
England	
James I	1603–1625
Charles I	1625–1649
Petition of Right	1628
Civil Wars	1642–1648
Commonwealth	1649–1653
Death of Cromwell	1658
Restoration of monarchy	1660
Charles II	1660–1685
Declaration of Indulgence	1672
Test Act	1673
James II	1685–1688
Declaration of Indulgence	1687
Glorious Revolution	1688
Bill of Rights	1689

(1660–1685), the son of Charles I. The restoration of the Stuart monarchy ended England's time of troubles, but it was not long before yet another constitutional crisis arose.

Restoration and a Glorious Revolution Charles was sympathetic to and perhaps even inclined to Catholicism. Moreover, Charles's brother James, heir to the throne, did not hide the fact that he was a Catholic. Parliament's suspicions were therefore aroused in 1672 when Charles took the audacious step of issuing a declaration of indulgence that suspended the laws that Parliament had passed against Catholics and Puritans after the restoration of the Anglican church as the official church of England. Parliament would have none of it and induced the king to suspend the declaration. Propelled by strong anti-Catholic sentiment, Parliament then passed the Test Act of 1673, specifying that only Anglicans could hold military and civil offices.

The accession of James II (1685–1688) to the crown virtually guaranteed a new constitutional crisis for England. An open and devout Catholic, his attempt to further Catholic interests made religion once more a primary cause of conflict between king and Parliament. In 1687, James issued a declaration of indulgence that suspended all laws that excluded Catholics and Puritans from office. Parliamentary outcries against James's policies stopped short of rebellion because members knew that he was an old man and his successors were his Protestant daughters Mary and Anne, born to his first wife. But on June 10, 1688, a son was born to James II's second wife, also a Catholic. Suddenly the specter of a Catholic hereditary monarchy loomed large. A group of prominent English noblemen invited the Dutch chief executive, William of Orange, husband of James's daughter Mary, to invade England. William and Mary raised an army and invaded England while James, his wife, and their infant son fled to France. With almost no bloodshed, England had undergone its "Glorious Revolution," not over the issue of whether there would be monarchy but rather over who would be monarch.

In January 1689, Parliament offered the throne to William and Mary, who accepted it along with the provisions of a bill of rights (see the box on p. 295). The Bill of Rights affirmed Parliament's right to make laws and levy taxes and made it impossible for kings to oppose or do without Parliament by stipulating that standing armies could be raised only with the consent of Parliament. The rights of citizens to petition the sovereign, keep arms,

THE BILL OF RIGHTS

In 1688, the English experienced yet another revolution, a bloodless one in which the Stuart king James II was replaced by Mary, James's daughter, and her husband, William of Orange. After William and Mary had assumed power, Parliament passed a bill of rights that specified the rights of Parliament and laid the foundation for a constitutional monarchy.

The Bill of Rights

Whereas the said late King James II having abdicated the government, and the throne being thereby vacant, his Highness the prince of Orange (whom it has pleased Almighty God to make the glorious instrument of delivering this kingdom from popery and arbitrary power) did (by the device of the lords spiritual and temporal, and diverse principal persons of the Commons) cause letters to be written to the lords spiritual and temporal, being Protestants, and other letters to the several counties, cities, universities, boroughs, and Cinque Ports, for the choosing of such persons to represent them, as were of right to be sent to parliament, to meet and sit at Westminster upon the two and twentieth day of January, in this year 1689, in order to such an establishment as that their religion, laws, and liberties might not again be in danger of being subverted; upon which letters elections have been accordingly made.

And thereupon the said lords spiritual and temporal and Commons, pursuant to their respective letters and elections, being now assembled in a full and free representation of this nation, taking into their most serious consideration the best means for attaining the ends aforesaid, do in the first place (as their ancestors in like case have usually done), for the vindication and assertion of their ancient rights and liberties, declare:

1. That the pretended power of suspending laws, or the execution of laws, by regal authority, without consent of parliament is illegal.
2. That the pretended power of dispensing with the laws, or the execution of law by regal authority, as it has been assumed and exercised of late, is illegal.
3. That the commission for erecting the late court of commissioners for ecclesiastical causes, and all other commissions and courts of like nature, are illegal and pernicious.
4. That levying money for or to the use of the crown by pretense of prerogative, without grant of parliament, for longer time or in other manner than the same is or shall be granted, is illegal.
5. That it is the right of the subjects to petition the king, and all commitments and prosecutions for such petitioning are illegal.
6. That the raising or keeping a standing army within the kingdom in time of peace, unless it be with consent of parliament, is against law.
7. That the subjects which are Protestants may have arms for their defense suitable to their conditions, and as allowed by law.
8. That election of members of parliament ought to be free.
9. That the freedom of speech, and debates or proceedings in parliament, ought not to be impeached or questioned in any court or place out of parliament.
10. That excessive bail ought not to be required, nor excessive fines imposed, nor cruel and unusual punishments inflicted.
11. That jurors ought to be duly impaneled and returned, and jurors which pass upon men in trials for high treason ought to be freeholders.
12. That all grants and promises of fines and forfeitures of particular persons before conviction are illegal and void.
13. And that for redress of all grievances, and for the amending, strengthening, and preserving of the laws, parliament ought to be held frequently.

How did the Bill of Rights lay the foundation for a constitutional monarchy in England?

have a jury trial, and not be subject to excessive bail were also confirmed. The Bill of Rights helped fashion a system of government based on the rule of law and a freely elected Parliament, thus laying the foundation for a constitutional monarchy.

The Bill of Rights did not settle the religious questions that had played such a large role in England's troubles in the seventeenth century. The Toleration Act of 1689 granted Puritan dissenters the right of free public worship (Catholics were still excluded). Although the Toleration Act did not mean complete religious freedom and equality, it marked a departure in English history in that few people would ever again be persecuted for religious reasons.

Many historians have viewed the Glorious Revolution as the end of the seventeenth-century struggle between king and Parliament. By deposing one king and establishing another, Parliament had destroyed the divine-right theory of kingship (William was, after all, king by grace of Parliament, not God) and confirmed its right to participate in the government. Parliament did not have complete control of the government, but it now had an unquestioned right to participate in affairs of state. During the next century, it would gradually prove to be the real authority in the English system of constitutional monarchy.

Responses to Revolution   The English revolutions of the seventeenth century prompted very different responses from two English political thinkers, Thomas Hobbes and John Locke. Thomas Hobbes (1588–1679), who lived during the English Civil War, was alarmed by the revolutionary upheavals in his contemporary England. His name has since been associated with the state's claim to absolute authority over its subjects, which he elaborated in his major treatise on political thought known as the *Leviathan,* published in 1651.

Hobbes claimed that in the state of nature, before society was organized, human life was "solitary, poor, nasty, brutish, and short." Humans were guided by animalistic instincts and a ruthless struggle for self-preservation. To save themselves from destroying each other (the "war of every man against every man"), people contracted to form a commonwealth, which Hobbes called "that great Leviathan (or rather, to speak more reverently, that mortal god) to which we owe our peace and defense." This commonwealth placed its collective power in the hands of a sovereign authority, preferably a single ruler, who served as executor, legislator, and judge. This absolute ruler possessed unlimited power. In Hobbes's view, subjects may not rebel; if they do, they must be suppressed.

John Locke (1632–1704), author of a political work called *Two Treatises of Government,* viewed the exercise of political power quite differently from Hobbes and argued against the absolute rule of one man. Like Hobbes, Locke began with the state of nature before human existence became organized socially. But unlike Hobbes, Locke believed that humans lived then in a state of equality and freedom rather than a state of war. In this state of nature, humans had certain inalienable natural rights—to life, liberty, and property. Like Hobbes, Locke did not believe that all was well in the state of nature, and people found it difficult to protect these rights. So they mutually agreed to establish a government to ensure the protection of their rights. This agreement established mutual obligations: government would protect the rights of people, and the people would act reasonably toward their government. But if a government broke this agreement—if a king, for example, failed to live up to his obligation to protect the people's rights or claimed absolute authority and made laws without the consent of the community—the people might form a new government. For Locke, however, the community of people was primarily the landholding aristocracy who were represented in Parliament, not the landless masses. Locke was hardly an advocate of political democracy, but his ideas proved important to both the Americans and the French in the eighteenth century and were used to support demands for constitutional government, the rule of law, and the protection of rights.

The Flourishing of European Culture

In the midst of religious wars and the growth of absolutism, European culture continued to flourish. The era was blessed with a number of prominent artists and writers.

The Changing Faces of Art

After the Renaissance, European art passed through a number of stylistic stages. The artistic Renaissance came to an end when a new movement called Mannerism emerged in Italy in the 1520s and 1530s.

Mannerism   The Reformation had brought a revival of religious values accompanied by much political turmoil. Especially in Italy, the worldly enthusiasm of the Renaissance gave way to anxiety, uncertainty, suffering, and a yearning for spiritual experience. **Mannerism** reflected this environment in its deliberate attempt to break down the High Renaissance principles of balance, harmony, and moderation. Italian Mannerist painters deliberately distorted the rules of proportion by portraying elongated figures that conveyed a sense of suffering and a strong emotional atmosphere filled with anxiety and confusion.

The Baroque   Mannerism was eventually replaced by a new movement—the **Baroque**—that dominated the artistic world for another century and a half. The Baroque began in Italy in the last quarter of the sixteenth century and spread to the rest of Europe. Baroque artists sought to harmonize the classical traditions of Renaissance art with the intense religious feelings fostered by the revival of religion in the Reformation. Although Protestants were also affected, the Baroque was most wholeheartedly embraced by the Catholic reform movement, as is evident at the Catholic courts, especially those of the Habsburgs in Madrid, Prague, Vienna, and Brussels. Eventually, the Baroque style spread to all of Europe and Latin America.

In large part, Baroque art and architecture reflected the search for power that was characteristic of much of the seventeenth century. Baroque churches and palaces featured richly ornamented facades, sweeping staircases, and an overall splendor intended to impress people. Kings and princes wanted their subjects—as well as other kings and princes—to be in awe of their power. The Catholic church, which commissioned many new churches, wanted people to see the triumphant power of the Catholic faith.

Baroque painting was known for its use of dramatic effects to heighten emotional intensity. This style was especially evident in the works of the Flemish painter Peter Paul Rubens (1577–1640), a prolific artist and an important figure in the spread of the Baroque from Italy to other parts of Europe. In his artistic masterpieces,

Peter Paul Rubens, *The Landing of Marie de'Medici at Marseilles*. The Fleming Peter Paul Rubens played a key role in spreading the Baroque style from Italy to other parts of Europe. In *The Landing of Marie de'Medici at Marseilles*, Rubens made a dramatic use of light and color, bodies in motion, and luxurious nudes to heighten the emotional intensity of the scene. This was one of a cycle of twenty-one paintings dedicated to the queen mother of France.

Artemisia Gentileschi, *Judith Beheading Holofernes*. Artemisia Gentileschi painted a series of pictures portraying scenes from the lives of courageous Old Testament women. In this painting, a determined Judith, armed with her victim's sword, struggles to saw off the head of Holofernes. Gentileschi realistically and dramatically shows the gruesome nature of Judith's act.

bodies in vigorous motion, fleshy nudes, a dramatic use of light and shadow, and rich, sensuous pigments convey intense emotions. The restless forms and sense of movement blend into a dynamic unity.

Perhaps the greatest figure of the Baroque was the Italian architect and sculptor Gian Lorenzo Bernini (1598–1680), who completed Saint Peter's Basilica and designed the vast colonnade enclosing the piazza in front of it. Action, exuberance, profusion, and dramatic effects mark his work in the interior of Saint Peter's, where Bernini's *Throne of Saint Peter* hovers in midair, held by the hands of the four great doctors of the Catholic church.

Less well known than the male artists who dominated the seventeenth-century art world in Italy but prominent in her own right was Artemisia Gentileschi (1593–1653). Born in Rome, she studied painting under her father's direction. In 1616, she moved to Florence

and began a successful career as a painter. At the age of twenty-three, she became the first woman to be elected to the Florentine Academy of Design. Although she was known internationally in her day as a portrait painter, her fame now rests on a series of pictures of heroines from the Old Testament, including Judith, Esther, and Bathsheba. Most famous is her *Judith Beheading Holofernes*, a dramatic rendering of the biblical scene in which Judith slays the Assyrian general Holofernes in order to save her besieged town from the Assyrian army.

French Classicism and Dutch Realism In the second half of the seventeenth century, France replaced Italy as the cultural leader of Europe. Rejecting the Baroque style as showy and overly passionate, the French remained committed to the classical values of the High Renaissance. French late classicism, with its emphasis on clarity,

© SuperStock, Inc./SuperStock (Rijksmuseum, Amsterdam)

Rembrandt van Rijn, *Syndics of the Cloth Guild*.   The Dutch experienced a golden age of painting during the seventeenth century. The burghers and patricians of Dutch urban society commissioned works of art, and these quite naturally reflected the burghers' interests, as this painting by Rembrandt illustrates.

simplicity, balance, and harmony of design, was, however, a rather austere version of the High Renaissance style. Its triumph reflected the shift in seventeenth-century French society from chaos to order. While rejecting the emotionalism and high drama of the Baroque, French classicism continued the Baroque's conception of grandeur in the portrayal of noble subjects, especially those from classical antiquity.

The supremacy of Dutch commerce in the seventeenth century was paralleled by a brilliant flowering of Dutch painting. Wealthy patricians and burghers of Dutch urban society commissioned works of art for their guild halls, town halls, and private dwellings. Following the wishes of these patrons, Dutch painters became primarily interested in the realistic portrayal of secular, everyday life.

The finest exemplar of the golden age of Dutch painting was Rembrandt van Rijn (1606–1669). Although Rembrandt shared the Dutch predilection for realistic portraits, he became more introspective as he grew older. He refused to follow his contemporaries, whose pictures were largely secular in subject matter; half of his paintings focused on scenes from biblical tales. Because the traditional Protestant hostility toward religious

pictures had discouraged artistic expression, Rembrandt stands out as the one great Protestant painter of the seventeenth century.

A Wondrous Age of Theater

In both England and Spain, writing for the stage reached new heights between 1580 and 1640. The golden age of English literature is often called the Elizabethan era because much of this English cultural flowering occurred during the reign of Queen Elizabeth. Elizabethan literature exhibits the exuberance and pride associated with English exploits at the time. Of all the forms of Elizabethan literature, none expressed the energy and intellectual versatility of the era better than drama. And of all the dramatists, none is more famous than William Shakespeare (1564–1614).

William Shakespeare   Shakespeare was the son of a prosperous glove maker from Stratford-upon-Avon. When he appeared in London in 1592, Elizabethans were already addicted to the stage. In Greater London, as many as six theaters were open six afternoons a week. London

WILLIAM SHAKESPEARE: IN PRAISE OF ENGLAND

*W*illiam Shakespeare is one of the most famous playwrights of the Western world. He was a universal genius, outclassing all others in his psychological insights, depth of characterization, imaginative skills, and versatility. His historical plays reflected the patriotic enthusiasm of the English in the Elizabethan era, as this excerpt from *Richard II* illustrates.

William Shakespeare, *Richard II*

> This royal throne of kings, this sceptered isle,
> This earth of majesty, this seat of Mars,
> This other Eden, demi-Paradise,
> This fortress built by Nature for herself
> Against infection and the hand of war,
> This happy breed of men, this little world,
> This precious stone set in the silver sea,
> Which serves it in the office of a wall
> Or as a moat defensive to a house
> Against the envy of less happier lands—
> This blessed plot, this earth, this realm, this England,
> This nurse, this teeming womb of royal kings,
> Feared by their breed and famous by their birth,
> Renowned for their deeds as far from home,
> For Christian service and true chivalry,
> As is the sepulcher in stubborn Jewry [the Holy
>   Sepulcher in Jerusalem]
> Of the world's ransom, blessed Mary's Son—
> This land of such dear souls, this dear dear land,
> Dear for her reputation through the world,
> Is now leased out, I die pronouncing it,
> Like a tenement or pelting farm.
> England, bound in with the triumphant sea,
> Whose rocky shore beats back the envious siege
> Of watery Neptune, is now bound in with shame,
> With inky blots and rotten parchment bonds.
> That England, what was wont to conquer others,
> Hath made a shameful conquest of itself.
> Ah, would the scandal vanish with my life,
> How happy then were my ensuing death!

Why is William Shakespeare aptly described as not merely a playwright but a "complete man of the theater"? Which countries might Shakespeare have meant to suggest by the phrase "the envy of less happier lands"?

---

theaters ranged from the Globe, which was a circular unroofed structure holding three thousand spectators, to the Blackfriars, which was roofed and held only five hundred. In the former, the admission charge of only a penny or two enabled even the lower classes to attend, while the higher prices charged in the latter attracted the well-to-do. Elizabethan audiences varied greatly, consisting as they did of nobles, lawyers, merchants, and even vagabonds—putting pressure on playwrights to create works that pleased all.

Shakespeare was a "complete man of the theater." Although best known for writing plays, he was also an actor and a shareholder in the chief performing company of the time, the Lord Chamberlain's Company, which played in theaters as diverse as the Globe and the Blackfriars. Shakespeare has long been recognized as a universal genius. He was a master of the English language, but this technical proficiency was matched by an incredible insight into human psychology. In both tragedies and comedies, Shakespeare exhibited a remarkable understanding of the human condition (see the box above).

Spain's Golden Century The theater was one of the most creative forms of expression during Spain's golden century. The first professional theaters founded in Seville and Madrid in the 1570s were run by actors' companies, as in England. Soon a public playhouse could be found in every large town, including Mexico City in the New World. Touring companies brought the latest Spanish plays to all parts of the Spanish Empire.

Beginning in the 1580s, the agenda for playwrights was set by Lope de Vega (1562–1635). Like Shakespeare, he was from a middle-class background. He was an incredibly prolific writer; almost one-third of his fifteen hundred plays survive. They have been characterized as witty, charming, action-packed, and realistic. Lope de Vega made no apologies for the fact that he wrote his plays to please his audiences. In a treatise on drama written in 1609, he stated that the foremost duty of the playwright was to satisfy public demand. He remarked that if anyone thought he had written his plays for fame, "undeceive him and tell him that I wrote them for money."

French Drama As the great age of theater in England and Spain was drawing to a close around 1630, a new dramatic era began to dawn in France that lasted into the 1680s. Unlike Shakespeare in England and Lope de Vega in Spain, French playwrights wrote more for an elite audience and were forced to depend on royal patronage. Louis XIV used theater as he did art and architecture—to attract attention to his monarchy. French dramatists cultivated a classical style that emphasized the clever, polished, and correct over the emotional and imaginative. Many of the French works of this period derived their themes and plots from Greek and Roman sources.

Jean-Baptiste Molière (1622–1673) enjoyed the favor of the French court and benefited from the patronage of the Sun King. He wrote, produced, and acted in a series of comedies that often satirized the religious and social world of his time. In *The Misanthrope,* he mocked the corruption of court society, while in *Tartuffe,* he ridiculed religious hypocrisy. Molière's satires, however, sometimes got him into trouble. The Paris clergy did not find *Tartuffe* funny and had it banned for five years. Only the protection of Louis XIV saved Molière from more severe harassment.

TIMELINE

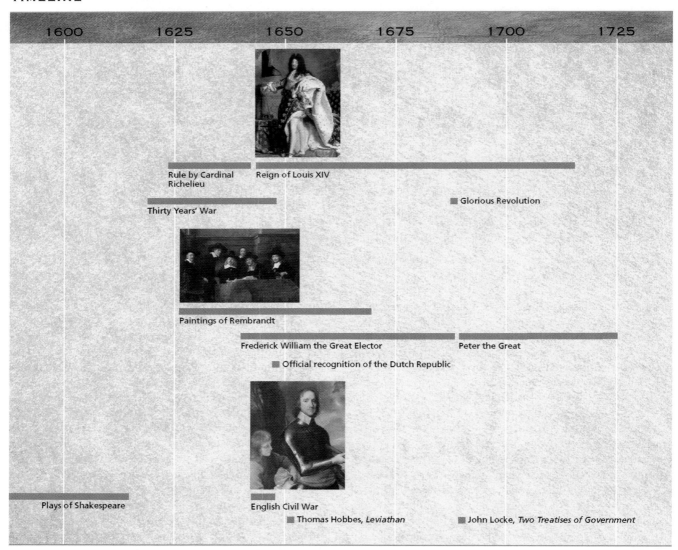

| 1600 | 1625 | 1650 | 1675 | 1700 | 1725 |

Rule by Cardinal Richelieu

Reign of Louis XIV

Thirty Years' War

Glorious Revolution

Paintings of Rembrandt

Frederick William the Great Elector

Peter the Great

Official recognition of the Dutch Republic

Plays of Shakespeare

English Civil War

Thomas Hobbes, *Leviathan*

John Locke, *Two Treatises of Government*

CONCLUSION

To many historians, the seventeenth century has assumed extraordinary proportions. The divisive effects of the Reformation had been assimilated, and the concept of a united Christendom, held as an ideal since the Middle Ages, had been irrevocably destroyed by the religious wars, making possible the emergence of a system of nation-states in which power politics took on increasing significance. The growth of political thought focusing on the secular origins of state power reflected the changes that were going on in seventeenth-century society.

Within those states, there slowly emerged some of the machinery that made possible a growing centralization of power. In those states called absolutist, strong monarchs with the assistance of their aristocracies took the lead in providing the leadership for greater centralization. But in England, where the landed aristocracy gained power at the expense of the monarchs, the foundations were laid for a constitutional government in which Parliament provided the focus for the institutions of centralized power. In all the major European states, a growing concern for power and dynastic expansion led to larger armies and greater conflict. War remained an endemic feature of Western civilization.

But the search for order and harmony continued, evident in art and literature. At the same time, religious preoccupations and values were losing ground to secular considerations. The seventeenth century was a period of transition toward the more secular spirit that has characterized modern Western civilization ever since. No stronger foundation for this spirit could be found than in the new view of the universe that was ushered in by the Scientific Revolution of the seventeenth century, and it is to that story that we now turn.

NOTES

1. Quoted in J. Klaits, *Servants of Satan: The Age of the Witch Hunts* (Bloomington, Ind., 1985), p. 68.
2. Quoted in ibid., p. 68.
3. Quoted in J. B. Wolf, *Louis XIV* (New York, 1968), p. 134.
4. Quoted in J. H. Elliot, *Imperial Spain, 1469–1716* (New York, 1963), p. 306.

SUGGESTIONS FOR FURTHER READING

For general works on the seventeenth century, see **D. H. Pennington, *Europe in the Seventeenth Century*,** 2d ed. (New York, 1989); **T. Munck, *Seventeenth-Century Europe, 1598–1700*** (London, 1990); and **R. S. Dunn, *The Age of Religious Wars, 1559–1715*,** 2d ed. (New York, 1979).

The story of the witchcraft craze can be examined in **J. Klaits, *Servants of Satan: The Age of the Witch Hunts*** (Bloomington, Ind., 1985); **J. B. Russell, *A History of Witchcraft*** (London, 1980); and **B. P. Levack, *The Witch-Hunt in Early Modern Europe*** (London, 1987).

The classic study on the Thirty Years' War is **C. V. Wedgwood, *The Thirty Years' War*** (Garden City, N.Y., 1961), but it needs to be supplemented by the more recent works by **G. Parker, ed., *The Thirty Years' War*,** 2d ed. (London, 1997); **R. G. Asch, *The Thirty Years' War: The Holy Roman Empire and Europe, 1618–1648*** (New York, 1997); and the brief study by **S. J. Lee, *The Thirty Years' War*** (London, 1991).

For a succinct account of seventeenth-century French history, see **J. B. Collins, *The State in Early Modern France*** (Cambridge, 1995). A solid and very readable biography of Louis XIV is **J. B. Wolf, *Louis XIV*** (New York, 1968), but also see **A. Levi, *Louis XIV*** (New York, 2004). A good general work on seventeenth-century Spanish history is **J. Lynch, *Spain Under the Habsburgs*,** 2d ed. (New York, 1981).

On the German states, see **P. H. Wilson, *The Holy Roman Empire, 1495–1806*** (New York, 1999), and **M. Hughes, *Early Modern Germany, 1477–1806*** (Philadelphia, 1992). On the creation of Austria, see **C. Ingrao, *The Habsburg Monarchy, 1618–1815*** (Cambridge, 1994), and **P. S. Fichtner, *The Habsburg Monarchy,***

1490–1848 (New York, 2003). On Austria and Prussia, see **P. H. Wilson, *Absolutism in Central Europe*** (New York, 2000). On Frederick William the Great Elector, see **D. McKay, *The Great Elector*** (Essex, 2001).

On Russian history before Peter the Great, see the classic work by **V. O. Klyuchevsky, *A Course in Russian History: The Seventeenth Century*** (Chicago, 1968). Works on Peter the Great include **L. Hughes, *Russia in the Age of Peter the Great*** (New Haven, Conn., 1998), and **M. S. Anderson, *Peter the Great*,** 2d ed. (New York, 1995).

Good general works on the period of the English Revolution include **M. A. Kishlansky, *A Monarchy Transformed*** (London, 1996); **G. E. Aylmer, *Rebellion or Revolution? England, 1640–1660*** (New York, 1986); and **A. Hughes, *The Causes of the English Civil War*** (New York, 1991). On Oliver Cromwell, see **R. Howell Jr., *Cromwell*** (Boston, 1977), and **P. Gaunt, *Oliver Cromwell*** (Cambridge, Mass., 1996). For a general survey of the post-Cromwellian era, see **T. Harris, *Politics Under the Late Stuarts*** (London, 1993). On Charles II, see the scholarly biography by **R. Hutton, *Charles II*** (Oxford, 1989). Locke's political ideas are examined in **J. H. Franklin, *John Locke and the Theory of Sovereignty*** (London, 1978). On Thomas Hobbes, see **D. D. Raphael, *Hobbes*** (London, 1977).

On the United Provinces, **J. Israel, *The Dutch Republic: Its Rise, Greatness, and Fall*** (New York, 1995), is a valuable but lengthy study. Of much value is **S. Schama, *The Embarrassment of Riches: An Interpretation of Dutch Culture in the Golden Age*** (New York, 1987).

A brief, readable guide to Mannerism is **L. Murray, *The Late Renaissance and Mannerism*** (New York, 1967). For a general survey of Baroque culture, see **M. Mainstone and L. Mainstone, *The Cambridge Introduction to Art: The Seventeenth Century*** (Cambridge, 1981), and **J. S. Held, *Seventeenth and Eighteenth Century Art: Baroque Painting, Sculpture, Architecture*** (New York, 1971). The literature on Shakespeare is enormous. For a biography, see **A. L. Rowse, *The Life of Shakespeare*** (New York, 1963). French theater and literature are examined in **A. Adam, *Grandeur and Illusion: French Literature and Society, 1600–1715*, trans.** J. Tint (New York, 1972). For an examination of French and Dutch art, see **A. Merot, *French Painting in the Seventeenth Century*** (New Haven, Conn., 1995), and **S. Slive, *Dutch Painting, 1600–1800*** (New Haven, Conn., 1993).

Thomson NOW! Enter *ThomsonNOW* using the access card that is available for *Western Civilization: A Brief History*. *ThomsonNOW* will help you understand this chapter with lesson plans generated for your needs. In addition, you can read the following documents, and many more, online:

John Locke, *An Essay Concerning Human Understanding*
King Frederick William, Welcoming the Huguenots to Prussia
John Milton, *The Tenure of Kings and Magistrates*
Jean Rousset de Missy, describing Russians in Western dress

16

TOWARD A NEW HEAVEN AND A NEW EARTH: THE SCIENTIFIC REVOLUTION AND THE EMERGENCE OF MODERN SCIENCE

CHAPTER OUTLINE AND FOCUS QUESTIONS

Background to the Scientific Revolution

☐ What developments during the Middle Ages and the Renaissance contributed to the Scientific Revolution of the sixteenth century?

Toward a New Heaven: A Revolution in Astronomy

☐ What did Copernicus, Kepler, Galileo, and Newton contribute to a new vision of the universe, and how did it differ from the Ptolemaic conception of the universe?

Advances in Medicine and Chemistry

☐ What did Paracelsus, Vesalius, and Harvey contribute to a scientific view of medicine?

Women in the Origins of Modern Science

☐ What role did women play in the Scientific Revolution?

Toward a New Earth: Descartes, Rationalism, and a New View of Humankind

☐ Why is Descartes considered the "founder of modern rationalism"?

The Spread of Scientific Knowledge

☐ How were the ideas of the Scientific Revolution spread, and what impact did they have on society and religion?

CRITICAL THINKING

☐ In what ways were the intellectual, political, social, and religious developments of the seventeenth century related?

The trial of Galileo

Erich Lessing/Art Resource, NY

𝓘N ADDITION TO POLITICAL, economic, and social crises, the seventeenth century witnessed an intellectual one. The Scientific Revolution questioned and ultimately challenged conceptions and beliefs about the nature of the external world and reality that had crystallized into a rather strict orthodoxy by the Later Middle Ages. Derived from the works of ancient Greeks and Romans and grounded in Christian thought, the medieval worldview had become almost overpowering. But the breakdown of Christian unity during the Reformation and the subsequent religious wars had created an environment in which Europeans became more comfortable with challenging both the ecclesiastical and political powers that be. Should it surprise us that a challenge to intellectual authority soon followed?

The Scientific Revolution taught Europeans to view the universe and their place in it in a new way. The shift from an earth-centered to a sun-centered cosmos had an emotional as well as intellectual effect on those who understood it. Thus the Scientific Revolution, popularized in the eighteenth-century Enlightenment, stands as the major force in the transition to the largely secular, rational, and materialistic perspective that has defined the modern Western mentality in modern times.

The transition to a new worldview, however, was far from easy. In the seventeenth century, the Italian scientist Galileo, an outspoken advocate of the new worldview, found that his ideas were strongly opposed by the authorities of the Catholic church. Galileo's position was clear: "I hold the sun to be situated motionless in the center of the revolution of the celestial bodies, while the earth rotates on its axis and revolves about the sun." Moreover, "nothing physical that sense-experience sets before our eyes...ought to be called in question (much less condemned) upon the testimony of biblical passages." But the church had a different view, and in 1633, Galileo, now sixty-eight and in ill health, was called before the dreaded Inquisition in Rome. He was kept waiting for two months before he was tried and found guilty of heresy and disobedience. Completely shattered by the experience, he denounced his errors: "With a sincere heart and unfeigned faith I curse and detest the said errors and heresies contrary to the Holy Church." Legend holds that when he left the trial rooms, Galileo muttered to himself: "And yet it does move!" In any case, Galileo had been silenced, but his writings remained, and they began to spread through Europe. The actions of the Inquisition had failed to stop the spread of the new ideas of the Scientific Revolution.

In one sense, the Scientific Revolution was not a revolution. It was not characterized by the explosive change and rapid overthrow of traditional authority that we normally associate with the word *revolution*. The Scientific Revolution did overturn centuries of authority, but only in a gradual and piecemeal fashion. Nevertheless, its results were truly revolutionary. The Scientific Revolution was a key factor in setting Western civilization on its modern secular and material path.✦

Background to the Scientific Revolution

To say that the **Scientific Revolution** brought about a dissolution of the medieval worldview is not to say that the Middle Ages was a period of scientific ignorance. Many educated Europeans took an intense interest in the world around them, regarding it as "God's handiwork" and therefore an appropriate subject for study. Late medieval scholastic philosophers had advanced mathematical and physical thinking in many ways, but the subjection of these thinkers to a strict theological framework and their unquestioning reliance on a few ancient authorities, especially Aristotle and Galen, limited where they could go. Many "natural philosophers," as medieval scientists were known, preferred refined logical analysis to systematic observations of the natural world. A number of changes and advances in the fifteenth and sixteenth centuries may have played a major role in helping "natural philosophers" abandon their old views and develop new ones.

Ancient Authors and Renaissance Artists

The Renaissance humanists mastered both Greek and Latin and made works by Ptolemy and Archimedes as well as Plato newly available. These writings made it clear that even the unquestioned authorities of the Middle Ages, Aristotle and Galen, had been contradicted by other thinkers. The desire to discover which school of thought was correct stimulated new scientific work that sometimes led to a complete rejection of the classical authorities.

Renaissance artists have also been credited with having an impact on scientific study. Their desire to imitate nature led them to rely on a close observation of nature. Their accurate renderings of rocks, plants, animals, and human anatomy established new standards for the study of natural phenomena. At the same time, the "scientific" study of the problems of perspective and correct anatomical proportions led to new insights. "No painter," one Renaissance artist declared, "can paint well without a thorough knowledge of geometry."[1]

Technological Innovations and Mathematics

Technical problems, such as calculating the tonnage of ships accurately, also served to stimulate scientific activity because they required careful observation and accurate measurements. Then, too, the invention of new instruments and machines, such as the telescope and microscope, often made new scientific discoveries possible. The printing press played a crucial role in spreading innovative ideas quickly and easily.

Mathematics, so fundamental to the scientific achievements of the sixteenth and seventeenth centuries, was promoted in the Renaissance by the rediscovery of the works of ancient mathematicians and the influence of Plato, who had emphasized the importance of mathematics in explaining the universe. Applauded as the key to navigation, military science, and geography, mathematics was also regarded as the key to understanding the nature of things. According to Leonardo da Vinci, since God eternally geometrizes, nature is inherently mathematical: "Proportion is not only found in numbers and measurements but also in sounds, weights, times, positions, and in whatsoever power there may be."[2] Copernicus, Kepler, Galileo, and Newton were all great mathematicians who believed that the secrets of nature were written in the language of mathematics.

Renaissance Magic

Another factor in the Scientific Revolution may have been magic. Renaissance magic was the preserve of the intellectual elite of Europe. By the end of the sixteenth century, Hermetic magic (see Chapter 12) had become fused with alchemical thought into a single intellectual framework. This tradition believed that the world was a living embodiment of divinity. Humans, who it was believed also had that spark of divinity within, could use magic, especially mathematical magic, to understand and dominate

ON THE REVOLUTIONS OF THE HEAVENLY SPHERES

*N*icolaus Copernicus began a revolution in astronomy when he argued that the sun and not the earth was at the center of the universe. Expecting controversy and scorn, Copernicus hesitated to publish the work in which he put forth his heliocentric theory. He finally relented, however, and managed to see a copy of it just before he died.

Nicolaus Copernicus, *On the Revolutions of the Heavenly Spheres*

For a long time, then, I reflected on this confusion in the astronomical traditions concerning the derivation of the motions of the universe's spheres. I began to be annoyed that the movements of the world machine, created for our sake by the best and most systematic Artisan of all, were not understood with greater certainty by the philosophers, who otherwise examined so precisely the most insignificant trifles of this world. For this reason I undertook the task of re-reading the works of all the philosophers which I could obtain to learn whether anyone had ever proposed other motions of the universe's spheres than those expounded by the teachers of astronomy in the schools. And in fact first I found in Cicero that Hicetas supposed the earth to move. Later I also discovered in Plutarch that certain others were of this opinion. I have decided to set his words down here, so that they may be available to everybody:

> Some think that the earth remains at rest. But Philolaus the Pythagorean believes that, like the sun and moon, it revolves around the fire in an oblique circle. Heraclides of Pontus and Ecphantus the Pythagorean make the earth move, not in a progressive motion, but like a wheel in a rotation from the west to east about its own center.

Therefore, having obtained the opportunity from these sources, I too began to consider the mobility of the earth. And even though the idea seemed absurd, nevertheless I know that others before me had been granted the freedom to imagine any circles whatever for the purpose of explaining the heavenly phenomena. Hence I thought that I too would be readily permitted to ascertain whether explanations sounder than those of my predecessors could be found for the revolution of the celestial spheres on the assumption of some motion of the earth.

Having thus assumed the motions which I ascribe to the earth later on in the volume, by long and intense study I finally found that if the motions of the other planets are correlated with the orbiting of the earth, and are computed for the revolution of each planet, not only do their phenomena follow therefrom but also the order and size of all the planets and spheres, and heaven itself is so linked together that in no portion of it can anything be shifted without disrupting the remaining parts and the universe as a whole....

Hence I feel no shame in asserting that this whole region engirdled by the moon, and the center of the earth, traverse this grand circle amid the rest of the planets in an annual revolution around the sun. Near the sun is the center of the universe. Moreover, since the sun remains stationary, whatever appears as a motion of the sun is really due rather to the motion of the earth.

What major new ideas did Copernicus discuss in this excerpt? What was the source of these ideas?

---

the world of nature or employ the powers of nature for beneficial purposes. Was it Hermeticism, then, that inaugurated the shift in consciousness that made the Scientific Revolution possible, since the desire to control and dominate the natural world was a crucial motivating force in the Scientific Revolution? Scholars debate the issue, but histories of the Scientific Revolution frequently overlook the fact that the great names we associate with the revolution in cosmology—Copernicus, Kepler, Galileo, and Newton—all had a serious interest in Hermetic ideas and the fields of astrology and alchemy. The mention of these names also reminds us of one final consideration in the origins of the Scientific Revolution: it resulted largely from the work of a handful of great intellectuals.

Toward a New Heaven: A Revolution in Astronomy

The cosmological views of the Later Middle Ages had been built on a synthesis of the ideas of Aristotle, Ptolemy (the greatest astronomer of antiquity, who lived in the second century A.D.), and Christian theology. In the resulting Ptolemaic or **geocentric conception**, the universe was seen as a series of concentric spheres with a fixed or motionless earth as its center. Composed of material substance, the earth was imperfect and constantly changing. The spheres that surrounded the earth were made of a crystalline, transparent substance and moved in circular orbits around the earth. Circular movement, according to Aristotle, was the most "perfect" kind of motion and hence appropriate for the "perfect" heavenly bodies thought to consist of a nonmaterial, incorruptible "quintessence." These heavenly bodies, pure orbs of light, were embedded in the moving, concentric spheres, which in 1500 numbered ten. Working outward from the earth, eight spheres contained the moon, Mercury, Venus, the sun, Mars, Jupiter, Saturn, and the fixed stars. The ninth sphere imparted to the eighth sphere of the fixed stars its motion, while the tenth sphere was frequently described as the prime mover that moved itself and imparted motion to the other spheres. Beyond the tenth sphere was the

Medieval Conception of the Universe. As this sixteenth-century illustration shows, the medieval cosmological view placed the earth at the center of the universe, surrounded by a series of concentric spheres. The earth was imperfect and constantly changing, whereas the heavenly bodies that surrounded it were perfect and incorruptible. Beyond the tenth and final sphere was heaven, where God and all the saved souls were located. (The circles read, from the center outward: 1. Moon, 2. Mercury, 3. Venus, 4. Sun, 5. Mars, 6. Jupiter, 7. Saturn, 8. Firmament (of the Stars), 9. Crystalline Sphere, 10. Prime Mover; and around the outside, Empyrean Heaven—Home of God and All the Elect, that is, saved souls.)

Empyrean Heaven—the location of God and all the saved souls. This Christianized Ptolemaic universe, then, was finite. It had a fixed outer boundary in harmony with Christian thought and expectations. God and the saved souls were at one end of the universe, humans at the center. Humans had been given power over the earth, but their real purpose was to achieve salvation.

Copernicus

Shortly before his death, Nicolaus Copernicus (1473–1543), who had studied mathematics and astronomy first at Krakow in his native Poland and later at the Italian universities of Bologna and Padua, published his famous book *On the Revolutions of the Heavenly Spheres.* Copernicus was not an accomplished observational astronomer and relied for his data on the records of his predecessors. But he was a mathematician who felt that Ptolemy's geocentric system was too complicated and failed to accord with the observed motions of the heavenly bodies (see the box on p. 305). Copernicus hoped that his **heliocentric** (sun-centered) **conception** would offer a more accurate explanation.

Copernicus argued that the universe consisted of eight spheres with the sun motionless at the center and the sphere of the fixed stars at rest in the eighth sphere. The planets revolved around the sun in the order of Mercury, Venus, the earth, Mars, Jupiter, and Saturn. The moon, however, revolved around the earth. Moreover, according to Copernicus, what appeared to be the movement of the sun and the fixed stars around the earth was really

explained by the daily rotation of the earth on its axis and the journey of the earth around the sun each year.

The heliocentric theory had little immediate impact; most people were not yet ready to accept Copernicus' thinking. But doubts about the Ptolemaic system were growing. The next step in destroying the geocentric conception and supporting the Copernican system was taken by the German scientist Johannes Kepler.

Kepler

The work of Johannes Kepler (1571–1630) illustrates the narrow line that often separated magic and science in the early Scientific Revolution. An avid astrologer, Kepler possessed a keen interest in Hermetic thought and mathematical magic. In a book written in 1596, he elaborated on his theory that the universe was constructed on the basis of geometric figures, such as the pyramid and the cube. Believing that the harmony of the human soul (a divine attribute) was mirrored in the numerical relationships existing between the planets, he focused much of his attention on discovering the "music of the spheres." Kepler was also a brilliant mathematician and astronomer who took a post as imperial mathematician to Emperor Rudolf II. Using the detailed astronomical data of his predecessor, Kepler derived laws of planetary motion that confirmed the heliocentric theory. In his first law, he contradicted Copernicus by showing that the orbits of the planets around the sun were not circular but elliptical, with the sun at one focus of the ellipse rather than at the center.

The Copernican System. The Copernican system was presented in *On the Revolutions of the Heavenly Spheres*, published shortly before Copernicus' death. As shown in this illustration from the first edition of the book, Copernicus maintained that the sun was the center of the universe and that the planets, including the earth, revolved around it. Moreover, the earth rotated daily on its axis. (The circles read, from the center outward: 1. Sun; 2. Mercury, orbit of 80 days; 3.Venus; 4. Earth, with the moon, orbit of one year; 5. Mars, orbit of 2 years; 6. Jupiter, orbit of 12 years; 7. Saturn, orbit of 30 years; 8. Immobile Sphere of the Fixed Stars.)

Kepler's work effectively eliminated the idea of uniform circular motion as well as the idea of crystalline spheres revolving in circular orbits. The basic structure of the traditional Ptolemaic system had been destroyed, and people had been freed to think in new ways of the paths of planets revolving around the sun. By the end of Kepler's life, the Ptolemaic system was rapidly losing ground to the new ideas. Important questions remained unanswered, however. What were the planets made of? And how does one explain motion in the universe? It was an Italian scientist who achieved the next important breakthrough to a new cosmology by answering the first question.

Galileo

Galileo Galilei (1564–1642) taught mathematics, first at Pisa and later at Padua, one of the most prestigious universities in Europe. Galileo was the first European to make systematic observations of the heavens by means of a telescope, thereby inaugurating a new age in astronomy. He had heard of a Flemish lens grinder who had created a "spyglass" that magnified objects seen at a distance and soon constructed his own. Instead of peering at terrestrial objects, Galileo turned his telescope to the skies and made a remarkable series of discoveries: mountains on the moon, four moons revolving around Jupiter, the phases of Venus, and sunspots. Galileo's observations seemed to destroy yet another aspect of the traditional cosmology in that the universe seemed to be composed of a material substance similar to that of earth rather than an ethereal or perfect and unchanging substance.

Galileo's revelations, published in *The Starry Messenger* in 1610, stunned his contemporaries and probably did more to make Europeans aware of the new picture of the universe than the mathematical theories of Copernicus and Kepler (see the box on p. 308). But his newfound acclaim brought Galileo the increasing scrutiny of the Catholic church. The Roman Inquisition (or Holy Office) of the church condemned Copernicanism and ordered Galileo to abandon the Copernican thesis. The Inquisition's report insisted that "the doctrine that the sun was the center of the world and immovable was false and absurd, formally heretical and contrary to Scripture, whereas the doctrine that the earth was not the center of the world but moved, and has further a daily motion, was philosophically false and absurd and theologically at least erroneous."[3] Thus the church attacked the Copernican system because it threatened not only Scripture but also the entire prevailing conception of the universe. The heavens were no longer a spiritual world but a world of matter. Humans were no longer at the center, and God was no longer in a specific place. All this the church found intolerable. In 1633, Galileo was found guilty of teaching the condemned Copernican system and was forced to recant his "errors".

The condemnation of Galileo by the Inquisition, coming at a time of economic decline, seriously undermined further scientific work in Italy, which had been at the forefront of scientific innovation. Leadership in science now passed to the northern countries, especially England, France, and the Dutch Netherlands. By the 1630s and 1640s, no reasonable astronomer could overlook that Galileo's discoveries combined with Kepler's mathematical

THE STARRY MESSENGER

The Italian Galileo Galilei was the first European to use a telescope to make systematic observations of the heavens. His observations, as reported in *The Starry Messenger* in 1610, stunned European intellectuals by revealing that the celestial bodies were not perfect and immutable, as had been believed, but were apparently composed of material substance similar to the earth. In this selection, Galileo describes how he devised a telescope and what he saw with it.

Galileo Galilei, *The Starry Messenger*

About ten months ago a report reached my ears that a certain Fleming had constructed a spyglass by means of which visible objects, though very distant from the eye of the observer, were distinctly seen as if nearby. Of this truly remarkable effect several experiences were related, to which some persons gave credence while others denied them. A few days later the report was confirmed to me in a letter from a noble Frenchman at Paris, Jacques Badovere, which caused me to apply myself whole-heartedly to inquire into the means by which I might arrive at the invention of a similar instrument. This I did shortly afterwards, my basis being the theory of refraction. First I prepared a tube of lead, at the ends of which I fitted two glass lenses, both plane on one side while on the other side one was spherically convex and the other concave. Then placing my eye near the concave lens I perceived objects satisfactorily large and near, for they appeared three times closer and nine times larger than when seen with the naked eye alone. Next I constructed another one, more accurate, which represented objects as enlarged more than sixty times. Finally, sparing neither labor nor expense, I succeeded in constructing for myself so excellent an instrument that objects seen by means of it appeared nearly one thousand times larger and over thirty times closer than when regarded without natural vision.

It would be superfluous to enumerate the number and importance of the advantages of such an instrument at sea as well as on land. But forsaking terrestrial observations, I turned to celestial ones, and first I saw the moon from as near at hand as if it were scarcely two terrestrial radii. After that I observed often with wondering delight both the planets and the fixed stars, and since I saw these latter to be very crowded, I began to seek (and eventually found) a method by which I might measure their distances apart....

Now let us review the observations made during the past two months, once more inviting the attention of all who are eager for true philosophy to the first steps of such important contemplations. Let us speak first of that surface of the moon which faces us. For greater clarity I distinguish two parts of this surface, a lighter and a darker; the lighter part seems to surround and to pervade the whole hemisphere, while the darker part discolors the moon's surface like a kind of cloud, and makes it appear covered with spots....From observation of these spots repeated many times I have been led to the opinion and conviction that the surface of the moon is not smooth, uniform, and precisely spherical as a great number of philosophers believe it (and the other heavenly bodies) to be, but is uneven, rough, and full of cavities and prominences, being not unlike the face of the earth, relieved by chains of mountains and deep valleys.

What was the significance of Galileo's invention? What impressions did he receive of the moon?

laws had made nonsense of the Ptolemaic-Aristotelian world system and clearly established the reasonableness of the Copernican model. Nevertheless, the problem of explaining motion in the universe and tying together the ideas of Copernicus, Galileo, and Kepler had not yet been solved. This would be the work of an Englishman who has long been considered the greatest genius of the Scientific Revolution.

Newton

Born in the English village of Woolsthorpe, Isaac Newton (1642–1727) showed little promise until he attended Cambridge University. In 1669, he accepted a chair of mathematics at the university. During an intense period of creativity from 1684 to 1686, he wrote his major work, *Mathematical Principles of Natural Philosophy*, known simply as the *Principia*, from the first word of its Latin title. In this work, Newton spelled out the mathematical proofs demonstrating his universal law of gravitation.

Newton's work was the culmination of the theories of Copernicus, Kepler, and Galileo. While each had undermined some part of the Ptolemaic-Aristotelian cosmology, no one until Newton had pieced together a coherent synthesis for a new cosmology.

In the first book of the *Principia*, Newton defined the basic concepts of mechanics by elaborating the three laws of motion: every object continues in a state of rest or uniform motion in a straight line unless deflected by a force, the rate of change of motion of an object is proportional to the force acting on it, and to every action there is always an equal and opposite reaction. In book three, Newton applied his theories of mechanics to the problems of astronomy by demonstrating that these three laws of motion govern the planetary bodies as well as terrestrial objects. Integral to his whole argument was the universal law of gravitation to explain why the planetary bodies did not go off in straight lines but continued in elliptical orbits about the sun. In mathematical terms, Newton explained that every object in the universe was

Isaac Newton. Pictured here is a portrait of Isaac Newton by Godfrey Kneller. With a single law of universal gravitation, Newton was able to explain all motion in the universe. His great synthesis of the work of his predecessors created a new picture of the universe as a great machine operating according to natural laws.

attracted to every other object with a force (gravity) that is directly proportional to the product of their masses and inversely proportional to the square of the distances between them.

The implications of Newton's universal law of gravitation were enormous, even if it took another century before they were widely recognized. Newton had demonstrated that one universal law, mathematically proved, could explain all motion in the universe. At the same time, the Newtonian synthesis created a new cosmology in which the world was seen largely in mechanistic terms. The universe was one huge, regulated, and uniform machine that operated according to natural laws in absolute time, space, and motion. Although Newton believed that God was "everywhere present" and acted as the force that moved all bodies on the basis of the laws he had discovered, later generations dropped his spiritual assumptions. Newton's world-machine, conceived as operating absolutely in space, time, and motion, dominated the modern worldview until the twentieth century, when the Einsteinian revolution based on a concept of relativity superseded the Newtonian mechanistic concept.

Newton's ideas were soon accepted in England but were resisted on the Continent, and it took much of the eighteenth century before they were generally accepted everywhere in Europe. They were also reinforced by developments in other fields, especially medicine.

Advances in Medicine and Chemistry

Although the Scientific Revolution of the sixteenth and seventeenth centuries is associated primarily with the dramatic changes in astronomy and mechanics that precipitated a new perception of the universe, a third field that had been dominated by Greek thought in the Later Middle Ages, medicine, also experienced a transformation. Late medieval medicine was dominated by the teachings of the Greek physician Galen, who had lived in the second century A.D.

Galen's influence on the medieval medical world was pervasive in anatomy, physiology, and disease. Galen had relied on animal, rather than human, dissection to arrive at a picture of human anatomy that was quite inaccurate in many instances. Even when Europeans began to practice human dissection in the Later Middle Ages, instruction in anatomy still relied on Galen. While a professor read a text of Galen, an assistant dissected a cadaver for illustrative purposes. Physiology, or the functioning of the body, was also dominated by Galenic hypotheses, including the belief that there were two separate blood systems, one controlling muscular activities and containing bright red blood moving upward and downward through the arteries, the other governing the digestive functions and containing dark red blood that ebbed and flowed in the veins.

Vesalius

Two major figures are associated with the changes in medicine in the sixteenth and seventeenth centuries: Andreas Vesalius and William Harvey. The new anatomy of the sixteenth century was the work of the Belgian Andreas Vesalius (1514–1564). After receiving a doctorate in medicine at the University of Padua in 1536, Vesalius accepted a position there as professor of surgery. In 1543, he published his masterpiece, *On the Fabric of the Human Body*. This book was based on his Paduan lectures, in which he deviated from traditional practice by personally dissecting a body to illustrate what he was discussing. Vesalius' anatomical treatise presented a careful examination of the individual organs and general structure of the human body. The book would not have been feasible without the artistic advances of the Renaissance and the technical developments in the art of printing. Together, these advances made possible the creation of illustrations superior to any hitherto produced.

Vesalius' hands-on approach to teaching anatomy enabled him to overthrow some of Galen's most glaring errors. He did not hesitate, for example, to correct Galen's assertion that the great blood vessels originated from the liver since his own observations made it clear that they came from the heart. Nevertheless, Vesalius still clung to a number of Galen's erroneous assertions, including the Greek physician's ideas on the ebb and flow of two kinds of blood in the veins and arteries. It was not until William Harvey's work on the circulation of the blood that this Galenic misperception was corrected.

Harvey

The Englishman William Harvey (1578–1657) attended Cambridge University and later Padua, where he earned a doctorate in medicine in 1602. His reputation rests on his book *On the Motion of the Heart and Blood,* published in 1628. Although questions had been raised in the sixteenth century about Galen's physiological principles, no major challenge to his system had emerged. Harvey's work, based on meticulous observations and experiments, led him to reject the ancient Greek's contentions. Harvey demonstrated that the heart was the beginning point of the circulation of blood in the body, that the same blood flows in both veins and arteries, and that the blood makes a complete circuit as it passes through the body. Although Harvey's work dealt a severe blow to Galen's theories, his ideas did not begin to achieve general recognition until the 1660s, when the capillaries, which explained how the blood passed from the arteries to the veins, were discovered. Harvey's theory of the circulation of the blood laid the foundation for modern physiology.

Chemistry

In the seventeenth and eighteenth centuries, a science of chemistry emerged. Robert Boyle (1627–1691) was one of the first scientists to conduct controlled experiments. His pioneering work on the properties of gases led to Boyle's Law, which states that the volume of a gas varies with the pressure exerted on it. Boyle also rejected the medieval belief that all matter consisted of the same components in favor of the view that matter is composed of atoms, which he called "little particles of all shapes and sizes" and which in various combinations formed the chemical elements. In the eighteenth century, the Frenchman Antoine Lavoisier (1743–1794) invented a system for naming the chemical elements, much of which is still used today. He is regarded by many historians as the founder of modern chemistry.

Women in the Origins of Modern Science

During the Middle Ages, except for members of religious orders, women who sought a life of learning were severely hampered by the traditional attitude that a woman's proper role was as a daughter, wife, and mother. But in the late fourteenth and early fifteenth centuries, new opportunities for elite women emerged as enthusiasm for the new secular learning called humanism encouraged Europe's privileged and learned men to encourage women to read and study

classical and Christian texts. The ideal of a humanist education for some of the daughters of Europe's elite persisted into the seventeenth century.

Margaret Cavendish

Much as they were drawn to humanism, women were also attracted to the Scientific Revolution. Unlike females educated formally in humanist schools, women interested in science had to obtain a largely informal education. European nobles had the leisure and resources that gave them easy access to the world of learning. This door was also open to noblewomen, who could participate in the informal scientific networks of their fathers and brothers.

One of the most prominent female scientists of the seventeenth century, Margaret Cavendish (1623–1673), came from an aristocratic background. Cavendish was not a popularizer of science for women but a participant in the crucial scientific debates of her time. Despite her achievement, however, she was excluded from membership in the

Margaret Cavendish. Shown in this portrait is Margaret Cavendish, the duchess of Newcastle. Her husband, thirty years her senior, encouraged her to pursue her literary interests. In addition to scientific works, she wrote plays, an autobiography, and a biography of her husband titled *The Life of the Thrice Noble, High and Puissant Prince William Cavendish, Duke, Marquess and Earl of Newcastle.* The autobiography and biography led one male literary critic to call her "a mad, conceited and ridiculous woman."

Royal Society (see "The Spread of Scientific Knowledge" later in this chapter), although she was once allowed to attend a meeting. She wrote a number of works on scientific matters, including *Observations upon Experimental Philosophy* and *Grounds of Natural Philosophy*. In these works, she did not hesitate to attack what she considered the defects of the rationalist and empiricist approaches to scientific knowledge and was especially critical of the growing belief that humans through science were the masters of nature: "We have no power at all over natural causes and effects . . . for man is but a small part . . . His powers are but particular actions of Nature, and he cannot have a supreme and absolute power."[4]

As an aristocrat, Cavendish, the duchess of Newcastle, was a good example of the women in France and England who worked in science. Women interested in science who lived in Germany came from a different background. There the tradition of female participation in craft production enabled some women to become involved in observational science, especially astronomy. Between 1650 and 1710, one in every seven German astronomers was a woman.

Maria Winkelmann

The most famous of the female astronomers in Germany was Maria Winkelmann (1670–1720). She was educated by her father and uncle and received advanced training from a local self-taught astronomer. When she married Gottfried Kirch, Germany's foremost astronomer, she became his assistant at the astronomical observatory operated in Berlin by the Academy of Science. She made some original contributions, including a hitherto undiscovered comet, as her husband related:

> Early in the morning (about 2:00 A.M.) the sky was clear and starry. Some nights before, I had observed a variable star, and my wife (as I slept) wanted to find and see it for herself. In so doing, she found a comet in the sky. At which time she woke me, and I found that it was indeed a comet. . . . I was surprised that I had not seen it the night before.[5]

When her husband died in 1710, she applied for a position as assistant astronomer, for which she was highly qualified. As a woman, with no university degree, she was denied the post by the Berlin Academy, which feared that it would establish a precedent if it hired a woman ("mouths would gape").

Winkelmann's difficulties with the Berlin Academy reflect the obstacles women faced in being accepted in scientific work, which was considered a male preserve. Although there were no formal statutes excluding women from membership in the new scientific societies, no woman was invited to join either the Royal Society of England or the French Academy of Sciences until the twentieth century. All of these female scientists were exceptional women because a life devoted to any kind of scholarship was still viewed as at odds with the domestic duties women were expected to perform.

Debates on the Nature of Women

The nature and value of women had been the subject of an ongoing, centuries-long debate. Male opinions in the debate were largely a carryover from medieval times and were not favorable. Women were portrayed as inherently base, prone to vice, easily swayed, and "sexually insatiable." Hence men needed to control them. Learned women were viewed as having overcome female liabilities to become like men. One man in praise of a woman scholar remarked that her writings were so good that you "would hardly believe they were done by a woman at all."

In the seventeenth century, women joined this debate by arguing against the distorted images of women held by men. They argued that women also had rational minds and could grow from education. Further, since most women were pious, chaste, and temperate, there was no need for male authority over them. These female defenders of women emphasized education as the key to women's ability to move into the world. How, then, did the Scientific Revolution affect this debate over the nature of women? As an era of intellectual revolution in which traditional authorities were being overthrown, we might expect significant change in men's views of women. But by and large, instead of becoming an instrument for liberation, science was used to find new support for the old, traditional views about a woman's "true place" in the scheme of things. New views were used to perpetrate old stereotypes about women.

An important project in the new anatomy of the sixteenth and seventeenth centuries was the attempt to illustrate the human body and skeleton. For Vesalius, the portrayal of physical differences between males and females was limited to external bodily form (the outlines of the body) and the sexual organs. Vesalius saw no difference in skeletons and portrayed them as the same for men or women. It was not until the eighteenth century, in fact, that a new anatomy finally prevailed. Drawings of female skeletons between 1730 and 1790 varied, but females tended to have a larger pelvic area, and in some instances, female skulls were portrayed as smaller than those of males. Eighteenth-century studies on the anatomy and physiology of sexual differences provided "scientific evidence" to

The "Natural" Inferiority of Women

Despite the shattering of old views and the emergence of a new worldview in the Scientific Revolution of the seventeenth century, attitudes toward women remained tied to traditional perspectives. In this selection, the philosopher Benedict de Spinoza argues for the "natural" inferiority of women to men.

Benedict de Spinoza, *A Political Treatise*

But, perhaps, someone will ask, whether women are under men's authority by nature or institution. For if it has been by mere institution, then we had no reason compelling us to exclude women from government. But if we consult experience itself, we shall find that the origin of it is in their weakness. For there has never been a case of men and women reigning together, but wherever on the earth men are found, there we see that men rule, and women are ruled, and that on this plan, both sexes live in harmony. But on the other hand, the Amazons, who are reported to have held rule of old, did not suffer men to stop in their country, but reared only their female children, killing males to whom they gave birth. But if by nature women were equal to men, and were equally distinguished by force of character and ability, in which human power and therefore human right chiefly consist; surely among nations so many and different some would be found, where both sexes rule alike, and others, where men are ruled by women, and so brought up, that they can make less use of their abilities. And since this is nowhere the case, one may assert with perfect propriety, that women have not by nature equal right with men: but that they necessarily give way to men, and that thus it cannot happen, that both sexes should rule alike, much less that men should be ruled by women. But if we further reflect upon human passions, how men, in fact, generally love women merely from the passion of lust, and esteem their cleverness and wisdom in proportion to the excellence of their beauty, and also how very ill-disposed men are to suffer the women they love to show any sort of favor to others, and other facts of this kind, we shall easily see that men and women cannot rule alike without greater hurt to peace.

What arguments did Spinoza use to support the idea of female inferiority? What was the effect of this line of reasoning on the roles women could play?

---

reaffirm the traditional inferiority of women. The larger pelvic area "proved" that women were meant to be childbearers, and men's larger skull "demonstrated" the superiority of the male mind. Male-dominated science had been used to "prove" male social dominance.

Overall, the Scientific Revolution reaffirmed traditional ideas about women's nature. Male scientists used the new science to spread the view that women were inferior by nature, subordinate to men, and suited by nature to play a domestic role as nurturing mothers. The widespread distribution of books—written primarily by men, of course—ensured the continuation of these ideas (see the box above). Jean de La Bruyère, the seventeenth-century French moralist, was typical when he remarked that an educated woman was like a collector's item "which one shows to the curious, but which has no use at all, any more than a carousel horse."[6]

Toward a New Earth: Descartes, Rationalism, and a New View of Humankind

The fundamentally new conception of the universe contained in the cosmological revolution of the sixteenth and seventeenth centuries inevitably had an impact on the Western view of humankind. Nowhere is this more evident than in the work of the Frenchman René Descartes (1596–1650), an extremely important figure in Western history. Descartes began by reflecting the doubt and uncertainty that seemed pervasive in the confusion of the seventeenth century and ended with a philosophy that dominated Western thought until the twentieth century.

The starting point for Descartes' new system was doubt, as he explained at the beginning of his most famous work, *Discourse on Method*, written in 1637:

> From my childhood I have been familiar with letters; and as I was given to believe that by their means a clear and assured knowledge can be acquired of all that is useful in life, I was extremely eager for instruction in them. As soon, however, as I had completed the course of study, at the close of which it is customary to be admitted into the order of the learned, I entirely changed my opinion. For I found myself entangled in so many doubts and errors that, as it seemed to me, the endeavor to instruct myself had served only to disclose to me more and more of my ignorance.[7]

Descartes decided to set aside all that he had learned and begin again. One fact seemed beyond doubt—his own existence:

> But I immediately became aware that while I was thus disposed to think that all was false, it was absolutely necessary that I who thus thought should be something; and noting that this truth *I think, therefore I am*, was so steadfast and so assured that the suppositions of the skeptics, to whatever extreme they might all be carried, could not avail to shake it, I concluded that I might without scruple accept it as being the first principle of the philosophy I was seeking.[8]

With this emphasis on the mind, Descartes asserted that he would accept only things that his reason said were true.

Descartes with Queen Christina of Sweden. René Descartes was one of the primary figures in the Scientific Revolution. Claiming to use reason as his sole guide to truth, Descartes posited a sharp distinction between mind and matter. He is shown here, standing to the right of Queen Christina of Sweden. The queen had a deep interest in philosophy and invited Descartes to her court.

From his first postulate, Descartes deduced an additional principle, the separation of mind and matter. Descartes argued that since "the mind cannot be doubted but the body and material world can, the two must be radically different." From this came an absolute dualism between mind and matter, or what has also been called **Cartesian dualism.** Using mind or human reason, the path to certain knowledge, and its best instrument, mathematics, humans can understand the material world because it is pure mechanism, a machine that is governed by its own physical laws because it was created by God—the great geometrician.

Descartes' conclusions about the nature of the universe and human beings had important implications. His separation of mind and matter allowed scientists to view matter as dead or inert, as something that was totally separate from themselves and could be investigated independently by reason. The split between mind and body led Westerners to equate their identity with mind and reason rather than with the whole organism. Descartes has rightly been called the father of modern **rationalism.** The radical Cartesian split between mind and matter, and between mind and body, had devastating implications

not only for traditional religious views of the universe but also for how Westerners viewed themselves.

The Spread of Scientific Knowledge

During the seventeenth century, scientific learning and investigation began to increase dramatically. Major universities in Europe established new chairs of science, especially in medicine. Royal and princely patronage of individual scientists became an international phenomenon. Of greater importance to the work of science, however, was the creation of a scientific method and new learned societies that enabled the new scientists to communicate their ideas to each other and to disseminate them to a wider, literate public.

The Scientific Method

In the course of the Scientific Revolution, attention was paid to the problem of establishing the proper means to examine and understand the physical realm. This creation of a **scientific method** was crucial to the evolution of science in the modern world. Curiously enough, it was an Englishman with few scientific credentials who attempted to put forth a new method of acquiring knowledge that made an impact on English scientists in the seventeenth century and other European scientists in the eighteenth century. Francis Bacon (1561–1626), a lawyer and lord chancellor, rejected Copernicus and Kepler and misunderstood Galileo. And yet in his unfinished work *The Great Instauration* (*The Great Restoration*), he called for his contemporaries "to commence a total reconstruction of sciences, arts, and all human knowledge, raised upon the proper foundations." Bacon did not doubt humans' ability to know the natural world, but he believed that they had proceeded incorrectly: "The entire fabric of human reason which we employ in the inquisition of nature is badly put together and built up, and like some magnificent structure without foundation."[9]

Bacon's new foundation—a correct scientific method—was to be built on inductive principles. Rather than beginning with assumed first principles from which logical conclusions could be deduced, he urged scientists to proceed from the particular to the general. From carefully organized experiments and systematic, thorough observations, correct generalizations could be developed. Bacon was clear about what he believed his method could accomplish. His concern was more for practical than for pure science. He stated that "the true and lawful goal of the sciences is none other than this: that human life be endowed with new discoveries and power." He wanted science to contribute to the "mechanical arts" by creating devices that would benefit industry, agriculture, and trade. Bacon was prophetic when he said that "I am laboring to lay the foundation, not of any sect or doctrine, but of human utility and power." And how would this "human power" be used? To "conquer nature in action."[10] The control and domination of nature became a central proposition of modern science and the technology that accompanied it. Only in the twentieth century did some scientists ask whether this assumption might not be at the heart of the modern ecological crisis.

René Descartes proposed a different approach to scientific methodology by emphasizing deduction and mathematical logic. Descartes believed that one could start with self-evident truths, comparable to geometrical axioms, and deduce more complex conclusions. His emphasis on deduction and mathematical order complemented Bacon's stress on experiment and induction. It was Newton who synthesized them into a single scientific methodology by uniting Bacon's empiricism with Descartes' rationalism. This scientific method began with systematic observations and experiments, which were used to arrive at general concepts. New deductions derived from these general concepts could then be tested and verified by precise experiments.

The Scientific Societies

The first of the scientific societies appeared in Italy, but those of England and France were ultimately of more significance. The English Royal Society evolved out of informal gatherings of scientists at London and Oxford in the 1640s, although it did not receive a formal charter from King Charles II until 1662. The French Royal Academy of Sciences also arose out of informal scientific meetings in Paris during the 1650s. In 1666, Louis XIV bestowed formal

recognition on the group. The French Academy received abundant state support and remained under government control; its members were appointed and paid salaries by the state. In contrast, the Royal Society of England received little government encouragement, and its fellows simply co-opted new members.

Early on, both the English and French scientific societies formally emphasized the practical value of scientific research. The Royal Society created a committee to investigate technological improvements for industry; the French Academy collected tools and machines. This concern with the practical benefits of science proved short-lived, however, as both societies came to focus their primary interest on theoretical work in mechanics and astronomy. The construction of observatories at Paris in 1667 and at Greenwich, England, in 1675 greatly facilitated research in astronomy by both groups. While both the English and French societies made useful contributions to scientific knowledge in the second half of the seventeenth century, their true significance arose from their example that science should proceed along the lines of a cooperative venture.

Science and Society

The importance of science in the history of modern Western civilization is usually taken for granted. But how did science become such an integral part of Western culture in the seventeenth and early eighteenth centuries? One cannot simply assert that people perceived that science was a rationally superior system. An important social factor, however, might help explain the relatively rapid acceptance of the new science.

Louis XIV and Colbert Visit the Academy of Sciences. In the seventeenth century, individual scientists received royal and princely patronage, and a number of learned societies were established. In France, Louis XIV, urged on by his minister Colbert, gave formal recognition to the French Academy in 1666. In this painting by Henri Testelin, Louis XIV is shown seated, surrounded by Colbert and members of the French Royal Academy of Sciences.

It has been argued that the literate mercantile and propertied elites of Europe were attracted to new science because it offered new ways to exploit resources for profit. Some of the early scientists made it easier for these groups to accept the new ideas by demonstrating how the ideas could be applied directly to specific industrial and technological needs. Galileo, for example, consciously sought an alliance between science and the material interests of the educated elite when he assured his listeners that the science of mechanics would be quite useful "when it becomes necessary to build bridges or other structures over water, something occurring mainly in affairs of great importance." At the same time, Galileo stressed that science was fit for the "minds of the wise" and not for "the shallow minds of the common people." This made science part of the high culture of Europe's wealthy elites at a time when that culture was being increasingly separated from the popular culture of the lower classes.

Science and Religion

In Galileo's struggle with the Holy Office of the Catholic church, we see the beginning of the conflict between science and religion that has marked the history of modern Western civilization. Since time immemorial, theology had seemed to be the queen of the sciences. It was natural that the churches would continue to believe that religion was the final measure of everything. The emerging scientists, however, tried to draw lines between the knowledge of religion and the knowledge of "natural philosophy" or nature. Galileo had clearly felt that it was unnecessary to pit science against religion when he wrote that

> in discussions of physical problems we ought to begin not from the authority of scriptural passages, but from sense-experiences and necessary demonstrations; for the holy Bible and the phenomena of nature proceed alike from the divine word, the former as the dictate of the Holy Ghost and the latter as the observant executrix of God's commands. It is necessary for the Bible, in order to be accommodated to the understanding of every man, to speak many things which appear to differ from the absolute truth so far as the bare meaning of the words is concerned. But Nature, on the other hand, is inexorable and immutable; she never transgresses the laws imposed upon her, or cares a whit whether her abstruse reasons and methods of operation are understandable to men.[11]

To Galileo, it made little sense for the church to determine the nature of physical reality on the basis of biblical texts that were subject to radically divergent interpretations. The church, however, decided otherwise in Galileo's case and lent its great authority to one scientific theory, the Ptolemaic-Aristotelian cosmology, no doubt because it fit so well with its own philosophical views of reality. But the church's decision had tremendous consequences. For educated individuals, it established a dichotomy between scientific investigations and religious beliefs. As the scientific beliefs triumphed, it became almost inevitable that religious beliefs would suffer, leading to a growing secularization in European intellectual life.

Many seventeenth-century intellectuals were both religious and scientific and believed that the implications of this split would be tragic. Some believed that the split was largely unnecessary, while others felt the need to combine God, humans, and a mechanistic universe into a new philosophical synthesis.

Pascal Blaise Pascal (1623–1662) was a French scientist who sought to keep science and religion united. An accomplished scientist and a brilliant mathematician, Pascal excelled at both the practical (he invented a calculating machine) and the abstract (he devised a theory of probability and did work on conic sections). After a profound mystical vision on the night of November 23, 1654, which assured him that God cared for the human soul, he devoted the rest of his life to religious matters. He planned to write an "apology for the Christian religion" but died before he could do so. He did leave a set of notes for the larger work, however, which in published form became known as the *Pensées,* or *Thoughts.*

In the *Pensées,* Pascal tried to convert rationalists to Christianity by appealing to both their reason and their emotions. Humans were, he argued, frail creatures, often deceived by their senses, misled by reason, and battered by their emotions. And yet they were beings whose very nature involved thinking: "Man is but a reed, the weakest in nature; but he is a thinking reed."[12]

Pascal was determined to show that the Christian religion was not contrary to reason: "If we violate the principles of reason, our religion will be absurd, and it will be laughed at."[13] To a Christian, a human being was both fallen and at the same time God's special creation. But it was not necessary to emphasize one at the expense of the other—to view humans as only rational or only hopeless. Pascal even had an answer for skeptics in his famous wager: God is a reasonable bet; it is worthwhile to assume that God exists. If he does, we win all; if he does not, we lose nothing.

Despite his own background as a scientist and mathematician, Pascal refused to rely on the scientist's world of order and rationality to attract people to God: "If we submit everything to reason, there will be no mystery and no supernatural element in our religion." In the new cosmology of the seventeenth century, "finite man," Pascal believed, was lost in the new infinite world, a realization that frightened him: "The eternal silence of those infinite spaces strikes me with terror" (see the box on p. 316). The world of nature, then, could never reveal God: "Because they have failed to contemplate these infinites, men have rashly plunged into the examination of nature, as though they bore some proportion to her.... Their assumption is as infinite as their object." A Christian could only rely on a God who through Jesus cared for human beings. In the final analysis, after providing reasonable arguments for Christianity, Pascal came to rest on faith. Reason, he believed, could take people only so far: "The heart has its reasons of which the reason knows nothing." As a Christian, faith was the final step: "The heart feels God, not the reason. This is what constitutes faith: God experienced by the heart, not by the reason."[14]

PASCAL: "WHAT IS A MAN IN THE INFINITE?"

*P*erhaps no intellectual in the seventeenth century gave greater expression to the uncertainties generated by the cosmological revolution than Blaise Pascal. Himself a scientist, Pascal's mystical vision of God's presence caused him to pursue religious truths with a passion. His work, the *Pensées,* consisted of notes for a larger, unfinished work justifying the Christian religion. In this selection, Pascal presents his musings on the human place in an infinite world.

Blaise Pascal, *Pensées*

Let man then contemplate the whole of nature in her full and exalted majesty. Let him turn his eyes from the lowly objects which surround him. Let him gaze on that brilliant light set like an eternal lamp to illumine the Universe; let the earth seem to him a dot compared with the vast orbit described by the sun, and let him wonder at the fact that this vast orbit itself is no more than a very small dot compared with that described by the stars in their revolutions around the firmament. But if our vision stops here, let the imagination pass on; it will exhaust its powers of thinking long before nature ceases to supply it with material for thought. All this visible world is no more than an imperceptible speck in nature's ample bosom. No idea approaches it. We may extend our conceptions beyond all imaginable space; yet produce only atoms in comparison with the reality of things.

It is an infinite sphere, the center of which is everywhere, the circumference nowhere. In short, it is the greatest perceptible mark of God's almighty power that our imagination should lose itself in that thought.

Returning to himself, let man consider what he is compared with all existence; let him think of himself as lost in his remote corner of nature; and from this little dungeon in which he finds himself lodged—I mean the Universe—let him learn to set a true value on the earth, its kingdoms, and cities, and upon himself. What is a man in the infinite? . . .

For, after all, what is a man in nature? A nothing in comparison with the infinite, an absolute in comparison with nothing, a central point between nothing and all. Infinitely far from understanding these extremes, the end of things and their beginning are hopelessly hidden from him in an impenetrable secret. He is equally incapable of seeing the nothingness from which he came, and the infinite in which he is engulfed. What else then will he perceive but some appearance of the middle of things, in an eternal despair of knowing either their principle or their purpose? All things emerge from nothing and are borne onward to infinity. Who can follow this marvelous process? The Author of these wonders understands them. None but He can.

Why did Pascal question whether human beings could achieve scientific certainty? What is the significance of Pascal's thoughts for modern science?

CONCLUSION

The Scientific Revolution marked a major turning point in modern Western civilization as the Western world overthrew the medieval, Ptolemaic-Aristotelian worldview and arrived at a new conception of the universe with the sun at the center, the planets as material bodies revolving around the sun in elliptical orbits, and an infinite rather than finite world. With the changes in the conception of heaven came changes in the conception of earth. The work of Bacon and Descartes left Europeans with the separation of mind and matter and the belief that they could understand and dominate the world of nature using reason alone. The development of a scientific method furthered the work of scientists, and the creation of scientific societies and learned journals spread their results. Although traditional churches stubbornly resisted the new ideas and a few intellectuals pointed to some inherent flaws, nothing was able to halt the replacement of the traditional ways of thinking by new ways that marked a more fundamental break with the past than that represented by the breakup of Christian unity in the Reformation.

The Scientific Revolution forced Europeans to change their conception of themselves. At first, some were appalled and even frightened by its implications. Formerly, humans on earth had been at the center of the universe. Now the earth was only a tiny planet revolving around a sun that was itself only a speck in a boundless universe. Most people remained optimistic despite the apparent blow to human dignity. After all, had Newton not demonstrated that the universe was a great machine governed by natural laws? Newton had found one—the universal law of gravitation. Could others not find other laws? Were there not natural laws governing every aspect of human endeavor that could be found by the new scientific method? Thus the Scientific Revolution leads us logically to the Enlightenment of the eighteenth century.

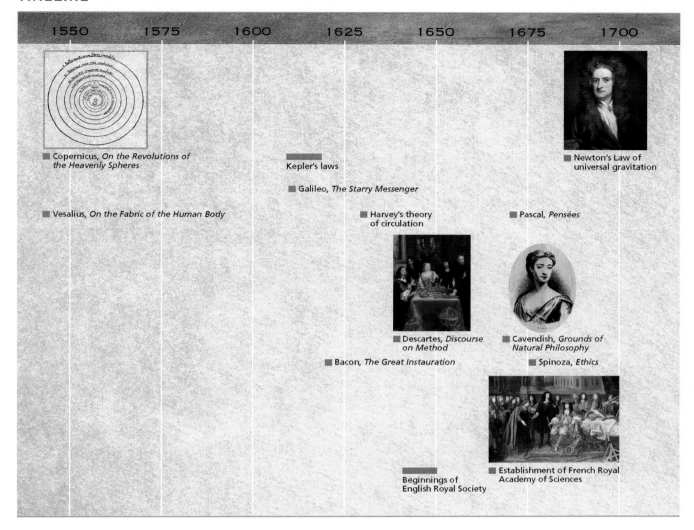

1550　　1575　　1600　　1625　　1650　　1675　　1700

■ Copernicus, *On the Revolutions of the Heavenly Spheres*

■ Kepler's laws

■ Galileo, *The Starry Messenger*

■ Newton's Law of universal gravitation

■ Vesalius, *On the Fabric of the Human Body*

■ Harvey's theory of circulation

■ Pascal, *Pensées*

■ Descartes, *Discourse on Method*

■ Cavendish, *Grounds of Natural Philosophy*

■ Bacon, *The Great Instauration*

■ Spinoza, *Ethics*

■ Beginnings of English Royal Society

■ Establishment of French Royal Academy of Sciences

NOTES

1. Quoted in A. G. R. Smith, *Science and Society in the Sixteenth and Seventeenth Centuries* (London, 1972), p. 59.
2. Quoted in E. MacCurdy, *The Notebooks of Leonardo da Vinci* (London, 1948), vol. 1, p. 634.
3. Quoted in J. H. Randall, *The Making of the Modern Mind* (Boston, 1926), p. 234.
4. Quoted in L. Schiebinger, *The Mind Has No Sex? Women in the Origins of Modern Science* (Cambridge, Mass., 1989), pp. 52–53.
5. Quoted in ibid. p. 85.
6. Quoted in P. Stock, *Better than Rubies: A History of Women's Education* (New York, 1978), p. 16.
7. R. Descartes, *Philosophical Writings*, ed. and trans. N. K. Smith (New York, 1958), p. 95.
8. Ibid. pp. 118–119.
9. F. Bacon, *The Great Instauration*, trans. J. Weinberger (Arlington Heights, Ill., 1989), pp. 2, 8.
10. Ibid. pp. 2, 16, 21.
11. S. Drake, ed. and trans., *Discoveries and Opinions of Galileo* (New York, 1957), p. 182.

12. B. Pascal, *Pensées*, trans. J. M. Cohen (Harmondsworth, England, 1961), p. 100.
13. Ibid. p. 31.
14. Ibid. pp. 52–53, 164, 165.

SUGGESTIONS FOR FURTHER READING

Three general surveys of the Scientific Revolution are **A. G. R. Smith, *Science and Society in the Sixteenth and Seventeenth Centuries*** (London, 1972); **J. R. Jacob, *The Scientific Revolution: Aspirations and Achievements, 1500–1700*** (Atlantic Highlands, N.J., 1998); and **J. Henry, *The Scientific Revolution and the Origins of Modern Science*** (New York, 1997). For a revisionist perspective, see. **S. Shapin, *The Scientific Revolution*** (Chicago, 1996). On the relationship of magic to science, see the pioneering works by **F. Yates, *Giordano Bruno and the Hermetic Tradition*** (New York, 1964) and ***The Rosicrucian Enlightenment*** (London, 1975). On the importance of mathematics, see **P. Dear, *Discipline and Experience: The Mathematical Way in the Scientific Revolution*** (Chicago, 1995).

The major figures of the revolution in astronomy are examined in **E. Rosen,** *Copernicus and the Scientific Revolution* (New York, 1984); **M. Sharratt,** *Galileo: Decisive Innovator* (Oxford, 1994); **S. Drake,** *Galileo, Pioneer Scientist* (Toronto, 1990); **M. Casper,** *Johannes Kepler,* trans. **C. D. Hellman** (London, 1959), the standard biography; and **R. S. Westfall,** *The Life of Isaac Newton* (New York, 1993). On Newton's relationship to alchemy, see **M. White,** *Isaac Newton: The Last Sorcerer* (Reading, Mass., 1997).

The standard biography of Vesalius is **C. D. O'Malley,** *Andreas Vesalius of Brussels, 1514–1564* (Berkeley, Calif., 1964). The work of Harvey is discussed in **G. Whitteridge,** *William Harvey and the Circulation of the Blood* (London, 1971).

The importance of Francis Bacon in the early development of science is underscored in **P. Zagorin,** *Francis Bacon* (Princeton, N.J., 1998). A good introduction to the work of Descartes can be found in **G. Radis-Lewis,** *Descartes: A Biography* (Ithaca, N.Y., 1998). The standard biography of Spinoza in English is **S. Hampshire,** *Spinoza* (New York, 1961).

For histories of the scientific academies, see **R. Hahn,** *The Anatomy of a Scientific Institution: The Paris Academy of Sciences, 1666–1803* (Berkeley, Calif., 1971), and **M. Purver,** *The Royal Society, Concept and Creation* (London, 1967).

On the subject of women and early modern science, see the comprehensive and highly informative work by L. Schiebinger, *The Mind Has No Sex? Women in the Origins of Modern Science* (Cambridge, Mass., 1989). See also **C. Merchant,** *The Death of Nature: Women, Ecology, and the Scientific Revolution*

(San Francisco, 1980). The social and political context for the triumph of science in the seventeenth and eighteenth centuries is examined in **M. Jacobs,** *The Cultural Meaning of the Scientific Revolution* (New York, 1988) and *The Newtonians and the English Revolution, 1689–1720* (Ithaca, N.Y., 1976).

Thomson NOW! Enter *ThomsonNOW* using the access card that is available for *Western Civilization: A Brief History.* *ThomsonNOW* will help you understand this chapter with lesson plans generated for your needs. In addition, you can read the following documents, and many more, online:

William Harvey, excerpts from *On the Motion of the Heart*
Isaac Newton, excerpts from *Principia*
René Descartes, excerpts from *Discourse on Method*
Blaise Pascal, exerpts from *Pensées*

WESTERN CIVILIZATION RESOURCES

Visit the Web site for *Western Civilization: A Brief History* **for resources specific to this book:**

http://www.thomsonedu.com/history/spielvogel

For a variety of tools to help you succeed in this course, visit the Western Civilization Resource Center at

http://history.wadsworth.com/spielvogel

Included are quizzes, images, documents, interactive simulations, maps and timelines, movie explorations, and a wealth of other sources.

GLOSSARY

abbess head of a convent or monastery for women.

abbot head of a monastery.

absolutism a form of government in which the sovereign power or ultimate authority rested in the hands of a monarch who claimed to rule by divine right and was therefore responsible only to God.

Abstract Expressionism a post–World War II artistic movement that broke with all conventions of form and structure in favor of total abstraction.

abstract painting an artistic movement that developed early in the twentieth century in which artists focused on color to avoid any references to visual reality.

aediles Roman officials who supervised the public games and the grain supply of the city of Rome.

Agricultural (Neolithic) Revolution the shift from hunting animals and gathering plants for sustenance to producing food by systematic agriculture that occurred gradually between 10,000 and 4000 B.C. (the Neolithic or "New Stone" Age).

agricultural revolution the application of new agricultural techniques that allowed for a large increase in productivity in the eighteenth century.

anti-Semitism hostility toward or discrimination against Jews.

apartheid the system of racial segregation practiced in the Republic of South Africa until the 1990s, which involved political, legal, and economic discrimination against nonwhites.

appeasement the policy, followed by the European nations in the 1930s, of accepting Hitler's annexation of Austria and Czechoslovakia in the belief that meeting his demands would assure peace and stability.

Arianism a Christian heresy that taught that Jesus was inferior to God. Though condemned by the Council of Nicaea in 325, Arianism was adopted by many of the Germanic peoples who entered the Roman Empire over the next centuries.

aristocracy a class of hereditary nobility in medieval Europe; a warrior class who shared a distinctive lifestyle based on the institution of knighthood, although there were social divisions within the group based on extremes of wealth.

Ausgleich the "Compromise" of 1867 that created the dual monarchy of Austria-Hungary. Austria and Hungary each had its own capital, constitution, and legislative assembly but were united under one monarch.

authoritarian state a state that has a dictatorial government and some other trappings of a totalitarian state but does not demand that the masses be actively involved in the regime's goals as totalitarian states do.

balance of power a distribution of power among several states such that no single nation can dominate or interfere with the interests of another.

Baroque an artistic movement of the seventeenth century in Europe that used dramatic effects to arouse the emotions and reflected the search for power that was a large part of the seventeenth-century ethos.

bicameral legislature a legislature with two houses.

Black Death the outbreak of plague (mostly bubonic) in the mid-fourteenth century that killed from 25 to 50 percent of Europe's population.

Blitzkrieg "lightning war." A war conducted with great speed and force, as in Germany's advance at the beginning of World War II.

Bolsheviks a small faction of the Russian Social Democratic Party who were led by Lenin and dedicated to violent revolution; they seized power in Russia in 1917 and were subsequently renamed the Communists.

bourgeoisie (burghers) inhabitants (merchants and artisans) of boroughs and burghs (towns).

boyars the Russian nobility.

Brezhnev Doctrine the doctrine, enunciated by Leonid Brezhnev, that the Soviet Union had a right to intervene if socialism was threatened in another socialist state; used to justify moving Soviet troops into Czechoslovakia in 1968.

Bronze Age the period from around 3000 to 1200 B.C. It was characterized by the widespread use of bronze for making tools and weapons.

caliph the secular leader of the Islamic community.

capital material wealth used or available for use in the production of more wealth.

cartel a combination of independent commercial enterprises that work together to control prices and limit competition.

Cartesian dualism Descartes's principle of the separation of mind and matter (and mind and body) that enabled scientists to view matter as something separate from themselves that could be investigated by reason.

centuriate assembly the chief popular assembly of the Roman Republic. It passed laws and elected the chief magistrates.

chansons de geste a form of vernacular literature in the High Middle Ages that consisted of heroic epics focusing on the deeds of warriors.

chivalry the ideal of civilized behavior that emerged among the nobility in the eleventh and twelfth centuries under the influence of the church; a code of ethics knights were expected to uphold.

Christian (northern) humanism an intellectual movement in northern Europe in the late fifteenth and early sixteenth centuries that combined the interest in the classics of the Italian Renaissance with an interest in the sources of early Christianity, including the New Testament and the writings of the church fathers.

civic humanism an intellectual movement of the Italian Renaissance that saw Cicero, who was both an intellectual and a statesman, as the ideal and held that humanists should be involved in government and use their rhetorical training in the service of the state.

civilization a complex culture in which large numbers of humans share a variety of common elements, including cities; religious, political, military, and social structures; writing; and significant artistic and intellectual activity.

civil rights the basic rights of citizens, including equality before the law, freedom of speech and press, and freedom from arbitrary arrest.

Cold War the ideological conflict between the Soviet Union and the United States after World War II.

collective farms large farms created in the Soviet Union by Stalin by combining many small holdings into large farms worked by the peasants under government supervision.

Columbian Exchange the reciprocal importation and exportation of plants and animals between Europe and the Americas.

commercial capitalism beginning in the Middle Ages, an economic system in which people invested in trade and goods in order to make profits.

common law law common to the entire kingdom of England; imposed by the king's courts beginning in the twelfth century to replace the customary law used in county and feudal courts that varied from place to place.

conciliarism a movement in fourteenth- and fifteenth-century Europe that held that final authority in spiritual matters resided with a general church council, not the pope; it emerged in response to the Avignon papacy and the Great Schism and was used to justify the summoning of the Council of Constance (1414–1418).

condottieri leaders of bands of mercenary soldiers in Renaissance Italy who sold their services to the highest bidder.

conquistadors "conquerors." Leaders in the Spanish conquests in the Americas, especially Mexico and Peru, in the sixteenth century.

conscription a military draft.

conservatism an ideology based on tradition and social stability that favored the maintenance of established institutions, organized religion, and obedience to authority and resisted change, especially abrupt change.

consuls the chief executive officers of the Roman Republic. Two were chosen annually to administer the government and lead the army in battle.

containment a policy adopted by the United States in the Cold War. Its goal was to use whatever means, short of all-out war, to limit Soviet expansion.

cosmopolitanism the quality of being sophisticated and having wide international experience.

cottage industry a system of textile manufacturing in which spinners and weavers worked at home in their cottages using raw materials supplied to them by capitalist entrepreneurs.

council of the plebs a council only for plebeians. After 287 B.C., however, its resolutions were binding on all Romans.

Crusade in the Middle Ages, a military campaign in defense of Christendom.

Cubism an artistic style developed at the beginning of the twentieth century, especially by Pablo Picasso, that used geometric designs to re-create reality in the viewer's mind.

cuneiform "wedge-shaped." A system of writing developed by the Sumerians that consisted of wedge-shaped impressions made by a reed stylus on clay tablets.

Dadaism an artistic movement in the 1920s and 1930s by artists who were revolted by the senseless slaughter of World War I and used their "anti-art" to express contempt for the Western tradition.

decolonization the process of becoming free of colonial status and achieving statehood; it occurred in most of the world's colonies between 1947 and 1962.

deconstruction (poststructuralism) a system of thought, formulated by Jacques Derrida, that holds that culture is created in a variety of ways, according to the manner in which people create their own meaning. Hence there is no fixed truth or universal meaning.

deism belief in God as the creator of the universe who, after setting it in motion, ceased to have any direct involvement in it and allowed it to run according to its own natural laws.

demesne the part of a manor retained under the direct control of the lord and worked by the serfs as part of their labor services.

destalinization the policy of denouncing and undoing the most repressive aspects of Stalin's regime; begun by Nikita Khrushchev in 1956.

détente the relaxation of tension between the Soviet Union and the United States that occurred in the 1970s.

divination the practice of seeking to foretell future events by interpreting divine signs, which could appear in various forms, such as in entrails of animals, in patterns in smoke, or in dreams.

domino theory the belief that if the Communists succeeded in Vietnam, other countries in Southeast and East Asia would also fall (like dominoes) to communism; cited as a justification for the U.S. intervention in Vietnam.

economic imperialism the process in which banks and corporations from developed nations invest in underdeveloped regions and establish a major presence there in the hope of making high profits; not necessarily the same as colonial expansion in that businesses invest where they can make a profit, which may not be in their own nation's colonies.

economic liberalism the idea that government should not interfere in the workings of the economy.

Einsatzgruppen in Nazi Germany, special strike forces in the SS that played an important role in rounding up and killing Jews.

encomienda in Spanish America, a form of economic and social organization in which a Spaniard was given a royal grant that enabled the holder of the grant to collect tribute from the Indians and use them as laborers.

enlightened absolutism an absolute monarchy in which the ruler follows the principles of the Enlightenment by introducing reforms for the improvement of society, allowing freedom of speech and the press, permitting religious toleration, expanding education, and ruling in accordance with the laws.

Enlightenment an eighteenth-century intellectual movement, led by the philosophes, that stressed the application of reason and the scientific method to all aspects of life.

entrepreneur one who organizes, operates, and assumes the risk in a business venture in the expectation of making a profit.

Epicureanism a philosophy founded by Epicurus in the fourth century B.C. that taught that happiness (freedom from emotional turmoil) could be achieved through the pursuit of pleasure (intellectual rather than sensual pleasure).

equestrians a group of extremely wealthy men in the late Roman Republic who were effectively barred from high office but sought political power commensurate with their wealth; called equestrians because many had gotten their start as cavalry officers (*equites*).

estates *see* orders.

ethnic cleansing the policy of killing or forcibly removing people of another ethnic group; used by the Serbs against Bosnian Muslims in the 1990s.

Eucharist a Christian sacrament in which consecrated bread and wine are consumed in celebration of Jesus' Last Supper; also called the Lord's Supper or communion.

evolutionary socialism a socialist doctrine espoused by Eduard Bernstein who argued that socialists should stress cooperation and evolution to attain power by democratic means rather than by conflict and revolution.

existentialism a philosophical movement that arose after World War II that emphasized the meaninglessness of life, born of the desperation caused by two world wars.

fascism an ideology or movement that exalts the nation above the individual and calls for a centralized government with a dictatorial leader, economic and social regimentation, and forcible suppression of opposition; in particular, the ideology of Mussolini's Fascist regime in Italy.

feminism the belief in the social, political, and economic equality of the sexes; also, organized activity to advance women's rights.

fief a landed estate granted to a vassal in exchange for military services.

Five Pillars of Islam the core requirements of the faith, observation of which would lead to paradise: belief in Allah and his Prophet Muhammad; prescribed prayers; observation of Ramadan; pilgrimage to Mecca; and giving alms (charitable contributions) to the poor.

Final Solution the attempted physical extermination of the Jewish people by the Nazis during World War II.

free trade the unrestricted international exchange of goods with low or no tariffs.

functionalism the idea that the function of an object should determine its design and materials.

genocide the deliberate extermination of a people.

gentry well-to-do English landowners below the level of the nobility. They played an important role in the English Civil War of the seventeenth century.

geocentric conception   the belief that the earth was at the center of the universe and that the sun and other celestial objects revolved around the earth.

glasnost   "openness." Mikhail Gorbachev's policy of encouraging Soviet citizens to openly discuss the strengths and weaknesses of the Soviet Union.

good emperors   the five emperors who ruled from 96 to 180 (Nerva, Trajan, Hadrian, Antoninus Pius, and Marcus Aurelius), a period of peace and prosperity for the Roman Empire.

Gothic   a term used to describe the art and especially architecture of Europe in the twelfth, thirteenth, and fourteenth centuries.

Gothic literature   a form of literature used by Romantics to emphasize the bizarre and unusual, especially evident in horror stories.

Great Schism   the crisis in the late medieval church when there were first two and then three popes; ended by the Council of Constance (1414–1418).

guest workers   foreign workers working temporarily in European countries.

guild   an association of people with common interests and concerns, especially people working in the same craft. In medieval Europe, guilds came to control much of the production process and to restrict entry into various trades.

Hadith   a collection of the sayings of the Prophet Muhammad, used to supplement the revelations contained in the Qur'an.

heliocentric conception   the belief that the sun, not the earth, is at the center of the universe.

Hellenistic   literally, "imitating the Greeks"; the era after the death of Alexander the Great when Greek culture spread into the Near East and blended with the culture of that region.

helots   serfs in ancient Sparta who were permanently bound to the land that they worked for their Spartan masters.

heresy   the holding of religious doctrines different from the official teachings of the church.

Hermeticism   an intellectual movement beginning in the fifteenth century that taught that divinity is embodied in all aspects of nature; it included works on alchemy and magic as well as theology and philosophy. The tradition continued into the seventeenth century and influenced many of the leading figures of the Scientific Revolution.

hieroglyphics   a pictorial system of writing used in ancient Egypt.

high culture   the literary and artistic culture of the educated and wealthy ruling classes.

Holocaust   the mass slaughter of European Jews by the Nazis during World War II.

hoplites   heavily armed infantry soldiers in ancient Greece who entered battle in a phalanx formation.

Huguenots   French Calvinists.

humanism   an intellectual movement in Renaissance Italy based on the study of the Greek and Roman classics.

ideology   a political philosophy such as conservatism or liberalism.

imperium   In the Roman Republic, the right to command troops that belonged to the chief executive officers (consuls and praetors); a military commander was known as an *imperator*. In the Roman Empire, the title *imperator* (emperor) came to be used for the ruler.

Impressionism   an artistic movement that originated in France in the 1870s. Impressionists sought to capture their impressions of the changing effects of light on objects in nature.

individualism   emphasis on and interest in the unique traits of each person.

indulgence   in Christian theology, the remission of part or all of the temporal punishment in purgatory due to sin; granted for charitable contributions and other good deeds. Indulgences became a regular practice of the Christian church in the High Middle Ages, and their abuse was instrumental in sparking Luther's reform movement in the sixteenth century.

inflation   a sustained rise in the price level.

intendants   royal officials in seventeenth-century France who were sent into the provinces to execute the orders of the central government.

interdict   in the Catholic church, a censure by which a region or country is deprived of receiving the sacraments.

intervention, principle of   the idea, after the Congress of Vienna, that the great powers of Europe had the right to send armies into countries experiencing revolution to restore legitimate monarchs to their thrones.

jihad   "striving in the way of the Lord." In Islam, the attempt to achieve personal betterment, although it can also mean fair, defensive fighting to preserve one's life and one's faith.

joint-stock company   a company or association that raises capital by selling shares to individuals who receive dividends on their investment while a board of directors runs the company.

justification   the primary doctrine of the Protestant Reformation, teaching that humans are saved not through good works but by the grace of God, bestowed freely through the sacrifice of Jesus.

Kulturkampf   "culture conflict." The name given to Bismarck's attack on the Catholic church in Germany, which has come to refer to conflict between church and state anywhere.

laissez-faire   "let (them) do (as they please)." An economic doctrine that holds that an economy is best served when the government does not interfere but allows the economy to self-regulate according to the forces of supply and demand.

latifundia   large landed estates in the Roman Empire (singular: *latifundium*).

lay investiture   the practice in which someone other than a member of the clergy chose a bishop and invested him with the symbols of both his temporal office and his spiritual office; led to the Investiture Controversy, which was ended by compromise in the Concordat of Worms in 1122.

Lebensraum   "living space." The doctrine, adopted by Hitler, that a nation's power depends on the amount of land it occupies; thus a nation must expand to be strong.

legitimacy, principle of   the idea that after the Napoleonic wars, peace could best be reestablished in Europe by restoring legitimate monarchs who would preserve traditional institutions; guided Metternich at the Congress of Vienna.

liberal arts   the seven areas of study that formed the basis of education in medieval and early modern Europe. Following Boethius and other late Roman authors, they consisted of grammar, rhetoric, and dialectic or logic (the *trivium*) and arithmetic, geometry, astronomy, and music (the *quadrivium*).

liberalism   an ideology based on the belief that people should be as free from restraint as possible. Economic liberalism is the idea that the government should not interfere in the workings of the economy. Political liberalism is the idea that there should be restraints on the exercise of power so that people can enjoy basic civil rights in a constitutional state with a representative assembly.

mandates   a system established after World War I whereby a nation officially administered a territory (mandate) on behalf of the League of Nations. Thus France administered Lebanon and Syria as mandates, and Britain administered Iraq and Palestine.

Mannerism   a sixteenth-century artistic movement in Europe that deliberately broke down the High Renaissance principles of balance, harmony, and moderation.

manor   an agricultural estate operated by a lord and worked by peasants who performed labor services and paid various rents and fees to the lord in exchange for protection and sustenance.

Marshall Plan   the European Recovery Program, under which the United States provided financial aid to European countries to help them rebuild after World War II.

Marxism   the political, economic, and social theories of Karl Marx, which included the idea that history is the story of class struggle and that ultimately the proletariat will overthrow the bourgeoisie and establish a dictatorship en route to a classless society.

mass education   a state-run educational system, usually free and compulsory, that aims to ensure that all children in society have at least a basic education.

mass leisure   forms of leisure that appeal to large numbers of people in a society, including the working classes; emerged at the end of the nineteenth century to provide workers with amusements after work and on weekends; used during the twentieth century by totalitarian states to control their populations.

mass politics   a political order characterized by mass political parties and universal male and (eventually) female suffrage.

mass society   a society in which the concerns of the majority—the lower classes—play a prominent role; characterized by extension of voting rights, an improved standard of living for the lower classes, and mass education.

materialism   the belief that everything mental, spiritual, or ideal is an outgrowth of physical forces and that truth is found in concrete material existence, not through feeling or intuition.

mercantilism   an economic theory that held that a nation's prosperity depended on its supply of gold and silver and that the total volume of trade is unchangeable; its adherents therefore advocated that the government play an active role in the economy by encouraging exports and discouraging imports, especially through the use of tariffs.

Middle Passage   the journey of slaves from Africa to the Americas as the middle leg of the triangular trade.

militarism   a policy of aggressive military preparedness; in particular, the large armies based on mass conscription and complex, inflexible plans for mobilization that most European nations had before World War I.

millenarianism   the belief that the end of the world is at hand and the kingdom of God is about to be established on earth.

ministerial responsibility   a tenet of nineteenth-century liberalism that held that ministers of the monarch should be responsible to the legislative assembly rather than to the monarch.

mir   a peasant village commune in Russia.

mobilization   the organization of troops and supplies for service in time of war.

Modernism   the artistic and literary styles that emerged in the decades before 1914 as artists rebelled against traditional efforts to portray reality as accurately as possible (leading to Impressionism and Cubism) and writers explored new forms.

monasticism   a movement that began in early Christianity whose purpose was to create communities of men and women who practiced a communal life dedicated to God as a moral example to the world around them.

monk   a man who chooses to live a communal life divorced from the world in order to dedicate himself totally to the will of God.

monogamy   the practice of being married to one person at a time.

monotheism   the doctrine or belief that there is only one God.

mutual deterrence   the belief that nuclear war could best be prevented if both the United States and the Soviet Union had sufficient nuclear weapons so that even if one nation launched a preemptive first strike, the other could respond and devastate the attacker.

mystery religions   religions that involve initiation into secret rites that promise intense emotional involvement with spiritual forces and a greater chance of individual immortality.

nationalism   a sense of national consciousness based on awareness of being part of a community—a "nation"—that has common institutions, traditions, language, and customs and that becomes the focus of the individual's primary political loyalty.

nationalization   the process of converting a business or industry from private ownership to government control and ownership.

nation in arms   the people's army raised by universal mobilization to repel the foreign enemies of the French Revolution.

NATO   the North Atlantic Treaty Organization, a military alliance formed in 1949 in which the signatories (Belgium, Canada, Denmark, France, Great Britain, Iceland, Italy, Luxembourg, the Netherlands, Norway, Portugal, and the United States) agreed to provide mutual assistance if any one of them was attacked; later expanded to include other nations.

natural laws   a body of laws or specific principles held to be derived from nature and binding on all human societies even in the absence of written laws governing such matters.

natural rights   certain inalienable rights to which all people are entitled, including the right to life, liberty, and property; freedom of speech and religion; and equality before the law.

natural selection   Darwin's idea that organisms that are most adaptable to their environment survive and pass on the variations that enabled them to survive, while less adaptable organisms become extinct; "survival of the fittest."

Nazi New Order   the Nazis' plan for their conquered territories; it included the extermination of Jews and others considered inferior, ruthless exploitation of resources, German colonization in the east, and the use of Poles, Russians, and Ukrainians as slave labor.

Neoplatonism   a revival of Platonic philosophy in the third century A.D., associated with Plotinus; a similar revival in the Italian Renaissance, associated with Marsilio Ficino, who attempted to synthesize Christianity and Platonism.

nepotism   the appointment of family members to important political positions; derived from the regular appointment of nephews (Greek, *nepos*) by Renaissance popes.

New Economic Policy   a modified version of the old capitalist system introduced in the Soviet Union by Lenin in 1921 to revive the economy after the ravages of the civil war and war communism.

new imperialism   the revival of imperialism after 1880 in which European nations established colonies throughout much of Asia and Africa.

nobiles   "nobles." The small group of families from both patrician and plebeian origins who produced most of the men who were elected to office in the late Roman Republic.

nuclear family   a family group consisting only of a father, a mother, and one or more children.

nuns   female religious monks.

old regime (old order)   the political and social system of France in the eighteenth century before the Revolution.

oligarchy   rule by a few.

optimates   "best men." Aristocratic leaders in the late Roman Republic who generally came from senatorial families and wished to retain their oligarchical privileges.

orders (estates)   the traditional tripartite division of European society based on heredity and quality rather than wealth or economic standing, first established in the Middle Ages and continuing into the eighteenth century; traditionally consisted of those who pray (the clergy), those who fight (the nobility), and those who work (all the rest).

organic evolution   Darwin's principle that all plants and animals have evolved over a long period of time from earlier and simpler forms of life.

Paleolithic Age   the period of human history when humans used simple stone tools (c. 2,500,000–10,000 B.C.).

pantheism   a doctrine that equates God with the universe and all that is in it.

papal curia   the administrative staff of the Catholic church, composed of cardinals who assist the pope in running the church.

paterfamilias   the dominant male in a Roman family whose powers over his wife and children were theoretically unlimited, though they were sometimes circumvented in practice.

patricians   great landowners who became the ruling class in the Roman Republic.

patronage   the practice of awarding titles and making appointments to government and other positions to gain political support.

Pax Romana   "Roman peace." A term used to refer to the stability and prosperity that Roman rule brought to the Mediterranean world and much of western Europe during the first and second centuries A.D.

perestroika   "restructuring." A term applied to Mikhail Gorbachev's economic, political, and social reforms in the Soviet Union.

perioikoi   in ancient Sparta, free inhabitants but not citizens who were required to pay taxes and perform military service.

permissive society   a term applied to Western society after World War II to reflect the new sexual freedom and the emergence of a drug culture.

philosophes intellectuals of the eighteenth-century Enlightenment who believed in applying a spirit of rational criticism to all things, including religion and politics, and who focused on improving and enjoying this world, rather than on the afterlife.

plebeians the class of Roman citizens that included nonpatrician landowners, craftspeople, merchants, and small farmers in the Roman Republic. Their struggle for equal rights with the patricians dominated much of the Republic's history.

plebiscita laws passed by the council of the plebs.

pluralism the practice of holding several church offices simultaneously; a problem of the late medieval church.

pogroms organized massacres of Jews.

polis an ancient Greek city-state encompassing both an urban area and its surrounding countryside; a small but autonomous political unit where all major political and social activities were carried out centrally.

political democracy a form of government characterized by universal suffrage and mass political parties.

politiques a group who emerged during the French Wars of Religion in the sixteenth century, placed politics above religion, and believed that no religious truth was worth the ravages of civil war.

polytheism belief in or worship of more than one god.

popular culture as opposed to high culture, the unofficial written and unwritten culture of the masses, much of which was traditionally passed down orally and centered on public and group activities such as festivals. In the modern age, the term refers to the entertainment, recreation, and pleasures that people purchase as part of the mass consumer society.

populares "favoring the people." Aristocratic leaders in the late Roman Republic who tended to use the people's assemblies in an effort to break the stranglehold of the *nobiles* on political offices.

Post-Impressionism an artistic movement that began in France in the 1880s. Post-Impressionists sought to use color and line to express inner feelings and produce a personal statement of reality.

Postmodernism a term used to cover a variety of artistic and intellectual styles and ways of thinking prominent since the 1970s.

Poststructuralism *see* deconstruction

praetor a Roman executive official responsible for the administration of the law.

praetorian guard the military unit that served as the personal bodyguard of the Roman emperors.

predestination the belief, associated with Calvinism, that God, as a consequence of his foreknowledge of all events, has predetermined those who will be saved (the elect) and those who will be damned.

price revolution the dramatic rise in prices (inflation) that occurred throughout Europe in the sixteenth and early seventeenth centuries.

principate the form of government established by Augustus for the Roman Empire; it continued the constitutional forms of the Republic and consisted of the *princeps* ("first citizen") and the senate, although the *princeps* was clearly the dominant partner.

procurator the head of the Holy Synod, the chief decision-making body for the Russian Orthodox church.

proletariat the industrial working class. In Marxism, the class that will ultimately overthrow the bourgeoisie.

propaganda a program of distorted information put out by an organization or government to spread its policy, cause, or doctrine.

psychoanalysis a method developed by Sigmund Freud to resolve a patient's psychic conflict.

Puritans English Protestants inspired by Calvinist theology who wished to remove all traces of Catholicism from the Church of England.

quadrivium arithmetic, geometry, astronomy, and music; four of the seven liberal arts (the others made up the *trivium*) that formed the basis of medieval and early modern education.

quaestors Roman officials responsible for the administration of financial affairs.

Ramadan the holy month of Islam, during which believers fast from dawn to sunset; since the Islamic calendar is lunar, Ramadan migrates through the seasons

rapprochement the rebuilding of harmonious relations between nations.

rationalism a system of thought based on the belief that human reason and experience are the chief sources of knowledge.

Realism a nineteenth-century school of painting that emphasized the everyday life of ordinary people, depicted with photographic accuracy.

Realpolitik "politics of reality." Politics based on practical concerns rather than theory or ethics.

real wages, income, and prices wages, income, and prices that have been adjusted for inflation.

Reconquista in Spain, the reconquest of Muslim lands by Christian rulers and their armies.

relativity theory Einstein's theory that, among other things, (1) space and time are not absolute but are relative to the observer and interwoven into a four-dimensional space-time continuum and (2) matter is a form of energy ($E = mc^2$).

relics the bones of Christian saints or objects intimately associated with saints that were considered worthy of veneration.

Renaissance the "rebirth" of classical culture that occurred in Italy between c. 1350 and c. 1550; also, the earlier revivals of classical culture that occurred under Charlemagne and in the twelfth century.

rentier a person who lives on income from property and is not personally involved in its operation.

reparations payments made by a defeated nation after a war to compensate another nation for damage sustained as a result of the war; required from Germany after World War I.

revisionism a socialist doctrine that rejected Marx's emphasis on class struggle and revolution and argued instead that workers should work through political parties to bring about gradual change (*see also* evolutionary socialism).

revolutionary socialism a socialist doctrine that violent action was the only way to achieve the goals of socialism.

rhetoric the art of persuasive speaking; in the Middle Ages, one of the seven liberal arts.

risorgimento a movement in Italy in the nineteenth century aimed at the creation of a united Italian republic.

Rococo an eighteenth-century artistic movement that emphasized grace, gentility, lightness, and charm.

Romanesque a term used to describe the art and especially architecture of Europe in the eleventh and twelfth centuries.

Romanticism a nineteenth-century intellectual and artistic movement that rejected the emphasis on reason of the Enlightenment. Instead, Romantics stressed the importance of intuition, feeling, emotion, and imagination as sources of knowing.

sacraments rites considered imperative for a Christian's salvation. By the thirteenth century, these consisted of the Eucharist or Lord's Supper, baptism, marriage, penance, extreme unction, holy orders, and confirmation of children; Protestant reformers of the sixteenth century generally recognized only two—baptism and communion (the Lord's Supper).

salons gatherings of philosophes and other notables to discuss the ideas of the Enlightenment; so called from the elegant drawing rooms (salons) where they met.

sans-culottes "without breeches." The common people, who did not wear the fine clothes of the upper classes and played an important role in the radical phase of the French Revolution.

satrap a governor with both civil and military duties in the ancient Persian Empire, which was divided into satrapies, or provinces, each administered by a satrap.

scholasticism the philosophical and theological system of the medieval schools, which emphasized rigorous analysis of contradictory authorities; often used to try to reconcile faith and reason.

scientific method a method of seeking knowledge through inductive principles, using experiments and observations to develop generalizations.

Scientific Revolution the transition from the medieval worldview to a largely secular, rational, and materialistic perspective that began in the seventeenth century and was popularized in the eighteenth.

scriptoria writing rooms for the copying of manuscripts in medieval monasteries.

scutage in the fourteenth century, a money payment for military service that replaced the obligation of military service in the lord-vassal relationship.

secularization the process of becoming more concerned with material, worldly, temporal things and less with spiritual and religious things.

self-determination the doctrine that the people of a given territory or a particular nationality should have the right to determine their own government and political future.

senate the leading council of the Roman Republic; composed of about three hundred men (senators) who served for life and dominated much of the political life of the Republic.

separation of powers a doctrine enunciated by Montesquieu in the eighteenth century that separate executive, legislative, and judicial powers serve to limit and control each other.

Shari'a a law code, originally drawn up by Muslim scholars shortly after the death of Muhammad, that provides believers with a set of prescriptions to regulate their daily lives.

skepticism a doubtful or questioning attitude, especially about religion.

social Darwinism the application of Darwin's principle of organic evolution to the social order; led to the belief that progress comes from the struggle for survival as the fittest advance and the weak decline.

socialism an ideology that calls for collective or government ownership of the means of production and the distribution of goods.

socialized medicine health services for all citizens provided by government assistance.

social security government programs that provide social welfare measures such as old-age pensions and sickness, accident, and disability insurance.

Socratic method a form of teaching that uses a question-and-answer format to enable students to reach conclusions by using their own reasoning.

Sophists wandering scholars and professional teachers in ancient Greece who stressed the importance of rhetoric and tended toward skepticism and relativism.

soviets councils of workers' and soldiers' deputies formed throughout Russia in 1917 that played an important role in the Bolshevik Revolution.

squadristi in Italy in the 1920s, bands of armed Fascists used to create disorder by attacking Socialist offices and newspapers.

stagflation a combination of high inflation and high unemployment that was prevalent in the United States and elsewhere from 1973 to the mid-1980s.

Stalinization the adoption by Eastern European Communist countries of features of the economic, political, and military policies implemented by Stalin in the Soviet Union.

Stoicism a philosophy founded by Zeno in the fourth century B.C. that taught that happiness could be obtained by accepting one's lot and living in harmony with the will of God, thereby achieving inner peace.

subinfeudation the practice whereby a lord's greatest vassals subdivided their fiefs and had vassals of their own, who in turn subdivided their fiefs, and so on down to simple knights, whose fiefs were too small to subdivide.

suffrage the right to vote.

suffragists advocates of extending the right to vote to women.

sultan "holder of power." A title taken by Turkish leaders who took command of the Abbasid Empire in 1055.

Surrealism an artistic movement that arose between World War I and World War II. Surrealists portrayed recognizable objects in unrecognizable relationships in order to reveal the world of the unconscious.

syncretism the combining of different forms of belief or practice, as, for example, when two gods are regarded as different forms of the same underlying divine force and are fused together.

tariffs duties (taxes) imposed on imported goods, usually to raise revenue and to discourage imports and protect domestic industries.

three-field system in medieval agriculture, the practice of dividing the arable land into three fields so that one could lie fallow while the others were planted in winter grains and spring crops.

tithe a portion of one's harvest or income, paid by medieval peasants to the village church.

totalitarian state a state characterized by government control over all aspects of economic, social, political, cultural, and intellectual life, the subordination of the individual to the state, and insistence that the masses be actively involved in the regime's goals.

total war warfare in which all of a nation's resources, including civilians at home as well as soldiers in the field, are mobilized for the war effort.

trade union an association of workers in the same trade, formed to help members secure better wages, benefits, and working conditions.

transformism the theory that societies evolve gradually.

transubstantiation a doctrine of the Roman Catholic church that during the Eucharist, the substance of the bread and wine is miraculously transformed into the body and blood of Jesus.

trench warfare warfare in which the opposing forces attack and counterattack from a relatively permanent system of trenches protected by barbed wire; characteristic of World War I.

triangular trade a pattern of trade in early modern Europe that connected Europe, Africa, and the Americas in an Atlantic economy.

tribunes of the plebs beginning in 494 B.C., Roman officials who were given the power to protect plebeians against arrest by patrician magistrates.

trivium grammar, rhetoric, and dialectic or logic; three of the seven liberal arts (the others made up the *quadrivium*) that were the basis of medieval and early modern education.

Truman Doctrine the doctrine, enunciated by Harry Truman in 1947, that the United States would provide economic aid to countries that said they were threatened by Communist expansion.

tyrant in an ancient Greek *polis* (or an Italian city-state during the Renaissance), a ruler who came to power in an unconstitutional way and ruled without being subject to the law.

ultraroyalists in nineteenth-century France, a group of aristocrats who sought to return to a monarchical system dominated by a landed aristocracy and the Catholic church.

uncertainty principle a principle in quantum mechanics, posited by Heisenberg, that holds that one cannot determine the path of an electron because the very act of observing the electron would affect its location.

unconditional surrender complete, unqualified surrender of a belligerent nation.

umma the Muslim community, as a whole.

utopian socialists intellectuals and theorists in the early nineteenth century who favored equality in social and economic conditions and wished to replace private property and competition with collective ownership and cooperation.

vassalage the granting of a fief, or landed estate, in exchange for providing military services to the lord and fulfilling certain other obligations such as appearing at the lord's court when summoned and making a payment on the knighting of the lord's eldest son.

war communism Lenin's policy of nationalizing industrial and other facilities and requisitioning the peasants' produce during the civil war in Russia.

War Guilt Clause the clause in the Treaty of Versailles that declared that Germany (with Austria) was responsible for starting World War I and ordered Germany to pay reparations for the damage the Allies had suffered as a result of the war.

Warsaw Pact a military alliance, formed in 1955, in which Albania, Bulgaria, Czechoslovakia, East Germany, Hungary, Poland, Romania, and the Soviet Union agreed to provide mutual assistance.

welfare state a sociopolitical system in which the government assumes primary responsibility for the social welfare of its citizens by providing such things as social security, unemployment benefits, and health care.

wergeld "money for a man." In early Germanic law, a person's value in monetary terms, paid by a wrongdoer to the family of the person who had been injured or killed.

zemstvos local assemblies established in Russia in 1864 by Tsar Alexander II.

ziggurat a massive stepped tower on which a temple dedicated to the chief god or goddess of a Sumerian city was built.

Zionism an international movement that called for the establishment of a Jewish state or a refuge for Jews in Palestine.

Zoroastrianism a religion founded by the Persian Zoroaster in the seventh century B.C., characterized by worship of a supreme god, Ahuramazda, who represents the good against the evil spirit, identified as Ahriman.

PRONUNCIATION

Abbasid ah-BAH-sid *or* AB-uh-sid

Abd al-Rahman ub-duh-rahkh-MAHN

Abu al-Abbas uh-BOOL-uh-BUSS

Abu Bakr ah-bu-BAHK-ur

Adenauer, Konrad AD-uh-now-ur, KOHN-raht

aediles EE-dylz

Aeolians ee-OH-lee-unz

Aequi EE-kwy

Aeschylus ESS-kuh-luss

Aetius ay-EE-shuss

Afrikaners ah-fri-KAH-nurz

Agesilaus uh-jess-uh-LAY-uss

Agincourt AH-zhen-koor

Ahlwardt, Hermann AHL-vart, hay-uh-MAHN

Ahuramazda uh-HOOR-uh-MAHZ-duh

Aix-la-Chapelle ex-lah-shah-PEL

Akhenaten ah-kuh-NAH-tun

Akkadians uh-KAY-dee-unz

Alaric AL-uh-rik

Alberti, Leon Battista al-BAYR-tee, lay-OHN bah-TEESS-tah

Albigensians al-buh-JEN-see-unz

Albuquerque, Afonso de AL-buh-kur-kee, ah-FAHN-soh day

Alcibiades al-suh-BY-uh-deez

Alcuin AL-kwin

Alemanni al-uh-MAH-nee

al-Fatah al-FAH-tuh

al-Hakim al-hah-KEEM

Alia, Ramiz AH-lee-uh, rah-MEEZ

al-Khwarizmi al-KHWAR-iz-mee

Allah AH-lah

al-Ma'mun al-muh-MOON

al-Sadat, Anwar el-suh-DAHT, ahn-WAHR

Amenhotep ah-mun-HOH-tep

Andreotti, Giulio ahn-dray-AH-tee, JOOL-yoh

Andropov, Yuri ahn-DRAHP-awf, YOOR-ee

Anjou AHN-zhoo

Antigonid an-TIG-uh-nid

Antigonus Gonatus an-TIG-oh-nuss guh-NAH-tuss

Antiochus an-TY-uh-kuss

Antonescu, Ion an-tuh-NESS-koo, YON

Antoninus Pius an-tuh-NY-nuss PY-uss

apella uh-PEL-uh

Aphrodite af-roh-DY-tee

Apollonius ap-uh-LOH-nee-uss

appartement uh-par-tuh-MUNH

Aquinas, Thomas uh-KWY-nuss, TAHM-uss

Arafat, Yasir ah-ruh-FAHT, yah-SEER

aratrum uh-RAH-trum

Archimedes ahr-kuh-MEE-deez

Argonautica ahr-guh-NAWT-uh-kuh

Aristarchus ar-iss-TAR-kus

Aristophanes ar-iss-TAHF-uh-neez

Aristotle AR-iss-tot-ul

Arsinoë ahr-SIN-oh-ee

artium baccalarius ar-TEE-um bak-uh-LAR-ee-uss

artium magister ar-TEE-um muh-GISS-ter

Aryan AR-ee-un

Ashkenazic ash-kuh-NAH-zik

Ashurbanipal ah-shur-BAH-nuh-pahl

Ashurnasirpal ah-shur-NAH-zur-pahl

asiento ah-SYEN-toh

Asoka uh-SOH-kuh

assignat ah-see-NYAH

Assyrians uh-SEER-ee-unz

Astell, Mary AST-ul, MAYR-ee

Atahualpa ah-tuh-WAHL-puh

Attalid AT-uh-lid

audiencias ow-dee-en-SEE-uss

Auerstadt OW-urr-shtaht

augur AW-gurr

Augustine AW-guh-steen

Aurelian aw-REEL-yun

Auschwitz-Birkenau OWSH-vitz-BEER-kuh-now

Ausgleich OWSS-glykh

auspices AWSS-puh-sizz

Austerlitz AWSS-tur-litz

Australopithecines aw-stray-loh-PITH-uh-synz

Austrasia au-STRY-zhuh

Autun oh-TUNH

Avicenna av-i-SENN-uh

Avignon ah-veen-YONH

Azerbaijan az-ur-by-JAN

Baader-Meinhof BAH-durr-MYN-huff

Babeuf, Gracchus bah-BUFF, GRAK-uss

Bach, Johann Sebastian BAKH, yoh-HAHN suh-BASS-chun

Baden-Powell, Robert BAD-un-POW-ul

Bakunin, Michael buh-KOON-yun

Balboa, Vasco Nuñez de bal-BOH-uh, BAHS-koh NOON-yez day

Ballin, Albert BAH-leen, AHL-bayrt

Banque de Belgique BAHNK duh bel-ZHEEK

Barbarossa bar-buh-ROH-suh

Baroque buh-ROHK

Barth, Karl BAHRT, KAHRL

Bastille bass-STEEL

Batista, Fulgencio bah-TEES-tuh, ful-JEN-see-oh

Bauhaus BOW-howss

Bayle, Pierre BEL, PYAYR

Beauharnais, Josephine de boh-ar-NAY, zhoh-seff-FEEN duh

Beauvoir, Simone de   boh-VWAR, see-MUHN duh

Bebel, August   BAY-bul, ow-GOOST

Beccaria, Cesare   buh-KAH-ree-uh, CHAY-zuh-ray

Bede   BEED

Beguines   bay-GEENZ

Beiderbecke, Bix   BY-der-bek, BIKS

Beijing   bay-ZHING

Belarus   bel-uh-ROOSS

Belgioioso, Cristina   bel-joh-YOH-soh, kriss-TEE-nuh

Belisarius   bel-uh-SAH-ree-uss

benefice   BEN-uh-fiss

Bergson, Henri   BERG-son, ahnh-REE

Berlioz, Hector   BAYR-lee-ohz, ek-TAWR

Berlusconi, Silvio   bayr-loo-SKOH-nee, SEEL-vee-oh

Bernhardi, Friedrich von   bayrn-HAR-dee, FREED-reekh fun

Bernini, Gian Lorenzo   bur-NEE-nee, ZHAHN loh-RENT-zoh

Bernstein, Eduard   BAYRN-shtyn, AY-doo-art

Bethman-Hollweg, Theobald von   BET-mun-HOHL-vek, TAY-oh-bahlt fun

Blanc, Louis   BLAHNH, LWEE

Blitzkrieg   BLITZ-kreeg

Blum, Léon   BLOOM, LAY-ohnh

Boccaccio, Giovanni   boh-KAH-choh, joh-VAH-nee

Bodichon, Barbara   boh-di-SHOHNH, bar-bah-RAH

Boer   BOOR *or* BOR

Boethius   boh-EE-thee-uss

Boleyn, Anne   BUH-lin *or* buh-LIN, AN

Bolívar, Simón   buh-LEE-var, see-MOHN

Bologna   buh-LOHN-yuh

Bolsheviks   BOHL-shuh-vikss

Bora, Katherina von   BOH-rah, kat-uh-REE-nuh fun

Borgia, Cesare   BOHR-zhuh, CHEZ-uh-ray

Bosnia   BAHZ-nee-uh

Bossuet, Jacques   baw-SWAY, ZHAHK

Botta, Giuseppe   BOH-tah, joo-ZEP-pay

Botticelli, Sandro   bot-i-CHEL-ee, SAHN-droh

Boulanger, Georges   boo-lahnh-ZHAY, ZHORZH

boule   BOO-lee

Bracciolini, Poggio   braht-choh-LEE-nee, POH-djoh

Brahe, Tycho   BRAH, TY-koh

Bramante, Donato   brah-MAHN-tay, doh-NAH-toh

Brandt, Willy   BRAHNT, VIL-ee

Brasidas   BRASS-i-duss

Brest-Litovsk   BREST-li-TUFFSK

Brétigny   bray-tee-NYEE

Brezhnev, Leonid   BREZH-neff, lee-oh-NYEET

Briand, Aristide   bree-AHNH, ah-ruh-STEED

Broz, Josip   BRAWZ, yaw-SEEP

Brumaire   broo-MAYR

Brunelleschi, Filippo   BROO-nuh-LESS-kee, fee-LEE-poh

Brüning, Heinrich   BROO-ning, HYN-rikh

Bückeberg   BOOK-uh-bayrk

Bulganin, Nicolai   bool-GAN-yin, nyik-uh-LY

Bund Deutscher Mädel   BOONT DOIT-chuh MAY-dul

Bundesrat   BOON-duhs-raht

Burckhardt, Jacob   BOORK-hart, YAK-ub

Burschenschaften   BOOR-shun-shahf-tuhn

bushido   BOO-shee-doh

Cabral, Pedro   kuh-BRAL

cahiers de doléances   ka-YAY duh doh-lay-AHNSS

Calais   ka-LAY

Calas, Jean   ka-LAH, ZHAHNH

Caligula   kuh-LIG-yuh-luh

caliph   KAY-liff

caliphate   KAY-luh-fayt

Callicrates   kuh-LIK-ruh-teez

Calonne, Charles de   ka-LUN, SHAHRL duh

Cambyses   kam-BY-seez

Camus, Albert   ka-MOO, ahl-BAYR

Canaanites   KAY-nuh-nytss

Capet, Hugh   ka-PAY, YOO

Capetian   kuh-PEE-shun

Caracalla   kuh-RAK-uh-luh

Caraffa, Gian Pietro   kuh-RAH-fuh, JAHN PYAY-troh

Caral   kuh-RAHL

carbonari   kar-buh-NAH-ree

Carolingian   kar-uh-LIN-jun

carruca   kuh-ROO-kuh

Carthage   KAR-thij

Carthaginian   kar-thuh-JIN-ee-un

Cartier, Jacques   kar-TYAY, ZHAK

Cassiodorus   kass-ee-uh-DOR-uss

Castiglione, Baldassare   ka-steel-YOH-nay, bal-duh-SAH-ray

Castro, Fidel   KASS-troh, fee-DEL

Çatal Hüyük   chaht-ul hoo-YOOK

Catharism   KA-thuh-riz-um

Catullus   kuh-TUL-uss

Cavendish, Margaret   KAV-un-dish, MAHR-guh-ret

Cavour, Camillo di   kuh-VOOR, kuh-MEEL-oh dee

Ceauşescu, Nicolae   chow-SHES-koo, nee-koh-LY

celibacy   SEL-uh-buh-see

cenobitic   sen-oh-BIT-ik

Cereta, Laura   say-REE-tuh, LOW-ruh

Cézanne, Paul   say-ZAHN, POHL

Chaeronea   ker-uh-NEE-uh

Chaldean   kal-DEE-un

Chandragupta Maurya   chun-druh-GOOP-tuh MOWR-yuh

chanson de geste   shahn-SAWNH duh ZHEST

Charlemagne   SHAR-luh-mayn

Chateaubriand, François-René de   shah-TOH-bree-AHNH, frahnh-SWAH-ruh-NAY duh

Chatelet, marquise du   shat-LAY, mahr-KEEZ duh

Chauvet   shoh-VAY

Cheka   CHEK-uh

Chiang Kai-Shek   CHANG ky-SHEK

Chirac, Jacques   shee-RAK, ZHAHK

Chrétien, Jean   kray-TYEN, ZHAHNH

Chrétien de Troyes   kray-TYEN duh TRWAH

Chrysoloras, Manuel   kriss-uh-LOHR-uss, MAN-yuh-wul

Cicero   SIS-uh-roh

ciompi   CHAHM-pee

Cistercians   sis-TUR-shunz

Claudius   KLAW-dee-uss

Cleisthenes   KLYSS-thuh-neez

Clemenceau, Georges   kluh-mahn-SOH, ZHORZH

Clovis   KLOH-viss

Codreanu, Corneliu   kaw-dree-AH-noo, kor-NEL-yoo

Colbert, Jean-Baptiste   kohl-BAYR, ZHAHN bap-TEEST

Colonia Agrippinensis   kuh-LOH-nee-uh uh-grip-uh-NEN-suss

colonus   kuh-LOH-nuss

Columbanus   kah-lum-BAY-nuss

comitia centuriata   kuh-MISH-ee-uh sen-choo-ree-AH-tuh

Commodus   KAHM-uh-duss

Comnenus   kahm-NEE-nuss

Comte, Auguste   KOHNT, ow-GOOST

concilium plebis   kahn-SIL-ee-um PLEE-biss

Concordat of Worms   kun-KOR-dat uv WURMZ *or* VORMPS

Condorcet, Marie-Jean de   kohn-dor-SAY, muh-REE-ZHAHNH duh

condottieri   kahn-duh-TYAY-ree

consul   KAHN-sul

Contarini, Gasparo   kahn-tuh-REE-nee, GAHS-puh-roh

conversos   kohn-VAYR-sohz

Copernicus, Nicolaus   kuh-PURR-nuh-kuss, nee-koh-LOW-uss

Córdoba   KOR-duh-buh

Corinth   KOR-inth

Corpus Hermeticum   KOR-pus hur-MET-i-koom

Corpus Iuris Civilis   KOR-pus YOOR-iss SIV-i-liss

corregidores   kuhr-reg-uh-DOR-ayss

Cortés, Hernán   kor-TAYSS *or* kor-TEZ, hayr-NAHN

Corvinus, Matthias   kor-VY-nuss, muh-THY-uss

Courbet, Gustave   koor-BAY, goo-STAHV

Crassus   KRASS-uss

Crécy   kray-SEE

Crédit Mobilier   kray-DEE moh-bee-LYAY

Croatia   kroh-AY-shuh

Croesus   KREE-suss

cum manu   koom MAH-noo

Curie, Marie   kyoo-REE, muh-REE

Cypselus   SIP-suh-luss

Daimler, Gottlieb   DYM-lur, GUT-leep

d'Albret, Jeanne   dahl-BRAY, ZHAHN

Dalí, Salvador   dah-LEE *or* DAH-lee, SAHL-vuh-dohr

Danton, Georges   dahn-TAWNH, ZHORZH

Darius   duh-RY-uss

Darmstadt   DARM-shtaht

dauphin   DAW-fin

David, Jacques-Louis   dah-VEED, ZHAHK-LWEE

Debelleyme, Louis-Maurice   duh-buh-LAYM, LWEE-moh-REESS

Debussy, Claude   duh-bus-SEE, KLOHD

décades   day-KAD

Decameron   dee-KAM-uh-run

decarchies   DEK-ar-keez

decemviri   duh-SEM-vuh-ree

de Champlain, Samuel   duh sham-PLAYN, sahm-WEL

Deffand, marquise du   duh-FAHNH, mar-KEEZ doo

de Gaulle, Charles   duh GOHL, SHAHRL

Delacroix, Eugène   duh-lah-KRWAH, ur-ZHEN

Delphi   DEL-fy

Démar, Claire   DAY-mar, CLAYR

demesne   duh-MAYN

Demosthenes   duh-MAHSS-thuh-neez

Denikin, Anton   dyin-YEE-kin, ahn-TOHN

De Rerum Novarum   day RAYR-um noh-VAR-um

Derrida, Jacques   DAY-ree-dah, ZHAHK

Descartes, René   day-KART, ruh-NAY

Dessau   DESS-ow

d'Este, Isabella   DESS-tay, ee-suh-BEL-uh

d'Holbach, Paul   DOHL-bahk, POHL

dhoti   DOH-tee

Diaghilev, Sergei   DYAHG-yuh-lif, syir-GAY

Dias, Bartholomeu   DEE-ush, bar-toh-loh-MAY-oo

Diaspora   dy-ASS-pur-uh

Diderot, Denis   DEE-droh, duh-NEE

Diocletian   dy-uh-KLEE-shun

Disraeli, Benjamin   diz-RAY-lee, BEN-juh-min

Djoser   ZHOH-sur

Dollfuss, Engelbert   DOHL-fooss, AYN-gul-bayrt

Domesday Book   DOOMZ-day book

Domitian   doh-MISH-un

Donatello, Donato di   doh-nuh-TEL-oh, doh-NAH-toh dee

Donatus   duh-NAY-tus

Donatist   DOH-nuh-tist

Dopolavoro   duh-puh-LAH-vuh-roh

Dorians   DOR-ee-unz

Doryphoros   doh-RIF-uh-rohss

Dostoevsky, Fyodor   dus-tuh-YEF-skee, FYUD-ur

Douhet, Giulio   doo-AY, JOOL-yoh

Dreyfus, Alfred   DRY-fuss, AL-fred

Dubček, Alexander   DOOB-chek, ah-lek-SAHN-dur

Du Bois, W. E. B.   doo-BOISS

Dufay, Guillaume   doo-FAY, gee-YOHM

Duma   DOO-muh

Dürer, Albrecht   DOO-rur, AHL-brekht

Ebert, Friedrich   AY-bert, FREE-drikh

ecclesia   ek-KLEE-zee-uh

Eckhart, Meister   EK-hart, MY-stur

Einsatzgruppen   YN-zahtz-groop-un

Einstein, Albert   YN-styn *or* Yn-shtyn, AL-burt

Ekaterinburg   i-kat-tuh-RIN-burk

encomienda   en-koh-MYEN-dah

Engels, Friedrich   ENG-ulz, FREE-drikh

Enki   EN-kee

Enlil   EN-lil

Entente Cordiale   ahn-TAHNT kor-DYAHL

Epaminondas   i-PAM-uh-NAHN-duss

ephor   EFF-ur

Epicurus   ep-i-KYOOR-uss

Epicureanism   ep-i-kyoo-REE-uh-ni-zum

episcopos   i-PIS-kuh-puss

equestrians   i-KWES-tree-unz

equites   EK-wuh-teez

Erasistratus   er-uh-SIS-truh-tuss

Erasmus, Desiderius   i-RAZ-mus, dez-i-DEER-ee-uss

Eratosthenes   er-uh-TAHSS-thuh-neez

eremitical   er-uh-MIT-i-kul

Erhard, Ludwig   AYR-hart, LOOD-vik

Estonia   ess-TOH-nee-uh

Etruscans   i-TRUSS-kunz

Euclid   YOO-klid

Euripides   yoo-RIP-i-deez

exchequer   EKS-chek-ur

Execrabilis   ek-suh-KRAB-uh-liss

Eylau   Y-low
Falange   fuh-LANJ
fasces   FASS-eez
Fascio di Combattimento   FASH-ee-oh dee com-bat-ee-MEN-toh
Fatimid   FAT-i-mid
Fedele, Cassandra   FAY-duh-lee, kuh-SAN-druh
Feltre, Vittorino da   FEL-tray, vee-tor-EE-noh dah
Ficino, Marsilio   fee-CHEE-noh, mar-SIL-yoh
Fischer, Joschka   FISH-ur, YUSH-kah
Flaubert, Gustave   floh-BAYR, goo-STAHV
Fleury, Cardinal   floo-REE, KAHR-di-nul
Floreal   floh-ray-AHL
fluyt   FLYT
Foch, Ferdinand   FUSH, fayr-di-nawnh
Fontainebleau   fawnh-ten-BLOH
Fontenelle, Bernard de   fawnt-NEL, bayr-NAHR duh
Foucault, Michel   foo-KOH, mee-SHEL
Fouquet, Nicolas   foo-KAY, nee-koh-LAH
Fourier, Charles   foo-RYAY, SHAHRL
Francesca, Piero della   frahn-CHESS-kuh, PYAY-roh del-luh
Frequens   FREE-kwenss
Freud, Sigmund   FROID, SIG-mund *or* ZIG-munt
Friedan, Betty   free-DAN
Friedland   FREET-lahnt
Friedrich, Caspar David   FREED-rikh, kass-PAR dah-VEET
Frimaire   free-MAYR
Froissart, Jean   frwah-SAR, ZHAHNH
Fronde   FROHND
Fructidor   FROOK-ti-dor
fueros   FWYA-rohss
Führerprinzip   FYOOR-ur-prin-TSEEP
gabelle   gah-BEL
Gaiseric   GY-zuh-rik
Galba   GAHL-buh
Galilei, Galileo   GAL-li-lay, gal-li-LAY-oh
Gama, Vasco da   GAHM-uh, VAHSH-koh dah
Gandhi, Mohandas (Mahatma)   GAHN-dee, moh-HAHN-dus (muh-HAHT-muh)
Garibaldi, Giuseppe   gar-uh-BAHL-dee, joo-ZEP-pay
Gasperi, Alcide de   GAHSS-pe-ree, ahl-SEE-day day
Gatti de Gamond, Zoé   gah-TEE duh gah-MOHNH, zoh-AY
Gaugamela   gaw-guh-MEE-luh
Gelasius   juh-LAY-shuss
Gentileschi, Artemisia   jen-tuh-LESS-kee, ar-tuh-MEE-zhuh
Geoffrin, Marie-Thérèse de   zhoh-FRANH, ma-REE-tay-RAYZ duh
Germinal   jayr-mee-NAHL
gerousia   juh-ROO-see-uh
Gesamtkunstwerk   guh-ZAHMT-koonst-vayrk
Gierek, Edward   GYER-ek, ed-VAHRT
Gilgamesh   GIL-guh-mesh
Giolitti, Giovanni   joh-LEE-tee, joh-VAHN-nee
Giotto   JOH-toh
Girondins   juh-RAHN-dinz
glasnost   GLAHZ-nohst
Gleichschaltung   glykh-SHAHL-toonk
Goebbels, Joseph   GUR-bulz, YOH-sef
Goethe, Johann Wolfgang von   GUR-tuh, yoh-HAHN VULF-gahnk fun

Gömbös, Julius   GUM-buhsh, JOOL-yuss
Gomulka, Wladyslaw   goh-MOOL-kuh, vlah-DIS-lahf
gonfaloniere   gun-fah-loh-NYAY-ray
Gonzaga, Gian Francesco   gun-DZAH-gah, JAHN frahn-CHES-koh
Gorbachev, Mikhail   GOR-buh-chof, meek-HAYL
Göring, Hermann   GUR-ing, hayr-MAHN
Gottwald, Clement   GUT-vald, kleh-MENT
Gouges, Olympe   GOOZH, oh-LAMP
Gracchus, Tiberius and Gaius   GRAK-us, ty-BEER-ee-uss and GY-uss
grandi   GRAHN-dee
Grieg, Edvard   GREEG, ED-vart
Groote, Gerard   GROH-tuh
Gropius, Walter   GROH-pee-uss, VAHL-tuh
Grossdeutsch   GROHS-doich
Groza, Petra   GRO-zhuh, PET-ruh
Guicciardini, Francesco   gwee-char-DEE-nee, frahn-CHESS-koh
Guindorf, Reine   GWIN-dorf, RY-nuh
Guise   GEEZ
Guizot, François   gee-ZOH, frahnh-SWAH
Gustavus Adolphus   goo-STAY-vus uh-DAHL-fuss
Gutenberg, Johannes   GOO-ten-bayrk, yoh-HAH-nuss
Guzman, Gaspar de   goos-MAHN, gahs-PAR day
Habsburg   HAPS-burg
Hadrian   HAY-dree-un
Hagia Sophia   HAG-ee-uh soh-FEE-uh
hajj   HAJ
Hammurabi   ham-uh-RAH-bee
Handel, George Friedrich   HAN-dul, JORJ FREED-rik
Hankou   HAHN-kow
Hannibal   HAN-uh-bul
Hanukkah   HAH-nuh-kuh
Harappa   huh-RAP-uh
Hardenberg, Karl von   HAR-den-berk, KAHRL fun
Harun al-Rashid   huh-ROON ah-rah-SHEED
Hatshepsut   hat-SHEP-soot
Haushofer, Karl   HOWSS-hoh-fuh, KAHRL
Haussmann, Baron   HOWSS-mun, BAR-un
Havel, Vaclav   HAH-vul, VAHT-slahf
Haydn, Franz Joseph   HY-dun, FRAHNTS YO-zef
hegemon   HEJ-uh-mun
Hegira   hee-JY-ruh
Heisenberg, Werner   HY-zun-bayrk, VAYR-nuh
heliaea   HEE-lee-ee
Hellenistic   hel-uh-NIS-tik
helots   HEL-uts
Herculaneum   hur-kyuh-LAY-nee-um
Herodotus   huh-ROD-uh-tuss
Herophilus   huh-ROF-uh-luss
Herzegovina   HURT-suh-guh-VEE-nuh
Herzen, Alexander   HAYRT-sun, ah-lek-ZAHN-dur
Herzl, Theodor   HAYRT-sul, TAY-oh-dor
Hesiod   HEE-see-ud
Hesse, Hermann   HESS-uh, HAYR-mahn
hetairai   huh-TY-ree
Heydrich, Reinhard   HY-drikh, RYN-hart
hieroglyph   HY-uh-roh-glif
Hildegard of Bingen   HIL-duh-gard uv BING-un

Hindenburg, Paul von   HIN-den-boork, POWL fun

Hiroshima   hee-roh-SHEE-muh

Hitler Jugend   HIT-luh YOO-gunt

Ho Chi Minh   HOH CHEE MIN

Höch, Hannah   HURKH, HAH-nuh

Hohenstaufen   hoh-en-SHTOW-fen

Hohenzollern   hoh-en-TSUL-urn

Hohenzollern-Sigmaringen   hoh-en-TSUL-urn zig-mah-RING-un

Holtzendorf   HOHLT-sen-dorf

Homo sapiens   HOH-moh SAY-pee-unz

Honecker, Erich   HOH-nek-uh, AY-reekh

Honorius   hoh-NOR-ee-uss

hoplites   HAHP-lyts

Horace   HOR-uss

Horthy, Miklós   HOR-tee, MIK-lohsh

Höss, Rudolf   HURSS, ROO-dulf

Hoxha, Enver   HAW-jah, EN-vur

Huayna Inca   WY-nuh INK-uh

Huguenots   HYOO-guh-nots

Husák, Gustav   HOO-sahk, goo-STAHV

Hydaspes   hy-DASS-peez

Ibn Sina   ib-un SEE-nuh

Ictinus   ik-TY-nuss

Ignatius of Loyola   ig-NAY-shuss uv loi-OH-luh

Il Duce   eel DOO-chay

Île-de-France   EEL-de-fronhss

illustrés   ee-loo-STRAY

illustrissimi   ee-loo-STREE-see-mee

imperator   im-puh-RAH-tur

imperium   im-PEER-ee-um

intendant   anh-tahnh-DAHNH *or* in-TEN-dunt

Isis   Y-sis

Issus   ISS-uss

ius civile   YOOSS see-VEE-lay

ius gentium   YOOSS GEN-tee-um

ius naturale   YOOSS nah-too-RAH-lay

Jacobin   JAK-uh-bin

Jacquerie   zhak-REE

Jadwiga   yahd-VEE-guh

Jagiello   yahg-YEL-oh

Jahn, Friedrich Ludwig   YAHN, FREED-rikh LOOD-vik

Jaufré Rudel   zhoh-FRAY roo-DEL

Jaurès, Jean   zhaw-RESS, ZHAHNH

Jena   YAY-nuh

jihad   ji-HAHD

Joffre, Joseph   ZHUFF-ruh, zhoh-ZEF

Journal des Savants   zhoor-NAHL day sah-VAHNH

Juana Inés de la Cruz, Sor   HWAH-nuh ee-NAYSS day lah KROOZ, SAWR

Judaea   joo-DEE-uh

Judas Maccabaeus   JOO-dus mak-uh-BEE-uss

Jung, Carl   YOONG, KAHRL

Junkers   YOONG-kers

Jupiter Optimus Maximus   JOO-puh-tur AHP-tuh-muss MAK-suh-muss

Justinian   juh-STIN-ee-un

Juvenal   JOO-vuh-nul

Ka'ba   KAH-buh

Kádár, János   KAH-dahr, YAH-nush

kamikaze   kah-mi-KAH-zay

Kandinsky, Wassily   kan-DIN-skee, vus-YEEL-yee

Kangxi   GANG-zhee

Kant, Immanuel   KAHNT, i-MAHN-yoo-el

Karlowitz   KARL-oh-vits

Karlsbad   KARLSS-baht

Kaunitz, Wenzel von   KOW-nits, VENT-sul fun

Kemal Atatürk   kuh-MAHL ah-tah-TIRK

Kenyatta, Jomo   ken-YAHT-uh, JOH-moh

Kerensky, Alexander   kuh-REN-skee, ah-lek-SAHN-dur

Keynes, John Maynard   KAYNZ, JAHN MAY-nurd

Khanbaliq   khahn-bah-LEEK

Khomeini, Ayatollah   khoh-MAY-nee, ah-yuh-TUL-uh

Khrushchev, Nikita   KHROOSH-chawf, nuh-KEE-tuh

Khubilai Khan   KOO-bluh KAHN

Kikuya   ki-KOO-yuh

Kleindeutsch   KLYN-doich

Kohl, Helmut   KOHL, HEL-moot

koiné   koi-NAY

Kolchak, Alexander   kul-CHAHK, ah-lek-SAHN-dur

Kollantai, Alexandra   kul-lun-TY, ah-lek-SAHN-druh

Königgrätz   kur-nig-GRETS

Kornilov, Lavr   kor-NYEE-luff, LAH-vur

Kosciuszko, Thaddeus   kaw-SHOOS-koh, tah-DAY-oosh

Kosovo   KAWSS-suh-voh

Kossuth, Louis   KAWSS-uth *or* KAW-shoot, LOO-iss

Kostunica, Vojislav   kuh-STOO-nit-suh, VOH-yee-slav

kouros   KOO-rohss

Koyaanisqatsi   koh-YAH-niss-kahts

Kraft durch Freude   KRAHFT doorkh FROI-duh

Kreditanstalt   kray-deet-AHN-shtalt

Kristallnacht   kri-STAHL-nahkht

Krupp, Alfred   KROOP, AHL-fret

Kuchuk-Kainarji   koo-CHOOK-ky-NAR-jee

kulaks   KOO-lahks

Kulturkampf   kool-TOOR-kahmpf

Kun, Béla   KOON, BAY-luh

Kundera, Milan   koon-DAYR-uh, MEE-lahn

Kursk   KOORSK

Kwasniewski, Aleksander   kwahsh-NYEF-skee, ah-lek-SAHN-dur

la belle époque   lah BEL ay-PUK

Lafayette, marquis de   lah-fay-ET, mar-KEE duh

laissez-faire   less-ay-FAYR

Lamarck, Jean-Baptiste   lah-MARK, ZHAHNH-bah-TEEST

Lancaster   LAN-kas-tur

La Rochefoucauld-Liancourt, duc de   lah-RUSH-foo-koh-lee-ahnh-KOOR, dook duh

Las Navas de Tolosa   lahss-nah-vahss-day-toh-LOH-suh

latifundia   lat-i-FOON-dee-uh

Latium   LAY-shee-um

Latvia   LAT-vee-uh

Launay, marquis de   loh-NAY, mar-KEE duh

Laurier, Wilfred   LOR-ee-ay, WIL-fred

Lavoisier, Antoine   lah-vwah-ZYAY, ahn-TWAHN

Lazar   lah-ZAR

Lebensraum   LAY-benz-rowm

Les Demoiselles d'Avignon   lay dem-wah-ZEL dah-vee-NYOHNH

Lespinasse, Julie de   less-pee-NAHSS, zhoo-LEE duh
Le Tellier, François Michel   luh tel-YAY, frahnh-SWAH-mee-SHEL
Lévesque, René   luh-VEK, ruh-NAY
Leviathan   luh-VY-uh-thun
Leyster, Judith   LESS-tur, JOO-dith
Licinius   ly-SIN-ee-uss
Liebenfels, Lanz von   LEE-bun-felss, LAHNTS fun
Liebknecht, Karl   LEEP-knekht, KAHRL
Liebknecht, Wilhelm   LEEP-knekht, VIL-helm
Lindisfarne   LIN-dis-farn
Lionne, Hugues de   LYUN, OOG duh
List, Friedrich   LIST, FREED-rikh
Liszt, Franz   LIST, FRAHNTS
Lithuania   lith-WAY-nee-uh
Livy   LIV-ee
Li Zicheng   lee-zee-CHENG
L'Ouverture, Toussaint   loo-vayr-TOOR, too-SANH
Louvois   loo-VWAH
Lucretius   loo-KREE-shus
Luddites   LUD-yts
Ludendorff, Erich   LOO-dun-dorf
Lueger, Karl   LOO-gur, KAHRL
Luftwaffe   LOOFT-vahf-uh
l'uomo universale   LWOH-moh OO-nee-ver-SAH-lay
Lützen   LOOT-sun
Luxemburg, Rosa   LOOK-sum-boork, ROH-suh
Lyons   LYOHNH
Lysias   LISS-ee-uss
Maastricht   MAHSS-trikht
Ma'at   muh-AHT
Machiavelli, Niccolò   mahk-ee-uh-VEL-ee, nee-koh-LOH
Maginot Line   MA-zhi-noh lyn
Magna Graecia   MAG-nuh GREE-shuh
Magyars   MAG-yarz
Maimonides   my-MAH-nuh-deez
Maistre, Joseph de   MESS-truh, zhoh-SEF duh
maius imperium   MY-yoos im-PEE-ree-um
Malaya   muh-LAY-uh
Mallarmé, Stéphane   mah-lahr-MAY, stay-FAHN
Malleus Maleficarum   mal-EE-uss mal-uh-FIK-uh-rum
Malthus, Thomas   MAWL-thuss, TAHM-uss
Manchukuo   man-CHOO-kwoh
Manetho   MAN-uh-thoh
Mao Zedong   mow zee-DAHNG
Marcus Aurelius   MAR-kuss aw-REE-lee-uss
Marcuse, Herbert   mar-KOO-zuh, HUR-burt
Marie Antoinette   muh-REE an-twuh-NET
Marius   MAR-ee-uss
Marquez, Gabriel Garcia   mar-KEZ, gab-ree-EL gar-SEE-uh
Marseilles   mar-SAY
Marsiglio of Padua   mar-SIL-yoh uv PAD-juh-wuh
Masaccio   muh-ZAH-choh
Masaryk, Thomas   MAS-uh-rik, toh-MAHSS
Mästlin, Michael   MEST-lin, mee-kah-EL
Matteotti, Giacomo   mat-tay-AHT-tee, JAHK-uh-moh
Mauryan   MAWR-ee-in *or* MOW-ree-in
Maxentius   mak-SEN-shuss
Maximian   mak-SIM-ee-un

Maya   MY-uh
Mazarin   maz-uh-RANH
Mazzini, Giuseppe   maht-SEE-nee, joo-ZEP-pay
Megasthenes   muh-GAS-thuh-neez
Mehmet   meh-MET
Meiji   MAY-jee
Mein Kampf   myn KAHMPF
Melanchthon, Philip   muh-LANK-tun, fil-LEEP
Menander   muh-NAN-dur
Mendeleyev, Dmitri   men-duh-LAY-ef, di-MEE-tree
Mensheviks   MES-shuh-viks
Mercator, Gerardus   mur-KAY-tur, juh-RAHR-dus
Merian, Maria Sibylla   MAY-ree-un, muh-REE-uh suh-BIL-uh
Merovingian   meh-ruh-VIN-jee-un
Mesopotamia   mess-uh-puh-TAY-mee-uh
Messiaen, Olivier   meh-SYANH, oh-lee-VYAY
Messidor   MESS-i-dor
mestizos   mess-TEE-ZOHZ
Metaxas, John   muh-tahk-SAHSS, JAHN
Metternich, Klemens von   MET-ayr-nikh, KLAY-menss fun
Michel, Louise   mee-SHEL, loo-EEZ
Michelangelo   my-kuh-LAN-juh-loh
Mieszko   MYESH-koh
Millet, Jean-François   mi-YEH, ZHAHNH-frahnh-SWAH
Milo_evi_, Slobodan   mi-LOH-suh-vich, sluh-BOH-dahn
Miltiades   mil-TY-uh-deez
Mirandola, Pico della   mee-RAN-doh-lah, PEE-koh DEL-uh
missi dominici   MISS-ee doh-MIN-i-chee
Mitterrand, François   MEE-tayr-rahnh, frahnh-SWAH
Moctezuma   mahk-tuh-ZOO-muh
Mohács   MOH-hach
Mohenjo-Daro   mo-HEN-jo-DAH-roh
Moldavia   mohl-DAY-vee-uh
Moldova   mohl-DOH-vuh
Molière, Jean-Baptiste   mohl-YAYR, ZHAHNH-bah-TEEST
Molotov, Vyacheslav   MAHL-uh-tawf, vyich-chiss-SLAHF
Monet, Claude   moh-NEH, KLOHD
Montaigne, Michel de   mahn-TAYN, mee-SHEL duh
Montefeltro, Federigo da   mahn-tuh-FEL-troh, fay-day-REE-goh dah
Montesquieu   MOHN-tess-kyoo
Montessori, Maria   mahn-tuh-SOR-ee
Morisot, Berthe   mor-ee-ZOH, BAYRT
Mozambique   moh-zam-BEEK
Mozart, Wolfgang Amadeus   MOH-tsart, VULF-gahng ah-muh-DAY-uss
Muawiya   moo-AH-wee-yah
Mudejares   moo-theh-KHAH-rayss
Mughal   MOO-gul
Muhammad   moh-HAM-mud *or* moo-HAM-mud
Mühlberg   MOOL-bayrk
mulattoes   muh-LAH-tohz
Müntzer, Thomas   MOON-tsur
Murad   moo-RAHD
Muslim   MUZ-lum
Mutsuhito   moo-tsoo-HEE-toh
Myanmar   MYAN-mahr
Mycenaean   my-suh-NEE-un

Nabonidas   nab-uh-NY-duss

Nabopolassar   nab-uh-puh-LASS-ur

Nagasaki   nah-gah-SAH-kee

Nagy, Imry   NAHJ, IM-ray

Nanjing   nan-JING

Nantes   NAHNT

Nasser, Gamal Abdel   NAH-sur, juh-MAHL ahb-DOOL

Navarre   nuh-VAHR

Nebuchadnezzar   neb-uh-kud-NEZZ-ur

Nehru, Jawaharlal   NAY-roo, juh-WAH-hur-lahl

Nero   NEE-roh

Nerva   NUR-vuh

Neumann, Balthasar   NOI-mahn, BAHL-tuh-zahr

Neumann, Solomon   NOI-mahn, ZOH-loh-mun

Neustria   NOO-stree-uh

Nevsky, Alexander   NYEF-skee, ah-lek-SAHN-dur

Newcomen, Thomas   NYOO-kuh-mun *or* nyoo-KUM-mun, TAHM-uss

Ngo Dinh Diem   GOH din DYEM

Nicias   NISS-ee-uss

Nietzsche, Friedrich   NEE-chuh *or* NEE-chee, FREED-rikh

Nimwegen   NIM-vay-gun

Ninhursaga   nin-HUR-sah-guh

Nivose   nee-VOHZ

Nkrumah, Kwame   en-KROO-muh, KWAH-may

nobiles   no-BEE-layz

Nogarola, Isotta   NOH-guh-rol-uh, ee-ZAHT-uh

Novalis, Friedrich   noh-VAH-lis, FREED-rikh

Novotny, Antonin   noh-VAHT-nee, AHN-toh-nyeen

novus homo   NOH-vuss HOH-moh

Nystadt   NEE-shtaht

Octavian   ahk-TAY-vee-un

Odoacer   oh-doh-AY-sur

Olivares   oh-lee-BAH-rayss

optimates   ahp-tuh-MAH-tayz

Oresteia   uh-res-TY-uh

Osama bin Laden   oh-SAH-muh bin LAH-dun

Osiris   oh-SY-russ

Ostara   oh-STAH-ruh

Ostpolitik   OHST-paw-li-teek

ostrakon   AHSS-truh-kahn

Ostrogoths   AHSS-truh-gahthss

Ovid   OH-vid

Oxenstierna, Axel   OOK-sen-shur-nah, AHK-sul

Pachakuti   pah-chah-KOO-tee

Paleologus   pay-lee-AWL-uh-guss

Panaetius   puh-NEE-shuss

Pankhurst, Emmeline   PANK-hurst, EM-muh-lyn

papal curia   PAY-pul KYOOR-ee-uh

Papen, Franz von   PAH-pun, FRAHNTS fun

Paracelsus   par-uh-SEL-suss

Parlement   par-luh-MAHNH

Parti Québécois   par-TEE kay-bek-KWA

Pascal, Blaise   pass-KAHL, BLEZ

Pasteur, Louis   pas-TOOR, LWEE

paterfamilias   pay-tur-fuh-MEEL-yus

Pensées   pahn-SAY

Pentateuch   PEN-tuh-took

Pepin   PEP-in *or* pay-PANH

perestroika   per-uh-STROI-kuh

Pergamum   PURR-guh-mum

Pericles   PER-i-kleez

perioeci   per-ee-EE-see

Pétain, Henri   pay-TANH, ahnh-REE

Petite Roquette   puh-TEET raw-KET

Petrarch   PEE-trark *or* PET-trark

Petronius   pi-TROH-nee-uss

phalansteries   fuh-LAN-stuh-reez

philosophe   fee-loh-ZAWF

Phintys   FIN-tiss

Phoenicians   fuh-NEE-shunz

Photius   FOH-shuss

Picasso, Pablo   pi-KAH-soh, PAHB-loh

Pietism   PY-uh-tiz-um

Pilsudski, Joseph   peel-SOOT-skee, YOO-zef

Piscator, Erwin   PIS-kuh-tor, AYR-vin

Pisistratus   puh-SIS-truh-tuss

Pissarro, Camille   pee-SAH-roh, kah-MEEL

Pizan, Christine de   pee-ZAHN, kris-TEEN duh

Pizarro, Francesco   puh-ZAHR-oh, frahn-CHESS-koh

Planck, Max   PLAHNK, MAHKS

Plantagenet   plan-TAJ-uh-net

Plassey   PLA-see

Plato   PLAY-toh

Plautus   PLAW-tuss

plebiscita   pleb-i-SEE-tuh

Pluviose   ploo-VYOHZ

Poincaré, Raymond   pwanh-kah-RAY, ray-MOHNH

polis   POH-liss

politiques   puh-lee-TEEKS

Pollaiuolo, Antonio   pohl-ly-WOH-loh, ahn-TOHN-yoh

Poltava   pul-TAH-vuh

Polybius   puh-LIB-ee-uss

Pombal, marquis de   pum-BAHL, mar-KEE duh

Pompadour, madame de   POM-puh-door, ma-DAM duh

Pompeii   pahm-PAY

Pompey   PAHM-pee

pontifex maximus   PAHN-ti-feks MAK-si-muss

populares   PAWP-oo-lahr-ayss

popolo grasso   PAWP-oo-loh GRAH-soh

Poseidon   poh-SY-dun

Postumus   PAHS-choo-muss

Potsdam   PAHTS-dam

Poussin, Nicholas   poo-SANH, NEE-koh-lah

Praecepter Germaniae   PREE-sep-tur gayr-MAHN-ee-ee

praetor   PREE-tur

Prairial   pray-RYAL

Pravda   PRAHV-duh

Primo de Rivera   PREE-moh day ri-VAY-ruh

primogeniture   pree-moh-JEN-i-choor

princeps   PRIN-seps *or* PRIN-keps

Principia   prin-SIP-ee-uh *or* prin-KIP-ee-uh

Procopius   pruh-KOH-pee-uss

procurator   PROK-yuh-ray-tur

Ptolemy   TAHL-uh-mee

Ptolemaic   tahl-uh-MAY-ik

Pugachev, Emelyan   poo-guh-CHAWF, yim-yil-YAHN
Punic   PYOO-nik
Putin, Vladimir   POO-tin, vlah-dyim-YEER
Pyrrhus   PEER-uss
Pyrrhic   PEER-ik
Pythagoras   puh-THAG-uh-russ
Qianlong   CHAN-lung
Qing   CHING
quadrivium   kwah-DRIV-ee-um
quaestors   KWES-turs
querelle des femmes   keh-REL day FAHM
Quesnay, François   keh-NAY, frahnn-SWAH
Quetzelcoatl   KWET-sul-koh-AHT-ul
Quran   kuh-RAN *or* kuh-RAHN
Racine, Jean-Baptiste   ra-SEEN, ZHAHNH-buh-TEEST
Rahner, Karl   RAH-nur, KAHRL
Rameses   RAM-uh-seez
Raphael   RAFF-ee-ul
Rasputin   rass-PYOO-tin
Rathenau, Walter   RAH-tuh-now, VAHL-tuh
Realpolitik   ray-AHL-poh-lee-teek
Realschule   ray-AHL-shoo-luh
Reconquista   ray-kawn-kiss-TAH
Reichsrat   RYKHSS-raht
Reichstag   RYKHSS-tahk
Rembrandt van Rijn   REM-brant vahn RYN
Renaissance   REN-uh-sahnss
Renan, Ernst   re-NAHNH, AYRNST
Ricci, Matteo   REE-chee, ma-TAY-oh
Richelieu   REESH-uh-lyoo
Ricimer   RISS-uh-mur
Rikstag   RIKS-tahk
Rilke, Rainer Maria   RIL-kuh, RY-nuh mah-REE-uh
Rimbaud, Arthur   ram-BOH, ar-TOOR
risorgimento   ree-SOR-jee-men-toe
Robespierre, Maximilien   ROHBZ-pyayr, mak-see-meel-YENH
Rococo   ruh-KOH-koh
Rocroi   roh-KRWAH
Röhm, Ernst   RURM, AYRNST
Rommel, Erwin   RAHM-ul, AYR-vin
Romulus Augustulus   RAHM-yuh-luss ow-GOOS-chuh-luss
Rossbach   RAWSS-bahkh
Rousseau, Jean-Jacques   roo-SOH, ZHAHNH-ZHAHK
Rurik   ROO-rik
Ryswick   RYZ-wik
Sacrosancta   sak-roh-SANK-tuh
Saint-Just   sanh-ZHOOST
Saint-Simon, Henri de   sanh-see-MOHNH, ahnh-REE duh
Sakharov, Andrei   SAH-kuh-rawf, ahn-DRAY
Saladin   SAL-uh-din
Salazar, Antonio   SAL-uh-zahr, ahn-TOH-nee-oh
Sallust   SAL-ust
Samnites   SAM-nytss
San Martín, José de   san mar-TEEN, hoh-SAY day
sans-culottes   sahnh-koo-LUT *or* sanz-koo-LAHTSS
Sartre, Jean-Paul   SAR-truh, ZHAHNH-POHL
satrap   SAY-trap
satrapy   SAY-truh-pee

Satyricon   sat-TEER-i-kahn
Schaumburg-Lippe   SHOWM-boorkh-LEE-puh
Schleswig-Holstein   SHLESS-vik-HOHL-shtyn
Schlieffen, Alfred von   SHLEE-fun, AHL-fret fun
Schliemann, Heinrich   SHLEE-mahn, HYN-rikh
Schmidt, Helmut   SHMIT, HEL-moot
Schönberg, Arnold   SHURN-bayrk, AR-nawlt
Schönborn   SHURN-bawn
Schönerer, Georg von   SHURN-uh-ruh, GAY-ork fun
Schröder, Gerhard   SHRUR-duh, GAYR-hahrt
Schurz, Carl   SHOO-utss *or* SHURTS, KAHRL
Schuschnigg, Karl von   SHOOSH-nik, KAHRL fun
Schutzmannschaft   SHOOTSS-mun-shahft
Scipio Aemilianus   SEE-pee-oh ee-mil-YAY-nuss
Scipio Africanus   SEE-pee-oh af-ree-KAY-nuss
scriptoria   skrip-TOR-ee-uh
Ségur   say-GOO-uh
Sejm   SAYM
Seleucid   suh-LOO-sid
Seleucus   suh-LOO-kuss
Seljuk   SEL-jook
Seneca   SEN-uh-kuh
Sephardic   suh-FAHR-dik
Septimius Severus   sep-TIM-ee-uss se-VEER-uss
serjents   sayr-ZHAHNH
Sforza, Ludovico   SFORT-sah, loo-doh-VEE-koh
Shalmaneser   shal-muh-NEE-zur
Shang   SHAHNG
Shari'a   shah-REE-uh
Sieveking, Amalie   SEE-vuh-king, uh-MAHL-yuh
Sieyès, Abbé   syay-YESS, ab-BAY
signoria   seen-YOR-ee-uh
sine manu   sy-nee-MAY-noo
Slovenia   sloh-VEE-nee-uh
Société Générale   soh-see-ay-TAY zhay-nay-RAHL
Socrates   SAHK-ruh-teez
Solon   SOH-lun
Solzhenitsyn, Alexander   sohl-zhuh-NEET-sin, ah-lek-SAHN-dur
Somme   SUM
Sophocles   SAHF-uh-kleez
Sorel, Georges   soh-REL, ZHORZH
Spartacus   SPAR-tuh-kuss
Spartiates   spar-tee-AH-teez
Speer, Albert   SHPAYR, AHL-bayrt
Speransky, Michael   spyuh-RAHN-skee, mee-kah-EL
Spinoza, Benedict de   spi-NOH-zuh, BEN-uh-dikt duh
squadristi   skwah-DREES-tee
Srebrenica   sreb-bruh-NEET-suh
stadholder   STAD-hohl-dur
Staël, Germaine de   STAHL, zhayr-MEN duh
Stakhanov, Alexei   stuh-KHAH-nuf, uh-LEK-say
Stasi   SHTAH-see
Stauffenberg, Claus von   SHTOW-fen-berk, KLOWSS fun
Stein, Heinrich von   SHTYN, HYN-rikh fun
Stilicho   STIL-i-koh
Stoicism   STOH-i-siz-um
Stolypin, Peter   stuh-LIP-yin, PYOH-tur
strategoi   strah-tay-GOH-ee

Stravinsky, Igor   struh-VIN-skee, EE-gor

Stresemann, Gustav   SHTRAY-zuh-mahn, GOOS-tahf

Strozzi, Alessandra   STRAWT-see, ah-less-SAHN-druh

Struensee, John Frederick   SHTROO-un-zay, JAHN FRED-uh-rik

Sturmabteilung   SHTOORM-ap-ty-loonk

Sudetenland   soo-DAY-tun-land

Suger   soo-ZHAYR

Suharto   soo-HAHR-toh

Sukarno   soo-KAHR-noh

Suleiman   soo-lay-MAHN

Sulla   SUL-uh

Sumerians   soo-MER-ee-unz *or* soo-MEER-ee-unz

Summa Theologica   SOO-muh tay-oh-LOG-jee-kuh

Suppiluliumas   suh-PIL-oo-LEE-uh-muss

Suttner, Bertha von   ZOOT-nuh, BAYR-tuh fun

Symphonie Fantastique   SANH-foh-nee fahn-tas-TEEK

Taaffe, Edward von   TAH-fuh, ED-wahrt fun

Tacitus   TASS-i-tuss

taille   TY

Talleyrand   tah-lay-RAHNH

Tanzania   tan-zuh-NEE-uh

Tenochtitlán   tay-nawch-teet-LAHN

Tertullian   tur-TUL-yun

Thales   THAY-leez

Theocritus   thee-AHK-ruh-tuss

Theodora   thee-uh-DOR-uh

Theodoric   thee-AHD-uh-rik

Theodosius   thee-uh-DOH-shuss

Theognis   thee-AHG-nuss

Thermidor   TAYR-mi-dor

Thermopylae   thur-MAHP-uh-lee

Thiers, Adolphe   TYAYR, a-DAWLF

Thucydides   thoo-SID-uh-deez

Thutmosis   thoot-MOH-suss

Tiberius   ty-BEER-ee-uss

Tiglath-pileser   TIG-lath-py-LEE-zur

Tirpitz, Admiral von   TEER-pits, AD-mi-rul fun

Tisza, István   TISS-ah, ISHT-vun

Tito   TEE-toh

Titus   TY-tuss

Tlaxcala   tuh-lah-SKAH-lah

Tocqueville, Alexis de   tawk-VEEL, al-lek-SEE duh

Tojo, Hideki   TOH-joh, hee-DEK-ee

Tokugawa Ieyasu   toh-koo-GAH-wah ee-yeh-YAH-soo

Tolstoy, Leo   TOHL-stoy, LEE-oh

Topa Inca   TOH-puh INK-uh

Torah   TOR-uh

Tordesillas   tor-day-SEE-yass

Trajan   TRAY-jun

Trevithick, Richard   TREV-uh-thik, RICH-urd

Tristan, Flora   TRISS-tun, FLOR-uh

trivium   TRIV-ee-um

Trotsky, Leon   TRAHT-skee, LEE-ahn

Troyes   TRWAH

Trudeau, Pierre   troo-DOH, PYAYR

Trufaut, François   troo-FOH, frahnh-SWAH

Tsara, Tristan   TSAHR-rah, TRISS-tun

Tübingen   TOO-bing-un

Tutankhamun   too-tahn-KAH-mun

Tyche   TY-kee

Uccello, Paolo   oo-CHEL-oh, POW-loh

uhuru   oo-HOO-roo

Ulbricht, Walter   OOL-brikkt, VAHL-tuh

Umayyads   oo-MY-adz

Unam Sanctam   OO-nahm SAHNK-tahm

universitas   yoo-nee-VAYR-see-tahss

Uzbekistan   ooz-BEK-i-stan

Valens   VAY-linz

Valentinian   val-en-TIN-ee-un

Valéry, Paul   vah-lay-REE, POHL

Valois   val-WAH

Van de Velde, Theodore   vahn duh VEL-duh, TAY-oh-dor

van Eyck, Jan   vahn YK *or* van AYK, YAHN

van Gogh, Vincent   van GOH, VIN-sent

Vasa, Gustavus   VAH-suh, GUSS-tuh-vuss

Vega, Lope de   VAY-guh, LOH-pay day

Vendée   vahnh-DAY

Vendemiaire   vahnh-duh-MYAYR

Venetia   vuh-NEE-shuh

Ventose   vahnh-TOHZ

Verdun   vur-DUN

Vergerio, Pietro Paolo   vur-JEER-ee-oh, PYAY-troh POW-loh

Versailles   vayr-SY

Vesalius, Andreas   vuh-SAY-lee-uss, ahn-DRAY-uss

Vespasian   vess-PAY-zhun

Vespucci, Amerigo   vess-POO-chee, ahm-ay-REE-goh

Vesuvius   vuh-SOO-vee-uss

Vichy   VISH-ee

Vierzehnheiligen   feer-tsayn-HY-li-gen

Virchow, Rudolf   FEER-khoh, ROO-dulf

Virgil   VUR-jul

Visconti, Giangaleazzo   vees-KOHN-tee, jahn-gah-lay-AH-tsoh

Visigoths   VIZ-uh-gathz

Voilquin, Suzanne   vwahl-KANH, soo-ZAHN

Volk   FULK

Volkschulen   FULK-shoo-lun

Voltaire   vohl-TAYR

Wafd   WAHFT

Wagner, Richard   VAG-nur, RIKH-art

Walesa, Lech   vah-WENT-sah, LEK

Wallachia   wah-LAY-kee-uh

Wallenstein, Albrecht von   VAHL-en-shtyn, AWL-brekht fun

Wannsee   VAHN-zay

Watteau, Antoine   wah-TOH, ahnh-TWAHN

Weill, Kurt   VYL, KOORT

Weizsäcker, Richard von   VYTS-zek-ur, RIKH-art fun

wergeld   WURR-geld

Windischgrätz, Alfred   VIN-dish-grets, AHL-fret

Winkelmann, Maria   VINK-ul-mahn, muh-REE-uh

Witte, Sergei   VIT-uh, syir-GYAY

Wittenberg   VIT-ten-bayrk

Wojtyla, Karol   voy-TEE-wah, KAH-rul

Wollstonecraft, Mary   WUL-stun-kraft, MAY-ree

Würzburg   VOORTS-boork

Wyclif, John   WIK-lif, JAHN

Yersinia pestis   yur-SIN-ee-uh PESS-tiss

Xavier, Francis   ZAY-vee-ur, FRAN-siss

Xerxes   ZURK-seez

Xhosa   KHOH-suh

Ximenes   khee-MAY-ness

Yahweh   YAH-way

Yangtze   YANG-tsee

Yeats, William Butler   YAYTS, WIL-yum BUT-lur

Yeltsin, Boris   YELT-sun, bur-YEESS

yishuv   YISH-uv

Zasulich, Vera   tsah-SOO-likh, VAY-ruh

Zemsky Sobor   ZEM-skee suh-BOR

zemstvos   ZEMPST-vohz

Zeno   ZEE-noh

Zenobia   zuh-NOH-bee-uh

zeppelin   ZEP-puh-lin

Zeus   ZOOSS

Zhenotdel   zhen-ut-DEL

Zhivkov, Todor   ZHIV-kuff, toh-DOR

ziggurat   ZIG-uh-rat

Zimmermann, Dominikus   TSIM-ur-mahn, doh-MEE-nee-kuss

Zinzendorf, Nikolaus von   TSIN-sin-dorf, NEE-koh-LOWSS fun

Zola, Émile   ZOH-lah, ay-MEEL

zollverein   TSOHL-fuh-ryn

Zoroaster   ZOR-oh-ass-tur

Zwingli, Ulrich   TSFING-lee, OOL-rikh

PHOTO CREDITS

C H A P T E R   1

1 © Nik Wheeler/CORBIS; 4 Erich Lessing/Art Resource, NY (Archaeological Museum, Amman, Jordan); **bottom** From Michael Roaf, *Cultural Atlas of Mesopotamia & the Ancient Near East*, published by Andromeda Oxford Limited, Oxford, England; 8 The Bridgeman Art Library International (British Museum, London, UK); **11 top** Hervé Lewandowski/Réunion des Musées Nationaux, Louvre, Paris, France/Art Resource, NY; 17 © British Museum, London, UK/HIP/Art Resource, NY; 18 © Will and Deni McIntyre/Photo Researchers, Inc.; **19 left** Werner Forman/Art Resource, NY (British Museum, London, UK); **19 right** Erich Lessing/Art Resource, NY (Tomb of Mennah, Sheikh Abd el-Qurna, Tombs of the Nobles, Thebes, Egypt)

C H A P T E R   2

23 Alinari/Regione Umbria/Art Resource, NY (Initial O, Ms. E2, *The Judgment of Solomon*, Archivio di Stato, Gubbio, Italy); 24 © Adam Woolfitt/CORBIS; 26 Erich Lessing/Art Resource, NY (British Museum, London, UK); 29 Bridgeman-Giraudon/Art Resource, NY (National & University Library, Jerusalem, Israel); 33 Werner Forman/Art Resource, NY (British Museum, London, UK); 35 The Art Archive/Dagli Orti; 37 Chuzeville/Réunion des Musées Nationaux/Art Resource, NY (Louvre, Paris, France)

C H A P T E R   3

40 British Museum, London, UK/The Bridgeman Art Library International; 43 © AAAC/Topham/The Image Works; 46 Scala/Art Resource, NY (Museo Nazionale di Villa Giulia, Rome, Italy); 53 © Art Resource, NY; 54 Scala/Art Resource, NY (Museo Archeologico Nazionale, Naples); 54 © Photodisc/Getty; 57 Erich Lessing/Art Resource, NY (Louvre, Paris, France)

C H A P T E R   4

60 Erich Lessing/Art Resource, NY (Museo Archeologico Nazionale, Naples, Italy); 61 © British Museum, London, UK/HIP/Art Resource, NY; 63 Erich Lessing/Art Resource, NY (Museo Archeologico Nazionale, Naples, Italy); 66 © Araldo de Luca/CORBIS (Museo Nazionale Romano (Palazzo Altemps), Rome, Italy); 69 Scala/Art Resource, NY (Museo Gregoriano Egizio, Vatican Museums, Vatican State); 70 © Araldo de Luca/CORBIS;

71 **left** Borromeo/Art Resource, NY (National Museum of Pakistan, Karachi, Pakistan); 71 **right** The Art Archive/Dagli Orti (Kanellopoulos Museum, Athens, Greece)

C H A P T E R   5

76 Dulwich Picture Gallery, London, UK/Bridgeman Art Library; 78 Scala/Art Resource, NY (Tomb of the Leopards, Tarquinia, Italy); 81 © Archivo Iconografico, S.A./CORBIS 84 Alinari/Art Resource, NY (Mostra Augustea, Rome, Italy) 85 Scala/Art Resource, NY (Forum Boarium, Rome, Italy) 86 Erich Lessing/Art Resource, NY (Museo Archeologico Nazionale, Naples, Italy); 91 Scala/Art Resource, NY (Museo Archeologico Nazionale, Naples, Italy)

C H A P T E R   6

96 Nimatallah/Art Resource, NY (Palazzo dei Conservatori, Rome, Italy); 97 Scala/Art Resource, NY (Braccio Nuovo, Vatican Museums, Vatican State); 101 © Vanni Archive/CORBIS; 102 The Art Archive/Bardo Museum, Tunis, Tunisia/Dagli Orti; 107 Scala/Art Resource, NY (Galleria Borghese, Rome, Italy); 108 Bildarchiv Preussischer Kulturbesitz (Johannes Laurentius)/Art Resource, NY (Antikensammlung, Staatliche Muséen zu Berlin '31329, Berlin, Germany); 111 Scala/Art Resource, NY (Catacomb of S. Domitilla, Rome, Italy)

C H A P T E R   7

115 Giraudon/The Bridgeman Art Library International (Fol.11r, detail of 192489, vellum, French School, 14th century, Bibliotheque Municipale, Castres, France); 118 Scala/Art Resource, NY (Palazzo dei Conservatori, Rome, Italy); 121 Bridgeman-Giraudon/Art Resource, NY (Ms Nouv. Acq.FR. 1098, Bibliotheque Nationale, Paris, France); 124 Snark/Art Resource, NY (Ms. lat. 10062, f. 98, Initial A, Bibliotheque Nationale, Paris, France); 128 Scala/Art Resource, NY (S. Vitale, Ravenna, Italy); 130 © Digital Vision/Getty Images; 131 Bibliotheque Nationale (Ar 5847 f.19 from *Maqamat*, "The Meetings," by Al-Hariri, vellum, Persian School, 13th century) Paris, France/The Bridgeman Art Library

C H A P T E R   8

137 Scala/Art Resource, NY (Bibliotheque de l'Arsenal, Paris, France); 141 Bridgeman-Giraudon/Art Resource, NY (Musée Goya, Castres, France); 143 Giraudon/The Bridgeman Art Library International (Castello di Issogne, Val d'Aosta, Italy); 145 The Pierpont Morgan Library (MS M.736, f.9v.), New York, USA/Art Resource, NY; 146 Alinari/The Bridgeman Art Library International (Museo Nazionale del Bargello, Florence, Italy); 148 © British Library (Queen Mary Psalter, early 14th century)/The Art Archive; 154 © Photodisc/Getty Images

CHAPTER 9

157 © Mary Evans Picture Library/The Image Works; **160** Art Resource, NY (R.G. Ojeda, Réunion des Musées Nationaux, Musée Condé, MS.340, f.303v, Chantilly, France); **161** Art Resource, NY (R.G. Ojeda, Réunion des Musées Nationaux, Musée Condé, Ms.65, f.4v, Chantilly, France); **166** Snark/Art Resource, NY (Bibliotheque de l'Arsenal, Paris, France); **168** Joerg P. Anders/Bildarchiv Preussischer Kulturbesitz/Art Resource, NY (Kupferstichkabinett, Min. 1233, Staatliche Muséen zu Berlin, Berlin, Germany); **171** © The Art Archive/Dagli Orti; **172** Scala/Art Resource, NY (Notre-Dame, Paris, France); **172** © The Art Archive/Dagli Orti

CHAPTER 10

175 © British Library (Harl.1498. Folio No 76 Min.), London, UK/HIP/Art Resource, NY; **176** Bridgeman-Giraudon/Art Resource, NY (Musée de la Tapisserie, Bayeux, France); **182** Giraudon/Art Resource, NY (Musée Condé, Ms.722/1196, f.392r, Chantilly, France); **185** Scala/Art Resource, NY (Sacro Speco S. Scolastica, Subiaco, Italy); **186** Archives Charmet/The Bridgeman Art Library International (Musée de l'Assistance Publique, Hopitaux de Paris, France); **188** © British Library (Cott Nero E II pt2 f.20v), London, UK/The Bridgeman Art Library; **193** © Bettmann/CORBIS

CHAPTER 11

196 Snark/Art Resource, NY (Bibliotheque Royale Albert I, Ms. 13076-77, c.24t, Fol. 24v, Brussels, Belgium); **200** Image Select/Art Resource, NY; **201** The Art Archive/Bibliothèque Nationale Paris/Eileen Tweedy; **202** Bridgeman-Giraudon/Art Resource, NY (Musée de l'Histoire de France aux Archives Nationales, Paris, France); **207** © British Library (Ms Add 23923 f.2), London, UK/The Bridgeman Art Library; **211** Scala/Art Resource, NY (Scrovegni Chapel, Padua, Italy); **212 top** Scala/Art Resource, NY (Palazzo Borromeo, Milan, Italy); **212 middle** The Art Archive/Bodleian Library (Douce 276 folio 124v), Oxford, UK; **212 bottom left** British Library (Roy 6 E VII f.67v), London, UK/The Bridgeman Art Library International; **212 bottom right** The Art Archive/Bibliothèque Universitaire de Mèdecine, Montpellier, France /Dagli Orti

CHAPTER 12

215 © Vatican Museums and Galleries, Sistine Chapel Ceiling (1508-12), Vatican City, Italy/Bridgeman Art Library; **220** Private Collection/The Bridgeman Art Library; **222** © AKG/Photo Researchers, Inc.; **226** Scala/Art Resource, NY (Brancacci Chapel, S. Maria del Carmine, Florence, Italy); **227 left** Scala/Art Resource, NY (Museo Nazionale del Bargello, Florence, Italy); **227 right** Scala/Art Resource, NY (San Lorenzo, Florence, Italy); **228** Scala/Art Resource, NY (S. Maria delle Grazie, Milan, Italy); **228** Erich Lessing/Art Resource, NY (Stanza della Segnatura, Stanze di Raffaello, Vatican Palace, Vatican State); **230 left** Scala/Art Resource, NY (Accademia, Florence, Italy);

230 right Erich Lessing/Art Resource, NY (National Gallery, London, UK); **231** Alinari/Art Resource, NY (Uffizi, Florence, Italy); **234** Scala/Art Resource, NY (Uffizi, Florence, Italy)

CHAPTER 13

237 Bibliotheque Nationale, Paris, France/The Bridgeman Art Library; **239** Scala/Art Resource, NY (Louvre, Paris, France); **242** Joerg P. Anders/Bildarchiv Preussischer Kulturbesitz/Art Resource, NY (Kupferstichkabinett, 1170, Staatliche Muséen zu Berlin, Germany); **244** Scala/Art Resource, NY (Alte Pinakothek, Munich, Germany); **247** © The Art Archive/University Library, Geneva, Switzerland/Dagli Orti; **251** Scala/Art Resource, NY (Il Gesu, Rome, Italy); **255** © Stapleton Collection/CORBIS

CHAPTER 14

257 Knud Petersen/Bildarchiv Preussischer Kulturbesitz/Art Resource, NY (Kunstbibliothek, Staatliche Muséen zu Berlin, Germany); **259** © Huntington Library/SuperStock (The Huntington Library, Art Collections and Botanical Gardens, San Marino, California, USA); **261** Erich Lessing/Art Resource, NY (Museo Navale di Pegli, Genoa, Italy); **265** © Bibliotheque des Arts Decoratifs, Paris, France/Archives Charmet/Bridgeman Art Library; **268 top** © Private Collection/Bridgeman Art Library; **268 bottom** © The Art Archive/London; **271** Arnaudet/Réunion des Musées Nationaux/Art Resource, NY (Musée des Arts Asiatiques-Guimet, MG 18653, Paris, France); **276** © Huntington Library/SuperStock (The Huntington Library, Art Collections and Botanical Gardens, San Marino, CA, USA)

CHAPTER 15

279 Hervé Lewandowski /Réunion des Musées Nationaux/Art Resource, NY (Louvre, 7492, Paris, France); **285** © Archivo Iconografico, S.A./CORBIS; **292** Joerg P. Anders/Bildarchiv Preussischer Kulturbesitz/Art Resource, NY (Gemaeldegalerie, 820B, Staatliche Muséen zu Berlin, Germany); **293** Jochen Remmer/Bildarchiv Preussischer Kulturbesitz/Art Resource, NY (National Portrait Gallery, 536, London, UK); **296 left** Jean Lewandowski/Réunion des Musées Nationaux/Art Resource, NY (Louvre, 1774, Paris, France); **296 right** Alinari/Art Resource, NY (Uffizi, Florence, Italy); **297** © SuperStock, Inc./SuperStock (Rijksmuseum, Amsterdam, The Netherlands)

CHAPTER 16

303 Erich Lessing/Art Resource, NY (Private Collection, New York, USA); **306** Image Select/Art Resource, NY; **307** Image Select/Art Resource, NY; **309** Jochen Remmer/Bildarchiv Preussischer Kulturbesitz/Art Resource, NY (National Portrait Gallery, London, UK); **310** © Bettmann/CORBIS **313** Hervé Lewandowski/Réunion des Musées Nationaux/Art Resource, NY (Chateaux de Versailles et de Trianon, MV 3464, Versailles, France); **314** Gerard Blot/Réunion des Musées Nationaux/Art Resource, NY (Chateaux de Versailles et de Trianon, Versailles, France)

Hominids, 2
Homo erectus, 2
Homo sapiens, 2
Homo sapiens sapiens, 2, *3*
Homosexuality
    Athenian, 57
    Greek, 57
    in High Middle Ages, 188
    Roman Catholic Church on, 142
Hondius, Henricus, *277*
Honorius II (pope), *182*
Hooch, Pieter de, 293
Hoplites, 44–45, *46*
Horace, 104
Horatius, 83
Horatius Defending the Bridge (painting), *76*
House of Commons, 177, 293
House of Lords, 177, 205, 293
House of Wisdom (Baghdad), 153
Housing
    in Greece, classical, 56–57, *57*
    in Mesopotamia, 10
    Neolithic, 4
    in Rome, imperial, 106
Huayna Inca, 264
Hudson, Henry, 272
Huguenots, 252–253, 284–285
Humanism, 222–224, 238–239, *239*
Humanists, scientific study and, 304
Humans, earliest
    hunter-gatherers of Old Stone Age, 2–3
    Neolithic Revolution, 3–5
Hundred Years' War (1337–1453), 201–203, *203*, *205*, 229
Hungary
    15th-century, 231, *232*
    17th-century, 291
    emergence of, 151
    High Middle Ages in, 181–182, *182*
    Magyars and, 145
Huns, 118, 150, 182
Hunter-gatherers, 2–3
Hunting, 2–3, *19*, 32, 33
Hus, John, 233
Hussite wars, 233
Hydaspes River, Battle of (326 B.C.), 63
Hyksos people, 18
Hymn to the Nile, 12, 13
Hymn to the Pharaoh, 13
Hymn to Zeus (Cleanthes), *72*, 72

Ibn al-athir, *192*
Ibn Fadlan, 152
Ibn Sina (Avicenna), 154
Ibn-Rushd, 169
Iceland, 145
Ides of March, *92*
Iliad (Homer), 43–44, 45
The Imitation of Christ (Thomas à Kempis), 239
Immortals (Persian army), 36, *37*
Imperator (emperor), 98
Imperialism. *See also* Colonization; European expansion and colonization
    Roman, 83–84
Imperium, 79
Inca Empire, 263–265
India
    Alexander the Great in, 63, *64*
    French and British in, 268–270
    Portuguese trade with, 260
    sculpture in, 70
Individualism, 222
Indo-European peoples, 24–25
Indulgence controversy, 240
Indus valley civilizations, 5, *5*

Industry
    in medieval cities, 166
    in Renaissance, 217–218
Inferno (Dante), 209
Inflation, 116
Inheritance laws, 19, 178
Innocent III (pope), 185, 187, 191
Inquisition (Holy Office)
    Albigensians and, 188
    Galileo and, 307
    Joan of Arc and, 202–203, 204
    Protestant Reformation and, 251
    Spanish Jews and Muslims and, 231
    witchcraft trials and, 281–283
Institutes of the Christian Religion (Calvin), 247
The Instruction of the Vizier Ptah-hotep, 20
Interdict, 185
Inventions. *See also* warfare
    in 14th-century Europe, 211–212
    carruca, 158
    telescopes, 307
    wheel, 7
Investiture Controversy, 184
Ionia, 43
Ionic columns, *53*
Iran. *See* Persian Empire
Iraq. *See also* Babylon
    first civilizations in, 1–2, 6
    Hellenistic kingdoms in, 64–65
    Mesopotamia, 7–12
    Persian Empire in, 32–33
Ireland
    monasticism in, 124–126
    Viking attacks on, 145
Irnerius, 167, 169
Iron, 30, 43, 158, 218
Irrigation
    in ancient Egypt, 13
    in Caral, Peru, 6
    in early China, 5
Isabella (Spanish queen), 261
Isabella d'Este, 221
Isabella of Castile, 230, *233*
Isaiah, 28, 30
Isias, letter to Hephaistion, 68
Islam. *See also* Islamic Empire; Muslims
    chronologies, 134, 153
    civilization in medieval Europe, 151–154, *152*
    defined, 131
    expansion of, 132–134, *133*, 153
    Muhammad and, 132–133
    Qur'an (Koran), 132
    rise of, 130–134
    Spain, expulsion of Muslims, *233*
    Sunnite and Shi'ite split, 133
    teachings of, 132
Islamic Empire, 130–134, 151–154
    Abassid dynasty, 151
    chronologies, 134, 153
    civilization in, 153
    Crusades and, 189–190, 191–192
    maps of, *133*, *152*
    translated Greek works in, 168–169
    Umayyad dynasty in, 133–134, 151, 153, *153*, *154*
Israel. *See also* Jews; Judaism; Semitic peoples
    Assyrian invasion of, 26
    Chaldean invasion of, 27
    chronology, 27
    divided kingdom in, 26–27
    map of, *26*
    spiritual dimensions of, 27–29
    united kingdom in, 25–26
Israelites. *See* Hebrews; Jews
Issus, Battle of (333 B.C.), 62–63, *63*
Istanbul. *See* Constantinople

Italy, ancient. *See also* Roman Empire; Roman Republic
    conquest by Roman Republic, 80–82
    Etruscans in, *77*, 78
    geography of, 77
    Greek settlements in, *77*
    maps of, *77*, *78*, *80*, *81*
    Roman roads in, 81
    Roman rule of, 80–81
Italy, medieval
    14th-century, 206, *206*
    Black Death in, 197, *199*
    German invasions, 13th century, 180–181
    Holy Roman Empire in, 180–181, *181*, *182*
    Justinian in, 128, 129
    maps of, *180*, *181*
    medieval, Carolingian Empire and, 138
    medieval trade in, 164
    Ostrogothic kingdom of, 119, *120*
Italy, Renaissance, 215–227
    art in, 225–228, *226*, *228*
    chronology, 222
    economic recovery in, 216–217
    education in, 224–225
    family and marriage in, 219–220, *220*
    general features of, 216
    humanism in, 222–224
    Italian states in, 220–221, *221*, 222
    Machiavelli in, 221–223, *222*
    social changes in, 218–220
    social classes in, 218
    trade in, 216–217
Italy, 17th- and 18th-century
    Baroque art in, 296–298
    Mannerism movement in, 296
    science in, 307–308, *308*, 314
Ivan III (Russian prince), 232
Ivan IV the Terrible (Russian tsar), 288

Jacquerie peasant revolt (1358), 200, *201*
Jamaica, *272*
James I (king of England), 292
James II (king of England), 294
James II (king of Scotland), 211
James VI (king of Scotland), 292
Jamestown, 273
Japan
    European expansion and, 271–272, *272*
    European trade with, 271, *271*
    Jesuits in, 275
Java, Dutch traders and, 267–268
Jerome, 127
Jerusalem
    Assyrian invasion of, 32
    Christianity and, 117
    Crusades and, 190–191, *191*
    under David and Solomon, 26
    destruction of, by Chaldeans, 26
    Judas Maccabaeus, uprising by, 73
    rebuilding of, 27
    Roman destruction of, 109, 111
Jesuits (Society of Jesus), 249–251, *251*, 271, 275, *276*
Jesus of Nazareth, 109–111, *111*
Jews. *See also* Anti-Semitism; Israel; Judaism
    Black Death and, 199
    Christianity, rise of, 109
    in Hellenistic world, 73
    High Middle Ages and, 190
    persecution of. *See* Anti-Semitism
    Persian Empire and, 26–27
    philosophers, 169
    prophets, 27–28
    Roman Empire and, 109
    Spanish expulsion of, 231
    spiritual dimensions of, 27–29
Jihad, 133